AQA An Introduction to
Philosophy
for AS level

AQA An Introduction to
Philosophy
for **AS level**

Gerald Jones
Jeremy Hayward
Daniel Cardinal

HODDER
EDUCATION
PART OF HACHETTE UK

Acknowledgements

The Publishers would like to thank the following for permission to reproduce copyright material:

Photo credits

Cover M.C. Escher's "Relativity" © 2007 The M.C. Escher Company-Holland. All rights reserved. www.mcescher.com; **p.9** The Bridgeman Art Library; **p.29** akg-images/Erich Lessing; **p.50** Published with permission of Universal Press Syndicate; **p.496** Published with permission of Universal Press Syndicate.

Written sources

p.302 Figure 4.11. A.N. Whitehead, B. Russell, *Principia Mathematica*, 1910, Cambridge University Press; **pp.483–4** © 1967 Siquomb Publishing Corp., USA, assigned to Westminster Music Ltd. of Suite 2.07 Plaza 535 Kings Road, London SW10 0SZ. International Copyright Secured. All rights reserved. Used by permission.

Every effort has been made to trace all copyright holders, but if any have been inadvertently overlooked the Publishers will be pleased to make the necessary arrangements at the first opportunity.

Although every effort has been made to ensure that website addresses are correct at time of going to press, Hodder Education cannot be held responsible for the content of any website mentioned in this book. It is sometimes possible to find a relocated web page by typing in the address of the home page for a website in the URL window of your browser.

Hachette's policy is to use papers that are natural, renewable and recyclable products and made from wood grown in sustainable forests. The logging and manufacturing processes are expected to conform to the environmental regulations of the country of origin.

Orders: please contact Bookpoint Ltd, 130 Milton Park, Abingdon, Oxon OX14 4SB. Telephone: +44 (0)1235 827720. Fax: +44 (0)1235 400454. Lines are open 9.00a.m.–5.00p.m., Monday to Saturday, with a 24-hour message answering service. Visit our website at www.hoddereducation.co.uk

First published in 2008
by Hodder Education,
An Hachette Company UK
338 Euston Road
London NW1 3BH

Impression number 5 4 3

Year   2012 2011 2010 2009

Illustrations by Richard Duszczak, Tony Jones and Tony Randell

Typeset in 11/13pt Galliard by Dorchester Typesetting, Dorchester, Dorset

Printed in Malta

A catalogue record for this title is available from the British Library

ISBN 978 0340 96525 2

Contents

Key to features

ACTIVITY — A practical task to help you to understand the ideas.

experimenting with ideas — Plays around with some of the concepts discussed; looks at them from different angles.

▶ criticism ◀ — Highlights and evaluates some of the difficulties in various ideas.

A direct quotation from a key thinker.

! more difficult — A more in-depth discussion of the ideas.

The series

This is the seventh book in a series aimed at students who are beginning to study philosophy. The books fill the middle ground between introductory texts, which do not always provide enough detail to help students with their essays and examinations, and more advanced academic texts, which are often too complex for students new to philosophy to understand.

All of the study guides are written around the themes and texts for the AQA AS/A2 level philosophy specification. In addition to this Introduction to AS level there are six other guides in the Philosophy in Focus series:

- *Plato's* Republic
- *Descartes'* Meditations
- *Sartre's* Existentialism & Humanism
- *Epistemology: the Theory of Knowledge*
- *Moral Philosophy: a Guide to Ethical Theory*
- *Philosophy of Religion*

The authors have substantial experience of teaching philosophy at A level. They are also committed to making philosophy as accessible and engaging as possible. The study guides contain exercises to help students to grasp the philosophical theories and ideas that they'll face in a meaningful way.

Feedback and comments on these study guides would be welcome.

Gerald Jones is Curriculum Development Manager for the Corporation of London.
Jeremy Hayward is a lecturer in Education at the Institute of Education, University of London.
Daniel Cardinal is a philosophy lecturer for the Faculty of Continuing Education, Birkbeck College, London.

Introduction

This A level may represent the first time you have formally studied philosophy, although you may well have debated many philosophical issues with friends, family or even with yourself. Unlike other A levels such as Mathematics, History, Business Studies or Biology, the nature of the subject is not immediately clear from the name alone. This is because the term *philosophy* is used to cover a great many things and is used differently by different people. To see this, you only have to wander into the philosophy section of your local bookshop or library, where the chances are you will find books covering such diverse topics as UFOs, tarot cards and personal therapy.

Even amongst philosophers themselves there is no clear consensus as to what the subject involves. Indeed John Campbell in his book *Philosophers* photographed over fifty philosophers and asked them each to describe the subject. Perhaps not surprisingly over fifty different answers were given. For example:

Philosophy is thinking in slow motion. It breaks down, describes and assesses moves we ordinarily make at great speed – to do with our natural motivations and beliefs. It then becomes evident that alternatives are possible

John Campbell, *Philosophers*

To add to this confusion, or possibly in an attempt to make things clearer, we sketch in this introduction our own account of the nature of the subject.

What is philosophy?

Below are six different human inventions or theories or techniques (we've called them discoveries) which have helped humans to make sense of the world. Read through these discoveries then think about, or go and find out, what each discovery is, when the discovery was made and how it might have helped us to learn about the world.

Discoveries

A The discovery and analysis of fossils and relics
B The invention of ground lenses
C The use of dissection on animals and humans
D The discovery of DNA
E Maxwell's theory of electromagnetism
F The theory that the earth's crust is divided into plates

Humans have long looked up at the stars in wonder and asked difficult and probing questions about the world we live in: where did we come from, why are we here, where are we going? Below are a list of some of the other puzzling questions about ourselves and the universe that humans have sought to answer:

Puzzling questions

1 Do other planets have moons?
2 What causes diseases?
3 What is it that all living things have in common?
4 What is light?
5 What happens to us when we die?
6 Did strange creatures ever walk the earth?
7 Why do earthquakes occur?
8 How does blood move around the body?
9 Have humans always existed?
10 Why does anything exist at all?
11 Why do children resemble their parents?
12 Why do certain metals attract one another?
13 Can we know anything for certain?
14 How old is the earth?
15 Why are kangaroos only found in Australia?
16 Why are certain diseases unavoidable?
17 Have humans always lived together?
18 Does every effect have a cause?
19 Should we dissect animals?
20 How do animals move?
21 How are mountains formed?
22 What is existence?
23 Why do batteries affect a compass?
24 Can a person think without a brain?
25 Is the earth the centre of the universe?
26 What is everything made of?

a) Now ask yourself for each puzzling question: 'could one of the discoveries help me to answer this?'

b) If you think one of them could help, then jot down on a bit of paper which discovery (from A–F) might help you to answer that question.

c) What questions do you have left over after considering all the puzzling questions listed above – i.e. which questions cannot be answered by any of the discoveries?

d) What do these left-over questions have in common?

This activity is designed to tease out a notable feature of philosophy, namely, how philosophical questions differ from other types of question. In Ancient Greece philosophy had a meaning very different from the one it has today. *Philos*, meaning 'love of', and *sophia*, meaning 'wisdom' gave rise to the word *philosophy* meaning 'love of wisdom'. But this love of wisdom encompassed nearly all fields of knowledge. If you were studying philosophy at Plato's Academy or Aristotle's Lyceum then you might find on your timetable maths, physics, chemistry, biology, geography, psychology, law, politics (although most of them would be grouped under the heading 'philosophy'). Philosophy was the study of everything that humankind wanted to gain knowledge about.

Over the centuries, from 400 BCE to the present day, many areas of thought have peeled away from philosophy and developed into separate disciplines: for example, chemistry, physics, biology (once termed 'natural philosophy'), and recently psychology, all became subjects in their own right, not merely subsidiaries of philosophy. Why was this so? Well, as the activity above might have shown, many subjects developed their own methodologies, their own tools and techniques enabling their own specific ways of answering the questions they were interested in.

How does this help us to understand philosophy? We could say that philosophy has always been the subject that asks the questions that humans cannot yet answer. In Greek times these included questions like 'what is light?' and 'do other planets have moons?' as well as questions like 'what is existence?' and 'can we know anything for certain?' As thinkers discovered and agreed upon techniques and tools that could address questions about the planets and light, then these questions became scientific rather than philosophical. So nowadays we think we have an answer for the first two questions, but philosophers continue asking questions like the last two.

Philosophy is therefore very difficult to define because it deals with the stuff left over – the questions which have no agreed method by which we can answer them. It can also appear frustrating, after all why are we asking the same questions that Plato and Aristotle asked over two thousand years ago – why hasn't there been any progress in philosophy?

■ Figure 0.1 *The categorisation of questions in ancient Greece*

In the beginning most questions were philosophical as there was no agreed method for solving them.

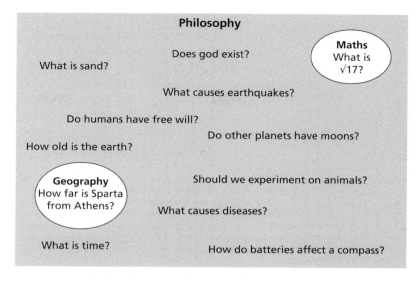

Philosophy

What is sand?

Does god exist?

Maths What is √17?

What causes earthquakes?

Do humans have free will?

Do other planets have moons?

How old is the earth?

Geography How far is Sparta from Athens?

Should we experiment on animals?

What causes diseases?

What is time?

How do batteries affect a compass?

One possible response is to say that there has been progress. Once upon a time all questions about the universe might have been classified as philosophical (see Figure 0.1); but we now have meaningful answers to around two-thirds of the questions in the activity above. Another response is that philosophy, by its very nature, addresses the questions we cannot answer. If we could definitively answer them, or at least agree on a methodology, then they would cease to be philosophical questions and would become scientific ones (see Figure 0.2). Yet another answer is to say that there has been progress in terms of the rigour with which philosophers answer questions, the critical testing from peers to which their answers are put, and the expanded knowledge base from which philosophers can begin their investigation.

■ Figure 0.2 *The categorisation of questions in the twenty-first century*

Over the centuries, aided by discoveries, we have agreed methods of answering certain questions. These are no longer considered philosophical but form part of a new discipline. Philosophy deals with the questions left over.

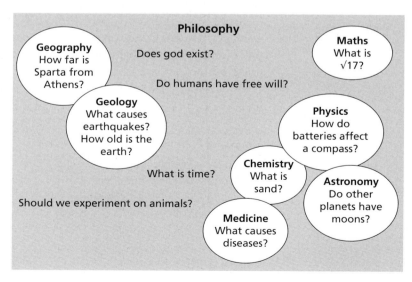

Philosophy

Geography How far is Sparta from Athens?

Does god exist?

Maths What is √17?

Do humans have free will?

Geology What causes earthquakes? How old is the earth?

Physics How do batteries affect a compass?

What is time?

Chemistry What is sand?

Astronomy Do other planets have moons?

Should we experiment on animals?

Medicine What causes diseases?

So what are these left-over 'questions'? Philosophy can be divided up into separate disciplines, each of which, even if not having its own methodology, does have its own area of interest and in many respects its own language. The three key areas are: metaphysics, the study of the ultimate nature of reality; epistemology, the study of what we can know; ethics, the study of how we should live and act. Underpinning all of these areas is a fourth discipline, which includes the skills of critical thinking, of analysis, and of logic.

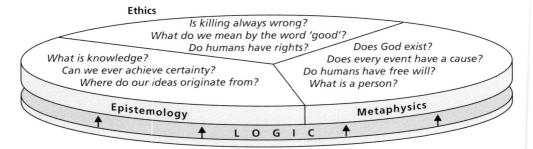

Ethics
Is killing always wrong?
What do we mean by the word 'good'?
Do humans have rights?

What is knowledge?
Can we ever achieve certainty?
Where do our ideas originate from?

Does God exist?
Does every event have a cause?
Do humans have free will?
What is a person?

Epistemology   Metaphysics

L O G I C

■ **Figure 0.3** *The different areas of philosophy*

Within these key areas there are further subdivisions: in metaphysics we will find questions grouped around the philosophy of mind (Do I have a soul? How does my mind work? What is consciousness?) and within this the question of persons (Who am I? Am I the same person I was ten years ago?). However, some of this categorisation is artificial, for example the concept of personhood will also raise epistemological and ethical issues. Some other subdivisions of philosophy include: philosophy of language, philosophy of religion, aesthetics, logic, and political philosophy.

Philosophy also deals with the cutting edge and abstract questions at the forefront of most other fields of knowledge. So there is a philosophy of history, critical theory (in English literature and the arts), philosophy of science, philosophy of maths and so on. Indeed, if you ask enough difficult questions about any aspect of the world, you will end up with a philosophical question.

Why did the car start?
Because I turned the key
But why?
Because it links the battery to the spark plugs which ignited the fuel
Why does this happen?
Because fuel ignites at a certain temperature
Yeah, but why?
Well that's the laws of physics
But why is that a law of physics?
Because that's the way the universe was made
And why was it made this way?

Eventually this discussion leaves science proper and drifts into the metaphysical and epistemological questions that make up the philosophy of science. Seen this way, philosophy is all around us; it's just a matter of asking the right questions. Most of the time though, we are happy to get on with our lives and so don't ask these difficult questions. As soon as we do, we start to realise that our explanations about life and the world come up a little short and we find ourselves philosophising. But why should we bother with these questions?

In one sense we can't avoid them. The unreflective life takes for granted common-sense assumptions which enable us to get on with the business of living. But these common-sense assumptions themselves represent answers to philosophical questions and so relying on these is still to rely on a particular philosophy. However, the common-sense approach is just one possible view of things and one which is often beset with inconsistencies that we ignore. If you scratch beneath the surface, problems can arise.

Consider someone who just wants to live their life and get on with things. Perhaps they want to get a job, earn some money, get a set of wheels and buy a house, and so on. But why does this person want to do these things? Is it because they think they it will make them happy? Do they think happiness is a goal worth pursuing? Is it achievable? Is the term even meaningful? If the person hasn't asked themselves these questions then it would seem they are just going about their life with no clear idea of what it is they are ultimately pursuing. We might want to ask: although such a life is possible, is it a good life? The Greek philosopher Socrates would say not:

The unexamined life is not worth living.

Socrates, *Apology*, 38a

Socrates

By avoiding these philosophical questions – all these questions still left hanging – our friends and neighbours are choosing to live the unexamined life. So congratulations for not hiding away from these issues and choosing to confront them head on. Congratulations for choosing to live the examined life.

Structure of the book

This book contains seven chapters which can each be placed under one of the three broad headings of philosophy outlined above, although once again each area throws up questions related to the other fields.

1 Why should I be moral – Ethics
2 The idea of God – Metaphysics
3 Persons – Metaphysics
4 Reason and experience – Epistemology
5 The debate over free will and determinism – Metaphysics
6 God and the world – Metaphysics
7 Knowledge of the external world – Epistemology

There is only one compulsory section in the AS Specification: the topic of 'Reason and experience'. However, epistemology is a highly abstract field, full of technical terms; as such it does not always make the best introduction to the subject. As is obvious from the way this book is ordered we would recommend starting with the chapter on ethics, as this may relate more closely to some of the philosophical issues that are thrown up by everyday life.

Each chapter covers the areas specified in the AQA specification, usually in the same order. At the end of each chapter we have provided a summary of the key points made. There is also a glossary of terms at the back of the book. In each chapter, the first time you encounter a word that is in the glossary it will be in SMALL CAPITALS.

Finally, philosophy is an unusual subject to study compared with some of the more heavily populated courses at A level and university. However, remember you are not alone in your studies; here is a short list of famous people who have studied philosophy. Feel free to add your name at the end!

Moby (musician)
Philip K. Dick (novelist)
J. Paul Getty (philanthropist)
Martin Luther King (political activist)
Woody Allen (comedian/actor/director)
Iris Murdoch (novelist)
Wes Anderson (director)
Wes Craven (director)
Harrison Ford (actor)
Steve Martin (comedian/actor)
Jake Gyllenhaal (actor)

Bill Clinton (politician)
Ethan Coen (director)
Joan Rivers (comedian)
Susan Sarandon (actress)
David Duchovny (actor)
Ricky Gervais (comedian/actor)
Matt Groening (creator of *The Simpsons*)
Larry Sanger (co-founder of Wikipedia)
Bill Hicks (comedian)
Bruce Lee (actor)
Bill Murray (comedian/actor)
Leo Tolstoy (novelist)

1

Why should I be moral?

Introduction

Gyges . . . found that every time he turned [the ring]
inward he became invisible, and when he turned it
outwards he became visible. Having made this discovery he
managed to get himself included in the party that was to
report to the king, and when he arrived he seduced the
queen, and with her help attacked and murdered the king
and seized the throne.
  Imagine now that two such rings existed and the just
man put on one, the unjust the other. There is no one, it
would commonly be supposed, who would have such iron
strength of will as to stick to what is right . . . For he would
be able to steal from the market whatever he wanted . . . to
go into any man's house and seduce anyone he liked, to
murder or to release from prison anyone he felt inclined,
and generally behave as if he had supernatural powers.

Plato, *The Republic*, 360a–d

What would you do if you found Gyges' ring? A ring that
meant that you could do whatever you liked without anyone
discovering it was you. You would be unobservable whenever
you chose to be: think of all the places you could go, the
people you could spy on, the conversations you could
eavesdrop, all the things you could take. Think of the power
that such stolen knowledge and secret thefts would bring and
what you could do with that power. Many of us would be
tempted to follow Gyges' lead, and to use the ring to
maximum advantage – for ourselves. But what reasons could
someone give to us, or to Gyges, *not* to use the ring in a way
that was purely selfish or that might harm others?

Read through the following scenario and answer the questions below.

A little fellow called Frodo Baggins has recently joined your
philosophy class. He confides in you that, just like Gyges, he has a
Ring of Power which, when he puts it on, makes him invisible. Frodo
seems like a nice enough chap but he has a strange look in his eye;
he admits that he sometimes uses the ring just to take what he wants.
Whilst he's talking, his face becomes half-twisted into a horrific smile.

1

He whispers to you that he's started to use 'unsound methods' to satisfy his desires, whatever harm this causes to other people. You shudder at what he means by 'harm' and 'unsound'. You decide to intervene, to convince Frodo that he should act in a moral way.

1 Why should Frodo be moral? Write down as many reasons as you can (aim for more than five).

2 Are there similarities between some of the reasons you have written down – and if so can you group them into 'clusters' of connected reasons?

3 Which reason, or cluster of reasons, do you think is the most persuasive?

4 Unfortunately most of us don't have Rings of Power or Invisibility, and so our actions, unlike those of Frodo and Gyges, are more likely to be noticed by other people.

What additional reasons could be given to the rest of us (i.e. those of us without magic rings) as to why we should be moral?

■ **Figure 1.1 *There are push and pull reasons for being moral***

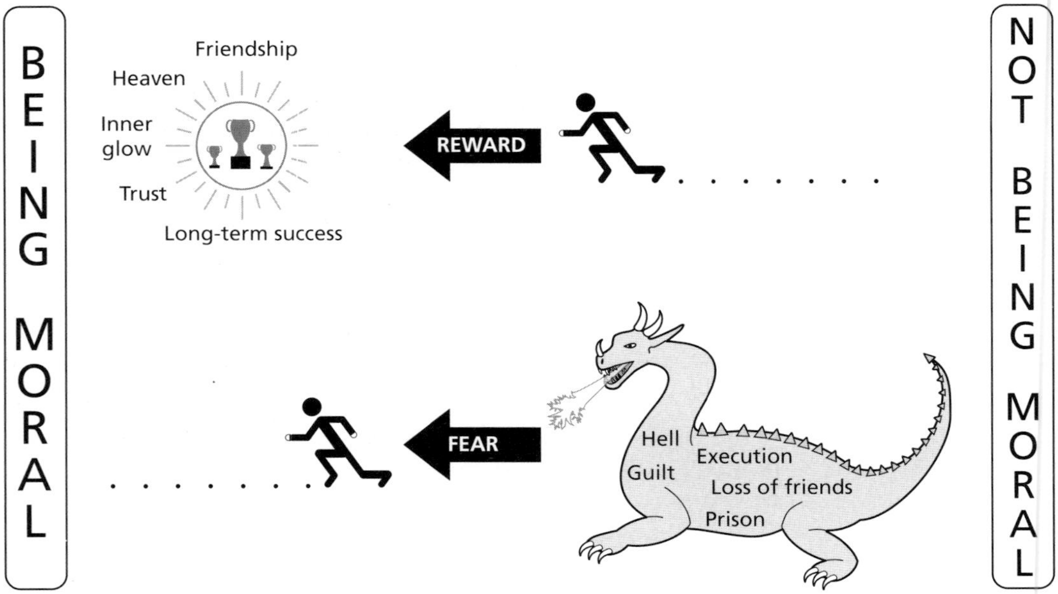

Being moral means doing the right thing, being a good person and, according to our common-sense understanding, this is generally thought to involve helping others and avoiding causing them harm. Moral behaviour, conventionally understood, is essentially ALTRUISTIC: that is, it involves unselfish concern for others. But, behaving altruistically can take a lot of effort for which there may be little obvious personal gain. What I *ought* to do is often in conflict with what I *want* to do. So morality may appear like a constraint on the realisation of your desires and so it seems reasonable to ask 'What's in it for me? Why *should* I be moral?' In other

BEING MORAL

Friendship
Heaven
Inner glow
Trust
Long-term success

REWARD

FEAR

Hell
Guilt
Execution
Loss of friends
Prison

NOT BEING MORAL

words, what possible reason could there be for acting morally?

In your answers to the activity above you might have given both 'push' and 'pull' reasons for behaving morally (Figure 1.1). The 'pull' reasons are ones that highlight the advantages of being moral and make it attractive to us: for example, people grow to like me; I feel good about myself; I might end up in heaven; people trust me; in the long run I'll do better by being moral. The 'push' reasons are ones that highlight things which we fear, for example legal punishments such as imprisonment, other forms of retribution, loss of friends and family, feelings of guilt, the possibility of eternal damnation. These threats can be avoided if we choose to be moral.

Both sets of reasons, the positive (how can I benefit from being moral?) and the negative (what nastiness do I avoid by being moral?), operate on us as powerful levers that influence our thought processes and affect our actions.[1] However, the bottom line seems to be that they both appeal to our self-interest. In other words we find it reasonable to be moral, and have reasons for being moral, only insofar as behaving morally benefits us individually.

For many of us this seems a strange conclusion. You might wonder whether it can be moral to act only out of self-interest; or whether performing a good act because it benefits you actually counts as a 'good act' at all. A philosopher might say that there is a tension between self-interest and morality – between doing what is good for us, and doing what is good full-stop – and that these two ideas pull in opposite directions. Imagine someone rescued you from your house when it was on fire, a brave and fine thing to do. Imagine that you later discovered that your rescuer had stared at the house whilst it was burning in order to make an assessment about **a** his chances of being killed and **b** his chances of getting a reward; and had only decided to rescue you because he judged **a** to be low (a little smoke, but no flames) and **b** to be high (semi-detached, nice car in the drive). Would your views on the rescuer and his action change? Perhaps it would occur to you that, if the flames had been fuller, the house terraced, or the car a different make, then you wouldn't have been rescued at all.

In the rest of this chapter we explore the tensions between self-interest, practical reason and morality. Our main goal is to examine some of the answers that philosophers have given to the question 'why should I be moral?' However, in the process, three subsidiary themes weave in and out of the narrative:

i)   Are we essentially self-interested creatures? Does human nature dictate the motives we can have for being moral?

ii) Does morality conflict with self-interest? Are self-interested reasons the very opposite to moral reasons, or are the two connected in some way?

iii) Is moral behaviour reached through reason? Is there another route to moral behaviour that does not depend on giving reasons?

The rest of this chapter is divided into three main parts, each of which looks at a different approach to the question of why we should be moral (see Figure 1.2).

1 *Morality as a social contract.* Here we look at those philosophers who accept that we are motivated by self-interest. However, my natural inclination to do what is best for me does not result in moral behaviour and leads to damaging conflict of interest for all of us. So we must come to some sort of agreement, or contract, which limits this conflict. Moral behaviour arises out of this agreement, which puts a limit on what we can do, but which ultimately optimises our self-interest. Morality, then, is like a social glue enabling society to function effectively. And, since we can all see the benefits of mutual cooperation, it is rational for us to adopt the moral code of society.

2 *Morality as constitutive of self-interest.* In this section we look at those philosophers, mostly from ancient Greece, who also believe that we are motivated by self-interest and should seek to satisfy this. However, it turns out that it is in our real self-interest to be moral and to develop a moral character. In this way we are able to flourish as human beings.

3 *Morality as overcoming self-interest.* In this final part we look at some philosophers who argue that self-interest has nothing to do with morality. The question then is what does motivate us to be moral? Duty itself is one possible motivator, as determined by reason. The final approach that we examine rejects reason altogether, claiming that it is our natural sympathy for others that motivates us to be moral.

In the conclusion to this chapter we look at the three subsidiary questions i)–iii) posed above and how the answers to these interconnect.

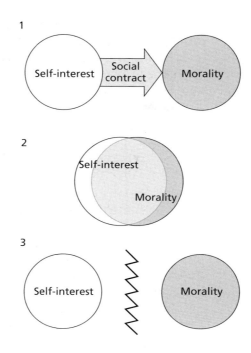

■ **Figure 1.2 *Three models of the relationship between self-interest and morality***

Morality as a social contract

Introduction

The idea that morality is a social contract offers an explanation of why it is reasonable to act in accordance with the dictates of morality; and so it provides us with an answer to the question 'Why should I be moral?' In order to see how this approach works let's consider a challenge posed above to the idea that we should be moral, not dissimilar to that posed by the example of Gyges, in another of Plato's dialogues, the *Gorgias.* There the figure of Callicles argues that behaving altruistically – that is, with the interests of others in mind – is a mug's game and that a sensible person should avoid doing so whenever they can. In other words, his answer to our question 'Why should I be moral?' is that I should not be moral. Instead I should break free of the constraints of conventional morality and be as 'immoral' as I need to be in search of what is good for myself regardless of the consequences for others.

Callicles' position is known as EGOISM: the view that I should always do what will promote my own greatest good. Callicles' way of thinking is based on the idea that human beings are naturally self-interested and therefore that the only good we can have any reason to pursue is our own good. It implies that the only reason I behave morally is in order to avoid the censure of others. If I can get away with it (as

Gyges can) I would, and should, behave in such a way as will bring maximum benefits to myself and ignore the 'agreements of men'. Inevitably this will mean behaving in a thoroughly immoral manner, at least according to our conventional understanding of 'moral'.

One way of dealing with Callicles' challenge is to accept the idea that we are all by nature incurably selfish creatures, but argue that the best way to achieve one's self-interest is actually to act according to the precepts of conventional morality. After all, as an egoist, whether I choose to behave selfishly will depend on whether I think such behaviour to be in my best interest. I may judge modesty, generosity and consideration for others to be the best long-term policy. I may, in other words, recognise the need to cooperate with others, and to act in a way which is traditionally regarded as moral, in order to serve my own interests. For example, I may judge it an unwise policy to lie, cheat and steal, for this will doubtless lead to my being distrusted and disliked, and to my having to give up the benefits of society. According to this way of thinking it is actually counterproductive to act in a manner which is openly egotistical. We are not all in the position of Gyges, and so, as a matter of practical necessity, we are forced to conform to moral behaviour. An egoist who reasons in this way, and so acts where necessary in a selfless way, is said to be an 'enlightened' egoist.

We return in the middle section of this chapter to look in some detail at what the ancient Greeks had to say about self-interest, and how their approach to ETHICS is very different from the approach that we might be used to.

Hobbes and the social contract

Plato considers a view similar to the enlightened egoist in the *Republic* where the figure of Glaucon puts forward the idea that moral rules are a convention agreed upon by people in order to avoid the extremes of harm that would result if everyone were permitted to do as they pleased. By submitting to conventional morality – Callicles' 'agreements of men' – we all stand to benefit. Plato himself rejects this view, arguing that living a virtuous or moral life is its own reward in that the virtuous individual is always happiest regardless of the external reward they may gain from their behaviour. (This is a position we will be examining in the next section, 'Morality as constitutive of self-interest'.) However, later thinkers revived the social contract approach to ethics, and among the most important of these was the seventeenth-century English philosopher Thomas Hobbes (1588–1679).[2] His position is that of an enlightened egoist, claiming that human beings are naturally self-interested but that it is rational for them to behave morally in order to maximise this self-interest.

◼ The state of nature

In his great work *Leviathan* (1651) Hobbes begins his account of the origins of morality by asking us to imagine the 'state of nature', that is, the condition humans would have enjoyed prior to any social organisation. Hobbes was persuaded that all human actions are motivated by the effort to satisfy our own desires and improve our own situation. Because human beings are naturally self-interested, in this state we all pursue what benefits ourselves without qualms, for there is no such thing as right and wrong: anything goes. However, the down side of everyone doing whatever they please is that there are no restrictions on how people may treat others. Given that resources are likely to be scarce, individuals will need to compete with each other, and this means everyone will live in constant danger of being robbed or killed. The upshot would be a kind of 'war of all against all' in which each of us would live in 'continual fear and danger of violent death'. Without the advantages that come from civil society, in Hobbes' famous phrase:

the life of man [would be] solitary, poor, nasty, brutish, and short.[3]

Hobbes

Given the fact that the state of nature is bad for everyone, Hobbes reckons it is rational for everyone to want to escape it. Since the only escape consists in following rules which require cooperation between people – a kind of social contract – it is rational for us to agree to follow such rules so long as we can rely on others to do so too. For example, I agree not to steal from other people on the understanding that they don't steal from me, and this is in all our interests. Hobbes is claiming that morality is purely conventional: that there is no such thing as right and wrong independently of what is agreed by people living in civil society.

► criticism ◄   ## There never was a conventional agreement

So did human beings ever live in a state of nature? And did a social contract ever actually take place? John Locke (1632–1704), who followed Hobbes in theorising about a state of nature in his *Second Treatise of Civil Government* (1689), believed the Native American peoples living at the time were fairly close to the 'natural' condition although, importantly, for him such a state was not one of perpetual war and involved familial groupings and loyalties. And the idea that human beings, who are everywhere cooperative and social animals, ever lived as solitary creatures is surely a fiction. There is certainly no historical evidence of any people making such an agreement. Moreover, the capacity to rear children successfully, to gather and hunt for food, to secure effective shelter and the other necessities of life would be impossible for our species without a high degree of cooperative behaviour. It seems that, like ants and wolves, humans are innately social, and living a solitary life is the exception rather than ever being the rule. If humans have always existed in social groups then the idea that we might have willingly contracted into them cannot be a historical reality. Indeed, the very idea of a contract could only make sense to people who are already socialised and so understand the practice of making contracts.

If the social contract never actually took place does this undermine the social contract approach to ethics? On the face of it, it certainly seems to. For if I haven't ever made any agreement to abide by moral laws, then surely there can be no obligation upon me to keep to them. No one actually asked me whether I wanted to accept conventional moral codes, and if I haven't promised to do so, then it seems I am free to do as I please and ignore them if it suits me.

◼ A tacit agreement

However, Hobbes himself did not want to suggest that people ever sat down and actually negotiated such a contract, but he still felt his approach was a sound one. For what he is asking us to consider is what life would be like if morality and laws were stripped away. His point is that if we had to confront life without moral obligations we would immediately want to buy into a contract with our fellow human beings, and this gives both an explanation and justification for why societies exist at all and why people behave morally. So long as we all recognise just how terrible the alternative would be and that it is to our mutual advantage to live according to a set of rules, then it is rational for each of us to agree to conform to these rules. Locke also argued that the agreement to abide by the rules is 'tacit', that is, we make it implicitly by the fact that we live in society. If, in other words, I am happy to reap the benefits of social life, then I implicitly agree to abide by its rules. He backs this view up with the claim that we are always free to leave if we so choose.

But can we? Is it a live option for you to leave a country simply because you don't accept its moral codes? Leaving a nation state, such as Great Britain, would require uprooting yourself from your home and way of life. It would also require a substantial sum of money, which you may not have access to. Moreover, where could you go? These days most other states would not allow you to move there anyway and, even if you did, you would simply be abandoning one set of conventional agreements in order to assume another. And the idea of living outside of any nation state is surely completely unrealistic. There are no readily available wildernesses beyond the reach of nations states where you could settle. But if leaving is not a real option, then it seems that any 'agreement' to live by social rules is effectively forced upon you. And if you do not willingly agree, then the whole idea of the social contract as a justification for moral behaviour fails.

If the state of nature was never a historical reality, there have nonetheless been times when society has broken down or a group of people become lost and must live without society and its laws. The chaos of England during the Civil War (see Figure 1.3 below) may be one example; contemporary Iraq another.

In R.M. Ballantyne's *Coral Island* three children are marooned on a desert island and must fend for themselves. Outside of society and in the absence of any authority figures, they maintain their moral sense and survive their many adventures because throughout they work together. William Golding's *Lord of the Flies* begins from the same premise, but the group quickly disintegrates into tribal feuding. Both books explore what human beings would be like in a 'state of nature', a state without government and without laws or anyone to police them, but the two writers' very different views of human nature produce two very different stories.

1 What do you think would really happen to such a group?
2 Would it maintain the basic moral codes that the group would abide by at home? Or would these be quickly abandoned as the group descends into mutual distrust and a war of all against all?

■ **Figure 1.3 *The horror of the English Civil War***

Hobbes lived through the English Civil War, a period of huge turmoil and social upheaval. This experience had a profound impact on his pessimistic view of human nature and on the importance he gave to a strong sovereign to ensure civil order.

experimenting with ideas

Read through the following then answer the questions below.

Helicopters suddenly appear above this street and announce the following news: THERE ARE NO MORE LAWS. REPEAT: ALL LAWS HAVE BEEN ABOLISHED. ANY ACTION YOU PERFORM WILL HAVE NO LEGAL CONSEQUENCE AS THERE ARE NO LAWS. THERE WILL BE NO POLICE OR MILITARY AS THERE ARE NO LAWS TO ENFORCE. THIS APPLIES AS OF NOW AND APPLIES THROUGHOUT THE WORLD. *All over the world, similar announcements are being made. There are no more laws, no legal system, no courts, no police, no Parliament, no punishment, no crimes – as of NOW.*

1 What would you do in the next ten minutes?
2 What would you do over the next few days?
3 What would be your long-term plan?

Such a lawless society would be in no one's interest. It would therefore be rational for us to enter an agreement with others and accept a set of laws and moral codes.

Would we honour the agreement?

If we are, as Hobbes claims, self-interested creatures, then even if we have made an implicit contract with everyone else in society, when it comes to the crunch surely we are going to break the contract before we risk our own skins! To see the point consider an example from Ian McEwan's novel *Enduring Love*. The novel begins in the Chiltern Hills with a man clinging to a hot-air balloon shouting for help. Inside the basket of the balloon is a child. Five strangers rush up and grab the ropes to bring the balloon and child back down to earth. But a sudden gust of wind takes the balloon up into the air, with the five men still hanging from the ropes. If every member of this makeshift crew holds on then their weight would be enough to bring the balloon back down – but the higher they go up the more chance they'll die from the fall.

I do not know, nor have I discovered, who let go first . . . What is certain is that if we had not broken ranks, our collective weight would have brought the balloon to earth a few seconds later as the gust subsided. Hanging above the Chilterns escarpment our crew enacted morality's ancient, irresolvable dilemma: us, or me. Someone said me, and there was nothing to be gained by saying us.[4]

Ian McEwan, *Enduring Love*

For all but one of these men, immediate self-interest won out over helping the group. The clear loser was the one who put others first and clung on, eventually falling to his death, suggesting that cooperation is a high-risk strategy. The fear and distrust of others means we are all highly likely to opt out rather than risk being the one left dangling. Does this not suggest that, even if we had made a Hobbesian contract to bind ourselves together with others, we are bound to resort to self-interest? Another way of raising the problem is to ask why I should behave morally if I can get away with not doing so? Clearly it is to my own advantage if others behave morally, but if I am given the opportunity to cheat or steal why not do so? But then, if it is in my interests to break the rules, then surely others will have reason to do the same, and so the system will quickly descend into anarchy.

■ The need for a strong sovereign

Hobbes' answer is that we need a powerful sovereign to enforce the law. The social contract, therefore, involves handing absolute power over to the state – his so-called 'Leviathan' – whose role it is to ensure we all honour our contractual obligations. It is only if we know breaking the rules is likely to lead to more harm than good for ourselves that we can be protected from our selfish natures and so gain from the benefits of cooperation. So it is reasonable for each of us to submit to the authority of the sovereign.

Some difficulties with the social contract approach

▶ criticism ◀ Are social agreements really to our advantage?
The kinds of obligation produced by a Hobbesian contract may not be precisely the same as those we would normally regard as our moral obligations. After all the stronger you are in the state of nature, the better your bargaining power in negotiating the contract. Not everyone has the same to gain from cooperation and from restrictions on their power. A strong individual might only enter a contract which seemed advantageous and would be able to dictate the terms of the contract. So the theory seems to allow that the weaker, for example the disabled, children, elderly, might become enslaved by the stronger. It appears entirely possible to have negotiated a contract which involves using children as slave labour, or executing those who no longer are able to work, or culling the old and infirm. But it seems intuitively clear that such contracts would not be truly moral.

▶ criticism ◀ Justice is the advantage of the stronger
Returning once more to Plato's *Republic* we find another significant argument advanced by the figure of Thrasymachus. Morality is indeed a matter of social convention, he argues, **11**

but it is not an agreement we would willingly make. Not, that is, if we fully understood what it entailed. Morality is in reality a means of social control, but one serving the interests of a minority rather than society at large. So long as the majority abides by moral regulations they can be readily exploited by those who would do so, namely the strong. Like Callicles, Thrasymachus therefore reckons that moral constraints on our actions are something to be overcome.

Karl Marx makes a similar argument when suggesting that morality is an expression of the ideology of the ruling class (see pages 159–165). Those in power regard certain behaviours as required by moral principles, namely those which serve their own class interest, such as the respect for private property. But the notion that this serves the interest of those required to abide by such principles is a deception. For Marx this is illustrated by the fact that the ruling class regard theft as a great evil precisely because they own the property. Social history is a history of class struggle in which the interests of the dominant class are expressed in the dominant ideology, which includes 'moral' values. The world views presented by moralists will typically reflect their class interests. This doesn't mean that when I act morally I recognise myself to be expressing class interests, but nonetheless this is the correct explanation of such actions since they tend to ensure social order by regulating behaviour and so serve to resist social change or revolution.

▶ criticism ◀ Why don't societies fall into anarchy?

Hobbes has shown us why it may be prudent to act according to the dictates of morality in a situation where we are likely to be caught and punished for breaking the contract. However, in most societies we have ample opportunity to break moral rules. So why don't all but the most totalitarian states fall into anarchy? While many may be tempted by relatively minor transgressions of moral rules, for example, avoiding a bus fare, serious crime is still a minority occupation and it doesn't seem plausible that the only reason people avoid mugging each other is simply to avoid getting into trouble. Also, if Hobbes is right and we are by nature selfish then we should have no problems with doing the wrong thing to make gains for ourselves. But we do have, suggesting perhaps that Hobbes is wrong to say we are by nature selfish creatures. Are we capable of caring about anything other than our own welfare? Surely people do all kinds of actions which are motivated by concern for others, and not for their own satisfaction. Consider here the actions of a parent raising their child, or of soldiers who are prepared to die to defend their country, or the many charity workers who devote their lives to caring for the poor. To deny that people are ever motivated to act altruistically seems to fly in the face of the facts. So perhaps Hobbes has an overly pessimistic view of human nature and that we can behave morally without the need for an authoritarian state surveying our every move. We shall see below (page 64) that David Hume believed that our sympathetic concern for others was at least as strong a feeling as self-interest.

This is a criticism made by other social contract theorists such as Locke and Rousseau. For Rousseau, Hobbes projected into the state of nature the failings of humans already corrupted by society. Society with its institution of private property encourages emotions such as jealousy, competitiveness and pride. In the natural state our natural aversion to the sight of the suffering of a fellow creature means we would live in relative peace, especially as Rousseau reckoned resources would be reasonably plentiful.

Locke argued that, while the state of nature was one of complete freedom, it was not one of license to do whatever one pleased, since humans were still bound by God-given moral laws not to 'harm another in his life . . . liberty, or . . . goods'.[5]

Nonetheless Locke agrees that conflicts of interest, particularly over rights to property, are bound to lead to disputes and feuding and so it is reasonable for the people to form a contract, handing over power to the government to punish those who transgress the fundamental moral laws. For these thinkers the contract agreed does not need to be enforced with the same totalitarian authority as Hobbes envisaged. In other words, the more optimistic one's view of human nature the less authoritarian the government needs to be, meaning we might be able to live morally in the absence of the constant threat of coercion.

One significant difficulty for us when considering who is right here is that if humans have always lived in social groups with moral codes, it is impossible to work out which aspects of our current behaviour are due to our socialisation, and which are, as it were, 'natural'. It seems that different philosophers' prejudices may determine their view of human nature without there being any objective basis for determining which view is more accurate.

▶ criticism ◀ Are our motives genuinely moral?
Another criticism of Hobbes' position asks whether he has really given an account of moral obligation at all. If he is right that we can only trust ourselves to act morally because of the

fear of being caught and punished, then, it may be argued, our motives are not genuinely moral. This criticism rests on the plausible contention that moral actions must be motivated by the desire to do good, and cannot be self-serving. After all, we normally suppose that for an action to be genuinely moral I cannot be doing it simply out of fear of the consequences. If I return a wallet that I find with the money inside, only because I fear I might have been caught on CCTV taking the money, then my actions are not morally praiseworthy. Hobbes is effectively saying that there is nothing inherently wrong with harming others – it is only imprudent – and that each of us stands to gain from a conventional agreement according to which it is 'wrong'. He is saying people are forced to behave morally, not because morality is a good thing in itself, but because they are constrained and cannot exercise power. If they did have the power, it appears, they would be perfectly justified in behaving immorally. But this is surely not what we ordinarily understand by morality. Moral demands are distinct from the demands of prudence. To say that it is wrong to steal does not mean that it is imprudent or unwise, but rather that it really is wrong.

So is there a way in which the social contract approach might operate without being grounded in the fear of punishment for failing to be moral? A contemporary social contract theorist, Gauthier, has argued that it is rational to act in the interest of others in order to serve one's own self-interest, and that this can be achieved without the need for coercion by an absolute Hobbesian authority. Before looking at this approach consider the discussion of the 'Prisoner's Dilemma' below.

The Prisoner's Dilemma

The argument of the enlightened egoist (i.e. that to act in my own self-interest is not ultimately to act immorally), is given support from 'game theory'. A good way in to an appreciation of the issues is to try playing the following game.

To play the game you will need an opponent (such as a friend, classmate or online at http://www.iterated-prisoners-dilemma.net/). It is a card game in which you try to get as a high a score as possible. You have two cards in your hands, a red one and a black one; so does your opponent. It is only the colour, not the number, of the card that is relevant in this game. You conceal these cards from your opponent, then select one and put it face down on a table. Your opponent does the same. You then each turn over your card to reveal its colour. This is repeated five times before you add up the score. You then move on to play another opponent. The scoring system (which will determine which cards you decide to play) is as follows:

If you both play black then you both get 3 points. If you play red and your opponent plays black, then you get 5 points and your opponent loses 2. Obviously if you play black, and your opponent plays red, then you lose the 2 points, while your opponent gets 5 points. However, if you both play red then you get zero and your opponent gets zero. This is summarised in the table below.

	She plays red	She plays black
You play red	<0, 0>	<5, −2>
You play black	<−2, 5>	<3, 3>

(Note that the first number represents the number of points you get, the second number represents the number of points your opponent gets. So <5, −2> means you get 5 points and she loses 2.)

■ The Prisoner's Dilemma and self-interest

The game described above is based on a well-known scenario used in game theory, called the Prisoner's Dilemma. Two people are arrested and held in separate cells by the police. The police do not have enough evidence to convict both, and so they make each prisoner the same deal: either the prisoner stays quiet, and trusts his friend not to betray him, or he betrays his friend, not caring what happens to her. The choices and outcomes are roughly the same as in this game, i.e. the betrayal is the more tempting option (there is the opportunity to go free), and staying quiet requires trust that the other prisoner will stay quiet. So, in the activity above, the selfless/selfish courses of action that confront the prisoners are represented as follows:

a selfish action   =   playing the red card
a selfless action   =   playing the black card

This activity can be used to illustrate how our innate self-interest may lead in the long-term to altruistic (selfless) behaviour. If the game has been understood and played properly then one thing that you will have realised is that the red card is the potentially higher scoring card:

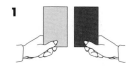

1 Selfish card v. selfless card – the selfish card wins and the selfless card loses.

The selfish (red) card also offers less risk as you can never actually lose points; the worst possibility is that you will score zero, but then your opponent will score zero too:

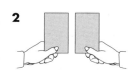

2 Selfish card v. selfish card – no one wins.

So, seen in terms of the outcome of each round, it seems more rational (and in our self-interest) to play the red card.

The black card on the other hand is the riskier one because it relies on trust – you have to hope that your opponent will play black, and not sting you with a red. But where there is this mutual trust then there is also a reward:

3 Selfless card v. selfless card – both win.

3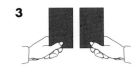

Those who play only red cards are thinking solely about themselves; those who play black are considering the overall outcome of the game for both themselves and for their opponent.

In the activity above, playing red all the time will eventually lead to failure. This can be shown by considering what would happen if this game is played many times ('iterated') among the same group of players. The more you play other friends, the more you learn to trust and cooperate with black-card players and penalise red-card players. Black-card players will start to do well, red-card players will start to suffer: either they will continue scoring zero or they will learn to play black. Taking this game as an analogy for society, it is possible to infer that, even in a state of nature, i.e. without any formal government or laws, we have the genesis of altruism (selflessness): you scratch my back and I'll scratch yours. So why should we be moral? Because in the long run being selfless (playing black) will bring us more benefits than selfishness. What this may be taken to suggest is that moral behaviour does not have to be motivated by selfless or altruistic motives. Its origins could simply lie in our own self-interest, namely the realisation that, in social groups, altruistic behaviour is more beneficial to the individual.

experimenting with ideas

Below are some examples of how you might reason in a self-interested way (like the people who let go of the balloon in Ian McEwan's novel, see page 10).

For each of the examples:
a) Describe what would happen if everyone acted in this way.
b) Describe whether the consequences of a) would damage what was in your interest.
c) What are the chances of everyone behaving in this way?
d) Having considered your answers to a), b) and c) would you say that it is still in your self-interest to behave in this way?

1 You are pushing a car up a hill with four other people and you think 'I could just pretend to be pushing, only three people are needed for this job', and so you stop pushing.
2 You go to the supermarket to buy some washing powder and buy the own-brand budget powder, because it is slightly cheaper than the environmentally friendly stuff.

3 Every Friday night you go out with friends for a drink. The idea is that everyone buys a round, but you have never bought a round and don't intend to – after all there are always plenty of other people who offer to buy rounds before you.

4 You want to listen to the latest CD by your favourite artists, but you don't want to actually buy it. Instead you borrow a CD from a friend and burn a copy for yourself.

5 It is the weekend before an important exam. You know that, because the exam room is so small, you'll be able to look at the work of the people sitting next to you and copy their answers. So you decide that you won't do any revision and that you'll cheat in the exam.

The activity invites you to consider what would happen if everyone behaved in a certain way, and what becomes clear is that everyone's behaving self-interestedly means they are all worse off. On this basis it has been argued (for example by David Gauthier[6]) that those of us who develop dispositions to altruism are going to be better off than those who remain short-sightedly self-serving in their behaviour. Thus with time we will all internalise the need for cooperative behaviour and thus willingly contract into moral behaviour without the need to be coerced by any authority. On this account, then, we can imagine human beings having genuinely altruistic motives, while at the same time the existence of such motives can be explained in terms of what best serves their individual as well as collective interest.

Altruism is in our genes

There is an alternative approach that has developed from the perspective of evolutionary biology. Altruistic behaviour amongst modern humans may be explained because it leads to greater evolutionary success. In other words, if strong altruistic instincts in an animal lead to its having more offspring than creatures who lack those instincts, then such instincts will be selected for. Richard Dawkins is one thinker who takes such a line.[7] Such animals, of course, never *chose* to be moral. There never was a conventional agreement struck in the understanding that this would be mutually advantageous. But the fact that it is mutually advantageous to behave morally means that the genes which tend to produce such behaviour will survive. So modern humans may well have genuinely altruistic motives which are hard wired precisely because this is an effective survival strategy, and those of our ancestors who were not so moral have died out.

► criticism ◄

Morality involves adopting an impartial perspective

Nonetheless, returning to a criticism we made earlier, any account of moral behaviour which explains why it is advantageous can still be accused of failing to understand what morality is really about. Morality, it is argued, necessarily involves taking an impartial perspective on matters. So, even if it turns out that moral behaviour is to my and others' advantage, this is not what *makes* it moral. Rather it is moral precisely to the extent that it is unconcerned with serving the advantage of any party, or, to put the point another way, because moral behaviour is good *in-itself*, irrespective of any good consequences that may follow from it.

We shall see below (pages 49–63) that the great German philosopher Immanuel Kant (1724–1804) argues along these lines, claiming that we are able to discover our moral duties by the use of reason and that these duties exist irrespective of any agreements made or advantages sought. Moral principles are applicable universally, that is, to all persons equally. This means that in order to discover them we have to adopt a point of view which is impersonal, from which we can consider all interested parties equally, rather than from the narrow perspective of self-interest.

A more recent version of the contract approach to ethics is found in John Rawls' influential work *A Theory of Justice*.[8] One difficulty for the Hobbesian approach is that individuals will not enter into negotiation over a contract on equal footing, meaning that, in the state of nature, those who are stronger are going to gain advantages over the others. However, for Rawls it is essential to a just social arrangement that each of us should be free from fear of having their rights violated and so, even if I happen to be in a minority, the majority cannot act in a way which benefits them at my expense. To ensure that we come up with a system of rules which doesn't unfairly benefit anyone, Rawls reckons the contract needs to be negotiated from a position of equality. To ensure this, the position from which we must negotiate the rules by which civil society is going to be organised must be one in which we are unaware of the place in society we are going to hold. In Rawls' words we must negotiate from behind a 'veil of ignorance' which ensures our impartiality. This approach sees moral reasoning as intrinsically to do with adopting an impartial perspective and emphasises the importance of fairness. So any inequalities can only be justified if they tend to benefit everyone including the least well-off.

► criticism ◄ Morality is not related to a social contract
Other thinkers would also argue that morality has nothing to
do with social agreements, and develop different accounts of
what it is that determines our moral obligations. Utilitarians,
for example, argue that the morally correct action is whatever
promotes the greatest happiness for the greatest number,
meaning that it may well be morally correct to break an
agreement if doing so is going to produce a net gain in
human happiness. If this is right, then social agreement
cannot constitute what is moral, but at best reflect it. Other
thinkers have regarded moral duties as given us by God, for
example in the Ten Commandments, and so as independent
of social conventions.

► criticism ◄ Certain things are wrong regardless of social convention
The approaches outlined above, while differing as to the
source of moral obligation, agree that there exist moral
principles which are binding on us irrespective of whether we
have agreed to them. In contrast, the view of morality as
social convention implies that whatever the agreements are
that a society happens to have made they must be moral. So,
if it happens that in the society in which I live it is regarded as
morally acceptable to keep slaves, then it would indeed *be*
morally acceptable to keep slaves. But surely, the objection
runs, whether or not certain things are morally right is
independent of whether people happen to believe they are
right and happen to have made an agreement that these
things are acceptable. Even in a slave-keeping society where
the citizens have agreed that keeping slaves is acceptable, it
would still be wrong to keep slaves.

► criticism ◄ The social contract approach presupposes moral
obligation
We asked earlier why anyone should be obliged to keep a
contract that they had not agreed to and we saw that the idea
of a tacit agreement could not account for moral obligation.
However, the problem here runs deeper. For even if I have
made a tacit agreement or promise, what is the status of this
promise? What kind of obligation could there be for me to
keep this promise? Presumably the answer would have to be
that I am *morally* obliged to do so. But if I have a moral
obligation to keep the contract, then the contract cannot be
used to explain where moral obligations come from. So it
seems social contract theories cannot explain the concept of

moral obligation since they presuppose it in saying that we ought to keep the promise to stick to the covenant. Some social contract theorists, such as Locke, regard the state of nature as one in which moral duties already exist, but in so doing theirs is no longer a theory of the origins of morality.

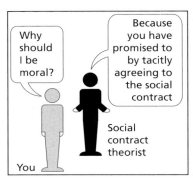

■ **Figure 1.4** *Two figures in dialogue*

What this dialogue shows is that the social contract theory must presuppose the existence of moral obligations before it can account for moral obligation. Someone who doesn't already accept the need for moral obligation cannot make sense of the idea of being obliged to keep the contract.

Can we articulate our self-interest independently of morality?

One of the most important considerations in favour of the social contract approach is the egoist's conviction that we are all motivated by self-interest. If this is right, then clearly we need to find some kind of explanation of how and why moral behaviour might appear. The notion of a contract can explain why it is rational for self-interested agents to restrict their freedoms. The claim that we are self-interested, however, needs to be handled with some care. One difficulty is that, on the face of it, there seem to be many examples of behaviour which seem to be motivated by genuine altruism. Why do people help others when they have nothing to gain? One response the egoist may make is that, while we may fool ourselves that we are being altruistic, in reality there is always a selfish – if unconscious – motive underlying the action. We do often gain satisfaction from helping others and so perhaps the real reason I give to charity is because it gives me a warm glow inside, or dispels my feelings of guilt. Perhaps the only reason people give up their seat on the bus is that it gives them a sense of moral superiority and self-satisfaction.

It is certainly true that we often feel good about ourselves because of having done the right thing. But it doesn't follow from this that such feelings of self-satisfaction represent the full explanation as to why we did that thing. It may well make me feel good to help others, but by itself this doesn't show that I only do it in order to feel good. After all, it may be that I feel good because I've done a good thing. In other words, the egoist can be accused of confusing the object of someone's desire with the satisfaction that results from obtaining it.

Egoists also face another difficulty if they insist that all motives must ultimately be egoistical. If every apparently altruistic act is ultimately a disguised egoistical one the egoist position threatens to degenerate into an empty claim. This is because the theory becomes irrefutable. Nothing will count as evidence against it. For any apparently altruistic act a selfish motive is posited. But if nothing can count against it, then the theory doesn't explain anything. For if in reality there are no altruistic acts then there is no longer any contrast to be drawn between altruistic and egoistic behaviour. If all acts are selfish then there is no difference between a selfish and an unselfish act. But if there is no such contrast, then the concept of a selfish act loses its meaning. It simply becomes synonymous with 'motivated'; for the very concept of a selfish act trades on the concept of an unselfish one. This shows that we cannot articulate the concept of self-interest independently of the concept of other-interestedness. This suggests that our ideas of what counts as self-interested behaviour can only be identified against a backdrop of cooperative behaviour. Thus any attempt to explain cooperative behaviour solely in terms of self-interested behaviour might be doomed from the start.

Morality as constitutive of self-interest

Introduction

In the previous section we looked at some theories which claim that self-interest is the primary driver of human action, and that it needs to be harnessed if people are going to behave morally. According to these theories self-interest does not naturally lead to moral action, and so an appeal to artificial devices (such as a social contract, or some other type of agreement) is necessary to make us care about other people and to consider them when we act. These artificial devices protect us from others and enable us to optimise, although not maximise, our self-interest.

However, there is an alternative ethical tradition that takes the same starting point, i.e. it places self-interest at the centre of human motivation, but which draws very a different conclusion about the relationship between self-interest and morality. Within this tradition, moral behaviour does not conflict with self-interested behaviour; rather morality flows from self-interest. This is very far from Hobbes' claim that

the pursuit of self-interest places human beings in a condition of universal war.[9]

Hobbes

The differences between this approach and the Hobbesian approach stem from differences in the account given of 'self-interest'.

For each of the following achievements:
a) Identify the goal the person was striving for.
b) Does the person consider that goal to be in their interests?
c) Do you think the goal is actually in their self-interest?
d) If it is not in their self-interest, why do you think the person has striven for something which isn't in their interests?

1 Paris had always wanted to be famous, it didn't matter to her what for. Eventually she appeared in a reality TV show about ordinary people who desired fame, and she became a star overnight.

2 Pete knew that his final exam was at least four weeks away. This gave him over 600 hours of potential revision time, so he partied as hard as he could for the first 50 of these.

3 Hilary flew round the world, speaking at conferences and universities throughout the year trying to convince people that global warming was a fiction.

4 Geremi published a book which, he claimed, demonstrated beyond doubt the non-existence of god and the falsity and futility of all known religions.

5 After a few drinks on a Friday night, Lewis would always try to break the land-speed record in his dad's souped-up motor, driving down the A10. This time he succeeded, clocking an incredible 764 miles per hour.

6 Howard had become a multi-millionaire and now devoted his life to guarding his millions in his small fortified apartment, which he never left.

7 Angelina was fed up of working, fed up of cooking, cleaning and tidying up after her children. She wished that she would never have to do another day's work in her life again. Her fairy godmother appeared and granted Angelina her wish. For the next fifty years she didn't have to do anything, and so she didn't.

8 There is a bird flu epidemic and it becomes law for everyone to be inoculated. Rihanna hates needles and claims it is a violation of her human rights. She wins her case and does not have the inoculation.

9   Gyges is a poor shepherd who finds a ring of invisibility. He puts it on, kills the king and marries the queen, becoming ruler of the kingdom.

10 Mr Creosote, a very large gentleman, has just finished a meal of pâté de foie gras, beluga caviar, eggs Benedictine, tart de poireaux, frogs' legs amandine, some quails' eggs on a bed of puréed mushroom all mixed up in a bucket and washed down with six crates of ale. He is offered a wafer-thin mint to finish off the meal. On eating it he explodes.

Some philosophers, including Hobbes, claim that what is in our interests is bound up with what we happen to desire at that moment.[10] But it makes sense to ask whether satisfying our current desires really is in our interest, and to question whether we can ever be mistaken about what is in our interests. There seems to be a difference between what we think or feel is in our interests and what is actually in our interests. We might chase after one desire then another without any consideration as to whether it's really in our interest; we might judge that something is good for us now, without considering whether it will be good for us in the long run; or we might simply be wrong about whether something is good for us.

So there is a distinction between a subjective account of self-interest (one in which self-interest is defined by what the individual thinks or feels is in their interest) and an objective account of self-interest (in which self-interest is defined independently of an individual's judgement). The ancient Greek philosophers we examine in this section argue in favour of the latter. Like Hobbes they put a high value on self-interest, but they also think we can be mistaken about what is in our self-interest. For Plato and Aristotle self-interest is defined by what is good, and so we must seek an objective understanding of what is good if we are to really to do what's best for us. Their analysis attempts to show that moral action is part of our good, and so it turns out that our true self-interests are best served by being moral.

Moral concepts in ancient Greece: happiness, function, virtue

Moral theories in ancient Greece drew on concepts that can seem strange to us today. But in order to understand the arguments of Plato and Aristotle, we need to understand these concepts, and how they connect with one another. Some of the most important ideas in Ancient Greek ethics are:

- happiness – *eudaimonia* (in ancient Greek[11])
- function – *ergon*
- virtue – *arete*

A central question for Greek philosophers from Socrates (469–399 BCE) through to Epicurus (341–270 BCE) and the Stoics (the Stoic school was founded in 300 BCE and became the dominant philosophy of the Roman Empire) was 'how should I live?' and for many of these thinkers the short answer is 'I should strive to be happy'. Both Plato and Aristotle believed that the ultimate goal in life was to reach EUDAIMONIA, in other words to be happy and live the good life. On the face of it this seems a very self-interested goal, and not far from the position of Hobbes. However, we can pick out at least three main differences between the Greek concept of happiness and our modern conception of it. First, 'happiness' in the ancient Greek sense of the word, does not mean pleasure or joy or contentment or some other emotional state that comes and goes. *Eudaimonia* is more permanent than any emotion and is a description applied to our lives as a whole. Secondly, happiness, or *eudaimonia*, is not something we can go out and get, or seek. *Eudaimonia* is something that arises out of all that we do, so we can't aim for it directly. Thirdly, happiness is not one component amongst many in a good life – *eudaimonia is* the good life. A far better translation of *eudaimonia*, as the term is used by Plato and Aristotle, is 'flourishing', in other words having a good life in all its different aspects: living well, reaching your goals and generally thriving. We shall see later how Plato and Aristotle believed happiness and the good life could be achieved.

For many ancient Greek philosophers, including Plato and Aristotle, the concept of 'good' and 'being good' was intimately connected with the idea of function, *ergon*: to be good meant fulfilling your function well. Even today there remains a connection (although we don't think of it as a moral connection) between calling something 'good' and recognising that it is fulfilling its function. This connection is drawn out in the activity below.

ACTIVITY   Consider each of the pairs below and answer the questions that follow.

1 A good can-opener; any old can-opener.
2 A good meal; an ordinary meal.
3 A good teacher; an average teacher.
4 A good video game; a mediocre video game.
5 A good person; an ordinary person.

a) What are the qualities and attributes that distinguish the good thing from the other, more ordinary, thing?

b) Which is better at fulfilling its function – the good thing or the more ordinary thing?

c) From the perspective of the ancient Greeks, what do you think makes something 'good'?

Being a good person and living the good life was linked to being good at whatever role you played in society. For example, if you were a farmer then you were good if you fulfilled your function well as a farmer. So striving to be good, in the ancient Greek sense of 'good', appears to be compatible with moral action – as you would be fulfilling your social and economic role in society and everyone would benefit. However, Aristotle believed that we had a function that went above and beyond the roles prescribed for us by society. For Aristotle we should strive to be good, and fulfil our function, because of the benefits it brings to us as human beings. So once again the ancient Greeks recommend behaviour that is self-interested rather than moral in its focus. We shall examine in more detail below exactly what Aristotle had to say about our function, how it could lead to the good life, and whether this way of life was one that we might recognise as a 'moral' life.

A third concept central to Greek moral thinking, particularly that of Plato and Aristotle, is *arete*, which is usually translated as 'virtue'. Unfortunately 'virtue' (derived from *virtu*, which was the Latin translation of *arete*) has certain connotations in modern times: it suggests a sort of piety or saintliness, or, even more narrowly, a kind of Victorian prudishness. But when thinking about Greek ethics it is important that we cast aside these connotations, since they have nothing to do with 'virtue' as Plato and Aristotle use the term. Instead we should think of 'virtue' in the sense of 'virtuosity' or 'virtuoso', in other words being brilliant or excellent in a particular area of life. In fact *arete* is better translated as 'excellence', but we shall follow the usual convention and refer to it as virtue. A virtue is a personal quality or habit or skill that has been highly developed, in a way analogous to achieving virtuosity in playing an instrument, through individual effort and engagement. We begin by asking 'what can I do to improve myself?' not 'what can I do to help others?' So the emphasis placed by Plato and Aristotle on developing virtues reinforces the view that self-interest is the primary motivation for action.

Now in the activity above you might have noticed that the good things had attributes or qualities that meant they were better able to fulfil their function – we can think of these qualities as virtues. So virtue (i.e. excellence) links the concepts of function and goodness for the Ancient Greeks: in order to be good you need to fulfil your function well; but in order to fulfil your function well you need to excel in the right ways – you need to possess virtues.

1. Function   2. Excellence/Virtue   3. Good

■ **Figure 1.5** *The connections between function, virtue and goodness*

So the moral vocabulary and concepts of the ancient Greeks were very different to those we have today. Some of the most common terms used in modern moral philosophy (words like right, good, morality, ethics) have no direct equivalent in ancient Greek philosophy. For example, we saw above that the Greek concept of 'good' was associated with functional performance, rather than with actions that helped others. The ancient Greeks did not have an exact equivalent word for 'right', i.e. a term that meant 'doing your moral duty' or 'following moral principles'. Even the term 'ethics' had a different meaning in ancient Greece: it is true that Aristotle wrote a book called *Ethics*, but in it he discussed the type of person we should be, i.e. how we should develop our character (in Greek *ethica*). Possibly the Greek term that comes closest to our concept of 'morality' is justice or *dikaiosune*. This word describes behaviour that is 'other regarding', which takes into account the impact of an action on others, or which intentionally benefits others. Both Plato and Aristotle thought it important to assess the part 'justice' had to play in our life and how it related to happiness.

We are now in a position to clarify the difference in perspective between the ancient Greeks' and our own view of morality. The ancient Greeks think of morality as centred around an individual: their character, their virtues, whether they fulfil their function, whether they are happy. So the judgements they make are first and foremost about the agent (the person who acts). However, we are more familiar today with moral theories, such as those of John Stuart Mill (1806–1873) and Immanuel Kant (1724–1804), that judge the actions first, not the person. Julia Annas characterises these two contrasting approaches as 'agent-centred' and 'act-centred' theories.[12] From within an act-centred theory, it seems straightforward to distinguish between actions that are self-interested and actions that are other-regarding. although we have seen with Hobbes' approach above that sometimes other-regarding actions have consequences that benefit ourselves. However, within an agent-centred theory the distinction between self- and other-regarding actions isn't so clearly made; indeed it appears as if all our motives (and all our actions) are focused on the self and are therefore self-interested. We look below at how self-interest is bound up with happiness, justice and virtue in the philosophies of Plato and Aristotle.

The works of Plato and Aristotle

Most philosophy books that you will read are ones in which the ideas of the writer are expressed and packaged together in fairly clear paragraphs, chapters or even numbered points. But Plato, who is thought of as the father of all Western philosophy, writes very differently. If you open a book by Plato it appears to be more like a play than a work of philosophy, with different characters engaged in arguments, short snappy exchanges or long speeches. These dialogues (as Plato's works are called) are the vehicle for Plato's ideas and were common devices at the time, used to explore a number of different concepts. This makes Plato's works accessible (because the conversations draw the reader carefully into the arguments) but difficult to interpret, because Plato never states 'this is what I believe, these are the criticisms of my theory, and these are my responses to those criticisms'. Instead we find Plato's theories emerging out of the discussions that the main speaker, Socrates, has with other characters from fifth-century Athens. Socrates, who had been Plato's teacher in real life, often acts as the mouthpiece for Plato's ideas; although on other occasions Plato's theories develop through the dialogue and the process of debate.

In several of his 'Socratic' dialogues Plato places Socrates in opposition to the sophists, the wandering scholars who taught students the art of persuasion and rhetoric. Sophists, such as

Socrates 469–399 BCE

↓

taught

Plato 427–347 BCE

↓

taught

Aristotle 384–322 BCE

Protagoras (c. 490–c. 420 BCE), argued that there were no absolute principles or moral rules which determined how we should live. It was common for the sophists to teach skills of public speaking and argument that would enable their students to win people over, and so get whatever they wanted in whichever culture they lived in. In two of Plato's most important books on ethics, the *Gorgias* and the *Republic*, the opponents of Socrates put forward compelling arguments that challenge our ordinary views about morality, self-interest and why we should be moral. These challenges, from opponents influenced by the sophists, lead Plato to express and refine his own views about the relationship between morality and self-interest. So Plato was influenced by his teacher, Socrates, and in turn his ideas filtered into the work of his student, Aristotle.

Aristotle's surviving writings are extensive, consisting of around thirty different treatises, but these represent only a fraction of what he originally produced. The surviving works appear to be lecture notes for his students rather than finished works for general consumption, and consequently, compared with Plato's dialogues, they are rather dull. This is unfortunate as Aristotle was known in the ancient world for the beauty of his prose, and the missing works, including many dialogues, represent one of the great losses to humanity. Aristotle wrote on a huge variety of subjects, from zoology and biology to logic and metaphysics, with detours via history, astronomy and psychology. In contrast to Plato's writings, Aristotle's are ordered and schematic, so that editors who have packaged his treatises into books have found it possible to divide his ideas up into chapters and sections.

Aristotle builds on many of the ideas introduced by Plato, but he often disagrees with his teacher and takes a different route when developing these ideas. In Raphael's painting (Figure 1.6) the artist has deliberately represented Plato and Aristotle as pointing in different directions, and these gestures indicate the direction they believe philosophy should be taking. Plato is pointing upwards to the sky; Aristotle's hand is stretched outwards, with his palm facing down. For Plato, philosophical wisdom and understanding lie away from this world, in the perfect, ideal world that is known as the world of the Forms. For Plato's pupil, Aristotle, the opposite is true and it is *this* world that provides us with wisdom and understanding. These differences underpin the differences between Plato's and Aristotle's moral philosophy. But there are important similarities, for example agreement as to what we are all striving for.

■ **Figure 1.6**
Detail of Plato and Aristotle from Raphael's painting School of Athens (1509–1510)

Knowledge lies in another world

Knowledge lies in this world

Plato

> *Don't all men desire happiness? And yet perhaps this is one of those ridiculous questions which I'm afraid to ask, and which ought not to be asked by a sensible man: for what human is there who does not desire happiness?*[13]

Aristotle

> *What is the highest of all goods? Well as far as the name goes there is pretty general agreement. 'It is happiness' say both ordinary and cultured people.*[14]

So although their perspectives differ in some very important respects, Plato and Aristotle both share the view that we are all striving to live the best possible life for ourselves, trying to secure what is in our best interests. We have seen that eudaimonia or 'happiness' is a shorthand way of saying that someone is living well, doing well in life and generally flourishing. We shall see later how Plato and Aristotle differ in the detail of what kind of life this would be, but from this starting point, their investigations have much in common:

1 The rejection of the view that our self-interests are best served by seeking pleasure or power or injustice

2 The belief that in order to know what the best life is for us we need to understand who we are (what our soul consists of)

3 The claim that developing our virtues (in each part of our soul) enables us to live the best possible life

4 The claim that the best possible life is determined by the ultimate 'Good'

The conclusion drawn by both Plato and Aristotle is that the best possible life includes behaving morally and justly. We shall now flesh out the four points made above, but in each section we distinguish between the arguments and approaches of the two philosophers.

◼ The rejection of hedonism, power-seeking and injustice

The truth, Socrates, is this: luxury and excess and freedom, if well supplied [are] virtue and happiness; those other things [morality], those agreements of men . . . those are rubbish, worth nothing.[15]

Callicles

Plato takes very seriously the claim that pleasure or power or immorality can serve our self-interest. In both the *Gorgias* and the *Republic* Socrates is confronted with these views and he responds to the challenge very carefully. The first two speakers in the *Gorgias* are the sophists Gorgias and Polus who present the view that rhetoric and sophistry are the tools by which we can obtain power and so live the best life. This seems, today as then, a plausible claim: after all, if you have the skills necessary to persuade people (your family, your partner, your work colleagues, the general public) that what you are saying is true, even if it isn't, then you should be in a strong position to get whatever you want. The cynicism that people often have about politics is grounded in the suspicion that politicians are skilled in sophistry, but that their messages are empty. But Socrates rejects the claim that sophistry (i.e. the verbal skills of persuasion) brings us any real power. Even though such a skill appears to benefit us, this is just an illusion, and the power is illusory. To Socrates sophistry is a form of 'pandering', in other words gratifying other people without any thought as to whether the satisfaction is a good thing or not. Taking Socrates' point forward, we can question our own political spin-doctors by asking 'who has the real power: the politician or the people they are so desperately trying to please?' Aristotle makes a similar point in the *Ethics*[16] when he says that winning the respect of others cannot be the key to living a good life. This is because he believes that the best possible life is not one which depends on the opinions of others; it should be self-sufficient.

Midway through the *Gorgias* a new character, Callicles, steps into the debate. We met him earlier in our discussion of egoism (on page 5) and have seen that he is prepared to push the debate about power and self-interest much further than is socially acceptable. He is dismissive of the constraints placed on people by 'social' morality, i.e. by the kinds of rules that people agree to under a Hobbesian contract. He thinks that morality, or justice, is a way of keeping strong men down, and that the truly strong will throw off the shackles of morality and do whatever they need to, however immoral, in order to satisfy their needs and wants. For Callicles the best kind of life is one in which we get as much pleasure as we can.

I tell you frankly that . . . the man who is going to live as a man ought, should encourage his appetites to be as strong as possible . . ., and be able by means of his courage and intelligence to satisfy them in all their intensity by providing them with whatever they happen to desire.

Gorgias 491–2

Callicles' claim that pleasure is the ultimate good is known as HEDONISM. Socrates undermines the hedonist position in a number of different ways. He asks us to consider the lives of two men, one who can control his desires and another who indulges all his desires. He uses the analogy of two people, each of whom has a number of storage jars (Figure 1.7). The first person has sound and full jars – once he has filled them up he gives them no more thought. The second person has leaky jars, and has to fill them up day and night. The question is, which life is happier: the life of someone who can control her desires, or the life of someone who is constantly having to satisfy them (the hedonist)? For Plato the answer is clear. The hedonist lives a life of constant craving, every desire that is satisfied is followed by a new desire that demands satisfaction.

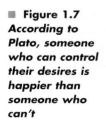

■ **Figure 1.7 According to Plato, someone who can control their desires is happier than someone who can't**

Temperate person – Satisfied   Intemperate person – Dissatisfied

Those people who can control their desires, i.e. temperate people, are happier than those who can't, the intemperate hedonists (we shall see below, why temperance is considered a virtue by both Plato and Aristotle).

Aristotle attacks hedonism on the grounds that humans have the potential for more than just satisfying our physical desires, and that this is what distinguishes our lives from those of other animals – we are not simply pleasure-seeking beasts like cows.[17] Even Callicles, who put forward an extreme form of hedonism, is forced to admit, under pressure from Socrates, that not all pleasures are good. Socrates suggests to Callicles that the pleasures of running away from battle are not good pleasures, and Callicles, who like many ancient Greeks believes that cowards are a disgrace, agrees. Socrates takes the point still further and asks Callicles whether he thinks someone who gets pleasure from itching and scratching, and spends all their life satisfying their desire to itch and scratch, is living a happy life.[18] Eventually Socrates forces Callicles to withdraw from his extreme hedonist position, and acknowledge that what we are really seeking is not pleasure, but whatever is good.

Plato revisits some of these ideas in his later dialogue, the *Republic*. In this book he uses the character of Thracymachus, another sophist, to pose the ultimate challenge to Socrates:

When a man succeeds in robbing the whole body of citizens and reducing them to slaves . . . they call him happy [eudaimon] and fortunate . . . So we see that injustice, given scope, has greater strength and freedom and power than justice . . . injustice is in the interest and profit of oneself.[19]

Thracymachus

Thracymachus is proposing that our real self-interest is served by ignoring the moral rules laid down by society and doing whatever it takes to get what we want. Those who are able to do this most successfully are the ones who live the best lives. This rather extreme position is put forward by both Callicles and Thracymachus, and they express unhealthy admiration for those bloodthirsty and ruthless tyrants who are able to ignore the moral rules of society to achieve their goals. But there is a more moderate, and commonly held, version of their 'immoralist' position which Plato treats carefully: that it is in our interests to do whatever we like to get what we want, so long as we appear to behave morally and we aren't caught – just as in the story of Gyges (above, page 1).

Socrates

> *We must proceed to the further question . . . whether the just live better and happier lives than the unjust . . . We must look at the question more closely. For it is not a trivial one; it is our whole way of life that is at issue.*[20]

As Socrates points out, the question of whether we should live moral or immoral lives is fundamental, affecting our whole way of life. According to both Plato and Aristotle people are often mistaken about what is really the best life to lead, what is in our true self-interests: we can be wrong both about the ends (what we should be aiming for) and about the means (the methods by which we get there). We have seen Plato and Aristotle identify some of the ends, or goals, that appear to be in our self-interest, but actually aren't, such as pleasure and power. But they also wish to show that Socrates is right, that it is better (for ourselves) to achieve these goals through moral, rather than immoral, means. In order to determine which goals, and what methods, are in our true self-interest both Plato and Aristotle believe we have to analyse what our true self consists of, and we examine this in the next section.

■ Function and psyche: understanding our selves

Aristotle

> *It is evident that the statesman ought to have some acquaintance with psychology, just as a doctor who intends to treat an eye must have knowledge of the body as a whole.*[21]

For Plato and Aristotle an understanding of our self is necessary if we are to identify the best possible life for us. This means examining what kind of creature we are, in order to determine what our purpose or function is – once we have determined our function then, the argument goes, we will know what kind of lives we are supposed to be leading.

experimenting with ideas

Shrik is an ogre who runs an advice service for fairytale creatures. These creatures come to Shrik's swamp from magical lands far and wide in order to ask what they are supposed to be doing with their lives. Read through the list of Shrik's customers below and then answer the questions that follow:

1 A handsome and brave prince
2 A magical walking can-opener
3 A donkey who could talk
4 A wicked fairy godmother
5 A dragon

For each creature,
a) write down what their function is
b) write down what they need to do in order to fulfil their function well
c) how do the answers to a) and b) help the creatures decide what sort of life they should be living?

If you happen to be a dog, then you have a doggy function, and your goals in life are very different from those of humans: to chase after balls, sleep as much as possible, yap all day, eat as much as you can and have lots of sex (perhaps they're not that different!). But what kind of thing is a human? For both Plato and Aristotle it is the type of soul we have that makes us human (soul in Greek is *psyche*, which is where we get our word 'psychology' from). Our function as human beings is determined by the make-up of our souls. So if we want to understand our function we need to understand our soul. But, as might be expected, Plato and Aristotle differ in their accounts of the composition of the soul.

In his book the *Republic*, Plato argues that our souls consist of three parts: reason, spirit and desires.[22] In the *Phaedrus*, Plato draws out the relationship between these three parts of the soul using the following analogy.

Plato

> *I divide the soul into three: two horses and a charioteer. One of the horses is good and the other bad.*[23]

So our soul, according to Plato, has two powerful impulses, desire and spirit, and something that can control these impulses, namely our reason. We function well as human beings only when each part of our soul is functioning well, and performing to its optimum. Now this does not happen when one of the impulses (desire or spirit) is out of control. If desire (the bad horse) gets out of control then we become indulgent hedonists with no real sense of what is good for us overall. If spirit (the good horse) gets out of control then we become headstrong impulsive types, always leaping into things and making snap decisions; again this is no recipe for functioning well. For Plato what these impulses need is the firm government of reason – the charioteer – which can control and shape these impulses so that we can use them to attain what is good for us (see Figure 1.8). By using reason to maintain a balanced and harmonious soul we are able to make the right decisions, and select the right goals, which enable us to live the best possible life and flourish. For Plato, the problem with hedonism (regarded as a better life by Callicles) is that reason is not in control and we pursue pleasures that are damaging in the short and the long term.

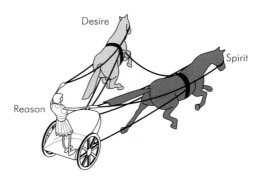

■ **Figure 1.8** *Plato's three elements of the soul*

Aristotle agrees with Plato's claim that reason should rule the soul, but he adds more detail to this claim. As well as being a philosopher, Aristotle was also one of the first biologists, someone who studied life in all its forms. He believed that everything in the world had a function, a purpose, and he saw the world around him in those terms (this is called a TELEOLOGICAL perspective). Like Plato, Aristotle holds that for humans our function is determined by our soul. However, he has a much more sophisticated, psychological view of the human soul. For Aristotle, it is a kind of 'blueprint' for a human being – the instructions for how we are going to develop in our lives. In Aristotle's book the *Ethics*, he describes the four parts of the soul: two non-rational parts (nutrition/growth being one, and desire/emotion being the other) and two rational parts (practical, day-to-day reasoning being one, and abstract, theoretical reasoning being the other).[24]

■ **Figure 1.9** *Aristotle's division of the soul*

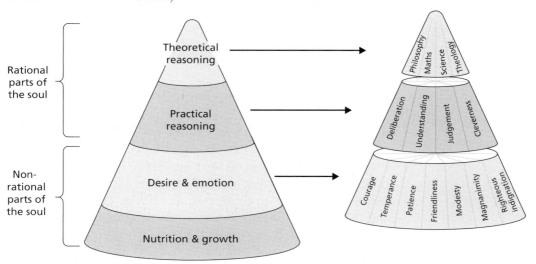

However, unlike Plato, Aristotle believes that each aspect of the soul (our psychological and physical make-up) can be subdivided into further parts that we can describe and analyse.

We shall see below how this more sophisticated conception affects Aristotle's theory of virtue.

From their analysis of the human psychology both Plato and Aristotle conclude that humans are meant to reason, and to reason well; this is the key to understanding what we need to do in order to live the best kind of life and flourish.

Virtue: the key to the good life

According to Plato and Aristotle, our goal in life is to achieve personal well-being and happiness (*eudaimonia*). Aristotle says that we achieve this through functioning well as human beings.[25] We saw in the activity above (page 24) how, in order to function well, something needs to possess all the necessary qualities (or virtues) that will enable it to do so. For example, a can-opener functions well insofar as it has whatever qualities are necessary in order to open cans efficiently, safely, ergonomically. For a plant to function well it needs those plant-like qualities that enable it to successfully grow, flower, reproduce. According to both Plato and Aristotle, a human being functions well through developing and refining the virtues that enable us to flourish as human beings. The focus on the virtues has meant that Plato's and Aristotle's moral theories are often labelled as 'virtue ethics' (a tradition kept alive in the writings of St Thomas Aquinas (1225–1274) and David Hume (1711–1776) and more recently by Alasdair MacIntyre (b. 1929)).

Aristotle

The function of a man is a kind of life, i.e. an activity or series of actions of the soul, implying a rational principle . . . the function of a good man is to perform these well and rightly.[26]

Both Plato and Aristotle identify reason as the primary characteristic of the human soul, and so reason takes a central place in their theories of what humans should be properly doing with their lives. However, we have seen that their conceptions of the soul differ slightly. Plato has a 'tripartite' theory of the soul: it is divided into three clear parts with reason the key to living a good life. Aristotle, however, sees human psychology in more complex terms: there is a rational and non-rational side to our soul, these sides are subdivided into many parts, each of which has a corresponding excellence of virtue, and each of which is important and necessary for our proper functioning (Figure 1.9).

Within Plato's tripartite division of the soul, the three elements (reason, spirit and desire) compete and jostle with one another for control. In the *Republic*, Plato explains how virtue, or excellence, in a human depends upon all the elements being in balance and 'each part of him is performing its proper function'.[27] For Plato this could happen if and only if reason was in control of all aspects of the soul. So spirit guided by reason carefully drives us to action; and desire, when tempered by reason, motivates us and enables us to live a healthy and satisfied life. So, for Plato, when reason is in control there are three virtues corresponding to each of the three parts of the soul:

- reason – wisdom
- spirit – courage
- desire – temperance (or self-control).

■ **Figure 1.10**
Justice emerges when each of the other three virtues is in place

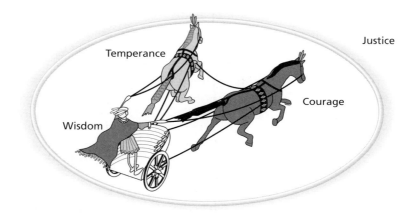

Now when all these three virtues are in place then a fourth virtue emerges, namely justice – which we have seen is roughly equivalent in value to our own concept of 'moral goodness'. So, for Plato, behaving morally, or justly, flows from developing our virtues by ensuring reason moderates our desires and our spirit. Justice is the most important virtue because it readies us for action:

When he [the just man] has bound these elements into a disciplined and harmonious whole . . . he will be ready for action of any kind . . . whether it is political or personal.[28]

Plato

Aristotle agrees with Plato that, in order to function well, we need to be virtuous (and excel) in all aspects of the soul, so we would expect to find in Aristotle's theory a virtue corresponding to each part of the soul. However, Aristotle believes that there are many virtues corresponding to the different parts, not just three as Plato maintained. As with Plato, the crucial thing for Aristotle is that the rational parts of the soul are in control, and this is the key to becoming virtuous. In the *Ethics*, Aristotle analyses in great detail the many aspects of our selves that need to be performing at the peak of their capacity (i.e. excelled at) if we are to function well as human beings. These include:

- excellences of character (controlling and shaping our desires and emotions)
- excellences of practical reasoning (having the skills to achieve those goals that are in our best interest)
- excellences of theoretical reasoning (being good at philosophy, maths, etc.).

Within each of these general virtues, or excellences, there are other virtues (see Figure 1.9 above). For example, the skills we need to excel at in reasoning about practical matters include:

- Deliberation – being able to plan a course of action
- Understanding – being able to see the 'Big Picture' of any situation
- Judgement – knowing what is the right thing to do in any situation
- Cleverness – the ability to execute our plan and accomplish our goal.

Aristotle also goes further than Plato in describing in detail what moral virtue (excellence of character) is and how we might acquire it. It is a type of characteristic, a personality trait, which we develop through practice, like learning to play the guitar. We are not born virtuous or excellent, but we become virtuous through developing good habits.

In the film *The Wizard of Oz* a young girl, Dorothy, encounters three creatures on her way to find the Wizard. Each of these companions is missing some virtue essential for their happiness: the Scarecrow lacks wisdom, the Tin Man lacks feelings, and the Cowardly Lion lacks courage. They misunderstand what these things are, and they believe that the Wizard of Oz, because of his powers, will be able to give them these qualities. When they finally confront the Wizard he can't do anything except give them tokens of virtue (an examination certificate, a clockwork heart, a medal). This was partly because the Wizard was a conman, and partly because virtue isn't something you can suddenly get; as Aristotle says, it is a habit that you develop. In the end, Dorothy's companions became virtuous by acting in a virtuous way: the Scarecrow had started to hatch plans, the Tin Man had started caring and the Cowardly Lion had begun to act bravely.

Aristotle argues that someone who is virtuous is someone who tends to avoid the extremes of over-reacting or failing to react in a particular situation. This means that when confronted with a situation we don't bottle up our emotions or suppress our drive for action (which would be deficient), but nor do we let our feelings come flooding out and completely over-react (which would be excessive). Instead we have to judge how far we should let a particular emotion affect us in this particular situation, and consider what would be the most appropriate response to this situation.

It is possible, for example, to feel fear, confidence, desire, anger, pity too much or too little; and both of these are wrong. But to have these feelings at the right times on the right grounds towards the right people for the right motive and in the right way . . . this is the mark of virtue.[29]

Aristotle

This description of the virtuous person is famously known as Aristotle's Doctrine of the Mean. 'Mean' here refers to 'middle', but Aristotle is not saying that we should take the 'middle way' in every situation, or act moderately in every situation. Clearly there are some situations where a more (or less) emotional response is required, for example when protesting against extreme injustices. But what Aristotle does believe is that if you look at the behaviour of a virtuous person over their whole life then they will tend to avoid over-reacting or under-reacting (avoid excess or deficiency).[30] The easiest example to use to illustrate the Doctrine of the Mean is the virtue of courage. This means getting the balance right between fear and confidence in the face of danger: if you tend to feel and respond with too much fear then you are cowardly; if you tend to feel and respond with too much confidence then you are rash or foolhardy; if you get the balance right, are able to temper your fear, but not do anything stupid through over-confidence, then you are courageous.

■ **Figure 1.11 Courage (digging in for a fight) is midway between rashness (taking on a whole army) and cowardice (running away)**

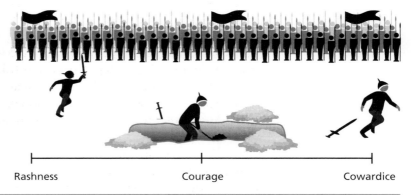

Rashness   Courage   Cowardice

experimenting with ideas

Write down what you would do when confronted by each of the following situations. Then answer the questions below.

1 At the end of your philosophy class you personally are asked to give a 10-minute presentation next week on some aspect of Aristotle.

2 After the class you have arranged to meet a friend, Alex, in a cafe. Jo, your partner, refuses to come along as Jo can't stand Alex. This means you have to walk to the cafe on your own. You walk down a deserted side street and you see a man lying face down on the pavement, his nose pressed into the concrete.

3 Your friend Alex is late arriving at the cafe and you nip to the toilet. On the floor of an empty cubicle you see a wallet.

4 You both order something to eat. Eventually Alex turns to you and asks why Jo is not there. 'Doesn't Jo like me?'

5 When you finally receive your bill you both think you have been overcharged by a small amount, but neither of you remembers exactly how much everything cost.

Now, for each situation, consider the following.

a) What would be an over-reaction or an excessive response?

b) What would be an under-reaction or a deficient response?

c) What would be, all things considered, the reaction that was the right or appropriate one, neither excessive nor deficient?

d) Which of the categories above (a, b or c) does your own reaction fall into?

Aristotle gives many other examples that fall under the heading 'excellence of character' (also translated as 'moral virtue'):[31]

- Bravery
- Justice
- Truthfulness
- Pride
- Ambition
- Temperance
- Friendliness
- Even-temperedness

So, for Aristotle, we become virtuous by becoming reflective, rational creatures and considering in each situation 'what is the right and appropriate thing to do here?' This means drawing on both moral and intellectual virtues. Now, deciding what is the right thing to do is a difficult judgement to make, but Aristotle believes that through moral education we are able to develop the wisdom that we need to make this judgement. Through hard experience, practice and by looking towards people we admire as role models, we can develop and fine-tune our decision-making capacities. Admittedly it is difficult to develop all these virtues, but Aristotle argues that it is only by doing so that we are able to live a properly good life and flourish.

Aristotle

> *The good for man is an activity of the soul in accordance with virtue.*[32]

We now have an understanding of our function, and of the virtues we must develop in order to function well. For both Plato and Aristotle this knowledge will enable us to reach the good, that which is in our true self-interest.

So what is 'the good'? What is the ultimate goal we are each striving for? We have seen that, according to Socrates, Plato and Aristotle, the good is *eudaimonia*, i.e. to be happy, to flourish and to lead the good life. We have also seen that Plato and Aristotle attacked hedonist theories of what is good, which located the good in the satisfaction of desire and seeking pleasure. But what is the difference between happiness in the sense of *eudaimonia* and happiness as a hedonist might conceive of it? The difference can be brought out through an anecdote about the football genius, George Best. He loved to tell the tale of how, in the early 1970s, a room-service waiter came into his hotel room one morning. The footballer was in bed with one of the most beautiful women in the world, surrounded by thousands of pounds in cash that he'd won at the casino, drinking champagne from the bottle. The waiter looked at him, shook his head and said 'George . . . where did it all go wrong?' And it was true, something had gone wrong. From being hailed as the best footballer in the world, George Best had turned into an alcoholic playboy – he failed to fulfil his real potential. In a hedonistic sense he was happy, but in Platonic and Aristotelian terms he was not happy – he was no longer flourishing, he was not fulfilling his function and he was not doing what was in his true self-interest.

For Plato we cannot understand what is truly good by studying this world, for example by analysing the actions of those we admire, or by looking to past heroes and how they behaved. Plato believed that this world was an imperfect copy of another more perfect world, and that everything in this world had a more perfect form in the other world. Plato refers to this other, perfect, world as the WORLD OF FORMS or ideals, and we grasp these perfect ideals with our intellect, not through our senses. Plato offers us a powerful analogy to help understand the difficulties of grasping the world of forms, as he describes the journey of a man from a world of shadows at the bottom of a cave – which represents the everyday physical world – up through the cave out into the blinding sunlight – which represents the world of forms. This journey, which we make through the tough and rigorous process of philosophising, eventually leads us to an understanding of the form of the Good.[33]

The world of forms

This world

■ **Figure 1.12**
Plato's simile of the cave describes the journey from this world (a world of shadows) to the world of forms where true knowledge lies

For Plato then, in order really to flourish, our reason needs first to be in control of our soul, and it must then turn us in the right direction: towards pursuing the right ends. We must use reason once again to make an intellectual journey towards understanding the form of the Good. Once you have grasped the Good, then for Plato it means you can never go wrong in life, or do wrong, such is the power of this moral compulsion. If people are unjust or behave immorally, then, for Plato, they are ignorant of what is good. This belief that 'no one willingly does wrong'[34] is one that Plato appears to have inherited from Socrates, but through his Theory of Forms Plato provides powerful metaphysical foundations for this claim.

Plato argues that it is through understanding the form of the Good that we are finally able to flourish. However, this means that only a tiny minority of humans, namely a rare breed of philosopher, can ever be virtuous and ever be truly happy. For Plato this has political implications: the best rulers of a country would be those who really know what is good for that country. Having such knowledge of the Good leads to an understanding of the true nature of justice, both in an individual person and in society as a whole. As we have just seen, for Plato, having knowledge of the Good also means being compelled to be good, to be just and to consider others in our actions. As it is only philosophers who have the necessary education and nature to reach this understanding of the Good, then it is philosophers who should rule the state.

We can now see more clearly how Plato responds to the claims of Thracymachus and Callicles, i.e. people who say that what is in our self-interest is to satisfy our desires, whatever the cost to others. Plato believes that people who adhere to any form of hedonism or immoralism, are actually damaging themselves and harming their self-interests. Such people are ignorant of the form of the Good; their reason is not in control; their soul is out of balance or harmony. For Plato what is in our real self-interest is developing a healthy and harmonious soul, and developing such a soul means becoming a just and moral person.

■ **Figure 1.13**
Plato's argument that morality is in our self-interest

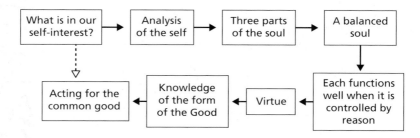

Unlike Plato, Aristotle did not believe in any mysterious world of forms and considered it to be an unrealistic and flawed philosophical view.[35] Aristotle argued that there was no single 'form' of the Good; rather there were as many 'goods' as there were individual creatures, objects and situations. The good for humans does not lie in some other mystical dimension, as with Plato, but lies within our grasp in the activities and projects of our daily lives. Moreover, the rejection of Plato's theory also meant that the Good did not have the same mystical compulsion for Aristotle as it did for Plato (remember that Plato believed that once we had grasped the Good then such is its power we could only do what was right). This led Aristotle to the rather more realistic view that we can know what is good, but fail to do it because we are weak-willed.

We have seen that, for Aristotle, what is good can be determined almost in a scientific way, by describing the kind of creature that we are, then identifying our function on the basis of this, then working out how we can excel at our function. We have been through these processes in the activity on page 24 and for Aristotle it was as simple as that. But, we may still ask, what on earth does being good in a functional sense have to do with living a good life, in the sense of striving for the Good and reaching *eudaimonia*?

Imagine you are a plant and you wish to flourish. Then, according to Aristotle's method, you must determine what your function is – let's say to grow, flower, reproduce, photosynthesise, etc. Now that you know what your function is as a plant, you follow Aristotle's advice by excelling (becoming virtuous) at your function. So you grow, flower, reproduce, etc. and become the brightest, bushiest plant in the forest. You are good (in a functional sense) at being a plant. But clearly you are also living the life of a good plant, you are striving for and reaching the Good: you are flourishing.

■ **Figure 1.14 The life of a good plant is identical to the good life for a plant**

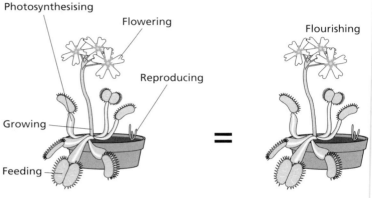

Photosynthesising
Flowering
Reproducing
Growing
Feeding

A life of a good plant

Flourishing

=

A good life for a plant

Aristotle held a teleological view of the universe: that is, he believed that everything, and in particular living things like us, have a purpose. Applying this teleological perspective to humans, we can identify our good by identifying what we were for and then becoming good at that. So being virtuous, which means being functionally good (a good human being), also means that we reach the 'good' and so lead a fulfilling and flourishing life. This means striving to develop myself as a good person, striving to shape my desires so that they are good for me, and striving to achieve those goals I set and the ambitions I have. This sounds much more plausible than Plato's view, and, more importantly, all of us are able to do this, not just philosophers (as Plato believed).

Aristotle's concept of virtue, and *eudaimonia*, sees our individual capacities (the parts of the soul) performing at their peak. So we become skilled thinkers in practical matters: we know what our goals should be, we can plan how we can achieve them and can execute that plan. We also become skilled intellectuals: we can theorise about the world, contemplate the nature of reality, and address difficult philosophical questions. Perhaps most significantly, we have emotional intelligence: we can temper our emotions, harness them to drive us towards our goal, and so make the right decision in each situation we encounter. Through developing our character in this way we become considerate, fair and reasonable people: Aristotle specifically lists as virtues friendliness, courage, truthfulness, justice, all of which drive other-regarding and moral behaviour. These moral virtues are also social virtues, and by flourishing we contribute to the flourishing and happiness of the whole community. If we fail to strive for virtue or excellence (and examples of such failure include habitual behaviour that we would label 'immoral', such as lying, killing and maliciousness) then we stand no chance of living a good life and flourishing. The hedonistic and immoralist recommendations of Callicles and Thracymachus are wrong-headed – there is no way, on Aristotle's account, that such behaviour can lead to happiness or be in our real self-interest.

However, this does not mean that pleasure and desire are rejected out of hand by Aristotle, as they seem to be by Plato (except a desire for understanding the form of the Good!). For Aristotle our desires need to be shaped so that they are for good (i.e. ultimately beneficial) things: this shaping has been described above as the development of the virtues. So accompanying the successful development of good habits are pleasures: the pleasures of doing something well, making the right decision, honing a skill, acting correctly – there are as many pleasures as there are virtues.

Despite their differences, however, Aristotle draws the same conclusion as Plato: that if we are virtuous then we will be both good (i.e. consider others) and live a good life (i.e. satisfy our self-interests and flourish).

■ **Figure 1.15**
Aristotle's argument that morality is in our self-interest

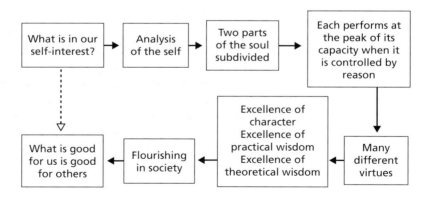

So Plato and Aristotle define self-interest, in the form of *eudaimonia*, in such a way that it is bound up with living what we would call a morally good life. Amongst the virtues are those that enable us to flourish within a community. So my happiness is inseparable from the people amongst whom I live, and it is inconceivable to Plato and Aristotle that I could be happy by harming that community and behaving immorally.

Criticisms of Plato's and Aristotle's theories

The most significant problem faced by both Plato and Aristotle is that their moral theories stand or fall on the success of their metaphysical theories.

Plato views the Good as a perfect ideal that exists, literally, in the world of forms. Knowledge of how to be truly virtuous is only possible once we have knowledge of the form of the Good. But, argues Plato, such is the power of the Good that once we have seen it then it is impossible for us to do wrong. Aristotle took issue with both Plato's claim that there is a single 'good' and with the claim that once you know what is good you can do no wrong. Aristotle is pointing out a META-ETHICAL problem with Plato's theory. Plato thought that the term 'good' refers to a single attribute that is possessed by all good things. For Aristotle there is nothing substantive in common between, say, a good doctor and a good football team; there is no single universal quality called 'good' which they both share. Instead Aristotle argues that everything is good insofar as it meets the standards or criteria for that particular area of expertise: so a good doctor meets all the standards of being a doctor, a good football team meets all the standards for playing football as a team, etc. We would probably agree with Aristotle that Plato was wrong in thinking that 'good' refers to some single ideal, existing in another realm.

If Plato is wrong on this point, and there is no form of the Good – no knowledge of what is absolutely and universally good – then his claims about virtue are damaged. Remember that Plato claimed that virtue is knowledge, and that knowing the form of the Good means knowing what is good for us, what is good for our community, and being unable to do anything other than what is good. If there is no such universal Good, then there is no such knowledge and Plato needs to seek elsewhere for an account of virtue.

Aristotle's theory, which does not hinge on the form of the Good, is not damaged by this particular criticism. But like Plato, Aristotle's ethics is vulnerable to criticism of his metaphysical assumptions, namely his teleological view of the universe. We know that Aristotle thought that everything had a function (everything was 'for' something), including humans. But Aristotle did not believe in a being who created the universe and created each thing inside the universe with a function in mind. For a religious philosopher such as St Thomas Aquinas (1224–1274) adopting Aristotle's view made sense as Aquinas believed that God had designed the world and given everything, including human beings, a purpose or function. However, for people who don't believe in God as a designer, or in God at all, it is harder to accept Aristotle's theory as a plausible one. If there is no Designer of the world then we can't base our ethical theory on what humans are 'for' or what our function is – because we simply don't have one. It might still be true, however, that thinking of our lives in Aristotelian terms (striving to flourish by excelling in what we do) does bring us happiness, does make us virtuous and does make us behave morally. But this wouldn't be because we were being 'good humans' in the functional sense that Aristotle understood.

Putting it another way, we might say that both Plato and Aristotle believe there is an objective answer to the question 'what is good for us – what is in our real self-interest?' For Plato this objective answer is determined by an understanding of the world of forms, in particular the form of the Good; for Aristotle it is determined by an understanding of human nature and function. But if there is no absolute Good, and no 'natural' function for humans then it becomes harder to say that there is an absolute 'good' that is really good for us and is in our real self-interest. Perhaps our self-interests are, in a Hobbesian way, determined subjectively and individually by each of us – depending on our own pleasures, pains, desires, hopes, wishes, etc.

A further criticism arises from the link that ancient Greek philosophers make between self-interest and morality – this connection sits uncomfortably with many of our ethical intuitions. Aristotle, in particular, seems to be interested in aspects of our character that have no connection with what we would consider 'moral' characteristics (ones that lead to actions that help others, prevent harm to others, bring positive benefits to others). Among the virtues he lists, and views as self-evidently valuable, are traits like practical wisdom, wittiness, proper pride, proper ambition – characteristics which might benefit the person who possesses them, but which have no obvious impact on helping other people. In the next section we look in detail at a moral theory which dismisses any attempt to link self-interest and morality.

Following from this is a criticism that has been frequently made of the supporters of 'virtue ethics' (including Aristotle and Aquinas), namely that they are simply describing the values of their social class and age, and their lists of virtues are the preferred characteristics of that class and age. There just don't seem to be any accepted criteria for determining what is a genuine virtue and what isn't. In fact it seems as if deciding what is a virtue, such as friendliness, or a vice, such as rudeness, is a matter of personal opinion, perhaps a highly informed one (Aristotle was one of the most widely read and travelled intellects of his age) but an opinion nevertheless.

Neither of these criticisms is fatal to virtue ethics. Plato and Aristotle have provided reasons for their judgements as to whether a particular character trait is a virtue or a vice. Aristotle assessed character traits according to whether they are required in order to flourish, live well and reach *eudaimonia*. Whether or not we agree with the reasons given depends in part on whether we buy into the rest of the theory. But in practical terms most of us do agree on what kinds of characteristics we would like to see in ourselves, our neighbours and colleagues, our children and fellow citizens: and the key virtues identified by both Plato and Aristotle would lead to a better, and more moral, community. If people were just, then we would all be treated more fairly; if people were more temperate, then we would have less to fear from their indulgence in drink, pleasure, violence, etc.; if people were more courageous, then we could trust in our neighbours to stand up and challenge the things we all feared; and if people we were wiser, then we would all benefit from their clearer insights and better decision making.

Morality as overcoming self-interest

We have looked at two answers to the question 'why should I be moral?', both of which locate the motive to behave morally in our self-interest. The first appeals to our self-interest by arguing that we would each be better off if we gave up the pursuit of some of our selfish goals, those which harm others, by signing up to a social contract which enforces moral behaviour and by agreeing to let some authority police this contract. The second response tried to show that moral behaviour is in our real self-interest, not as a means but as an integral part of what enables us to flourish and live the good life. In this section we examine a third response: it is not self-interest, but something else, which motivates us to be moral. Much of this section examines Immanuel Kant's theory which states that our motive for behaving morally is a stand-alone motive – that of duty, or as Kant puts it: 'the moral law within'.

Kant

Two things fill the mind with ever new and increasing admiration and awe, the oftener and more steadily we reflect on them: the starry heavens above and the moral law within.[36]

At the end of this section we briefly examine a theory, put forward by David Hume (1711–77), that is the virtual opposite of Kant's. Hume, like Kant, believes that the source of moral motivation is not located in self-interest. However, unlike Kant, Hume believes that our natural dispositions and feelings are the true source of moral behaviour.

Immanuel Kant

Immanuel Kant (1724–1804) was writing during a period of intense intellectual activity in Europe, a period that became known as the ENLIGHTENMENT. Thinkers of this 'age of reason' were beginning to liberate themselves from the restrictive ties to the Church that had characterised most of the Middle Ages, and which had still been felt by the father of modern philosophy, René Descartes (1591–1650). There was a confidence in human reason, boosted by the growing successes of 'natural philosophy' (what we now call science) in explaining the physical laws of the universe. Religious authority could no longer determine what people ought to think about the nature of the universe nor about what is right or wrong. Human beings, it appeared to many, had come of age and were sufficiently 'enlightened' to realise that they had to discover their values for themselves rather than expect them to be delivered by a higher power.

Kant was sceptical of the optimistic claims made by some 'rationalist' philosophers about the extent to which human reason alone could grasp truths about the universe. He was also critical of the more pessimistic claims of the Scottish philosopher David Hume that human reason could tell us nothing very interesting about the universe at all. Kant's project was to offer a 'critique' of reason: sketching its limits while showing that human reason could arrive at some truths about the universe after all. (See pages 320–38, 'Conceptual schemes', for more on Kant's project.) Part of this critique extended to practical reason, i.e. the application of reason to the question 'how should we live?' Kant explained his ethical theory in two important works, *Groundwork for the Metaphysic of Morals* (1785) and the longer *Critique of Practical Reason* (1787).

Good will, not self-interest, is the source of moral action

Kant's ethical theory is known as a DEONTOLOGICAL theory, in that he believes a moral action is one which we are duty-bound to perform, and an action is only genuinely moral if it is prompted by a recognition of our duty. ('Deon' is an ancient Greek term which carries the sense of 'obligation' or

■ **Figure 1.16 *The problem with self-interest*[37]**

'duty'). Fundamental to Kant's approach is the conviction that morality is absolute and that moral judgements are objective and so apply to all people equally. However, it is clear that self-interested motives are subjective. They are particular to the individual, and so often in conflict with the interests of others. As Calvin discovers in Bill Watterson's cartoon above, a Calliclesean approach to morality ('might is right', 'the end justifies the means', ethics is for losers) is fine when you're the only one adhering to these guidelines, but very annoying when others start doing so too. Genuinely moral motives on the other hand are objective and universal insofar as they apply to all individuals no matter what differences in personal circumstances, character, desires, preferences, etc.

Thus, to the extent that I act for any other reason, for example out of prudence, self-interest, or even from having a compassionate disposition (or virtue), the act is not strictly a *moral* one. Kant argues that, because people have different emotional reactions, these reactions cannot be significant in evaluating the moral worth of an act. For a rational determination of our duties will be impartial and so will determine the same duties for everyone.

What this implies is that if I behave in a way which we

would normally recognise as morally praiseworthy – for example, I regularly donate to charity – and if I do so simply because it has become a habit, or because I feel like it, or because I hope that if I'm ever in trouble someone will be similarly generous, then this action is not properly speaking a *moral* act. Moreover, according to Kant, someone who, through the use of dispassionate reason, recognises her duty to help others in distress even though she has no compassion for her fellow human beings, is more praiseworthy than someone who would have helped others whether it were his duty or not, because of a compassion for others. For the former must act, as it were, against the grain of her inclinations, while the latter is slavishly led by his emotions.

There are occasions when prudence and duty coincide: in other words where the same action is required both by what we morally ought to do and by what it is in our self-interests to do. Kant gives the example of a shopkeeper who has a fixed price for each of the goods in his shop, even when he could get away with ripping off naïve customers by overcharging them.

Kant

Thus people are served honestly; but this is not nearly enough to justify us in believing that the shopkeeper has acted in this way from duty or from principles of fair dealing; his interest required him to do so . . . the action was done neither from duty nor from immediate inclination, but solely from purposes of self-interest.[38]

For Hobbes this would be an example of how being moral is in our self-interest (customers keep coming back). However, Kant would claim this is not really moral at all – it is the mere appearance of morality: it is not what we do that makes an action a moral one, but the grounds on which we do it. In the case of the honest shopkeeper the only thing that could make his honest action a moral action is that he was motivated solely by duty (Figure 1.17).

The moral worth of an action does not depend upon the results expected from it.[39]

Kant

So far as Kant is concerned, it is our motive which determines the moral worth of an act. The genuinely moral motive for action, i.e. a recognition of our duty, is what Kant terms the 'good will'. A good will is the only motive which is intrinsically or unconditionally good. That is to say, an act which proceeds from the good will is good in itself and not good because of its consequences.

■ **Figure 1.17**

Honest John charges everyone the same because it's good for his business. Dutiful Dave charges everyone the same because it's his duty. According to Kant only Dave is acting morally.

Our duties, or the judgements of the good will, are determined by reason alone. For Kant's goal is to show that we should act morally to the extent that we are rational, i.e. according to reason alone and not on the basis of feelings. This, as we have seen, means that our moral obligations are not in any way determined by our SYMPATHY for others, or our inclinations to flourish, to fulfil our desires or any other purely psychological motive. For these types of motive only have value *conditionally* and not for their own sake. Moreover, for Kant, if we are swayed in our actions by emotions then we are not acting freely. If we submit to the urgings of our feelings we are like slaves, simply doing the bidding of forces outside our control. And being a rational being means being able to deliberate autonomously about how to act, and not – as an animal does – simply follow our primitive impulses. Truly to be free, therefore, means acting purely according to the dictates of reason. To act out of a recognition of duty, motivated by the good will, is to exercise our freedom. (See the discussion of 'What is a person?' on page 199.)

ACTIVITY   Which of the following actions, if any, are done from good will alone (and without a self-interested motive)?

1 Josie saves someone from drowning in order to impress the gorgeous lifeguard whom she's been flirting with all summer.
2 Every Saturday Colin works four hours in his local Youth Centre. He doesn't really enjoy it but feels that he should put something back into society.

3 In the weeks running up to his birthday Marlon always makes an extra special effort helping out his parents, checking they're okay and whether they need anything, etc.

4 Mel decides that eating one more triple-choc cookie will make her sick, and so she puts the rest of the biscuits she 'borrowed' from her flatmate back into his cupboard.

5 Leonie gives Friends of the Earth £1 because she loves watching the coins whirl round and round the hole before falling into the charity box.

6 Samsia notices a large, unaccompanied rucksack by the door of a train, and asks the crowded carriage who the owner of it is.

7 Jane keeps her promise to show off her latest dance moves to her philosophy class, despite just having been promoted to Head of Department.`

Categorical and hypothetical imperatives

Kant believes that morality is experienced as a command or 'imperative'; in other words it tells us what we *ought* to do. An imperative is an inner 'tug' on our will, a compulsion to act in one way rather than another. But there are two different types of imperative, which is to say, two distinct senses of the term 'ought':

All imperatives command either hypothetically or categorically.[40]

Kant

One kind of 'ought' is a conditional, or (in Kant's terminology) a HYPOTHETICAL IMPERATIVE. An example of this use might be 'If you want your pudding, then you ought to eat your greens.' Note that this kind of 'ought' depends upon your having a certain goal or desire, namely getting some pudding. The first part of the statement gives us the condition; the second part tells us what to do to meet this condition. In other words, the ought is dependent or conditional upon the existence of a certain desire. All such conditional (hypothetical) imperatives will involve an 'if' at the beginning as not everyone will want to follow the imperative. So if you want X then you ought to do Y. For example if you don't want any pudding, then there is no earthly reason why you ought to eat your greens. Many of the imperatives we encounter in life are based on this type of self-interested, or prudential, reasoning: first of all we identify things that we think are in our self-interest (e.g. satisfying our desire for eating something sweet, tasty and crunchy), then we figure out what we must do in order to get this thing (eating something green, tasteless and chewy).

Children are constantly being given hypothetical imperatives of this sort, as they have to learn what is good for them, or at least what adults think is good for them. To assist in this socialisation, parents will often use fairy stories and fables which speak of disobedient boys and girls not doing what they are told and suffering the consequences – traditionally this seems to involve being eaten by a wolf. A particularly terrifying set of bedtime hypothetical imperatives (aimed at satirising the whole morality tale genre, but terrifying nonetheless) can be found in the nineteenth-century tales of *Struwwelpeter*, translated usually as 'Shockheaded Peter', because of the story of the monstrous freak, Peter, who refused to comb his hair![41] Here children find that if they don't want their thumbs chopped off by the psychotic Scissor-man then they ought not to suck them. They also discover that if they don't want to drown in the canal, then they ought not to walk around gazing at the sky. Another hypothetical imperative is found in the story of 'Augustus who would not have any soup'; and, as you might have guessed, the clear moral here is that if you don't want to die of starvation then you ought to eat up all your soup.

However, Kant isn't interested in this sort of conditional or hypothetical imperative. The imperatives that Kant thinks are central to morality are ones that are *not* dependent on any set of conditions. These types of oughts are unconditional and absolute, or (in Kant's terminology), CATEGORICAL IMPERATIVES. An example might be 'You ought to respect your mother and father.' Note that this use is not dependent on any goals or aims you may have – the 'if you want X' bit of the imperative disappears, leaving only 'you ought to do Y'. These sorts of imperatives tell us that we have a certain obligation or duty regardless of the circumstances. This is what is meant by saying they are unconditional or categorical. And it is this sort of ought which Kant regards as the only genuinely *moral* ought.

ACTIVITY Read the following commands and answer the questions below.

a) I should do more sit-ups.
b) I ought to be more loyal to my friends.
c) I should pay more attention to my charming philosophy teacher.
d) I ought to buy flowers and grapes for my sick aunt.
e) I ought to start revising soon.
f) I ought to give more money to Children In Need.
g) I shouldn't lie as much as I do.
h) I ought not to kick my little brother on the shins.
i) I should get up earlier.
j) I should stop eating tuna fish.

1 Which commands are in the interests purely of my self?

2 Which commands are hypothetical imperatives? (For example, 'I should do more sit-ups' is a conditional or hypothetical imperative.)

3 For those you have identified as hypothetical imperatives, state the conditions they are dependent upon. (For example, 'I should do more sit-ups' could have the condition 'if I want to get rid of all this flab'.)

Using your intuition

4 Which commands are moral commands?

5 Which commands are unconditional or categorical imperatives?

6 What connection, if any, is there between the answers you gave for 1 and 3, and 4 and 5?

Using the 'categorical imperative' to determine our duties

We have now seen the central idea behind Kant's approach to ethics, namely that in moral terms we are bound by categorical imperatives – these are our duties.

Kant

An action done from duty has its moral worth, not in the purpose to be obtained by it, but in the maxim according with which it is decided upon.[42]

Kant suggests that we can think of there being a general principle of action, or a MAXIM, underlying the intention to perform any act. This is a rule of conduct, that is to say a reason why someone elects to act in a certain way or an expression of their motive to so act. But, to be moral, an act must have the appropriate maxim underlying it, namely (as we have seen) one which expresses our duty to perform the act. So my actions to help the homeless or to obey my parents, i.e. to be moral, must be grounded in a maxim such as 'Always help others (just because it is your duty)', or 'Always respect your father and mother (just because it is your duty)', and not in a conditional one such as 'Always respect your father and mother (if you want your inheritance money)'.

Since categorical imperatives are unconditionally binding, they are equally applicable to all people because of their status as 'rational beings', which is to say beings which can freely deliberate about their actions. They must, in other words, be universal. It follows from this that the basic categorical imperative is that:

Kant

I should never act in such a way that I could not will that my maxim should be a universal law.[43]

In other words we must always act in accordance with a maxim which is binding for everyone. This is the principle of UNIVERSALISABILITY, a version of the religious GOLDEN RULE to treat others as you would like them to treat you.[44] This principle contrasts starkly with the view put forward by Calvin (Figure 1.7 above) who wants one rule for himself ('the ends justify the means') but does not want everyone else to follow this rule. For Kant you cannot make an exception of your own case when making moral judgements and so whenever we make a judgement about a particular immoral act we implicitly commit ourselves to saying that a similar act would be wrong in a similar situation. For example, if I argued today that it is wrong for me to eat beef it suggests (all things being equal) that it would also be wrong tomorrow. It also suggests that it would be wrong for anyone else to eat beef. Put the other way around, if I claim that it is wrong to eat beef today but that it is not wrong tomorrow, I am committed to there being some morally relevant difference between today and tomorrow. Or, if I argue that it is wrong for me but not for you, then I am committed to finding some relevant difference between my situation and yours. Note that the principle of universalisability implies that any moral reasoning must involve espousing rules or principles which bind us all.

Kant believes that the categorical imperative can help us to determine what these principles are. It will allow us to distinguish truly moral maxims from amoral or immoral ones. In one illustration Kant supposes that someone (let's call him Tony) makes a promise but is ready to break it if this suits his purposes. Tony's maxim then may be expressed thus: 'When it suits my purposes I will make promises, intending also to break them if this suits my purposes.' But Tony cannot consistently will this maxim to be universally acted on, says Kant.

Kant

Could I say to myself that everyone makes a false promise when he is in difficulty from which he otherwise cannot escape? I immediately see that I could will the lie but not a universal law to lie. For with such a law [i.e. with such a maxim universally acted on] there would be no promises at all. . . Thus my maxim would necessarily destroy itself as soon as it was made a universal law.[45]

What Kant means by a maxim *destroying itself* is that it would entail a contradiction or inconsistency. Such maxims cannot be moral. By contrast the maxim underlying a moral duty is one that can be made universal *without* any inconsistency. For example, Tony was following the maxim 'I can break promises when it suits me'; but what happens if everyone follows this maxim? Kant would argue that if Tony's maxim were universalised then the very institution of promise-making would collapse, since there would be no genuine promises at all. The possibility of making promises depends on there being some general agreement about what making promises involves, and if there is no such agreement then I cannot make or break them. So Tony's maxim is self-defeating; it 'destroys itself' since universalising it would undermine the possibility of making promises which the maxim presupposes. For this reason, according to Kant, we can recognise that this maxim is not moral and cannot be a duty.

Kant offers four illustrations of the types of duty that the categorical imperative entails.[46] The types of duty that Kant discusses are duties to ourselves and duties to others; and within each of these we find there are perfect duties (ones which have no exceptions) and imperfect duties (ones which may admit of exceptions). Each of the following examples shows how a particular maxim underpinning an action can (or cannot) be universalised, thus demonstrating whether or not that maxim is a duty.

1 *Perfect duty to ourselves.* Someone miserable is contemplating committing suicide, and Kant shows how the categorical imperative entails that the person has a duty not to commit suicide (no matter how miserable they are).

2 *Perfect duty to others.* Someone wants to borrow money on the promise that they'll pay it back, but they know that they will never be able to afford to pay it back within the agreed time limit of the loan. We have already seen that Kant believes the categorical imperative to show that making false promises cannot be universalised; it cannot be a duty and is morally wrong.

3 *Imperfect duty to ourselves.* Someone with natural talents lets them go to waste because they are lazy. Here Kant uses the categorical imperative to show that it is wrong for us to waste our natural talents – we must at least choose to develop some of them (this is why it is an imperfect duty, because we can choose to let some of our talents rust).

4 *Imperfect duty to others.* Someone who is doing pretty well in life is considering helping out other people. Kant shows that although it is possible to universalise the maxim '*don't* help others', it is not possible to 'will' this to happen – because we would not want to be in a situation where we need assistance and yet no one wants to help us.

Kant also expresses the categorical imperative in other ways. One version states that others should be treated as *ends* in themselves and never as *means* to an end.[47] This entails that you should never simply use other people to further your own goals. Rather you ought always to respect other people's desires and goals. This is because a rational being is not just valued as a means to some end. Rather they are valued for their own sake, or unconditionally. The Realm of Ends is an ideal community that Kant imagines in which everyone would treat one another as 'ends in themselves', in other words with respect for them as persons.

Using only Kant's categorical imperative you must decide what would be the right course of action in each of the following situations:
i) Determine what the maxim is underpinning each course of action.
ii) Determine whether it is possible to universalise this maxim without contradiction or inconsistency.
iii) Work out which maxims can and can't be universalised.

1 You promise to take your nephew (Little Johnny) to the park to play on Saturday. But on Wednesday your friend calls up with two tickets for a Cup Final/top West End musical/Richard Dawkins lecture. Little Johnny is away camping until Saturday morning.
a) Do you break your promise?
b) Do you keep your promise?

2 You are helping out your Auntie by taking her dog, Rooney, for a walk to the newsagents. Suddenly the dog's fur catches fire, from the flick of someone's cigarette butt. Rooney is in pain, but there is no water available, only two pints of milk on No. 32's doorstep.
a) Do you steal the milk?
b) Do you leave the milk?

3 Your friend who recently developed an eating disorder asks you if her bottom looks lumpy in her new tight trousers. It does.
a) Do you lie?
b) Do you tell the truth?

4 You are standing on the roof of a building, hauling a piano up to the third floor. Suddenly you hear gunshots. A man directly below the piano is shooting at a passing parade of local dignitaries.
a) Do you drop the piano and kill him?
b) Do you let him carry on shooting?

5 With your partner away working a two-year stint on an oil rig, your very attractive yet terminally ill neighbour confesses undying love for you and asks for one romantic night together before the illness finally takes its toll. You cannot contact your partner.
a) Are you unfaithful?
b) Do you remain faithful?

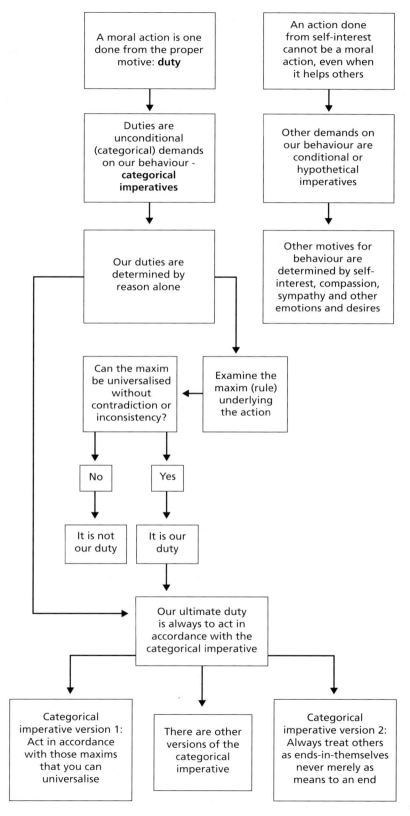

Some criticisms of Kant's theory

■ What makes an act a moral act?

A major difficulty for Kant's theory is that it seems that not every universal maxim is a moral one. It could be trivial or amoral. And this shows that not every maxim that passes his test of universalisability is a duty. The problem is that Kant does not tell us precisely how we are to distinguish moral duties from absurd imperatives, for surely there is nothing to stop me from universalising the maxim 'never step on the cracks in the pavement'. It is certainly not *inconsistent* to will that everyone do so. Similarly, it is not clear how Kant could distinguish moral obligations from social etiquette. I could easily will that everyone eat with a knife and fork and be outraged at the thought that some adults use their hands or just spoons. It is not hard to imagine my consistently regarding bad table manners as the height of depravity, for here there is no contradiction. But in so doing surely I would betray nothing more than my own bigotry. There are other, apparently innocent, examples of maxims which cannot be universalised and hence, on Kant's account, must be morally wrong. For example, 'using contraception when having sex' is a maxim that someone might have if they don't want children. But it cannot be universalised, because there would soon be no human species, and hence it appears to be morally wrong. This will be counter-intuitive many, and so may indicate that something is problematic within Kant's theory. (Of course, a Catholic might embrace the consequence and insist that contraception is indeed morally wrong precisely because it cannot be universalised.)

Moreover it is also not clear that Kant's principle rules out certain *immoral* maxims, such as the maxim of never helping anyone. For surely there is nothing inconsistent with my willing this to be acted on by everyone. It may be that Kant can defend himself against this criticism by pointing to one of the alternative formulations of the categorical imperative, the one that says we should treat people as ends in themselves, and never solely as a means to an end. So, using this version of the categorical imperative, Kant might argue that never helping anyone at all involves treating others as means (because we all need a community in which to grow, be educated and survive) and not as ends in themselves (i.e. as people who have needs just like us).

■ It doesn't fit with our intuitions

There are aspects of Kant's theory that fall clearly outside of our 'moral intuitions', i.e. with what we are pre-theoretically inclined to say. Kant uses Plato's example from the *Republic* of the madman who wants to reclaim a lent weapon in order to show that we have a duty not to lie, no matter what the circumstances.[48] So imagine you've borrowed an axe from an acquaintance to chop down a tree, and one night he knocks on your door, looking and sounding like he wants to murder someone, and he demands his axe back. Plato uses this example to show that an account of morality which requires us to return the axe in these circumstances must be a flawed account. Kant, however, drawing on a similar example (although in his example the madman already has the axe and simply wants to know whether the intended victim is in your house), thinks that we still have a duty to tell the truth to the madman, even though we suspect this will lead to a murder. Plato seems to be right here, and Kant's use of the example brings out a problematic inflexibility in his position.

■ It doesn't tell us how to act

A related objection is that Kant's approach is impractical as it provides no concrete advice on how to behave. While providing a framework, it provides no substantive help in making moral decisions when we are faced with moral dilemmas. This is particularly telling when Kant comes to apply the categorical imperative to everyday life. The categorical imperative goes some way in this direction but if we encounter conflicts between different duties it appears there is no way for us to choose. Jean-Paul Sartre criticises Kant by using an example from his own experience during the Nazi occupation of France (*Existentialism and Humanism*, Methuen, p. 35). Here a young man is torn between his duty to his country, which impelled him to join the resistance and which would probably lead to his death, and his duty to care for his mother, who had already lost her other sons to the war. Kant's ethical theory is of no use in helping him to resolve this conflict since both imperatives are categorical and yet they pull in different directions. Kant seems to have believed that genuine moral dilemmas of this sort could not occur, but the reality of our everyday experience shows that this is not the case.

W.D. Ross (1877–1971) tries to address the problems levelled at Kant's deontological theory that it is counter-intuitive and impractical.[49] Ross believes that through a process of experience and intuition we build up a collection of moral principles: rules concerning what's right and what's wrong. Ross calls these principles '*prima facie* duties' and they include all the usual suspects: beneficence (the obligation to promote the welfare of others), non-malevolence (the obligation not to harm others), justice, promise-keeping, honesty, etc. What is important is that these duties cannot be drawn from one single principle and Ross recognises all these *prima facie* duties as basic and irreducible. Sometimes, as we have seen, we are confronted with conflicting duties. We use the term 'moral dilemma' to refer to those real-life situations in which we do face a conflict of duty, where two duties seem to have equal weight and yet point in opposite directions (e.g. in our on-going confrontation with the mad axe murderer, we have a duty to be honest, but also a duty to prevent harm to others). The problem for Kant was that he believed our duties are absolute, so we are compelled to obey the command of each duty; where these duties conflict, Kant provides no procedure for resolving this conflict. But for Ross it is crucial that *prima facie* duties are not absolute; this is why he calls them *prima facie* (a Latin term which means roughly 'at first sight'). *Prima facie* duties are the ragbag of obligations that we know from experience are usually right. On Ross's account of duties, when we are faced with a moral dilemma in which these *prima facie* duties clash we don't have the problems that Kant faced, since these duties are not absolute: we simply have to decide for ourselves which duty should be adhered to, and which placed to one side. In the case of the mad axe murder, our actual duty will probably be our duty not to harm others, and so it would be justifiable to lie to him. Treating our moral principles in this way (as rough and ready, but which can be prioritised according to the individual situation) resolves the problem of conflicting duties that Kant faced.

experimenting with ideas

The mad axe murderer is back again, and this time he's really mad. He has brought video evidence that he lent you his axe and on the same tape you can clearly hear that you promised to give him the axe back again. However, you know that he hasn't been taking his medication recently and that his old desire to 'kill them all' is resurfacing.

What would be the relevant *prima facie* duties in this situation? Well, we know that we ought to 1) keep our promises and 2) tell the truth, but we also know that 3) we have a duty not to harm others. So there are three *prima facie* duties involved. According to Ross, intuition tells us that our actual duty in this case would be 'not to harm others', so we would break our promise to the axe murderer (we wouldn't give him his axe back) and we'd also probably lie to him about where the axe was.

Now refer back to the activity on page 58 above. (You promise to take your nephew to the park etc.). Read through the situations. Then, for each situation carry out the following tasks:

a) Write down the relevant *prima facie* duties (these may well be the two duties that apparently conflict, but you might think of others too).

b) Which of these *prima facie* duties does your moral intuition tell you is your actual duty in this situation? In other words which moral principle would be the right one to follow in this situation?

■ It doesn't acknowledge the role of emotion

A further objection to Kant is that he encourages a cold and calculative approach to ethics by demanding that we put aside our feelings for the fellow suffering of others. In fact Kant's claim that emotions are irrelevant, and that the only appropriate motive for a moral action is a sense of duty, seems to be at odds with our intuition that certain emotions have a moral dimension, such as guilt and sympathy, or pride and jealousy. Don't we regard the possession of such emotions itself as morally praise- or blame-worthy?

Moreover we may doubt whether it is even possible for us to set aside our self-interest and the concerns and desires that make us individuals, and to think of ourselves, as Kant wants us to, as purely rational autonomous beings engaged in universal law-making. Bernard Williams argues that the impartial position that Kant wishes us to adopt may be possible for factual considerations, but not for practical, moral deliberations.[50] For example, if I ask 'I wonder whether strontium is a metal?' it is possible to remove the personal 'I' from this question, and seek an answer that is independent of my own perspective on the world. This kind of deliberation means that it is possible for anyone to take up my question and be given the same answer; there is what Williams calls a 'unity of interest' in the answer. This is because deliberation about facts is not essentially personal, but is an attempt to reach an impersonal position (where we all agree that these are the facts). In contrast, Williams maintains that practical deliberation is essentially personal and it does make a difference whether it is me, or someone else (for example, the madman's mother, his intended victim, the victim's life insurer or the madman himself) asking the question 'Should I give this man his axe back?' We cannot and should not strive for the same impersonal position as in the factual case. With moral deliberations there is no longer a 'unity of interest', and a different person, with a different set of desires and interests, who is now standing in my shoes, might seek a different answer. The position from which we ask this practical question is a personal position, and the answer will affect us very much. Williams argues that Kant is wrong and that we cannot adopt an impersonal perspective (the perspective of the categorical imperative), because by doing so we lose our place in the world, our interests and any sense of self.

63

David Hume and sympathy

Hume

Sympathy is the chief source of moral distinctions.[51]

Like Kant, David Hume (1711–76) rejects self-interest as the source of moral action. But unlike Kant, Hume views our emotions – our natural sympathy for others – as the real origin of morality. Because of its emphasis on the development of certain character traits, David Hume's moral theory is more in line with the agent-centred virtue ethics than with the act-centred approach of Kant. As with Plato and Aristotle, Hume is interested in the virtues (or dispositions) of a good person, and what the origins of moral virtue are. His answer to the question 'why should we be moral?' is one based on our natural sympathy, which gives most of us a fundamental desire to *be* moral.

Hume's most famous book on morality, *Enquiry Concerning The Principles Of Morals* (1752), is more of an investigation into origins of moral judgements than a normative theory guiding how we should act. Hume's main concern throughout the *Enquiry* is to discover the principle underlying morality; in particular he wishes to understand on what basis we call some character traits 'virtuous' and other traits 'vicious'.

Hume on the place of reason in ethics

Before writing the *Enquiry*, Hume had laid out his philosophical stall very clearly in his *Treatise of Human Nature* (1752). This work establishes his EMPIRICIST credentials (see Chapter 4) but it also sets out his beliefs about the source of morality. Hume, a famous sceptic, was sceptical about the role that reason had in informing our moral decisions and would have rejected Kant's austere account of the rational origins of morality. Reason can be seen to support morality in two ways. First, 'practical' reason helps us to get what we want (as, for example, when you plan your examination revision), so we use practical reason to select the *means* towards our ends (our goals). Secondly, reason at a more abstract and contemplative level enables us to find out what our *goals* should be (for example, what we need in order to flourish). So we can reason about ends as well as the means to those ends. However, Hume puts forward a convincing case that we cannot reason about ends, about the things we want, or what our goals are. We can only reason about means. This is because our ends, the things we want, are determined by our 'passions', which are non-rational motivators that we have no control over. For Hume it's a truth about human psychology that we begin with our passions (our wants and desires) and use reason to work out how to satisfy these passions. But we cannot work the other way round, i.e. we cannot use reason to shape our wants and desires; that's just not how our minds work. Two famous passages from the *Treatise* sum up Hume's position:

Hume

> *Reason is . . . the slave of the passions and can never pretend to any other office than to serve and obey them.*[52]
>
> *'Tis not contrary to reason to prefer the destruction of the whole world to the scratching of my finger.*[53]

The latter quote is particularly shocking, and not at all what we'd expect to hear from a moral philosopher.[54] But all Hume is saying is that it is possible for my preferences to be geared towards my own interests rather than towards the interests of the rest of the world. This is not to say that these desires are a good thing – only that they are not *irrational*, because according to Hume our preferences or desires come first and they cannot be derived from any sort of reasoning, such as a calculation of what would be the most beneficial outcome.

So where does Hume's conclusion leave us? The ethical theories we have examined up to now provide us with different motivating reasons to be moral: for Hobbes we are motivated to agree to a social contract so that we might ultimately benefit; for Plato and Aristotle we are motivated to develop our moral virtues so that we would benefit; for Kant we are motivated to do our duty because it is rational to do so. But, if Hume is right, and reason cannot motivate us to be moral, then how can we be moral and why should we be moral?

Moral motivation lies in our natural sympathy

In contrast to the rational approach of the ancient Greeks, Hobbes and Kant, Hume believes there to be a non-rational source of morality. Because of his claims about the limits of reason as a motivator, Hume cannot link virtues to knowledge, like Plato, nor can he tie them strictly to function and excellence, like Aristotle and Aquinas. For Hume we must build up our moral theory on the basis of the preferences and natural dispositions that human beings happen to hold in common, and particularly on those qualities that we find in people that we approve of.

Hume

Take any action allowed to be vicious: wilful murder for instance. Examine it in all lights and see if you can find that matter of fact or real existence, which you call vice . . . In whichever way you take it, you find only certain passions, motives, volitions and thoughts . . . Here is a matter of fact, but it is the object of feeling, not of reason. It lies in yourself, not in the object.[55]

Hume argues that when we make a moral judgement we are not talking about some feature of the world 'out there' that is good or right or virtuous. If we think carefully about the moral judgements we make then we discover that they are derived only from a feeling inside us. When someone does something kind, or generous or courageous, we have a general feeling of approval for such behaviour. So, for Hume, morality isn't really a (rational) judgement at all; it's more of a gut feeling, or, as Hume says, a 'perception in the mind' rather than a 'quality in the object': morality is in me, not 'out there'.

In the *Enquiry* Hume continues his investigation into ethics by seeking to discover the origins and basis of morality. For Hume, morality is simply based on our (and everyone else's) reactions to people's behaviour, and it is these reactions that tell us whether someone is virtuous or not. Does this make morality a matter of personal opinion? Not according to Hume, because he believes that in actual fact our moral reactions are all pretty similar, that we can all recognise virtuous actions when we see them, and that we have a common concern for other people. This conformity of response results from the natural disposition that each of us has to feel sympathy for one another. Sympathy lies at the heart of Hume's moral philosophy; he thinks of it as a kind of moral trigger that all of us (except perhaps psychopaths) possess.

Hume

Would any man, who is walking along, tread as willingly on another's gouty toes, whom he has no quarrel with, as on the hard flint and pavement?[56]

Sympathy is the connection we have with other people, and our appreciation of their pains and pleasures. Our natural disposition for sympathy motivates us to be moral, and makes it difficult for us to treat people as mere objects or as means. Hume is right, most of us just couldn't walk on someone lying on the ground as if they were another bit of pavement.

However, he does recognise that our sympathy diminishes in proportion to the (emotional and physical) distance to us of the people concerned. So we may feel less concerned about an earthquake that happened thousands of miles away than about the car accident a friend was in. And Hume also recognises that sympathy competes with self-interest (another natural disposition that we all share) as a motivator for action, although, for Hume, sympathy overcomes self-interest in most cases.

This tension between self-interest (or 'self-love' as Hume called it) and sympathy is brought out in Hume's discussion of the 'sensible knave' in the concluding paragraphs of the *Enquiry*. A knave is someone who is a bit of a scoundrel, a cheat who will try to get away with whatever he can. The sensible knave accepts, for example, that 'honesty is the best policy' but there are many exceptions and the knave, who is motivated purely by self-interest, will take advantage of all those exceptions in order to get what they want. In Laclos' scandalous novel of sexual intrigue, *Dangerous Liaisons* (1782), one of the main characters is a scheming and amoral aristocrat named Valmont – the kind of 'sensible knave' that Hume might have had in mind.

I summon the tax-collector, and yielding to my generous compassion pay him £56, for the lack of which sum five persons were to be reduced to living on straw and despair. You cannot imagine the shower of blessings this simple action brought down upon me from those present . . . My eyes were moist with tears and inside I felt an unwonted but delicious emotion. I was astonished at the pleasure to be derived from doing good, and I am now tempted to think that what we call virtuous people have less claim to merit than we are led to believe.[57]

Laclos, *Dangerous Liaisons*

For the most part, Valmont is a vicious and nasty piece of work; he has no interest in virtue and is driven only by hedonistic self-interest. Yet on the surface he displays all the virtues he needs to get by as a respected aristocrat – as on this occasion when he gives some money to the poor (and finds it astonishing that charity could be a source of pleasure – which suggest to him the amusing possibility that virtuous people are really just hedonists like him!). Such behaviour appears to be a problem for Hume's belief that sympathetic feelings overcome self-interested ones, because it seems that the rewards gained by a sensible knave who plays the system like

Valmont are greater than those gained by someone who is disposed to be selfless. But for Hume, as for Plato and Aristotle, these gains are merely apparent and such a person's lack of virtue will remain a barrier to their happiness. Such people

Hume

will discover that they themselves are the greatest dupes and have sacrificed the invaluable enjoyment of a character . . . for the acquisition of worthless toys and gewgaws.[58]

Two types of virtue

Hume thought that there are basically two kinds of virtue, or dispositions, based on two sets of qualities that we value in people. The first set is clustered around how useful someone's behaviour is (the pains and pleasures it generates) which Hume calls its UTILITY. The second set is based on whether someone's behaviour pleases us, which Hume terms its *agreeability*. These qualities (of utility or agreeability) may either be extended to ourselves, or to other people. This is the principle that Hume believes governs morality: that we value those qualities which are 'useful or agreeable to the person himself or to others'.[59] Qualities that are neither useful nor agreeable to ourselves or others are not virtues. Hume gives as an example of such qualities the so-called 'monkish' virtues, which are tainted by 'superstitious and false religion': celibacy, fasting, self-denial, silence, solitude, etc.[60] Below is a table of some examples of the virtues (or qualities), classified according to Hume's principle:

	To others	To ourselves
Qualities that have utility	Justice, benevolence, humanity, generosity, charity, gratitude, friendliness, honesty, fidelity, mercy, moderation	Industry, frugality, caution, willpower, wisdom, memory, economy, prudence, patience, judgement
Qualities that are agreeable	Good manners, wit, ingenuity, eloquence, affability, modesty, decency, politeness, cleanliness	Cheerfulness, magnanimity, courage, dignity, tranquillity, delicacy, serenity

ACTIVITY
1 Do you agree with Hume's classification of the virtues?

2 Do you think we still recognise and value all the virtues on this list? Why/Why not?

3 Are there any virtues that Plato and Aristotle acknowledge, but which Hume misses out from his list?

4 Are there any virtues that you think could be added to this list?

Hume makes a clear distinction between social virtues (which he also calls 'artificial virtues') and natural virtues. Natural virtues are ones that we all possess innately, perhaps as a result of our biological make-up (although Hume was writing before Darwin and did not have a theory of how dispositions might be 'hardwired' through natural selection). Hume gives BENEVOLENCE as an example of a natural virtue. Social virtues on the other hand are virtues that we gain through growing up and living in a community. Justice, the fair distribution and ownership of property, is an example of this type of virtue.[61] The social virtues act as essential moral glue for large societies, binding us together; this is because in a large society our natural sympathy towards fellow citizens diminishes as many more of them are strangers to us.

Criticisms of Hume's ethics

The account of morality that Hume gives in the *Enquiry* is based on a kind of empirical investigative approach; he even says that he is adopting an 'experimental method'.[62] Hume thinks that by taking examples of dispositions that we all agree are valuable (i.e. virtues) and then by analysing these qualities to see what they have in common we are engaging in a science of ethics. But is this really science? A science in its most basic form is generally thought to consist of evidence gathering and constructing hypotheses based on this evidence, then testing the hypothesis against new pieces of evidence. But the virtues that Hume has identified do not appear to be based on any concrete evidence in the sense that we now understand it (e.g. qualitative research questionnaires from a sample of representative people). Perhaps if Hume were around today he would be conducting interviews as part of his research into the psychology of ethics, but you get the feeling that when he wrote the *Enquiry* he was making a slightly more personal selection of virtues.

Following from this Hume seems to think that we would in fact all agree that the qualities he picks out are universally valued. So, for Hume, morality is common to all humankind, and by definition a moral virtue is a disposition approved of by everyone. But is this so? For many of these qualities (e.g. chastity, sobriety, secrecy) Hume seems to be describing what he and his peers value, rather than virtues that are universally valued. If this is so then Hume's investigation must be one that is limited to his own historical era and possibly his own social class.

Moreover Hume seems optimistic in thinking that vicious, non-virtuous people will always be disapproved of by the majority of people. The sensible knave now seems to be the default position for many people. At the more extreme end of non-virtuousness, we need only look to the history of genocide in the past hundred years to find out how frequently vicious (i.e. non-virtuous) behaviour becomes normal amongst a majority, thus enabling a group systematically to kill those who fall outside of it.[63]

A further criticism is that it appears as if Hume is already assuming what he is setting out to prove. Hume wishes to know what principle of morals we follow. In order to do this he examines qualities we all admire. His conclusion is that these qualities are all based on utility or agreeability. This is his principle of morals. But when faced with a counter-example (the 'monkish virtues' of poverty, chastity, humility and obedience) he dismisses them because they are not useful (and nor are they agreeable). However, if he is sincere in his empirical approach then he should try to understand *why* so many people do value these qualities. These qualities are counter-examples that go against his original principle of utility, and so either Hume must amend his principle, or say why they are not genuine counter-examples. Because he dismisses them outright, he must already be assuming that his principle is correct, even before his investigation has begun, which is hardly in the spirit of empiricism.

The implications of Hume's theory for ethics

What are the consequences for ethics if Hume is correct, i.e. if our motivation to be moral is simply a reflection of our natural sympathy? In this section we look at how Hume's ideas influenced a theory of ethical language known as EMOTIVISM, which stated that moral statements are just expressions of an emotion: there can be no truth about moral statements, and therefore no debate or discussion about moral statements. So the ultimate implication of Hume's claim – that morality is based on sympathy – is that morality doesn't exist outside of human emotion. This means morality is at best subjective and at worst non-existent.

Realism and anti-realism

Ralph leapt to his feet.
'Jack! You haven't got the conch! Let him speak.'
Jack's face swam near him.
'And you shut up! Who are you anyway? Sitting there –
telling people what to do.' . . .
'The rules!' Shouted Ralph, 'you're breaking the rules!'
'Who cares?' . . .
Ralph summoned all his wits. 'Because the rules are the only
thing we've got!'[64]

William Golding, *Lord of the Flies*

Ralph and Jack are in trouble – they are twelve years old, they
are rivals who hate one another, they are on a desert island and
there is nothing and no one to stop them slashing each other's
throat or worse (and on this island there is much, much worse).
Ralph is right, the rules are all they've got, or at least all they
have to prevent their fragile little society from shattering. The
question is, where do the rules come from? Ralph's rule, that
you can only speak at an assembly if you're holding a conch
shell, is something transported from another culture, another
country, far, far away. In this new context the rule is as fragile as
the shell he holds. Jack's rule, the rule of physical power, is one
that he develops as a hunter and exploits to terrifying effect as
the new chief. In the end the culture that turns the boys into a
unit is a culture based on fear, on hatred of outsiders, on
superstition and violent ritual. These boys are making up their
moral principles as they go along, and it's not pretty.

The question is do we discover or do we create the moral
rules and principles that we feel bound by? Are Ralph, Jack
and the rest simply discovering principles that other cultures
have discovered, or are they inventing them? Philosophers
known as REALISTS believe that moral values are real things
that can be discovered or intuited – Kant, for example,
believed that we could discover the moral law through the use
of reason. ANTI-REALISTS on the other hand do not believe
that morality is something real – instead they argue that
humans create it themselves.

In our discussion of virtues in the previous sections two
different views have emerged about what 'virtue' refers to, i.e.
about what we are judging when we say that something is a
virtue. Aristotle thought of virtues as referring to particular
character traits: courage, self-control, practical wisdom, etc.
This seems to be common sense: if I say that you are virtuous
then I'm talking about your behaviour, the way you are
disposed to act. But Hume disagreed, arguing that our
judgement of someone's behaviour as virtuous did not spring
from their behaviour, but from *our feelings* about their

■ **Figure 1.19** *The differences between Aristotle's and Hume's view of what 'virtue' means*

behaviour. So when I say that you are virtuous I am expressing my feelings of approval about your behaviour; I am not referring to anything intrinsic in your behaviour itself. One way of putting this might be to say that, for Aristotle, our term 'virtue' reflects something 'out there' (in people's behaviour), whereas, for Hume, 'virtue' reflects something 'in here' (the feelings of sympathy provoked by people's behaviour).

■ The influence of Hume on anti-realism

Hume's claim that morality refers to something inside ourselves, rather than out there in the world, does not make him an anti-realist. After all, Hume certainly believed in the reality of the human sentiment of sympathy. However, certain comments he made proved to be influential on anti-realism, which had a direct effect on the status of morality, as we shall see. As he claimed in his *Treatise of Human Nature*:

Where a passion is neither founded on false suppositions, nor chooses means insufficient for the end, the understanding can neither justify nor condemn it.'Tis not contrary to reason to prefer the destruction of the whole world to the scratching of my finger.[65]

Hume

For Hume, reason cannot provide us with a motive for action. However, this approach need not imply that moral judgements are made on the basis of a simple examination of the facts revealed to us through experience. We cannot see, hear, smell, etc. good or evil. In his *Treatise* Hume argues that an empirical examination of a vicious act, of murder for instance, can never reveal to us anything we can term 'vice'. That is, there is nothing about the event itself, no fact which we can observe, which constitutes its being wrong. So where do ethical judgements come from? We have seen that Hume argues that all our preferences, including our moral ones, must be based upon passions, i.e. our basic feelings and desires.

Hume

So that when you pronounce any action or character to be vicious, you mean nothing, but that from the constitution of your nature you have a feeling or sentiment of blame from the contemplation of it. Vice and virtue, therefore, may be compared to sounds, colours, heat and cold, which, according to modern philosophy, are not qualities in objects, but perceptions in the mind.[66]

Thus ethical judgements are grounded in experience, not reason; in other words, they are a matter of our own feelings and dispositions. While in this sense they are subjective or mind-dependent, Hume argues that they are objective insofar as they are rooted in facts about human nature. We do not choose these dispositions; they are simply given to us by our biological heritage. We are just the kind of creature that has the feelings that we do, and it is these shared feelings which constitute morality: our ethical nature is characterised by the capacity for sympathy, or the disposition to feel with (empathise with) others. On such an account any variations in moral codes must be a consequence of differing social conditions, while ultimately all such codes must express some fundamentals which humanity shares. However, thinkers in the twentieth century who rediscovered Hume found that his comments about feelings and dispositions led them to a definite, *anti-realist*, conclusion. To philosophers like A.J. Ayer and C.L. Stevenson, what seemed obvious was that moral terms were simply an expression of our personal feelings and emotions, and that morality refers to nothing real at all – a philosophy known as 'emotivism'.

So, by locating morality in our feelings rather than in anything outside of us, Hume led the way for philosophers who wished to deny the meaningfulness of moral statements, and the purpose of moral discussion.

■ A.J. Ayer and emotivism

Ayer

> *In every case in which one would commonly be said to be making an ethical judgement, the function of the ethical term is purely emotive. It is used to express feelings about certain objects, but not to make any assertion about them.[67]*

The strongest statement of emotivism as a moral theory came from A.J. Ayer (1910–1989). He was a British philosopher who was very much under the influence of a group of Austrian philosophers known as LOGICAL POSITIVISTS, who in turn had been influenced by David Hume. These philosophers were angered by the gibberish that they thought many philosophers, particularly in the nineteenth century, had a tendency to spout. Language, they said, was only meaningful when it referred to the world; if we go beyond this then we venture into nonsense. Ayer was greatly affected by this idea and in 1936 he wrote a book called *Language, Truth and Logic* that popularised logical positivism in Britain and America. The theory of meaning that is now associated with Ayer is the VERIFICATION PRINCIPLE and it is a kind of test that sentences must pass if they are genuinely meaningful (we revisit this principle again in Chapter 4, page 255). The Verification Principle states that:

A sentence is meaningful if and only if
either (a) it is a *tautology* (i.e. true by definition)
  or   (b) it is verifiable through sense experience.

What the principle is saying is that in order to say something meaningful we must know what makes our statement true. Ayer believed that if a statement wasn't a tautology (i.e. true by definition), and if there was no empirical way of discovering its truth, then it was meaningless. Like all positivists, Ayer put a lot of faith in science and in our observations of the world. He used the verification principle as a tool to sort out the good from the bad, the philosophical sheep from the metaphysical goats.

experimenting with ideas

Read through the following sentences and decide for each whether or not it meets A.J. Ayer's verification principle (i.e. whether it is capable of being true or false).

1 Stealing money is wrong.
2 There is life after death.
3 A bachelor is an unmarried man.
4 It is good to give money to charity.
5 It is your duty to tell the truth.

6 There are invisible pixies that live in my fridge who disappear without trace as soon as I open the door.

7 The universe is expanding.

8 Bondi beach contains more than 1 billion particles of sand.

9 It is wrong to abort a 20-week-old foetus.

10 The sunset over Victoria Falls is the most beautiful sight on Earth.

So what did Ayer have to say about judgements of value, which include such terms as 'right' and 'good'? He agreed with those who claimed that these terms were un-analysable, but that is because he said there is nothing to analyse. 'Good' and 'right' are what Ayer calls 'pseudo-concepts': they don't refer to anything at all. So if they do not refer to any property of the world, then moral judgements are not propositions and are not capable of being true or false. According to Ayer's verification principle, moral judgements are therefore meaningless. Given the frequency of moral judgements in our everyday lives, and their importance to us, what then does Ayer think is behind moral language? He concludes that moral terms are simply expressions of emotions or feelings, like going 'boo!' or 'hooray!' So when I say

Ayer

'Stealing money is wrong' I produce a sentence with no factual meaning . . . It is as if I had written 'Stealing money ! !' – where the shape and thickness of the exclamation marks show . . . that a special sort of moral disapproval is the feeling which is being expressed.[68]

Now this 'emotive' account of moral terms was not new; its origins lie in David Hume's theory, and the philosophers Ogden and Richards had said almost the same thing thirteen years previously in their book *The Meaning of Meaning* (1923) writing that '"good" . . . serves only as an emotive sign expressing our attitude'.[69] So emotivism claims that moral assertions express attitudes or feelings. By arguing that all ethical statements are simply expressions of emotion, a bit like expletives, Ayer is taking an anti-realist stance towards moral terms. 'Good' doesn't refer to anything in the world, but is only an expression reflecting something in me. It is important to emphasise that, unlike Hume's position outlined above, emotivism denies that moral expressions *describe* feelings or emotions any more than they describe other empirical facts. This is what leads Hume back into a realist view of ethics. But on an emotivist account moral terms *express* a feeling, much as a frown or an angry tone of voice does.

The American philosopher C.L. Stevenson went a step further than Ayer in analysing the emotive meaning of moral judgements. He argued that moral judgements which employed terms like 'good' and 'right' were not simply expressions of a feeling, as Ayer had maintained. More importantly, thought Stevenson, they were also attempts to influence other people, to persuade them to feel as we feel and to have the same attitude that we have. So Stevenson might say that when we say 'that's a good film' we mean 'I like this film; you should do so as well.' Similarly if we say 'abortion is wrong' we mean 'I disapprove of abortion and so should you.' So Stevenson is able to give an account of how moral terms motivate our action – they do so on the power of the emotion behind the words like someone shouting or urging us to do something.

experimenting with ideas

Revisit sentences 1, 4, 5 and 9 on pages 74–75 and write down the emotive meaning that Stevenson would find in them.

The disagreement between anti-realists (like Ayer) and realists (like Plato, Kant and Aristotle) turns on their analysis of simple ethical propositions. Consider the following propositions (illustrated in Figure 1.20): Boris is big, and Boris is bad.

■ **Figure 1.20 Do moral terms refer to a real property in the world?**

According to the emotivist, it is a mistake to think there must be something in the world corresponding to the expression 'is bad'

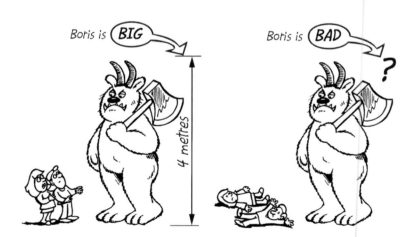

Both these propositions have the same basic grammatical form. They both have a subject term ('Boris') which picks out an individual in the world (Boris himself). And both statements have a predicate term ('is bad' and 'is big') which says something about Boris. Now, the realist claims that what is ascribed to Boris in both these statements is a property which we can discover in the world. Both bigness and badness are real properties of people, albeit natural and non-natural ones respectively. And it is here that the emotivist takes issue with realism. The emotivist claims that although these two propositions are superficially similar, in reality they are very different. While the first does indeed ascribe a real property to Boris, the second does not. Badness is *not* really a property of people or actions at all. This means that the second proposition is deceptive as it leads us to look in the world for something corresponding to the word 'bad'. But in reality, says the emotivist, there is no such thing. For the real meaning of 'Boris is bad' is closer to 'Avoid Boris!' or 'Boris, yuk!', that is to say, it expresses disapproval and does not ascribe any objective property to him at all.

◼ The implications of emotivism

One conclusion that can be drawn from emotivism is that value judgements are not rational and so no rational agreement is possible on ethical matters. Different people feel differently about different things and each has equal right to their opinion: I like strawberry ice cream, you like chocolate ice cream; I feel 'ugh!' when I think about capital punishment for terrorists, but you feel 'hurray!' There is no point in having a moral discussion, since two people cannot really contradict each other when they appear to be expressing a disagreement over some moral issue.

► criticism ◄   The immediate difficulty with this conclusion is that it appears to misunderstand the true character of moral judgements. When I claim that 'abortion of a 20-week-old foetus is wrong' I intend to contradict your claim that 'abortion of a 20-week-old foetus is permissible'. For when we disagree on a moral issue we argue with reasons and it seems as if we are literally contradicting each other; we are not just expressing conflicting ethical attitudes or feelings. Emotivism appears to make such rational moral argumentation impossible. If moral judgements were purely subjective it would be senseless for me to condemn someone who professed a different moral attitude.

This objection, however, need not be fatal, and an important lesson needs to be drawn from the emotivist's defence. For emotivism can allow for rational dispute over matters of fact (for example, whether or not a 20-week-old foetus can feel pain, or can survive outside of the womb), and over the definition of terms (for example, whether a foetus is a person, or a potential person). So if we are in disagreement over some issue, it may not be irrational to argue so long as our disagreement concerns something objective, such as a factual belief about the world, or a confusion over the meaning of the terms we are using. The rational approach is adopted, according to the emotivist, in order to seek out any shared values that we have and use these as leverage in the argument. In the case of the argument over the abortion of a 20-week-old foetus, we may both share the view that harming innocent human beings is wrong. If I can demonstrate that the foetus is a human being (for example, by showing that a foetus has complex responses, can survive outside of the womb with special care, has all the necessary body parts in place, etc.) and that it can be harmed (because it feels pain), then the other person may come to agree with me on this argument. What has happened here is that the pro-abortionist did not initially realise that their moral position was actually inconsistent, because they were unaware of certain facts.

Despite this, while particular value judgements may be a matter for rational debate ultimately, on an emotivist account, the criteria on which we base such judgements boil down to the expression of feelings. And in the final analysis any reasons I may offer for why something is wrong can only reduce to some gut feeling for which no justification can be offered. So Hume's theory, as adopted by Ayer, implies that there is no rational basis for our moral disputes.

We mentioned above Stevenson's emotivist account of how moral terms motivate action. So ethical statements may be instruments for the control and redirection of social behaviour etc. But so are advertisements, political speeches, bribes, blackmail, orders and so forth. In order to influence someone's behaviour, in other words, I may engage in moral exhortation, but I may also threaten, plead or bribe them. This observation raises the question of what, if anything, is distinctive about purely *moral* discourse, for according to emotivism it would seem that it is 'ethical' to deploy any effective means to persuade someone to adopt a certain kind of behaviour. The implication is that there can be no way of saying whether a moral argument is good or bad, but only whether or not it has the desired effect and thus ethics appears to be on a par with propaganda and rhetoric.

▶ criticism ◀ Emotivism is mistaken in claiming that moral discourse always involves itself in trying to change attitudes or influence action. For it is possible to condemn someone's behaviour, without holding out any hope of influencing it. Moreover moral discourse can be meaningful without its being any expression of an emotional state. I can express a moral opinion without being emotionally excited, for example when giving someone moral advice. Indeed often it is regarded as important to be dispassionate in evaluating a moral dilemma, since our emotions can cloud our ability to make moral decisions.

► criticism ◄   Kantian theorists may turn to the principle of universalisability to resist the claims of emotivism. For, following Kant, they may insist on the need for the element of *reason* in moral conduct. In other words, there is a crucial difference between saying that something is right or wrong, and expressing a liking or dislike for it. If I do something because I ought to do it, I will be prepared to act the same way if the same circumstances arise. But this is not true of feelings. If I do something because I feel like it, not because I ought to, there is no commitment to acting in a similar way in similar circumstances. Moral judgements, in other words, refer beyond the particular case in a way that feelings or emotions do not. Further they involve not just how I ought to behave in certain circumstances, but how anyone ought to behave in such circumstances. What this means is that to make a moral judgement implies having principles; and while non-rational beings can have feelings and express them, only a rational being can hold universal principles of this kind.

Conclusion: the three subsidiary questions

We mentioned above (pages 3–4) that there were three themes that criss-crossed the different answers given to the main question 'why should I be moral?' They were:

i)   Are we essentially self-interested creatures? Does human nature dictate the motives we can have for being moral?
ii) Does morality conflict with self-interest? Are self-interested reasons the very opposite to moral reasons, or are the two connected in some way?
iii) Is moral behaviour reached through reason? Is there another route to moral behaviour that does not depend on giving reasons?

Below we illustrate, in diagrammatic form, how the different theories we examined above give different answers to these questions.

■ **Figure 1.21** *Are we essentially self-interested?*

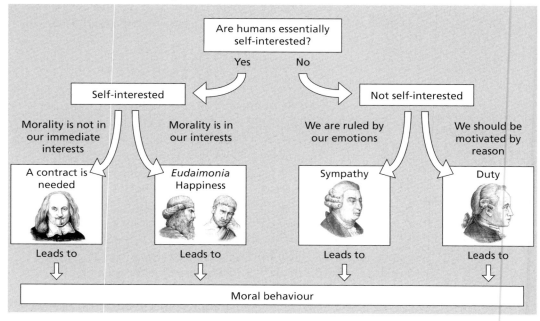

■ **Figure 1.22** *Does morality conflict with self-interest?*

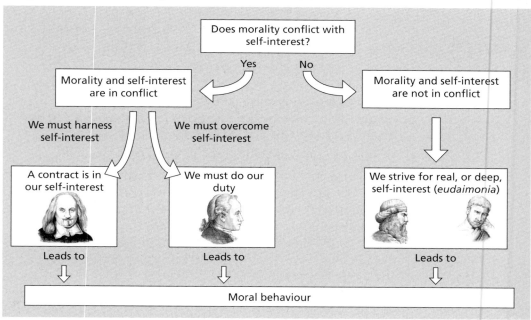

■ **Figure 1.23** *Is moral behaviour reached through reason?*

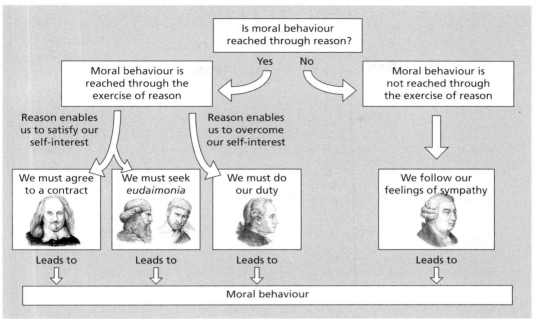

Key points: Chapter 1

What you need to know about **Why should I be moral?**

1 There is a tension between acting in a way that considers
only myself (egoism) and acting in a way that considers
others (altruism). Being moral means acting in ways that
consider the goals, desires and interests of others, with a
view to not harming them, and helping them to flourish
and be happy. Being self-interested means acting in ways
that meet my own interests, desires and goals. The
question is: if we are self-interested then why should we be
moral?

2 One answer to this question is that in fact it is in our
interests to behave morally. Imagine a world in which
everyone thought only of themselves, and there were no
laws to prevent people from doing whatever they wanted to
get what they wanted. Hobbes says in such a world our
lives would be nasty, brutish and short. Very few of us
would be able to pursue our self-interests in such a world.
It is far better if we agree to follow rules, and give some of
our freedom away to the government who can enforce

these rules. These rules demand that we think of others, but also that others think of us when they act. A social contract of this type, which forces us to behave in a moral way, is mutually advantageous for all of us. So moral behaviour is a simply means to achieving, as far as possible, what is in our self-interests.

3 A different approach to the question 'why should I be moral?' can be found in the philosophy of the ancient Greeks. Greek philosophers like Socrates, Plato and Aristotle had a view of morality which centred on the individual person. They all agree that each of us is trying to be happy and flourish. However, this cannot be achieved by seeking money or power or pleasure. What is in our true self-interest is determined by what kind of being we are and what our function is. Plato and Aristotle explore the different aspect of our selves, our souls, and argue that reason should be in control of all that we do. Letting reason rule our souls will lead to happiness. However, letting reason rule also leads to the development of the virtues – character traits like justice and courage that not only benefit ourselves but others too. So it turns out that moral behaviour flows from our true self-interest.

4 Connecting morality with self-interest, as Hobbes and the ancient Greeks did, seems strange, as the two seem directly opposed. Kant rejects the idea that self-interest, or anything approximating it, has any bearing on morality. For Kant a moral action is one done by a free agent, which means we must set to one side all our emotions and interests (including feelings of compassion that might lead to moral action). The only truly moral motivation is that of duty – following a command (the categorical imperative) because we ought to. We can use reason to calculate our duties: these are actions which can be universalised (or rather the maxim underpinning them can be universalised) without contradiction or inconsistency.

5 There is another type of theory which rejects self-interest as a motivator of moral behaviour, but which also rejects reason. David Hume proposed that reason cannot give us the motivation to act. Instead reason should be seen as a calculating tool employed to achieve an outcome that is set by our desires, feelings, etc. In moral terms we are motivated, not by self-interest, nor by duty, but by our natural sympathy for the pain and suffering of others. Our sense of what is beneficial and useful to us, or what is beneficial or useful to others, gives us a marker against which we can judge people's characters. So we value those

characteristics, or virtues, which are beneficial or useful to ourselves or others.

6 The implications of David Hume's arguments appear to be quite damaging to ethics. Aristotle and Plato use moral terms (such as 'good') to refer to something outside of ourselves. However, Hume says that moral terms or virtues are ascribable internally to ourselves – to our feelings of sympathy. So when Aristotle says someone is virtuous he means that 'virtue' really does exist independently of me; but when Hume says someone is virtuous he does not think this concept exists independently of him. For A.J. Ayer and the emotivists, Hume's theory leads to the conclusion that morality is subjective, referring only to our own emotions. According to Ayer's verification principle this implies that moral terms (such as 'good') are meaningless: they cannot be verified.

2 The idea of God

Introduction

It is incomprehensible that God should exist and incomprehensible that God should not exist.[1]

Pascal

God said to Moses: I am what I am.

Exodus 3:13

Philosophers tend to be inquisitive meddlers, poking their noses into all aspects of human life, and trying to clarify our ideas about the world, about how we should live and what we should believe. Religion offers philosophers a rich vein of puzzling ideas that they can tap into: thinking about God ties people up in intellectual knots, and leads to strange, confusing statements as the quotations above from Pascal and the Bible illustrate.

What particularly excites philosophers is investigating the beliefs that people have about the world, and the way we think we ought to live. Because religion deals with both these issues it is no surprise that philosophers have had much to say about religion and God over the past two thousand years. A rich body of philosophical work has built up in Western philosophy around the religious traditions of Europe and the Middle East. This 'philosophy of religion' has dealt with questions such as: who is God? Can his existence be proved? How can God let innocent people suffer so much pain? What place does faith have in our belief in God? Where does our idea of God come from? In this chapter, and in Chapter 6, we start to address these questions and more.

- In the first section of this chapter we look at what philosophers have had to say about the nature of God, and whether their description is a coherent or meaningful one.
- In the second section we take a short diversion into philosophical proofs and arguments, looking at how arguments are constructed and the different ways in which it is possible to prove that something exists.
- From there we move in the third section on to a specific attempt to prove the existence of God by analysing the

nature of God – this is known as the ontological argument for God's existence.

■ In the fourth section we examine Descartes' claim that the idea of God is 'innate', something we each possess at birth.

■ In the final section we look at the claims of atheists that the idea of God is a human construction, arising from fear and ignorance, from other psychological mechanisms, or from social necessity.

The attributes of God

Many debates in the philosophy of religion revolve around proving the existence of God, and we look at one such proof in this chapter (the ONTOLOGICAL ARGUMENT) and a further proof in Chapter 6 (the ARGUMENT FROM DESIGN). But before trying to prove *that* something exists it seems sensible to understand *what* it is that you are trying to prove. After all, if you don't know what you're looking for then how will you know when you've found it? As David Hume puts it:

The question is not concerning the being but the nature of God.[2]

Hume

This section looks at what philosophers and religious believers have had to say about the nature of God, and whether their description of the attributes, or characteristics, of God are coherent and meaningful. We begin by looking at two contrasting approaches to finding out about God – REVEALED THEOLOGY (based on revelation) and NATURAL THEOLOGY (based on human reason and experience) – and at their origins in ancient Greek philosophy. We then look at some of the most frequently ascribed characteristics of God, including his OMNIPOTENCE, OMNISCIENCE and BENEVOLENCE, and ask whether they are coherent. Finally we assess how far it is possible to describe a being that is so utterly beyond human comprehension.

Two approaches: revealed theology and natural theology

A promising place to start our investigation into the nature of God is the sacred texts on which religions are based, such as the Torah, the Bible or the Qur'an. We should first say that because the philosophers we examine in this chapter, and in Chapter 6, are predominantly Christian we have chosen to use only examples from the revealed texts of Christianity, namely the Old and New Testaments. These books record the foundations of the religion through the REVELATIONS of certain individuals. These individuals, it is claimed, had some direct or indirect contact with God, and may be best positioned to reveal something of God's nature. However, it could be argued that, as philosophers, we should be sceptical of religious texts because they tend to assume that the revelations they record are genuine and that their interpretation of God is the only true one. Yet it is precisely these assumptions that we are trying to investigate.

An alternative starting point for our investigation into the nature of God would be to look around us at the universe he is said to have created. By analysing the various features of this universe (the types of things that exist, the laws that govern it, human behaviour, etc.) we might hope to establish what God must be like. If we start here we might at least avoid the charge of bias when we make our first report on the nature of God, since we wouldn't be looking at the text of any particular religion. This approach is characterised by the attempt to use reason, and so has been of particular interest to philosophers since ancient Greek times.

Religious philosophers and theologians have taken both these approaches: the first is called revealed theology, because it trusts sacred texts to reveal religious truths and an understanding of God; the second approach is called natural theology, because it stresses the possibility of understanding God via human reason and observation alone. There is a tension between these two methods or approaches: as potential philosophers we are naturally drawn to reason, but as potential believers we cannot put aside faith, and the goal of many religious philosophers down the ages has been to resolve the tension between these two.

ACTIVITY

1 Write down as many words that you can think of associated with the idea of 'God'.

2 Which of these words or categories do you think come from a religious text (e.g. the Bible) and which come directly from people's experience?

The influence of ancient Greek philosophy

Before we look in more detail at what revealed and natural theology have to say about the nature of God, we should first say something about how theology and the philosophy of religion have been influenced by the pagan philosophers of ancient Greece, in particular Plato and Aristotle.

Philosophy competes with religion in our search for answers to those ultimate questions that humans ask about the universe: Why are we here? How should we live? What is the meaning of life? What happens to us when we die? Since its birth in ancient Greece, philosophy has always been concerned with such questions but unlike religious thought it approaches them with reasoned argument. Inevitably, the relationship between philosophy and religion has often been uneasy. St Paul, for example, writes to the Colossians warning them about the philosophy of the ancient Greeks. To a Christian like Paul, the philosophical approach, with its emphasis on reasoned argument, is misguided and can serve only to distract us from the truths of religious teachings about God and the world.

Take care that no one leads you astray by philosophy and useless misleading teaching.

Colossians 2:8

However, even St Paul acknowledged that philosophy could offer some insight into the nature of God and the universe, when he addressed a group of Athenian philosophers:

It is in [God] that we live and move and have our being, as some of your own writers have said.

Acts 17:28

The opening section of John's gospel, in the New Testament of the Bible, also owes a debt to ancient Greek philosophy. 'In the beginning was the Word [*logos*], and the Word was with God, and the Word was God' (John 1:1). John deliberately uses the concept of *logos*, usually translated in this context as 'word', but which has the broader philosophical meaning, used by both Plato and Aristotle, of 'rational account' or 'explanatory principle' or 'source of order'. So what John may be saying in these mysterious lines is that God is that which gives rise to and explains the existence of the universe.

Moving beyond the apostles, theologians have from the beginning of Christianity used ancient Greek philosophy as an ally to support religious belief. Plato's belief in an immortal soul distinct from the physical body, his proposal that we are rewarded or punished in the afterlife, his speculations about the origins of the universe, the central THEORY OF FORMS and the mystical idea of the mind's union with the form of the Good (see Chapter 1, page 42), have all found themselves appropriated by Christianity. The Christian religion owes such a debt to Plato that Schopenhauer was led to describe it as

Platonism for the masses. Plato's 'forms' exist outside of space and time, are IMMUTABLE (never changing) and perfect: concepts that we shall see are mirrored in the attributes ascribed to God. In his dialogue the *Laws,* Plato made a distinction between things that had the power to move or change both themselves and others (which he called *primary movers*) and things that could only move or change others once they had been moved (called *secondary movers*). For Plato, primary movers are the ultimate source of change, as they alone possess the power to cause motion spontaneously. Plato argued in the *Laws* that only souls can be primary movers, and that whatever causes the whole universe to change and move must also be a soul. Plato's suggestion that the universe is dependent on some ultimate, intelligent, primary mover was hugely influential on later proofs of the existence of God.

Shall we say then that it is the soul which controls heaven and earth.[3]

Plato

Like Plato, Aristotle also believed that all changes in the universe must come from some ultimate source. In the *Metaphysics* he put forward an argument to prove that there must be an 'unmoved mover' who is the ultimate cause of the universe. His argument asks us to consider two competing claims: that the universe has an ultimate cause, and that the universe has no ultimate cause. By showing that the second claim is not possible, he leaves us with only one option, namely that there is an ultimate cause.

The series must start with something, since nothing can come from nothing.[4]

Aristotle

Since these beginnings, philosophers down the centuries have used philosophy as an ally of their belief. St Augustine drew on the Greek philosopher Plotinus (c.205–270), who had been heavily influenced by Plato, in order to throw light on Christian beliefs. Medieval theologians built further on the work done by Plato and Aristotle, showing that the unmoved, or prime, mover who created the world, and on which its continued existence depended, was God. These proofs of God's existence are known as COSMOLOGICAL arguments, and amongst Christian philosophers it was St Thomas Aquinas who explored the proofs in most detail. Aquinas made it his life's work to show how the theories of the pagan philosopher Aristotle could be reconciled with, and enrich, Christian teachings,[5] and he incorporated Aristotle's ideas in his own account of the concept of God.

So, with the influence of the ancient Greeks as a backdrop to the investigation, let us now turn to see how God has been described, what attributes have been given to him, by religious thinkers: first from the perspective of revealed theology, then in more detail from the perspective of natural theology.

Revealed theology: The God of Abraham, Isaac and Jacob

I am . . . the God of Abraham, the God of Isaac and the God of Jacob.

Exodus 3:6

God of Abraham, God of Isaac, God of Jacob, not the God of the philosophers and scholars.

Pascal, unpublished note

In a note found after his death, the seventeenth-century mathematician and philosopher Blaise Pascal distinguishes between 'the God of the philosophers' and the God as revealed in the Bible. The implication of Pascal's words is that if we seek to know and experience God then we should turn to the Bible, and not to those religious philosophers who go far beyond the Bible in their quest to understand God. We shall see in the pages that follow how different the 'God of the philosophers' is from the 'God of Abraham'; and a question that believers might need to ask is 'is the God of the philosophers the God whom I actually worship?' Pascal thought not, but plenty of other philosophers have disagreed. In the rest of this section we focus almost exclusively on the words and thoughts of philosophers on God. But first we shall follow Pascal's advice and see what we can glean about the nature of God from the Bible.

The God of the Bible is a God whose character varies in its description according to the changing fortunes of his people. Various periods can be found within the Bible, and the personality and attributes of God develop over these periods. The pre-prophetic period (before 900 BCE) was a time of optimism when Moses and his descendants established their roots in Canaan, and their God was placed above all the many competing gods of the region. During the prophetic period (900–500 BCE) prophets such as Isaiah responded to the religious and political threats of their neighbours by describing their God, who is called Yahweh, as the only true God. In the post-exilic period (following the release of the Jews from captivity in 500 BCE) the

Jewish concept of God was refined further, perhaps influenced by the philosophical beliefs of the Persian and Greek occupiers of Canaan. Finally, the character of God takes on different nuances in the New Testament, as certain attributes are emphasised (his love, his participation in the world) and others are set aside (his wrath and his exclusivity to one group of people). What remains constant throughout these different periods is that the God of the Bible is the object of worship, and is the only being worthy of worship.

Below are some of the main characteristics of God that emerge from the descriptions of him given in the Bible.

■ The only God

For much of the opening books of the Bible, Yaweh is thought of only as the God of Israel, with other nations and tribes having their own gods. The first commandment states: 'You shall have no other gods besides me' (Exodus 20:3) but it does *not* say 'I am the only God.' It is several hundred years later (around the prophetic period in the eighth century BCE) that the existence of other gods is ruled out altogether: 'I am the Lord and there is none else. Besides me there is no God' (Isaiah 45:5). By the time of the New Testament, God has become universal. Now he is the only god, and one to be worshipped by all people, not just by the people of Israel.

■ The creator

God is described throughout the Bible as the creator. The opening lines are 'In the beginning God created the heavens and the earth' (Genesis 1:1). This is reiterated in the opening verses of the last gospel: 'All things were made through him' (John 1:3). As the creator, in the Old Testament God is described as intervening in the world regularly: for example, he walked with Adam (Genesis 3:8); he caused the sun to stand still to help Joshua win a battle (Joshua 10:13); he created floods (Genesis 6:13) and destroyed cities (Genesis 19:24) when he was displeased with his creation. However, God becomes increasingly absent from his creation, and many Psalms are laments about this absence and pleas for God to reveal himself (e.g. Psalm 102). An interesting consequence of God being the creator of the universe – and hence of space and time – is that God seems to have to be outside of space and time. This is the kind of corollary (logical consequence) that philosophers are interested in teasing out, and we shall see more of these below.

■ A personal God

'God created man in his own image' (Genesis 1:27). The God of the Old Testament is full of emotion and action that is recognisably human. He has his favourites, the Hebrews, and he encourages them to wage war against the other tribes of Canaan; for example, Moses calls God 'a man of war' (Exodus 15:3). Although his military disposition fades through the Old Testament other personal qualities remain, but these are guided by his righteousness rather than his favouritism for Israel (see the book of Amos). God is vengeful; he is jealous; he is a law-maker who watches over and protects all people so long as they are faithful to him and his laws; he is a judge who punishes those who break his laws; but he is also 'merciful and gracious, slow to anger and abounding in steadfast love' (Psalms 103:8). God's positive and compassionate qualities are emphasised in the New Testament, with God portrayed more often as a father or a shepherd than a law-maker and judge. It is only at the very end of the Bible, in the letters of John, that we find all God's attributes summed up by the single word: 'love' (1 John 4:16ff).

It is belief in God as a person, and one who has an ongoing relationship with his creation, that identifies a believer as a THEIST. A *deist*, in contrast, believes that there was a supernatural creator of the universe (perhaps a 'demiurge' as described by Plato[6]) but that this creator no longer has a relationship with the universe – God was a starting mechanism, as it were. Deism became popular amongst thinkers of the Enlightenment, Voltaire (1694–1778) being a famous supporter of this view, which prioritised human reason and effort, whilst encouraging religious tolerance.

A holy God

The term HOLY captures all that is felt about the special nature of God and his relationship with humans. It is used throughout the Old and New Testaments, it is what sets God apart from everything else and it indicates God's uniqueness not just as a creator or as a supreme power, but as a being who should be worshipped (and feared): 'Be holy, for I am holy' (Leviticus 11:44); 'Holy, holy, holy is Yahweh' (Isaiah 6:3); 'The Lord of hosts you shall regard as holy, let him be your fear, let him be your dread' (Isaiah 8:13). God's holiness is bound up with his spiritual and moral perfection (Isaiah 5:16), and to believers it thus has the power to overcome their sins. The effect of God's holiness on those who experience it is analysed in some detail by Rudolf Otto in his article 'The Numinous'.[7] Otto invented the word NUMINOUS to describe the 'shudder' of awe and dread that people feel when they encounter God.

The God as described above will be familiar to many believers. However, these features of God have not usually taken a central position in the writings of philosophers. Instead philosophers have chosen to focus on certain technical attributes of God, which are informed by his status as a perfect, unique and holy creator. We should remember that there is a tension between revealed theology (where believers study and accept the truths of the Bible) and natural theology (where philosophers try to make sense of the conceptual undercurrents of the Bible and its interpretations). For example, the theologian Colin Gunton warns 'it is not a matter of what *we attribute* [to God], but of what he *reveals himself* to be'.[8] The problem for philosophically minded believers is that what God has revealed himself to be is sometimes unclear (does he know everything or not?), sometimes contradictory (is he full of love or wrath or both?) and sometimes uncomfortable (why in the Old Testament does he appear to be such an advocate of ethnic cleansing?). The 'God of the philosophers', in Pascal's phrase, is an attempt to clarify and make more coherent the concept of God, and is the product of thinkers who harness their devout and sincere faith alongside all the analytic and critical tools of philosophy.

Natural theology: the God of the philosophers

Augustine

. . . one God, who is the author of this whole universe . . . immaterial . . . incorruptible . . . who is, in fact, our source, our light, our good.[9]

St Augustine

Anselm

God is that, than which nothing greater can be conceived.[10]

St Anselm

Descartes

By the word 'God' I mean a substance that is infinite, independent, supremely intelligent, supremely powerful, and the Creator of myself and anything else that may exist.[11]

René Descartes

A person without a body, present everywhere, the creator and sustainer of the universe, able to do everything, knowing all things, perfectly good . . . immutable, eternal, a necessary being, and worthy of worship.[12]

Richard Swinburne

Pascal thought that God was infinitely beyond our comprehension, and he wondered who would dare to think they could know what he was or whether he existed.[13] Despite this, philosophers down the centuries have dared to imagine they could tell us something specific about the nature of God, and the quotations above, which span over 1500 years of religious philosophy, are representative of the theistic philosophical tradition. What all these quotes emphasise is God's greatness and perfection. God is the most perfect and greatest of beings and hence he is supremely good, knowing and powerful, he cannot change and is eternal. At the same time he is the source of all other beings: the creator of the universe.

In this section we take a brief look at some of the characteristics that philosophers have ascribed to God, and the problems associated with these characteristics. These concepts have taken on technical philosophical meaning that has become part of the language of the philosophy of religion: but we should remember that these concepts have their origin both in the work of pre-Christian philosophers such as Plato and Aristotle, as well as in the Bible. Because the writings of philosophers of religion, working in a Christian tradition, can sometimes seem very far removed from the original 'revealed' texts, we have taken care to locate the origin of these concept in specific quotes from the Bible. The eight attributes we examine are:

- omnipotence
- omniscience
- benevolence
- immanence
- transcendence
- eternal
- everlasting
- immutability

God's infinite power: omnipotence

The God of Abraham was able to do anything; this was the message behind the countless examples in the Bible of what God could and did do: 'He will not grow tired or weary, and his understanding no one can fathom. He gives strength to the weary and increases the power of the weak' (Isaiah 40:28–30); 'With God all things are possible' (Matthew 19:26); 'For with God nothing is impossible' (Luke 1:37). The power of God to do anything was termed 'omnipotence' by philosophers (from the Latin *omni* meaning 'all' and *potens* meaning 'power') and it takes a central position in God's perfection. There has long been a question mark over the meaning of omnipotence; can God literally do anything?

▶ criticism ◀ Some philosophers, such as J.L. Mackie,[14] have been eager to point out the incoherence of the concept of 'omnipotence', and hence the incoherence of the idea of 'God', and we will be examining 'the problem of omnipotence' in the next section. In defence of omnipotence, religious philosophers have been prepared to offer limits to God's power. In *Summa Contra Gentiles* 2:25 Aquinas lists twenty types of things that God can't do, for example he can't do what is logically impossible such as create a married bachelor. Similarly he cannot alter what has already happened; or force us to choose something freely. Many have felt God cannot change the laws of mathematics (he cannot, for example, make 2 + 3 equal to 6) or act in a way that goes against his fundamental nature (e.g. do something EVIL). We examine the problem of omnipotence below (page 101) and the problem of evil in Chapter 6.

■ God's infinite knowledge: Omniscience

By the nature of their profession, philosophers place a high value on knowledge, and we shouldn't be surprised to find that religious philosophers consider perfect knowledge to be an aspect of God's perfection. As with omnipotence, God's omniscience (from the Latin *omni* meaning 'all', *scientia* meaning 'knowing') is illustrated in the Bible by examples, rather than stated explicitly. Psalm 139:4 tells us that 'even before a word is on my tongue, O Lord, thou knowest it altogether', Hebrews 4:13 says 'nothing in all creation is hidden from God's sight. Everything is uncovered and laid bare before the eyes of him'. However, in some parts of the Bible God's knowledge does not seem to extend so far: 'But the Lord God called to the Man [Adam] and said to him "Where are you"?' (Genesis 3:9).

Philosophers are interested in how far God's omniscience extends. Is God's knowledge only *propositional*, meaning it involves 'knowing that . . .' something is true, such as knowing that the world will come to an end on 26 May 2010, or that Adam has eaten forbidden fruit? Does it involve having *practical* knowledge of how to do things, such as how to ride a bike or create human beings out of clay? If God is INCORPOREAL, i.e. he lacks a body, or TRANSCENDENT, existing outside the universe, then it does not make sense to say that God knows *how* to engage in physical activity, although a theologian might wish to say that God knows the full set of truths about the activity.[15] Other questions we might wish to ask are 'can God know what it is logically impossible to know, for example the area of a round square?' and 'does God know what I'm freely about to do?' We examine the problem of free will and omniscience on pages 101–102.

■ God's supreme goodness: Benevolence

'O give thanks to the Lord, for he is good, for his steadfast love endures for ever' (Psalm 106:1, and 107, 117, 118, 136, etc.). In the Bible, God's benevolence (from the Latin *bene* meaning 'good', *volens* meaning 'will') is recognisable and familiar to humans. It is a goodness full of passion, based on righteousness; and it carries the consequence of angry retribution to those who disobey him. In the New Testament, God's goodness becomes focused through the expression of love and mercy: 'God so loved the world that he gave his one and only Son' (John 3:16); '[God's] mercy extends to those who fear him' (Luke 1:50). It is these personal aspects of goodness that ordinary, non-philosophical, believers emphasise.

The account of God's goodness provided by religious philosophers is more abstract and less personal, and influenced by the two giants of ancient Greek philosophy, Plato and Aristotle. For some theologians such as Aquinas, who follow Aristotle's philosophy (see Chapter 1), goodness is a form of perfection, meaning that there is no flaw or deficiency and that all the necessary qualities are present. In this sense God's goodness is not just an extra characteristic (like omniscience or omnipotence), but it is *the* single property that includes all other properties. God's goodness means he is complete and perfect, containing all the attributes (such as those described by Descartes) necessary for perfection.

Some philosophers have taken God's goodness in an ethical sense: God is the moral standard and the origin of all moral goodness. On this interpretation God's goodness is seen as the source of all goodness, just as Plato's form of the Good is the source for all the other forms. According to philosophers like St Augustine, God's goodness filters down through all of his creation, but all goodness has its origins in God: 'this thing is good and that good, but take away this and that, and regard good itself if you can: so you will see God . . . the good of all good'.[16] However, there is a problem that arises if God is seen to be the source of all *moral* goodness – this is known as the EUTHYPHRO DILEMMA, and we examine it on pages 103–106. In its narrower sense God's goodness could also refer to God's own moral character, and is exemplified in his love, his justice and his wisdom. Even the writers of the Old Testament recognised that God's benevolence had to be reconciled in some way with the horrific pain and suffering that exists in this world. We shall look at this, the so-called PROBLEM OF EVIL, in Chapter 6.

■ God's relation to the world: immanence and transcendence

We saw above that the writers of the Bible proclaim God both as the creator of the world, and as having a personal relationship with this creation. Unlike the gods of most other ancient religions (such as Baal in Canaan, Purusha in India, Zeus in Greece and Osiris in Egypt) the God of Israel, Yahweh, came to be seen as a unique God, one who controlled the direction and history of the whole world – not just one who shaped nature and interfered in the lives of humans. This positioned Yahweh apart from the universe or, as philosophers say, transcendent – a term which means going beyond, or existing outside of, a limit or boundary: 'You, whose name is Lord, are Most High over all the earth' (Psalms 86:18). God's transcendence is in keeping with his role as the creator of the universe and of space and time – if he were in space and time then it would be difficult, even for the sharpest of minds, to conceive how he could have created these dimensions.

In contrast to God's transcendence, the story of the Old Testament, and certainly of the New, is a story of God's engagement in his creation, and of there being a two-way relationship: humans (particularly prophets) communicate with God, and God directly acts on the world through miracles. The term philosophers use to capture God's participation in his creation is IMMANENCE, which refers to God's presence and on-going engagement with the world: 'Do not I fill heaven and earth' (Jeremiah 23:24). For Christians this immanence is most powerfully recognised in the figure of Jesus, who is at once both God and God's son: 'for in Christ all the fullness of the Deity lives in bodily form' (Colossians 2:9).

▶ criticism ◀

To a non-believer these two attributes (transcendence and immanence) seem mutually contradictory – both cannot be ascribed to one being – and so one or the other must be given up. However, for theists within a Christian tradition it is crucial that God is understood to be a personal God who is both present in the world (immanent) whilst also being beyond the world (transcendent). Paul writes that there is 'one God, who is over all and through all and in all' (Ephesians 4:6). If theists give up the belief that God is immanent, then they become *deists* (holding the belief that God is an impersonal creator); if they give up their belief that God is transcendent then they will become *pantheists* (holding the belief that God is the world and no more).

A further problem with God's immanence arises if God is thought to be benevolent. The world, as poets, historians and the tabloid press constantly tell us, is full of horror, evil, pain and suffering. If God is in the world, then his goodness is also in this horrific pain and suffering, which appears contradictory, unless the evil, pain and suffering is viewed in some way as illusory. We return to this problem when we examine the problem of evil in Chapter 6.

God's relation to time: eternal and everlasting

Aspects of the Bible, taken together with some of the perfect characteristics already attributed to God earlier, point towards the conclusion that God is timeless and eternal. In other words, God exists outside of, or independent of, time. For example, God in his capacity as creator of the universe (Genesis 1:1–5) must exist outside of the universe in order to create it. As the universe consists of space and time, God must exist outside of space and time: 'The one who is high and lifted up, who inhabits eternity, whose name is Holy' (Isaiah 57:15). Aquinas illustrates how this might be possible. Imagine someone sitting on top of a hill, watching people travel along a road beneath them. From the point of view of someone on the road, there will be people in front and people behind. But from the view of the observer on the hill, everyone on the road can be seen simultaneously.[17] In a similar way, all of time is simultaneously present to a timeless God (see Figure 2.1). This timeless or eternal aspect of God mirrors God's position as a transcendent being, existing beyond the universe. It was this account of God's relationship with time that was held by scholastic philosophers from Augustine to Aquinas.

It's impossible to imagine what 'seeing time' from the perspective of a timeless being might be like, as it is so different from our limited experience of time. Kurt Vonnegut tries to describe the difference in his novel *Slaughterhouse 5*. The Tralfmadorians, a super-intelligent and advanced alien species from the planet Tralfmadore, see the past, present and future simultaneously, and they find it difficult to understand what it must be like to see time in

■ **Figure 2.1 *God is outside of time***

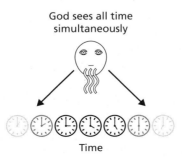

God sees all time simultaneously

Time

the limited, sequential way that Billy Pilgrim experiences it (Billy is a human whom they've kidnapped for their zoo). This is how the Tralfmadorian guide tries to explain the difference to the visitors at the zoo:

The guide invited the crowd to imagine that they [the Tralfmadorians] were looking across a desert at a mountain range on a day that was twinkling bright and clear. They could look at a peak or a bird or a cloud, at a stone right in front of them . . . But among them was this poor Earthling and his head was encased in a steel sphere . . . There was only one eyehole through which he could look, and welded to that eyehole was six feet of pipe . . . He was also strapped to a flatcar on rails, and there was no way he could turn his head or touch the pipe . . . Whatever poor Billy saw through the pipe, he had no choice but to say to himself, 'That's life.'[18]

▶ criticism ◀ Understanding God as timeless sits uneasily with God's immanence, i.e. his participation and presence in the world. If God is timeless then how does God act on the world, for example through miracles, or when communicating with prophets, as such events take place in time?

There is a way to avoid this problem, and to describe God's relationship with time in a way that better fits the lay-person's understanding of God. Throughout the Old Testament, God is described as without a beginning and without an end (Genesis 21:33, Deuteronomy 33:27, Isaiah 57:15) and, although this is consistent with God being timeless, there is another interpretation – namely that God is everlasting. 'Before the mountains were born or you brought forth the earth and the world, from everlasting to everlasting you are God' (Psalm 90:2). In this sense God has always existed, and always will, but lives alongside and through his creation. An everlasting God is one who, for Christians at least, is more obviously capable of a personal relationship with humans and of love for them and the world. There is a question, though, of whether this limits God's knowledge and undermines his omniscience and omnipotence. Unless God existed outside of time he could not have created time (this is one of Augustine's arguments for God's timelessness[19]), in which case God cannot be omnipotent. But if God exists in time, as an everlasting God, then this suggests he doesn't know what's on the horizon, as it simply hasn't happened yet, in which case God cannot be omniscient.

There is a further problem with describing God as timeless, which is that he must know what we are about to do, and this appears to imply that we have no choice in our actions. This is a difficulty that we will return to below (page 101).

■ God's unchanging nature: immutability

If something never changes, and cannot change, then it is termed 'immutable'. As with the previous attributes, the idea of God's enduring (immutable) nature has its origins in the Bible. 'They will perish, but you will endure; they will all wear out like a garment . . . but you will remain the same and your years will never end' (Psalm 102:26–27); 'For I, the Lord, do not change' (Malachi 3:6). Immutability is more difficult to understand than God's goodness, power or knowledge, because there is nothing analogous to it in our usual understanding of a person. The concept may make more sense when we consider that change only occurs in things that can be divided up into 'parts'. So, for example, people are made up of many different parts both mentally and physically, and these parts change (e.g. through getting older, or through injury). But God does not have any parts either in space (God does not have a body; he is incorporeal) or in time (God does not exist over different periods of time; he is eternal); in other words God is said to be 'simple'. Because God is not made up of parts, and because he is perfect, he cannot change and does not need to change – Matthew wrote 'Be perfect, therefore, as your heavenly Father is perfect' (Matthew 5:48). This also suggests that God's attributes cannot be separated from one another. So it's not the case that God is omniscient *and* omnipotent *and* benevolent etc. Instead we should think of these as just different aspects of the same thing, namely God's essential nature: his 'Godness'.

■ **Figure 2.2** *All God's attributes are one*

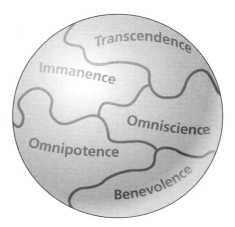

Are God's attributes coherent?

We have now looked at the main characteristics of God and sketched some of the problems with these. Combining these attributes gives rise to further problems, and ultimately to the charge that the idea of God (the God of the philosophers) is an incoherent one. In this section we examine in more detail some of the challenges that most threaten the coherence of the concept of God. These challenges are:

- The problem of omnipotence
- The problem of free will
- The Euthyphro Dilemma
- The problem of divine action and creation
- The problem of evil

The table on page 103 shows which attributes, when combined, lead to inconsistencies or contradictions that need to be addressed by the believer. (Obviously these inconsistencies are not a concern for non-believers, or ATHEISTS, and can be seen as further evidence that 'God' is not a term that refers to anything in, or out of, the universe.)

In the left-hand column below are some of the properties attributed to God by believers; in the right-hand column are properties attributed to the universe by believers.

1 Try to think up as many potential problems with the concept of God as you can by combining properties from either column (e.g. 2 and D). You may find that a single property is problematic in itself or you may combine three or four properties together to create a problem.

2 How might a believer go about resolving these problems?

Properties of God	Properties of the universe
1 God is omnipotent	A Evil exists in the world
2 God is omniscient	B Humans have free will
3 God is omnipresent	C There is evidence of God in the world
4 God is benevolent	
5 God is beyond understanding	D Humans can have private thoughts
6 God has free will	
7 God defines morality	E God intervenes in the world
8 God is outside of time	F The universe is governed by physical laws
9 God acts morally	
10 God is immaterial	G The universe exists in space and time

The problem of omnipotence

There is an issue with the claim that God is all-powerful or *omnipotent*. J.L. Mackie, amongst others, argues that if we examine the idea of being literally all-powerful we quickly find that it is incoherent.[20] To see why, we need to recognise that being all-powerful means being able to do literally anything. So, consider the task of creating a stone so large that God himself could not lift it. Can God perform this task or not? Well, if he *cannot* then there is at least one thing he cannot do, and so he would not be omnipotent. But, on the other hand, if he *can* successfully perform this task, then there is something else he cannot do, namely lift the stone he has created. So either way there is something an omnipotent being cannot do. It seems to follow that it is impossible to be literally all-powerful. There just have to be limits to the power a being has to perform certain tasks, and if so then omnipotence isn't a possible attribute of any being.

Possibly the swiftest solution to this problem comes from St Thomas Aquinas who argues that God's power is bound by what is logically possible, but he is still omnipotent. He cannot perform actions which contradict reason. This means he cannot create round squares, or married bachelors; and in the same way he cannot create stones that he cannot lift. But within the limits of the logically coherent his power is indeed boundless.

The atheist may ask more problematic questions, such as 'Can an omnipotent God create something that later he will have no control over?': for example, humans that have free will. This is a more serious problem for the believer since it touches on our own nature and our relationship to God. If God is truly all-powerful, then surely we would not have any power over our own actions. Everything would be under his control. On the other hand, if he were truly all-powerful he should be able to give us power over our own actions. So, once again, either way there is a limitation on his power.

The problem of free will

There is also a problem arising from God's omniscience (the claim he is all-knowing) when combined with the claim that human beings have the freedom to choose their own course of action, at least some of the time; in other words, the claim that humans have FREE WILL (for more on the idea that humans have free will, see Chapter 5). If God really knows literally *everything*, then it seems as if he must know the future, and, in particular, he must know what choices we are going to make. But if God knows what action I will perform before I decide to do it, then I cannot have chosen to do otherwise than I did. But if we cannot choose otherwise, then the actions we appear to choose are not really freely chosen at all. I may feel as though I freely choose to drink tea rather than coffee with my breakfast, but God knew all along that I would choose tea. I couldn't have done otherwise than 'choose' tea, and so, it seems, this choice was predetermined. It follows that the feeling of free choice is just an illusion.

Now, faced with this dilemma, the believer could give up their commitment to human freedom. Perhaps we are all just robots living out our predetermined lives. But this view of human kind does not sit at all well with the notion that we are responsible for our actions, and with the associated claim, so crucial to most religious systems, that we are accountable to God for our choices. In Christian theology, for example, it is often said that at judgement day we will have to account for our actions before Christ, and that if we are found wanting we will be subject to eternal damnation. Now, if I have no genuine choice about the sins I have committed, then I appear to have good reason to feel aggrieved by this arrangement. If God knew I would sin, and made me so that I would sin, then what do my sins have to do with me? If I couldn't help it, why punish me? Surely God is the only person responsible for all the crimes of humanity!

Clearly then, denying humans free will has not been a popular option for believers, since it appears to put the blame for all sin onto God. But neither do believers normally wish to surrender claims to God's omniscience. So how can the problem be resolved? One approach is to say that God's omniscience arises because he is outside of time, so he is able to survey the whole of time in one go. This means that for him there is no future or past; or rather, future and past co-exist on a continuum laid out before his gaze. Human actions are not predetermined and we freely choose to act as we do. But, at the same time, God is able to see what actions we do, as it happens, choose. So, just because God knows what I will do, this doesn't mean that I was somehow forced to do it. To see this thought, consider our own knowledge of the past. Think back to a choice that you made recently, say to have tea rather than coffee with your breakfast this morning. You now know that you chose tea; but the fact that you know that you chose tea, doesn't mean that you didn't freely choose tea. You might have chosen coffee. In the same way, the thought goes, the fact that God can know what our choices will be doesn't mean that they couldn't be otherwise. He may know that I will choose tea with my breakfast tomorrow. But when the choice comes, I am still freely choosing tea over coffee, and it is still true to say that I could, if I wanted, choose coffee.

	OMNISCIENCE	OMNIPOTENCE	BENEVOLENCE	TRANSCENDENCE	IMMANENCE	ETERNAL	EVERLASTING
OMNISCIENCE	–	–	Problem of evil	Problem of free will	Inconsistent (If God is in the world how can he know everything?)	Problem of free will	Inconsistent (If God is in time then how can he know the future?)
OMNIPOTENCE		Problem of omnipotence	Problem of evil	Problem of divine action	Problem of creation	Problem of divine action	Problem of creation
BENEVOLENCE			Euthyphro Dilemma	Problem of divine action	Inconsistent (If God is in the world then he is in evil)	–	–
TRANSCENDENCE				–	Inconsistent (God can't be both in and out of the world)	–	Inconsistent (If God is outside the world then he is outside of time)
IMMANENCE					–	Inconsistent (If God is in the world then he is not eternal)	–
ETERNAL						–	Inconsistent (God can't be both in and out of time)
EVERLASTING							–

■ **Figure 2.3**
Some of the problems associated with the attributes of God

■ The Euthyphro Dilemma

Plato

> *Is what is pious loved by the gods because it is pious, or is it pious because it is loved?*

Euthyphro, 10a

In his dialogue the *Euthyphro* Plato shows that there are problems with viewing God's goodness as moral goodness. In short, is God good because he sets the standard for moral goodness, or because he follows perfectly an independent moral standard? In the dialogue the character Euthyphro attempts to define morality as that which is the will of the gods, or, in his phrase, that which is 'loved by the gods'. Socrates raises the question of whether everything that the gods command must therefore be moral, or whether everything the gods command is 'moral' because they are following some external moral authority. This choice has become known as the Euthyphro Dilemma, and as a dilemma it offers two unpalatable options to a theist:

1 Every action that God commands us to do (even cruel and despicable ones) is good.
2 Every action that God commands us to do is good because it accords with some other moral authority.

■ **Figure 2.4 *The two horns of the Euthyphro Dilemma***

God's commands are good simply because they come from God

God's commands are good because they conform to an external moral source

Let's examine the consequences of each option.

The first option assumes that God is the source and standard of all moral goodness, and that whatever he commands will automatically be good. So God could command us to do completely trivial things (such as not stepping on the cracks in the pavement) and these would be morally good. God could even have commanded us to perform cruel, dishonest or unjust acts, which run counter to our moral intuitions. But, according to this interpretation of God's goodness, a believer would be obliged to do these things and they would be morally right because God had commanded them. It is possible to find many examples in the Old Testament of God's commands that seem to us to be morally questionable, for example the command to Moses to commit acts of genocide whilst on the journey to Canaan (Deuteronomy 3:2; Numbers 31), or the command given to Abraham to sacrifice his own son Isaac:

God tested Abraham and said to him 'Abraham . . . Take your son, your only son Isaac whom you love, and go to the land of Moriah and offer him there as a burnt offering.'

Genesis 22:2

In the original dilemma given to Euthyphro, Socrates asks why should we worship a God who could command us to do horrific acts. But this interpretation of God's goodness forces us into a position where any act, however terrible, is good when it is commanded by God. This is a conclusion we might wish to avoid, as Job says.

It is unthinkable that God would do wrong, that the Almighty would pervert justice.

Job 34:12

However, Søren Kierkegaard (1813–1855) is quite prepared to accept that God may tell us to commit acts that require us to suspend our ethical beliefs, and that we would be obliged to carry out those acts. In *Fear and Trembling*, Kierkegaard defends Abraham's decision to kill his son, on the grounds that God has commanded it as proof of his faith.[21] In doing so Kierkegaard challenges the assumption that ethical values should be placed above all other values. For Kierkegaard there is a higher value, known only by God, and yet we must have faith in God's will if he commands us to perform an apparently unethical act. Such faith cannot be rationally explained, nor supported by evidence, yet faith may, in some situations, require the suspension of our ethical beliefs. It was just so with Abraham: he was, as Kierkegaard says, a 'knight of faith' and was prepared to murder his own son in the faith that he was doing it for some higher purpose or 'telos'. Kierkegaard refers to this as the 'teleological suspension of the ethical', where the will of God comes above mere ethics.

But Kierkegaard's position is also one that many believers would be uncomfortable with. Both Aquinas and St Augustine believed that God cannot will evil because he is perfectly good, in an ethical sense. It seems tempting to reject an account of moral goodness which implies that God could tell us to do anything and it would by definition be good. In which case, what makes God's commands good?

Moving back to the dilemma, the other option, and the preferred choice of Plato, is that good is independent of God's will; so what makes him good, and everything he says good, is that these conform to some external moral authority. In this case God doesn't issue commands which then automatically become 'good'; instead God issues commands which are good only insofar as they comply with a moral code that lies outside of God. This approach conforms with Plato's metaphysical theory of forms in which the good has objective reality discoverable by reason. However, for the traditional theist this is a problematic way of accounting for the goodness of God's commands. For if the moral law lies beyond God then we can by-pass God if we wish to be moral, and we can also wonder, why we should worship a God who is bound by the same moral rules as ourselves? So to many believers the second horn of the dilemma seems as unacceptable as the first.

The Euthyphro Dilemma, when applied to Christianity, challenges the view that God's commands form the basis of ethics. Both options given by the dilemma are unpalatable to the believer: the first, because it makes acts of genocide and infanticide morally good; the second because it places morality beyond God.

■ The problem of divine action and creation

Two fundamental tenets of Christian belief are that God created the universe and that since that creation God has acted in the universe (for example, through miracles, responses to prayer and communications with prophets). But there is a tension between these two beliefs: the claim that 'God is a creator' puts God in the position of being transcendent and eternal, i.e. as outside of the universe and time. However, the belief that God is an agent who cares about the world and acts in the world puts God in the position of being immanent and everlasting, i.e. as immersed in the world.

The accepted doctrine of creation is that God created the universe *ex nihilo* – out of nothing. This is not how Plato thought of creation; for him the demiurge (not the God of the Bible) fashioned the universe out of pre-existing matter. But, for Christians, God started with nothing, and he created space and time from nothing. If God is to be the creator of space and time in this way, then it makes sense to think of him as outside of the universe – as transcendent – and as outside time – as eternal or atemporal. From this position as an eternal, transcendent being, God's immutability then also makes sense: God remains a perfect being who doesn't change and is affected by nothing. We have seen that this is the view of Christian philosophers influenced by the metaphysical theories of the ancient Greeks, such as St Anselm, St Augustine and St Aquinas. Anselm writes:

You exist neither yesterday, nor today, nor tomorrow but are outside all times.[22]

Anselm

But if God does indeed 'transcend' his creation, then how is he able to intervene in the world? If God is not in time, and he is not composed of ordinary physical matter, then how can he enter into the spatio-temporal universe and make things happen in space and time? To be atemporal and immaterial yet act on matter and in time seems impossible, in which case divine action in the form of miracles, response to prayers, revelations would be impossible – a conclusion which is very troubling to the believer. Miracles lie at the heart of Christian belief, firstly in the virgin birth of Jesus, and secondly in his resurrection after his crucifixion. Both of these events confirm that Jesus was not a mere prophet or spiritual leader but the Son of God. So any challenge raised regarding the impossibility of divine action on the world is an important one and must be met by the believer.

One solution is to say that because God is omnipotent there are no limitations on what he is capable of doing. Through his omnipotence, God is able to act on the world, and perform miracles, despite being outside of time. Another solution takes the line of deism, by saying that a timeless God created the universe, along with all the laws governing the universe, and he 'built into' his creation certain miraculous events that seem to go against these laws – much like a computer programmer can design a word-processing package that contains a few surprises for the user (such as the head of the Queen popping-up the millionth time that the '£' key is pressed).

Finally a believer might insist that God is in the world (immanent). This means that God exists in time and hence is able to act upon the universe. God's immanence also entails that he can sustain a personal (rather than impersonal) relationship with human beings, which again is important for believers, who believe it is possible to pray and to communicate with God in a meaningful way. But if God is to be a creator and a personal deity, then he must be both immanent and transcendent. And if God is immanent, then he must exist in time (because the world exists in time, and an everlasting God is in the world), in which case how could he have created time? The point when believers start to happily accept contradictions is the point when non-believers start questioning whether the language of religion is meaningful (we look at this in the next section and in Chapter 6). Below, on pages 158–59, we look at the explanation given by the German philosopher and atheist Feuerbach (1804–1872) as to why there is this fundamental tension in theism between God's transcendence/eternality and God's immanence/everlasting nature.

■ The problem of evil

The final and most significant challenge to the coherence of the idea of God is the problem of evil. This is one of the oldest and most pressing concerns faced by the believer. How is it possible that an omnipotent, omniscient and benevolent God allows such horrific pain and suffering to exist within his creation? It seems as if God, who created a universe with all this horror, must be responsible for it, and if so this would seriously undermine his perfection and his status as a being worthy of worship. We examine this problem in detail in Chapter 6.

ACTIVITY

Consider the problems below. How might a philosophically minded believer respond to each of them?

1 God cannot do what it is logically impossible to do (e.g. make a stone so large that he can't move it). Therefore God is not omnipotent.
2 God cannot create a being whom he can control yet who has genuine free will. Therefore God is not omnipotent.
3 God cannot know what a being with genuine free will is about to do. Therefore God is not omniscient.
4 God has created beings whom he knew would do evil to one another. So ultimately God is to blame for our wicked acts. Therefore God is not good.
5 God is outside of space and time. Therefore God cannot intervene in the world, and he cannot perform miracles.
6 God is present in the world, existing inside of space and time. Therefore he cannot have created space and time and cannot have created the universe.
7 God is present in the world, existing in all parts of it, including all that is evil and horrific. Therefore God is not perfectly good.
8 Ultimately, the God as described by the philosophers (omnipotent, benevolent, omniscient, etc.) cannot possess all the properties they ascribe to him. The very concept of God is an incoherent one, and belief in such a God is irrational.

Aquinas on applying these attributes to God

The attributes of God that we have been examining were first discussed by scholastic philosophers of the Middle Ages, and the greatest of these, St Thomas Aquinas, offered an influential and enduring analysis of religious language. The problem, as Aquinas saw it, was that when we apply attributes like 'goodness' and 'powerful' to God, we are not using these terms in the same way as when we apply them to ordinary things. For example, when the author of Psalm 31 described God as his 'rock' and his 'fortress',[23] he did not imagine God to be constructed from stone. And when we read in Exodus that 'The Lord is a great warrior: Almighty is his name'[24] this does not mean that God is triumphant in warfare over other gods (which is the meaning that the ancient Greeks might have intended when referring to Zeus as a great warrior).

Despite the difficulties of knowing anything about God, Aquinas is still confident that we can talk about God in a positive and literal way.[25] He is opposed to the *VIA NEGATIVA* (i.e. the claim that God can only be spoken of by saying what he is not), although he does accept that the words we use to describe God only do so in an imperfect way. He is also opposed to the idea that we can only speak of God in a non-literal way (for example, through metaphors like 'rock' and 'lion'). The question for Aquinas is how can we talk about God in a substantial way, when God is beyond experience, and our language cannot describe what is beyond experience?

Aquinas' solution to the problem of talking about God rests on his identification of three ways of using words:

1 Univocal use: if I use a word univocally in two sentences then it has the same meaning in both those sentences. For example, in the statements 'There's a rat in the kitchen' and 'You look like a drowned rat' the word 'rat' has the same meaning, and is being used univocally.
2 Equivocal use: if I use a word equivocally in two sentences then it has different meanings in both those sentences. For example, in the sentences 'He was feeling a bit down after his disappointing exam result' and 'She told her sister to climb down from the electric pylon' the word 'down' has different meanings, so in these cases it is being used equivocally.
3 Analogical use: if I use a word analogically in two sentences then there is a similarity between the meanings of the two words. For example, if I say that 'Lassie was faithful to her owner' and 'Mr Smith was faithful to his wife' then I am applying the word faithful to the dog in a way that is analogous (similar) to the faithfulness of Mr Smith. In other words there is a resemblance between the behaviour (and perhaps thoughts) of a dog and a human. Aquinas refers to this resemblance as 'proportion', because there is a sense in which the faithfulness of the dog is proportioned to the faithfulness of a human being. The proportion of faithfulness in the dog is less than that in the human, because it is a less complex type of creature.

For the second sentence of each pair, identify whether the word in **bold** is being used in an equivocal, a univocal or an analogical way as the same word in the first sentence.

1 a) His eyes stayed focused on the window across the street.
  b) The eyes are a **window** to the soul.

2 a) The guards fought the thieves in order to protect the crown.
  b) The king fought a bloody war in order to protect his **crown**.

3 a) The artist drew a blank white square on the canvas.
  b) The detective drew a **blank** when interviewing the suspect.

4 a) The fresh air had brought a healthy glow to her cheeks.
  b) He had a very **healthy** appetite for a two year old.

5 a) Nottingham Castle was a stronghold for the oppressed.
  b) God is a **stronghold** for the oppressed (Psalms 9:9).

Aquinas goes on to analyse whether the words that we use to describe God are being used equivocally, univocally or analogically. He says that when we say 'God is good' we cannot be using the word in the same way that we use it when we are talking about humans. God is so different from any other being that it is impossible to apply to him the same attributes that we apply to humans or other creatures. So we cannot use words like 'good', 'wise' or 'compassionate', univocally of both God and human beings. However, this does not mean that we are therefore using these terms in a completely different (equivocal) way when we talk about God. Aquinas believes that there is a resemblance between the meaning of the words that we use to describe God, and the meaning of the words we use to describe his creation (and the creatures that inhabit it).

So Aquinas rejects the view that terms applied to God are identical to those applied to everyday beings, i.e. the univocal use. He also rejects the view that the words we use to talk about God (like goodness) bear no relation to the words we use to talk about humans, i.e. the equivocal use. Instead Aquinas argues that when we talk about God we are generally using words analogically. This means that there is a resemblance between the meaning of 'faithfulness', 'wisdom', 'goodness', etc. when applied to God and the meanings of these terms when applied to humans. But it is only a resemblance, and our words cannot come close to accurately describing God, such is the extent of the difference between God's perfections (which are unified and indivisible from one another) and our own flawed virtues (which do not come altogether as a single package).

This failure of words accurately to describe God arises because words 'apply primarily to creatures, not God'.[26] So we are taking a tool (language) which has been developed to do one particular task, namely to talk about the world around us, and we are using this tool to do a task for which it isn't equipped, namely to talk about God. For example, we are comfortable using the word 'love' to describe the fiery, finite and jealous emotion that humans feel for each other. But the same word hardly conveys at all the power and depth of God's love, which is held to be infinite, all embracing and an inseparable part of his essence. However, we can see that there is a sort of resemblance between God's love and our own feeble love, and so for Aquinas the word 'love' can be used to talk about God in a literal sense. The words we use to describe human thoughts, feelings and actions are the only ones we have available to us when it comes to talking about God. We just have to remember that, with religious language, we are using these words in an analogical way.

▶ criticism ◀ But there is a difficulty with claiming that we can talk about God, even in an analogical way. In Stanislaw Lem's novel *Solaris*, human beings have discovered a planet, called Solaris, covered by an ocean which seems to be alive, which moves and extends its 'tendrils' out into the atmosphere, and which might even have a mind. For decades scientists investigate the behaviour of this living planet, and countless theories are proposed as to what Solaris is: a psychic ocean, a dying organism, an introverted hermit, an inorganic fluid, the cradle of a new god . . . Because Solaris is beyond anything humans have experienced, the scientists are only able to express their theories through the language of analogy: by finding correspondences between the apparently purposeful activities of the planet and the purposeful activities that we already know about and understand, namely human or animal behaviour. But ultimately the scientists cannot explain or predict the purpose or meaning of the planet's behaviour. As Lem puts it:

Transposed into any human language, the values and meanings involved lose all substance; they cannot be brought intact through the barrier.[27]

The inner workings and consciousness of Solaris lie completely beyond human understanding and words. Because Solaris remains inexplicable and incomprehensible to humans, the analogical language we use to describe it becomes meaningless: the scientists can never know whether Solaris is 'like' a human in any respect. The problem that Lem's scientists face on Solaris is the same as that faced by believers in the real world: how can we be sure whether our analogical descriptions of God (as good, or wise, or loving) actually refer to any real attribute of God? If God is so utterly different from humans, then even analogical language might fail to describe him in any significant way. Perhaps, as St Paul said, we shall have to wait until the next life in order to know exactly what we're talking about when we speak of 'God'.

For now we see through a glass, darkly, but then face to face; now I know in part; but then shall I know even as also I am known.

Paul, 1 Corinthians 13:12

A brief diversion into philosophical proofs

We have seen how philosophers have attempted to analyse *who* God is; now we turn to look at their attempts to prove *that* God is. In Woody Allen's short story 'Mr Big', a private detective is hired to find God and his first lead is Rabbi Wiseman:

'You ever see Him?'

'Me? Are you kidding? I'm lucky I get to see my grandchildren.'

'Then how do you know He exists?'

'How do I know? What kind of question is that? Could I get a suit like this for fourteen dollars if there was no one up there? Here, feel [the cloth] – how can you doubt?'[28]

Careful reasoning in support of a belief or theory is a fundamental part of the tradition of Western philosophy. It is not surprising then that when philosophers turn their attention to religion they often wish to supplement sacred texts and revelation with their own arguments in support of their religion. The use of human reason and arguments to determine truths about God is central to natural theology, and Christian philosophers have sought to demonstrate that God exists by a process of reasoning since at least the time of St Augustine (354–430). The Vatican Council of the Catholic Church has declared that God can be known with certainty, and through the natural power of human reason.[29] This declaration was made in part on the basis of a passage in the New Testament which claims that if we attend properly to the nature of the world around us we will notice that it must have been created by God.

Ever since God created the world, his invisible qualities, both his eternal power and his divine nature, have been clearly seen; they are perceived in the things that God has made.

Romans 1:20

Rational demonstrations of God's existence reached their zenith with the medieval philosopher St Thomas Aquinas, who offered five ways to prove God's existence. During the Enlightenment of the eighteenth century, proofs of God's existence began to fall from favour with religious thinkers and philosophers alike. David Hume (1711–1776) and Immanuel Kant (1724–1804) are often credited with doing permanent damage to the classical arguments for the existence of God. However, religious philosophers have continued to reason for the existence of God, and the past century has witnessed a resurgence in this area.

As we are going to be looking in detail at two of the main arguments for God's existence (the ontological argument and the argument from design in Chapter 6), it is worth making a few points about arguments in general.

How are arguments structured?

When we talk about arguments we are not referring to a quarrel, or some kind of personal battle of words involving a denial of everything the other person says, combined with gentle sarcasm and incisive put-downs. An argument, in the sense we're interested in, consists of one or more statements offered in support of a further concluding statement. The supporting statements, the ones that provide the justification, are referred to as the PREMISES of the argument, and the concluding statement is obviously referred to as the CONCLUSION. If a passage contains the words 'and so', 'therefore' or 'hence' then this is a good indication that a conclusion is being drawn and that an argument has been made to support the conclusion. The premises may need to be combined in order to support the conclusion, or they may support the conclusion individually.

The goal of most arguments is to convince us of the truth of the conclusion, and so to persuade us to believe it. As the conclusion rests on the supporting premises it is essential that every premise in an argument be true. This means that when constructing, or evaluating, arguments we must pay careful attention to each premise. There are various types of premise which can combine to provide grounds to support the conclusion, for example:

- general observations (e.g. 'politicians have always done whatever it takes to keep themselves in power')
- statements of fact (e.g. 'there were only enough lifeboats on the *Titanic* to save half the passengers')
- theoretical assumptions (e.g. 'everything in the world has a purpose or function')
- definitions (e.g. 'God is a perfect being')
- hypothetical statements (e.g. 'if you eat carrots then you'll be able to see in the dark')

It is helpful to make the premises explicit when evaluating or constructing an argument, so that each one can then be weighed up and considered. As arguments usually take the form of densely written prose, you may have to tease out each premise, and many philosophers do this by assigning the premises numbers, and presenting them as a list. We have tried to do this when looking at the ontological argument below and the TELEOLOGICAL ARGUMENT in Chapter 6. Hopefully breaking down the arguments in this way will make them easier to understand and evaluate.

As well as paying attention to the truth of each premise, we also need to consider the overall structure of the argument. You might like to think of the list of premises as a sum that 'adds up' to the conclusion. If the premises correctly add up to the conclusion, that is, if by accepting them we are forced to accept the conclusion, then the argument is termed 'valid'. However, as with any human calculation, there is always the chance that mistakes have been made. An invalid argument is one where the premises do not add up to the conclusion, in other words the argument falls short of fully justifying the conclusion. This may be because the argument is flawed or because the argument is an inductive one (see below).

Deductive and inductive arguments

Aquinas

Demonstration [of God's existence] can be made in two ways: One is through the cause, and is called a priori . . . The other is through the effect, and is called a demonstration a posteriori.[30]

Valid arguments are known as DEDUCTIVE or 'deductively valid'. In a deductive argument the truth of the premises guarantees the truth of the conclusion, so long as no errors have been made. The key word here is 'guarantee'. With a deductive argument, if we accept the premises to be true then we absolutely must accept the conclusion to be true. If, as we've claimed, the goal of an argument is to persuade people to believe its conclusion, then deductive arguments must be a powerful tool: after all, if we can guarantee the truth of a conclusion, we have good reason to believe it. However, this great strength can also appear as a weakness. For deductive arguments can't establish anything new with their conclusions: they simply reveal what is already contained in the premises. For this reason, they don't really get us beyond what is already known. Another weakness is that, whilst we can know that the conclusion must follow *if* the premises are true, we still can't guarantee that the premises actually are true. Knowing that the conclusion has to follow from the premises is all very well, but it simply passes the buck and we still have find a way to establish the truth of the premises. To make clearer the strengths and weakness of such arguments, take the following standard example of a deductively valid argument:

1 All men are mortal.
2 Socrates is a man.
3 (Conclusion) Therefore Socrates is mortal.

Here, if we accept the two premises, then the conclusion follows necessarily. The great strength of the argument is that it appears to be impossible to deny the conclusion once we've accepted that the premises are true. We might say that so long as we accept the premises to be true then we can work out the truth of this conclusion in an *A PRIORI* manner, in other words prior to any further experience or fact-finding, simply by teasing out what is implicit in what is already given in the premises. Everything can be done in our heads. However, this also means that we haven't really learned anything new here. The conclusion says nothing more than was already contained in the premises. Moreover, whilst we know that Socrates must be mortal *if* he is a man, and *if* all men are mortal, we have still to find a way of establishing that these other facts are actually true. So deductive arguments appear to leave us with further questions to address, namely how to establish the truth of the premises.

INDUCTIVE ARGUMENTS are often contrasted with deductive ones because they strive to reveal something new in their conclusion. This is one of the strengths of such arguments. However, because this means they have to go beyond the information contained in their premises, they lose the power to guarantee the truth of their conclusions. This means that no inductive argument can be fully valid, and at best their conclusions are only ever probably true, even if the premises are certainly true. Typically, induction occurs where an argument moves from what is known (e.g. facts about the past, or particular observations) to what is unknown (e.g. speculations about the future, or generalisations). Induction is frequently used in the sciences and social sciences, whenever we move from empirical data to theories about the data. A typical inductive argument might be:

1 Every raven I've ever seen has been black.
2 There are 100 ravens kept at the Tower of London.
3 (Conclusion) Therefore it is likely that all 100 ravens in the Tower are black.

Even if we accept the premises as definitely true, this conclusion doesn't necessarily follow. This is because there might be whole families of London-born white ravens, which I don't know about, or it might be that for every 100 black ravens in a population two of them will be white. Just because I have only ever seen black ravens doesn't establish that they must all be black. Note that, just as with deductive arguments, we still have to accept the premises as true before the argument can be at all convincing.

Another example of an inductive argument is one where we draw a conclusion from a finite set of instances:

1 John 'Stumpy' Pepys used to play drums for Rock'n'Roll legends Spinal Tap but he died in mysterious circumstances.
2 Eric 'Stumpy Joe' Childs used to play drums for Spinal Tap but he too died in mysterious circumstances.
3 Peter 'James' Bond used to play drums for Spinal Tap but he eventually died in mysterious circumstances.
4 Mick Shrimpton now plays drums for Spinal Tap.
5 (Conclusion) So it is likely that Mick Shrimpton will one day die in mysterious circumstances.

Here we have observed that these drummers are all similar to each other in one respect (they were members of Spinal Tap), and concluded that the new drummer must be similar to the others in some further respect (he will die in mysterious circumstances). Of course, the conclusion does not follow necessarily from the premises. Mick Shrimpton may be different from the others; he may evade the Grim Reaper of Rock and live to a ripe old age. So, like other inductive arguments, this one cannot establish its conclusion with absolute certainty. Here the strength of the argument will depend on how strong the similarities are between each case of drumming tragedy. We will be looking later on at the strengths and weaknesses of a particular type of inductive argument when we come to the design argument in Chapter 6.

ACTIVITY   Read through the following arguments, asking yourself:
a) What is the conclusion of each one?
b) Which are inductive arguments, and which are deductive?
c) Which arguments do you think work, and which don't?

1   I've split up with every person I've ever been out with, so the relationship I'm in at the moment is bound to end too.

2   Men are incapable of driving safely, because they are prone to uncontrollable hormonal changes that can lead to road rage.

3   If you don't believe in God you will go to hell. Stuart doesn't believe in God. So Stuart will go to hell.

4   Philosophers spend much of their time sitting around and thinking, which means their muscles weaken, and so none of them is any good at strenuous exercise such as lifting weights.

5   Paul says he had a vision of the Virgin Mary in his bedroom last night. Paul is known to be a trustworthy person and so it likely that the Virgin really did appear to him.

6   It's wrong to kill innocent people. But babies are people too, even when they're in the womb. So it's wrong to have an abortion.

7   The evil dictator denies he has any weapons of mass destruction. But we know from his denials in the past that he's a liar. So he must have them somewhere, and we should keep looking until we find them.

8   My little sister is three and she loves the adverts for toys, so your three-year-old sister should enjoy them too.

9   If God exists then he would have created a world without suffering and evil. However, examples abound of terrible suffering and evil in the world. So God cannot exist.

10 No England football team for the last 40 years has got through to the final of a major competition. So they will obviously fail in the next World Cup.

A *priori* and *a posteriori* knowledge

We saw that the strength of both deductive and inductive arguments will ultimately depend on the plausibility of their premises. If the premises are obviously false, then the arguments cannot be any good. So how do we establish the truth of the premises of an argument? One obvious answer is through experience. To return to the examples above: the claim that all the ravens I've observed are black is based on my own experience. Such knowledge seems fairly straightforward and unassailable. I should know, after all, what I have experienced. Similarly, knowing that Socrates was a man comes from experience, albeit indirect experience via the testimony of others. I may have read about him in a book, or heard about him from a teacher. Knowledge that is acquired in this kind of a way is known as *A POSTERIORI*, meaning that it depends on, or comes *after*, experience. To know such things I have to have experience of them.

But philosophers have also been very interested in another way of establishing their premises that does not require reference to anyone's experiences of the world around them. Such knowledge is known as *a priori*, meaning it does not depend on experience. Examples of such knowledge come from mathematics – '2 + 3 = 5' can be known just by working it out in your head. Its truth doesn't depend on doing any experiment counting real-life objects. Of course, I do need to learn the meanings of the terms involved in the expression of this sum, but that is the sole extent of the role of experience here. Other examples of *a priori* knowledge are statements that have to be true because of the definitions of the words they use, such as 'You can't steal your own property', or 'Abel's brother was male'. So long as I understand the meanings of the words in such a sentence I can be sure that it is true. In other words, I can work it out in my head, just by thinking about it, and I don't need to go out into the world, as it were, to check that this is true. For more on the distinction between *a priori* and *a posteriori* knowledge see Chapter 4 (page 292).

Summary

When we come to examine the arguments for the existence of God we need to bear in mind what has just been said about arguments in general. This means thinking about the following types of questions:

- What are the premises?
- Are there any hidden premises (or assumptions)?
- Are the premises true?
- Are there any flaws in the reasoning?
- Do the premises support the conclusion?
- Does the conclusion go beyond the premises?
- With inductive arguments, is the probability of the conclusion high, or are there alternative conclusions we can draw from the evidence?

The ontological argument

Introduction

We now turn to look at a specific proof of the existence of God, one that is based on the very idea of God, and is known as the ontological argument. We examine a number of different ontological arguments and the criticisms made of them as they developed from the time of St Anselm through to Descartes. We shall also briefly look at modern perspectives on the arguments.

Ontological arguments for God's existence are supposed to be deductively valid. In other words, if we accept their premises as true, the conclusion is said to follow necessarily. Such arguments, if successful, would clearly represent an incredible achievement for human reason, for they promise to establish God's existence with absolute certainty! However, before we can be certain that they succeed we need to be sure that the premises used in such arguments are true. But ontological arguments also claim that their premises are unassailable since they concern only definitions and the analysis of concepts, and specifically the analysis of the concept 'God'. Because we can examine the concept of God in a purely *a priori* manner it represents a firm starting point for our argument. Thus an ontological argument should establish the existence of God with the same degree of certainty as is to be found in mathematics.

But how can an argument that proves the existence of something begin from premises that are knowable purely *a priori*? Surely, we would need to begin with some experience of the world before we could establish the existence of anything. If we want to know whether the Black Panther of Bodmin Moor exists then we examine eye-witness accounts, assess the video footage, carry out autopsies on the savaged lambs, and perhaps even recruit thousands of foolhardy students to trawl across the barren hills searching for panther droppings and paw prints.[31] On the basis of the empirical data (the experiences) that we have gathered we then build up a case for, or against, the existence of the beast. So here the proof of the existence of the Black Panther begins with evidence obtained *a posteriori*. However, an ontological argument claims to establish the existence of something (namely God) without drawing on any observation, evidence or experience. How is this possible?

Unpacking concepts

The ontological argument works by analysing the concept of God. This process of analysing a concept can be thought of metaphorically, as 'unpacking' the concept. In other words we must discover all the ideas that are essential elements of the concept. For example, Figure 2.5 illustrates how we might 'unpack' the concept of 'triangle'. We find it contains the following ideas: it is a shape with three sides, the sides are straight lines connecting to form angles, and those internal angles add up to 180 degrees.

■ **Figure 2.5**
Unpacking the
concept of 'triangle'

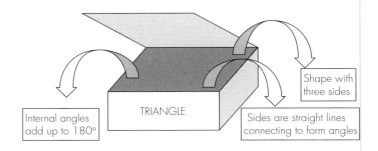

experimenting with ideas

Unpack each of the following concepts into their component parts (the characteristics or ideas that make up each concept).

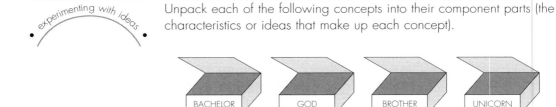

Let us now look at how we might unpack a statement about the world in order to reveal an *a priori* truth. Take the claim that *Elvis' mother was female*. Without knowing anything about Elvis, his mother, or their stormy relationship, we can safely conclude that the claim is true. We do this through unpacking the essential elements of the key term 'Elvis' mother', as shown in Figure 2.6.

■ **Figure 2.6**
Unpacking the
concept of Elvis'
mother

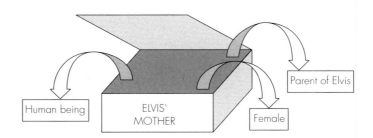

Our analysis, or unpacking, reveals that 'Elvis' mother' is the human, female parent of Elvis. So we can now see the obvious truth that *Elvis' female parent was female*.

This statement has a structure similar to the structure of many other claims, for example that 'terrorists are a threat to national security', or that 'love of money is the root of all evil'. To assist our analysis it is useful to identify two distinct parts of such statements (or PROPOSITIONS):

1 the SUBJECT (the thing the statement is about, e.g. 'love of money')
2 the PREDICATE (the properties we're claiming that the subject has, e.g. 'is the root of all evil').

ACTIVITY   For each of the following propositions identify which part is the subject and which the predicate.

1 The Beast of Bodmin Moor is black.
2 Britney loves Prince William.
3 Tabloid newspapers aim to educate rather than titillate.
4 Noah counted the animals two by two.
5 The cow jumped over the moon.
6 Humans could fly too if only they could flap their arms fast enough.
7 God exists.
8 The earth is about to enter another Ice Age.
9 Cain's brother was male.
10 This triangle's internal angles add up to 180 degrees.

Once we have identified the subject and the predicate we can then ask whether the claim is true. This usually means gathering empirical evidence, for example that Britney really does love the Prince and is not just in it for his mother's fabulous jewellery. However, statements 9 and 10 are special cases, as they are both true by definition. With a little analysis the predicate (e.g. 'was male') can be shown to be already contained in the subject (e.g. Cain's male sibling). And saying 'this triangle's internal angles add up to 180 degrees' is very uninformative to people who know what a triangle is: they know it is true by definition. This means that it is possible to know that some propositions are true *a priori* and these do not need any further empirical investigation.

So, to return to the question, one way of justifying a claim *a priori* is to show it is true by definition through analysing the concepts used in the proposition; in other words to show that the subject already contains within its meaning the property we're claiming that it possesses. With an ontological proof of God's existence a similar process takes place: by analysing, and fully understanding, what 'God' means, we shall see that the proposition 'God exists' is true by definition and hence that God must exist.

St Anselm's first ontological argument

Anselm

Why then has the fool said in his heart, There is no God (Psalm 14.1), since it is so evident, to a rational mind, that thou dost exist in the highest degree of all? Why, except that he is dull and a fool?

Proslogion, Ch. 3

St Anselm (1033–1109) is widely credited with inventing ontological arguments in his book the *Proslogion* (meaning 'the discourse'). He writes in the preface that he was searching for a single proof of God's existence, one that would not only demonstrate that God existed, but also reveal his existence as the supreme good, depending on nothing else. In the *Proslogion* St Anselm offered at least two versions of this proof, later dubbed the 'ontological' argument by Immanuel Kant (ontology is the study of existence). Both proofs rely on the analysis of a particular definition of God; by fully understanding this definition we come to recognise that God must exist.

Although Anselm addresses his proof to God almost as a prayer, it may be easier for us to grasp if we present it in a standard philosophical form: with a list of numbered premises leading to a conclusion.

1 God is the greatest possible being (or as Anselm puts it 'that than which nothing greater can be conceived').[32]
2 Even a fool (someone who doesn't believe in God) can understand that God is the greatest possible being.
3 (From Psalms 14 and 53) The fool says there is no God in reality.
4 (From 2 and 3) The fool is convinced that God, the greatest possible being, exists only in his understanding and not in reality.
5 It is greater to exist both in the understanding and in reality, than merely in the understanding.
6 (From 5) The greatest possible being, if it is genuinely the greatest, must exist both in the understanding and in reality.
7 (Conclusion from 1 and 6) Therefore God exists both in reality and in the understanding. Moreover (from 4 and 6), the fool really is a fool, as he is denying the existence of the greatest possible being, i.e. a being which must exist if it is genuinely the greatest!

Anselm's argument can be made clearer if we take out his passages about the fool. These passages are meant to show that the atheist is guilty of an absurdity, namely believing that something that must exist (God) doesn't exist! However, Anselm's argument works just as well if we focus only on those parts that prove God exists (and leave out the parts that reveal the fool to be a fool). There are two crucial aspects to Anselm's argument: first his definition of God as the greatest possible being, secondly his assumption that existing in reality is greater than existing in the understanding. From these two premises it becomes clear why St Anselm believes 'So truly, therefore, thou dost exist, O Lord, my God, for thou canst not be conceived not to exist' *(Proslogion 3)*. We can present the essence of Anselm's argument in standard philosophical form thus:

1 God is the greatest possible being.
2 It is greater to exist in the understanding and in reality rather than in the understanding alone.
3 Therefore the greatest possible being, God, must exist in the understanding and in reality.

Who is the greatest? Have a look at the two different scenarios in Figure 2.7.
There are two possibilities. Either God, the greatest possible being, exists only in our minds, or he exists in our minds and in reality as well.
1 Which scenario do you think is true? (Which universe do we live in?)
2 Which scenario do you think contains the greater being?
3 Are your answers to 1 and 2 the same? If they are different how can you account for the difference?

■ **Figure 2.7**

Scenario 1: The greatest possible being only exists in people's understanding

Scenario 2: The greatest possible being exists in people's understanding and in reality

In Scenario 1 people can imagine a powerful being, God, who has created and designed the world, who can perform miracles, who is the source of all morality, and who is omnipotent. Unfortunately, in this scenario, God exists only in people's imagination, and hasn't really created the world. Compare this with Scenario 2 where people can also imagine such a powerful being, except in this scenario the being actually exists, and has in fact created and designed the world, performed a few miracles, and so on. The question St Anselm might ask is: which scenario has described the greater being: Scenario 1 or 2? Atheists (Anselm's fools) allege we live in Scenario 1, where the greatest possible being exists only in our imagination. But Anselm's point is that an imaginary greatest possible being cannot be the *greatest*, because it is possible to conceive of an even greater being, namely one which actually exists and so is actually able to perform miracles and create the world,[33] as in Scenario 2. By comparing these two possibilities, a God who is imaginary and a God who really exists, we begin to understand that God, in order to be genuinely the greatest, must exist in reality. Another way of making the point is to consider that a God who didn't exist wouldn't be the greatest possible being so to be genuinely the greatest he just has to exist.

The activity above brings out some of the reasons why Anselm thinks it's greater to exist in reality than merely in the understanding (the imagination). But here is another activity that might also bring out why Anselm's assumption is a plausible one.

Imagine your perfect partner.
1 Write down all the amazing qualities such a person would have. Now suppose that there is someone, somewhere in the world, who corresponds to your fantasy.
2 Would you rather go out with the real person, or with the purely imaginary one? Why? Why not?

If, in the activity above, you decided that you'd rather go out with someone who has all the qualities of your perfect partner and actually exists in flesh and blood as well (rather than make do with a perfect but imaginary partner) then it may seem that you are agreeing with Anselm that it is better to exist in reality rather than simply in the mind.

We have seen that Anselm's ontological argument for God's existence springs from his understanding of God. By analysing what 'God' means (the greatest possible being) Anselm comes to realise that he must exist, because he is the greatest, and that those who deny his existence don't really understand the kind of being he is.

1 The philosopher Arthur Schopenhauer (1788–1860), referred to the ontological argument as a 'sleight of hand trick' and 'a charming joke', and the argument strikes many people as suspicious in some way. Have a look at each premise and each step in Anselm's argument: where, if anywhere, do you think the trickery lies in his argument?

2 What other things could you prove the existence of, using an argument like St Anselm's? Try the following format to prove the existence of whatever you like:

1 So-and-so is the greatest possible such-and-such.
2 It is greater to exist in reality and in the understanding.
3 Therefore so-and-so, if it is to be genuinely the greatest such-and-such, must exist.

Gaunilo's criticism

Before we look at Anselm's second ontological argument, it is worth examining a criticism made by one of his contemporaries, the monk Gaunilo of Marmoutier. Gaunilo suspected that something was amiss with Anselm's argument and rejected it in his work entitled 'On Behalf Of The Fool'. Gaunilo truly believed in God, but objected to Anselm's move from 'understanding God to be the greatest possible being' to the conclusion that 'God must exist in reality'. Gaunilo argued that we can use this method to define anything we like into existence, so long as we claim it has the property of being the 'greatest' or 'most excellent'.[34] But the real existence of such things, even of God, would always be doubtful without further evidence.

Gaunilo

For example: it is said somewhere in the ocean is an island . . . And they say that this island has an inestimable wealth . . . it is more excellent than all other countries . . . Now if someone should tell me that there is such an island, I should easily understand his words . . . But suppose that he went on to say . . . 'since it is more excellent not to be in the understanding alone, but to exist both in the understanding and in reality, for this reason [the island] must exist'.

'On Behalf of the Fool', Section 6

Gaunilo uses his counter-example of the perfect island to undermine Anselm's proof, and we can summarise it as follows.

125

1 We can imagine an island which is the greatest possible island.
2 It is greater to exist in reality than merely in the understanding.
3 Therefore the greatest possible island must exist in reality.

We can see Gaunilo structures his argument in the same way as Anselm's, but it leads to a questionable conclusion: there may be no such island (despite what worshippers of Ibiza may say). For Gaunilo, using an ontological argument to prove that a perfect island exists doesn't actually work, as the existence of the island is always going to be in doubt until we find real evidence for it. The fact that we can imagine such an island (and as Anselm would say it then exists in my understanding) has no bearing on whether the island does in fact exist. Instead, according to Gaunilo, we must demonstrate as a 'real and indubitable fact' the excellence and greatness of the island. The same doubts can be raised over Anselm's argument for the existence of God. The fact that we can conceive of the greatest possible being does not imply that it actually exists, and the fool is right to say he can conceive God as not existing. Gaunilo goes on to say that the fool would be right to demand that we must prove that God is *in fact* (and not just by definition) the greatest possible being.

St Anselm's second ontological argument

Anselm wrote a *Reply to Gaunilo* in which he defends his ontological argument, and draws upon his second version of it. This revolves around an extension to his definition of God, namely that he cannot be thought of as non-existent.

Anselm

God cannot be conceived not to exist . . . That which can be conceived not to exist is not God.

Proslogion, Ch. 3

To help us understand why Anselm makes this claim, let us once again compare two conceptions of God and ask which is the greater being: 1) a God who *can* be conceived of as not existing, or 2) a God who *cannot* be conceived of as not existing? To Anselm it is pretty clear that the second conception of God is greater: because God is the greatest possible being, it must be impossible to conceive of his non-existence. In fact the idea of a non-existent greatest possible being is a contradiction in terms, claims Anselm, and so only a fool could think that God existed only in his or her mind.

This goes some way to defeating Gaunilo's counter-example. Gaunilo is right to say an island, or any other physical thing, can be imagined not to exist: for example, we can imagine the sea level rising, or volcanic activity making the island disappear. However, it is impossible to imagine the greatest possible being, God, as not existing: for if you could you wouldn't be imagining the *greatest* being. The implication here is that an island, or any other physical thing, is dependent upon other physical things for its existence: if those things were to change then the island might not exist. However, God's existence is not dependent upon anything, and so no variation in the universe could cause God not to exist.

Philosophers employ two rather technical terms to distinguish between these two types of existence, although Anselm himself didn't use these terms. Islands, and all physical things, have a CONTINGENT existence, in other words they depend upon other physical things for their existence. This means that for any physical thing certain changes in the state of other physical things could mean it would no longer exist. So, as we saw, the existence of any island depends on the sea level of the water around it, and the tectonic plates supporting it. If these were to change then the island might cease to exist. In fact it is logically possible for any physical thing not to exist. Now, Gaunilo seems to be suggesting that God, like an island, has a contingent existence in this sense and so he too can be imagined not to exist. However, Anselm's definition of God states that his existence is NECESSARY. Because he is the greatest possible being he depends upon nothing else for his existence. This means that he would have to exist no matter what the world happened to be like and so no changes in the state of other things will have any impact on his existence.

Gaunilo attempted to undermine Anselm's ontological argument by using it to show that all manner of perfect things, including God, could exist, but they could easily be imagined not to exist. However, Anselm claims Gaunilo's attempt fails because he doesn't understand that God is a necessary being, i.e. God (and only God) cannot be conceived of as not existing. Once again Anselm believes that he has shown that the very nature and meaning of God entails that God must exist.

Consider the proposition 'God exists'. (You may want to refer back to page 121.)
1 What is the subject of this proposition?
2 What is the predicate?
3 From Anselm's perspective, in what sense might you say the subject contains the predicate?

► criticism ◄ The theological genius of the Middle Ages, St Thomas Aquinas (1225–1274), rejected Anselm's proof in favour of his own five ways of proving of God's existence.

Because we do not know the essence of God, the proposition ['God exists'] is not self-evident to us.

Summa Theologica 1:2:1

Aquinas

Aquinas agreed that some things were self-evident, and could be known to be true *a priori*: for example, that 'man is an animal'. But in order to know these things we must be able to define both the subject (man) and the predicate (being an animal). However, humans have a limited intellect, and it is impossible for them to understand or define the nature of God. According to Aquinas, Anselm is overstepping the mark when he claims to know that God is the greatest possible being. Our minds cannot truly grasp what it means to call God this. Now, if the concept of God is not one that we can genuinely understand, then Anselm's argument cannot get off the ground. For if we can't really grasp the idea of God in the first place, then we are hardly in a position to know what must or must not follow from that idea, so Anselm's ontological argument fails.[35]

Descartes' ontological argument

Perhaps because of the success of Aquinas' own cosmological proof of God's existence, ontological arguments lay abandoned for several centuries. They were eventually revived by René Descartes (1596–1650). In the *Meditations on First Philosophy* Descartes sought certain and indubitable knowledge, and he began by subjecting all his beliefs about the world to extreme doubt (see pages 303–305). He famously discovered that he could not doubt his own existence, and so he knew he existed, but he wanted to go further than this in his search for knowledge. He believed that if he could prove the existence of God then this should provide the secure foundations for his beliefs about the world. However, because he didn't trust his own senses, he would have to prove God's existence to be true *a priori*, and this meant using an ontological argument.

ACTIVITY Go back to pages 92–99 above and remind yourself of the attributes that the God of the philosophers was said to possess. Would you say that 'existence' should be included as one of his attributes?

We do not know whether Descartes was familiar with Anselm's proof, but the one he constructed took a very similar form. We can reconstruct Descartes' argument in the following way:

1 God is the supremely perfect being.
2 A supremely perfect being contains all supreme perfections.
3 Existence (as well as omnipotence, omniscience, benevolence, etc.) is a supreme perfection.
4 (Conclusion, from 2 and 3) Therefore God, a supremely perfect being, exists.[36]

As with Anselm's argument, Descartes' argument relies upon a particular definition of God, in this case that he is 'a supremely perfect being'. Descartes then analyses this concept of God and notes that a supremely perfect being would have to be perfect in every possible way, in other words, he would have to possess every possible perfection. So he would have to be all-powerful, all-good, all-knowing, etc. Now, it seems clear to Descartes that existence is a perfection just as being all-powerful, all-good, and so on are. In other words, as Anselm argued, it is better or more perfect to exist than not to exist. And so it follows that 'existing' must be an essential property of the perfect being. In his proof Descartes brings out what Anselm presupposes, namely that an ontological argument assumes that 'existence' is a predicate (or a property) that belongs to the concept of 'God'. By making this assumption both Descartes and Anselm are able to conclude that 'God exists' is true by definition, because the subject ('God', who contains all perfections) already contains the predicate ('exists', which is a perfection).

From the fact that I cannot conceive of God without existence, it follows that existence is inseparable from him, and hence that he really exists.

Meditations 5

Descartes

Descartes also agrees with Anselm on the type of existence God must have: God is a necessary being. Descartes argued that it is impossible to imagine God as not existing, just as it is impossible to imagine an uphill slope existing without a downhill slope, or imagine a triangle without its internal angles adding up to the sum of two right angles. God's existence is a part of his essence as the supremely perfect being. Because God is perfect his non-existence is impossible, in other words God necessarily exists.

In the eighteenth century, Immanuel Kant, himself a religious believer, claimed to have conclusively refuted the type of argument put forward by Anselm and Descartes.[37] In his *Critique of Pure Reason* Kant coined the term 'ontological argument' to refer to this kind of proof. He offers two main objections to the argument: first, that, even if existence is a necessary property of God, that doesn't entail that God actually exists; secondly, that existence cannot be a property of God nor of anything else. Let's examine the criticisms in the order they appear in the *Critique*.

Kant's first criticism

Kant begins by provisionally granting Descartes' claim that 'existence' is a part of the meaning of 'God'; in other words the proposition 'God necessarily exists' (let's call this P_1) is true by definition, or ANALYTIC. But, says Kant, it does not follow from the fact that this proposition is true by definition that God actually exists in reality. Kant believes that it is possible to accept a proposition as true by definition (in other words to accept that the subject and predicate are inseparable) and yet to deny that there is anything in the world to which the subject refers.[38] Figure 2.8 gives one way of imagining the inseparability of various subjects and some of their essential predicates. For example, a shape, in order to be a triangle, must necessarily have three sides; if the shape lost the property of 'having three sides', then it would no longer be a triangle.

■ **Figure 2.8**
Inseparable predicates

All the black segments are inseparable predicates: if we try to take them away from the concept of the subject, the subject ceases to be what it is

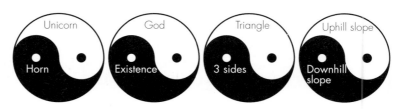

Figure 2.9 gives some examples of predicates that are separable from their subject. So the essence of the subject isn't affected if you take away or change any of these predicates. You could see a unicorn that's manically happy, or deeply depressed, but it would still be a unicorn. However, if

■ Figure 2.9
Separable predicates

you saw a unicorn without a horn you'd have every right to say 'Hey, that's not a unicorn, that's a horse'. Having a horn is an essential (an inseparable) feature of being a unicorn; suffering from manic depression isn't.

So, looking at the proposition (let's call it P_2) 'Unicorns are horned horses', we know this is true by definition because 'a horse with a horn' forms part of our definition of 'unicorn'. But of course it does not follow from this that there are any unicorns; that is to say, we can deny that there are any horned horses in the world. As Kant puts it, with propositions that are true by definition,[39] we cannot separate the subject from the predicate but we can still deny the existence of both the subject and the predicate together. The most we can infer about reality from P_2 is that '*if* unicorns do exist then they necessarily have horns'.

For Kant it is the same case with P_1 'God necessarily exists'. We might accept, along with Descartes, that 'necessary existence' forms an essential part of our definition of 'God', because it is one of his perfections. But it does not therefore follow that there is a God, as we can deny that there are any necessarily existing beings in the world. The most we can infer from P_1 is that '*if* there is a God then he must necessarily exist'.

So what Kant is arguing here is that we cannot move from the realm of definitions and concepts to reality in the manner that ontological arguments attempt. It is one thing to talk about our concepts and a very different one to talk about what exists in the real world. Descartes is free to define God however he likes, and it may well be that the proposition 'God exists' is true by definition. But that tells us only about the definition of the *word* 'God' and nothing about the *existence* of God in the world. Nothing in the definition can ever bridge the gap to tell us what must exist in reality.[40]

Kant's second criticism

Kant, however, was not satisfied with this criticism and sought to destroy the most important assumption made by ontological arguments: namely the claim that existence can be a part of our definition of God. To do this he tries to show that existence cannot be a property of God, because it is not a property of anything.

'Existence' is obviously not a real predicate.[41]

Kant

To begin to see what Kant means by this, try the following exercise.

1 Imagine a piece of paper.

2 Picture it in detail in your head: what does it look like, where is it, what is it made of, how big is it? Write down a description of the paper, starting with the phrase 'The piece of paper I'm imagining is . . .'

3 Now add the following features to your picture-image of the paper:

- is splattered with chip grease and batter
- is made of eye-catching lime green paper
- says the words 'Congratulations, you've won a trip of a lifetime' at the top
- is scrunched up in a gutter
- exists.

4 Which of these further features changed your image of the paper?

In the exercise your initial description of the paper contained a number of predicates, to which we invited you to add some more. These additional predicates should have enriched your original idea of the paper: in other words, they have added to the concept by giving it new properties. However, what happens when you add the last feature and imagine the scrunched-up, greasy paper *existing*? Does this make any real difference to your idea?

Kant thinks not. He proposes that a genuine predicate is one that really does *describe* the thing we're talking about and so adds a descriptive property to it and enriches our concept of it. However, 'existence' does not do this: it adds nothing to our concept of a subject, and hence cannot be a genuine predicate. If I think of something as existing, the idea is the same as if I think of it as not existing. The properties it has are the same in both cases. So Kant is saying that a genuine predicate describes the subject. Since the predicate '. . . exists' does not describe its subject it is not a genuine predicate. This means that existence is not a property that a thing can either have or not have.

Kant makes his point by asking us to imagine 100 Thalers, coins used as the currency of his day: we might think of them as gold, heavy, round, musty, old. According to Kant's rule, these are all genuine predicates as they all change our concept of the '100 Thalers'. However, if we now add the concept of 'existence' to our description then nothing changes: there is no difference between our idea of '100 coins' and of '100 coins that exist'. In contrast, if we add the words 'covered in pink anti-theft paint' to the description then our concept definitely changes.

Kant concludes that 'existence' (unlike 'covered in pink anti-theft paint') is not a genuine predicate. If he is right, then ontological arguments fall apart because we cannot treat existence as one of the properties that God has. It is essential to the ontological arguments of both Anselm and Descartes that 'existence' is a part of what we mean by 'God'. But, if existence is not a predicate, then 'existence' does not belong to our definition of 'God', and ontological arguments fail.

Russell's criticisms of ontological arguments

The second criticism proposed by Kant anticipates a problem raised by philosophers of language in the first part of the twentieth century. Philosophers such as Gottlob Frege (1848–1925) and Bertrand Russell (1872–1970) thought that there was a real difference between the surface structure of language and the true logical structure that underlies it, and that we must be careful not to confuse the two. For example, on the grammatical surface a statement like 'Nothing matters' seems to have a straightforward subject–predicate structure. However, on closer inspection we find that the term 'nothing' doesn't name or refer to anything, and is not a genuine subject. So sometimes what appears on the surface to be a subject (or a predicate), can be shown by further analysis not to be a genuine, logical subject (or predicate).

Russell

Existence quite definitely is not a predicate.[42]

The suggestion is that there is a similar deceit when it comes to the word 'exists'. 'Exists' seems to function as a normal predicate, appearing as a verb after a subject, so just as we can say that 'Bill laughs', 'Jesus saves', 'the lion sleeps', we can also say 'God exists'. However, Frege and Russell would agree with Kant that 'exists' is not a genuine predicate, as it does not describe a property of the subject. Frege argued that 'exists' is really just a shorthand way of saying 'there are *some* objects in the world that this concept refers to'; in other words to say that lions exist is to say that there are things in the world to which the concept of 'lion' corresponds. It is not to say that lions have a very special property known as existence.

Take another example. When we say 'A moon-jumping cow exists', we are not adding something new to our description of 'cow'. We are not saying 'A cow is a four-stomached ruminant which jumps over moons *and exists*.' All we are saying is that the description 'four-stomached ruminate which jumps over moons' identifies some object in the real world. Figure 2.10 represents how Russell might analyse the claim that 'The cow that jumped over the moon actually exists.'

■ **Figure 2.10** *How Russell might illustrate the meaning of 'exists' in the statement 'A moon-jumping cow exists'*

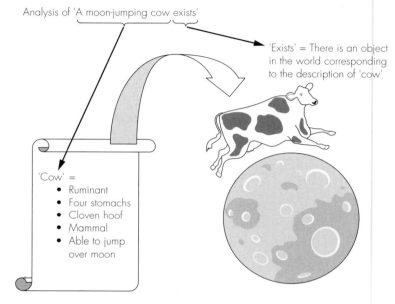

Analysis of 'A moon-jumping cow exists'

'Exists' = There is an object in the world corresponding to the description of 'cow'

'Cow' =
• Ruminant
• Four stomachs
• Cloven hoof
• Mammal
• Able to jump over moon

Another way to see the point is to contrast propositions like 'All cows eat grass' with 'All cows exist'. Whilst the predicate 'eat grass' tells us something meaningful about the habits of cows, the apparent predicate 'exist' seems oddly tautological. For obviously all the cows that there are must exist, otherwise they wouldn't be all the cows. Similarly, compare 'Some cows are mad' with 'Some cows exist'. Again, using 'exists' in this way is rather odd. The oddness seems to come from the fact that this sentence treats existence as a real predicate; suggesting that there are cows, some of which happen to have the property of existence, and others of which don't. But we can't properly describe some cows as existing, as though there were others that don't, because, of course, there aren't any others. There just aren't any non-existent cows. These observations suggest that to say that something exists isn't to describe it or to ascribe a special kind of property to it, but rather simply to say that there is such a thing in the world.

If Russell is correct then 'existence' is not a predicate, but is simply a term that informs us that there is something in the world corresponding to a particular description. When we say

'God exists' we are simply saying 'there is something in the world corresponding to our concept of "God": namely a being who is omnipotent, omniscient, benevolent, etc.' (see Figure 2.11).

■ **Figure 2.11** *How Russell might illustrate the meaning of 'exists' in the statement 'God exists'*

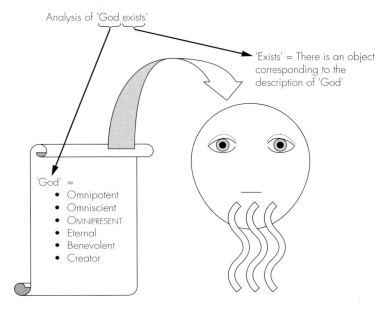

Russell's analysis of 'existence' profoundly damages the ontological arguments of Descartes and Anselm. These sought to show that 'God exists' was true by definition because 'existence' was a property and so part of the meaning of 'God'. We now find that 'existence' cannot be a property of God, or of anything. In order to show 'God exists' is true we need to find something in the world corresponding to our description of 'God', and this means producing empirical evidence for such a being.

ACTIVITY   **1** Re-read Anselm's and Descartes' ontological arguments. Then re-read the criticisms of these arguments.

2 For each criticism identify which parts of Anselm's or Descartes' argument it undermines: for example, which premise does the criticism try to show as false, or which step does it show as invalid?

Modern revivals of ontological arguments

more difficult

Because of their beauty and potential power, ontological arguments have continued to intrigue and inspire philosophers of religion. In the twentieth century there have been versions or interpretations by Norman Malcolm (1911–1990), Alvin Plantinga (1932–) and Karl Barth

(1886–1968) amongst others. Both Malcolm and Plantinga focus on claims about God's status as a necessary being, i.e. one who must exist. It is difficult to do any justice to the complexities of Malcolm's and Plantinga's arguments here. However, we have tried to give a brief summary of them below.

Malcolm believes that St Anselm got things right in his second version of the ontological argument. As with this version, Malcolm's argument rests on the claim that God's existence is necessary, although this claim is ambiguous. It may mean that the proposition 'God exists' is a necessary truth (in the same way '2 + 2 = 4' is a necessary truth). Or it may mean that God's existence is necessary in that he possesses a special quality called 'necessary existence'. This ambiguity is a possible source of criticism against Malcolm.

We can think about Malcolm's ontological argument in the following way. Consider four possibilities concerning God's existence:

1 God's existence is *necessarily false* – it is logically impossible for any being that has God's properties to exist.
2 God's existence is *contingently false* – it is possible that a being with the properties of God could exist, but it just so happens that there isn't such a being.
3 God's existence is *contingently true* – it is possible that a being with the properties of God could exist, and it just so happens that there is such a being.
4 God's existence is *necessarily true* – it is logically necessary that any being with the properties of God exists.

Malcolm would argue that 2 and 3 simply cannot apply to a being like God. This is because God is the greatest possible being, and as such he must be unlimited, independent and eternal. However, 2 and 3 suggest that his existence is contingent, i.e. limited by and dependent upon other factors. For example, for Malcolm there is a crucial difference between an eternal being, and a being who just happens (contingently) to exist forever: eternity is a quality of God whereas eternal duration is not. Malcolm argues that, because God is the greatest possible being, God's existence cannot be contingent, and thus the claim that 'God exists' cannot be contingently true (or false).

This leaves either 1 or 4 as the remaining possibilities. Statements that fall under category 1 are logically contradictory propositions, such as 'This square is round' or 'That bachelor is on his fifth marriage'. Malcolm argues that there is nothing logically contradictory about the claim that 'God exists'. This leaves 4 as the only remaining possibility:

God's existence is necessarily true. For Malcolm this doesn't mean that 'existence' is a predicate of 'God', instead it means that 'necessary existence' is a predicate of 'God'. Malcolm believes he has shown that because God is the greatest possible being he must be a necessary being, and therefore he must exist.

▶ criticism ◀   Plantinga criticises Malcolm's argument, and offers his own ontological argument in its place.[43] Plantinga's objection to Malcolm is that it is possible for God to exist contingently (possibility 3 above) without God losing his independence or his unlimited or eternal qualities.

Plantinga's own ontological argument takes a slightly different approach to Malcolm's. What we mean when we say that 'God necessarily exists' is that God exists in every possible universe: i.e. there is no possible universe that doesn't contain God. Why is this so? Well, as with all ontological arguments, Plantinga accepts the definition of God as the greatest possible being (a being with 'maximal greatness' is Plantinga's phrase). A God that exists in all possible universes is greater than one that exists in only some universes. Therefore God, in order to be the greatest, must exist in every possible universe. This is the same as saying that God necessarily exists.

Conclusion

Ontological arguments can be seen in two ways: first as proofs that establish the existence of God with absolute certainty; secondly as an expression and exploration of what 'God' means to the believer. It is unlikely that the arguments will sway an atheist. Critics of the arguments have strived to show that you cannot define something into existence, no matter how clever your definition.

However, ontological arguments may be more fruitfully read from within the framework of the believer. To the reflective believer the argument reveals what 'God' means, or who God is. Once you begin to understand God then you see that God's existence is of a different order to the existence of the rest of the universe. For the believer, God is a being unlike anything else because his existence stems from his own nature, and not from any external cause. His existence, as Descartes has it, is part of his essence and is therefore 'necessary' which suggests it is unlimited, independent, without a cause, without a beginning, and without an end.

Karl Barth argues that St Anselm's ontological argument should be read more as an exploration of faith than a proof of

God's existence. Barth points out that Anselm's argument is framed at the beginning and the end as a prayer. As St Anselm says at the beginning of the *Proslogion*:

Anselm

I do not seek to understand so that I may believe, but I believe in order to understand.

Proslogion 1

This seems to suggest that for Anselm philosophical analysis (in the form of his ontological argument) takes a back seat to faith. He does not use philosophy in order to prove to himself that God exists; instead he uses philosophy to help him explore and understand his own faith.

Origins: the idea of God is innate

Introduction

In the first section of this chapter we looked at some of the key attributes ascribed to God, and saw how many of these qualities had their origins in revealed texts – the Old and New Testaments of the Bible in the case of Christianity. Building on these attributes, in particular the idea of God's perfection, St Anselm and others tried to show how a being who was perfect had to exist (as a part of his perfection). In this section we look at where the idea of 'God' generally originates: is it innate, as Descartes claims, or is it something we learn?

In Chapter 4 we examine the claim that the mind at birth is like a blank slate, completely empty of thoughts or concepts and that all our ideas come to us through our experience of the world. We also examine the opposed claim, associated with rationalist philosophers, that at least some of our ideas don't need to be learned or acquired since they are with us at birth. Candidates for such innate ideas include those of substance and attribute of numbers, of moral good and evil, and – importantly for our purposes in this chapter – of God. To claim that we are born with an idea already in our minds does not need to imply that we must be consciously aware of it from infancy. For it may lie dormant or, as it were, implicit within one's mind waiting to be activated or drawn out. Thus while we have come to hear about God in this life from our parents or preachers, this is not the ultimate origin of the idea. It is rather something that has always lain within each of us waiting to rise to the surface of consciousness.

The claim that the idea of God is innate in this sense is central to the philosophical project of the father of modern philosophy, René Descartes. He hoped to uncover a set of beliefs that would be free from doubt and upon which he might build a system of certain and enduring scientific knowledge. One of his books, the *Meditations*, attempts to bring his philosophical project to a wide audience and it consists of a journey from uncertainty through to knowledge. Most famously, Descartes finds his first point of certainty in his belief that he exists. He cannot meaningfully doubt that he exists or, as he puts it in another of his books, the *Discourse*, 'I think therefore I am'. That he exists cannot be doubted, because it is so clear and distinct. However, for Descartes this single point of certainty is only the beginning, and he wishes to show that other 'clear and distinct' ideas are also true.

But there is a problem: Descartes could be deceived by a powerful EVIL DEMON (or living in a virtual world, as in the film trilogy *The Matrix*) into thinking that an idea is clear and distinct. To erase the possibility of this kind of global deception, Descartes feels he needs to prove that God exists; if he can do this, then he can be certain that his clear and distinct ideas are in fact true. We have already seen above (pages 128–30) Descartes' ontological argument for the existence of God, but before that, in the *Meditations*, Descartes offers another argument, known as the Trademark Argument, based on the claim that God is an idea that is innate.

Descartes set out to formally *prove* that we have an innate idea of God. To do justice to this formal proof we need to explore in detail the arguments he presents in *Meditation 3*. It may be an idea to get hold of a copy of the *Meditations* to accompany this section.

Descartes' Trademark Argument

The basic point of the argument is to try to show that Descartes' idea of God can only have appeared in his mind if there really is a God. Much like the trademark on a piece of clothing reveals the maker, so the idea of God within his mind reveals its maker, namely God himself (see Figure 2.12). To show this, Descartes argues that the idea of an infinite being (i.e. God) cannot be produced from within the mind of a finite being like himself or anyone else. The cause of such an idea, he argues, can only be a being which really is infinite.

Below is an outline of the argument, which follows its development through the text of the *Meditations*. If you have a copy of Descartes' *Meditations* then you could read the summary of each point below, then read what Descartes has

■ **Figure 2.12**
A designer imprints his clothes with his logo. God has 'imprinted' the concept of God in our minds

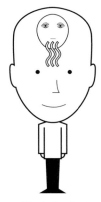

Made by Logo   Made by God

to say; this will help you to follow the development of his thought. All page references are to the Penguin Classics edition of the *Meditations*.[44]

■ An outline of the Trademark Argument

1 I know that ideas exist in my mind, but I don't know whether what they represent really exists outside of my mind (*Meditations* pp. 115–16).

2 I am led to think my ideas of material things represent real physical things, but this judgement is made by a 'blind and rash impulse' not by the natural light of reason (*M* p. 118).

3 So can I prove there is anything outside of my mind (*M* p. 118)?

4 Yes. My ideas have degrees of 'objective reality', that is to say what they represent can be thought of as being more or less 'perfect'. For example, my idea of a *substance* is less perfect than my idea of a *human*, which in turn is less perfect than my idea of *God* (*M* p. 119).

5 '[T]here must be at least as much reality in the efficient and total cause as in its effect.' In other words, any effect cannot be greater than what caused it: it cannot be more 'perfect' or contain more 'reality' than its effect (*M* p. 119). (We will call this Descartes' *causal principle*.)

6 It follows that, since our ideas must come from somewhere and so must be caused by something, their causes must contain at least as much reality or perfection as the ideas themselves (*M* pp. 119–21).

7 So if I can be sure that I cannot be the cause of one of my ideas, then I shall know that there must be something other than me in the world (*M* p. 121).

8 Now, I could well be the cause of my idea of physical substances (e.g. a goat, a rock or a tree) since I am myself substance (i.e. a thinking substance). I may not be aware

that I am the origin of such ideas, but then it is quite possible that perceptions come from some unknown part of me. So I cannot prove that physical things really exist outside my mind (*M* pp. 121–23).

9 But what of God? Well, my idea of God is that of an 'infinite substance' with 'great attributes'. Since I am only a finite substance (which I must be since I make mistakes) I am not sufficiently perfect to create this idea myself. So I cannot be the cause of my idea of God (*M* pp. 123–24).

10 Since the cause of my idea of God must be at least as perfect as the idea, the only thing that can be the cause of it is God himself.

And so it follows that God exists.

ACTIVITY If you have a copy, read through *Meditation 3* and identify where each of the above premises can be found in the text.

Here is a formal version of the essential steps of the argument.

Premise 1 The cause of anything must be at least as perfect as its effect.
Premise 2 My ideas must be caused by something.
Premise 3 I am an imperfect being.
Premise 4 I have the idea of God which is that of a perfect being.
Intermediate conclusion 1 I cannot be the cause of my idea of God.
Intermediate conclusion 2 Only a perfect being (i.e. God) can be the cause of my idea of God.
Main conclusion God must exist.

■ **Figure 2.13**
Descartes is moving from knowledge of his idea of God in his mind, to the cause of that idea outside of his mind. This cause must be God, and so God must exist

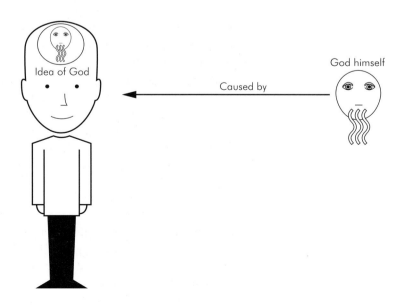

Idea of God

Caused by

God himself

■ Interpretation of the argument

more difficult

If you managed to read through Descartes' original text you may feel rather confused about the details of his argument and in this section we will work through the argument in greater depth to try to clarify some of the intricacies. However, if you grasp the outline versions above, you have understood the important ideas.

Ideas and sensations are like pictures: they have 'representational content'

Descartes' argument for the existence of God has to begin by looking into his own mind and the thoughts it contains. This is because all he can be certain of is the existence of his own thoughts and experiences. As he begins this examination he observes that:

Descartes

> *Among my thoughts, some are, as it were, the images of things, and it is to these alone that the name idea properly belongs; as when I represent to myself a man, a chimera, the sky, an angel or God himself.*[45] (M p. 115)

What Descartes is saying is that some of his thoughts, what he terms 'ideas', are a bit like pictures or images, in that they seem to represent things. For example, if I think of a goat or Jupiter, my idea is a kind of picture of a goat or Jupiter. And this is true whether or not such things actually exist outside of my mind. So even though a chimera (a mythical creature) doesn't exist I can still have the idea or image of it in my mind.

Similarly, my sensations appear to represent objects outside of me. They too seem to picture something beyond themselves. They too are like images. Another way of expressing this point is to say that ideas and sensations have 'representational content'.

Ideas and sensations cannot be false

Descartes showed earlier in the *Meditations* that often ideas and sensations do not accurately represent things outside of me and I can make mistakes. It may even be that there is *nothing* outside of me, and all my ideas and sensations represent nothing in reality at all but only seem to. But even if this is true, ideas and sensations in themselves cannot strictly be termed 'false', but only the judgement made on their basis concerning the nature of things outside of me. So, as long as we confine ourselves to ideas, as they appear in the mind, without making any judgements about what is outside of us, we cannot go wrong. As Descartes puts the point:

Descartes

Now, concerning ideas, if they are considered only in themselves, and are not referred to any other thing, they cannot, strictly speaking, be false; for whether I imagine a goat or a chimera, it is no less true that I imagine the one than the other. (M p. 116)

So his point here is that, whatever the real world turns out to be like, and whether it exists or not, my ideas are real and I can't be mistaken about what they are like. Mistakes can only creep in once I make *judgements* about the world beyond my mind. The judgement that sensations and ideas resemble and are caused by physical objects is subject to error, but the sensations and ideas considered in themselves are not. So whilst sensations are not subject to our will, in other words we can't control what we see, hear or smell, this doesn't show that they must come from outside of us. They could be produced from some part of ourselves of which we are unaware, as they seem to be in dreams.

Only the clearly and distinctly perceived properties are likely actually to exist

At this point Descartes reminds the reader that he discovered earlier in the *Meditations* that, when we analyse an object (the example he uses is wax), some qualities such as colour, sound and odour are experienced in what he calls a 'confused' and 'obscure' way, whilst other qualities, e.g. those of magnitude, substance, motion, duration are clear and distinct. And so, argues Descartes, these latter qualities may really exist in objects, if, that is, objects do actually exist. His reasoning here is that because sensation is 'confused' we cannot know what sort of thing it might represent in the physical world, if anything. What he means by this is that we can't tell simply by examining our experience what may have caused it. For example, Descartes writes:

Descartes

the ideas I have of cold and heat are so unclear and indistinct that I cannot discern from them if cold is only a privation of heat, or if heat is a privation of cold; or if they are both real qualities or not. (M p. 122)

So from my experience of heat I can't tell what kind of a thing causes me to feel it. Similarly, when I sense red, or smell chocolate I cannot tell what kind of a thing in the world might be causing such sensations. I can form no clear answer to the question of what it is about chocolate that makes it taste chocolatey.

But when it comes to sizes, shapes etc., I *can* tell what kind of a thing might be causing me to have such sense experiences. If I see something square, I know what kind of a thing in the world might cause this experience, namely something square. So, as far as the clear and distinct ideas he has of CORPOREAL things are concerned, it is at least possible that they accurately represent real qualities of objects (although, of course, this is yet to be established since there is nothing about these ideas which means that they cannot have been produced by myself).

Here Descartes is clearly alluding to the primary/ secondary quality distinction (see pages 526–31). Whether or not the world exists, my perceptions of secondary qualities must be inaccurate in their representation of reality. They don't have any clear representational content; that is, I have no idea what being red really amounts to for an object. However, my perceptions of primary qualities do have clear representational content. I know exactly what they picture. Part of Descartes' idea here is that the primary qualities lend themselves to geometric description and so can be clearly and distinctly grasped by the understanding. This suggests that they may actually be real. Our sensations of colour, smell, sound and so on cannot be described in the clear and distinct language of geometry, and so cannot be grasped by the intellect, and so cannot be real. This claim needs also to be read in the light of Descartes' observations about the wax, namely that its essence is intuited by the mind. This essence is describable in geometry: it is extended and malleable. The outer clothing of the wax is apprehended only confusedly by the senses.

The table shows some of the physical objects that Descartes mentions perceiving in the *Meditations*. Next to these objects (in the second column) are some qualities that Descartes perceives in the objects.

For each quality, decide if it is a 'real quality' or not. To do this, consider whether

a) Descartes would claim he could perceive it clearly and distinctly, i.e. would Descartes know what it is in the real world that would cause such a perception?

b) Descartes would claim this was an unclear and indistinct perception, i.e. he cannot know what it is in the world that might cause this perception.

Object	Ideas that Descartes forms from encountering the object	Do these ideas represent a 'real quality' of the object (yes or no)?
The sun	Yellow	
	Hot	
	Small	
	Far away	
A piece of wax	Cylindrical	
	Malleable	
	Light	
	Smooth	
The fire	Hot	
	Bright	
	In front of him	
	Yellow	

The causal principle

Descartes now introduces a general principle which he thinks is self-evident. He writes:

Descartes

> *Now it is manifest by the natural light that there must be at least as much reality in the efficient and total cause as in its effect. (M p. 119)*

What Descartes is saying here is that the cause of anything must, in some sense, be *adequate* to its effect. So, you can't cause something to happen unless the cause is sufficient to make the effect. A corollary of this principle is that 'nothingness cannot produce anything' (*M* p. 119). The thought here is plausible enough: if something occurs, what caused it has to have enough power or *oomph*, as it were, to produce the effect.

To illustrate the basic idea, imagine that a window shatters. Now, we can tell that whatever caused it to shatter must have had enough power – what Descartes here calls 'reality' – to make it shatter. So, it couldn't have been shattered by something too small or weak, such as a grain of sand or a fly. It would have to have been something big and powerful enough, or with sufficient 'reality', or *oomph*, such as a brick or an escaping criminal.

Descartes gives us his own example to illustrate his point. He asks us to consider the production of a stone. Whatever it was that caused a stone to come into existence would have to be sufficient to have produced it. This means that the stone cannot come into existence 'unless it be produced by something which has . . . everything that enters into the composition of a stone, in other words which contains in itself the same properties as those in the stone, or others superior to them' (*M* p. 119). Similarly something cannot be made hot, Descartes claims, unless it is caused to do so by something 'which is of an order, degree or kind, at least as perfect as heat' (*M* p. 120).[46]

What must have caused my ideas?

Armed with his causal principle Descartes now proceeds to consider the possible causes of his various ideas. Our ideas, after all, must be caused by something, and the causal principle suggests to Descartes that this cause will have to have at least as much reality as the ideas themselves. In other words our ideas cannot be more perfect than what has caused them. If Descartes can show that he doesn't have the resources within himself to produce one of the ideas he has, then this idea will have to have been caused by something else.

Descartes argues that his ideas of humans, animals or angels could be made up by himself out of his ideas of material things and of his idea of God, even if these things didn't exist. The thought here is that, so long as he has an idea of physical things, he can make up men and animals in his imagination,

■ **Figure 2.14 Descartes' causal principle**

Descartes' causal principle says that the cause of anything must be sufficient to produce the effect. Since ideas must be caused by something, if he can show that he is not himself sufficient to produce them, this will show that something else must have caused them. And this means that something other than himself must exist.

Ideas in the mind

Where do my ideas come from? If I could not have made them up myself, they must have come from outside of me.

just as we make up the idea of a unicorn. The idea of angels, although far greater than that of humans, is lesser than his idea of God, and so could be invented as a lesser version of God. Moreover, the idea of physical things themselves could also be made up. For there is no reason to think that he, being himself a thinking substance, couldn't be the cause of the idea of physical substances. So it is quite possible that perceptions come from some unknown part of himself. So he cannot prove that physical things really exist (*M* pp. 121–23).

ACTIVITY Descartes claims to have a very clear and distinct idea of God, and of the qualities or attributes that he possesses. Before we look at his idea, consider your own idea of God.

List the main qualities or attributes that you think God possesses. Note that this should be possible whether or not you believe God exists, for here all you are doing is analysing your idea or concept of God.

This just leaves Descartes' idea of God, i.e. the idea of:

Descartes

an infinite substance, eternal, immutable, independent, omniscient, omnipotent, and by which I and all the other things which exist (if it be true that any such exist) have been created and produced. (M pp. 123–24)

Descartes reckons that God's attributes:

Descartes

are so great and eminent, that the more attentively I consider them, the less I am persuaded that the idea I have of them can originate in me alone. And consequently I must necessarily conclude from all I have said hitherto, that God exists; for, although the idea of substance is in me, for the very reason that I am a substance, I would not, nevertheless, have the idea of an infinite substance, since I am a finite being, unless the idea had been put into me by some substance which was truly infinite. (M p. 124)

What Descartes is saying here is that since the cause of my idea of God must have at least as much reality as the idea has reality, the only thing that can be the cause of it is God himself. For the idea of an infinite substance could not have originated from within me, who is only a finite substance. The only cause with sufficient reality to produce the idea of an *infinite* being, would have to be an infinite being. It follows that the idea of God must have been planted in me by God himself, and so God must exist.

Moreover, Descartes elaborates, the notion of the infinite must *precede* that of the finite (i.e. the notion of God must precede that of myself) since the latter could only be recognised by contrasting it to the former (*M* p. 124). Thus the idea I have of God:

Descartes

> *was born and produced with me at the moment of my creation. And, in truth, it should not be thought strange that God, in creating me, should have put in me this idea to serve, as it were, as the mark that the workman imprints on his work.* (M *p. 130*)

In other words, his idea of God is *innate*.

We have followed Descartes through some fairly complex reasoning, and it will not be surprising if you have found it difficult to follow. Having made the effort to make sense of what he is trying to say, you may have your suspicions that, despite the complex language, there are some fairly obvious difficulties with Descartes' thinking.

ACTIVITY   Before turning to the evaluation of his argument below, look again at the outline of the main steps of the argument, and see whether any of them strike you as implausible. Try to explain what you think is wrong with them and take a note of your objections.

■ Evaluation of the Trademark Argument

► criticism ◄   The Cartesian Circle
This first criticism is not related specifically to Descartes' proof of God's existence but rather concerns the overall strategy taken in the *Meditations*, and so can be skipped if you are not studying this book as a set text. Descartes is primarily concerned with establishing knowledge that can be held with absolute certainty – in other words knowledge that is impossible to doubt. The proof of God outlined above plays an important role in his quest for certainty, as once God existence is established then other important doubts can be cast aside.

In order to establish certainty Descartes sets out by doubting everything he knows. Anything that remains can then be considered doubt-free. He starts with some fairly ordinary doubts about vision and so on but soon progresses to the fanciful idea that there might be a powerful demon setting out to systematically deceive him (see page 304 onwards). If this is a possibility, however remote, then it would seem that we cannot be absolutely certain of anything. After some debate Descartes eventually concludes that even if there is a demon, he can still be absolutely certain that he exists (the famous 'I think therefore I am'). From this small starting point of certainty Descartes then wants to establish that there is a God and so remove the possibility of an evil demon deceiving him. God's existence will also enable him to trust ideas that he knows with real clarity and distinction, as a good God would not have made humans to have really clear and distinct ideas that are not true.

However, it is argued that his proof of God appears too soon in the Meditations. Descartes' proof involves the use of logic, memory and several ideas (such as the causal principle) all of which might be illusions or distortions created by the evil demon. In other words the demon could have fooled Descartes into thinking he had proved the existence of God when in fact he hadn't. In trying to prove that God exists Descartes uses element and ideas that at this stage in the *Meditations* had not been proved to be beyond doubt. As such the proof itself cannot be considered to be beyond all doubt – however convincing you think each stage of the argument is.

Descartes' reasoning here appears to be circular: that is, it presupposes what it sets out to prove. He wants to prove that judgements he understands clearly and distinctly must be true, and to do this he needs to prove God's existence. Yet the argument he uses to prove God's existence depends upon the truth of the judgements made in its construction. So until he has proved that these judgements are reliable he cannot prove God exists, and he cannot prove God exists until he knows these judgements are reliable. Descartes' whole enterprise seems to have stalled: caught in the double bind known as the Cartesian Circle.

■ **Figure 2.15 *The Cartesian Circle***

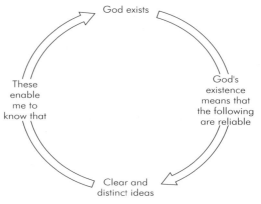

A more familiar example of such a circular justification occurs in the following chain of reasoning:

Q How do you know that God exists?
A *Because it says so in the Bible.*
Q How do you know the Bible is true?
A *Because it's the word of God.*

We could construct a similar line of reasoning from the above passage of the *Meditations*, as follows.

Q How do you know that God exists?
A *Because I proved his existence using clear and distinct ideas.*
Q How do you know that clear and distinct ideas are reliable?
A *Because a non-deceiving God exists.*

This criticism was levelled at Descartes' *Meditations* soon after they were written, and so Descartes had the opportunity to reply to it. What Descartes needs is a way of establishing the reliability of clear and distinct ideas which doesn't rely on clear and distinct ideas in the first place.

► criticism ◄ Is the causal principle true?

Descartes' causal principle states that 'there must be at least as much reality in the efficient and total cause as in its effect' (*M* p. 119). Descartes clearly believes this is self-evidently true. Part of his thinking is that you cannot get more out of the effect than was already in the cause, otherwise you would be getting something for nothing. Since it is self-evident that nothing can come from nothing, this must be impossible. However, when looking at the world, there do – on the face of it at least – appear to be all kinds of examples where it does seem possible to produce something with more perfection or reality than there was originally in its cause. Can we not light a bonfire with a match? Or cause an avalanche with a whisper? Here the causes appear to have markedly *less* reality than what they are able to produce. Chaos theory also suggests that great effects can follow from small causes, as in the standard example of a butterfly's wing-flap causing a hurricane (see page 364). Consider also the effects of a long process such as evolution. Incremental changes over billions of years can produce complex creatures such as ourselves out of disorganised matter. Here the effect surely has vastly more 'perfection' than the original cause. Quantum physics may also be cited as evidence against Descartes' principle, with its denial of the principle that all events have causes which are adequate to them. The precise position of electrons is thought to be truly random and uncaused. If these are genuine counter-examples to Descartes' causal principle then the Trademark Argument cannot rely on the principle and it may well be possible to produce the idea of God from pretty humble beginnings. In the next section we will consider some ways in which this might happen.

► criticism ◄ Hume on causation

David Hume famously argued that we cannot determine the cause of anything simply by examining the effect, and in so doing he is effectively attacking Descartes' causal principle. If I see a window break I cannot deduce what kind of thing must have caused it. We said earlier that we can know that something big enough to have broken it must have impacted with the pain of glass, but how do we know this? Not by reasoning *a priori*, claims Hume, but rather by reference to our past experience of shattering glass. We have learned exclusively from experience which kinds of thing can succeed in breaking windows; if we were to encounter a window breaking for the first time, we could have no idea what caused it. I can only learn that cold weather causes water to freeze by observing water freezing in cold weather. I cannot deduce it *a priori* from observing a puddle of water and thinking very hard about what might happen if the temperature drops.

So the only way we can tell what the cause of something is, Hume says, is by observing it in conjunction with its effect. If he is right, then it seems to follow that, by simple consideration of my idea of God, I cannot know what must have caused it. To find out, I would have to observe its coming into existence.

ACTIVITY Compare the idea you had of God (activity on page 86) with Descartes' idea of God (page 147).

1 In what ways, or in what qualities, does your idea of God differ from Descartes' idea?

2 If your idea of God does differ from Descartes' (e.g. you do not have a clear idea of God as immutable or infinite), then what implications might this have for Descartes' Trademark Argument (i.e. is it important for Descartes' argument that everyone has the same idea of God)?

► criticism ◄ Do we really have an idea of an infinite being?

A premise of Descartes' argument is that he has the idea of God: 'the idea by which I conceive a God who is sovereign, eternal, infinite, unchangeable, all-knowing, all-powerful and universal Creator of all things outside himself' (*M* p. 119). But can we really grasp such an idea? Even theistic philosophers (e.g. St Thomas Aquinas) have expressed doubts about whether the human mind can actually frame a positive idea of God (see page 109 above). He may be just too great for us to understand. So, it can be argued that Descartes is able to use the word 'God' without having a genuine corresponding idea in his mind. The idea of an infinite being, like that of infinity, may be something we can express in words, but not truly understand. If I try to conceive of infinity my mind fails me; the idea is really only a negative one, namely the opposite of finite. Now if this is right, and we don't really have the idea of an infinite being, then the issue of where the idea comes from doesn't arise, and so the Trademark Argument doesn't get off the ground.

► criticism ◄   ## The idea of God is incoherent
Another reason for thinking that we don't have a proper idea of God in the first place is that it is contradictory. Note that in Descartes' account of his idea of God, he mentions that God is all-powerful. We have seen above (pages 100–107) that this is problematic: can God set himself a task that he cannot perform? If he *can*, then there is a task he cannot perform; and if he *cannot* there is a task he cannot perform (namely set himself a task that he cannot perform) and so either way he cannot be all-powerful. This paradox in the very notion of omnipotence suggests that Descartes' idea of God is unclear; and obviously the cause of an unclear idea need not be that great, and certainly need not be caused by God himself. It would be far more likely to have originated within Descartes himself.

ACTIVITY   Descartes has an idea of God as an infinite, supremely intelligent, supremely powerful, creator of the world. List all the possible causes of these ideas – where might Descartes (or any other believer) have got these ideas from?

► criticism ◄   ## The idea of an all-powerful God is not universal
It often occurs to those encountering this argument for the first time to point out that people from other religions don't have an idea of an all powerful God. And if they don't have such an idea then Descartes is surely wrong to say that it is planted in our minds. Similarly, it can be argued on empirical grounds that we know that the origin of the idea of an

omnipotent God is not divine since it has a historical genesis around 500 BCE in Palestine. We can imagine how the idea of an all-powerful being came about, as competing tribes each claimed their own god to be more powerful than those of the others. Eventually one tribe hit upon the idea that their own god was *all-powerful,* thereby trumping the competition: no other tribe can ever again claim to have a god more powerful still. This interesting account of the human origins of 'God' is suggested by Hume (page 156 below).

Descartes would not be overly impressed by such an argument as he can explain how it can be that people don't always appear to have the idea of God, even though it is innate. For all this shows is that people don't always think hard enough about metaphysical issues. Compare this with mathematics where we often fail to learn many of its truths, and yet these truths are still universal. We can point to the historical discovery of π but this doesn't mean that it is not a universal constant discoverable *a priori*. Nonetheless, if we put this objection next to our questioning of the causal principle above, it does give us an alternative account of how such an idea might evolve from origins far less than divine.

► criticism ◄ Empiricist accounts of the origin of our idea of God
Empiricists argue that all our concepts come from experience, and so have an account of how we can generate the idea of God from experience. The basic idea, argued for by Hume among others, is that we can observe the relative virtues in other people, and so recognise that there are degrees of goodness, or power, or benevolence. Having observed this, we can imagine extending the degree of goodness indefinitely until we reach the idea of infinite goodness, infinite power or infinite benevolence. In this way we arrive at the idea of an infinite being, perfect in every way, but the cause of the idea is not in the least infinite or perfect. In this section we have explored Descartes' argument that we all have an innate idea of God within us. If the empiricist account is correct, then the idea of God is not innate, contrary to Descartes' claim.

In the final section of this chapter we look at some of the most significant empirical and naturalistic accounts of the origin of our idea of God.

Origins: the idea of 'God' is a human construction

Introduction

He was a wise man who originated the idea of God.[47]

Euripides

Russell

Religion is based, I think, primarily and mainly upon fear . . . fear of the mysterious, fear of defeat, fear of death.[48]

Russell

We have now looked at several potential sources of the idea of 'God': in the revelations of the Bible; in the metaphysical writings of the ancient Greeks; in the individual minds of each of us as an innate idea. In the final section of this chapter we look at the claims made by atheist thinkers that God is a human creation, born out of distinctly human needs and desires. Such accounts of the concept of 'God' are termed 'naturalistic' as they reject any supernatural explanations and deny that 'God' refers to any spiritual or non-material being.

There is both a constructive and destructive, or critical, side to the atheist's project. The critical project consists of the attack on religious beliefs, which might include a demonstration of the following: that the problem of evil is fatally damaging to the theist's conception of God; that all the arguments for the existence of God fail; that religion has hindered, rather than helped, the progress of individuals or societies; that religious language is meaningless; and that the concept of God is incoherent. The most sustained and successful critique of religion probably comes from David Hume in his works *Dialogues Concerning Natural Religion*, *An Enquiry Concerning Human Understanding* (particularly Section 10) and *The Natural History of Religion*.[49]

But it is not enough for atheists simply to take a critical stance towards God and religion. Even if atheists are successful in their critical commentary on religion, and show that it is unreasonable and undesirable to believe in God, they still have much explanatory work to do. The constructive atheistic project includes showing: that morality and moral behaviour is possible, and meaningful, in the absence of religious justification; that a scientific study of the universe, its origins, laws and its future, has no need for religion and is more successful without it; that a philosophical investigation into the meaning and purpose of life needs no reference to God; that religious experiences and miracles have sound naturalistic explanations. In particular, atheists need to give an explanation as to why people throughout history have believed in supernatural, or non-natural, beings such as God.

Read through the following descriptions of rare phenomena and answer questions a)–d) below.

1 The sky to the far north is filled with walls of rippling lights in intense bright colours reaching hundreds of metres in the air. These lights form the Bifröst Bridge, where the Valkyries wait to escort fallen warriors to the halls of Valhalla in the afterlife.

2 In front of a crowd of thousands at Wembley Stadium an American evangelical miracle worker invites the Holy Spirit into the body of a woman with a limp; immediately she can walk normally again.

3 In 1995 in New Delhi a granite statue of Ganesha, the elephant-headed God of Wisdom, was seen to drink milk from a spoon that was held in front of it. This miraculous event was repeated on several occasions.

4 You wake up in the middle of the night certain that you are being watched from the door. In the morning you can see what looks like a handprint on the door frame (later you find out that a woman was murdered in the room a hundred years ago). The handprint fades as the room heats up, until it eventually evaporates completely.

5 In 1917 in the Portuguese village of Fatima two children saw the figure of the Virgin Mary in a field. A crowd of thousands gathered in anticipation of a further visitation by the virgin. Eye-witness reports gathered by journalists 20 years later speak of the increasing excitement of the crowd, and of the hysteria which greeted the spectacle of the sun spinning violently and then falling from the sky.

6 In New York state in 1827 a man claims to have found, buried in a field, a long-lost book of the Bible, which records the ancient journey of a tribe of Israelites to America. An angel led the man to the buried pages, and also to the stones which helped him translate them.

7 In Nebraska in 1950 a church choir all arrived 10 minutes late for their weekly practice, something that had never happened before. Choir members arrived separately and each had their own individual reason as to why they were late. When they came to the church they found it utterly destroyed by an explosion that happened five minutes earlier. This explosion would have killed anyone who had arrived on time.

For each description:
a) What is the best explanation for the phenomenon described?
b) Is the explanation a natural or a supernatural one?
c) If you think it is a natural explanation, what evidence could be taken to support it?

d) If you think it is a supernatural explanation, can you think of an alternative, naturalistic explanation which might also account for the event?

In this section we look at a number of naturalistic answers to the question regarding the widespread belief in God. These fall into two broad categories: psychological explanations, which locate the origins of God in human mental processes (as a response to conscious or subconscious needs or fears or wishes, or as an evolved by-product of some other process); and sociological explanations, which view belief in God and religion as emerging from social structures and pressures.

Hume: God is a response to human fear and ignorance

The primary religion of mankind arises chiefly from an anxious fear of future events.[50]

Hume

David Hume, in his *Natural History of Religion* (published in 1757), investigates the origins and evolution of human beings' belief in gods and in God. His theory mirrors his arguments about morality (see page 66), namely that it is our emotions and feelings, rather than reason, that are our primary motivators for action and belief. The irrational forces that are at work in humans, and which give rise to a belief in supernatural beings, are a product of the chaotic, dangerous and unpredictable world that our ancestors found themselves in. Hume argues that POLYTHEISM (the belief that there are many gods in existence, as in the religions of ancient Greece, Rome and Egypt) helps to make sense of an apparently senseless world. Our ancestors were ignorant of the causes of natural disasters, of the changing weather systems, of disease, of the seasons. Hume goes on to say that we invent *unknown causes* in order to avoid the unpleasant emotions that we otherwise have to live with – as Hume puts it 'we hang in perpetual suspense between life and death, health and sickness, plenty and want'. So the original cause of the idea of gods lies in

the anxious concern for happiness, the dread of future misery, the terror of death, the thirst of revenge, the appetite for food and other necessities[51]

Hume

But what are these 'unknown causes'? Hume highlights human beings' tendency to anthropomorphise the world, in other words to see the world as if it were made up of things like humans, and ascribe human properties to the world. Hume says that this tendency leads us to see human faces in the moon, armies in the clouds and to personify nature. This personification of nature means viewing volcanoes, clouds, rivers and forests as if they were persons, with all the whims, desires, anger and love of real people. But, to our ancestors, these mountain-spirits and sky-gods were real people, only ones you couldn't see. So, in order to explain the unpredictability of nature, our ancestors posited the existence of a number of 'invisible agents' – gods. Because each god had his or her own interests and desires, and each tribe had their own gods, the resulting conflict between the gods matched the occasional chaos of the world, and helped explain (although not predict) why events sometimes went very well and sometimes very badly. The crucial thing is that we pray to these gods, and hope that they're listening – for when they do then our crops will flourish, the rains will arrive, the snows will melt and all will be well.

These ancient religions, Hume acknowledges, do not have the philosophical refinements of theistic religions: the anthropomorphic qualities of the polytheistic deities are too close to the qualities of real human beings. In other words their gods are basically trumped-up humans who squabble and murder, and who have petty arguments, jealous relationships, and sexual relations with each other. But Hume goes on to explain how polytheism (the belief in many gods) leads to theism (the belief in one god). He is careful to note again that this progression is not due to the triumph of reason over superstition, but once again has its origins in 'the ignorance and stupidity of the people'. Within polytheism there may be many different sects, each with its own temple or oracle or place of worship. According to Hume, there is a kind of arms race amongst the differing sects, with each proclaiming its god to be more powerful than the others. Out of this arms race, one god gradually rises above the pantheon (Figure 2.16) to become a more powerful god with more refined and excellent human qualities (our god is wiser, stronger, more courageous than yours): Zeus in Greece, Jupiter in Rome, Yahweh in Canaan.[52] But by 'swelling up the titles of his divinity', in other words ascribing more and more power to this god (of courage, of strength, of wisdom, of goodness) eventually, as in a playground game, the point of infinity is reached (our god is infinitely courageous, wise, strong, good, etc). The messy, anthropomorphic pantheon of

Figure 2.16
**Hume's account of
the origins of theism**

gods in polytheism becomes the refined, universal and perfect god of theism. We sketched a process similar to this above (page 90) when we looked at the evolution of the God in the Bible.

A pantheon of gods | A pantheon of gods with one chief among them | One God

Feuerbach: God is the projection of a human ideal

> *Man first unconsciously and involuntarily creates God in his own image.*[53]

Feuerbach

A hundred years after Hume concluded that humans created the gods in their image, the German philosopher Ludwig Feuerbach (1804–1872) arrived at a similar conclusion in *The Essence of Christianity*, although via a very different route from Hume. Feuerbach states that humans come to an understanding of themselves by projecting themselves, or externalising themselves, into the idea of God. God is a kind of 'wishful illusion', a being that we hope exists but which we in fact create ourselves. By objectifying ourselves in the form of God, and ascribing God with certain characteristics, we come to know ourselves and understand our essential nature. So the attributes of wisdom, love and mercy, which we ascribe to God in a purified form, are really attributes of humanity. For Feuerbach this is problematic: by ascribing to (a fictional) God these qualities we are denying ourselves these qualities, even though they are only meaningfully ascribed to ourselves – Feuerbach calls this process of denial and mistaken ascription ALIENATION. Alienation means estrangement, becoming separate from or removed from something which we should be in harmony with. By looking outwards to (a non-existent) God we are failing to connect with our own humanity and with one another as fellow humans. What we need to do is replace our love of God with love of humankind, and replace faith in God with faith in humanity.

Feuerbach goes on in *The Essence of Christianity* to identify many of the contradictions in the concept of God that we looked at above (pages 100–107), in particular the contradiction between God as impersonal, metaphysical and transcendent, and God as personal, loving and present. These attributes are fundamentally incompatible (which isn't a problem for Feuerbach as, for him, God doesn't exist) because they are projections of two distinct parts of our essential self – our rational and emotional self.

The lasting importance of Feuerbach lies in the fact that, unlike Hume, he explicitly proclaimed himself as an atheist and wished to account for the idea of God from a purely atheistic perspective. So the study of religion and God was removed from religious philosophers, theologians and priests, and became the proper subject of anthropology. Feuerbach's legacy was this release, or prising, of religion from those who are religious, and it profoundly affected a whole generation of German thinkers (including Marx and Engels) and changed the way that atheists could think and talk about God. Feuerbach made it possible for what we've termed the 'constructive atheist project' to go ahead, and he set a precedent for atheists to give a serious account of religion and the origins of God.

Marx: religion is an ideology

Man makes religion, religion does not make man.[54]

Marx

Karl Marx (1818–1883) transformed the political landscape of the twentieth century and was one of the most influential philosophers who ever lived, striving for and achieving social impact: 'Philosophers have only interpreted the world . . . the point is to change it.'[55] Marx's views on the origins of religion and of the idea of God emerge from his works on politics, economics and history. Marx saw his work as that of a scientist uncovering the laws of society, examining the evidence available and extrapolating from this to conclude that human societies were structured in the same way, progressed according to a specific pattern, and that this progression was inevitable and determined. Although Marx was more interested in religion as a whole than in the concept of God, he did see 'God' as a human construction that played an important role in the structure of society.

For Marx and his close collaborator Friderich Engels (1820–1895) the foundation of all societies is not religion, or politics or philosophy; these are merely the layers of justification that are added after a particular type of society has been established. The real foundations of any society lie in the relationship between the world, the tools employed to exploit the world and the people needed to work the tools (what Marx calls the 'means' of production). Humans, tools and materials: everything follows from the differing relations between these three things, what Marx calls the 'relations' of production. This could mean hunting and gathering, farming and mining, or it could mean the destruction of rain forests and the creation of new silicon technology. But in every stage of society some people own the means of production (the land, the materials, the tools) and some people don't, and the discrepancy between these two groups leads to distinct social classes: those with power and those without. However, Marx predicts that the current Western set of economic relations, which he terms capitalism, will lead to a dramatic collapse and the establishment of a classless society in which everyone owns the means of production – this he called communism. The table below shows the classes in each of the main 'epochs' (periods) that Marx identifies.[56]

The class relationships in the five main economic epochs:

Epoch	Owners of the means of production	Non-owners
Primitive communism	Patriarchs (male heads of family)	Everyone else
Ancient despotism	Slave-owners	Slaves
Feudalism	Aristocracy	Serfs
Capitalism	Bourgeoisie	Workers
Communism	No classes	No classes

As societies advance, the technologies change, the environment changes and the economic relationships change, but everything is still grounded in the fundamental 'relations of production'. For Marx we cannot understand politics or philosophy or religion until we grasp these fundamental economic relationships between human beings. The changes that move a society from one epoch to the next come about for many reasons, for example the use of a new technology that creates a powerful lobbying group which demands, and fights for, more power. History follows an inevitable path as the tensions in the two classes eventually lead to a crisis, such as the political revolutions seen in Europe in the eighteenth and nineteenth centuries. This crisis is resolved through an often violent readjustment of economic relations, and two fresh classes emerge in this new epoch – but there is still one group with the power, one without. According to Marx, until the advent of communism, this conflict is the pattern of all past and present societies:

The history of all hitherto existing society is the history of class struggles.[57]

Marx

Built on top of this economic foundation is what Marx calls the legal and political superstructure: the laws that enforce the economic relations, and the governmental systems that sanction these laws (see Figure 2.17). Again these change over time, but they depend for their content on the relations of production, so ancient primitive societies have different laws and political structures to modern capitalist societies. Emerging from this superstructure are the intellectual justifications for this particular social set-up, and these justifications come in many forms: through a society's philosophy, art, literature and, of course, its religion. So, according to Marx, the features most explicitly valued by societies (ethics, religion, culture, etc.) are mere side effects of their economic and productive relations. Marx calls these features the IDEOLOGY of a given society. A society's ideology does not bring about social change (we saw that this comes only from the foundations, through a change in the relations of production), but it is a set of controlling messages propagated by those in power to maintain their own interests, and to make it appear that what is in the interests of the ruling class is in the interests of everyone.

■ **Figure 2.17 The structure of society according to Marx**

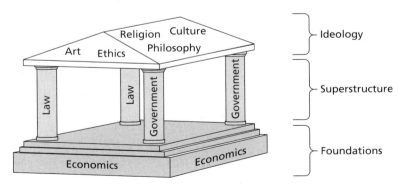

ACTIVITY

1 How do you think religion has been used in the past to control people and keep them happy?

2 Why might religion have been used in this way – whom did it benefit?

3 How might you set out to prove, or disprove, Marx's claims about the function of religion?

Plato suggested a notorious philosophical example of an ideology in the *Republic*, in which he describes and justifies the structure of the ideal state.[58] Such a state is run along strictly hierarchical lines, and who fits where in the hierarchy is determined by which aspect of an individual's soul has dominance – see page 34). In the *Republic* Socrates suggests that the rulers will need to develop a myth so that citizens buy-in to this vision of the ideal state. This myth or 'Noble Lie' explains how people in the different strata of society have been fashioned out of different types of metal by God – gold, silver and bronze – with each type of metal being appropriate to a particular position in society. The myth is in effect a piece of propaganda, in Marx's terms an 'ideology', designed to ensure that people accept their lot, stick in their place, and work within their class to serve the whole community. An even more sinister method of ideological conditioning and acceptance of inequality can be found in Aldous Huxley's novel *Brave New World*: as children sleep they listen to propaganda that has been selected according to their class (Alpha, Beta, Gamma, etc.). Here's what Beta children listen to:

Alpha children wear grey. They work much harder than we do, because they're so frightfully clever. I'm awfully glad I'm a Beta, because I don't work so hard. And then we are much better than the Gammas and Deltas. Gammas are stupid . . .[59]

We have seen that Marx believed that all forms of society have been divided into the haves and the have-nots (in early 21st-century Britain this has become the chavs and the chav-nots[60]): the class who own the means of production (the tools, the factories, the land) and the class who don't. So, for Marx, all societies up till now have contained class inequalities, exploitation and oppression. The influence of Feuerbach on Marx can now be felt, as Marx believes that both classes are in a state of alienation and that religion contributes to this. We saw that Feuerbach made two radical claims: that humans create God (not the other way round) and that this prevents us from valuing ourselves, meaning we remain alienated from our own humanity. But Feuerbach also thought that religion was part of the solution – for the attributes we currently ascribe to God (of wisdom, benevolence, mercy, strength) should really be ascribed to ourselves. Marx agrees with Feuerbach that humans are alienated from their true nature, but fundamentally disagrees with the claim that religion has a positive role to play in connecting us with our nature. Religion is part of a social ideology, and as with all ideology its primary function is to keep the ruling classes in power and ensure that the rest of us are happy with that. For Feuerbach, religion was part of the solution but, for Marx, religion is a part of the problem.

ACTIVITY

Alienation refers to our estrangement from something that we should naturally feel ownership of, and a close connection with. Below is a list of some significant aspects of our lives.

a) Which of these areas of life would you say you felt alienated from?

b) For each area that you do feel alienated from, what are the main reasons and causes for this alienation?

c) Again for each area that you do feel alienated from, try to imagine and then describe what it might be like not to be alienated from that area.

1 Your job
2 Your community
3 Your partner (boyfriend/girlfriend)
4 Your work for school or college
5 Your family
6 Your society
7 Your art, or music, or other creative projects.
8 Your religion

Marx

Religion is the sigh of the oppressed creature, the heart of a heartless world, as it is the spirit of spiritless conditions. It is the opium of the people.[61]

There is a particular ideological role that religion plays in every society. However oppressed or alienated or disillusioned we are by our economic position in society, religion deceives us into thinking that our lives have dignity, purpose and meaning. God loves us, he is watching over us, he has given us a purpose and will give us the opportunity for eternal life, he will judge and punish wrong-doers. In this sense belief in God is a drug, it soothes us and stops us from panicking or from seeing the world as it really is. But religion damages all of us, both the haves and the have-nots, by ensuring that we remain alienated from our true nature – which is to work, to love and to feel connected with the products of our labour. Marx wishes to raise our awareness of this, to destroy the 'false consciousness' that we have had up until now, to teach us to see all ideology including religion for what it really is, and to strive for a classless society in which we are fulfilled instead of alienated. As Marx wrote:

Marx

► criticism ◄ There is an issue about the scientific status of Marx's claims (similar to questions raised about Freud's theory that we examine below). One problem with Marx's theory is that it seems to have been falsified. Marx's predictions about the direction of capitalism turned out to be incorrect: at least in developed nations, there has not been a widening in the wealth of the two classes, with fewer and fewer people owning more and more. Although the gap between the richest and the poorest has remained, Marx's predictions of a crisis in capitalism have not been borne out; instead there has been an expansion of prosperous middle classes in the West. The political movement of communism, which had its origins in Marx's theories, led to an effort in some countries to artificially precipitate a change in epoch – leap-frogging from feudalism to communism through a process of painful revolution. In the last century, countries all over the world experienced violent upheavals which led to the creation of a communist state; these include China, Russia, Cuba, North Korea, Laos, Vietnam and most Eastern European countries. However, these experiments in communism, with everyone having equal economic status and power, were largely failures from the perspective of Marx. Most communist countries are both totalitarian, with a small elite having much of the power, and bureaucratic, with higher-ranking state employees living lifestyles that resemble those of capitalists. Most importantly, people in communist countries are not free from alienation, as Marx hoped and predicted.

However, the historical evidence has not led all Marxists to abandon Marx's theory. For example, they might account for the failure of communist states to live up to the ideals of a classless society by saying that the Soviet Union and Communist China weren't really communist. Or they might explain why there hasn't been a revolution in Western, developed, capitalist societies by redefining capitalism to mean 'global capitalism' and by identifying the two conflicting classes as the developed world and the developing world – with inequalities which are getting wider, just as Marx predicted. But such theoretical foot-shuffling raises the question of whether there is anything that we could observe in the world which would lead a Marxist to say that Marx's theory was false. Karl Popper points out that Marxists are very good at finding confirming instances everywhere that support Marx's theory of class struggle, social structures and ideology.[63] However, when it comes to examples that appear to undermine, or prove false, Marx's theory, Popper found that there is always some interpretation that ensures that the theory isn't falsified. For Popper (see page 167), it is the mark of a scientific theory that it is falsifiable; so if Marx's theory cannot be falsified then it is not a scientific theory at all.

Freud: God arises from our subconscious wish for a father

Freud

> *The derivation of religious needs from an infant's helplessness and the longing for a father seem to me incontrovertible.[64]*

Sigmund Freud (1856–1939) is known as the father of psychoanalysis, a therapeutic process he initially devised to treat patients with mental illnesses, tics and neuroses that had their origins in the unconscious. Although Freud did not 'discover' the unconscious, he certainly popularised the view that subconscious processes are constantly at work behind the scenes in our minds and have an impact on much, if not all, of what we do, say and think. He also put forward the theory, which we now take as commonplace, that our dreams are symbolic to us as individuals and provide clues to our unconscious desires. Over a period of fifty years Freud developed and modified his theory of the workings and structures of the subconscious mind. Most significantly he argued that we have the capacity to repress certain desires and impulses (e.g. sexual ones), and that what has been repressed is transformed into some other (potentially damaging) activity. Freud claimed it is possible to trace the origins of this repression back to our childhood, and the therapeutic process of psychoanalysis often involves the patient talking about their childhood memories, anxieties and scarring events.

Freud's analysis of religion is informed by his theories of the unconscious, of repressed desires, and of our capacity for deluding ourselves. Freud's view on the origin of religion echoes that of Hume – our belief in God arises from our terror of nature, the cruelty of fate, and it compensates for the sufferings of our life. When we were children, Freud argues, we had the same helplessness and the same lack of control over our environment, but we had our parents (specifically our father to protect us, according to Freud). A father, to a small child, seems all-powerful, all-knowing, all-loving and just. As adults we are confronted with the same feelings of helplessness, but our father can no longer protect us: either because he is not around or because we realise he cannot protect us from all the horrors of the world. So, faced with these feelings of helplessness as adults, we regress to our childlike self, and try to reconstruct our omnipotent father in the form of God:

Freud

God is the exalted father and the longing for the father is the root of the need for religion.[65]

But God is simply wish fulfilment, the construction of a comforting illusion, believed by millions, but an illusion nonetheless. The illusion fulfils our wish for protection, and staves off our fear of an indifferent and hostile natural world, and the terror of the finality of death. So, when we speak of the attributes of God, we are not referring to a being who actually exists, but to an idealised, imaginary father who can protect us from all the cruelties, injustices and uncertainties of the world.

Freud

[Religious beliefs] are illusions, fulfilment of the oldest, strongest and most insistent of wishes of mankind; the secret of their strength is the strength of these wishes.[66]

► criticism ◄

Responses to Freud's theories about the subconscious, buried memories and repressed sexual desires are often extreme and immediate. In the drama series *The Sopranos*, Tony Soprano, the godfather of a New Jersey mafia family, says to his therapist:

That crap about Freud, and every boy wanting to have sex with his mother – that's not going to fly here.[67]

This scepticism about Freud's theories is commonplace. Tony Soprano's blunt outburst refers to an aspect of Freud's theory known as the Oedipus Complex. Freud derived the name from the ancient Greek myth of Oedipus who, as predicted by the oracle, grew up (unknowingly) to kill his father and marry his mother. According to Freud all boys go through a stage of development in which they experience their fathers as rivals in the love for their mother. But Freud's belief that psychoanalytical theory is universal has been challenged through research into the social and familial structures of other societies. For example, the Polish anthropologist Bronislaw Malinowski claimed through years of careful study that the Oedipus Complex was not to be found in the

Polynesian societies of the Trobriand islanders and could not be regarded as universal.[68] If Freud's theories carry weight then perhaps they apply not universally but only to people living in European nuclear family units in the nineteenth century.

► criticism ◄ Freud's claims that his theories are universal are further undermined by his failure to acknowledge non-paternalistic religions. The emphasis in Western monotheistic religions is on God as the father, as a paternal figure with many of the positive and negative features of that archetype (protector, authority figure, wrathful, merciful). Freud's theory attempts to capture the origins of belief in this paternal being. But there are many polytheistic religions in which there are both male and female gods; and in Buddhism there isn't even a single god, although there is a belief in reincarnation after death – and Freud's theory as it stands cannot account for this range of beliefs. Moreover, in Europe there is a strong tradition of belief in maternal supernatural authorities, in particular the Virgin Mary, which Freud's theory does not touch on. This omission, noted by feminist critiques, is typical of Freud's default position, namely that the male is the norm on which his psychoanalytic theory was built. In the example of the Oedipus Complex, Freud eventually twists the theory to fit the case of girls only by claiming that, initially at least, girls also compete with their fathers for the love of their mothers. This assumption that the male experience and mental processes are the norm should make us suspicious of Freud's claims to having discovered universal laws of the unconscious.

► criticism ◄ Freud's belief that his theory was a scientific one has also been attacked, most famously by Karl Popper (1902–1994). Popper grew up and studied in Vienna where, at the time, Freud worked and Einstein lectured. Popper was impressed by the differences between Einstein's highly risky theory of relativity (which made predictions about the universe that, had they turned out to be false, would have sent all Einstein's claims tumbling) and Freud's theory, which didn't seem to make any predictions that could be shown to be false. Freud's universal claims for his theory, that it could account for and explain every aspect of human behaviour, is for Popper a significant weakness. We have seen that Popper drew a line between genuine science and non-science, or pseudo-science: theories that fail to make genuine predictions (ones that could

Origins: the idea of 'God' is a human construction

be shown to be false) or which fail to acknowledge falsifying instances (as in the case of Marxism) are not scientific theories. Freud's theory, according to Popper, is unfalsifiable and unscientific because it does not make any precise predictive claims; it is too vague to be testable.

[Freud's] theories describe some facts, but in the manner of myths. They contain most interesting psychological suggestions, but not in a testable form.[69]

Popper

Dawkins: God is an evolutionary by-product

I am one of an increasing number of biologists who see religion as a by-product of something else.[70]

Dawkins

The atheist's account of the psychological origins of God has been revived in recent years by the work of the evolutionary biologist Richard Dawkins (1941–). His contribution to the atheist's case has been a circuitous one, beginning with his most important work *The Selfish Gene* (1976). In this book Dawkins argued that the central unit of evolutionary selection is the gene. Charles Darwin (1809–1882) had first proposed the theory of evolution by natural selection in his book *On the Origin of Species* (1859). Darwin argued that there is 'natural selection' for characteristics that enables an organism to survive. In turn this means more offspring that share these advantageous characteristics which themselves have more offspring, and so the characteristic, over a number of generations, becomes more common throughout the species. Hence a species becomes more adapted to its environment (followers of Darwin are often referred to as adaptationists). For example, in Victorian London, light-coloured peppered moths were replaced by dark-coloured peppered moths as pollution got worse. This was because lighter moths were easier to see and catch by predators (see Figure 2.18). However, as London became less polluted in the last century, darker moths became easier for predators to catch, and the moth population eventually became predominantly lighter-coloured once again. This on-going natural selection means a species is continually adapted to its environment, and gives rise to the appearance of design, an issue we return to in Chapter 6 on pages 436–51.

Dark-coloured moths are rare in this environment, as they are vulnerable to predators

The industrial revolution causes the moths' environment to change

In the new environment dark-coloured moths survive, while light-coloured moths are eaten

■ **Figure 2.18** *As the environment changes so does the frequency of light/dark-coloured moths*

In *The Selfish Gene* Richard Dawkins argued that natural selection works at a genetic level (not at the level of groups of organisms, or the physical traits of individual organisms) by showing how genes 'out-replicate' each other. So, in the case of the peppered moths, the gene (or rather the allele) for light-coloured wings was widespread in the population until the industrial revolution caused the trees on which the moths rested to become darkened with soot. Moths carrying the light-coloured-wing gene (allele) were eaten before they had a chance to reproduce, whilst moths carrying the dark-coloured-wing gene survived and replicated this gene in the next generation, and so on until the majority of peppered moths had the gene for dark wings.

So a crucial task for an adaptationist is to examine the features that organisms have, and through 'reverse engineering' try to work out what benefit they must have been to the species. Reverse engineering is a term used to refer to the practice of working backwards from an unknown object, such as one that's been found on a archaeological site, to try to establish the origins and purpose of the object. So the critical question that an adaptationist has to ask herself when looking at an organism is: How does this feature (e.g. dark-coloured wings) benefit the gene/s which gave rise to it? Or to put it shortly: 'What is its survival value?'[71]

There is a complication, in that an organism not only needs to survive; it also needs to have offspring in order for its genes to be replicated. So the choice of sexual partner that individuals make works as part of natural selection, determining the number of offspring an organism has, and hence how widespread a feature becomes in a population.

Features such as a peacock's tail, which appear to be a severe hindrance to a peacock fleeing from a swift-moving predator, spread through the population because they are advertisements of the peacock's strengths: 'I'm tough enough to survive even though I have this ridiculous and cumbersome tail, so mate with me.' So features that promote success in reproduction, as well as ones that promote survival, eventually appear throughout a population.

Dawkins notes that there is a further complication, in that some features do not seem to have any survival value at all. For example, moths commit suicide near candles, an activity that does not obviously yield any great advantage to the (now destroyed) genes that caused them to behave in this self-immolatory fashion. However, the behaviour of moths in response to the stimulus of light is, in many other contexts, beneficial. Moths evolved to navigate in the dark using the light of the moon, and maintaining a 30° angle to it enables them to steer through the night. Replace the light source of the moon with the light source of a candle and we see the moth fly round in circles, closer and closer to the candle, until it is burnt in the flame. So the moth's behaviour in a candle-lit room is an unfortunate, and fatal, by-product of behaviour that is normally beneficial. The adaptationist's critical question ('What is a feature's survival value?') therefore needs to be supplemented with a further question: 'If this feature does not have any survival value, then is it a by-product of a feature which does?'

In recent years some psychologists, such as Steven Pinker, have started to view our mind as a product of evolution and ask: 'How does this mental process benefit the gene/s which gave rise to it?' Or rather, because evolution operates over such large time periods (except in unusual and neat cases such as peppered moths), an evolutionary psychologist asks: 'How did this mental process benefit the genes of my ancestors?' For adaptationists like Pinker our mind is a highly adapted system of modules designed to figure out how the world works – success in this project meant success for my ancestors and success for whichever gene, or combination of genes, gave rise to the relevant mental process. According to evolutionary psychologists, the mental systems of humans are as much the product of evolution as the wings of peppered moths. But how does religion fit into all this? Pinker asks (thinking about the sky-gods of our ancestors):

What kind of mind would do something as useless as inventing ghosts and bribing them for good weather?[72]

Pinker

Dawkins takes up this question in his book *The God Delusion*: why is it that so many humans, across so many cultures past and present, believe in God? Religious belief is a strikingly common feature of our species that needs an explanation. Dawkins notes that, on the face of it, the religious rituals which accompany a belief in God are time-consuming (all that praying), energy-consuming (building all those huge churches, pyramids, etc.) and endanger the lives of those who believe (through martyrdom, war and countless examples of murderous intolerance). Moreover, religions hardly have a track record of teaching useful, or true, facts about the physical world (the sun is not at the centre of the universe; the earth is not flat; the earth does not go round the sun; there are no gods in the mountains, rivers or skies; there are no witches; the earth was not created in six days; dinosaurs existed, although they are not mentioned in religious texts; and pigs, shellfish and cows – each prohibited by one religion or another – are all safe to eat if cooked properly). So he asks: 'What is it all for? What is the survival value of religion?'[73]

Dawkins' hypothesis is that religious belief is a by-product of a mental process which *is* advantageous to any human organism that possesses it. The tendency for us to believe in God (or angels, or ghosts) is an unfortunate by-product of our propensity to believe what others say when we are children.

Dawkins

More than any other species, we survive by the accumulated experience of previous generations, and that experience needs to be passed on to children for their protection and well-being.[74]

It is theoretically possible, Dawkins says, that children could learn for themselves not to stand near cliffs, or eat deadly nightshade berries, or play with crocodiles. But there is a clear evolutionary advantage for children who don't have to work things out from first principles, because they possess the mental equipment and systems which enable them to believe, trust and obey human adults. So natural selection works to make children's brains gullible, in the sense they will believe anything adults tell them. But a by-product of this very useful gullibility is that we also believe things that are false and/or unhelpful (although usually not fatally so). There is no way for a child to distinguish the good advice that adults offer ('don't go near that crocodile-infested swamp') from the bad advice ('don't forget to sacrifice a goat, otherwise the rains will fail' which, as Dawkins notes, is a waste of both time and goats). Baseless and arbitrary beliefs are passed down from generation to generation along with useful and justifiable beliefs – but so long as the latter are a recipe for evolutionary success, the former will hitch a ride on our gullibility. So religious belief, for Dawkins, is the useless by-product of a very useful mental mechanism.

Dawkins acknowledges that other explanations for religious belief can be found within evolutionary psychology. The philosopher Daniel Dennett identifies three stances that we adopt towards the world: the design stance, the physical stance and intentional stance (for more on this see pages 423–24).[75] These stances are strategies that we use in order to try to make sense of and predict behaviour. So, for example, we use the 'design stance' when we try to understand things, like can-openers and alarm clocks, that appear to have a goal and a purpose. This strategy is a shortcut, as it means we don't worry about the mechanics or internal physical processes of the alarm clock; we just think about what it's trying to do (wake us up) and act accordingly (move it as far away from the bedroom as possible). We adopt the intentional stance when we are making predictions about something that looks like it is an agent (it seems to have beliefs and desires and it acts on these). This shortcut is very useful when it comes to predicting quickly how a tiger, or a crocodile, or a malicious robot might behave.

■ **Figure 2.19**
Daniel Dennett's three stances, which we can adopt towards the world

Stance	Explanation of stance	What this stance means in real life
Physical (or mechanical)	View something as driven by purely mechanistic processes	Spend time working out how it works, what's wrong with it, what is driving it at a micro-level (e.g. its physical or chemical make-up). This takes time but, in principle, makes for accurate predictions
Design	View a thing (and its component parts) as having a function or purpose	Ask the question 'What is this for?' Try to work out what its function is – what each bit does. This is quicker to do than the approach of the physical stance
Intentional	View a thing as having intent like us – it is driven by its beliefs, desires, fears, etc.	Treat it as if it has a mind. What's it trying to do? What does it want? Why is it doing that?

Religious belief could be a by-product of either the design or the intentional stance. According to Dawkins both of these strategies have a 'survival value' in that they speed up our responses to the world, and mean we can second-guess the behaviour of potential predators or mates. Individuals who have the mental systems that support these strategies are more successful than ones that don't, and so they are more likely to be replicated in the next generation and spread throughout our species. But crucially, as Dawkins points out, both stances lead to religious belief as a by-product. An over-extension of the design stance means we have a tendency to see the universe, and everything in it, as designed – a natural mistake made by Aristotle, as well as by religious believers throughout the world who conclude that the (imagined) designer is God. We assess the strength of this design argument in Chapter 6. The by-product of the success of the intentional stance means we have a tendency to anthropomorphise nature. We assign human-like beliefs, desires, emotions to the creatures around us, and this makes us very successful in predicting the behaviour of human and other animals. But we can't stop ourselves from extending our attribution of human qualities, and this leads, as Hume showed, to the belief in spirits, deities and God.

▶ criticism ◀ One of the standard criticisms made of evolutionary biology and psychology is that it is guilty of creating 'just-so' stories. Rudyard Kipling's *Just So Stories* are origin tales for children that explain how things have turned out just the way they have: how the elephant got his trunk, how the leopard got his spots, etc. These narratives have no explanatory power or evidential basis, but then they're not supposed to; they're simply stories. The criticism made of Dawkins and other evolutionary biologists, particularly by believers in INTELLIGENT DESIGN, such as Michael Behe and William Dembski, is that Darwinian accounts of adapted features are just-so stories[76] (we return to Intelligent Design on pages 448–51). In other words the explanations for a particular feature are pulled out of a hat and have no substantive evidence behind them.

Worse than that, critics say that evolutionary explanations are unverifiable, insofar as it is impossible for us to fast-forward through time to see whether a particular feature does evolve in a species in the way that biologists claim. Moreover, evolutionary biologists are accused of being guilty of the cardinal sin of science by treating their theory as unfalsifiable (the same criticism that cut so deeply into Freud's and Marx's theories). No matter what maladaptive or useless feature an evolutionary biologist encounters, it appears as if she will always find an evolutionary explanation for it, rather than seeing the useless feature as evidence that natural selection is false. We saw what looks like an example of this above, when Dawkins admits that not all features have a survival value, and that some (like the suicidal behaviour of moths) might be 'by-products' of a feature that does have a survival value. As Dawkins himself writes in another, related, context:

Dawkins

One can almost hear the baying chorus of 'Unfalsifiable! Tautological! Just-so story!' [77]

So perhaps Dawkins' explanation of the origins of religious belief is an unverifiable and unfalsifiable just-so story.

However, Dawkins, Steven Pinker, Stephen Gould and other evolutionary biologists and psychologists are well aware of the dangers of just-so stories. As Pinker says, there is no shortage of after-the-fact stories that we could tell and bad evolutionary 'explanations' we could find: 'why do men avoid asking for explanations? Because our male ancestors might have been killed if they approached a stranger.' More amusingly, why is our hair brown? Because it enabled our monkey ancestors to hide amongst the coconuts (see below). [78]

■ **Figure 2.20 Why is our hair brown?**

The response of thinkers like Dawkins and Pinker to these criticisms is to say that, like any science, evolutionary biology is dependent on the strength of the available evidence and of the explanatory causal links. Bad evolutionary explanations are bad because they are not supported by evidence (we don't all have brown hair), or because they depend on other puzzling features that simply defers the need for an explanation (why did our ancestors have to hide predominantly amongst coconuts?), or because there is no demonstration of cause and effect (that success in hiding amongst coconuts leads to success in survival and reproduction). As Dawkins says 'we [scientists] believe in evolution because the evidence supports it, and we would abandon it overnight if new evidence arose to disprove it.'[79] Dawkins' explanation for belief in God remains a tentative hypothesis, albeit a persuasive one for many atheists; but as a scientific hypothesis it is only the hard graft of scientists (not theologians or ideologists or pseudo-scientists) that will show it is anything more, or less, than that.

Key points: Chapter 2

What you need to know about **the idea of God:**

1 The idea of God, in a Christian sense, is derived from the revealed texts of the Bible, and filtered through Greek philosophy. So the 'God of the philosophers' (as Pascal describes it) has its origins in the 'God of Abraham', i.e. the Holy Creator described in the Bible, who loves the world. The God of the philosophers is generally attributed with the following characteristics: omnipotence (all-powerful), omniscience (all knowing) and benevolence (possessing supreme goodness). God is also described both as transcendent (existing outside of the universe) and immanent (existing in his creation); as atemporal or eternal (existing outside of time) and as being everlasting (existing in time, but without an end).

2 Some of these attributes of God are problematic in themselves, and some combinations appear to be incoherent. The idea of omnipotence is damaged when we consider whether an omnipotent being can create something that later on he can't control (if he can, then he's not omnipotent; if he can't then he's not omnipotent). If God is omniscient then he would know what were going to do before we actually did it – but this undermines our free will. God's goodness is equally mysterious – is anything he commands good by definition (because good means 'commanded by God') or are God's commands good because they conform to an external standard of ethics? In either case, God's authority seems diminished. The problem of evil arises when we attempt to reconcile all three of these main attributes (omnipotence, omniscience and benevolence) with the existence of pain and suffering in the world (we look at this problem in Chapter 6). It also seems hard to understand how a being can exist both transcendentally and immanently at the same time, yet this is required by religious texts which claim God created space and time (meaning he is outside of space and time) and yet that God walks with his creation (meaning he must be in

space and time). Perhaps, as Aquinas says, we can't apply these attributes to God directly but only by analogy, which recognises the immeasurable difference between our goodness, for example, and God's goodness.

3 Arguments for God's existence consist of reasons put forward to support a conclusion. In a deductive argument the reasons, if true, guarantee the truth of the conclusion. In an inductive argument the reasons give good grounds for accepting the probable truth of the conclusion. The reasons, or propositions, that support an argument may be known to be true a priori (without further need for empirical evidence or observation) or a posteriori (on the basis of observation and experience).

4 Ontological arguments for God's existence are deductive arguments, and their premises are alleged to be a priori. A typical ontological argument works as follows: We can define God as 'the greatest being imaginable'; it is, of course, greater to exist in reality than simply in the imagination; therefore, in order for God to be the greatest possible being he must exist in reality. In other words it is part of the essence of God that he exists. Unfortunately it seems as if ontological arguments can be used to prove the existence of the 'greatest possible anything', even things like islands. The problem seems to be that they treat 'existence' as if it were just another property of an object, like being red or round. In objecting to this, philosophers of language, such as Russell, have argued that 'existence' is not an additional property of X, but tells us whether there is anything in the world that corresponds to X. Recent revivals of ontological arguments have focused on the idea of God's necessary existence.

5 Descartes believes that the idea of God is innate. He uses this to prove that God must exist. Descartes' proof hinges on the causal principle, the idea that the cause of anything must have at least as much reality as the effect. Since all of his ideas must have causes, Descartes can enquire into the cause of his idea of God. And since the cause of his idea must have at least as much reality as the effect, Descartes is able to argue that neither he nor any finite thing could be the cause of his idea of an infinite being. Only a being which is *actually* an infinite being could be the cause. It follows that an infinite being must exist, and that he placed the idea of himself within Descartes' mind in the same way that an artisan places his 'trademark' onto an artefact.

6 Over the past two hundred years there has been increasing scepticism about the existence of God, and thinkers have tried to find a 'naturalistic' solution as to the origin of the idea of God. David Hume thought our idea of God

emerged from our tendency to see things in the world (rivers, clouds, animals) as if they had beliefs and desires just like humans. This, combined with our fear of the future and of nature, leads us to believe in gods who lived in the world and who could care for us and protect us. To Feuerbach, God was a human invention – and we mistakenly attributed properties to him that should properly be attributed to human beings. Marx argued that the invention of God is part of the ideology of any society – it is the opium of the people – a key part of the system of beliefs that keep those with power in power, and those without power oppressed. Like Hume, Freud thought that the idea of God arose from childhood fears continuing into adulthood. As children we have a father who can protect us from those fears; but as an adult we turn to God, who performs the same function. Finally there are a number of explanations from evolutionary biology that account for our belief in God. An adaptationist like Richard Dawkins would look to 'reverse engineer' features that we currently have, in order to trace them back to characteristics that would have helped our ancestors become more successful. Drawing on the work of evolutionary psychologists Dawkins suggest that our natural, evolved, gullibility as children (which is very useful when we are children) leads us to believe in things that are useful and true ('fire burns') but also in things that are not so useful or true ('God exists').

Persons

Introduction

The concept of persons has been the focus of considerable philosophical attention in recent years. Interest has focused on two linked questions which we are going to tackle separately in this chapter; the first concerns what it is to be a person; and the second what makes an individual the *same* person at different times. These questions have links with issues discussed at A2 in Moral Philosophy (Unit 3) including rights and responsibilities, and in particular in applied ethics and the discussions of the moral difficulties surrounding euthanasia, abortion and our treatment of non-human animals. There are also important connections with the concept of personal autonomy explored in the AS Tolerance module (Unit 2) and with issues in Political Philosophy (Unit 3) studied at A2, in particular the determination of human nature and the concept of rights. The issues explored here are also particularly pertinent to the discussion of the nature of the mind, self and consciousness in Descartes' *Meditations* (Unit 4), which are further explored in the Philosophy of Mind (Unit 3) both of which can also be studied at A2.

What are the characteristics of personhood?

To begin reflecting on the first of our questions have a go at the thinking exercise below.

ACTIVITY **What is a 'person'?**

Consider the following individuals and decide whether you think they are persons. For the purposes of the exercise, don't concern yourself with whether the individuals actually exist or not. Rather, simply ask yourself whether – if they did exist – they would be persons.

Once you have answered, reflect on why you answered as you did. What is it that makes some individuals persons and others not?

1 Your best friend
2 A cave dwelling Neanderthal
3 A new-born baby
4 A chimpanzee in the zoo

5 Your pet dog
6 A talking parrot
7 Mr Spock from *Star Trek*
8 CP30 from *Star Wars*
9 Your mobile phone
10 God

What do we mean by a person?

What exactly is a person? How are persons to be distinguished from other kinds of being? This is not simply a question of how we happen to use the word 'person', but rather of how we ought to. So we are asking which individuals can be included within the group of beings we typically call persons and why. What are the important characteristics of personhood which someone needs to have in order to be deemed a person?

Probably the most obvious answer is that a person is a member of a particular species, namely *homo sapiens*, and this gives us an initial definition to consider:

'A person is a human being.'

This definition has some initial plausibility. After all, it is likely that all of the persons you know are humans, and that all the humans you know are persons. And if you found that, in the activity above, all and only the human beings counted as persons, then it will seem reasonable for you to hold that they are indeed the same things. Let us suppose for the moment that this is indeed the case. Would this settle the matter? Does this mean that a person can be defined as a human being?

Perhaps rather surprisingly, there are good reasons to think that it does not. Even if it is true that, as a matter of fact, all humans are persons and all persons are humans, this still wouldn't establish that the two terms 'person' and 'human being' have the same *meaning*.

To see this, consider that all apes that walk upright have opposable thumbs, and all apes with opposable thumbs walk upright; but, despite this, the expressions 'ape that walks upright' and 'ape with opposable thumbs' clearly have different meanings. This example shows that different terms can *refer* to the same things without having the same *meaning*, and this means that our concept of a person can be different from our concept of a human being even though, as a matter of fact, the two terms may refer to the same group of individuals.

Apes that walk upright →

← Apes with opposable thumbs

■ **Figure 3.1**

These two terms refer to the same group of things, namely human beings. But they have different meanings. In the same way it could be that the terms 'human being' and 'person' refer to the same group of things while their meanings are different.

We owe the distinction between what a term *refers* to and what it *means* to the German philosopher and logician Gottlob Frege (1848–1925). According to Frege the reference (*Bedeutung* in German) of a term is the thing or things in the world to which it refers, while the meaning (*Sinn*) is the way in which the thing is presented to the mind. In a now-famous example used to illustrate the point, he noted that the terms 'morning star' and 'evening star' have clearly different meanings. (This example first appeared in Frege's paper 'On sense and reference' in 1892.) And it was an important astronomical discovery that these two stars are in fact one and the same planet, Venus. So these terms turned out to have the same reference, while retaining distinct meanings. Our example of apes that walk upright and apes with opposable thumbs makes the same point. Even though it may be that all apes that walk upright have opposable thumbs and vice versa, it is easy for us to imagine a world in which things were different. Indeed there may have been a point in evolutionary history when our ancestors had opposable thumbs but did not walk upright or vice versa.

In the same way if 'human being' and 'person' have different meanings we would expect to be able to imagine persons who are not members of our species. And we can. Robots which can speak, and intelligent extra-terrestrial life forms, are frequent visitors to science fiction films, and from an early age we are familiar with stories about animals and toys which can think and talk. Moreover, in the past there may well have been creatures, Neanderthals perhaps, whom we would consider persons, but which are not genetically human. Now, while, so far as we currently know, no such non-human persons actually exist, the fact that we can conceive of them is itself enough to show that our idea of a person cannot be the same as our idea of a human being. If the two words meant the same thing, then the very idea of a non-human person would be a contradiction in terms, something we could not imagine. So while – as a matter of fact – it may be the case that only human beings are persons, this appears to be a *contingent* fact about our world. To say it is contingent is to say it just happens to be the case and that things might well have been otherwise. It may be that you have to be human to be a person in this world, but not in other possible worlds that we can readily imagine and which might have been.

Locke's parrot

The seventeenth-century English philosopher John Locke tells a story of a parrot he heard of which could speak fluent Portuguese and which appeared able to respond intelligently to a range of questions put to it.[1]

Imagine that a rational talking parrot was discovered in South America and brought over to Britain. Its owner might start doing television appearances and chat shows where the parrot showed it was not just capable of mimicking human speech but could actually hold down a conversation with a chat-show host on a range of topics. Suppose that after a while the parrot began to demand a share of the profits made from its TV appearances, opened a bank account, and started attending classes to educate itself in British history and culture.

Would you consider this parrot a person? Do you think it should be allowed to apply for British citizenship?

Is being human sufficient for being a person?

While at present we can only imagine persons who are not humans, there is a case for saying that there are humans who are not persons, meaning that merely being human would not be sufficient for being a person. For example, a recently fertilised human ovum is, genetically speaking, an individual human being, but we may be reluctant to grant it full-fledged 'person' status because it lacks what we tend to regard as the necessary features – whatever these may turn out to be. Most obviously, when a person dies they somehow absent themselves from their dead body, and yet their corpse remains human. We talk in terms of the person's body as though the physical remains and the person were distinct; as though the body had ceased to be the person. In a similar way, someone in a permanent coma may have lost what is needed for being a person and so might be considered an ex-person.

We can see from this discussion how the question of what a person is, and at what point something becomes or ceases to be one, bears upon questions in practical ethics, in particular those involved in discussions of the rights and wrongs of abortion and euthanasia. This is because it is generally agreed that killing persons, however we end up defining the term, is morally worse than killing non- or ex-persons. So, determining when a foetus becomes a person has been regarded as key to determining whether abortion can be morally justified. Pro-life campaigners have tended to argue that a newly fertilised human egg is a person and therefore that killing it must be wrongful. Those in favour of a woman's right to choose will often argue that foetuses do not have the necessary qualities to count as full-fledged persons and so do not have the same rights to life as other human beings. And similarly, it is argued, the question of whether and when someone's life can rightfully be terminated hinges on whether they qualify as a person. A human being in a coma from which there is no prospect of recovery, for example, might be permitted to die, since they have lost necessary qualities for personhood.

◼ Necessary and sufficient conditions

Returning to the question at hand, what we are trying to discover here is not which things happen to be persons, but what the essential characteristics of personhood are. In other words, we are trying to work out what the features are that anything must have in order to count as a person or attempting to analyse the concept of a person. In addressing questions such as this, philosophers often try to determine what the necessary and sufficient conditions are for the use of the term 'person'. To get clearer about what this means we need to begin by drawing a distinction between these two sorts of condition.

To understand what a NECESSARY CONDITION is, consider the following example.

1 Being at least 18 years of age is a condition of being eligible to vote in Britain.

What this means is that someone has to be at least 18 in order to vote. And if that person is not at least 18 they cannot vote. This is termed a *necessary* condition because it is necessary that one be at least 18 if one hopes to vote. Now, note what this sentence does *not* mean. It does not mean that if you are 18 you will automatically be able to vote; because it is quite possible that you'll be debarred from voting for some other reason. For example, you may be a prisoner, or be insane, or be a dog. So while being 18 is *one* condition it is not the *only* condition for being able to vote. Simply being 18 is not enough to guarantee one the vote, or as philosophers say, it is a *necessary* condition but it is not by itself a SUFFICIENT CONDITION.

Now consider a second example:

2 Having your head chopped off is a condition for dying.

What this means is that if you have your head chopped off then you will die. This is a *sufficient* condition since losing your head is enough, or sufficient, for dying.

Now, once again, note what this sentence does not mean. It does not mean that if one has *not* had one's head chopped off then one is *not* dead. For it is quite possible to die by some other means, for example you might die in an accident, or of bird flu. So you don't have to have your head chopped off in order to die. In other words, losing your head is not a *necessary* condition for death, but it is a *sufficient* condition.

Some conditions are both necessary *and* sufficient. For example, to win a game of football it is necessary to score more goals than the opposing team. For if you don't score more then you can't win. But it is also sufficient, because if you score more goals then you will have won. (We are ignoring aggregate scores here.)

Often the occurrence of something may have more than one condition. In our first example we saw that a necessary condition for being able to vote in Britain is being 18. But this is not the only condition. There are others. One also must be sane, human, British and so on. These conditions are also necessary. So if we try to analyse what is necessary for being able to vote in Britain we will need to list *all* the necessary conditions.

1 Being over 18
2 Being human
3 Being British
4 Being sane
5 Not being in prison

Everyone who hopes to vote must satisfy all of these conditions. Each one is necessary or, as we might say, each is *individually necessary.*

Now, if there are no other conditions that need to be satisfied, then together these conditions will also be *sufficient.* In other words, if someone is over 18, human, British, sane, etc., then they will be eligible to vote. What this shows is that if we succeed in listing *all* the individually necessary conditions for something then they will be *jointly sufficient.*

experimenting with ideas

Identifying necessary and sufficient conditions

For each of the things or states in the third column identify whether the conditions given in the first column are necessary, sufficient, both necessary and sufficient, or neither necessary nor sufficient. Copy and complete the table.

Conditions	Necessary / sufficient / both / neither	States or things
Having three sides		Being a triangle
Having a horn		Being a unicorn
Needing a filling		Going to the dentist
Having grandchildren		Being a grandmother
Going to college		Being a student
Killing somebody		Being a murderer
Having more than three people		Being a party
		Being a mother
Being female		Being fat
Eating too much		

With all this in view it should be clearer what philosophers are attempting when they try to analyse the concept of a person: they are trying to determine what the individually necessary and jointly sufficient conditions are for saying that some individual is a person. If such conditions could be found, it is thought, we will have analysed and clarified our concept of a person. And the attempt to provide such conditions for the proper deployment of a concept is termed a *logical analysis* of it.

Before reading on, make sure you are clear on the following points to avoid confusion later.

1 To show that A isn't a *necessary* condition of B all we need to do is think of an example when you get B without A. So, to determine whether alcohol is a necessary condition of a good party, we have to try to think of a good party without alcohol. If we can, then alcohol cannot be a necessary condition for a good party.

2 To show that A isn't a *sufficient* condition for B, all we need to do is to think of an example when you can have A without B. So, to work out whether having a lot of money is a sufficient condition for being well liked, we have to

think of someone who has a lot of money but is not well liked. If we can, then having a lot of money cannot be sufficient for being liked.

With these points in mind try the next activity.

ACTIVITY

One approach to determining what we mean by a person is to discover what the necessary and sufficient conditions are for the use of the term. In other words, what are the required features we look for in an individual in deciding whether they count as a person, and which of these together are enough to guarantee someone is a person?

Consider the following list of features. For each one decide whether it is necessary to being a person. In other words, would it be possible to be a person if you didn't possess this feature? If not, the feature is necessary.

Then consider which of these features would be needed to guarantee someone is a person. In other words, which conditions would together be enough to ensure the individual counts as a person? These conditions would be jointly sufficient.

1 Being human
2 Being able to reason
3 Being able to form relationships with other persons
4 Being able to talk
5 Being able to plan for the future
6 Being able to recall the past
7 Being capable of consciousness
8 Having a brain
9 Being able to appreciate music
10 Having awareness of a range of sensations
11 Having a body

If you selected option 1 'Being human' as either a necessary or a sufficient condition make sure you have understood the arguments made so far in this chapter. What these have tried to establish is that being human is not *necessary* for being a person. This means that you don't have to be a human being to be a person, in the sense that it is conceivable that someone could be a person without being a human, for example if they are an intelligent extra-terrestrial life form. The second point we have tried to establish is that being human is not *sufficient* for being a person either. This means that being a human being is not by itself enough to ensure you are a person: for example, you might be a zygote or a corpse.

The characteristics of personhood

We said that simply being a member of a species can't determine what being a person is, but it also seems likely that most if not all other animals are not persons. So why not? What is it that makes humans persons? A plausible view is that being a person has something to do with the complexity of our psychology when contrasted with other animals. But what about this complexity precisely?

Rationality

Aristotle, the great Ancient Greek philosopher and student of Plato, identified our ability to use reason, our 'rationality', as the characteristic that distinguishes us from other animals. He believed that our capacity to use language reflects, or perhaps even constitutes, this rationality. (Indeed included amongst the meanings of the word for 'reason' that Aristotle used, namely *logos*, are speech and thought.) One skill our use of language reveals is a capacity to weigh up the reasons for performing our actions. In a mundane example, you might be faced with a decision to make as to whether to go to the cinema or to spend the evening in the pub; or whether to get out of the bed now, or turn over for another forty winks. Coming to a decision may involve reflecting on the pros and cons of either course of action and weighing them up in your mind. This isn't to say that we are always rational. Persons may well behave irrationally much of the time; the point is simply that our capacity for rational deliberation is a key element of our personhood.

More significant for Aristotle is the ability to engage in moral deliberation and to reflect on the best way to live one's life. It's likely that at some point in your life you have had to face a dilemma about what the morally right course of action is – Is it morally justifiable to eat animals? Should I take illegal drugs? – or whether you would rather do what is to your own advantage – Shall I hand the wallet I have just found straight in to lost property, or take the money first? Making decisions like these involves being able to think about your own motives, feelings and interests.

Possession of a network of beliefs

Our rational nature is also what enables us to form beliefs about the world on the basis of reasons, and to reflect upon the strength of the evidence for these beliefs, as for example in deciding whether to accept a scientific hypothesis, such as that the earth goes round the sun. We also form a whole network of beliefs about the world based largely on our own experiences and what people tell us, such as concerning the state of the weather, the current prime minister, the date of the Battle of Hastings and so forth. It is often argued that this capacity to form beliefs which we can explicitly reflect upon and be conscious of is distinctive of persons. Other animals may well believe things in the sense that their past experience will influence future behaviour – a dog may avoid eating chocolate because of a bad experience devouring a whole box – but it is doubtful that the dog is able consciously to hold the belief in mind that 'chocolate makes me sick'. Certainly, human beliefs form a far more complex network of beliefs than we have any reason to think can exist in other animals. I have beliefs about the history of the universe, of life on earth, and of human kind; beliefs concerning the kinds of plants and animals there are; I know various facts about the earth's oceans, seas and mountains, and about countries and cities I have never visited. At the same time I have beliefs about the best route to work, the price of the bus fare, and how much milk is left in my fridge. Such a complex array of interrelated beliefs gives our mental life a level of complexity which may be cited as essential to genuine personhood.

Autonomy

These abilities, so central to being human, mean, according to Aristotle, that we are not governed by our instincts as other animals are. In deciding what to believe and do, it appears that a person is not determined by their basic animal drives, but is able to rise above these and take a measure of control over his or her life. A dog does not reflect on whether to bark at the stranger in the street, or continue to loll quietly in the shade; a lion does not agonise over whether it is right to target the tasty young antelope in a hunt rather than an older one who has at least had a good life. By enabling us to reflect on how to act, reason gives us some mastery over our passions, and elevates us above the level of creatures of instinct. Thus the capacity to reflect and reason gives us a measure of AUTONOMY or self control, and this autonomy is often cited as a key characteristic of being a person. (Note: the concept of personal autonomy is closely connected to that of free will, which we examine in detail in Chapter 5.)

Being a social animal

For Aristotle, as for Plato before him, it is through reason that we can reflect on how we ought to live; it is by the cultivation of our reason that we can discover the best way to live and so hopefully come to live a good life. The good life, however, is not something I can achieve in isolation, for we are able to reflect not only on our own lives and our various motives and feelings but also on those of other human beings.

As Aristotle pointed out, we are inherently social or political animals,[2] and it may be argued that being a person necessarily involves forming and maintaining a range of social relationships with other persons, from the intimate bonds formed with family and loved ones, through friendships, work ties and so forth. Our ability to communicate enables us to form complex social and political communities within which each of us adopts a series of social roles. The Latin term *persona*, from which the modern word 'person' developed, originally denoted the mask worn by an actor in a play, and the origins of our use of the word lie in the idea of social and legal roles rather than the individuals who occupy them. We identify ourselves through social roles, close relationships, membership of certain groups, our work, cultural origins, nationality, and so on. One's identity as a particular person is, it may be argued, in large part constituted by this network of social relations. Here we can relate our discussion to the philosophy of mind and the so-called problem of other minds. It may be that the ability to recognise oneself as a person with his or her own perspective on the world, and his or her own motives, beliefs, experiences and so forth, is made possible because of a prior awareness of the existence of other such persons.

The individual

But this emphasis on our social role does not capture an important aspect of our modern conception of personhood with its emphasis on the distinctiveness of the individual. It is in Roman times that this modern sense of the word 'person' developed. The philosopher and statesman Cicero was the first to emphasise the uniqueness of each of us, arguing that the individual person is defined not so much by their shared human essence as by the particular characteristics of his or her own nature. In law it is the individual who is held legally responsible for actions and on whom rights are conferred, and it is sometimes said that the idea of the self as a source of action, and as an autonomous agent responsible for his or her conduct, really emerged in Roman thought because of their advanced legal system. This meant that individuals who were not conferred legal rights, such as women and slaves, might be considered less than full persons; but with the adoption of Christianity by the Roman Empire there developed the idea of universal possession of an immortal soul guaranteeing personhood for all human beings.

And yet the importance of individuality is not exclusively a development within a particular culture. Human beings in all societies give themselves proper names which uniquely identify them as an individual, and some philosophers have argued that it is a natural tendency for all human beings to construct a unique personality, complete with preferences, habits, character traits and foibles, much as it is natural for a spider to spin a web.[3] In adolescence we spend much energy negotiating the tensions between the need both to belong and to differentiate ourselves from the group, and the process of developing our own individual selves is perhaps part of our biological endowment. To appreciate how important differentiating oneself as an individual is to our idea of a person, it is perhaps instructive to imagine what we might think of someone who failed to do so. Suppose someone adopted all her mother's beliefs, preferences, habits and so on. She would only ever watch the TV programmes her mother watched, and only espouse the political views her mother held. She would wear the same clothes, make-up, hairstyle and so on, and never choose for herself in even the most mundane aspect of her life. Someone such as this, we might reckon, falls short of full personhood because of a failure to differentiate herself as an individual. This suggests that forging an independent character is part of becoming a full-fledged person and that it is a natural part of growing up. This way of viewing the process of becoming a mature person suggests that personhood is a matter of degree rather than an all-or-nothing affair. A person is something that gradually evolves as the individual develops sufficient autonomy and individuality. Since, on this account, children are not yet full persons, this explains why they do not enjoy the same legal rights as adults.

■ Self-creation

ACTIVITY[4] Imagine you land a well-paid job, but on your first day your new boss asks you to change the following aspects of your lifestyle:
- your clothes
- your hair style
- the TV programmes you watch
- the music you listen to
- your posture
- the company you keep
- where you take your holidays
- your voting intentions

At what point would you object? Why?

You may have found that you would be reluctant to give up many of the things on the list, even for a good salary. Why is this? It seems we are protective of our individuality and put great store by our freedom to choose for ourselves what we want to be like.

Roman thought is sometimes identified as the source of the notion that each of us possesses an autonomous self. Cicero also argued that life should be lived in an attempt to be true to our real self. And from here it is a short step to the idea that the individual creates him or her self by forging goals and blazing a path through life. Nietzsche argued that great individuals create themselves through actively choosing the characteristics they want to have and who they want to be, and to some extent we can see the same process occurring in all persons. We make choices about ourselves through which we can fashion the kind of person we become.[5] We have seen that the desire to be an individual distinct from others appears to be integral to human beings. The decisions we make about what we wear, the career we pursue, the friends we keep, and so on, form part of a complex web of traits which make up the individual we are.

Nonetheless, how important the individual person is when compared with the family, tribe, nation, etc. is clearly culturally relative, and it is argued with some plausibility that contemporary 'Western' societies, particularly British and American, give an unusual degree of importance to the individual person.

Being a moral being

The idea of each of us being unique and individual is closely related to the value we place upon the life of persons. If a child loses a cuddly toy, it can be replaced. Nothing much hangs on the fact that the replacement is not precisely the same as the original. Even with the death of a pet goldfish, for example, a child is likely to be placated if we buy her a new one. The goldfish is, to a degree, replaceable (although the goldfish might disagree). But this is clearly not the case with persons. It is often said that a human life is sacred, or that its value is inestimable, and part of the idea here is that, when a human being dies, something significant is lost forever. If your fiancé(e) dies, it's little consolation to be told they have a brother or sister you might marry instead, who looks pretty much the same. Of course a slave owner might well consider one slave as equivalent to another and feel no compunction about replacing them when they wear out, but to treat other human beings as property is precisely to ignore their personhood and for this reason is normally regarded as morally offensive.

The great German thinker Immanuel Kant's moral philosophy provides a framework by which we can make sense of these intuitions (see Chapter 1). Kant regards our ability to use reason to reflect dispassionately on how we ought to act, and to use moral principles to determine our actions, as what defines us as moral beings. We are able to recognise what our duties are and choose whether to act in accordance with them. So he agrees with the notion that it is our autonomy which enables us to escape being a slave to our animal instincts. But with this ability comes responsibility for our actions. So if we freely choose not to act morally, then we are responsible for this and can be brought to account.

Central to Kant's moral philosophy is the importance of the recognition of the intrinsic value of other persons. A rational being does not have merely *conditional* worth, that is to say, we should never use other people to further our own goals. They are not worthwhile merely as a means to some end but rather they are valuable unconditionally and for their own sake. In Kant's language this means we must respect other autonomous agents as 'ends in themselves' and never treat them as a 'means' to our own ends. Respect for other persons' desires and goals means they have the right to make their own life choices, and should be left freely to choose their own destiny. The idea that we should treat others as 'ends in themselves' is one formulation of the central concept of Kant's moral philosophy, the so-called CATEGORICAL IMPERATIVE (which is looked at in Chapter 1, pages 48–62). What it is saying is that the moral community operates through a mutual recognition of the personhood of others. Persons, on this view, are those beings that are autonomous and so responsible and accountable for their actions.

Speech

We've seen that Aristotle saw speech and reason as closely associated. And more recently, Donald Davidson[6] has argued that language is necessary for the possession of genuine desires and beliefs about the world. Without language an animal can only follow instincts but not reflect on its own mental states or on how the world is. While a cow may well be hungry and desire to eat grass, it is not self-consciously aware *that* it is hungry, or *that* it wants to eat grass. Without words for hunger or grass, a cow cannot possess the concepts of these things and so cannot frame any thoughts about them. A cow is not self-conscious of its own mental states.

Davidson's argument for this claim is that to have a concept of grass one needs to have a reasonably complex network of beliefs *about* grass, for example, that it is the principal diet of cows, can be dried to make hay, requires water and soil to grow, can be continually cropped by grazing without dying, and so forth. Full possession of the concept, in other words, can occur only if it is embedded within a network of other related beliefs. Since a cow surely does not hold these various other beliefs it follows that it cannot have the concept of grass.

However, we may object that Davidson's argument cannot support quite so strong a conclusion. It may well be that a cow doesn't possess quite the detailed concept of grass that we do, enmeshed as it is within a genuinely complex set of other concepts and beliefs. However, it may be part of a more simple network, a network relevant to the life of a cow. What precisely these cow-beliefs would be like is obviously going to be difficult if not impossible to state, but this should not lead us to conclude that it has none. Having concepts and beliefs may be a matter of degree, with some animals having fairly primitive ones, and most adult humans far more detailed ones. If this is right we should expect the process of developing concepts and beliefs to be a gradual one in the development of a child. A two-year-old child, left by his mother at nursery, may be said to believe that his mother has gone to the bank and be able to say as much. Yet, having no other beliefs about banks, the sense in which he really possesses this concept is limited. Nonetheless it is surely wrong to say that he cannot believe his mother is at the bank. This belief is enmeshed in a fairly primitive network of beliefs and concepts, but nonetheless it surely still counts as a belief. And, as the child grows, his concepts will become more detailed and his belief system more complex.

ACTIVITY   What beliefs would you need to hold in order to have a concept of

- cheese
- football
- communism
- pens?

Make a list of all these related beliefs.

Of course a great advantage that a child has over a cow in developing a complex network of beliefs is its capacity to acquire a language. And philosophers have often pointed to the significance of language use in distinguishing us from animals and so in identifying what is distinctive about us as persons. Descartes, for example, wrote that animals 'never use words or other constructed signs, as we do to declare our thoughts to others'.[7] For Descartes this ability to use signs demonstrates that we, unlike animals, have a spiritual dimension. As well as a physical body, humans possess a soul or mind, which is the seat of consciousness. Other animals are mindless, unthinking, machines: purely material beings bound by their natures to behave in specified ways. Notoriously, this view led Descartes to claim that animals have no conscious awareness at all and are therefore incapable of sensations such as pain. Few philosophers have gone so far as to claim this, but the ability of the human mind to understand unfamiliar ideas, and to create genuinely new thoughts; to act and react in unpredictable ways, our capacity for novelty and creativity have seemed an important point of contrast with other animals. And no activity reveals this ability better than our manipulation of language. Each of us is able to generate an indefinite number of sentences and understand ones we have never heard before. For example: the sentence 'There are fifteen hungry crayfish in the living room' has doubtless never been written before, and yet, you are able to read and understand its meaning immediately. Any human conversation involves a dynamic exchange in which we are continually making sense of novel utterances and responding appropriately in original ways. For Descartes and others this ability is a defining characteristic of personhood.

Whatever the extent to which language is required before one can form beliefs and concepts, it is clearly of great importance to our advanced abilities to think about situations which we are not currently experiencing, to reflect on the past and plan for the future. Without language it is also surely impossible to engage in extended chains of reasoning, such as are involved in science and mathematics; or in ethical or political discussions; in preparing a battle campaign; or even in fairly mundane activities like organising a party. Without language it is impossible to give directions on how to locate a distant house, or follow a recipe. And if a creature is not able to represent its future states to itself it is unable freely to choose different courses of action or decide autonomously how best to live its life.

ACTIVITY

Try to imagine what your mental life would be like if you had never learnt a language.

1 When looking at the many things in the world around you, such as trees, dogs and cars, what would be going on in your mind?
2 Would your experience be confined to your immediate sensations, feelings and urges?
3 Would your experience be similar to that of an animal such as a cow?

The capacity to consider one's own future involves the recognition, probably unique to humans, that one's life will come to an end. Some have argued that knowledge of death means humans can value their own lives; indeed, that the ability to value their own lives actually contributes to making their lives more valuable than those of animals. An animal may instinctively fight to survive, and its death may be a loss in so far as it will no longer be able to enjoy life. But it is unable to suffer from the contemplation of is own death, or have a conscious investment in its future. Someone who cannot see beyond the present moment cannot recognise the consequences of their actions, cannot make social commitments or promises, nor plan for or value their futures, and so lacks a key dimension in what we take for granted in persons.

Self-awareness

Descartes reckoned that speech and reason are functions of minds, and what essentially characterises a mind is consciousness. To say that a person is conscious is to say that he or she is aware, that he or she enjoys a range of experiences of different sorts such as sensations and desires. As we have seen, for Descartes, other animals don't have minds and so are not sentient in this sense. They do not experience anything. For Descartes, an animal is nothing more than a very complex machine. This would certainly mean that animals cannot be persons, but few today would follow Descartes in denying that they can experience pain. Does this mean we must disagree with Descartes about animals not being persons? Is simply being aware either a necessary or a sufficient condition for being a person?

Most would agree that sentience is not sufficient, for, although it seems reasonable to suppose, contrary to Descartes, that mammals such as dogs and dolphins are sentient – that is they experience sensations and emotions of various kinds – since they lack many of the other complexities of human psychology and social communication that we've discussed, it seems they cannot be persons. More particularly, for Descartes and others, it is the human capacity for *self-consciousness* which is particularly significant. I am not just aware that there are experiences and thoughts occurring, but also that it is me to whom they are occurring. It is the ability to say 'I', that is, to be able to reflect upon oneself and recognise one's self as a subject of experience, which Descartes regarded as the essence of the mind. In other words, the ability to recognise that my various experiences, motives, desires and so forth are indeed *mine* is essential to being a person.

And these experiences are not just possessed by a self in the present moment but to a self which endures through time. In his important discussion of personal identity, Locke defined a person as follows.

Locke

a thinking intelligent Being, that has reason and reflection, and can consider it self as it self, the same thinking thing in different times and places; which it does only by that consciousness, which is inseparable from thinking, and as it seems to me essential to it.[8]

In other words, the person must be self-conscious, but also aware of itself as the same over time.

■ **Figure 3.2**

It is likely that other animals are consciously aware of what they perceive within both their bodies and their environment. Human beings may be unique in also being aware of themselves as a particular point of view upon the world. Self-awareness is often cited as a necessary condition for personhood. The lion is aware of the antelope but the human hunter is also self-aware.

■ Possessing an emotional life and an aesthetic sense

We have seen that self-consciousness involves being able to reflect on our own mental states. Moreover possession of a language enables us to plan and reason about our own and others' mental states, and the upshot of this is that human emotional life is of a more complex nature than that of animals. The feeling we have for a loved one involves consideration of what is best for them, an understanding of their desires, a respect for their interests, and so on. Such complexity and depth within our emotional lives is something we value highly in ourselves and others, and it is likely that you would regard its loss as an attack on an essential aspect of your person, so that it is likely you may regard it as an essential characteristic of anyone's being a person. Similarly the nature of our aesthetic sense is surely also far more complex than might be found in other animals, in large measure because of our ability to reflect on art, its purpose, construction, effects, etc.

■ The soul

Descartes produced one of the most systematic and influential dualist accounts of human nature, which can be studied at

A2. He argued that I am in essence a conscious being, insisting that only mental attributes such as thoughts, beliefs, desires and sensations can properly be applied to my self. This means that my physical attributes – where I am in space, my weight and size, the colour of my eyes and hair, and so on – do not, strictly speaking, characterise my true self, but rather just the body to which I happen to be attached. So, while Descartes recognised that in this life I am a compound of mind and body, he denied that the body was essential to being the person I am. In support of this view he used a version of an argument dating back to the great Arab commentator on Aristotle, Avicenna (980–1037), which we will examine below. Avicenna had argued that it is possible to imagine oneself fully rational but without any awareness of one's body or physical attributes. In Descartes' version he says that it is possible that the body is an illusion, the product of a kind of dream. In imagining I have no body I would still be certain of my own existence and so the word 'I' must refer to my mind alone, not the body. The conclusion drawn by Avicenna and Descartes is that my body cannot be necessary to being the person I am, my true self is not a physical thing and does not depend on the body to exist and so I can continue to exist once my body is destroyed, perhaps to enjoy the afterlife.

The concept of persons as primitive and a natural phenomenon

The view that the self is distinct from the body and can be separated from it at death has a long history extending at least as far back as the pre-Socratic philosophers such as Pythagoras (lived around 530 BCE) and Empedocles (lived around 450 BCE). It became particularly popular amongst Christian thinkers as it appeared to be a good way of explaining how it is possible for a person to survive bodily death and be resurrected. However, the idea that the body is not an integral part of who I am sits uneasily with our everyday understanding of what a person is. In everyday life we recognise people as being the same by their bodies. Your friends and family members are flesh and blood beings, not disembodied souls. And if they lost their bodies you would be unable to recognise them. So, for example, my students recognise me as the same person who taught them last week because I have the same face. If next week someone turned up to teach them with a different face and different body, doubtless they would conclude that it was a different person. I doubt that they would be persuaded that it was really me, no matter what the person said. This may be taken to suggest that wherever someone's body goes they go, and that their body is an essential component of who they are. We cannot detach ourselves from our bodies and take off as disembodied spirits to roam another plane, or to hitch up with a new body. These things, while common in fiction, just don't happen. This suggests that without my body I would cease to be, and that bodily death is the end of the person.

■ **Figure 3.3**
The teacher identifies the students in her class by their bodies. If after the register is taken one student complained that he had been marked absent when he had been present in spirit alone, it is unlikely the teacher would adjust the register, since the presence of the student's body is in such everyday contexts a necessary condition for the presence of the person. Indeed, one way of questioning whether it is possible for someone to survive as a pure consciousness is to ask how they would be recognised and identified. Without the use of a body it is unclear how this could be done.

Moreover, how could one tell what a person was thinking or feeling if they were not to be identified by their body? Would we be able to ascribe mental states to disembodied souls? It certainly seems that to be able to say that so-and-so is happy, or rational, I need first to look at their behaviour or hear them speak, both of which require them having a body. Souls, it seems, are not detectable in ordinary experience, and so we cannot ascribe mental states to them.

Bernard Williams argues that psychological states alone cannot be sufficient to distinguish one person from another, meaning that we have to use the body to do so.[9] The argument begins by pointing out that any psychological state, such as a memory of watching the film *Casablanca*, or the hope that I will win the lottery, can be shared by different persons. Now, suppose that there were two minds that shared *all* their psychological states. They have the same set of memories, the same hopes, beliefs and so on. In asking you to imagine this, Williams does not mean to imply that this could ever actually happen, but just that it is a logical possibility. Now the question becomes: how could these two persons be distinguished? Clearly, they could not be distinguished by appeal to the states of their minds, since they are, according to the scenario we are asked to imagine, psychologically indistinguishable. However, we know that bodies do allow for clear distinctions to be made between individuals – I do not share my body with anyone else after all – and so the body is the only candidate for making the distinction. (We will return to this argument, often called the Reduplication Argument, later in our discussion of personal identity over time.)

P. F. Strawson famously argued that dividing persons into minds and bodies in the manner of Descartes is a mistake since persons are essentially the kinds of things that can be spoken of both in terms of mental and physical characteristics.

Strawson

The concept of a person is the concept of a type of entity, such that both predicates ascribing states of consciousness and predicates ascribing corporeal characteristics, a physical situation & co. are equally applicable to a single individual of that single type.[10]

So *both* mental and physical attributes are ascribable to the one person, rather than these attributes being applicable to two distinct things, the mind and body. Strawson regards the concept of a person as 'primitive'. That is to say, it cannot be analysed into anything more simple; it cannot be reduced to the physical or the mental. For, as we have been seeing, in identifying persons and attributing mental states to them, we don't search the world for their minds – we wouldn't be able to find them. To ascribe mental states to anything it must be possible to identify the thing, but the only way to identify any individual, according to Strawson, is spatio-temporally, that is, via their body. So to attribute a mental state to someone is to presuppose that they are a subject of experience and that they have a body.

On this view the search for necessary and sufficient conditions for the concept of a person must ultimately be in vain. This is because this is an attempt to render the concept of a person in terms of other concepts, but if, as Strawson maintains, the concept is 'primitive' or basic, then it cannot be analysed in this way. Any attempt to reduce the concept will involve returning to that very concept once again.

The importance of the brain

Belief in an immaterial soul has, however, been in retreat in recent years, in large part because of a reduction in the influence of religious considerations on philosophers' reflections on the issue of what a person is. The mounting evidence from modern neuroscience, which suggests that much of our mental life depends on our brains, has also tended to make the soul appear redundant to an account of what a person is. Indeed, the various psychological factors we

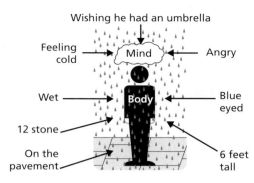
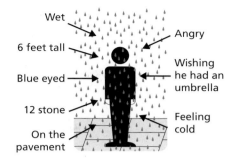

■ Figure 3.4

The person is not divisible into two substances, a mind and a body, to which mental and physical attributes belong. Rather the person is a simple or primitive concept which cannot be broken down further. It is the kind of individual to which both mental and physical characteristics can be applied.

have identified as being necessary for personhood – the ability rationally to deliberate about what to do, self-consciousness, language learning and so forth – do appear to require a well-functioning human brain. Magnetic resonance imaging techniques can now pinpoint which parts of the brain are active when we are engaged in a great range of different mental activities such as imagining colours, recognising faces, listening to music, or making mathematical calculations. Disrupt the operations of the brain with drugs or physical trauma and all these mental functions can be radically affected. The dependence of mind on brain suggests that the destruction of the brain must destroy consciousness, implying that the person cannot survive the death of the body and that the person is not distinguishable from it, or perhaps more particularly, their brain.

In this section we have explored several ideas as to what it is that makes an individual a person. Most of these features are closely interrelated, so that you can't have one without the others. Being a rational agent involves being autonomous and is closely associated with being a moral being. Self-awareness seems to require the ability to consider and plan for the distant future. So it is likely that none of these features is sufficient for personhood on its own. However, as a cluster of concepts they give flesh to our notion of a person.

What is a person?

Having explored the necessary characteristics associated with being a person, we can now turn to determining which things in the actual world count as persons. After all, we generally identify persons before applying the above criteria and tend to identify all and only humans and persons. So here we will be examining whether this approach is justified by asking firstly whether all humans are indeed persons, and secondly whether all persons are human beings.

Are all human beings persons?

ACTIVITY   Imagine losing some of your faculties. Which would you consider severe enough to mean you had lost something essential to being the person you are?

1 Your memories
2 Your self-awareness
3 Consciousness
4 The ability to experience emotional attachments
5 The ability to appreciate beauty

We saw in the opening section that there are good reasons to think that not all human beings are persons, or in other words, that species membership is not a sufficient condition for personhood. An unconscious human being in a coma with no prospect of recovery does not possess the features that we value in them and that made them the person they were.

One argument for denying such a human being personhood would be to consider whether you would prefer to be dead, or be in such a coma. If you would accept that there is no obvious reason to prefer being alive in such a condition to being dead, then this suggests that whatever it is that I value in myself as a person would be lost as much in a coma as in death. Consciousness then appears to be a necessary condition for being a person.

However, a difficulty with this way of thinking is that it implies that sleeping and unconscious people are not persons. Descartes was aware of this problem for his identification of personhood with consciousness and adopted the rather implausible solution that we are always, even in the womb or in deepest sleep, to some degree conscious. Another response is to say that while we are unconscious we are indeed not persons, but that we regain personhood when we regain consciousness. This, however, suggests that being a person is an intermittent business and that I do not genuinely exist as the person I am when I'm asleep in my bed at night. My body is there, but I am somehow temporarily absent. This is certainly an odd way of talking and so it may be preferable to respond that I remain the person I am so long as I can expect to regain consciousness. This would mean that people in comas may or may not be persons depending on whether they are likely to recover, and this may not be at all clear.

What of self-awareness? Would you still be a person if you lost the ability to say 'I' and to recognise yourself as the subject of your experiences? One way to think about this question is once again, to consider whether you would have any interest in continuing to exist with the mental ability of, say, a cow, that is, without any self-awareness, but reduced to a basic level of brute awareness. Would you rather live on, self-consciously aware even if unhappy, or live contented but with the mental ability of a cow?

If the former, this suggests that what we value in personhood includes self-awareness and this gives us a reason to suppose that it should be considered a necessary condition. Recall here that it is likely that our ability to reason, our autonomy and moral agency and the general complexity of our psychology are all closely associated with self-awareness and that together these are necessary for being a person. Without consciousness of self an animal cannot reflect on its desires and think about future desires, and so be able to decide to do the shopping for tomorrow's dinner. They will also be unable to recognise a conflict between desires, for example to smoke cigarettes, or to have a healthy old age, and adjudicate between them. Such abilities are key to planning. This, of course, implies that babies and the senile would not count as persons. A baby which has no self-awareness, no ability to use reason and plan for its future, no conception of its future states, is not a person. It is, however, a potential person and will naturally develop into one, but the precise moment at which it becomes one cannot be specified since it is a gradual process. Similarly, someone with Alzheimer's disease, who over time loses the mental capacities associated with personhood, will gradually diminish as a person. So it seems that being a person is not an all-or-nothing affair, but a matter of degree and so there can be no clear dividing line between a person and non-person but a range of diminished persons in between.

Another candidate for someone who might fall short of personhood, is someone who lacked a moral sense or lacked the ability to form genuine emotional attachments. Are sociopaths full persons?

Some are uncomfortable at the prospect of excluding the mentally impaired, foetuses, babies and children, because it might be seen to countenance a loss of proper respect for them, and the consequences of this might well be morally abhorrent. However, it is important to note that excluding an individual from being a person need not involve denying them rights. After all, diminished persons may still be worthy of moral consideration. For example, it may be argued that what is most significant in assessing the moral worth of an individual is its capacity to suffer rather than to think and reason. Even if such moral concerns can be dealt with, some people's intuitions are that any human being ought to be included within the club of persons, perhaps because of their potential to develop the features typically associated with personhood, as in the case of foetuses and children, or because, even if they no longer have this potential, they are nonetheless members of a species which typically do have such psychological attributes.[11] Certainly we generally identify persons first before we consider whether they have any of the psychological criteria we have discussed here, suggesting that we presuppose the reality of persons instantiated in the figures of other living human beings.

Could some non-human animals be persons or have some of the characteristics associated with personhood?

In the previous section we looked at whether being human was a sufficient condition for personhood. In this and the next section we will return to the issue of whether it is necessary. Now, we have already seen that there is no principled reason why a non-human animal might not be a person. Being a member of our species is not what *defines* us as persons. Moreover, we have seen that the features we have identified as being necessary to personhood admit of degrees. This suggests that, in the same way as babies and children develop gradually into persons, it must also possible that some other animals might have some or all of the mental capacities associated with personhood to a greater or lesser degree, meaning that we should consider them at least partial-persons, if not the full-blown thing.

We have seen that rationality, involving as it does the ability to weigh up reasons for actions, plan for the future, and act as an autonomous agent, is an important if not necessary feature of personhood. So are animals capable of reason? Certainly, there are good reasons for many of the actions they perform and this suggests an ability to plan ahead. Birds fly south to escape the harsh northern winters. Squirrels collect and bury nuts to eat when food is scarce. Some species of ants raise and tend aphids in order to feed on their honeydew.

The great Scots philosopher David Hume thought that animals were capable of reason:

no truth appears to me more evident, than that beasts are endowed with thought and reason as well as men.[12]

Hume

The example he used was of 'a bird that chooses with such care and nicety the place and materials of her nest'.[13] What better evidence can there be of intelligence and reason than intelligent, rational behaviour?

But we need to be careful here. Do birds, squirrels and ants recognise as we do the reasons for their behaviour, or are they simply driven by instinct? One reason to be sceptical that they are reasoning about their actions is that these creatures are unable to modify their behaviour when it ceases to be reasonable in light of their interests. For example, some birds migrate directly across regions at the same time each year, even though many of them are shot and killed by human beings. If these birds really recognised the reasons for their migration, they would surely also be able to think twice about repeatedly flying over such a dangerous section of the route and take a detour. The fact that they carry on blithely flying directly into the line of fire year after year suggests they are blindly following instincts programmed into them by evolution.

Nonetheless, the possibility that other creatures may be capable of abstract thought and a complex psychology cannot be ruled out of hand, and it may be that we will increasingly come to see other creatures as possessing at least some of the features we associate with human persons. Certainly, in the light of Darwin's theory of the evolution of species through natural selection, it is much harder to draw any precise dividing line between ourselves and other animals. Darwin's *On the Origin of Species* (1859) argued that different species of animal are not created fully formed but have gradually developed from common ancestors. More recently, investigations into the genetic make-up of animals have shown close affinities between them, which suggest we share around 99 per cent of our DNA with chimpanzees. Thus, while they may not share all of our psychological and social complexity, other animals, chimpanzees perhaps, may well possess some of the criteria for personhood to some degree.

So how might we determine whether or not an animal is actually capable of some degree of rational deliberation? The problem here, as we have seen, is that behaviour can seem rational when it is purely instinctive and it is not obvious how we are going to get inside the mind of an animal to see what, if anything, it is thinking. If only we could talk to the animals, then surely we would be able to tell just how clever they are! If we could understand their languages we might be able to see just how far their reasoning abilities extend.

For this avenue of exploration to work we would have to suppose that animals actually do have languages. Certainly animals have methods of communication of some sort, yet it currently seems unlikely that these are 'languages' in the full sense of the term. What is so important to our abilities to reason through the use of linguistic signs is that we can represent states of affairs that are not actual, that is we can talk about what would be the case *if* something else happened; what may or may not happen in the future; or what happened in the past. A language has a finite number of words, but because they can be combined in different ways according to grammatical rules it is possible to generate an infinite number of sentences. Are animals capable of manipulating signs in such ways and so to reason?

It is often said that animals probably do have language, but that we cannot understand it. Perhaps the songs of whales and the clicks and buzzes of dolphins are languages as sophisticated as our own. It is *possible* that animals do have such languages, even though we have not yet been able to translate them, but it has to be said that there is little positive evidence for this and the simplest explanation is that their communication systems involve none of the complexity of our own.

Nonetheless, could animals perhaps be taught to use a language like ours? Certainly parrots are able to mimic human speech remarkably accurately, but of course there is more to language use than being able to mimic speech. What a parrot would need to be able to do, to demonstrate some degree of rationality, is hold down some kind of conversation. If Locke's story about the 'rational parrot' discussed above (page 181) – an animal not only able to mimic speech, but to engage in discussion[14] – turned out to be true we would have to think of the parrot as a person despite the fact that it is not human. Unfortunately, it is unlikely that the story was actually true. Parrots just don't have the capacity to do more than mimic human speech, but what of other animals? It appears that, in the wild, the great apes' communication is limited to genetically programmed cries, gestures and facial expression. However, in the 1960s and 1970s, some apes in captivity were taught to use hand gestures and symbols. A chimpanzee named Washoe was taught to use over 200 different words in American Sign Language. Washoe was able to communicate not only with humans but with four other chimps and apparently even taught her own son to sign. Researchers claim Washoe was capable of combining signs to express new ideas, such as in calling a watermelon a 'drink-fruit'.[15]

It is a controversial matter as to how far such research genuinely demonstrates an ability to use human language as a means to generate new ideas using grammatical rules. It may be that these apes are merely imitating humans and while they may understand individual signs any abilities they have for generating new concepts or sentences, by combining these signs, appear to be limited. Note that for a creature to show genuine abilities to plan, it must be able to use a future tense, and to consider what is not actual it must be able to make conditional claims, that is, to talk about what would be the case *if* something else were the case. It would also need to express general claims, that is, articulate what generally happens.

Figure 3.5
Wittgenstein reckoned that if a lion could talk we would not be able to understand what it was saying. The way a lion would categorise its world, the nature of its wants and interests, would mean its network of beliefs and concepts would be so alien from ours as to be incomprehensible. Perhaps a necessary condition for being a person is sharing a certain form of life which is distinctively human and which makes mutual understanding possible.

Good morning!

Growl!

Wittgenstein famously said that if 'a lion could speak, we could not understand him'.[16] If this is true, one reason may be that the complexity of the belief system it would be able to form would be so limited as to fall short of what we would be able to make sense of. Alternatively, it might be that its way of life and the concepts it formed would be so different from ours that we simply could not translate its language into ours. If so, could a talking lion still be a person?[17]

The famous conservationist John Aspinal responded by saying that Wittgenstein had clearly not spent much time with lions. To suppose that we are so different from them as to find communication impossible is to insist on a fundamental discontinuity in nature between us and the rest of the animal kingdom. We may like to consider ourselves as very different from other animals but, if Darwin is right, perhaps we need to get over it.

The moral implications of these discussions have concerned ethicists such as Peter Singer, some arguing that to be consistent we need to include animals in the moral community, that they must count as persons; others that mentally impaired humans are morally equivalent to animals.

Lacking autonomy is often regarded as making someone a diminished, marginal person.

Note that as we saw above with respect to humans that are not persons, to say that an individual is a diminished person is not to say that they should have no moral consideration afforded them. It is perfectly consistent to argue that animals are not full persons, but nonetheless that they have some rights, rights appropriate to the various kinds of being that they are. For example, some moral philosophers argue that merely being able to experience pain and pleasure is sufficient for us to include such a being within our moral deliberations. On this view, causing pain is an evil no matter what creature experiences it, but this is not to say that this makes the animal a person.

Could some machines be persons or have some of the characteristics associated with personhood?

■ Turing's test

We say that a computer has a certain amount of 'memory', that it processes information, searches for files, responds to questions and commands and so forth. Computers can beat grand-masters at chess, correct our grammar and spelling and far outstrip any human in the speed at which they can make mathematical calculations. On the face of it, it seems that computers perform many of the same functions carried out by rational self-conscious beings, and often far better. So should we regard at least some of them as persons? And if not yet, could there come a day when there would exist artificial persons?

We have seen that many philosophers have regarded linguistic competence as a defining characteristic of being a person because of its close association with rationality and the capacity for complex abstract thought. The logician and pioneer of computing Alan Turing (1912–1954) famously suggested that a machine that was indistinguishable from a human being in terms of linguistic competence should be regarded as genuinely intelligent.[18] In other words, if a computer could be programmed to have a conversation with you via a keyboard so that you could be fooled into thinking it was a person, then it would pass Turing's test, meaning we should accept it as genuinely intelligent and in possession of the same mental abilities as normal human beings. Turing is following Hume's thought about animals, namely that if they exhibit intelligent behaviour we should consider them intelligent. Is Turing right? Would such a machine be a person?

■ **Figure 3.6 *The Turing test***

If a computer could fool you into thinking it was a person, when communicating with you via screen and keyboard, Turing argued it would be intelligent.

No machines currently are able to fool us for long in such a test, yet it is possible to engage in a limited conversation with a computer, which we might take to suggest they possess a degree of intelligence even if it falls short of our own. However, many philosophers have disagreed with Turing, arguing that even a machine that could hold down a complex conversation would not have any genuine understanding of what it was talking about. For example, if I access the National Rail Enquiries computer via their website, it is possible to engage a computer in a 'conversation' of sorts about where I want to go, the most suitable train to catch, the price and so forth. I tell the computer where and when I want to go, and it will give me a series of options. However, what is clear in this example is that the computer doesn't really understand anything about train journeys. It is simply programmed to respond in set ways to the questions put to it. Now our question is: would anything different be going on if the computer could respond appropriately in a more complex conversation? If I could go further and discuss with the computer what the view would be like from the window, if it could recommend a good restaurant in the town I was travelling to, and what it thought of last night's football match, would this demonstrate real understanding? Probably not, as even here the computer might still be responding in pre-programmed ways. It cannot really understand what the view is like or what makes for a good restaurant or a disastrous football result because it has no way of enjoying food, or watching football. So, arguably, in order to have some grasp of the meaning of the signs it manipulates, a machine would need to have information about the world around it. Learning to use a language in all its complexity would necessarily involve a grasp of what words like 'restaurant' and 'football' referred to in the world, and so the computer would need to be equipped with some form of sensory apparatus, as in C3P0 in *Star Wars* and Data in *Star Trek, The Next Generation*. It would also need to have desires and be able to represent its own desires and other people's beliefs and desires to itself so as to be able to discuss what you might like to do and be able to make plans. For this, as we have seen, self-awareness would also be necessary.

So while this may be taken to mean we should regard some machines as having some of the characteristics of personhood, currently they clearly fall short of what we have said must be the most important features, namely rationality, self-awareness and the capacity to enter into meaningful emotional relationships with other rational agents. But this does not rule out the future possibility of the development of artificial persons.

Personal identity

Introduction: What secures our personal identity through time?

So far we have been engaged with the question of what it is to be a person. In this section we will be concerned with what it is that makes us the *same* persons at different times, despite the various changes we undergo. What makes me the same person today as I was yesterday? Suppose that since then I have had a haircut, and caught a cold and had some bad news. While yesterday I was shaggy, healthy and happy, today I am clean cut, feverish and miserable. Over longer periods of time persons change even more radically. Our whole character can change, our bodies change, sometimes beyond recognition. Indeed, it is said that over a period of seven years or so the body replaces all its cells so after this time you are composed of a completely new collection of atoms. However, we normally reckon ourselves to be the same persons despite these changes. But, if I have changed, in what sense can I be said to be the 'same' person? Isn't it contradictory to say I am different but the same?

ACTIVITY   How much have you changed from the person you were eight years ago?

1 Make a brief note of some of the main changes – both physical and psychological.
2 Is there a case for saying you are still the same person as back then?
3 Is there a case for saying that you are not the same person as back then?

One slightly confusing aspect of these questions is that there are two distinct senses in which we use the word *same*. Consider the following sentences:

1   Your TV is great; I have the *same* one at home.
2   At the cinema I sat on the *same* chair as I did last week.

In the first sentence 'having the *same* TV' implies having the same make of TV: one that looks the same; in other words, one that has the same features and qualities. This type of 'sameness' is called QUALITATIVE IDENTITY. Identical twins, for example, are more or less qualitatively identical, as they share most of the same features.

In the second sentence 'sitting on the *same* chair' implies *exactly* the same chair. All of the chairs in the cinema are qualitatively identical. In the sense in the paragraph above, they are all roughly the same. But here we mean something different. We mean we sat in exactly the same chair – for example, row H seat 14. This is termed NUMERICAL IDENTITY. It is a harder concept to define, but it may help to remember it if you think of every single object in the universe having its own unique serial *number* – hence its own *numerical* identity.

Each of the two identical twins has their own numerical identity. The twins may look the *same* (qualitative identity) but they are not the *same* person (numerical identity). In one sense I may have the *same* TV as you, but in another sense I can't have the *same* TV. Unless of course I've stolen it.

Corresponding to these two senses of identity are two corresponding types of change. I was given a nice bike for my birthday by Auntie Nora. Unfortunately, after a month of solid use it got a bit scratched. These scratches meant that it was no longer qualitatively identical to when it was new, which is to say it has undergone some small *qualitative change*. It is, however, still the same bike – its numerical identity has not changed. Because of the scratches I decided to paint it a new colour and, while I was at it, put on some new tyres. Again, it has undergone some more qualitative changes but remains the same numerical bike. However, after a silly altercation with the village blacksmith, the bike ended up in a very hot furnace and what emerged was a large blob of metal. The bike was no more. It had undergone a radical change in its qualities, but this time the bike has also undergone a *numerical* change. It has ceased to be. (A numerical change is more usually referred to as an EXISTENTIAL change.)

These concepts of numerical and qualitative identity and change might help shed light on the question of whether you are still the same person as you were eight years ago. There is a sense in which we change every second of every day. We acquire new memories, haircuts and the like, which means that we qualitatively change, in small ways, all the time. However, there is a sense in which, through all these (usually gradual) changes, we remain one and the same person. We retain our numerical identity.

These concepts can also help to frame the central concern of this section, namely what it is that makes us able to retain our *numerical* identity over time. What makes us the same person despite our qualitative changes? The answer to this is naturally related to the converse question of what has to happen for a person to undergo an existential change whereby they are no longer the same person. Going back to the bike, some of the qualitative changes had no impact on the numerical identity of the bike – it remained the same bike. However, when the qualitative change was radical, the bike ceased to be. In terms of persons the question is: what qualitative changes might occur for us to say that an existential change has occurred?

Some of the answers to this question will focus on our psychological qualities. The claim is that if certain mental qualities radically change then so do we, and it is precisely these qualities that allow us to be the same person through all our changes in life. Other answers will focus on something material, suggesting that if key physical changes occur then we are no longer the same person, and that it is these physical qualities that enable our continuity over time. We will look at both sets of answers; the psychological and the physical in turn. Before we start this analysis it is worthwhile noting a few more features of numerical identity.

It appears that the name matters. The bike mentioned above did not retain its numerical identity through the furnace incident. However, instead of focusing on the object as a bike, consider this question: Is it still the same lump of metal through all the changes? You could argue that it was – that the lump of metal retained its numerical identity. Likewise imagine a friend asked you to look after her pet caterpillar while she went on holiday for two weeks. Lo and behold it turned into a butterfly! What would you tell your friend when she asked for her caterpillar back? You no longer have the same *caterpillar*, although you have the same *animal*. Described as a caterpillar, it has undergone an existential change – the caterpillar is no more. Described as an animal, although it has undergone a radical qualitative change, it has retained its numerical identity.

This is a key concept to hold on to. For some humans, perhaps those who have sustained severe mental injuries or acute cases of senile dementia, they remain the same human, the same animal, while it can be argued that the person they were no longer exists. The person has undergone an existential change but it is still the same numerical human.

When trying to account for how we can remain the same through continual change it is tempting to look for some aspect of the person that remains exactly the same. However, there is no need for anything constant to remain. Consider the case of a river. The water is constantly changing, and the route it takes, over time, gradually changes too. Indeed if the water did not change then it would no longer be a river; it would be a lake. The changing nature of the water is a key element in the river retaining its numerical identity. Football teams are another example of things which continually change. The players change, the owner and manager change, the stadium changes even the name of the team changes sometimes. Nothing remains the same, yet it is the same team in the eyes of most fans. Notice though that if all of these changes occurred at once, then for many their team would have ceased to be. It is the gradualness of the change that enables its numerical identity to be retained.

Part of the interest of this question to philosophers has been its importance for our moral thinking. This is because one condition of holding someone responsible for their actions is that they are the same person. After all, we wouldn't punish one twin for what the other twin did. Also if people change such that they are no longer the same person then to what extent can we hold the new person responsible for the actions of the old? For example, in 1993 two ten-year-old boys, Jon Venables and Robert Thompson, were convicted of killing two-year-old James Bulger. The case received wide media attention which was in part caused by the fact that the killers were so young. They spent eight years in prison and after much legal argument were released in 2001 under new identities. Some people, including some elements of the media, feel that their sentences were too lenient and that they should be punished further. Others feel that the punishment was appropriate. The question of personal identity, along with that of diminished responsibility, comes into play here. To what extent would keeping the killers in jail for longer be punishing the same people who committed the crime? They will have undergone radical psychological change since the time of the crime to the extent that some would not consider them to be the same persons.

Beyond morality the question has significance for the belief in life after death. After all, if what survives death does not fill the criteria set out for personal continuity then it cannot really be the same *person* that lives on. Pagan thinkers such as Plato tried to give arguments to show that we can survive death, and later Jewish, Christian and Muslim thinkers have all tried to make sense of their religious commitments to the possibility and so have tried to explain how one's personal identity might be maintained through this process.

ACTIVITY

In normal situations it isn't difficult to tell whether someone is the same person at one time as at another. But to begin to think about what it is that makes us the same, have a look at the following more unusual scenarios in which it may be less obvious.

a) Read through each scenario and answer the question at the end. Once you have finished, look back over the scenarios and ask yourselves why you chose as you did. What reasons underlie your decisions? In other words, what principle or criterion informed your choice?

b) Take note of all the criteria that occur to you.

1 Myrtle married Reg when they were both very young. In those days Reg was handsome, witty and charming. Above all he was always extremely considerate of others and would never raise his voice in anger. Now, however, he has grown ugly, and has nothing of interest to say. He is loud and aggressive and is concerned only with himself. Myrtle despairs of her lot and wants a divorce. 'This is not the same man that I married!' she declares.
   ● Is it the same person that Myrtle married?

2 Karl-Heinz is a peaceable old man living in Hanover. He is a committed liberal-democrat with no sympathy for the Nazi regime or its ideology. Nonetheless, one day he is arrested for war crimes committed during the Nazi occupation of Poland. The documentary evidence shows that, as a young man, he did commit these crimes and he is found guilty. Sitting in jail contemplating his fate, Karl-Heinz is horrified by the thought of the actions in question. He can barely remember performing them, and has no comprehension of what could have motivated the young man to do them.
   ● Is Karl-Heinz the same person who committed the war crimes?

3 Josephine is very interested in 'new age' healing methods. One day she decides to undergo hypnosis to see who she was in her past life. Under hypnosis, memories of the life of a great queen come flooding back. She remembers bathing in asses' milk, falling in love with Mark Anthony and many other wonderful adventures ruling over Egypt. These memories are as real to her as the memories of her present life as a traffic warden in Orpington, Kent. She is convinced that she is the reincarnation of Queen Cleopatra.
   ● Are Josephine and Cleopatra the same person?

4 Twin brothers Boris and Igor are crossing the road when they are involved in a terrible accident. Poor Boris' body is badly squashed, but luckily his brain remains virtually unscathed inside his skull. Igor is killed outright in the incident but, other than serious brain damage, his body hasn't a mark on it. The two are rushed to hospital where a (crazed) surgeon decides that the best option in the circumstances is to transplant Boris' brain into Igor's body. The operation is a great success. The next morning the patient wakes up.

● Who is the patient?

5 Barnaby is happily married with three fine children. One day he goes to the woods to collect berries but never returns. His family is devastated. Ten years on, his wife Hilda and the children happen to take a trip to the neighbouring valley to sell their cheeses. Suddenly to Hilda's amazement she spots Barnaby in the crowd. She rushes up to him saying, 'Barnaby, where have you been all these years? I've been worried sick!' The man explains that he has no knowledge of any 'Barnaby', that he calls himself Solomon and that he has no memories of any life prior to one day ten years ago when he found himself lost in the woods with a bump on his head. Since then he has got married and is living happily with three fine children.

● Is Solomon the same person as Barnaby?

6 Absent-minded genius, Dr Jekyll, often works late in his lab concocting frothy, smoking potions in a vain effort to cure all known diseases. Late one particularly frustrating night, Jekyll confuses his bedtime hot cocoa for one of his vile potions and drinks several gulps. By the time he realises his mistake it's too late and he is already turning into a rabid monster. He runs out of his lab and into the street where he commits several hideous crimes. The next morning Jekyll wakes up in bed with no memory of the night's events.

● Did Jekyll commit the crimes?

Psychological continuity

■ Descartes and the soul

One answer to the question of what it is that maintains personal identity over time is that despite the changes there is a core or essence which remains: the soul. This view has been very influential within Western philosophy in large measure because it appears to give support to the Christian belief that we survive death. For, if we are to sustain our personal identity despite the destruction of the body, one way this might occur is if the true essence of what we are does not decay when the body does.

In the modern era this view has been given important support in Descartes' philosophy. In his famous 'cogito' argument he follows St Augustine in pointing out that it is possible to imagine oneself without a body, but that we cannot imagine ourselves existing without having a mind, that is, without being conscious in any way. Descartes supplemented this thought with the observation that what I observe when I look into my own mind is something very different from what I observe when I look at my body. The former is a realm of beliefs, desires, thoughts, feelings and so forth, while the body is a physical object composed of flesh and blood and taking up space. These two seem so radically unlike each other, Descartes reasoned, that they just had to be different types of thing altogether.

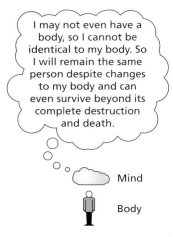

■ **Figure 3.7**
According to Descartes, I remain the same person despite changes to my body and can even survive its complete destruction at death.

I may not even have a body, so I cannot be identical to my body. So I will remain the same person despite changes to my body and can even survive beyond its complete destruction and death.

Mind

Body

Descartes concluded that my essence must therefore be non-physical. My true self, in other words, is not a part of my body, but a purely spiritual substance. According to Descartes, for there to be thought or consciousness, there has to be a thinker. And it is this thinker or mind to which the word 'I' refers. Each thinker has direct awareness of his or her own mind or *self*. Since I am essentially a thinking *substance*, I endure through time, in much the same way as any kind of substance must. This essence – thought or consciousness – is the principle of identity: the condition that is necessary for being who one is. And all modifications that occur in that substance – i.e. all one's experiences – are one's own precisely in virtue of occurring in or to one's substantial self.

This way of thinking chimes well with some of our common views about the self and our personal identity. What I am, we often suppose, is not reducible to my physical aspect, so that we think people shallow if they judge others merely on their physical appearance rather than on psychological or mental characteristics, such as their personality and character. My true self, in other words, is not discoverable by investigating my physical body.

Moreover, this view of personal identity makes sense of our responses to certain thought experiments in which the body changes radically, but we judge the person to remain. We have already spoken, for example, of the fact that the body replaces all its physical material over a period of some years, and yet we suppose ourselves to remain the same person. We are also used to supposing that someone remains the same person despite losing parts of their body. We might be given prosthetic legs and arms and still think of ourselves as essentially unchanged. Indeed, many would regard a completely new body, as in the example of Boris and Igor in the activity on pages 212–13, as still not changing one's personal identity.

More radically it is possible to imagine being transported into a completely new body as in the film *Freaky Friday*, where a mother and daughter wake up to find themselves occupying each other's bodies, or in Kafka's novella *Metamorphosis* in which Joseph K wakes up to find himself transformed into a giant beetle. If you woke up and looked into the mirror to find your mother's face looking back, you would, the thought goes, still be you, not your mother, meaning that I am not identical to my body and that it is a purely CONTINGENT fact that one has the body one does. Locke makes the point in his discussion of personal identity, which we will be examining shortly.

Locke

Should the soul of a prince, carrying with it the consciousness of the prince's past life, enter and inform the body of a cobbler, as soon as deserted by his own soul, every one sees he would be the same person with the prince, accountable only for the prince's actions . . .[19]

Descartes also had an argument, originally found in Plato, to suggest that the mind is indestructible and will survive bodily death. Consciousness, he points out, is not a thing which we can divide up in the way we can always, at least in principle, divide up a piece of physical stuff, such as my body. This is because the self, that to which we refer with the word 'I', is, as we might say, a unitary centre of consciousness. In other words, it makes no sense to think of dividing *my* consciousness so that it might occupy two places at once. It seems that there can only ever be one me. And although I may have different experiences they are all united by belonging to the one thing which is me.

Another way of making this sort of point about the mind is to consider that mental things, like beliefs, desires and thoughts, cannot be thought of as having any size or shape. In other words, they do not seem to be the kinds of thing we can think of as being extended in space. This means that I cannot say that my belief that it is raining is two inches long, or triangular, or to the right of my desire for a beer. It also means that it makes no sense to talk about dividing a belief into parts. So mental life, again, seems to be unextended and indivisible.

These observations about the unity of consciousness led Descartes and others to the claim that the mind must be indestructible. The thought here is that if you cannot divide something, you cannot decompose it or take it apart. And if you can't take it apart then you can't destroy it. On this way of thinking, only composite things like our bodies can decompose. So minds must be immortal and must survive the destruction of the body. More importantly for our purposes here, this argument suggests that I can undergo any number of physical changes through a lifetime and still maintain personal identity, since the self cannot die.

▶ criticism ◀ There are, however, various difficulties with the Cartesian or DUALIST account of personal identity. Firstly Descartes' arguments for dualism are not without their problems. The fact that I can conceive of myself without a body doesn't mean that self and body are separable in reality. *Imagining* myself philosophising as a pure disembodied consciousness may be possible, but this doesn't show that it is a genuine possibility. And the fact that you can doubt the body's existence, but not your mind's existence doesn't show that they must be different things or that the one doesn't depend upon the other. The mind and body may well seem very different, but this doesn't mean that they must be different things. It is quite possible for one thing to appear in two different ways.

experimenting with ideas

Try to imagine yourself without a body, as a pure consciousness, a disembodied soul. To do this you might try to imagine leaving your body.

How successful were you? Could you eliminate any awareness of sensation and of your body? Could you disappear from the physical world entirely?

▶ criticism ◀ Descartes and others have thought it is perfectly possible to continue to exist without a body, but others have asked whether our apparent ability to imagine such a state is a deception. Do we not make implicit reference to our bodies as we attempt to imagine this? As I imagine floating out of my body I am imagining myself occupying a position in space but to do this I must have some kind of body. And to place myself in space I must be able to sense my surroundings, but again this presupposes being able to see or touch things, and so having sense organs or limbs of some kind.

▶ criticism ◀ The supposed unity of consciousness and the implication that it cannot be divided has been questioned by modern neuroscience. Patients who have had the connection between the two hemispheres of their brains cut appear literally to have their minds split in two, meaning that one hand may perform a task, while the person is unable to account for its behaviour. One surgeon describes the effect as revealing 'two independent spheres of conscious awareness, one in each hemisphere, each of which is cut off from the mental experience of the other',[20] which seem to show that there is no unitary self; rather we are a set of integrated systems which produces the illusion that they are all owned or belong to one 'me'.

Also, the fact that it makes no sense to talk about splitting the self doesn't show that it is a special kind of indivisible stuff. It may simply be that the concept of divisibility doesn't apply to the self. We can't talk about dividing beauty or music either, but this doesn't mean they are indestructible substances. Similarly with mental states: many physical states, such as running or being wet, cannot be divided into parts, but they are still physical.

▶ criticism ◀   There are strong arguments to suggest that I am dependent on my brain for my conscious life. Damage to the brain, and drugs, have a profound effect on consciousness, emotion, and our ability to use language and to reason. Even a sharp blow to the head has a profound effect on consciousness; all of which suggests an intimate dependence of the mind on brain function. All this makes perfect sense if reason, emotion and consciousness are activities of the brain, and very little if they are activities of something else entirely. While Descartes' view of the mind and brain in causal interaction can account for the connection between brain states and mental states which have to do with sensation and imagination, there is no explanation for why activities of pure thought or intellect should have any neurological correlate. For Descartes, reasoning, thinking about mathematics, acts of affirming and denying, willing and not willing are purely mental and need no physiological basis. And yet modern brain imaging techniques show that these activities are invariably correlated with very specific sorts of neurological activity. Moreover there is a puzzle for dualism as to why we have such a complex organ as the brain at all, if all our conscious life goes on in something else entirely. In other words, dualism seems to leave the brain without a function.

▶ criticism ◀   There is now very good evidence that the human species is the product of a wholly physical process of evolution. Like many other species we have a nervous system which is itself a physical system and which is distinguished from those of other species only in degree of complexity and power, not in kind. If we accept evolution then we are committed to seeing humans as appearing in the world by a purely material process. Thinking this way makes the appearance of a non-physical mind look like an anomaly. Where did it come from? How did it suddenly become attached to our brains? The theory of evolution suggests that the mind evolved in the same way as everything else and that it is therefore a product of the increasing complexity of our brains, and not something else entirely. Such considerations have moved most contemporary philosophers to embrace the view that we are purely material beings and therefore that the person's identity over time must be grounded in physical continuity, not something immaterial.

Despite these difficulties, Descartes' basic approach, which involves the idea that what makes me what I am is something mental, something to do with my beliefs, thoughts, memories and character rather than my physical body, has had an enduring appeal. This approach has been attractive since, from the first person perspective – my perspective – it seems obvious that I am the same person I was yesterday because I am conscious of being the same. And this certainty would remain even if I woke up with a new body, or even in a disembodied state. There is a level of certainty about this that seemed to Descartes a reasonable basis on which to found self-knowledge and with it personal identity.

ACTIVITY

Imagine that a 17-year-old called Romesh, studying for his A levels, goes to sleep in his bed as normal. That night there is a freak electric storm and something funny happens to Romesh's brain. His entire set of memories is erased and they are replaced with the entire set of memories of the football legend George Best, who died that night. All the games, the famous girlfriends, the battles with the bottle, the liver replacements, and so on, are mysteriously etched on Romesh's brain while he sleeps.

Who is the person who wakes up?
a) Romesh
b) George Best
c) Someone new

To help answer this question consider some of the following:
■ Would the person be shocked when they looked in the mirror?
■ Who would the new person think they are?
■ Romesh didn't like sugar in his tea, whereas George Best likes four sugars. How many sugars would this person put in their first cup of tea, and would they like the taste?
■ Who would Romesh's family think the person is?

- Would the new person want to live with Romesh's family or George Best's?
- Would Romesh's family happily let him leave?
- Would George Best's family happily welcome him in?
- Would the person be able to convince anyone that he was George Best?
- Would the person be substantially better at football than before?
- Would George Best's wife love the new person, as a person (ignoring the physical aspects)?
- If you think that the person is no longer Romesh, does that mean you believe that memory is the key to the psychological continuity of the person?

Locke's memory theory

Locke is perhaps the first philosopher to raise serious objections to the Cartesian account of personal identity. In the chapter 'Of identity and diversity' in his *Essay Concerning Human Understanding* (1690) he argued that being the same *substance* is not a sufficient condition of being the same *person*. So, even if it were established that we do indeed have a soul which endures throughout our lives, this in itself could not establish identity of the person. Locke argues that we are completely in the dark as to what substance sustains our consciousness, and it is conceivable, for example, that it changes every night. Perhaps a soul is worn out after a day's work, and so God provides us with a brand new one onto which he 'downloads' all the psychological states of the previous one. So long as we still wake up with the same consciousness and memories we would be none the wiser.

Another consideration of Locke's involves reflecting on what we would say about an apparent case of reincarnation.

Let anyone reflect upon himself and conclude that he has in himself an immaterial spirit, which is that which thinks in him and in the constant change of his body keeps him the same and is that which he calls himself; let him also suppose it to be the same soul that was in Nestor or Thersites at the siege of Troy (for souls being, as far as we know anything of them, in their nature indifferent to any parcel of matter, the supposition has no apparent absurdity in it), which it may have been, as well as it is now the soul of any other man; but he now having no consciousness of any of the actions either of Nestor or Thersites, does or can he conceive himself the same person with either of them? Can he be concerned in either of their actions, attribute them to himself, or think them his own, more than the actions of any other men that ever existed?[21]

Locke

Locke's answer is that he cannot. Even if your soul is numerically the same as Nestor's, this doesn't make you the same person as Nestor, since our notions of what makes us the person we are depend upon having continued consciousness and memory. It is worth recalling here Locke's definition of a person as 'a thinking intelligent Being, that has reason and reflection, and *can consider it self as it self, the same thinking thing in different times and places*, which it does only by that consciousness, which is inseparable from thinking, and as it seems to me essential to it' (our italics). It would follow from this definition that I cannot be the same person if I have no consciousness or memory of my former life.

So Locke's own view is that it is through consciousness or memory that identity is secured. After all, it would seem clear that I know that I am the same person who went to bed last night, because I can *remember* doing so, or at least could recall doing so if asked. Moreover those experiences which I consider *mine* are those that I can remember having. He supports this approach with further thought experiments such as that already discussed of the consciousness of a prince entering the body of a cobbler. In such a case, it is the memories of his past life as a prince which would determine him as being the prince despite his having miraculously turned up in someone else's body. He also asks us to consider the possibility of two distinct consciousness occupying the same body, rather like in the Robert Louis Stevenson story of Jekyll and Hyde, arguing that they would be two different persons. There are documented cases of so called multiple-personality disorder in which it appears that the person has indeed been fractured into two or more distinct personalities in which each may have limited or no memory of those episodes where the other is present. On Locke's account these would indeed be different persons despite sharing a body. So that it would be wrong to hold one responsible for what the other had done.

Locke

. . . to punish the same Socrates waking for what sleeping Socrates thought, and waking Socrates was never conscious of, would be no more of right, than to punish one twin for what his brother twin did.[22]

But there is a another slightly different point about psychological continuity worth making here, namely that what matters to me about survival is absent in this case. For if I, in a future incarnation, have no recall of my previous life then there is no reason for me to want to be that person.

Another implication of Locke's theory is that radical mental discontinuity, or radical amnesia or coma, would mean the person had ceased to occupy a particular body. Also, he argues that if I do remember doing something then it must be me who did it. In other words, memory is not just a necessary condition for being the same person, but it is also sufficient.

Locke

> *Had I the same consciousness that I saw the ark and Noah's flood, as that I saw an overflowing of the Thames last winter, or as that I write now; I could no more doubt that I who write this now, that saw the Thames overflowed last winter, and that viewed the flood at the general deluge, was the same self.*[23]

Problems for the memory theory

▶ criticism ◀ **Forgetting**

Locke anticipates what is perhaps the most obvious objection. He writes:

Locke

> *But yet possibly will it be objected, suppose I wholly lose the memory of some parts of my life beyond a possibility of retrieving them, so that perhaps I shall never be conscious of them again: yet am I not the same person that did those actions, had those thoughts that I once was conscious of, though I have now forgot them?*[24]

The force of this objection can be brought out through an example. Suppose one evening you get horribly drunk and commit some terribly embarrassing act in front of your friends and family. If Locke is right, then, so long as you have no possibility of recalling your actions, then it was not really you who did it. In which case, why be embarrassed about it? The fact that you might well be terribly ashamed suggests that you identify with the person who so acted even though you can't remember being them. The point here is that common sense tells us that it is possible to lose irretrievably our memory of past deeds without thereby ceasing to be the person who did them. After all, we might ask, if I didn't do it, who did?

Moreover, we do tend to hold people responsible for their actions even when they have no recall of doing them. If Locke were right we would surely have to let people off for crimes they have forgotten committing – perhaps because they were drunk, or because they have suffered amnesia in an accident – since they would not be the same person as the one being prosecuted. Worse, it would seem that all the things I forget in the ordinary course of life, like turning off the gas this morning or locking the door on the way out of the house, weren't done by me. Again, we might wonder who did them.

To meet this objection Locke draws an important distinction between what he calls the 'man', which is to say the particular human being, and the 'person'. As we have seen, the person is essentially a psychological entity for Locke, a rational being able to consider themselves as themselves over time. In contrast, the human being is a particular physical animal. Now, in the case of forgetfulness, it is true to say that it is the same *human being* which committed the embarrassing act, says Locke, but not the same *person*. We tend in everyday life to confuse these two, in large part because most of the time if an individual is the same human being they are also the same person. This means that we tend to feel embarrassed for forgotten actions, but strictly this is a mistake. In the case of holding someone responsible for forgotten actions, Locke also points out that we tend to do so because forgetting is relatively rare so we tend to assume the person is lying. If we were to accept having forgotten committing a crime as completely absolving someone of responsibility it would become an easy excuse. And, because it is very hard to prove someone has forgotten, it is not an excuse we can in practice take seriously.

Nonetheless, Locke is committed to saying that if it could be shown that someone had indeed forgotten, then they should be let off. And this is not always as implausible as it sounds. There are cases of people who commit crimes while sleep walking and for whom it is very likely they genuinely have no recall of what they did. In such cases, while it is clearly the same human being which committed the crimes, it does seem unreasonable to hold them responsible, and a plausible explanation for this is that it is not the same person. In the case of drunkenness there is also another way round Locke's problem. It may well be right that I am not the same person who drunkenly drove home and caused a serious accident, but so long as I remember choosing to get drunk, perhaps I can at least held be responsible for setting a chain of events in motion which led to an individual driving dangerously. Nonetheless, in the case of accidents it is quite often that people will have no memory of what happened for quite a period before the accident, and so it seems, on Locke's account, such a person could not be held responsible for causing an accident by reckless driving if they had no recall of, say, breaking the speed limit. Here Locke's account does seem to jar with our intuitions, and we may be inclined to want to say that the person who chose to behave irresponsibly does have important psychological continuity with the person we want to prosecute, even if they can now no longer recall making the decision. Perhaps if they were the kind of person who was likely to drive recklessly, and they can remember being that person, then they can still be held responsible.

Consider now another way of bringing out the problem. Suppose someone studies history in school and learns that Napoleon crowned himself Emperor of France in 1804. Suppose that in later life the same human being is able to confirm this date, thereby demonstrating that this person has learned it, but has no recollection of the occasion when they learned it. On Locke's account the later person cannot be the person who learned the date in school. But in that case how can Locke explain how they came to believe that Napoleon crowned himself Emperor in 1804? This suggests that the kinds of psychological connection I need to a past self need not involve any explicit memory of actions performed or events witnessed by that self. They might involve processes of learning or other kinds of psychological effects caused in later life. Repressed childhood traumas would be another example of this. It is still me who experienced the traumatic events in childhood, even though now I cannot recall them, because they have had a psychological influence on the person I am as an adult.

The Scottish philosopher Thomas Reid (1710–1796) neatly brought out the problem we have been examining above in his famous Brave Officer Paradox.

Reid

Suppose a brave officer to have been flogged when a boy at school for robbing an orchard, to have taken a standard from the enemy in his first campaign, and to have been made a general in advanced life; suppose, also, . . . that, when he took the standard, he was conscious of his having been flogged at school, and that, when made a general, he was conscious of his taking the standard, but had absolutely lost the consciousness of his flogging.

These things being supposed, it follows, from Mr. Locke's doctrine, that he who was flogged at school is the same person who took the standard, and that he who took the standard is the same person who was made a general. Whence it follows if there be any truth in logic, that the general is the same person with him who was flogged at school. But the general's consciousness does not reach so far back as his flogging; therefore, according to Mr. Locke's doctrine, he is not the person who was flogged. Therefore the general is, and at the same time is not, the same person with him who was flogged at school.[25]

Figure 3.8
The old man remembers gaining the standard as an officer, and the officer remembers stealing apples as a boy, but the old man has forgotten stealing the apples.

What Reid brings out in this example is that Locke's theory leads to a contradiction. To see this we need to understand that identity is what is termed a 'transitive relation'. Transitive relations between individuals are such that they are passed along from individual to individual. So, for example, 'bigger than' is transitive in that if Dan is taller than Gerald and Gerald is taller than Jeremy then Dan must be taller than Jeremy. Similarly with identity if person A is identical to person B and person B is identical to person C then person A and person C must also be identical. But the brave officer example shows that Locke's memory criterion violates the transitivity of identity, since the fact that the general is identical to the brave officer and that the brave officer is identical to the young boy does not guarantee that the general is identical to the boy.

▶ criticism ◀   Can we deal with this objection by modifying Locke's theory? Perhaps we need to modify the memory criterion to say that, even though we forget episodes from our lives, they can still count as episodes in the same life in virtue of having indirect connections to present memories: in other words, so long as there is a continuous chain of linked memories extending back to our earliest years, much like a piece of string in which no one strand extends along the whole length, but every strand is indirectly linked to every other. On this view, memories would be like a rope.[26] Parfit supports a Lockean view of continuity and connectedness of memories and other psychological states.[27]

In a tug of war we normally say that the two teams are holding on to the same piece of rope. Indeed, if they were not, then surely they would fall over. However, the rope itself

is made up of very many strands of fibre, each overlapping with many others but none extending the whole length of the rope. The identity of the rope is a function of a large collection of distinct but overlapping strands held together by friction. In the same way perhaps we should consider the identity of the person as constituted not by any single thread of memory extending throughout a person's life and including every episode, but rather as by a series of overlapping strands of memory. So long as memories overlap with each other, so that there is a continuous series with no breaks, then they are part of the life history of a single person.

▶ criticism ◀   **Butler's circularity objection**

However, the main objection against any theory which uses memory as the criterion of personal identity is that the notion of memory itself *presupposes* that of personal identity, and so cannot be used in an account of what constitutes it without circularity. The thought here, developed first by Joseph Butler[28] and again by Thomas Reid,[29] is that Locke's theory gets things the wrong way round; he confuses the criteria for personal identity with the means by which we discover it. Clearly memory is indeed an important part of the evidence used to determine which experiences are mine, argues Butler. I remember eating sausages and going to bed last night and this makes me confident that these things really did happen to me. However, this doesn't mean that it is memory that *makes* these experiences mine. It is not *because* I remember going to bed last night that is was indeed me, but the other way around: I remember it because it was me.

Locke's mistake is to think that memory could have some special power of making some past person me whereas all it really does is record which past persons are me. Memory cannot *make* some experience a part of my life if they weren't already something I really had experienced. The fact that it doesn't work this way is shown by the fact that if we have good evidence to think that something I appear to remember just couldn't have happened to me, we tend to conclude that the memory was some sort of illusion. That people can have so called *false* memories is now well documented. For example, suppose you had a clear memory of visiting Whitstable with your family one summer holiday. It then turns out that the only holiday they took to Whitstable occurred before you were born. Suppose this could be fairly conclusively demonstrated with your mother's diaries and clearly dated holiday snaps. In such a circumstance you would probably be forced to conclude that you couldn't really have been to Whitstable. This shows that for us to judge something a genuine memory we have to suppose the person did actually have the experience and therefore, contrary to Locke, our concept of memory actually presupposes that of personal identity.

So what criteria are we using in deciding that you could not have been to Whitstable that summer? Presumably it is the fact that your *body* was not in existence which is determining our decision, meaning it is physical continuity which is of greater importance than subjective memories in making judgements of personal identity over time. Physical continuity clearly has greater objective validity than first person expressions of memory. Consider again the case of Josephine remembering being Cleopatra. When confronted with this example, many people are inclined to say that Josephine is deluded. If I told you I could remember fighting at the battle of Waterloo, you would be more likely to judge me crazy than think I really was at the battle because you know I could not physically have been there. So while from a first-person perspective I may be completely convinced that I was at Waterloo, this doesn't guarantee that I really was. Indeed, even I, reflecting dispassionately on this apparent memory, might well be inclined to regard it as some sort of illusion, given that the physical form I am used to taking just could not have been present.

Quasi memory
We can defend the psychological continuity approach by accepting that our normal concept of memory does indeed presuppose that of personal identity, but that we can define a new concept, 'quasi-memory', which does not. Quasi-memory is like ordinary memory in all respects except that it does not necessarily entail being right. So I can quasi-remember going to bed last night without this meaning I definitely did – it could be an illusion. Quasi-memory and other kinds of psychological continuity with my former self will then constitute personal identity over time.

► criticism ◄

more difficult

The reduplication argument

Bernard Williams in an important article 'Personal identity and individuation'[30] makes similar points against the memory theory using the example of apparent reincarnation. If we can imagine one person, call him Charles, having memories of events from the life of a historical figure, say Guy Fawkes, then there is no reason why we can't also imagine a second person, Robert, having the same memories. But in such a situation how would we judge which one, Charles or Robert, really was Guy Fawkes? Clearly there is nothing to distinguish between the two psychologically, meaning that they both have equal claim, according to the memory theory, to be Guy Fawkes. But obviously they can't both be Fawkes since then they would be the same person, which clearly they are not (since there are two of them). Williams concludes that the best description of what has happened is that they have mysteriously, perhaps clairvoyantly, acquired these apparent memories. And if this is the right description of both it should also be the right description of either of them if they alone had acquired these apparent memories. For nothing changes in the relationship between Charles and Guy Fawkes by the appearance Robert, so what we must say of Charles if Robert exists we must also say if he does not. Williams concludes that anyone who appears to have memories of someone who is not physically continuous with them cannot be regarded as the same person, and the only criterion we can use to determine which really is Guy Fawkes will be the bodily one.[31] We must ask, which of the two is physically continuous with Fawkes?

■ **Figure 3.10**

If both Charles and Robert have the same memories of Guy Fawkes' life, which would we say was the true reincarnation of Fawkes? Since both candidates are equally good and two people cannot be one – that is, Charles and Robert can't both be Guy Fawkes – neither can be. But if neither can be Guy Fawkes, then merely having the same memories of being someone cannot be sufficient for really being them.

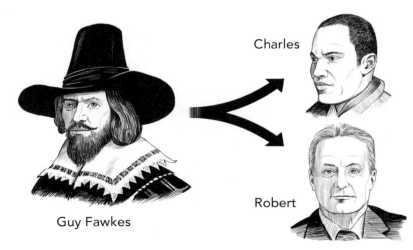

Charles

Robert

Guy Fawkes

Williams' reduplication argument can be summed up quite simply. *Memory is replicable, but personal identity is not.* If we relate this point to the activity on page 218, we can ask what would happen if two people were to wake up with George Best's memories? Surely they couldn't both be George Best. But if they can't both be then having George Best's memories cannot be sufficient for being George Best.

Considerations such as these have led many philosophers to turn to the third-person perspective and its observations of our bodily continuity as the ultimate ground for our judgements about personal identity. However, what the arguments we have so far examined seem to show is only that physical continuity may be a necessary condition for our ordinary ascription of personal identity over time, not a sufficient condition. For it remains the case that some form of psychological continuity has an important role to play in enabling us to re-identify ourselves. It would seem, in other words, that to recognise oneself upon waking as the same person who went to bed is to recognise some form of memory or psychological connectedness between the two states. If someone were to suffer complete amnesia about their former life it is certainly not clear in what sense we could meaningfully speak about them being the same person. Moreover, even from the third-person perspective we may look for psychological continuity in others in order to be confident about considering them the same person, and this continuity may be interpreted more broadly than just memory. For example, we may want to include personality, character traits, habits, belief systems and abilities. Persistence of such features of a person are certainly what we would normally expect to find in the same person. Also the ability to formulate intentions about one's future self and to carry these out, for example when making a promise, is a form of psychological connectedness over time which may be involved. So we might argue that personal identity would be maintained so long as there is a sufficient amount of connectedness of these sorts between former and later selves. This of course allows for a vague boundary to exist between past and future selves, so that if in dementia the connectedness broke down sufficiently one would eventually have to say the person had ceased to survive, although precisely when this happens need not be clear.

Hume's bundle theory

Another argument that can be made against the Cartesian view of the self as a substance comes from Hume. He suggested that if you examine your own mind in search of your self you will not find it. There is nothing in consciousness, in other words, which corresponds to the word 'I'. I never experience the owner of my experiences but only the experiences. He writes:

Hume

> *There are some philosophers who imagine we are every moment intimately conscious of what we call our self; that we feel its existence and its continuance in existence . . . For my part, when I enter most intimately into what I call myself I always stumble on some particular perception or other, heat or cold, light or shade, love or hatred, pain or pleasure. I never can catch myself at any time without a perception, and never can observe anything but the perception.[32]*

Since the self is not an item within consciousness it doesn't really exist. What I mean by the word 'I' therefore is no more than the sequence of experiences and there is nothing independent of this sequence. Thus all that we have reason to believe on the basis of *introspection*, that is, looking into the mind, is in the existence of the stream of consciousness itself, and not of any underlying subject in or to which the stream occurs.

On the back of this view of the self, Hume argues that there is no such thing as personal identity. It is merely a psychological illusion. For since, strictly speaking, no two experiences are ever the same, then there can be no real continuity within a stream of experiences that could justify our claim to be the same person. So where do we get the idea that we are the same person from? Hume's answer is that different experiences belong to the same person if they are linked together by relations of causation and resemblance. In other words if one experience *causes* another experience to come to mind then they are linked, and it is the network of such links which makes all these experiences belong to what we think of as one person's life. In this way, although Hume treats the idea of personal identity as a mistake, he nonetheless gives us an account of how this mistake arises, that is, of how we come to believe in a continuous self, and this account is not unlike Locke's in regarding psychological connectedness or continuity as the key.

▶ criticism ◀   Arguments against the bundle theory

more difficult

1 If the mind is merely a bundle of states and events, then it must be logically possible for the various elements to exist on their own. Thus it should be conceivable for there to be free-floating pains. But this, this objection claims, is absurd.

Experiences are clearly *properties* of something, just as colours are. And just as colours cannot float free of objects, neither can experiences float free of minds. This intuition seems to lie behind Descartes' thinking when he assumes the existence of a thinker on the basis of the existence of thoughts.

But is it absurd? Is there any reason why we should not imagine a pain existing independently of any other experiences? Surely there is no logical inconsistency in the idea, and therefore, if it is true that pains always occur in bundles with other experiences, this is merely a contingent fact.

2 What criteria of identity for persons can Hume appeal to? What, in other words, *unites* the series of experiences that makes a person? If there is no self which 'has' the experiences, what makes certain experiences mine and not yours? Surely there must be some permanent thing, the self, which remains identical through time and to which experiences occur. And clearly I do not just *perceive*, I perceive experiences as happening *to me*, or as being *mine*.

This line makes appeal to the need for some enduring *substance* if we are to make sense of true identity and we have already considered Locke's objection to this line. Hume's own response, as we have also seen, is provided in terms of the notions of *resemblance* and *causality*. In his view it is the resemblance of the different conscious states to one another, and the causal relations between them, which bind them together in a single bundle. However, it would seem that we can have experiences which are *not* related to each other in either of these ways, and which we can only explain as being part of the same bundle by saying that they are possessed by the same individual self. Thus, for example, there would seem to be no relation of resemblance or of causation between my philosophising, having a headache and smelling breakfast, and yet they all seem to happen to *me*.

3 On the Humean view, minds are constructs out of thoughts and experiences, since particular minds are merely bundles of particular conscious states. If this is so, then our notions of the particularity (numerical identity) of any given conscious state must be logically prior to our notion of the particularity of any given particular mind. However, this order of priority is the wrong way round. For we do not *first* establish that we are dealing with two distinct but exactly similar experiences, and *then* settle the question of whether those experiences belong to two distinct minds or only one. Rather, the question 'Are there two exactly

similar experiences here, or only one?' can only be answered in terms of whether or not the experiences belong to two different experiencing things (persons or selves), or only one.

4 As we have seen, it is often argued that consciousness is necessarily *unitary*. Descartes, for example, claims that it makes no sense to speak of dividing the self. I cannot be half a mind or half a person. Either I am or I am not. But if Hume is right then I would be nothing more than a series of different experiences and so I would be divisible into these various experiences. So, it may be argued, Hume's theory is inconsistent with the facts.

However, we may be less than impressed by the Cartesian claim that the self is truly unitary. Split-brain experiments suggest that consciousness can be divided, as has already been discussed above.[33]

◼ Problem cases for the criterion of psychological continuity

Certain thought experiments suggest limitations on the credibility of either memory or a Humean conception of psychological continuity as a criterion of personal identity over time.

Consider firstly the example of the matter transporter in *Star Trek*, in which people travel across space by having the molecules from which they are composed disassembled and reassembled. Would I survive such a process as the same person? Here the continuity in the arrangement of my bodily parts has been interrupted while my memories stay intact. But the fact that Captain Kirk had no qualms about using this method of transport might be taken to suggest that *psychological* rather than *bodily* continuity constitutes personal identity.

However, consider the example of 'tele-transportation', whereby a machine reads off the entire make-up of my body and in the process destroys it, only to produce an exact replica on another planet. The person appearing on the other planet has all my memories and believes himself to be me. But is he? Here again there would appear to be psychological continuity without bodily continuity, and yet we are less inclined to think that personal identity has been retained.

1 You are a guest on the Starship Enterprise and Captain Kirk invites you to take a trip to a local planet in their matter transporter. The machine will decompose your body into its constituent atoms, channel them along a laser beam across space and recompose you on the planet's surface.

If you stepped into the matter transporter do you think you would arrive safely on the planet surface as the same person?

2 Suppose that the matter transporter doesn't operate over great distances, but that luckily the ingenious technicians on the Enterprise have invented a tele-transporter. The tele-transporter works by first decomposing your body and recording the precise pattern of the constituent atoms. It then transmits the pattern to the distant planet where another machine recomposes you out of local materials. Keen to cross the galaxy you agree to step into the machine. The person appearing on the other planet believes they are you.

Do you think you would arrive safely on the planet surface as the same person?

3 Is your answer the same for the matter transporter? What differences are there between the two cases?

4 Consider a tele-transporter which does not destroy your original body, but simply creates a copy out of local materials on the planet so that now there are two of 'you'. Which one would be the real you and why?

5 Finally suppose that you have been convicted of a terrible crime and are offered the choice of being hanged, or of being given a drug which induces total amnesia and then being tortured to death. Which would you choose?

If you believe that psychological continuity is the only criterion of self-identity, then you would not believe the torture victim to be the same person as you, and so the rational thing to do (assuming you care only about your self) would be to opt to take the drug. However, most people given this choice would opt for hanging, suggesting that they do not regard psychological continuity as the only criterion of self-identity.

Physical continuity

We examined some of the difficulties with taking psychological continuity as the criterion of personal identity and so we will now turn to the idea that personal identity involves the persistence of something physical. In moving to a physical criterion we are moving away from a subjective account, which has been traditional in much 'modern' philosophy since Descartes, towards a third-person account which focuses on evidence available to all. The view that a person's identity is constituted by the identity of their body is perhaps the most natural one to take.

■ **Figure 3.11**

Imagine you are looking at a photo of yourself as a six year old. You may ask yourself, how can I be sure that this is a photo of me? The natural way to explain this is to imagine you could retrace all your steps backwards in time. There would be a continual journey in space and time from when and where you are now, looking at the photo, to eventually a younger you standing in front of the camera having their photo taken.

However, the idea that spatio-temporal continuity of the body constitutes personal identity faces an immediate difficulty. How can we speak of identity of the body over time given that the parts of which it is composed are gradually replaced so that the matter constituting my body today is completely different from the matter constituting it ten years ago? The classic statement of this problem uses the example of a ship belonging to Theseus, the mythical king of Athens, which he retained in service over many years, gradually replacing its parts as they wore out. After a period of time all the parts of the original ship had been substituted and so the question arises as to whether it was the same ship.

Consider in a parallel way the identity of physical organisms such as animals and plants. The fact that the actual atoms and molecules of an organism are gradually replaced doesn't mean that it has changed its identity. We can even imagine two trees over a period of years swapping all the molecules of which they are made. But such a swapping of the material *substance* which composes them doesn't mean that the *trees* have changed places. These considerations suggest that the criteria of identity in these cases is not identity of substance, and it may be that living things are similar with artefacts such as ships. It remains the same ship even though the stuff of which it is made has been replaced.

How are we to make sense of the idea that something can remain the same even when nothing of which it is made is the same material? Locke has an answer to this question when it comes to living things. So long as there remains the same organisation between the parts, then it will remain the same. So, for example, the identity of a human being (as opposed to a person) or any animal or plant is not a matter of the persistence of any piece of material stuff. So long as there is an uninterrupted maintenance of organic unity or, as Locke has it, 'vital union', then we think of it as the same organism, and the same logic may be extended to complex artefacts such as watches or ships. So we could, in principle, track the identity of the thing through space and time and as long as there were no radical breaks; for example, if it was completely dismantled, then it might be regarded as the same, despite the on-going changes to its component parts. This give us a fairly robust and objective basis for determining the identity of a human being over time and so can be the basis for our discussion of whether bodily continuity is necessary or sufficient for *personal* identity over time.

Bodily continuity

When considering psychological continuity above we looked at the science fiction example of the matter transporter from *Star Trek*. Let's consider the example again now and how it bears upon the idea that it is bodily continuity that constitutes personal identity. The issue here is that spatio-temporal continuity and the continuous 'vital union' has been broken. Christian scholars since the early days of the Church have wrestled with the problem of how personal identity is to be retained when we are resurrected given that we know our bodies decompose at physical death. The early Christian thinkers[34] were materialists and so believed that personal identity was constituted by physical identity of the body and they argued that, so long as God recomposes you in exactly the same way as before, using precisely the same atoms and molecules in the same arrangement, then you are numerically identical with the original you. For these thinkers, identity is ensured so long as your body is made out of the same stuff and so I can have intermittent existence and still preserve identity. Irenaeus, for example, used the analogy of a statue which is recast in the same mould using the same metal, arguing that the new statue would be the same.

However, the analogy of the statue suggests that without continuity in space and time there can be no numerical identity. We are likely to conclude that this is an exactly similar statue but, because of the radical break, not the same, and by analogy recomposing me after my death would amount to creating a replica, not resurrecting the original me. It is plausible to say, with Locke and others, that numerical identity can only be retained if the body traces an unbroken path through space and time so that the unity of the organism is not destroyed. If there is a radical break, as in the matter transport example, then the new me may be thought to be nothing more than a precise copy, qualitatively identical, but numerically distinct.

▥ Figure 3.12

A statue is melted and recast in the same mould. Is it the same statue or merely a replica?

At the end of the third *Alien* film the character played by Sigourney Weaver, Ripley, is killed only to be 'resurrected' by cloning her from a piece of her genetic material. Would this be a genuine case of personal survival? She could have been cloned while she was still alive, and this new person would clearly not be Ripley. So why should it be her if the cloning took place after her death? Replicating someone is not the same as them actually surviving.

Consider once again the tele-transporter from the activity on page 231 in which you survive the process while a duplicate or clone of you appears on a distant planet. This can be taken to show that numerical identity cannot be retained without physical continuity through space and time. The only difference between the matter transporter and the tele-transporter is that the actual atoms from which you will be recomposed are different. But this shouldn't make any real difference since one carbon or hydrogen atom is much the same as another. And yet in the tele-transporter case it is clear that the clone is not numerically identical precisely because it is possible for there to be two survivors. Suppose that when the tele-transporter reads off the positions of the atoms composing you it fatally weakens you. As you lie dying on Earth you would certainly consider the person on the other planet to be a qualitatively identical copy, rather than the real you, and you probably wouldn't gain much comfort from the idea that this other person was going to take over your life. If this is right, then any process which might allow for more than one survivor cannot sustain personal identity and so it appears that organic unity cannot be broken for personal identity to be preserved.

1 Consider a tele-transporter, as before, which destroys your body in the process, but creates more than one replica of you on another planet. Which would be you? Could you survive as more than one person?

2 Suppose that God does indeed resurrect people at the end of time and let's suppose he decides to bring Socrates back. Socrates lived for 80 years and so over his lifetime he shed enough physical material to make around eight different Socrateses at age 10, 20, 30, and so on. Suppose God, in his wisdom, decides to bring all eight back. Which would be the real Socrates?

Williams' reduplication argument, which we considered above on page 227, is instructive when reflecting on these cases. Williams pointed out that if any survivor of person P could be duplicated so there were more than one candidate with as good a claim to be P, then neither of them could be identical with P. In the tele-transportation case, it is always possible to duplicate survivors and so the conclusion seems to be that I cannot survive the process. Making a copy, no matter how precise can only ever be a copy.

If we apply the same logic to the example of recomposing eight different Socrateses out of the original materials of Socrates at different stages of his life, the conclusion must be that none of them is the real Socrates. And this again suggests that personal identity cannot endure through radical decomposition and re-composition of the body, even if the same materials are used.

Problems for bodily continuity

We have already examined some of the arguments to show that bodily continuity cannot be sufficient for personal survival. If I fall into a permanent vegetative state, the person I was has ceased to exist, even though my body remains alive. The more interesting question, however, is whether bodily continuity is a necessary condition, and we have already seen why some philosophers have thought it is when examining some of the difficulties with the idea that psychological continuity is necessary.

Brain criterion

We have looked at replacing the cells of the body gradually, but what of more radical changes to our physical constitution? Clearly we can lose a limb without ceasing to be the same person and we might replace various organs of the body with donated or artificial ones. If someone were to have their limbs replaced, given a new heart, liver, kidneys and so forth, would we still consider them to be the same? Presumably we would, suggesting that much of the body is dispensable. And we can readily push the thought experiment further and ask about replacing the whole body either piece by piece or all at once. At what point would they cease to be the same person?

Many would argue that it is possible in principle to replace the whole of the body and still preserve identity, not because they believe in an immaterial soul, but because they regard the brain as the true seat of the necessary features of personhood. Recalling the example of the brain transplant in example 4 of the activity on page 212, most would agree that the patient waking up is Boris because it is his brain and so his consciousness. If consciousness, memory and the other psychological features of personhood depend on the brain, then ultimately it will be the brain which we will identify as the organ which preserves personal identity.[35] What this suggests is that bodily continuity is not necessary for the identity of the person, but rather that the brain is. This is still something physical, of course, so we are still dealing with physical continuity, but not of the whole body.

Brain damage

The natural next step of his line of inquiry is to ask how much damage to the brain a person might survive while being the same person? If they were to lose some or all of the characteristics we have identified as required of a person, then they would surely cease to exist as the person they are, indeed as a person at all. However, developments in our understanding of the brain in the last century have shown that a considerable amount of the brain can be lost to accidental or stroke damage while the person retains their memories, personality traits, habits and so forth. It is even possible for one hemisphere to be destroyed and yet for the other to maintain the essential functions of both, including a full array of psychological connections to the person's past life. Now if we accept the brain criterion discussed above, it seems we must also accept that half a brain in such cases is also sufficient for personal identity. This may lead us to accept a version of the physical criterion which requires that just some of the brain is necessary.

Objections to the brain criterion

1 You will recall Williams' reduplication argument discussed earlier. Williams' target was the idea that psychological continuity might be sufficient for personal identity, but some philosophers have felt the argument has a wider application. One such is against the idea that someone might survive the destruction of half of their brain.

Suppose you are kidnapped by aliens who, for the furtherance of their scientific understanding of human beings, decide to remove your brain, cut it in two and transplant each hemisphere into two other human beings' (recently evacuated) skulls. The question they want to answer is which of the two will be you? One of the survivors? Both? Or neither?

Williams' reduplication argument can be put to work on this example in the following way. Since both the survivors of this experiment have an equal claim to be you, and yet they cannot both be you, we must conclude that neither is you. But if neither is you in this scenario, then you could not survive even if half your brain were destroyed and the other half transplanted, since whether the other half of your brain has been transplanted or destroyed should make no difference. Therefore you cannot be identical with someone who survives with half your brain.[36]

2 A second objection to the idea that survival of part or all of the brain is a sufficient condition for personal identity involves consideration of further thought experiments.

1 Suppose that a device were invented which could record and store the entire contents of someone's brain. Such a device might be used to safeguard your memories just in case you were to suffer amnesia, in which case they could be downloaded once more onto your brain. Imagine now that you suffer an accident in which you lose much or all the information stored in your brain, and that you have this information restored to you via the device.
   ● Would you be the same person?·
2 Now suppose that you didn't physically survive the accident but that the device was used to download the information from your brain onto someone else's brain,
   ● Would you have survived?

These scenarios are obviously science fiction, but there doesn't seem to be anything in principle to say that this couldn't be done. And one answer to these questions is that, so long as you recovered all the abilities, habits, personality traits, memories, and so on that you had before, you would retain your personal identity through both these processes. But this response goes against the idea that the brain, or even some part of the brain, is necessary for personal identity, which might perhaps return us to the idea of psychological continuity.

3 We have already seen that it is conceivable that there are beings which we would consider persons even though they are not human. Suppose there was a Martian which behaved much like us with respect to its rationality and so forth but which, instead of a human brain, had something akin to spaghetti hoops in its skull. Now, in such a case we would doubtless want to grant the Martian personhood, even though it doesn't have a brain, suggesting that having a brain cannot be necessary to our idea of being a person and so cannot be a necessary condition for personal identity over time.

Other accounts of personal identity

■ Personal identity is what it is

Butler and Reid were led by their rejection of Locke's arguments about psychological continuity to return to a Cartesian position, namely that personal identity is not analysable in terms of anything else. Their thought was that psychological continuity is evidence for personal identity, but does not constitute it. They also believed, as did Descartes, that physical continuity could also not constitute personal identity. The person is in fact identifiable with a spiritual substance which remains strictly identical over time. Persons are primitive: they are what they are, and not anything else, such as a body, a brain, or a stream of continuous psychological states.

On this view, personal survival is an all-or-nothing affair, and this gives a basis for dealing with the reduplication problem raised by Williams. If someone does survive such a duplication process, we may not be able to determine who it is, but nonetheless it can only be one person. So, while the evidence may be indeterminate, there remains a fact of the matter of where the soul has gone. After all, in the fission cases we have imagined, where there are two candidates claiming to be me, our intuitions suggest that only one of them can be. I cannot be in two places at once or survive as two halves of my original self.

Personal identity is indeterminate

Contrasting with this approach we may be inclined to wonder whether there really are definite answers to the question of whether someone has survived in the cases we have been examining here. Are we looking for a definite answer when in fact our concept of personal identity is not as precise as we tend to think? Recall here the example of Socrates being recomposed at different states. What this thought experiment shows is that a person could, in principle, be duplicated at any point in their life both physically and psychologically. But if so, this implies that they cannot be strictly identical over any stretch of time, much as Hume argued. Whether or not we decide to say that someone is the same is, then, not something which has a definite answer, but will depend on the nature of the case. On this view the identity of persons is something we may have to adjudicate on as a matter of convention, much as in we do in many examples of physical objects.

If a church burns down and is rebuilt on the same site using the same materials, is it the same church? Is there a fact of the matter in deciding the issue? Or is it really a matter of convention or how we choose to use words like 'same' and 'identical' in such cases?

Perhaps identity of persons is more like the case of identity of churches in the example given. It is a matter of how we *choose to use words* like 'identical person' and not a matter of what is actually the case *in reality*.

It may be that different people have different views on whether identity is preserved. Recall how football clubs change over time (page 211). In 2004, when Wimbledon Football Club moved location and changed their name to Milton Keynes Dons, many fans saw this as the end of their old team and refused to support what they saw as a new club. Some of the old fans, however, thought the club had continued and believed MK Dons to be the same club they had supported since a child. Interestingly, after much discussion, MK Dons eventually agreed to hand back the trophies won by the old Wimbledon to be kept by the London borough of Merton, where the old team were based.

Identity is not what matters in survival

If we become sceptical about the very idea of the continued existence of persons over time, we may be led to question why it is that we are so interested in surviving. If I will not be the same person tomorrow as I am today, then why do I have any concern for this future person's welfare?

To address this question let's return to Williams' reduplication argument and its application to the case of the aliens planting the two hemispheres of your brain into two other people's skulls. The argument says that, since both the people waking up have an equal claim to be you, and they cannot both be you, then neither can. It follows that if this happened you would cease to exist. Does this mean you should face the fission prospect below in the same way as you would face your death?

Return to the alien spaceship as you face the 'fission' operation in which the two hemispheres of your brain are to be transplanted into two different skulls. You know that people have survived the loss of one hemisphere and maintained psychological continuity with their former selves. But you are also familiar with the reduplication argument, according to which personal identity cannot survive such a process.

1 Do you face the operation with the same alarm as you would your imminent death? Do you consider this to be the complete end of you?

2 Do you try to persuade the aliens to transplant only one hemisphere so as to avoid the duplication problem?

If you are not as alarmed by the prospect of the operation as you would be by that of your imminent demise, then it seems we are left saying that we have an interest in a kind of survival as two people, which does not involve strict personal identity. This is a line of reasoning followed by Parfit.[37] He argues that we are not really interested in strict personal identity over time, but rather with the survival of persons who are continuous with my current self. These continuers need not be identical with me, but any degree of survival of my psychological states is something in which I have some interest in securing. In everyday life the best way of securing this is to avoid death. But in the puzzle cases this is not the case.

One reaction to this is to deny that we are ever dealing with genuine numerical identity when discussing issues of personal survival, not just through such radical changes as in the examples above, but in the ordinary course of someone's life. In other words, a lesson we might take from this is that there is no real personal identity over time at all. We are constantly changing and, while we may like to concoct a sense that there is a genuine 'self' which endures, this is an illusion. Parfit argues that it is a matter of convention how we make judgements that someone is the same, but the reality is that each successive individual in the course of a normal life has a degree of continuity with the previous one such that features of one will survive. But survival as a concept admits of degrees in the way that identity does not. Thus which survivor in a fission case is the real me is a matter of determining which has greater psychological and perhaps physical continuity with my former self.

Key points: Chapter 3

What you need to know about **persons:**

1 The concepts we have of person and human being are distinct, so that it is possible that there exist non-human persons and humans that are not persons. So if being human is not a necessary or sufficient condition for personhood, what is? There are a whole range of characteristics typically associated with persons, including rationality; the ability to reflect on one's own experiences; the possession of a network of beliefs and the ability to make plans for the future; the capacity for self-awareness; autonomy; individuality; being a language user and a moral and social being which can form meaningful relationships with other persons.

2 The dualist idea of an immaterial soul as what constitutes the essence of the person implies that our physical make-up is not necessary, and yet this conflicts with our common-sense use of the concept of personhood to refer to flesh and blood beings. The belief in a soul has, however, been in retreat in recent years, in large measure because of the increased recognition of the importance of the brain to our various psychological attributes. Strawson claims that the concept of a person is primitive, that is, it cannot be further reduced to either mental or physical characteristics.

3 If being a human being is not a sufficient condition for being a person, what attributes do we require for an individual to count as a person? The likely features discussed at 1 above all admit of degree, and so being a person appears not to be an all-or-nothing affair. We can make sense of the ideas of diminished person (e.g. dementia sufferers), potential persons (e.g. babies) and ex-persons (e.g. coma victims).

4 Moreover, some non-human animals or machines might be considered persons if they were to possess these characteristics to sufficient degree. Some have argued for animals' abilities to reason and hold beliefs, and there is some evidence to suggest that apes may be able to acquire a basic grasp of language. However, their abilities suggest

they fall far short of the kind of psychological complexity normally associated with human persons. Turing's test for machine intelligence treats competence in the use of language as the key; however, Searle and others have argued that it is possible to manipulate signs without actually understanding their meaning. Before a machine might be considered a person, it may be essential for it to have access to some form of sensory apparatus so that it might'have an understanding of the world around it.

5 What secures my personal identity through time despite the various changes I undergo? One suggestion is that I am an immaterial substance: a soul or mind. Locke countered this view by highlighting our intuition that what makes me think of myself as the same as my past selves is that I can *remember* being them. Psychological continuity, for him and many subsequent thinkers, is the necessary condition for personal survival rather than that of any substance, be it material or immaterial. However, the theory of psychological continuity has various difficulties which have led some to defend a materialist position: that what sustains personal identity is the body, or possibly some part of the body such as the brain. Others have suggested that there is no real personal identity over time: that survival is a matter of degree as successive selves gradually metamorphose into each other.

Reason and experience

Introduction

We all claim to know various facts about the world – the price of tomatoes, who wrote *Hamlet*, our birth dates, that 2 + 3 = 5. But where does this knowledge ultimately come from? In other words what are the basic sources of knowledge? Take the example of *Hamlet*. Perhaps I learned who wrote *Hamlet* from a teacher at school. But where did the teacher gain their knowledge? Perhaps they got it from a book. But this simply leads us to the further question of where the author of the book gained their knowledge? In the end it seems there has to have been an original source of this piece of knowledge. Searching for the ultimate sources of knowledge has been a central quest of that branch of philosophy known as either EPISTEMOLOGY or the theory of knowledge.

ACTIVITY   **Where does knowledge come from?**

1 Using the word 'know' in its everyday sense, write down four things that you know.
2 For each of these things try to trace the knowledge back to its origin.
3 Have a look at the origins of knowledge you have identified. Do they have anything in common? Are there any 'ultimate' sources of knowledge?

Traditionally philosophers have identified four ultimate sources of knowledge: experience, revelation, reason and INNATE IDEAS.

Experience as the source of knowledge: empiricism

EMPIRICISM is the view that the ultimate source of knowledge is experience. Empiricists argue that we are born knowing nothing. Everything we know, they claim, comes to us through our five senses. All our knowledge, indeed all our thoughts, must ultimately relate to things we have seen, smelled, touched, tasted or heard. The spirit of empiricism is embodied in literature and myth in the figure of the wise traveller: someone who has set out and explored the world, has had many great and varied adventures, and finally returns with the wisdom of experience.

Revelation as the source of knowledge: gnosticism

Another view of the origins of human knowledge claims that genuine wisdom is only to be gained by means of divine revelation (page 89). This view is sometimes called gnosticism. Again, we find this idea personified in myth and literature in the figure of the mystic: a wise and deeply spiritual person to whom special knowledge is given, neither through the senses nor through reason, but from some supernatural source.

Reason as the source of knowledge: rationalism

RATIONALISM is the view that the ultimate source of knowledge is reason. Rationalists often look to the world of mathematics as a template for their theory. Mathematical knowledge can be gained with reason alone and without the direct use of the senses. Alone in a room, cut off from the world, in theory it would be possible for me to work out substantial truths about geometric shapes and numbers just by thinking very hard. The knowledge that is gained in this way somehow appears to be eternal, or outside of time. In other words, while everything in the physical world comes in and out of existence, 2 + 3 will always be 5. Moreover, mathematical knowledge seems to have a kind of certainty that exceeds other forms of knowledge. Knowledge that 2 + 3 = 5 appears unshakable; it's difficult to see how one could be wrong about it. For these reasons, many rationalists thought that the model of mathematical knowledge, with its clarity and certainty, should be applied to all human knowledge. Through the application of reason, they argued, it would be possible to understand a significant body of knowledge about the world and how it operates. This knowledge, like that of maths, would be certain, logical and endure for all time. The evidence of the senses should agree with the truths of reason but it is not required for the acquisition of these truths.

The idea that the rationalists embody is also reflected in literature and myth. It is encapsulated in the image of the wise hermit who withdraws from the world and contemplates deep questions of life and the universe. Through the application of reason and thought alone, the hermit slowly uncovers essential truths about the world or the universal moral principles of life and so becomes exceedingly wise. The knowledge gained is not tainted by the ordinary concerns of everyday life and so has a kind of purity and eternity.

Innate ideas as the source of knowledge

Some philosophers believe that we are born knowing certain things, in other words we are born with INNATE KNOWLEDGE. Is this true? It is undeniable that we are born with certain instincts: to suckle, to cry when hungry, and so on. However, whether these count as knowledge is debatable. After all, do swallows know that they must fly south in autumn? Do squirrels know that the winter is coming and that they should store nuts? It seems likely that they have no explicit understanding of these facts, but simply act instinctively. However, believers in innate knowledge argue that beyond instinct certain other elements, such as a moral sense, a knowledge of God, of abstract principles, or of mathematics, may also be known innately. The belief in innate knowledge is traditionally associated with rationalism, since rationalists often felt that reason revealed knowledge that we were born with buried within our minds. If we include the notions of instinct then this idea of knowledge is embedded in literature and art in the concept of the genius, in particular that of the child prodigy – someone born with a seemingly innate ability to write music, to draw, or to dance.

In this chapter we will be focusing on these important questions of where our ideas come from and how we acquire knowledge of the world around us.

Mind as a blank slate or *tabula rasa*

The idea that the mind can be compared to a *tabula rasa*, which is Latin for blank tablet or slate, goes back to the early days of Western philosophy where we find it in the writings of Aristotle.[1] On this view we are born knowing nothing. Our minds are void of thoughts or ideas and it is only through the imprint of sense experience on the blank slate of the mind that our knowledge of the world is built up.

Such a view has considerable intuitive appeal. After all, it does seem that we have to learn what we know about the world through our life experiences. A new-born baby knows nothing of colours, sounds, tastes and smells, except perhaps what it recalls of its limited experiences in the womb. It gradually learns to recognise faces, where to find milk, which foods it likes, and so on. What we as adults consider the most basic pieces of knowledge about our world, such as that objects fall downwards, or that day follows night, would at one point in our lives have been novel discoveries.

The philosophical view that all our ideas and knowledge come from the senses is known as empiricism, and so the *tabula rasa* thesis is primarily associated with empiricist philosophers. The earliest of these in the modern era is the English philosopher John Locke (1632–1704). The first book of his main work in the theory of knowledge, the *Essay Concerning Human Understanding* (1690), is devoted to refuting the view – associated with rationalist philosophers – that we are born with certain 'innate ideas', ideas that exist in the mind but which have not been derived from experience. The subsequent books try to show how the human mind is able to acquire the knowledge and ideas of which it is capable exclusively from sense experience and from the mind's ability to reflect upon itself and its own operations.

Sense impressions and concepts

To see how this is supposed to work we need first to make clear an important distinction between sense experiences and CONCEPTS. Much of what we are conscious of is what we are actually sensing. So I am now aware of the tea I am drinking because I am actually seeing, tasting and smelling it. But I am also able to think about tea when I am not actually in its presence. This is an important ability since without it we would only ever be conscious of what we are sensing at the present moment. If we couldn't think about tea while we were not actually experiencing it, then we could not recognise it on the next occasion, nor could we hold any beliefs about it, such as that it is a good drink to wake up to, or that it is made by pouring boiling water onto dried leaves. So concept formation is crucial to knowing about the world. Understanding its mechanism is going to be central to any theory of knowledge.

Empiricism claims that all our concepts, like that of tea, are formed out of sense experiences. It's only because I have encountered tea that I can have the concept of tea, and so can form beliefs about it. We also have various inner impressions ranging from physical sensations of pleasure and pain to emotions such as jealousy or sadness. These are also an important source of concepts. At first glance, this view seems inadequate to account for the complexity of the mind, since we surely possess all kinds of concepts of things we have never experienced.

For example, we are able to imagine all kinds of fantasy creatures, such as unicorns and dragons, that don't exist in reality and which we have never encountered. I am able to imagine green aliens with eyes on stalks and spiky legs, which I have never actually witnessed with my senses. However, on closer inspection I have to concede that the elements out of which I have composed my imaginary alien do indeed come from my own experiences. Its colour is derived from my perception of grass and leaves; the antennae are obtained from seeing butterflies; and its spiky legs are stolen from crabs I have caught on the beach. It seems that all the elements of my imaginary alien friend have, in one way or another, come from my sense experience of the world. The only novel thing is the arrangement of the elements. And so it goes, argues the empiricist, with anything I can imagine or conceive.

Locke and the other empiricists, notably David Hume (1711–1776), distinguished between simple and complex concepts or what they called 'ideas'. Simple ideas consist of a single element such as the idea of red. Complex ideas involve various simple ideas – for example, a gold mountain or a unicorn. All simple ideas must ultimately derive from simple impressions. For example my idea of red must have come from my SENSE IMPRESSIONS of red. Hume claimed that we have inward impressions (feelings) and outward impressions such a seeing a tree. In other words, not all impressions are sense impressions; my emotions such as anger or feeling of pain, for example, count as impressions too. And my idea of anger will come from my impression of anger. So not all our ideas are derived from sense experience, as some ideas, such as sadness, will be derived from our inward impressions.

■ **Figure 4.1 *Where our ideas come from***

Following the arrows backwards we can see that all ideas, both complex and simple, derive from impressions.

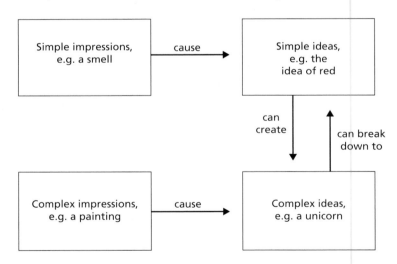

One important consequence of this theory is that all of our ideas, our concepts, thoughts and imagination must have come from our impressions. This is, of course, the central claim of empiricism. But, for a moment, consider its consequence. The claim is that everything in our imagination must have come from an impression. We cannot imagine anything that has not ultimately come from our impressions.

To help you consider the theory of empiricism, try the questions below.

1 Is it possible to imagine a brand new colour you have never experienced before?

2 Do you think someone who is colour blind from birth could ever know what red is?

3 Construct your own alien or made-up creature and then identify how your construction is derived from experience.

4 Can you think of any ideas that are not ultimately derived from experience?

5 Do your answers to these questions tend to support empiricism? Or do they raise difficulties with it?

We have seen that the traditional empiricism of Locke and Hume claims that our imaginations can rearrange the basic elements we acquire from experience but that we cannot invent these elements for ourselves. We can now flesh out the details of this picture of how our minds work. We have, on the one hand, simple impressions, that is, the information gained through experience, typically via the senses (sometimes called SENSE DATA). These are the basic elements that come into the mind, which cannot be broken down further into smaller elements. Examples of simple impressions might be the sight of red, the smell of tea, or the sound of a trumpet.

On the other hand, we can also think about the things we experience when we are not actually perceiving them. I can think of the colour red or a nice cup of tea even when I'm not presently experiencing them: in other words I can form concepts. To do this, according to the empiricist, the mind retains the basic sense experience as a kind of copy or image. This copy is stored in the mind so that we can think about things we are not experiencing and recognise them when we encounter them. For example, I acquire the concept of red from first observing it and my mind stores the concept as a kind of image of the original sensation. Armed with this concept, I am able to recognise some new experience as being an experience of red.

In the same way, my concept of tea is formed from the various sense experiences I have had of tea from seeing, smelling and tasting it. My concept of tea, therefore, unlike that of red, is complex, since it is formed out of the various simple elements of its smell, colour, taste and so forth. Once I possess the tea-concept, the next time I encounter some tea I can recognise it. Having the concept of tea also enables me to distinguish it from coffee, biscuits and everything else. Simple concepts, like red, can be acquired only if one has experienced the relevant impression and so for every simple concept there must correspond a simple sense experience. This means a person born blind cannot have the concept of red, or any other colour because they haven't had the simple impression of red. But, as we've seen, I can concoct new, complex concepts of things I have never experienced by rearranging simple elements.

■ **Figure 4.2 *No concepts without impressions***

The tabula rasa *thesis is saying that all our ideas or concepts are derived from impressions, so that there can be nothing in the mind that does not originate with impressions.*

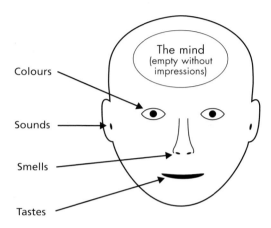

To see if this theory of no concepts without impressions works, try to trace the following complex ideas back to the impressions from which they derive.

1 Sherlock Holmes
2 Dragons
3 Chocolate pizza
4 Friendship
5 God
6 Beauty

Are some of the ideas harder than others? Later we will discuss some of the difficulties with the empiricist account of concept formation that this activity raises.

Hume's empiricism

So empiricism claims that all of our concepts, ideas and imaginings must ultimately be derived from our impressions. Hume believed that this picture of the mind gives us a means to clarify our thinking on a range of philosophical issues by allowing us to make our concepts more precise. The process of tracing concepts back to experience, Hume believed, could be used to reveal their true nature, often demonstrating that they are rather different from what we had supposed. Since philosophical progress can only be made once we are clear about the concepts we are using, the investigation of the origins of our concepts became in Hume's hands a starting point for his investigations into several important philosophical issues.

These investigations, however, sometimes seemed to show that a concept cannot be traced back to experience, suggesting that it cannot be a genuine concept at all. So what is it then? Hume's answer is that it is a kind of error. We may think we have a concept because we have a word, and the word seems to be the sign for a concept. But when we look closely we may discover that it was not a concept at all. Such apparent concepts are to be treated with suspicion and rejected as confusions.

This point is most obvious if we consider a made-up word like 'wagglytoth'. We have no idea of what a wagglytoth is because we cannot trace any such concept back to sensations or emotions. We have nothing to 'picture', as it were, when we use the word, and so the word is meaningless. On other occasions, however, we may use words which seem to have concepts attached to them. In such cases, Hume argues, we should ensure that there is indeed a lineage we can trace back to experience and so establish that there really is a concept there. If we fail, we must reject the concept as empty or non-existent. In this way the empiricists' idea that all knowledge comes from experience becomes a critical tool by which to reject certain sorts of concept as unthinkable, and hence reject certain areas of enquiry as unknowable.

To see how this critical tool works in practice let's consider some of the philosophical problems Hume hopes to solve with it.

What is God?

To deal with this question, Hume asks where our concept of God, as a supremely powerful, infinitely wise, all-loving being, comes from. Clearly we haven't encountered God, and so it cannot come directly from him. So the concept must have come from our experiences of powerful, wise and loving people that we have encountered. Having encountered such qualities in people, we then imagine them being extended without limit. Thus, although God may have made man in his own image, the concept of God is made in man's own image according to Hume (see page 156). This invites the conclusion, radical in Hume's day, that God doesn't exist.

Who am I?

What does the word 'I' refer to? The idea of my self, Hume claims, cannot be based on any one sensation – the smell of tea, the memory of falling off a bike, the feeling of anger – as these feelings and emotions change constantly. If you look into yourself you never find any impression of something which corresponds to your idea of your self. But if the idea has no source in sensation, then it cannot be a proper concept. Hume concludes that the idea that I have a self is a kind of illusion (see page 228). The words 'I' or 'self' are really just the name for the entire series of sensations and thoughts that make up your life. There is no thing, no essential me, existing independently of the sum of conscious experiences which constitute my mind.

What is morality?

Hume points out that our concepts of good and bad cannot be traced back to any particular sensations. After all, you can't see the evil of an action, or smell the goodness of someone's character. So where do we get such concepts from? According to Hume, they come from the 'inner' sensations that are our own emotions (page 66). We condemn and praise different actions ultimately because of the way they make us feel. This insight is the basis for Hume's moral theory, which shows how our concepts of good and bad stem from our emotions.

Thus Hume engages with many of the big debates in philosophy, using the simple principle of empiricism. How successful he was in each of these areas is debatable, but in the philosophical discussions of religion, the self and morality Hume remains a very important figure. However, it is his treatment of the concept of causation that has led to the most discussion.

Hume on causation

We are all aware of causes and effects. A dog's tails knocks a glass, the glass falls over. The dog has caused the water to spill. The water in turn causes the ink on the essay to run, and so on. Every minute we can witness multiple examples of causation all around us, but where does the concept come from? What would an empiricist say? At first sight it seems obvious. We can see that the dog has caused the water to spill. We can see the effect of the water on the ink. We observe the one thing causing the other and, like anything else, the concept of causation derives from sensation.

However, Hume points out that things are not as simple as we might suppose. Using his example, consider observing one billiard ball approaching another, striking the second and the second moving off. Here it seems we have a clear case of observing one ball causing the other to move. So surely this must be the origin of our concept of causation? However, when we look more closely at this experience, it becomes clear that all we ever saw was one ball approach and come into contact with another; we heard a sound and saw the second move off; we never actually witnessed any sense datum corresponding to the cause. Imagine that all the time there were elaborate magnets under the table and that these moved the first ball up to the second, and then a separate magnet moved the second ball away, such that the first ball did not cause the second to move at all. Would this look any different? The answer must be no; but if there is no difference between the first and the second case, then we must conclude that indeed a cause is not something we actually experience in the sense impressions themselves, as the sense impressions are the same whether or not there was a cause.

So it seems that the concept of cause is not drawn from the senses. So where does it come from? Rationalists might conclude that the idea is innate. Obviously, as a good empiricist, this is not Hume's solution. An empiricist must either deny that we really have such a concept, or attempt to redefine it. Hume actually elects to do both. He claims that we tend to use the word 'cause' to link together experiences that frequently occur together. In other words, we notice patterns that repeat themselves and come to regard them as governed by causal laws. This is something that our minds do automatically for us. Imagine you clap your hands and a split second later you hear thunder in the distance. You would probably think nothing of it. Imagine the same thing happens again a minute later. Again, you would put it down to coincidence. But imagine the same thing happens a third, fourth, fifth and sixth time. Eventually you would begin to suppose that your clapping was causing the thunder. But this supposition cannot be based simply on the sense impressions involved for there is nothing different about the first clap than about the sixth. The only difference is in the repetition, the constant occurrence, of the two events. By the sixth clap your experience of the event feels very different; it now starts to feel like a causal event. Thus Hume suggests that what we mean and experience as cause and effect is really just the constant conjunction of events. The feeling of one event inevitably following the other is the result of repetition, and is little more than custom or habit. Instead of claiming that the concept of causation is meaningless, Hume suggests that it refers to the feeling of anticipation that arises in our minds when we come to expect one event to follow another, because it has done in the past. In this way he is able, true to his empiricist convictions, to trace the source of our concept of cause back to experience: in this case, not an experience of something external to us, but the internal feeling of expectation we develop that one event will follow another.[2] Empiricism claims that all of our ideas are derived from

■ **Figure 4.3**

If every time you clapped your hands you heard a thunder clap, it wouldn't be long before you developed the conviction that the one was the cause of the other. According to Hume, the feeling of anticipation you would have of an imminent thunder clap whenever you clapped your hands is the source of our ordinary idea of causation.

impressions. Hume used this simple idea to examine some of the central questions in philosophy. In each case he took a difficult concept and looked to find out from which impressions it was derived. If he could not find such impressions then he suggests we should treat the concept with suspicion.

Logical positivism

ACTIVITY   Which of the following sentences do you think are meaningful?

1 Water boils at 100°C on the surface of the earth.
2 There is life after death.
3 It is always wrong to kill innocent persons without good reason.
4 The cat has just got off the bed.
5 Jesus is the Way, the Truth and the Light.
6 My love is a red rose.
7 The sunset over Victoria Falls is beautiful.
8 One day computers will be conscious agents and worthy of moral rights.
9 The obvious design and purpose of the natural world can only have God as its cause.
10 The toys in the toy cupboard move whenever you're not looking.
11 Colourless blue dreams sleep furiously.
12 Twas brillig and slithy toves did gire and gimble in the wabe.

more difficult

Some philosophers have taken Hume's approach and turned it into a theory about meaning. They have argued that sentences are only meaningful if they are connected in some way to the world. Such sentences describe the world either truly or falsely. For example,

The teacher of the class is a tall man with a beard.

is meaningful because it tries to tell us something about the world. It is irrelevant for this theory of meaning whether a sentence is actually true; false sentences are still meaningful because they still 'paint a picture' of the world.

▪ A.J. Ayer and the Verificationist Theory of Meaning

Please note that much of the following section is adapted from text in Chapter 1.

A.J. Ayer (1910–1989) was a British philosopher who was influenced by the philosophy of the young Ludwig Wittgenstein (1889–1951) and a group of Austrian philosophers known as the Vienna Circle. These philosophers (known as *logical positivists*) wanted to clarify what could be meaningfully said and written. They argued that language was only meaningful if it confined itself to discussing what was within human experience. Once we step beyond the realms of what we can experience then we venture into nonsense.

Ayer was greatly affected by this idea and when he was in his mid-twenties wrote a book called *Language, Truth and Logic* that popularised logical positivism in Britain and America. In this book he used the ideas of the Vienna Circle and applied them to all aspects of philosophy. He defended what is known as the *Verification Principle*, which is a kind of test that a sentence must pass if it is genuinely meaningful. The Verification Principle states that:

> *A sentence is meaningful if and only if*
> either (a) it is a tautology, i.e. true by definition;
> or (b) it can hypothetically be proved to be true or false, i.e. it is verifiable.

What the principle is saying is that in order to say something meaningful we must know what would make what we say true. If a PROPOSITION isn't a tautology, and there is no possible empirical way of discovering its truth, then it is meaningless. The principle is suggesting that propositions make claims about the world; they claim that world is *this way* or *that way*. However, if upon reading a proposition we are unsure what the world would be like if the proposition were true as opposed to false, in other words if we did not know what would count as verifying it, then the proposition doesn't appear to be making a claim about the world after all. It is factually insignificant and meaningless.

So, for example, the claim that it snowed in London on Christmas Day 2000 is clearly meaningful because it could be verified by contemporary observations from London on that day. However, what of scientific claims such as that water boils at 100 degrees Celsius? The problem here is that the truth of general claims is that they can never be conclusively proved, since we can't boil all the water in the universe to confirm that it always boils at 100 degrees. This would be a serious difficulty for the principle as so far formulated since most scientific claims are of this general sort. So Ayer's principle needs to be modified so that a proposition is meaningful just if we know what observations would count towards its verification.

Note also that much of science deals with entities which are not directly observable, for example quantum particles such as protons and quarks. Ayer gets round these problems by differentiating between a *strong* and a *weak* version of verification, with scientific theories fulfilling the weaker conditions:

- The *strong* version states that a statement is meaningful if we could verify it by our own observation – and therefore establish its truth/falsity for *certain*.
- The *weak* version states that a statement is meaningful if there are some observations that could establish the *probable* truth of the statement.

Another point that needs to be made is that there are claims which appear meaningful, but which we cannot in practice verify. For example, it is meaningful to say that there is life on a planet orbiting Alpha Centuri, even though at present we have no means of verifying this claim. For Ayer, such claims are meaningful because we could in principle verify them. In other words, we know the kinds of things we would need to do (travel to Alpha Centuri in a space ship and take a look, for example) to determine whether they are true. So the Verification Principle isn't saying that we can as a matter of fact verify all meaningful propositions, just that we could do so in principle.

The Verification Principle is also useful in identifying statements that look as if they are meaningful but are in actual fact word games, grammatical errors or simply incoherent. For example:

There is an invisible, intangible, odourless, tasteless and silent rabbit in this room.

According to Ayer's Verification Principle this sentence would be meaningless because it cannot be verified. It *appears* to be making claims about the world, but when you look at it closely you see that whether it is true or false (i.e. whether the world is the way it says it is) makes no difference to our experience. In other words, the sentence is not *factually significant*.

ACTIVITY   Go back to the list of propositions in the previous activity. Which of the statements are meaningful according to Ayer's Verification Principle?

For Ayer only sentences 1, 4, and 10 are verifiable and therefore meaningful. And 10 is only verifiable if we allow the idea that the toys' movement might be caught on camera or some such.

One of the most significant consequences of Ayer's theory is that it appears to make many claims about religion and about God meaningless, as well as most claims about morality and most use of metaphor. This is because for Ayer every religious claim is ultimately about something transcendent, that is to say, about objects which lie beyond human experience, whether it is God, the afterlife or Heaven. But, talk about what lies outside experience is, according to the Verification Principle, meaningless. So statements such as 'God loves the world' or 'God is the Father, the Son and the Holy Ghost' appear to be telling us something about someone. But when we look more closely we see that we would not know how to check their truth. There are no experiments or observations we could carry out to prove them and so such statements are not factually significant. Importantly, then, Ayer does not regard the claim that 'God exists' as false, but rather as meaningless.

Summary

So we can see that this simple idea at the heart of empiricism – that all ideas must derive from impressions – can in turn generate a powerful theory of meaning. It can provide us with the criteria to decide what it is for a sentence to be meaningful. By this means it has been thought possible to solve many of the great puzzles of philosophy by showing that the claims and thoughts are in fact meaningless.

However, much of the analysis relies on the *truth* of the claim that all of our ideas can be derived from our experiences, in other words of the idea of the *tabula rasa*. And later we will turn our attention to some issues that might make us doubt the truth of this central claim.

Claims about the world must ultimately be justified by sense experience

For now we will explore the theory of empiricism further. So far we have discussed the claim that our ideas are based on impressions. Now this theory may be true but yet our ideas may still tell us nothing about the world. All that has been discussed so far is the relationship between ideas and impressions. If there is no clear link between impressions and the world then our ideas cannot constitute knowledge of the world.

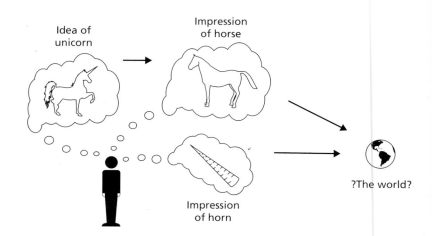

The empiricists have argued that all ideas are derived from our impressions. However, they need to show that impressions relate to the world in order to claim that our sense experience can account for our knowledge of the world.

Consider this science fiction story:

It's the year 2560. Scientists know an enormous amount about the workings of the human brain to the point where they are able to keep brains alive suspended in a vat of chemicals and nutrients. One fiendishly clever (yet slightly mad) scientist is working on a pet project of his own. He has acquired a brain which he plays with in his secret laboratory. With the brain kept alive in the vat of chemicals, the scientist has carefully wired up the brain's input and output nerves to a powerful computer. The computer is able to send a complex array of electrical impulses which mimic precisely those that a normal brain-in-a-body would ordinarily receive from its environment through its senses. The computer interacts with the brain in such a way as to maintain an illusion that the brain is in fact a complete human being with arms and legs etc. living a normal life. Further the brain is fooled into believing that it is living in the early part of the twenty-first century and that it has been alive in this period all of its 'life'. The brain is fooled into believing that it has friends, eats food, speaks English, and so on, and that right at this very moment it is reading a strange science fiction story in a book on philosophy.

In fact this is not a science fiction story. The story is true, and you are that brain. You have been deceived about every single aspect of your entire life. The year is really 2560 and everything you thought you knew about yourself and the world is false.

Is this plausible? Is it a remote possibility? Well, however remote, if it is indeed a possibility then you cannot know for certain that anything you think is real actually exists, nor that anything you've done has actually happened.

If this is true then none of our beliefs about the world constitute knowledge, as none of the ideas that make up our beliefs would be linked with reality. Note, however, that even if this were the case it still could be argued that one of the central claims of empiricism is true – that all our ideas may be derived from our impressions. It is just that, if I am a brain in a vat, my sense impressions do not relate to any external reality.

In this section we will consider whether our sense experience can account not only for our ideas but also for our knowledge of the world. To aid this discussion we will introduce the concept of foundationalism.

Foundationalism

We claim to know lots of things about the world: what date our birthday is; that Madonna is the best singer in the world; that water boils at 100°C; that you are reading this now; that 2 + 2 = 4; that the Amazon crocodile cannot stick its tongue out; and so on. Few of us, however, would count all of the claims as examples of genuine knowledge.

Often when a friend claims to know something that you consider a bit unlikely you ask them for their reason. For example, imagine a friend claimed that Gordon Brown is in fact a woman. After your initial surprise, you would doubtless respond by saying something like: 'I don't believe you!' or 'How do you know that?' In other words, you would be sceptical about your friend's claim, and would ask her to offer some evidence or JUSTIFICATION for it. In response, your friend might well attempt some form of justification. For example, she might say one of the following:

> 'I read it in the *Sunday Sport*.'
> 'A friend told me, and he's studying politics at college.'
> 'I saw a very detailed photograph on the internet.'

Once again, consider how you would respond to your friend at this point. Probably, you would still not be persuaded that Gordon Brown was a woman. But why not? A plausible initial answer is that none of these three responses represents a good enough justification for your friend's claim. In each case a new source is being introduced to justify the claim about Gordon Brown, but each of them can easily be doubted. Consider the first justification, that she read it in the *Sunday Sport*.

Most people would discard the claim because the justification is not strong enough. In this case the justification seems

Belief: Gordon Brown is a woman

↓

Justification: I read it in the *Sunday Sport*

to rely on an unstated belief that everything that is published in the *Sunday Sport* is true, and most people would question that belief. You don't believe that Gordon Brown is a woman as the claim relies on a suspect belief about the veracity of the *Sunday Sport*. However, what if your friend added: 'But I know the journalist, Dean Jenkins, and he wouldn't lie; he simply sold the story to the highest bidder.' In this case a further justification is given to support the truth of the article in the *Sunday Sport*.

Would this make you more likely to believe the story? The question rests on whether you are prepared to accept this new belief as true or not. If so, then you are prepared to count

Belief: Gordon Brown is a woman

↓

Justification: I read it in the *Sunday Sport*

↓

Justification: Dean Jenkins wrote the article and he doesn't lie

it as a good enough reason for the claim about Gordon Brown to count as knowledge. Other people might still be a bit sceptical, however. Consider the following exchange:

Laura: *Here's an amazing fact. Did you know that the Amazon crocodile cannot stick its tongue out?*

Luke: *I don't believe it! How do you know?*

Laura: *I saw it on Nature Watch on the telly.*

Luke: *How can you possibly regard Nature Watch as a reliable source of information? Don't you realise that it is in the pay of Brazilian coffee producers who have a vested interest in spreading disinformation about crocodiles!*

Laura: *Ah, I thought you might say that, so I've cross-checked with a reputable encyclopaedia which stated quite clearly that Amazon crocodiles cannot stick their tongues out.*

Luke: *But that evidence is also unreliable. You should realise that this myth about crocodiles has been perpetrated for some time and that all the experts have been taken in. So it wouldn't be surprising if the vast majority of reputable encyclopaedias carried this error.*

Laura: *Well, actually I have been to South America and checked for myself. I examined several crocodiles along the Amazon and none of them could stick their tongues out.*

Luke: *Ah, but it's always possible that the coffee producers saw you coming and somehow engineered it so that you would only encounter crocodiles without tongues.*

There are several things to note about this dialogue. What strikes people immediately is the silliness of Luke's doubts. Luke appears interested in being sceptical simply in order to irritate Laura. Moreover he has no good evidence for supposing that there is an elaborate coffee conspiracy. His sceptical scenarios are increasingly unlikely as the dialogue progresses and so his argument is not one we would be inclined to take seriously. While all this is true, it misses the philosophical points that the dialogue is intended to illustrate. For scepticism in philosophy is a peculiar thing and not at all like scepticism in ordinary life. Luke is really testing Laura to see if she can claim her fact about crocodiles for *certain*. For Luke believes that we should only count claims as knowledge if the claim can be shown to be true for certain, if we cannot show this then we should consider such claims to be mere beliefs. Not everyone, however, would agree with Luke's need for absolute certainty, and we will discuss this issue later.

Note also that Laura's claim about crocodiles, as with the claim about Gordon Brown, was justified by another belief, which was in turn justified by another. However, each of these new beliefs, it seems, could be doubted. Does this process go on for ever?

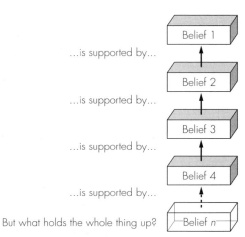

■ **Figure 4.5 The infinite regress of justification**

For a belief to be known it must be supported by a good reason, and the reason will be something else we believe. This second belief must also be supported by some further reason. This leads to an infinite regress, and it seems that there can be nothing to give any ultimate support to our knowledge claims. So a sceptic might conclude that nothing can be known.

...is supported by...   Belief 1

...is supported by...   Belief 2

...is supported by...   Belief 3

...is supported by...   Belief 4

But what holds the whole thing up?   Belief n

Now, if we are ever going to achieve certainty for any claim, we must eventually end up with a belief that cannot itself be doubted: a belief that does not need to be justified by appeal to any further beliefs, in other words, one that is self-evident or self-justifying. This approach to epistemology leads to the position known as FOUNDATIONALISM. Foundationalism is the view that divides our beliefs into two sets: those that need no further justification – the foundational ones – and those that do. We can call the ones that need further justification SUPERSTRUCTURAL BELIEFS, simply meaning those that are built on top of the foundations. Some empiricists would claim that foundations for all our beliefs about the world are the impressions gained from the senses.

■ **Figure 4.6**
Empiricist
foundationalism

The empiricist
foundationalist regards
knowledge of sensations
or sense impressions as
the basis for all our factual
knowledge about the
world. Knowledge of
sense impressions is
immediate and
incorrigible. On this basis
we infer the existence of
the physical world. So all
our knowledge of the
physical world is ultimately
justified in terms of
knowledge about our own
sense impressions.

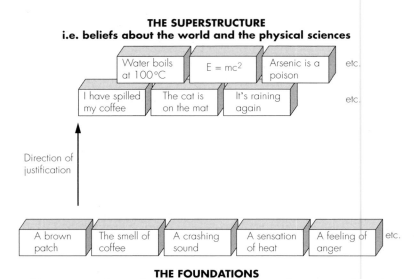

THE SUPERSTRUCTURE
i.e. beliefs about the world and the physical sciences

Water boils at 100°C | $E = mc^2$ | Arsenic is a poison | etc.
I have spilled my coffee | The cat is on the mat | It's raining again | etc.

Direction of justification

A brown patch | The smell of coffee | A crashing sound | A sensation of heat | A feeling of anger | etc.

THE FOUNDATIONS
Things we are immediately aware of such as colours, sounds and smells, as well as emotions and feelings; sometimes referred to as sense impressions, 'sense data' or the 'given'.

This claim that there are beliefs about sense impressions that can be known with certainty is at the heart of the empiricist claim that sense experience can act the foundation for our knowledge of the world.

■ Sense experience as the foundation for our knowledge of the world

Empiricists would argue that, as it accounts for our *ideas*, sense experience is the ultimate source of our *knowledge* of the world. One reason for thinking this is right is that we appear to know nothing as babies and have to learn about the way the world is by living in it. Empiricists also stress the point that we tend to appeal to our own experience when trying to justify our claims to know things. If I want to convince you that I know there is chicken across the street, a good way is to appeal to the fact that I can see one.

Scepticism about the senses

However, the reliability of our senses as a source of knowledge of the world was something that philosophers had been subjecting to serious doubt ever since the Ancient Greeks had first begun to produce philosophy some two millennia earlier. Sceptics would point out that our senses are often unreliable and so ask how we can trust them as a basis for knowledge. A standard example of sense deception is that of a straight stick which appears bent when half immersed in water. If I see a bent stick, when it is in reality straight, then sensation is misleading me about how the world is. But if sensation is misleading me, then the empiricist project to ground knowledge of the world in sensation looks flawed. The possibility of hallucinations is also problematic for the empiricist, for, if I can seem to see a snake slithering across my desk when there isn't really one there, how can I be sure that any of the things I appear to see around me are real? For more discussion of the fallibility of our senses in providing information about the world see Chapter 7.

In the century before Locke was writing, Descartes had famously revived the ancient sceptics' concerns, pointing once again to the senses' susceptibility to error. He also noted that when we dream we are normally unaware of the fact and take our experiences to be part of real life. How then can I be sure I am not dreaming now? And if it is possible that I am dreaming now, then I cannot be sure that any of the things I appear now to perceive are really there. Descartes went as far as to question whether we can use the senses to make knowledge claims about anything we appear to perceive, including our own bodies. The whole system of beliefs about our world might be founded in a grand deception.

ACTIVITY

Descartes' dreaming argument (*Meditation 1*)

On occasion you dream that you are engaged in the normal activities of everyday life. For example, you may dream that you wake up, have a shower, eat breakfast and so forth. You may even dream that you travel to college, go to a philosophy class and ponder deep problems; or are reading about scepticism, much as you are now. While having such a dream there is nothing within the dream which you could point to which would show that it was a dream and not waking life. Everything in the dream happens just as it does when you are awake. Since the experience within such dreams is indistinguishable from waking life, you cannot be sure that you are not dreaming *now*. But if it is possible that you are currently dreaming, then you cannot be sure that any of the things you are experiencing is real. It follows, therefore that *you do not know for certain that this room or any of the people and things in it exists.*

1 Is it possible you are dreaming now?
2 How might you be able to tell if you were dreaming?
3 When you are having a dream does it feel as if you are not dreaming?
4 Can you be certain you are not dreaming now?

So it seems that, despite what we might ordinarily think, our own experience of the evidence of the senses is not a firm bedrock upon which to ground knowledge of the world.

However, even if we accept that our senses may deceive us about the world, it seems impossible to deny that we are actually having sense experiences. Whether or not the world exists, I remain conscious of having various sensations. I may be hallucinating or be in a virtual reality machine and thus the purple curtains I seem to be staring at may not actually exist, but despite all this it is impossible to deny that I am having a purple-curtain-like experience. I'll grant the sceptic that the physical world is a figment of my imagination, but the sceptic still cannot take away the fact that I am now having an experience of purple.

As Descartes puts it, even if I am dreaming,

Descartes

all the same, at least, it is very certain that it seems to me that I see light, hear a noise and feel a heat; and this is properly what in me is called perceiving.[3]

Thus, to the extent that sensation or 'perceiving' is treated purely as an aspect of conscious experience, and any judgement about the nature of the world beyond it is suspended, then it has a kind of certainty. This means that, while I can doubt the existence of the physical universe, I cannot doubt the existence of the sensations which present themselves to me.

This is a crucially important move for the development of modern philosophy. Descartes' genius was to recognise that even if the entire physical world is a dream none the less sensations can be viewed purely as an aspect of consciousness. This means that the experience of sensation need not commit us to any beliefs concerning the material things which we may normally associate with it, i.e. our bodies' sense organs and the effects made on them by physical objects. So I can know I'm experiencing sensations regardless of whether or not objects or even my body really exist. Indeed, Descartes would even say that I can know with absolute certainty that I have a headache, even though I may not know that I have a head!

The incorrigibility of sensation

Now, if my own sensations are certain, regardless of any doubts that may be raised about their origin, then it seems that I cannot be led to change my mind about them. In other words, there is no new evidence that could come to light which could lead me to correct my claim to know that I am having a sensation of a certain sort – be it seeing a purple patch, experiencing a smell of lavender, or suffering from a headache. I know I am having them whether or not purple things, lavender or even my own head exist. I cannot be brought to doubt that I have a headache no matter what sceptical scenarios one might raise. And the question 'How do you know you have a headache?' seems a silly one.

It is on the basis of our sensations that we infer the existence of objects and events, mostly without being aware of doing so. I open the fridge and have a yellow and round visual experience – from this I infer that there is a grapefruit before me. I have a barking aural experience, and infer the existence of a dog outside. In these cases we move from our basic sense experience to a belief about the world. In moving from one to the other there is the possibility of error: it may be a toy grapefruit; it may be a dog impersonator outside my window. I may even be dreaming. Because there is an inference involved, there is always room for doubt. But when it comes to experiencing the sensations themselves no inference is necessary. They are presented immediately to my mind and so knowledge of them allows no room for error. That I am experiencing a yellow, round shape cannot be doubted, regardless of what is actually causing it.

It seems that we have indeed found a bedrock of beliefs. Those about our own sensations are immune from sceptical doubts and for this reason are often termed INCORRIGIBLE; meaning that they are not correctable. I would not under any conceivable circumstances give them up. In other words, they require no further justification; they are, as it is often put, simply GIVEN. Sensations treated simply as aspects of consciousness are often termed SENSE DATA or sometimes *the given* and are roughly equivalent to what we have been calling sense impressions.

The empiricists agreed with Descartes' assessment that sense impressions were incorrigible, and figured that this gave them the starting point from which to build up knowledge of the world. The difficulty, as the sceptic is keen to point out, is how we can ever be sure that the judgements we make on the basis of our sense impressions are sound.

Knowledge of sense impressions

This chapter is not primarily concerned with an analysis of the concept of knowledge. However, it is worth now looking as the different sorts of knowledge that there are, for the kind of knowledge that we have of sense impressions is, in an important way, unlike other sorts of knowledge.

One sort of knowledge involves believing facts, expressed in sentences, and so is usually called factual knowledge (sometimes it is called propositional knowledge – a proposition being another word for a factual sentence). For example, I might know that snow is made of crystals, or that Elton John's real name is Reginald Dwight. Such knowledge is often gained from books, teachers or TV. As such we infer the knowledge from the relevant sources or from our other beliefs. However, our knowledge of sense impressions is different in that it is immediate and present, and not inferred from anything else. We may subsequently use the awareness of the sense impressions to infer the existence of objects and things, but the sense impressions themselves are given immediately to us – they do not have to be inferred. We are immediately acquainted with them and so I can know I am having a certain sense impression without having to justify it by reference to any other claim. So we have here a distinction between FACTUAL KNOWLEDGE, which is inferred, and KNOWLEDGE BY ACQUAINTANCE, which is not.

Now, we can use this distinction between inferred and immediate knowledge to clarify what the empiricist is saying. Essentially, the idea is that the knowledge one has of one's own sense impressions is incorrigible because one is directly acquainted with it. It is the bedrock on which all other knowledge must be based since it involves an immediate awareness. For this reason I cannot be mistaken into thinking that I am acquainted with a certain smell when in fact I am not. Notice however that such knowledge does not require that we are able to say anything about the experience in question. Thus, if I have toothache I am intimately acquainted with a pain, but I may not know that I have a wisdom tooth coming through. That is, I may know very little about my condition. Knowledge by acquaintance in itself remains incommunicable since it lacks what is often called PROPOSITIONAL CONTENT. In other words, while factual knowledge can be expressed in a *proposition* (a type of sentence) – knowledge by acquaintance need not be. So I can know I have a toothache simply by being acquainted with it, but not be able to say anything about it. A dentist, on the other hand, may know all kinds of things about my toothache and be able to communicate them to me and others in the form of propositions. In this sense, factual knowledge appears to be objective, while knowledge by acquaintance is subjective. So the empiricist's idea is that factual knowledge about the world can be built on top of the incorrigible knowledge by acquaintance, which constitutes subjective experience.

Summary

So far we have explored two of the central tenets of the empiricist philosophy that is strongly associated with the idea of the *tabula rasa*: firstly the claim that

> all ideas are derived from sense experience

and secondly the broader assertion that

> our claims about the world must ultimately be grounded and justified by sense experience.

We will now explore criticisms of these claims. We will start by focusing on the first claim, although criticisms that undermine this will undermine both. We will then end by exploring criticisms that relate more directly to the second claim.

Criticisms of the claim that all ideas are derived from sense experience

■ Criticism 1: Does the concept of 'simple ideas' make sense?

Locke and Hume gave examples such as red, cold and sadness as examples of simple impressions and defined them as concepts that could not be broken down or analysed into anything simpler. But how precisely are complex concepts like that of a unicorn to be analysed into these simple ones? In the case of a unicorn the initial answer must be a horn and a horse, but it appears that these can be further analysed. The concept of a horn might be composed of simpler concepts perhaps including hard and pointy; the concept of a horse would be composed of a kind of bundle of innumerable simple concepts derived from various impressions one can have of horses, including those of neighing and snorting, galloping and trotting, of hooves, nostrils, shanks, manes, and so on. Are the parts of which the horse is composed – the hooves, the mane – simple? Or must we analyse these into elements? Perhaps a mane is a complex concept, somehow composed of a bunch of the hair-concept. The trouble with this suggestion, however, is that a mane doesn't necessarily appear to the senses as a collection of hairs, not unless we examine it closely. So how closely do we need to examine such things to determine the point where analysis stops and we have found simple impressions? And even a horse hair appears not to be a simple concept, since it is in turn analysable into the concepts of its colour, texture, length and so on. The qualities of the hair – say, dark, coarse, thin – may be very different from those of the mane – shiny, wavy and thick. So it doesn't seem that we can straightforwardly move from the hair concept to the mane concept. What of neighing? Is it a simple concept? Presumably it needs to be analysed into its constituent sounds and it is certainly true that I can hear different tones in the neigh of a horse. And yet the sense impression which gives us the concept of a horse neighing seems complete in itself and if we were to break it down into moments of sound we would appear to lose the essence of the concept. What of galloping? Is this is a complex concept? What are the simple ones of which it is composed? Such questions begin to show some of the difficulties empiricists are going to have to address when working out the details of their theory that concepts derive from impressions and which impressions are to count as simple.

ACTIVITY   Consider the following concepts. Which do you think are simple? That is, which do you think cannot be analysed into any simpler concepts? What do your reflections suggest about the feasibility of discovering absolutely simple ideas?

1 Moon
2 Triangle
3 Beauty
4 The sound of a G chord on a guitar
5 Fairness
6 Poetry
7 The number two
8 The taste of an apple
9 Mother
10 The colour orange

■ Criticism 2: Do all simple ideas come from sense experience?

Firstly we should note that if by sense experience we mean via the five senses then it is fairly obvious that many of our simple ideas do not come from this route. Ideas such as joy, melancholy and headaches come from our own feelings and moods, not from the outward senses. As mentioned earlier Hume counts these among what he terms 'impressions', so for the purposes of criticism we too will consider sense experience to include this inner sense.

An important consideration in favour of the empiricists' account is that someone who has not experienced, for example, the colour blue, perhaps because they were born blind, cannot have an idea or concept of it. But suppose now a person born blind were to regain their sight and on first opening their eyes were to stare straight into the bright blue sky. Having seen sky-blue are they then able to form the *general* concept of blue, in all its varieties – including aqua marine, navy blue, turquoise – or are they confined to a grasp of the sky-blue they have so far experienced? Is it possible to imagine any shade of blue having only seen one? Hume discusses a similar case where someone has seen a range of blues from which one is missing and asks whether they would be able to form the concept of the missing shade (we have used grey to illustrate the point):

■ **Figure 4.7**

Is there a missing shade of grey? Can you imagine a shade of grey or blue that you have never seen?

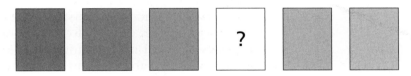

The problem here for the empiricists is that if they say that you can form the concept of the missing shade of blue it means that it is possible to form a concept which has no corresponding impression, and this goes against their principle that nothing can exist in the mind that has not come through the senses. And yet it does seem plausible to suggest that one would be able to imagine the missing shade. Indeed Hume actually allows this to be an exception to the general rule, but in doing so he is often taken to have undermined this most basic tenet of empiricism. If we can form this concept without having had an impression, why shouldn't we be able to form others?

An alternative response to this question, open to the empiricist, is to say that we can form the concept of this shade because it is actually a *complex* one. On this view, the missing shade would be formed from the simple concept of blue-in-general and the concepts of dark or light. In the imagination we could somehow mix some light with the adjacent shade of blue and so form the missing shade. The problem with this response is that all our concepts of shades of blue would then become complex ideas: mixtures of light and dark with the general concept. But this makes it difficult to see how we form the simple concept since it is no longer straightforwardly derived from any particular sense impression. Also, we do not experience an impression of, for example, sky-blue as complex. While we may be able to produce sky-blue by mixing paints, this is not the same as experiencing the impression itself as complex. There is also here the problem of how we move from the particular experiences of different blues, to the concept of blue in general? It can't be by 'copying', as Hume held, since a copy of a sense impression of blue will have to be of a particular shade. And how can a copy of particular shade come to represent all blues? In other words, how does the specific image recorded in the mind come to function as a general concept? Moreover, if my general concept of blue is indeed somehow identifiable with a copy of a particular shade of blue, how am I to distinguish this general concept of blue from the concept of the specific shade?

Another option open to the empiricist is to insist that we cannot form the concept of the missing shade, and the implication of this is that we must have millions of different concepts of every colour, one corresponding to every shade we have ever experienced. Maybe my concept of blue-in-general is a complex concept formed from the collection of all the shades of blue I have experienced. This of course implies that I wouldn't be able to form the concept of a shade of blue not so far encountered, which Hume certainly found counter-intuitive. Other odd implications appear to be that most of us probably don't have the full concept of blue; that the concept is constantly evolving as we encounter new blues; and that each of us, having experienced a different array of blues, has a slightly different concept of blue. Another puzzle concerns how we are able to recognise unfamiliar shades when we encounter them. If I haven't yet encountered a particular shade of blue then it does not form part of my concept of blue-in-general. But if it is not part of my concept of blue, then how can I recognise it as blue? The fact that we have no problem recognising unfamiliar shades of colour, suggests we already have a full-blown concept which includes all possible shades. But this just returns us to the problem of how the general concept is derived from particular experiences.

ACTIVITY

1 If you had only seen crimson, could you imagine scarlet and magenta?

2 If you had never seen pink or purple, could you imagine them on the basis of having seen red, white and blue?

3 Do you think a child who has never seen blue and yellow paint mixed can predict what colour they will make? Could you imagine green if you had only ever seen blue and yellow?

4 Do you think a child who has never seen yellow and red mixed can predict what colour *they* will make? If this case is different from the blue/yellow case, how is it different?

On a related point, you may think that that the empiricists' claim that we cannot imagine a colour we have never seen is fairly plausible. However, this is not the same as to say that we cannot form the *concept* of this colour. To see the point, take the example of ultra-violet, a colour in a wavelength too short for the human eye to detect. Now, we are able to form the concept of such a wavelength of light even though we can't see it, suggesting that the concept here is not to be identified with a copy of any sense experience. In a similar way a blind person could form the concept of red as being that colour which occurs in a particular part of the light spectrum, without ever being able to imagine what it is like to see this colour. So, again, the concept need not be identified with a copy of any impression.

Criticism 3: Do all complex ideas/concepts relate to sense experience?

Concepts don't have to relate to experience

Other difficulties arise when we consider that we seem able to have a concept of something without ever having experienced it. I can have the concept of tea even if I haven't tasted it, and, similarly, I can form the concept of Spain even though I have never been there. Consider also the concept I have of an atom, something that is too small for us ever to have any sense experience of. How is this concept formed? Certainly, while such concepts might have their source in experience, the way in which they are derived from experience seems to be more complex than a simple matter of copying sense impressions, whether they be inner or outer. With the concept of Spain, it seems implausible to say that my concept is a series of images of Spain gleaned from travel brochures and trips there, and when it comes to abstract concepts the difficulties get worse. How do I acquire the concept of justice or freedom? It seems very difficult to relate such concepts merely to patterns within experience and ultimately to patterns of sense impressions. After all, neither justice nor freedom looks or smells like anything; nor can they be equated with inner emotions or feelings. In fact, they don't seem to be things that we have sense experience of at all.

Note here that it is possible that you have some sort of image in your mind when you think of justice, the scales of justice perhaps, or a wise-looking judge in a wig. Similarly, the thought of justice might produce a certain feeling within you, a warm righteous glow in the chest perhaps. But even if you do enjoy such images and feelings when contemplating the concept of justice, they cannot be identified with it since the concept involves all kinds of connections with other concepts which cannot be explained in terms of such impressions. Indeed, it is quite likely that other people will have very different images and feelings in mind when they think of justice, and yet they still have the same *concept* as you. So it seems that what we *imagine* when thinking of justice is not the same as what we *think of* and therefore that the concept is not reducible to a copy of any impression of inner or outer sense. Again this brings us up against the obscurity of the relationship between the concept and experience.

An empiricist could argue that the fact that it is very difficult to explain abstract concepts in terms of sense experience is why such terms are notoriously vague. They could claim that if we could pin them more closely to experience then we would have greater clarity, and this is what Hume argues when conducting his examinations of concepts such as God, self and cause. With a concept like justice there might be a complex route back to experience, one terribly hard to trace, but nonetheless somehow it would find its origins in observation of just acts, and hearing about just judgements in law courts, and the associated inner feelings produced. The empiricist might also argue that if we lived in a world without just behaviour of any kind, in some kind of anarchic dystopia, we would be unable to form the concept precisely because we would have no experience of it. However, the fact that the justness of an act doesn't look, sound or smell any specifiable way and that there is no specifiable inner emotion which is the feeling of justice may leave us with the suspicion that the concept may not be traceable to experience, and the burden of proof lies with the empiricist to show how this might be done.

Do relational concepts derive from impressions?

■ **Figure 4.8**

I have sense impressions of a cat and sense impressions of a mat, but what impression relates to the on-ness?

Further difficulties arise for relational concepts such as being near or far, next to or on top of. If I form the concept of a cat from seeing a cat, then how do I form the concept of the cat being on the mat? I can't actually see the 'on-ness'; all that appears in sensation is the cat and the mat. Obviously it is on the mat, but the recognition of this fact and the understanding of the relationship involved is not something we acquire by copying any sense impression. When we term someone 'a sibling' this again does not relate to any specific quality the person has; rather it describes a relation between two people. We can all think of people who are siblings to someone, but there is no sense impression that they have in common. The concept doesn't seem to be derived from impressions; indeed someone who had never seen a sibling would be able to acquire the concept.

Some ideas are innate

As we have seen, for many of our everyday concepts it is extremely hard to uncover their origins in sense experience. For rationalist philosophers this is inevitable, since many concepts that might at first glance appear to be learned from experience are actually innate. However, rather than explore this claim here as a criticism of empiricism the theory of innate ideas will explored as a topic in its own right in the next section of this chapter.

■ Criticism 4: Language doesn't have to relate to sense experience to be meaningful

Hume wanted to argue that philosophers who discuss concepts which cannot be derived from sense impressions were ultimately talking nonsense. Meaningful talk had to have its roots in reality, which is to say, in our actual experience. We saw this idea taken a stage further by a movement called logical positivism outlined earlier, whose Verification Principle claimed that a proposition is only meaningful if it is true by definition or hypothetically verifiable.

With regard to Hume we have seen above that it is hard to see how all of our ideas are derived from sense impressions. Concepts like infra-red and ultra-violet, or abstract concepts like society or beauty, seem not to relate to impressions in a simple way, yet seem to be perfectly meaningful. One criticism is that underpinning Hume's claim about the meaning of terms is a misguided view of how language works. Hume can be seen as suggesting that the meaning of a word is given by a series of images or other sense impressions, but this doesn't seem to be the case. After all, as you are reading this sentence now, are there a flood of related images in your mind? Possibly not – yet the sentence seems to be meaningful. Take this last sentence, what images, or sense impressions might be related to the words *the, possibly, seems, not, yet, to, be* or *meaningful*? Language itself has been a major focus of philosophical study since the time of Hume and no recent theory holds a word-impression account of meaning. After all, what sense impressions does the term *empiricism* relate to!

Logical positivism focuses on sentences rather than just words in its account of meaning and so is immune to the criticism above. However, this theory too faces some difficult questions.

The first criticism is that the Verification Principle seems far too strong since it not only outlaws religious language from the realm of the meaningful, but it also makes much of what humans speak and write about meaningless as well, including art, beauty, metaphors, poetry and our inner sensations. It makes all ethical judgements a matter of personal feeling and it makes most philosophical speculation nonsense. This need not be a problem, but it certainly suggests that Ayer's notion of meaning is very different from the one we operate with in everyday life.

A second, telling criticism of verificationsim is that the principle is meaningless according to itself. The principle claims that *for any proposition to be meaningful it must be hypothetically verifiable or true by definition.* This itself is a proposition about the world, so to be meaningful we must be able to imagine how we could verify its truth (as it is not true by definition). However, it is hard to imagine how the world would differ if the principle were true or false and so difficult to see what could count as verifying its truth. The principle is meaningless according to itself!

Summary

In this section we have raised a host of problems for the traditional empiricist picture of how we form concepts. The fundamental problem seems to be with the idea that concepts are ultimately *images* or *copies* of sense impressions. While we may be persuaded that most or even all of our concepts require some experience before we can develop them, this is a far weaker claim than to say that they must all be copied from sense impressions.

We will now turn to criticisms that are specifically related to the second tenet of empiricism, that *our claims about the world must ultimately be grounded and justified by sense experience.*

Criticism 5: The trap of solipsism

Recall the problem described earlier of the brain in a vat. Is it possible that you are such a brain? If so, does that mean that you can never be certain of anything about the world?

A key difficulty with the empiricist position is that it threatens to lead us into the trap of SOLIPSISM. To understand the difficulty we need to be aware that empiricists, such as Locke, follow Descartes in claiming that we perceive the physical world only indirectly, via the senses. They hold to a theory of perception called REPRESENTATIVE REALISM, which is discussed in detail in Chapter 7.

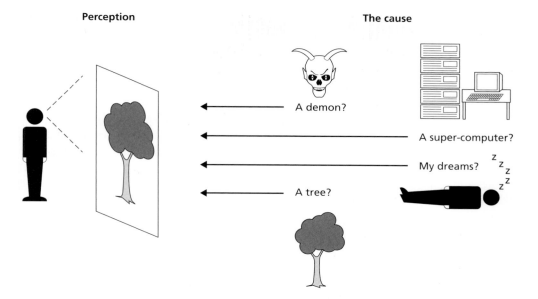

Perception

The cause

A demon?

A super-computer?

My dreams?

A tree?

■ **Figure 4.9 The trap of solipsism**

If I don't perceive the world directly then what causes my sense impressions? The world? A super-computer? My dreams? A powerful demon?

But if it is right that we don't perceive the world directly, then how do I get from the immediate knowledge I have of my own sense impressions to knowledge of anything beyond them, namely the physical world? If all I can be absolutely certain of is that I experience sense impressions, then it seems I can never be certain that anything else exists after all.

Beliefs founded in one's own personal experience appear to be incurably subjective, and inferred beliefs about physical objects are always vulnerable to sceptical attack. Moreover, if I can't be sure that the physical world beyond my mind exists, then I can't be sure that minds other than my own exist either. It seems that I may be completely alone! This sceptical position is known as solipsism. It is the idea that all that we can really be certain of is our own existence and experience. It could be that nothing and no one else exists.

Dealing with the problem of solipsism became a central concern of eighteenth-century epistemology. The credibility of the empiricist project hangs on whether or not it can be solved. If Locke is unable to escape the trap of solipsism – and many argue he can't – then his epistemology will amount to the claim that knowledge of the physical universe is impossible: a sceptical conclusion which we surely have good reason to try to avoid.

Although it might be possible that you are a brain in a vat do you really think it likely? Most would say it's highly unlikely. The problem of solipsism only occurs if, like Luke in the dialogue above (page 260), you are seeking an account of our knowledge of the world that guarantees absolute certainty. If we drop this quest for certainty then the empiricist claim resembles this: we can be certain that we are having sense impressions and from these we can be *reasonably* certain of some the claims that we make about the world. For example, I am having sense impressions of a red and round variety right now and as a result I can reasonably infer that there is an apple on my table in front of me.

This *reasonably certain* criterion would conform to most people's use of the word 'know'. After all if I claim to know that Arsenal won the FA Cup in 2002 most people would not retort 'You don't *really* know that as it's possible that you might be a brain in a vat and the whole world an illusion.' Most people would happily concede that I do know who won the FA Cup in 2002, and this is because most people don't expect absolute certainty to underpin our claims for knowledge.

As a point of interest Descartes thought that we *could* be certain of our knowledge of the world. He claimed that God, being good, would not have set things up in such a way that it looks as though the world exists when it doesn't really. However, this might not convince everyone, as his prior arguments for the existence of God are problematic.

In another attempt to overcome this doubt a philosophical movement called PHENOMENALISM claimed that we don't need to believe that the world exists beyond our sense experience. Phenomenalists claimed that when we talk about the world and the objects in it we are really just talking about patterns of sense data that we perceive anyway, and these we can be certain of. For more on this see Chapter 7.

Finally even the weaker claim – that we can be reasonably certain of the inferences we can draw from our sense impressions – is open to many criticisms. To defend the claim it would be necessary to give a general account of how our sense impressions relate to the world. In other words, it would be necessary to give a theory of perception, and this forms the focus of Chapter 7.

Criticism 6: Scepticism about the future and the past

I'm sitting in a room and have sense impressions of a cup of tea, I pick up the cup and drink the tea. When dealing with the immediate world around me the idea that my knowledge is based on my sense experience seems reasonable enough. But what about knowledge of the future and the past? If the empiricists are to claim that all our knowledge of the world is derived from current sense experience they must give an account of how we know about the future and the past.

Scepticism about knowledge of the future

In our ordinary lives there are certain things about the world which we take for granted. For example, I expect the sun to rise in the morning, objects to fall when dropped, the neighbour's dog to bark as I leave the house and not suddenly start speaking French, and so forth. But what evidence do we have for these beliefs? Why do we suppose we know that dogs won't suddenly start to speak to us in French, or that gravity won't suddenly work in reverse?

The obvious answer is that gravity has always worked that way, and dogs have never spoken French, and so we have no reason to think that such things will change now. But is this a good response? Notice that it presupposes that the future resembles the past, since it is saying that dogs will continue to behave as they always have and that objects will fall down just as before. But why should we suppose that the future will resemble the past? Perhaps things will be very different tomorrow. After all, think of a poor turkey fed grain for 364 days, who wakes up on Christmas morning expecting the same again, only this time to be tragically disappointed. In blindly assuming that the future must resemble the past we may well end up as disappointed as this turkey.

In response to this one might accept that it is *possible* that things will change, but none the less insist that, generally speaking, the past is a good indicator of what the future will hold. After all, this supposition has worked well so far, so it's sensible to stick with it. Unfortunately, the fact that (generally speaking) the future has resembled the past *in the past*, goes no way to establishing the claim that it will continue to *in the future*. To think it does is once again to use evidence from the past to make claims about the future, and this move is the very thing being questioned. So our general belief that past experience can be a reliable guide to the future cannot be justified, since any appeal to past experience inevitably presupposes what it is trying to prove. In other words, it amounts to saying that the future resembles the past because the future resembles the past and argues in a circle. Therefore we can have no certain knowledge of the future. This is known as the problem of INDUCTION: the problem of justifying our belief in the future based on how the world has worked in the past. (See page 114 for more on induction.)

Scepticism about knowledge of the past

How do we acquire knowledge about the past? Well, we have fossil records, written records, and of course our own memories, all of which provide evidence of what happened yesterday, last year or thousands of years ago. However, these records are not always accurate. For example, we can have false memories created under hypnosis. Or people may invent events that never happened and write them down. Or fossils may be fabricated by unscrupulous pranksters. So how can we be sure that any of the evidence we have about the past is reliable? Indeed, it is conceivable that the world came into existence only yesterday complete with apparent memories, history books and fossil records, all as a cosmic prank made up by some unthinkably powerful deity. Since we can't know that this hasn't happened, we can't have knowledge of the past.

These sceptical arguments work by pointing out that knowledge of both past and future has to be based on an inference. This is because neither can be observed directly – neither is an immediate part of our present sense experience. The thrust of the sceptical argument lies in their insistence that genuine knowledge must come from immediate and present experience or from acquaintance with sense impressions. If we insist on this, then it is a short step for all other kinds of knowledge, knowledge inferred from sense impressions, to appear less than certain and even, in the final analysis, unknowable. If this is right, then empiricism leads us further into scepticism and so appears inadequate as an account of how human knowledge is justified.

However, once again this might only be a problem if we are interested in how our sense experience can give us *certainty* about the future or the past. The simple answer is that it can't. It is perfectly possible that at any second the laws of the universe may simply stop holding and that all matter just floats away. The empiricist can argue that our sense experience can give us beliefs that are *reasonable*, as opposed to certain, about the future. After all, we have no other guide to the future that could be considered to be more reasonable. The empiricist will then need to give an account of what counts as reasonable and why.

■ Criticism 7: What is the relationship between concepts and impressions?

more difficult

Empiricism suggests that our sense impressions, which cannot be doubted, are the building blocks for all our knowledge. However, one objection to this seeks to undermine the supposed certainty of our sense impressions. The critic claims that sometimes we can be unsure as to how to characterise much of our immediate experience. For example, I may see a flashy car and be unsure of whether the colour is metallic purple or magenta. Moreover I can make mistakes. I may believe that I am eating smoky bacon crisps, when in fact the crisps are paprika flavoured. But surely, the objection runs, if immediate experience is certain I could never be in such a position?

The empiricist may feel that she has been cheated here. The obvious defence is that any uncertainty does not concern the appearance to me of the sense impressions. Rather the error here has to do with how I categorise or describe them. Since these are examples of possibly mis-describing what one perceives, the defence goes, they do not touch the certainty one can have of the immediate sense impressions themselves prior to any description. I may not be sure of what this colour or taste is called, but I can none the less be certain of what it is like here and now for me.

Another way of making the point is to say that we can avoid error so long as we resist the inclination to 'translate' the immediacy of experience into categories, or to put them into words. While we may go wrong in trying to conceptualise such experience, surely the immediacy of present sensation remains indubitable. The empiricist maintains that this original pre-conceptual given is the ground for any ordered experience.

However, without some sort of interpretation it is difficult to see how such experience could be anything more than what the American philosopher William James (1842–1910) called a 'blooming, buzzing confusion': an undifferentiated stream of sensations. It is only by placing what is given – the stream of sense impressions – within certain categories that beliefs can be held and knowledge claims made *about* one's experience. You would be acquainted with your sense impressions, but not have any factual knowledge about them. In other words, we need some kind of conceptual scheme in place before we can make sense of experience. Kant pushed this thought further, summing his position up in the well-known statement:

Kant

Thoughts without content are empty; intuitions without concepts are blind.[4]

Kant is saying that sense impressions (which he terms intuitions) prior to any form of conceptual ordering cannot yet form any part of experience. The mind would be 'blind' to them because they have not yet been classified.

The idea that some form of conceptual organisation of sensations is needed for any meaningful experience gives rise to a further series of related criticisms.

Not all our concepts are derived from sense experience
If the human mind must have a conceptual scheme already in place in order for any data received by the body to be classed as an experience of some kind, then how is it possible to have had any experience in the first place? Presumably there would

have to be some kind of a conceptual scheme already in place, prior to any experience, which makes that experience possible. But if this is the case then it appears that not all of our concepts can be derived from the senses. The details of this attack on empiricism will be explored later (page 324) when we look at Kant's account of knowledge.

A similar point has been made Noam Chomsky (1928–). He claims that it would be impossible for any human to learn language simply on the basis of what they hear as they grow up if their minds didn't already possess certain innate organising principles. He argues that we have an innate capacity to learn language, which enables us to pick up the structure and grammar of language much more quickly than would otherwise be possible. The mind, in other words, brings an innate structure, a type of conceptual scheme, to our experience and is not formed exclusively out of sense impressions as the *tabula rasa* thesis claims.

Are beliefs about our sense impressions incorrigible (free from correction)?

Another criticism attacks the empiricist conviction that beliefs about our own sense impressions must be incorrigible. Beliefs about sense impressions can be corrected in the light of new evidence and therefore are not self-justifying after all. To demonstrate this take as an example my suddenly discovering that the crisps I have been enjoying come from a pack labelled 'paprika'. Up until this discovery I had thought I was experiencing smoky bacon, but now I may well decide that I have been mistaken and I may even start to experience the taste of the crisps differently. In cases like this it seems the nature of the actual experience can be changed because of changes in our beliefs about the physical objects causing them. Thus, contrary to the assumptions of traditional empiricism, we can alter our beliefs about our sense impressions in the light of our beliefs about physical objects.

At the core of this criticism is the idea that there is no such thing as a simple sense impression that we experience. The very act of experiencing the sense impression is an act of interpreting. It is not a question of a 'given' or set experience that we then interpret, but rather the experience has already been interpreted by our conceptual scheme. This amounts to saying that there is no such thing as a 'fixed' foundation to the world that we all experience. Rather the world as we experience it is already figured by our interpretation of it in terms of the concepts and beliefs that we already hold. (This claim is explored again in Chapter 6, pages 483–512 where we discuss the view that a belief in God gives a believer a radically different way of viewing the world from the non-believer.)

We cannot claim sense impressions are 'certain' as they are not the sort of thing that could be meaningfully doubted in the first place

While Kant argued that experience of the raw, uninterpreted 'given' is impossible, other philosophers have wanted to hold on to the idea that we can access this pre-conceptual, unorganised experience. But even if we can be aware of sense experience prior to conceptual ordering, it is certainly hard to see how we can say anything meaningful about it. For any attempt to describe such experience would have to use words and so would have to translate the experience into conceptual categories.

Moreover, without conceptual organisation there can be no knowledge about our own sense impressions. It would seem that we cannot even claim certainty for the proposition that a colour looked like magenta or that the taste seemed like smoky bacon to me, here and now, since to do so is to go beyond the immediacy of the moment. This is because to describe the way something appears to you involves categorising it along with other similar experiences. Perceptual beliefs depend (if they are to be intelligible) on our being able to connect them with past experiences that are alike in a certain respect. The word 'magenta' functions to connect the present experience with many others that are not present, and to treat it as equivalent to the others in the relevant respect. In other words, the very effort to identify the immediate data of one's private experience necessarily involves going beyond what is immediate. This reference to what lies beyond the experience that is being described opens up any such statement to the possibility of error or mis-description. It may turn out that the present experience is not of the sort we had supposed it to be.

These considerations are supposed to establish that the possibility of error accompanies any attempt to place things within conceptual categories. Even apparently basic reports about our sense impressions such as 'I smell thyme' or 'I see magenta' are embedded within larger frameworks. Consequently, factual knowledge must by its very nature be open to doubt and correction, and the idea that there could be an indubitable bedrock of beliefs about our own sensory states is to be rejected. Acquaintance with what is given in sense experience does not constitute any kind of factual knowledge, since factual knowledge concerns propositions *about* sense impressions, not simply those impressions themselves. Before receiving conceptual ordering or classification, the given cannot have any propositional form and so it cannot be either true or false. This means that, since the given is not the kind of thing that admits of doubt, it cannot be the kind of thing that admits of certainty either, because to acquire knowledge we must run the risk of error. Therefore, it becomes meaningless to say that sense impressions are indubitable since only propositions about them can be doubted or not doubted. Sense impressions just 'are'.

■ Criticism 8: Reason alone can provide knowledge of the world, independently of experience

So far we have been examining how the *tabula rasa* thesis deals with how we acquire knowledge of the physical world around us. It claims that we are born knowing nothing and that all our ideas and knowledge about the world must come from the senses. However, others would claim that we can acquire knowledge of the world using reason, as opposed to the senses. For example, it would seem that I can know in advance that if I place two feathers next to three feathers that I will have five feathers. If I draw a triangle, I know, without having to do any measurements, that the sum of the internal angles will be 180°. I may need to have had *some* sense impressions to have the ideas of feathers and triangles in the first place, but the knowledge that 2 + 3 = 5 and that the angles of a triangle make 180° is not *derived* from experience but from reason.

Such knowledge is termed A PRIORI, meaning that it can be recognised *prior* to, or independently of, any experience of the world. This is contrasted with knowledge which can only be justified via experience. Such knowledge is termed A POSTERIORI (see page 292).

A strict empiricist, such as John Stuart Mill, would claim that all of our knowledge must come from experience – that it is all *a posteriori*. A less strict empiricist might claim that some knowledge can indeed be gained *a priori*, such as the knowledge of maths, but that this knowledge is not really knowledge about the world. After all 2 + 3 = 5 would be true if there were no world so in some sense can't be making any specific claim about the world. In this way empiricists can still claim that all our knowledge about the world must come from the senses.

Some philosophers, known as RATIONALISTS, would claim that it is possible to gain fundamental knowledge about the world through reason alone, in other words *a priori*. As we have seen, most empiricists would naturally disagree, and this debate will be carried on in the next section, which turns its attention to the sorts of knowledge we can acquire *without* experience.

Innate knowledge

So far we have explored the idea of the *tabula rasa*. Using this concept, empiricists have sought to show that all of our ideas, and subsequently all of our knowledge, must be derived from our experience of the world. In this section we will explore the opposing view: that some of our ideas, and subsequently some of our knowledge, do not derive from our experience of the world. Note that this view is not, strictly speaking, the opposite of the *tabula rasa* view. While some empiricists would claim that *all* of our ideas come from experience, very few philosophers would claim that *all* of our ideas come from other sources. Most would acknowledge that many of our ideas do indeed come from experience. However, some philosophers, while acknowledging that many *ideas* may be derived from the senses, would go so far as to say that none of our *knowledge* comes via this route. These *rationalist* philosophers suggest that all knowledge must come from reason, not experience, as only reason can guarantee the certainty required for true knowledge. Before we explore this last suggestion we will turn first to the claim that not all of our ideas come from experience.

Innate ideas

Locke defines *innate ideas* as

Locke

some primary notions . . . Characters as it were stamped upon the Mind of Man, which the Soul receives in its very first Being; and brings into the world with it.[5]

A range of different thinkers disagree with the idea of the *tabula rasa* and claim that at least some of our concepts and some of our knowledge is in-born and discoverable without reference to experience. In this section we will explore different candidates for the types of knowledge and ideas that might disprove the *tabula rasa* theory. These are collectively known as the doctrine of innate ideas, which is sometimes referred to as *innatism*.

It is often supposed that if innate ideas exist they will be universally held by all humans. Whereas everyone in life has different experiences and so different empirical ideas, ideas that are innate are to be found in us because of our nature as human beings and so should be in us all equally. This claim for universality can be used as an argument both for and against the existence of innate ideas: some claim that the universal nature of certain ideas shows that they cannot be derived from human experience; others claim that such ideas are not in fact universally held and so cannot be innate.

One of Locke's arguments from Book I of the *Essay Concerning Human Understanding* is that if there were ideas that all of us were somehow born understanding then we could expect everyone, including children and 'idiots', to accept them. However, if you ask a young child whether they believe that something can both be and not be, they are likely to be lost for an answer. Similarly for knowledge of geometry or the idea of God: a child who has not been taught geometry, according to Locke, will not be able to answer questions on it, and one who has not learned about God will have no idea of him. This shows, he argued, that such ideas cannot be innate. We will examine below how seriously the proponents of innate ideas need to take such arguments.

In this section we outline some of the possible candidates that might count as innate ideas and also explore some of the claims that we can have innate knowledge of the world.

◼ Some instincts are innate

A baby knows how to suckle from its mother, it knows to cry when hurt. It seems that there are many things that a baby knows how to do that cannot be derived from experience. Do these count as innate ideas or as types of genuine knowledge?

Hume claims that if we are to regard such things as ideas then we are using the term 'ideas' very loosely indeed, and suggests that we should leave it to refer to thoughts rather than instincts. The question of knowledge is harder to dismiss. Claiming that a baby knows how to suckle doesn't seem, at least on the face of it, to be an unreasonable use of the verb 'to know'. There are, of course, limits to how the word can be meaningfully pushed. Do birds know when to migrate? Does a heart know how to beat? Do rain drops know how to make the pavement wet? We need to have some sort of criteria for what we are to count as knowledge and what is simply an ability or function. Part of the problem might be that there are at least three distinct senses of the verb 'to know' in use in the English language: know how; know by acquaintance; and know that.

1 Practical knowledge – *know how*

Firstly there is *practical* knowledge, that is, knowledge of *how* to do something. For example, we talk of knowing how to swim, of how to speak Russian, or of how to bake a soufflé. Such knowledge involves a capacity to perform a certain kind of task, but may not involve having any explicit understanding of what such a performance entails. In other words, I may *know* how to swim without being able to *explain* how. I may know how to tie my shoe-laces, while giving verbal instructions would be virtually impossible. So it is possible to know how to do things, without being able to articulate our knowledge, suggesting that practical knowledge can be independent of any ability to communicate it in language or of having any conscious knowledge of just what one knows.

2 Knowledge by acquaintance

Secondly there is knowledge by *acquaintance*, that is, knowing in the sense of knowing a person, place or thing. So, for example, we often speak of knowing somebody because we have met them, or knowing Paris in virtue of having visited it, or knowing the taste of pineapple having tried it. As with practical knowledge, knowledge by acquaintance need not involve any capacity to give a verbal report of what it entails. I may know the taste of pineapple without being able to describe it and without knowing any facts *about* it. We saw in the last section that empiricists regard knowledge by acquaintance with our own sense impressions as the foundation of all empirical knowledge. The claim is that factual knowledge is always an inference from the impressions that we know through acquaintance.

3 Factual knowledge

Finally there is *factual* knowledge, that is, knowing *that* something is the case. So for example, we speak of knowing that squirrels collect nuts in autumn, that the earth orbits the sun, or that Socrates was a philosopher. Unlike the other two types of knowledge, when we know some fact, what we know can, in principle, be expressed in language. Thus if someone claims to know that Socrates was a philosopher, he or she claims that the sentence 'Socrates was a philosopher' is true. As we have seen, what is asserted by a sentence, that is to say, what it means or affirms about the world, is called a *proposition* and for this reason factual knowledge is often called *propositional* knowledge.[6]

It's interesting to note that knowledge by acquaintance and factual knowledge are distinguished in many languages. French, for example, has *connaître* and *savoir*, German has both *kennen* and *wissen*, whereas English just has *to know*.

ACTIVITY   Which kind of knowledge is each of the following?

1 John knows London like the back of his hand.
2 A baby knows how to suckle.
3 I've known Mary for a long time.
4 I know the difference between right and wrong.
5 Marvin knows how to do well in exams.
6 Nerris knows her onions.
7 Ian knew that hard work is the only way to succeed.

This activity might show that the distinctions outlined above are not always clear-cut. Take, for example, 'John knows London'. Does this mean he is well acquainted with the city? That he is able to get around the city quickly? Or that he knows lots of street names and facts about London? Or a combination of all three?

Most people though would classify the baby's suckling as a clear-cut example of practical knowledge. This may give empiricists a way of salvaging their theory from the claims of innate knowledge. They can acknowledge that the baby knows how to suckle, but deny that this counts as knowledge of the world. It is simply an instinct to behave. There is no factual knowledge accompanying the suckling, such as that a woman has breasts or that breasts contain milk. The empiricist can still maintain that all of our knowledge of the world must be derived from experience and at the same time allow that humans are born with certain instincts to behave in certain ways.

However, this empiricist defence might not satisfy all. Some behaviourist philosophers have claimed that all forms of knowledge really amount to practical knowledge. After all, it is the ability to behave in a certain way that makes us inclined to attribute knowledge to anyone in the first place. For example, factual knowledge can be seen as the ability to answer certain questions or to do well in exams. Scientific knowledge is the ability to make accurate predictions about the world. The claim is that all knowledge is the knowledge of how to behave in a certain way. Now the empiricist is trying to defend their theory by claiming that the baby's knowledge is not about the world in the way that factual knowledge is. However, if all our knowledge is really knowing how to behave, then the distinction between the knowledge of the baby and the scientist is less clear. It should be noted though that the behaviourist's account of knowledge is not widely accepted.

God

Descartes believed that the idea of God was planted in our minds by God himself; he argued this on the basis that that the concept of God, by which he meant a being that is perfect in every way, could not be acquired from experience. Part of his thinking here is that nothing in experience is ever perfect, so if we weren't born with the idea of a perfect being we could never produce it ourselves. Descartes' argument that the concept of God is innate is explored in more detail in Chapter 2, pages 138–53.

■ Conceptual schemes

Causation

We looked earlier at the claim that there must be conceptual schemes in place prior to anything counting as an experience. In the final section of this chapter we will explore the ideas of Immanuel Kant, who claims our knowledge of causation is not directly derived from the world but rather forms part of the conceptual scheme through which we experience the world. In this way Kant might be said to claim that we have innate knowledge of, for example, causation.

Deep grammar

As previously mentioned, Chomsky has argued that our ability to learn language is not simply derived from our experiences. He argues that we have an innate capacity to learn language, which enables us to pick up the structure and grammar of language on the basis of rather limited evidence. He also claims that all languages share the same deep grammatical structure and uses this to support the thesis that a language-learning faculty is a universal aspect of our biological make-up. In other words, he makes use of the universality argument outlined above.

■ Morality

Another area in which philosophers have thought we may have innate concepts is morality. It may be that we have an innate sense of what is right and wrong so that we can all recognise when something is fair or unfair, for example, without the need for it being taught. Is a moral conscience the voice of God within us? Does a child have an innate recognition of the correct way to divide a cake between three equally greedy mouths? A glance at playground disputes might make us sceptical of this view. On the other hand, do we then acquire our moral sense from socialisation, from our parents and schooling? Is it based in our inner impressions, our feelings of sympathy as Hume argued? (For more on Hume's moral theory see Chapter 1, pages 64–73.)

Several moral theories claim that our moral concepts cannot be derived from our sense experience. In this regard they must be considered innate. One of the most important of these theories is INTUITIONISM.

Moral ideas are known intuitively – G.E. Moore

Moral 'intuitionism' has had a long history, and the great debate amongst these moral philosophers was over where our intuitions come from. Some philosophers, such as Francis

Hutcheson (1694–1746), said our moral intuitions stemmed from an internal, god-given, moral sense (analogous to our other five senses) through which we could intuit what was right and wrong. Others said our intuitions stemmed from a rational faculty in our mind that had the power to grasp moral truths (analogous to our capacity to grasp mathematical truths).

The British philosopher G.E. Moore (1873–1958) provided some powerful arguments to suggest that our moral concepts cannot be based on things that we see in the world. Morality cannot be equated with anything from our sense experience. So what do we mean by 'good'? The answer that Moore reached by the end of his seminal work *Principia Ethica* is that 'good' cannot be defined, but is known intuitively. This is why his approach is known as intuitionism. Because 'good' is indefinable it cannot be reduced to elements that we can observe in the world, such as 'the greatest happiness', or to 'what people desire', or any other such non-moral good. In order to clarify what he means by indefinable Moore likens the word 'good' to 'yellow'. If we try to say that 'yellow' means 'light travelling at a particular frequency' then we are simply wrong – yellow refers to what we see when we see yellow objects, not to 'light-vibrations'. So for Moore 'yellow' is clearly comprehensible to us, yet we are not able to define it in terms of anything else. The same goes for 'good': we know what it is when we see it, but we cannot define it in any other terms. But for Moore it is important to note that moral properties are unlike natural properties such as 'being yellow', as we do not observe them through our ordinary senses. Moral judgements are evaluative rather than factual and so cannot be justified by purely empirical observation. Moral terms are *self-evident* and can only be known by what Moore calls INTUITION.

The Open Question Argument

The problem, as Moore sees it, is that most philosophers down the years have been wrong to try to define 'good' in other terms: they have failed to see that 'good' is indefinable. In order to support this view Moore presents us with a dilemma. When we ask the question 'What is good?' Moore says that we are faced with three possibilities:

1 'good' is indefinable
2 'good' is definable
3 'good' means nothing at all and 'there is no such subject as ethics'.[7]

The last option is given short-shrift and rejected almost out of hand. This leaves us with only two options, either good is definable or it is not. To show that good cannot be defined, Moore offers an argument which has become known as the Open Question Argument. Consider the argument this way:

> Any theory which attempts to define 'Good' is saying something equivalent to:
> '"Good" means X (where X is some fact or set of facts).'
>
> But for any such definition it will always make sense to ask:
> 'But is X really good?'

So, for example, if a UTILITARIAN says 'Good means maximising pleasure and minimising pain for the majority' it still makes sense to ask 'But is it really good to maximise pleasure and minimise pain for the majority?' Not only does this question makes sense, but it's a question we would want to ask when some innocent person is being punished on utilitarian grounds (e.g. to placate an angry mob).

Moore goes on: If good can be defined as X, then it shouldn't make any sense to ask 'but is X really good?' We can see this by looking at another definition, such as 'a bachelor is an unmarried man'. It just doesn't make sense to then ask 'but is an unmarried man really a bachelor?' as we would then be asking 'but is bachelor really a bachelor?', which is an absurd question. But asking a utilitarian 'but is maximising happiness really good?' *is not* the same as asking 'but is good really good?'. Yet if the utilitarian were right then the first question would be trivial: it *would* be like asking whether good is good. So the proposed definition must be inadequate: it must mean that 'good' and 'maximising happiness' are not the same.

For Moore. we can always meaningfully pose the question 'but is X really good?' for every definition of good, including all naturalistic ones. It remains an open question whether or not it really is good. Moore believes that this Open Question Argument shows that good is not definable, ruling out option 2. This leaves only option 1, namely that good is indefinable.

▶ criticism ◀ It may be objected to Moore's Open Question Argument that the question only appears to remain open because the meaning of a word like 'good' is unclear in ordinary usage. So when the philosophers do provide a definition of 'good' it is not surprising that we don't immediately recognise its accuracy. In other words, the reason we may wonder whether the promotion of pleasure really is good, is only because we are still unclear in our minds about the proper meaning of the term 'good'. So we could then argue against Moore that strictly speaking it does *not* make sense to ask whether an action that (for example) leads to the general happiness is in fact 'good'.

Hume put forward a theory of morality that has some innate elements. Hume agrees that our moral ideas are not derived from sense impressions; instead he claims they are derived from our sentiments, in particular from our emotion of sympathy. It is our feelings of sympathy that give rise to our moral ideas and intuitions. For Hume, however, our emotions are still impressions – inner impressions. It may be true that our emotional responses to the world are to some degree innate, in the same way that the baby's suckling response is innate; but our responses are not the same thing as having moral ideas. We are not born with moral ideas. We are born with emotional faculties and, upon having certain sense impressions, these may generate emotions and it is from these that we later derive from our moral ideas.

■ Numbers

Plato argued that our concepts of numbers are innate on the grounds that we never have any sense experience of them. The number two is not a thing you can encounter with your five senses. We encounter couples, pairs of gloves, braces of pheasants and so forth, in the world, but never the number two itself. It is as though what we experience is always an *example* of 'two-ness', but never the real thing. If the number is not something encountered in the physical world, Plato concluded, it must be something we encounter in some other realm, a realm of pure thought which is independent of the senses (see page 42).

The empiricist response to this is to say that we can acquire the concepts of different numbers by abstracting from the experiences of collections of objects in the world. After several encounters with objects in threes I can work out what they have in common. The concept of three is some kind of copy of this common denominator. However, this still leaves us with the problem of how we acquire the concepts of numbers which we haven't encountered. I have the concept of 5,381 and yet I may well never have encountered a group with this many members. Descartes makes a powerful argument against the empiricists along similar lines in his *Meditations on First Philosophy* where he points out that we can form the image of geometric shapes such as triangles and pentagons in our mind's eye, suggesting the possibility that our concept of these shapes derives from a sense experience of them copied into an image retained in the mind. But, he points out, I am equally capable of understanding the concept of a figure with a thousand sides, and yet I can form no clear image of this shape in my mind. He concludes that geometric shapes are conceived not in the imagination as kinds of copies of sensations, but rather by the intellect. Like Plato, he argues that our grasp of numbers and geometric shapes is not grounded in the senses.

Beauty

Plato went further, arguing that concepts like 'beauty' or 'justice' are not things we ever perceive in the world. We encounter beautiful things or just acts, but never *beauty* or *justice* as such. He concludes that we must acquire these concepts from somehow observing the essential nature of beauty or justice with our minds and not with our senses.

Plato also points out that our ability to recognise an action as just or a person's face as beautiful appears to require that we understand what beauty and justice are. However, if the *tabula rasa* thesis is true, at birth we can have no such understanding. But this means that we would be unable to recognise a beautiful face the first time we saw one. Not yet having acquired the concept of beauty seems to imply that we could never recognise beautiful things. How then could we ever hope to learn what beauty was from experience?

Reason as a source of knowledge about the world

Perhaps the major criticism of empiricism is the claim that reason alone, independently of the senses, can generate knowledge about the world. This is most clearly seen in mathematics where the fields of arithmetic and geometry, amongst others, seem to be pointing out fundamental truths about the physical world, and these truths cannot derived from the senses. We will state this claim briefly here before exploring it in detail in the next section.

As we have seen, there are good reasons for thinking that there is a category of knowledge – known as *a priori* knowledge – which can be acquired independently of experience. I don't need to check whether triangles have three sides by first finding a triangle and then counting the sides. I can tell what the answer will be before (i.e. *prior* to) conducting any such experiment. Similarly I can know in advance that no matter what pattern I arrange five feathers in (in two groups of 4 and 1; two groups of 2 and 3, or three groups of 2, 2 and 1, and so on) the total feathers will remain five. Of course, I have to know the meanings of the terms involved here to recognise such truths, but this is all. Truths which are not from mathematics or geometry can also be known *a priori*. One example concerns colour. We can know that if an object is blue all over it cannot also be orange. It is essential to colour that if a place on a surface is one colour it cannot simultaneously be another and this can be known without our needing to check. In all these cases we seem to have examples of truths that can be discovered by reason alone, and yet they also appear to tell us substantive things about the world.

A quick criticism of this claim is that the all the examples given rely on concepts derived from the senses and so are not really examples of innate knowledge. After all you can't do any theorising about triangles without having the concept of a triangle and this must have come from experience. And what of theorising about shapes we have never seen, such as Descartes' thousand-sided shape. The empiricist might still claim that the idea of a thousand-sided shape is still derived from the senses – it is just an extension of other shapes we have seen. However the innatists would claim that all this is missing the point – the truths that are reached in mathematics are derived from reason; they are not like generalisations from the senses.

Some key philosophical terms

Before exploring this issue in more depth we need to introduce some new philosophical terms as well as reminding ourselves of some old ones. We will look at three pairs of terms that will have a bearing on the debate as to whether reason can provide us with truths about the world independently of the senses:

- *a priori* and *a posteriori* knowledge
- analytic and synthetic truths
- necessary and contingent truths.

We will then briefly outline two different ways of reasoning, induction and deduction.

A priori and *a posteriori* knowledge
The terms *a priori* and a *posteriori* refer to the way in which we acquire knowledge.

Truths that can be known independently of experience, without the use of the senses, are said to be *a priori*. The term can also be applied to the truths themselves: an *a priori* truth is one which can be known *a priori*. Truths that can only be known via the senses and so are dependent on experience are termed *a posteriori*. The claim of innatisim is that *a priori* knowledge of the world is possible. The strict empiricist, on the other hand, claims that all knowledge is derived from the senses and so is *a posteriori*.

Analytic and synthetic truths
You can tell that some sentences are true simply through an examination of the meanings of the terms involved. Such truths are termed ANALYTIC or *tautological*. An analytic truth is true by definition, and so is a tautology, which cannot be

denied without contradiction. For example, it is analytically true that a square has four sides. To say that a square does not have four sides is to contradict oneself. That a bachelor is unmarried is also an analytic truth. I can tell this is true just by looking at the terms involved; I do not need to go out into the world and conduct a survey of actual bachelors. Contrasted with analytic truths are SYNTHETIC truths, which are not true simply by definition and can be denied without contradiction. For example, it is a synthetic truth that the dinosaurs died out, or that John, a 43-year-old bachelor, is miserable. Dinosaurs might have continued to dominate the earth if the asteroid that ultimately wiped them out had been on a slightly different course. John might not have been miserable if he had won the lottery the night before. These possibilities are conceivable since there is no contradiction in them.

Analytic truths are also known by other names – *tautologies* or *logical truths* – and, as with *a priori* truths, they do not seem to rely on the senses to be known.

Necessary and contingent truths

There are competing definitions of NECESSARY and CONTINGENT truths, but one way of seeing the distinction is to imagine there are worlds just like this one, but each different in one or more ways. No matter how much these worlds differ, some propositions will have to be true in all of

Table 4.1 *Different ways in which propositions can be known or can be true*

Term	What does it apply to?	What distinction does it pick? out?
A priori	Knowledge or truths	Knowledge/truths that can be known independently of the senses, via reason
A posteriori	Knowledge or truths	Knowledge/truths that can be known only via the senses
Analytic (sometimes called tautologies or logical truths)	Truths	Propositions that are true because of the meanings of the terms alone Propositions whereby the opposite implies a contradiction
Synthetic	Truths	Propositions that are not true because of the meanings of the terms alone Propositions whereby the opposite implies no contradiction
Necessary	Truths	Propositions that are true in all possible worlds Propositions whereby the opposite is impossible
Contingent	Truths	Propositions that are only true in this world (and maybe some others, but not all) Propositions whereby the opposite is possible

them, for example that $2 + 3 = 5$ or that water is H_2O. These truths are termed necessary. Necessary truths are truth since there is no world possible in which they are false. Some propositions, however, will only be true of some worlds, for example that Tony Blair was the prime minister in 1999. It is possible to imagine a world in which another politician was the leader. Such truths are termed contingent, because they could have been otherwise.

One feature that may immediately strike you is that these terms all seem to be saying similar things. In other words doesn't all *a priori* knowledge simply consist of analytic truths, which in turn are the same as necessary truths?

There is no easy answer to this question, and philosophers have held very different positions. For example, innatists would claim that we can have *a priori* knowledge of the world – in other words that not all knowledge of the world comes via the senses. However, empiricists may claim that the only things we can know *a priori* are analytic truths, and these tell us nothing about the world, as they would be true even if there were no world. We will pick up this discussion in the next section.

ACTIVITY   Read through the following statements and see for each of them whether they are
a) *a priori* or *a posteriori*
b) analytic or synthetic
c) necessary or contingent.

1 Everyone wants what is good.
2 The square root of 81 is 9.
3 All bachelors are unmarried men.
4 Some bachelors have penthouses and throw wild parties.
5 Mammals exist which have beaks like ducks, and which lay eggs.
6 God exists.
7 All things eventually decay and die.
8 Material objects occupy space.
9 Two parallel lines will never meet.
10 Nothing can come from nothing.
11 Water is H_2O.

Induction and deduction
Another useful distinction drawn by philosophers is between two forms of reasoning: DEDUCTION and INDUCTION (see pages 114–117). In deductive reasoning if the PREMISES are true the CONCLUSION must be true. In other words, if we accept the reasons of a deductive argument we are forced into

accepting the conclusion as well: it is impossible for the reasons to be true and the conclusion to be false. Such arguments are also called 'deductively valid', or simply 'valid'. For example, If I know that Abby is taller than Brian and I know that Brian is taller than Collette then I can work out through reason alone that Abby is taller than Collette. I don't have to make any further inquiries to tell that this is true and so this conclusion has to follow from the reasons. I may need to rely on the evidence of the senses to work out that Abby is taller than Brian and again that Brian is taller than Collette but that Abby is taller than Collette was deduced by reason alone. Deductive arguments are attractive since they are so strong. If we accept the reasons we cannot but accept the conclusion too and so they give absolute support to their conclusions. However, since deductive validity is only a matter of the relationship between reasons and conclusions, a deductive argument need not have reasons or conclusions that are actually true. Moreover, a deductive argument doesn't tell you anything in the conclusion that wasn't already contained implicitly in the premises and so deductive reasoning cannot tell us anything new.

Inductive reasoning offers to overcome these limitations. It is based on the idea that unobserved cases are likely to resemble observed cases. For example, having observed that the apples have ripened on the apple tree in your own garden, you might conclude that it is likely that the apples have also ripened on the apple tree in a friend's garden. Such reasoning involves generalising from the evidence and, since it goes beyond the given evidence with such arguments, it is possible for the reasons or evidence to be true but the conclusion to be false. In this example, it is conceivable that the apples on your friend's tree have failed to ripen this year. So the reasons go some way to support the conclusion, but cannot demonstrate that it must be true. This means that the strength of inductive arguments is not an all-or-nothing affair as it is with deductive arguments, but rather a matter of degree. In other words, such arguments can be strong or weak. However, inductive arguments do tell us something new in their conclusions that wasn't already contained in the premises.

What can be known through reason alone?

In this section we will examine the view that some fundamental claims about what exists can be grounded in and justified by *a priori* intuition and/or demonstration – in other words without the aid of the senses.

ACTIVITY Imagine that you are suddenly kidnapped, bundled into an alien spacecraft and taken to a dark room on another planet. You are asked to provide as much knowledge as you can about the Earth and how things work on the planet to someone who knows nothing about the universe, including the planet Earth. However, you have to follow some important rules. You have to be able to demonstrate that the information you give is true just by talking about it, and you will only be believed if you have demonstrated your claims beyond doubt. Further, you cannot do any experiments, such as dropping a pen, to show that a claim about gravity is true; you can only use words to make your points.

1 Would you be able to convince the aliens that London is the capital of England?

2 How much would you be able to convince them? Could you convince the aliens of anything at all?

3 How much can we know about the world just using reason alone?

Rationalists would claim that the aliens could be convinced on a range of matters. For a start they would claim that truths of mathematics and of logic can be demonstrated by reason alone; in other words they could be demonstrated *a priori*. But they would also claim something further, namely that reason can establish substantive truths about the empirical world as well. Before we look at their claims in more detail we will briefly consider what this might mean for the idea of the *tabula rasa*.

A priori knowledge and the tabula rasa

Can *a priori* knowledge tell us about the world? The empiricist would say no, as this would seem to undermine the *tabula rasa* thesis, which claims that all our knowledge must come from the senses. There are two different ways in which the empiricist might deny the claim to *a priori* knowledge:

- claiming that all knowledge is in fact *a posteriori* and that *a priori* knowledge doesn't exist
- claiming that *a priori* knowledge does exist but it tells us nothing about the world.

There is no *a priori* knowledge
Strict empiricists such as John Stuart Mill (1806–1873) have claimed that we obtain all our knowledge, including mathematical knowledge, via experience, and that there is therefore no *a priori* knowledge. They claim that we observe that two apples and three apples make five apples, that two lizards and three snakes make five reptiles, and so on, and it is from such observations that we can generalise that 2 + 3 = 5. The argument is that mathematical laws are discovered in much the same way as other laws about the world are. For example,

just as we see the sun rise each morning and thus generalise that it will rise every morning, or observe that delicate objects dropped from certain heights tend to break, so we observe how objects behave when grouped together and make empirical generalisations, which are the laws of addition. The difference between mathematical truths and other empirical truths is only that the evidence for them is more consistent. As we have seen, using the past as a guide to the future is called inductive reasoning. And the claim here is that maths is another form of induction: we observe how the world has worked in the past and then believe it will work that way in the future again.

▶ criticism ◀ However, this conclusion is not very satisfactory. It places mathematical claims on the same level as empirical generalisations and it seems clear that this is wrong. For example, on the basis of my previous experience, I might conclude that the number 3 bus will probably take 30 minutes to get me to work today, but I'm not very certain about this. I do, however, feel very certain that if I give the driver £1 and a 50 pence piece then I will have given the driver £1.50. Of this I am sure.

Not every delicate object is certain to break when dropped from a height, and eventually the sun may not rise. And even if delicate objects did always break, and the sun did always continue to rise, it is at least *conceivable* that this might not be the case. Yet surely 2 plus 3 will always be 5, and we just can't imagine waking up one morning and finding that they were now 6. Such an idea appears to make no sense: 2 plus 3 just has to make 5.

From this we can see that the truths of maths don't have the same features as truths gained by induction. The former are certain and impossible to conceive otherwise; the latter are not certain and possible to conceive otherwise. The reason for this difference, argue the rationalists, is that the truths of maths are not empirical generalisations: they are not inductions based on the evidence of the senses but are deductions based on logical reasoning. As they are deductions, they can be demonstrated to be true and so are beyond doubt.

We can never be certain that the future will resemble the past, as often it doesn't. So our inductive reasoning about the future – it might rain tomorrow; the tomatoes should be ripe soon – is no guarantee of that future. However, our deductive reasoning seems far more reliable. Two and two make four today, and will do tomorrow and the day after that. Here our reasoning seems to guarantee the truth.

For reasons such as this, the claim that mathematical truths are inductions based on past experience is no longer held by many, if any, philosophers.

A *priori* knowledge does exist but it tells us nothing about the world

As we saw above, analytic truths are true in virtue of the meaning of the terms. Because of this they can be known *a priori*. Take for example the proposition: 'All bachelors are unmarried'. I don't need to conduct a survey of bachelors to justify my belief that this is true. I would be wasting my time if I did. I can know that it is true *prior* to any experimental evidence simply in virtue of understanding the terms involved.

To take another example, contrast the proposition: 'No one can steal the Queen of England's property' with 'No one can steal his or her own property'. In the first case, to establish whether or not it is true I would have to make various enquiries into the security surrounding the Queen. So establishing its truth would involve more than just thinking about the meaning of the proposition. But in the second case, I can see that it must be true just by understanding what the terms involved mean. It is impossible to steal one's own property just because stealing *means* taking someone else's property (without permission).

Some empiricists argue that all *a priori* truths are analytic; and, as they tell us only about the meanings of the symbols, such truths are condemned as being able to tell us nothing of interest.

So an empiricist may recognise that there are truths of reason, but regard them as empty of empirical content and so useless as a basis for knowledge about the physical universe. In so doing the empiricist can retain the basic point that it is only experience that can provide interesting or new information about the world. Reason's usefulness lies in unpicking implications and truths that are already present in the knowledge we have. So, for example, if I knew that Shakespeare wrote *Hamlet* and I later found out that *Hamlet* was a tragedy, I would be able to deduce, by reason alone, that Shakespeare wrote at least one tragedy. However, in doing so I would not be gaining any new knowledge but merely teasing out facts I knew implicitly already.

Can reason provide us with new knowledge about the world?

Is this claim of the empiricist true? Is *a priori* knowledge limited to analytic truths and the unpicking of the implications of truths already known, or can it tell us new facts about the world?

To answer this we will consider:

- the relationship between mathematics and the world
- whether rationalism can generate knowledge beyond the mathematical and the analytic.

Mathematics and the world

The relationship between mathematics and the world is not easy to describe and represents a significant philosophical problem in itself. In this section we can only summarise some of the main positions and see the implications for the claim that we can gain significant knowledge of the world *a priori*.

Geometry

One of the easier areas to discuss is that of geometry – the study of shapes – and it is here that we will begin our brief foray into the world of mathematics.

The foundations of geometry were established by the seminal Greek mathematician Euclid. In his book the *Elements*, Euclid sets out what is known as an axiomatic system, that is to say, a system in which all the propositions are derived from a small set of initial axioms and definitions. These initial axioms and definitions are thought to be self-evident. For example, among those in Euclid's axioms are the following:

> All right angles equal one another.

> A circle is a plane figure contained by one line such that all the straight lines falling upon it from one point among those lying within the figure equal one another. (Meaning a circle is a single line whereby every point on it is the same distance from the centre.)

From these Euclid then proceeds to prove a host of further propositions, for instance:

> If a straight line falling on two straight lines makes the alternate angles equal to one another, then the straight lines are parallel to one another.

Through the careful use of reason, Euclid is able to establish a large and systematic body of truths all derived from his initial axioms and definitions.

Euclid's system was undoubtedly the inspiration behind many of the rationalists' attempts to gain knowledge through reason. First establish a series of truths that cannot be doubted (axioms) and then build from this point to establish a complete system of truths. Descartes, for one, saw this as much more than a mathematical procedure but as something that could be applied to the whole of science and philosophy.

Descartes

These long chains of perfectly simple and easy reasonings by means of which geometers are accustomed to carry out their most difficult demonstrations had led me to fancy that everything that can fall under human knowledge forms a similar sequence.[8]

Regarding geometry it would seem that the truths established through reason do indeed apply to the world. We are able to construct bridges and buildings that rely on matter and space behaving in the ways described by geometry. We can even correctly predict the angles and properties of shapes that have never before existed. Geometry seems to be telling us new facts about the nature of physical space, facts that have genuine application and are not just true by definition. So it would seem that with geometry we have an example of how we can gain knowledge of the world independently of the senses.

► criticism ◄

However, is this really the case? It can be argued that geometry is simply working out the logical implications of a given set of initial assumptions. Once these axioms have been established then the other truths can be analytically deduced. These other truths follow deductively from the axioms. They are essentially claiming conditional truths along the following lines:

> Given that a straight line is the shortest distance between two points and that parallel lines never meet, triangles and squares will have certain properties x, y and z.

So perhaps geometry is not adding any new facts beyond the initial assumptions; it is simply working out their implications. And, where did we get these initial assumptions from? If they are ultimately derived from experience, then the whole system is grounded in experience after all and we are not gaining any new knowledge *a priori*.

Further, the truths established by Euclid's geometry aren't even true of the world. In most instances they are simply very good approximations. It seems to be the case, following the

■ **Figure 4.10
Euclidean and non-
Euclidean space**

In Euclidean space parallel lines never meet and stay the same distance apart. However, this is not true in other possible geometries such as hyperbolic and elliptic. Further it is also suggested that the world itself is not Euclidean, it merely appears to be on the scale relevant to the human eye.

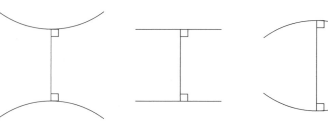

Hyperbolic   Euclidean   Elliptic

work of Einstein and others, that the world is in fact non-Euclidean – which means that the axioms that Euclid based his theories on are not actually true. It turns out that, in real space, parallel lines do actually cross; it is just that this can't be observed on the scales that the human eye deals with.

It seems that we need to carry out experiments and careful measurements in order to determine the actual properties of space, and that they can be worked out by reason alone. There are many different possible geometries that would each follow from a different set of axioms and all of them are perfectly intelligible. This means that the axioms of any geometry are not true by definition (analytically true) as the opposite is conceivable. It seems we have to actually look at the world using our senses and see which of the many possible geometries actually applies to the universe we live in.

Algebra

Unlike geometry, numbers themselves don't seem to be describing anything as tangible as space. However, the truths of numbers seem to apply to almost every aspect of the universe. But what do these numbers actually describe? There are a range of possible answers of which we outline only three:

1 *Platonism*. Earlier we saw Plato suggest that numbers describe ideal entities that exist independently of the human mind. As he believed they exist outside of the mind, Plato was a *realist* about numbers (see Chapter 7, page 516 for more on realism). On this view mathematicians are trying to work out the relationships between these various entities (numbers) and these seem to apply to the world we inhabit too. Despite being over 2000 years old Platonism is still one of the main theories in the philosophy of maths. If true it would imply that reason can tell us about the world independently of the senses.

2 *Empiricism*. As described above, empiricism is the view that mathematical truths are just generalisations from experience. This is not widely held today, but if true would imply that mathematics can only be known *a posteriori*.

3 *Logicism*. Bertrand Russell and Alfred Whitehead, following the work of other philosophers, attempted to show that it is possible to derive the truths of mathematics from a set of more basic truths about logic – for example, that 'A or not A' is necessarily true. Their masterpiece *Principia Mathematica* famously contains a proof that 1 and 1 makes 2, which is several pages long. In this view, numbers are defined by possible sets of objects: the number 2 describes the set of all possible pairs of objects.

Like Euclid's, Russell and Whitehead's approach is axiomatic. It assumes some basic truths – in this case a few laws of logic – and shows that the truths of mathematics can be logically derived from these. It should, however, be noted that axiomatic attempts such as Russell's to explain mathematics have run into a major problem known as *Gödel's incompleteness theorem*, which states that in any such system there will always be mathematical statements that are true but that are not derivable from the axioms of the system.

If logicism was right it would show that the truths of mathematics can be derived from the truths of logic. The question that then arises, however, is whether the truths of logic themselves are derived from the senses or known innately.

■ **Figure 4.11 Part of a mathematical proof that 1+1=2**

$*54\cdot43.\quad \vdash:.\,\alpha,\beta\,\epsilon\,1\,.\,\supset\,:\alpha\cap\beta=\Lambda\,.\equiv.\,\alpha\cup\beta\,\epsilon\,2$

Dem.

$\vdash.*54\cdot26.\supset\vdash:.\,\alpha=\iota`x\,.\,\beta=\iota`y\,.\,\supset:\alpha\cup\beta\,\epsilon\,2\,.\equiv.\,x\neq y\,.$

$[*51\cdot231]\qquad\qquad\qquad\qquad\qquad\qquad\equiv.\,\iota`x\cap\iota`y=\Lambda\,.$

$[*13\cdot12]\qquad\qquad\qquad\qquad\qquad\qquad\equiv.\,\alpha\cap\beta=\Lambda\qquad\quad(1)$

$\vdash.(1).*11\cdot11\cdot35.\supset$

$\qquad\vdash:.(\exists x,y)\,.\,\alpha=\iota`x\,.\,\beta=\iota`y\,.\,\supset:\alpha\cup\beta\,\epsilon\,2\,.\equiv.\,\alpha\cap\beta=\Lambda\qquad(2)$

$\vdash.(2).*11\cdot54.*52\cdot1.\supset\vdash.\text{Prop}$

From this proposition it will follow, when arithmetical addition has been defined, that 1 + 1 = 2.

Summary

Mathematical truths would seem to be a clear example of *a priori* knowledge. We are able to generate such truths in a way that is very different from empirical generalisations, using deduction, rather than induction. What is less clear is whether these truths constitute new truths about the world, or whether they constitute a set of analytic truths from assumptions that have been derived from the senses.

■ Can rationalism generate knowledge beyond the mathematical and the analytic?

Many philosophers thought that the model of mathematical knowledge, with its clarity and certainty, should be applied to all human knowledge. Through the application of reason, they argued, it would be possible to understand a significant body of knowledge about the world and how it operates. This knowledge, like that of maths, would be certain, logical and endure for all time. The evidence of the senses should agree with the truths of reason, but they are not required for the acquisition of these truths. As we have seen, these philosophers are called rationalists, and perhaps the most famous rationalist was René Descartes.

René Descartes

Descartes (1596–1650) was born in France and educated at a Jesuit college. Thereafter he travelled Europe extensively, for some of this time as an officer in the army. When he was a young man, on consecutive nights, he had strange and vivid dreams, which would shape his life. His dreams told him that it was his mission to seek the truth using reason – and he spent the rest of his life doing this. As well as being famous for his writings in philosophy, Descartes is also an important figure in mathematics. Many students will keenly remember plotting lines and shapes on x–y axes, using Cartesian coordinates (Cartesian means 'of Descartes'). Throughout his life, Descartes was fond of lying in bed of a morning, 'thinking'. In his later life he was persuaded to move to Sweden to teach Queen Christina. The Queen required her philosophy lessons to begin at five in the morning. Descartes died after about six months of this new regime.

Following his mission to seek the truth through reason Descartes examined many of his beliefs. He noticed that the beliefs he had held from an early age had turned out to be false, and that his ordinary belief system appeared to be full of errors and contained little of which he could be certain. He felt he needed to start again to see if he could build a system of beliefs that was completely certain. The best way to do this, he decided, would be to tackle scepticism head on. If he could defeat it, then he would have good reason to claim to have knowledge. So he used a method which begins by employing the most radical sceptical arguments he could think of. This method – the so-called 'method of doubt' – tries to suspend judgement about *all* the things he previously took for granted. Everything that can possibly be doubted is treated as false for the purposes of argument. So the very possibility of doubt about something was, for Descartes, sufficient for treating it as false. If, after following this method, he arrived at something which cannot be doubted, i.e. something which is INDUBITABLE, then he would have reached a point of absolute certainty. At that point, he hoped, he might start to rebuild a new system of beliefs which would be free from errors.

In this book the *Meditations* Descartes begins this process of doubting by noting that his senses have sometimes deceived him. For example, he has, from time to time, been the victim of illusions. In accordance with his method of doubt, he therefore resolves not to trust his senses any more, for 'it is prudent never to trust entirely those who have once deceived us.'9 To this sceptical move Descartes considers the objection that this is a rather extreme reaction to the fact of the occasional illusion. Surely, only a mad person wouldn't trust their senses? But, continues Descartes, are we not equally deluded as a mad person when we dream? When dreaming we often believe ourselves to be people, and to be in places which we are not. And how can I be sure that I am not dreaming now? If this could be a dream, then I cannot be sure that anything appearing around me is real. Nonetheless, Descartes reckons, whether or not I am dreaming it remains the case that the things I am dreaming about must have some basis in reality. So is there anything in my dream that must have existence? Perhaps I can only be sure that shapes and colours are real. It is at this point that Descartes introduces his most radical sceptical scenario.

The evil demon

Descartes

> *I shall suppose, therefore, that there is, not a true God, who is the sovereign source of truth, but some evil demon, no less cunning and deceiving than powerful, who has used all his artifice to deceive me. I will suppose that the heavens, the air, the earth, colours, shapes, sounds and all external things that we see, are only illusions and deceptions which he uses to take me in.*

Meditations, p. 100

A powerful demon such as this could make anything appear to be the case. Your whole life could have been a fiction created by the demon. Descartes came up with the idea of a deceiving demon nearly 400 years ago, and it can seem rather far-fetched to the modern imagination. Yet the central insight can be readily made with more up-to-date scenarios, for example in *The Matrix* or the idea of a brain in a vat (page 258).

Can you be 100 per cent sure that you are not being deceived in this way? If you concede that this is a possibility, however absurd or remote, then surely you can never be 100 per cent certain of anything again. Nothing is certain – perhaps you don't even exist at all. At this point Descartes produces a response that is probably the best-known philosophical argument of all.

My own existence cannot be doubted because, when I attempt to doubt it, I recognise that there must be something doing the doubting, and that something is me. So at the time of thinking, Descartes cannot in fact be nothing. His own existence can be known for certain in the face of his most radical doubts. Here Descartes discovers the first principle, the first certainty that he has been searching for, what is often termed the COGITO, after the Latin formulation from Descartes' *Principles of Philosophy* (1644), namely: *cogito ergo sum*, meaning 'I am thinking therefore I exist', or 'I think therefore I am.'

Descartes

> *While we thus reject all that of which we can possibly doubt, and feign that it is false, it is easy to suppose that there is no God, nor heaven, nor bodies, and that we possess neither hands, nor feet, nor indeed any body; but we cannot in the same way conceive that we who doubt these things are not; for there is a contradiction in conceiving that what thinks does not at the same time as it thinks, exist. And hence this conclusion I think, therefore I am, is the first and most certain of all that occurs to one who philosophises in an orderly way.*[10]

The *cogito*

So Descartes was looking for a way of defeating the sceptic, something that could not be doubted, and it looks as if he has found it. It is impossible to doubt your own existence, for the very fact that you are doubting implies that you exist.

What is so significant about the *cogito* is that we can know it to be true just by thinking it. It is knowable *a priori* and tells us about something that actually exists, myself. Here my conviction in my own existence appears unshakable. It doesn't depend for its truth upon anything else, and so appears to justify itself. And this is precisely what we were looking for: a self-justifying belief.

But has Descartes really defeated the sceptic? And, if so, what exactly has he established?

Focusing on the latter question, Descartes is claiming to have established that 'I am, I exist'.[11] But what exactly is this *I*? Descartes himself realises that he has not yet established the existence of himself as a human being, for the evil demon could still be deceiving him as to his earthly form. He may not even have a body. But he claims, however, that the *I* must be something, and that the very least it must be is a thing that can think – a thinking thing, or, in other words, a conscious being. Of this he feels sure that any demon could not deceive him.

But is this so? Some commentators feel that Descartes has only established the existence of some thoughts or conscious experiences; can Descartes assert that these experiences belong to any self or *I*?[12] Perhaps thoughts can exist by themselves not owned by any thinker? This is the line, you will recall, that Hume takes in his critique of the concept of the self (on page 252). If thoughts can exist on their own then Descartes is overreaching in claiming 'I am'.

In any case, the *cogito* is a fairly limited place to start to rebuild a body of knowledge. Descartes needs further truths which also have this character of being self-justifying and which can be known just by thinking about them. Are there any other truths that have this quality? Descartes thinks there are and he calls them CLEAR AND DISTINCT IDEAS. These ideas, we are told, are ideas that can be 'intuited' by the mind by what he calls the 'light of reason'. They are truths of reason, truths that can be known with the mind alone. Descartes' examples of self-justifying beliefs are the basic claims of logic, geometry and mathematics. Such knowledge, it is claimed, resists any sceptical attack, since we recognise its truth immediately. Our faculty of intuition permits us to recognise the truth of such propositions without allowing any room for doubt or error. There is no point in asking how I know that triangles have three sides. Such knowledge is given in the very act of understanding the terms involved. There is no further evidence I could appeal to which could justify such knowledge.

Contemporary philosophers would call Descartes' clear and distinct ideas articles of *a priori* knowledge, knowledge that can be acquired without reference to experience. So here Descartes may have found the foundations for which he was searching. From this bedrock Descartes thought it would be possible to deduce further truths and from these build out a whole series of truths about the world – including scientific laws. The experience of the senses would also confirm the truth of the laws, but they would be known with certainty as they were deduced via reason and not induced via the senses.

■ **Figure 4.12**
Descartes'
foundationalism

All knowledge is based on a foundation of beliefs which are knowable a priori, and which are self-justifying. The rest of our beliefs, principally those about the physical world, are to be justified in terms of these basic beliefs. So any belief which is not ultimately based on reason is not justified and so is not knowledge. The view that all genuine knowledge is grounded in reason is termed rationalism.

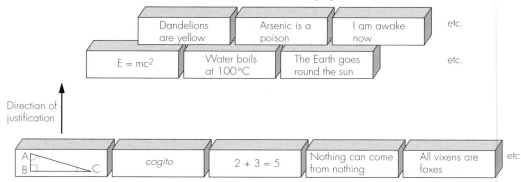

THE SUPERSTRUCTURE
i.e. knowledge of the world and the physical sciences

| Dandelions are yellow | Arsenic is a poison | I am awake now | etc. |

| $E = mc^2$ | Water boils at 100°C | The Earth goes round the sun | etc. |

Direction of justification

| A B C | cogito | 2 + 3 = 5 | Nothing can come from nothing | All vixens are foxes | etc. |

THE FOUNDATIONS: 'CLEAR AND DISTINCT' IDEAS
i.e. knowledge of my existence, of maths and geometry; truths of reason and analytic truths

This plan sounded grand, but the problem for Descartes was developing further truths on top of the *cogito*. After all, he still hasn't got rid of the idea that there is an evil demon; he has simply established that he exists. From this point Descartes tries to prove that God exists (see page 139). Then he argues that, as a good God wouldn't deceive us, we can trust our senses and our judgements as long as we proceed with suitable care and attention. For many readers of the *Meditations*, Descartes' elaborate system of certainty starts and ends with the *cogito*.

Plato and the theory of forms

Descartes was not alone in thinking that reason could provide important truths about the world. The fascination with *a priori* truths, especially those of mathematics and geometry, and the tendency to regard them as in some way superior to *a posteriori* truths has a long philosophical history. To regard such knowledge as having a privileged status, and to hold it as a benchmark for all other knowledge claims, is one of the main features of rationalism. In this Descartes is in the good company of Plato.

Plato (c. 428–347 BCE) is regarded by many as the most important of the Ancient Greek philosophers and as the father of the whole of Western philosophy. Both he and Descartes, two thousand years later, contended that knowledge had to involve self-evidence, and this possibility is fulfilled most effectively by beliefs acquired *a priori*. What particularly impresses rationalists about a geometric proof, for example, is that once we see its truth we also recognise that no further evidence could undermine it. It is a truth that appears unchanging and eternal and which couldn't be otherwise. For example, consider the following proof that Plato employs in his dialogue, the *Meno*:

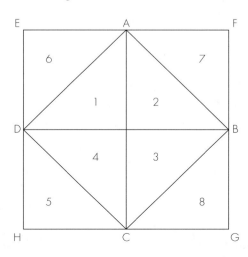

■ **Figure 4.13**
Socrates' experiment with the slave in Plato's Meno

This diagram shows that the total area of the square EFGH is twice that of the square ABCD. This can clearly be seen since each of the four triangles (1, 2, 3 and 4) which divide ABCD is equal in area and equal to each of the eight triangles (1, 2, 3, 4, 5, 6, 7 and 8) which divide EFGH, and eight is twice four.[13]

Once we understand the proof, we recognise it to be true not just of the particular square drawn on the page but of all squares, indeed of squares as such. This suggested to Plato that such knowledge cannot derive from our experience, since our experience is only ever of particular squares. So how is such an understanding possible? Plato's answer was that my mind sees the essential nature or FORM of the square and recognises truths about this, rather than about the particular example of a square I see with my eyes. Like Descartes, he thought that we have an innate faculty which recognises such truths as eternal and necessary. This furnishes us with genuine knowledge. By contrast, our understanding of empirical truths learned *a posteriori* lacks certainty. They are only ever contingently true, that is to say, they might not have been true and only happen to be true. For this reason, we can only have beliefs about them.

Moreover, the precise properties of geometric and mathematical ideas are never found among physical objects, since never in the physical world do we encounter perfect circles or squares, or numbers. At some level of detail, all examples of circles are only approximately circular. Only the form of 'circle' is perfectly or unqualifiedly circular. All threesomes come and go in the physical world, but the number three is timeless and eternal. It does not exist in time or space and so cannot undergo any changes. By contrast, even the most enduring of physical objects is both located in space and subject to change over time. This kind of consideration leads Plato to suppose that mathematics and geometry attain precision and certainty to the extent that they do not correspond to objects in the physical world. Since he thinks they must none the less apply to something, he posits a realm of intelligible objects which is more real than this world of imperfect, changeable objects.

In this way Plato draws a distinction between a world of ideal forms – the object of knowledge – and the physical world of which only belief or opinion is possible. But in Plato's mind knowledge isn't restricted to maths and geometry. We can acquire knowledge of the essential nature of moral and aesthetic concepts, such as justice and beauty, in the same way, by contemplating the essential nature of them with the mind. This is because the idea or form of beauty exists independently of any particular beautiful things, just as the form of the square exists independently of square things. Physical things may be beautiful to some degree, but cannot be completely or perfectly beautiful. Their beauty comes and goes, and always depends on factors such as the state of the perceiver, the context, and so forth. Yet we can acquire knowledge of the eternal and unchanging form of beauty by reasoning about the concept in an *a priori* manner.

Plato contrasts forms and sensible objects by saying the former are 'forever', or 'always are', whereas the latter 'wander in generation and decay',[14] meaning that, while objects are subject to change, the form is unalterable. Plato uses a variety of metaphors to describe the relation that obtains between the two worlds. Sometimes he speaks of the form being 'present' in an object, or of the object 'sharing in' the form. Alternatively, he speaks of the object as an 'approximation', 'copy' or 'imitation' of the form.[15] The form may also be thought of as like a mould or blueprint determining what a set of objects of a certain kind have in common, while no two particulars need ever be identical. It is our recognition of the form in the particular which enables us to see that it belongs to a certain class of thing.

The problem for Plato, as it was for Descartes some two thousand years later, was trying to actually establish what these *a priori* truths are. Plato tell us that the forms exist and that we can reach them through thought alone. However, he fails to offer up a single form for us to scrutinise. Perhaps the apprehension of a form is not the sort of thing one can discuss using language? But, until these forms are established they cannot really count as examples of *a priori* knowledge of the world.

Scepticism about the nature and extent of rational knowledge

Few philosophers today would agree that we can acquire the precision of mathematical knowledge in aesthetics or morals. Concepts of justice and beauty are (relatively speaking) vague and may vary between individuals and cultures. But what of scientific knowledge? Descartes reckoned it would be possible to work out basic physical laws with mathematical certainty simply by reasoning from indubitable first principles without empirical observation. However, this project now seems overly ambitious. His difficulty was how to move from knowledge of his own existence and of *a priori* truths to that of the physical world. Mathematical truths may be eternal and necessary, but they can't be used to overcome scepticism about the existence of the world, nor can maths and geometry alone tell us how the world behaves. To know that if I have two marbles and then add three more marbles that I will have five marbles tells me nothing about whether or not there are marbles. The price of demanding that all our knowledge come through reason seems to be that we end up not knowing very much.

The lack of progress that pure reason has made in telling us about the world seems to support the earlier claim that reason alone can tell us only about analytic truths and that all truths about the physical world, all empirical truths, are synthetic.

As noted, analytic truths are true by definition, and the denial of an analytic truth is always an impossible contradiction. For example, a two-sided triangle or a married bachelor is impossible. However, it is always possible that things in the world could have been different. The truths of the world are not true by virtue of the meanings of the terms themselves and their opposites do not imply a contradiction. There is no logical contradiction in supposing that there are two suns or mice that speak. Even the laws of physics could have been different. Scientists can model aspects of the universe with different laws. If reason alone can only provide analytic truths then it can tell us nothing about the world, as no denial about a fact in the world would seem to imply any contradiction. So, I cannot work out the laws of physics, just as I cannot work out what colour the sky is, by reason alone. Such things can be found out only by observation. This is an argument put forward Hume. It is important because, if it is right, it shows that deductive reasoning by itself is of limited use. Experience can be the only true source of knowledge about the physical universe, and deductive reasoning can only help to work out the implications of this knowledge.

Other rationalists

Hume's claim is that the rationalist enterprise must fail. It fails because reason will provide us only with analytic truths – truths by definition – whereas knowledge of the world involves knowledge of synthetic truths – truths that could have been otherwise. However, Descartes was not the only rationalist of the modern era. Others followed in his footsteps and took up the challenge of establishing knowledge through reason. Two of these, Leibniz and Spinoza, avoid Hume's criticism to some extent since both of them claimed that all empirical truths are necessary truths, and that these, in principle, can be established by reason alone.

Leibniz

Gottfried Wilhelm von Leibniz (1646–1716), like Descartes, was another great polymath. Most of his life was spent working in the courts of various European royalty and consequently his studies in philosophy, maths and science were all conducted in his spare time. Much of his philosophy was carried out with correspondents through the exchange of letters – he wrote over 16,000 in his lifetime. He was also a great mathematician and discovered calculus at the same time as Isaac Newton. Leibniz established a complex and contained metaphysical view of the world and it is very easy to misrepresent his views by presenting small segments of his philosophy in isolation. Leibniz believed that God existed necessarily and that by definition God is all-good, all-powerful and all-knowing. He subscribed to a version of what is known as the ONTOLOGICAL argument for the existence of God. In outline, this argument claims that if we understand the concept of God properly we will recognise that he just has to exist, that is, his existence is necessary (see Chapter 2). Since this necessary being is all-good and all-powerful, it follows that the world he created would have to be the best possible world there could be. It would be nonsensical for an all-good and all-powerful God to create a less than perfect world. So the world we live in, and every event that takes place in it, takes place necessarily as part of the divine plan to maximise the good.[16]

This may seem implausible initially. We can see perfectly well that a lot of what goes on in the world is not good. We can certainly imagine far better worlds than this one – for example, worlds without famine, or the suffering of innocent children. Leibniz defends himself against this objection by arguing that the apparent imperfections in this world appear only because we have a limited view of the whole of God's creation. Each local piece of evil is necessary in order to maximise the overall perfection of the world (see page 476). So some suffering is required so that more good can be realised, just as we must sometimes endure the discomfort of taking unpleasant medicine in order to recover from an illness. If we had the mind of God and could grasp the bigger picture, we would see that these apparent imperfections are necessary and so could understand the reason for everything in the universe. So, in principle at least, all empirical truths about the world could be worked out *a priori*, just by thinking about them. So, we wouldn't need to do any empirical research to know whether there will be a white Christmas this year. We could work it out, just by thinking about whether a white Christmas would be part of God's plan to produce the best possible world. Of course, in reality, humans are not up to the task of working out truths like this by reason alone. Our finite minds can't see whether snow or no snow would be best. This is why we have to do empirical research and why such truths appear contingent.

Spinoza

Benedict de Spinoza (1632–1677) was born in Amsterdam. He lived an austere life, refusing to accept his inheritance and earning his living as a humble lens-grinder. He died of consumption, probably triggered by the fine glass dust that he inhaled every day. While grinding he would contemplate philosophical ideas, often discussing his thoughts with friends and intellectuals who would frequent his workshop. Spinoza, like Descartes and Leibniz, adopted the rationalist view that the essential truths about the world should be established through reason and thus could attain the certainty of maths and geometry. His great work, *The Ethics*, starts by stating a series of definitions and axioms that he believes cannot be doubted. Inspired by the geometric method of Euclid who, using a few axioms and definitions, proves various geometrical propositions, Spinoza proceeds to try to deduce in the same manner all sorts of general or metaphysical truths. As *The Ethics* develops, Spinoza arrives at a strange and complex metaphysical picture of the world. Spinoza was a PANTHEIST, believing that God is one and the same as the universe and, like Leibniz, he claimed that all truths are necessary, and nothing is contingent. The appearance of contingency is the result of the fact that our minds are not powerful enough to see why everything is the way it is. Forming only a small part of the universe, each human fails to see how every part of the universe, i.e. God, is connected, and it is from this that the feeling of contingency arrives. So while it may seem to me that some events in the universe just happen to be the case, in fact all are necessary. I had to have the cup of tea I've just finished, as this was a necessary event. I couldn't have had a cup of coffee instead.[17]

Reason and necessary truths

The rationalist views adopted by both Leibniz and Spinoza attempt to avoid Hume's criticism by claiming that the truths about the world are necessary and suggesting that because of this they could, in theory, be discovered by reason. However, these attempts at the rationalist enterprise raise further difficulties. Chiefly, both depend on their conception of God as a necessary being, who, in turn, confers necessity on the world and all the events in it. As such, they rely on the existence of God, and although both attempt to prove his existence using reason alone, neither of their versions of the ontological argument is generally considered successful.

However, we could try to imagine a modern-day version of rationalism, which posits a necessary universe that does not rely on the existence of God. We can already predict successfully the movements of the moon and the planets by applying the relevant scientific laws to some initial starting positions. We can also predict the outcome of thousands of chemical reactions in the same way. Now, imagine this predictive power extended a million-fold, such that the behaviour of every atom could be predicted using the laws of nature and initial starting conditions. (Let us assume that there is no random element in nature, and that we are able to surmise initial starting conditions of particles down to the sub-atomic level.) Imagine further that we can somehow find out the exact starting conditions of the universe at the Big Bang. We would have a situation where, theoretically, some sort of super-computer could predict how every event in the universe subsequently took place, right up to and including the event of your reading this now.

This thought experiment suggests a way that reason (albeit through a computer) could indeed work out all truths about the universe. However, even this scenario (which contains many dubious assumptions) fails to live up to the rationalist ideal. How could reason alone work out the laws of nature and the initial starting conditions of the universe? These would have to be established through the senses, through observing how the universe works. An out-and-out rationalist would have to claim that these too could be established using reason alone, by claiming that there is only one logically possible universe and set of natural laws that could exist. Yet this view is hard to believe – surely this isn't the only possible universe. Things could have been different. It is hard to see how a universe in which I drank a cup of coffee five minutes ago instead of the cup of tea I in fact had, is logically impossible. Further, current science even suggests that universes with different laws of nature may be possible. So it seems that, no matter how hard we push the case, it is simply not possible to prove substantial truths about the universe and the way it works by using reason alone.

Claiming that truths about the world are necessary doesn't seem to help the cause as firstly the claim is questionable and secondly reason alone is not sufficient to establish all necessary truths – only those that are also analytic. For example, that water is H_2O is not considered to be analytic by some, as it was a discovery by science as opposed to someone looking into the meaning of terms. However, it is claimed that, once established, water must be H_2O in all possible worlds and so is necessary. There may be worlds with things that look, feel, sustain life and quench thirst like water. However, these will not actually be water unless they are H_2O. So that water is H_2O is a necessary truth, but this fact was never going to be discovered by reason alone. The source of this knowledge had to be our experiences of what the world is actually like.

Is 'certainty' confined to introspection and tautologies?

So far both the foundationalist approaches of the empiricists and the rationalists have failed to provide a system of beliefs that can be known with certainty. For the empiricist, the fact that we are having sense impressions seems certain, along with our inner impressions such as pain and happiness. It is certainly hard to see how we could be mistaken about these, although some of the criticisms on pages 280–81 do indeed question their indubitable nature. Extending our knowledge beyond these is a challenge for the empiricist as we cannot be absolutely certain as to what is causing these impressions; it is possible after all that we may be brains in a vat. So, although I may be certain that I'm having a warm, wet tea-tasting experience, I can't be absolutely certain that I'm drinking tea. The certainty seems limited to the elements of my mind – the sense impressions. Another way of saying this is that certainty is limited to introspection – introspection being the ability to look at the content of your mind.

Rationalism fares a little bit better in the certainty stakes. Descartes seems able to establish the *cogito* through reason alone. The truths of mathematics can be known with certainty along with analytic truths. Beyond this there seems to be little that reason alone can tell us.

Is this our lot? Are our own existence, knowledge of our own sense impressions, and a host of analytic truths or tautologies all we can know about for certain? Beyond this are we condemned to a life of uncertainty? Has the sceptic lost a few battles over maths and impressions, but overall won the war?

Maybe scepticism is not as powerful as it first appears and we can find further ways of resisting its advance. Below we now examine other attempts at establishing certainty.

Ways of defeating the sceptic and establishing certainty

1 Are there more arguments like the *cogito*? – Transcendental arguments

The *cogito* is one of the most scrutinised philosophical arguments of all time. One of the big concerns has been to determine what sort of argument it is. How exactly does it work as an argument? Although there is no universal agreement (there rarely is in philosophy) many argue that the important point is that it defeats doubt about my own existence by showing that if I don't exist it is impossible to doubt. In other words, existence is a necessary condition for doubt to occur, and so the very act of doubting actually proves my existence. The attempt to doubt my own existence, in other words, is self-defeating. Arguments that have this sort of structure are called TRANSCENDENTAL arguments (a term first used in this way by Kant). Such arguments ask what the conditions of possibility are for something's being the case. Here, my own existence is a condition of possibility for my doubt. Perhaps my existence is not the only thing that defeats doubt in this way. What other things must be the case for doubt to occur?

ACTIVITY   Below is a list of beliefs that you probably hold.

- Go through each of them in turn and try doubting it.
- What difficulties are encountered in attempting to doubt it? Take note of any difficulties that occur to you.

A Language exists.
B You are aware of having experiences.
C You hold beliefs.
D You can doubt various things.
E Your reasoning ability is reliable.
F Knowledge is possible.

Here are some possible answers to the activity. Note that there are numerous other possible answers you may have found, but those given here all have something in common. Can you put your finger on what it is? Do you think this defeats the sceptic?

A *Language exists.* If you were seriously to doubt that language existed, how would you express or formulate your doubts? Presumably they could only really be formulated in language. You would have to think or say something like 'I doubt language exists.' But in the act of formulating your doubts you are using language, the very thing you are supposed to be doubting. So such a doubt would appear to defeat itself as soon as it was expressed.

B *You are aware of having experiences.* Focus on a particular experience you are having and try to doubt that you are having it. For example, if you are seeing a white page before you with dark letters printed on it, try to doubt that you are having this experience. It would seem impossible to do. It is certainly possible to doubt that the page itself and the writing exist. But it seems impossible to doubt you are having the experience of the letters. Whether this experience is caused by a demon, hallucinogens or even by reality, you are still having the experience. It's as though in the very having of an experience you are directly aware that you are having it, and can't doubt that you are having it. Indeed to doubt at all you would seem first to have to be conscious and so to have experiences.

C *You hold beliefs.* To doubt that you hold beliefs is to believe that it is possible that you don't have any beliefs. But this is itself a belief. So if you believe this you have at least one belief, and so you cannot consistently doubt that you hold beliefs.

D *You can doubt various things.* To doubt that you can doubt things involves doubting. So you can't consistently doubt that you can doubt.

E *Your reasoning ability is reliable.* If you doubt the reliability of your own reasoning abilities then you won't be able to make any progress in any argument whatsoever. Any piece of reasoning is suspect. This would mean that you would have to doubt the validity of the arguments that led you to doubt your reason in the first place.

F *Knowledge is possible.* If you deny that knowledge is possible, then you can't know anything, including the claim that knowledge is not possible.

2 A difference that makes no difference

Consider again Descartes' evil demon scenario. Imagine that we argue with Descartes that if there really were a demon we should be able to catch it out. For example, we might try to open a drawer unexpectedly, or turn the wrong way down a side road. If we did so quickly enough, perhaps we could get a glimpse of the real world, before the demon had a chance to create the illusion of the inside of the drawer, or scenery in the side road.

It is clear what Descartes' response would be. He would say that we have missed the point. The demon is so powerful and cunning that there is nothing that we could do, no possible means by which to detect its shenanigans. The demon is undetectable *in principle*.

This response raises a difficulty, however. Some philosophers have complained that the possibility that we are being so radically deceived is empty. For if there is no possible way of detecting the deception, not even in principle, then there is no effective difference between being deceived and living an ordinary life. In other words, because it can make no practical difference to our lives, it is not a supposition that we should take seriously. The supposed difference between the real world and the world created by the demon is not one that we can actually draw. And so some philosophers suggest that if there is no way of drawing the difference, then there isn't any real difference to draw. If so we can eliminate those doubts caused by the evil demon possibility. However, it is not entirely clear what new certainties arise after this as other modes of doubt may come into play.

3 Doubting the very nature of belief

Another limitation on what can consistently be doubted concerns our beliefs about the nature of belief itself. It is significant that Descartes never questions the notion that he actually holds certain beliefs, but just that these beliefs can be true or false, that they can be justified or unjustified, be certain or uncertain, and so on. The reason for this is that the exercise of doubt is only possible if one buys into the idea that beliefs are the kinds of thing that can be doubted, be supported by evidence, be certain, be true and so forth. Without accepting these basic ideas about the nature of belief itself, no serious scepticism can get going. What this shows is that we need to take some assumptions for granted in order to doubt others: at the bare minimum we need to assume that we can have doubt about or conviction in beliefs, and that beliefs can be true or false. In other words, we need certain minimal beliefs about the nature of belief, evidence, certainty, truth, and so on, in order even to call beliefs into question.

Actually Descartes is not unaware of this fact about the very possibility of doubt. In the *Rules for the Direction of the Mind* he writes:

Descartes

If, for example, Socrates says that he doubts everything it necessarily follows that he understood at least that he is doubting and hence that he knows that something can be true or false etc. for there is a necessary connection between these facts and the nature of doubt.[18]

It is important therefore to realise that Descartes' scepticism cannot be as all-encompassing as the opening lines of the *Meditations* might be taken to suggest. For he is obliged to retain the basic framework of beliefs concerning the nature of doubt, certainty and evidence which allow his method to operate.

This consideration loosens somewhat the stranglehold of doubt, although, as yet, no substantive certainties have emerged about anything beyond the mind and its thoughts.

4 The appeal to ordinary language

Philosophers spend a lot of time pointing out that people often say they *know* something, when in fact they don't. However, in everyday life we are happy to say that we are *certain* or that we *know*, for example, that grass is green, that dogs don't speak French, and that Everest is the tallest mountain on Earth, and we are rarely challenged when we do so. It is only philosophers who question our use of such words as 'know', and 'certain' in these and other contexts. They often claim that we need to refine our concepts of certainty and knowledge, and give them a philosophically strict meaning.

In the last century, however, so called 'ordinary-language philosophers' questioned this approach and in so doing hoped to find an alternative route to defeating the sceptic. So how does ordinary-language philosophy attempt to overcome scepticism?

To answer this question let's begin with the example of the term 'certainty'. Remember that the sceptic claims that I cannot be 'certain', just because I see a table before me, that there really is a table before me. The possibility that there exist Cartesian demons or mad scientists deceiving us shows, according to the sceptic, that we can never be certain about the nature or existence of the physical world. In other words, the sceptic argues that, because it is possible for me to be mistaken, I cannot be certain that I am not mistaken.

Notice, however, that in ordinary language the merest possibility of error does not warrant avoiding the use of the word 'certain'. For in everyday life we say we are certain of all kinds of things about which it is at least conceivable that we could be mistaken. For example, if in the ordinary course of things someone were to ask you if you are certain that there is a table before you, you would doubtless think she was joking. But if she were insistent that your certainty might be ill founded you might be led to make some straightforward checks. You might make sure that it was no hologram by rapping your finger against it; or you might pick it up to ensure that was indeed made of solid wood and not a fiendishly clever fake fashioned out of paper. Having conducted these tests you would – according to the ordinary use of the word – be quite justified in pronouncing yourself *certain* that this thing was indeed a table. For this is just the kind of situation in which the word 'certain' is typically used. If the sceptic insists that you still cannot be certain, even after these various checks have been made, then she is inviting us to buy into a radical departure from the way the word 'certain' is normally used.

What this shows is that the philosophical tradition uses the concept of certainty (and those of knowledge, doubt, etc.) in a different way from our ordinary usage. For Descartes, for example, certainty involves extremely strict criteria such that there could be no possibility of being mistaken. But, ordinarily speaking, to see a table is good enough reason for affirming that one is certain of its existence.

Having made this clear, the ordinary-language philosopher can now claim that traditional sceptical arguments only have force if we accept this departure from our ordinary usage of terms like 'certain'. But, the argument goes, the sceptic has given us no reason to accept this new usage. And if we continue to use language in the ordinary way, then the sceptical arguments lose their force. Instead of responding to the sceptic by trying to prove that we really are certain – even according to the new stricter definition of certainty – the ordinary language philosopher insists on keeping the old definition, and so can claim to be certain according to it.

But why should the ordinary usage of words like 'certain' be preferable? The ordinary-language philosopher claims that such words actually acquire their meaning from their use in everyday contexts. To rip them from those contexts and try to make them do work for which they are not designed is literally to start talking nonsense. Imagine trying to use the word *biscuit* to do the work of the word *the*. In doing so you very quickly start talking gobbledygook. And it's the same with philosophers who try to use words in the wrong way. In claiming to have grave doubts about the existence of physical objects, we have departed radically from ordinary usage of the word 'doubt' and in so doing we have raised confusions about how the word works. The sceptic is no longer talking about *doubt, certainty* and *knowledge,* but rather about some peculiar *philosophical* versions of them.

In sum, philosophical doubt, by trading on the mere possibility of being mistaken, has little to do with the original or proper meaning. And if we stick to the generally accepted understanding of the concept then the sceptic's argument is invalid. Part of the point here is that we have no reason to suppose that there is an evil demon deceiving us and so there is nothing to undermine the normal sense in which we can be certain. The mere possibility of a demon is not sufficient for it to be reasonable to doubt the existence of a world of physical objects. So it is just not true that I am not certain of something because it is possible that I am mistaken. If I can't be said to be certain that there is a table before me then 'certainty' would be meaningless. Since it is clearly not

■ Figure 4.14 Language goes on holiday

Words like 'doubt' or 'know' begin life as ordinary words used in ordinary contexts. When being used in these contexts – when they are at home getting on with their everyday work – everyone understands perfectly well how to use them, and no puzzles arise. However, when words like these are taken out of their ordinary context – when they are taken off 'on holiday' by unscrupulous philosophers – they are no longer able to do the work for which they are suited, and all sorts of confusions arise. The sceptic is no longer talking about the same thing when talking about 'knowledge' as what we are ordinarily talking about.

Ordinary language user

Philosopher

Here, the word 'doubt' is at home.

But here doubt has gone on holiday, which can lead to confusion.

meaningless then this must count as certain. It is senseless for the sceptic to press further on this matter, for she has misunderstood what being certain means.

Wittgenstein (see page 503) claimed that all manner of philosophical muddles could be avoided if only people paid more attention to how language works in ordinary contexts. Philosophical difficulties arise when, as he put it, language is allowed to go on holiday, that is, when terms become used in inappropriate ways (see Figure 4.14).

■ Certainty isn't everything

The quest for certainty can seem appealing. However, there is very little difference in the feelings accompanying my claiming to know that 2 plus 3 is 5, and my claiming to know that I am sitting in my chair now. One may be slightly more immune to philosophical doubt than the other, but this is hardly distinguishable in my mind and would not change the fact that I would claim to know both. Do I know them both?

The concept of knowledge is a disputed one. With similar evidence one person may be inclined to say they know a fact whereas another may be less so. Some people think that to truly know something you must be absolutely certain, whereas others are less strict. Either way you should note that most philosophers, and non-philosophers for that matter, do not equate knowledge with certainty. To know something, they claim, does not require you to be absolutely certain. It is worth remembering this because when we consider sceptical arguments we can have a tendency to search for certainty as a way of overcoming them, and this, in turn, can lead to a tendency to think that to know something you must be absolutely certain of it. But these tendencies can be avoided.

If you can be 100 per cent certain of something then you must, indeed, know it. But it does not then follow that in order to know something you must be 100 per cent certain of it. To claim this would be to take a particular stance on the nature of knowledge: a stance that would mean that the human race as a whole knew very little at all.

Conceptual schemes

Introduction

Lord Macauley once recorded in his diary a memorable attempt – his first and apparently his last – to read Kant's Critique.

'I received today a translation of Kant . . . I tried to read it but found it utterly unintelligible, just as if it had been

written in Sanskrit. Not one word of it gave me anything like an idea except a Latin quotation from Persius.'
... What sort of writing was it that Macauley was called upon to read? I quote a single fairly typical sentence:
'Because a certain form of sensuous intuition exists in the mind a priori *which rests on the receptivity of the representative faculty, the understanding, as a spontaneity, is able to determine the internal sense by means of the diversity of given representations, conformably to the synthetical unity of the apperception of the manifold of sensuous intuition* a priori, *as the condition to which must necessarily be submitted all objects of human intuition.'*[19]

Immanuel Kant is generally considered to be one of the greatest philosophers of all time. Unfortunately, as the quote above illustrates, his masterpiece, the *Critique of Pure Reason*, is formidably hard to understand. Part of the complexity is due to the new terminology that Kant introduced, but also to Kant's convoluted style. Indeed, the density of his style is such that it is said that some German scholars actually prefer to read his work in the English translation.

Kant's work has implications for the *tabula rasa* theory and the claim that deductive reasoning can only yield analytic truths. However to see these implications we will need to take a brief journey into some of the ideas within the *Critique*.

The *tabula rasa* revisited

Let us start by revisiting the *tabula rasa* thesis. Is the idea that all of our concepts and ideas are derived from our senses really believable? The eighteenth-century French philosopher Condillac (1715–1780), a disciple of Locke, certainly believed so, and tried to prove it through a thought experiment. He asked his readers to imagine a statue that is organised like a human on the inside but devoid of any sensations. In his book *A Treatise of Sensations* (1756), Condillac described the process whereby the statue experiences a series of sensations and is brought from having no ideas at all to forming concepts and acquiring beliefs about itself and the world around it. Is this believable?

ACTIVITY   Imagine a human-sized statute. It is made of marble and at the moment can't let any sensations in. Then imagine that we add the five senses and place basic structures inside the head, for example the statute now has a memory and can store copies of the sensations it starts to receive.

1 Would this statue eventually be able to develop all the concepts you have? Can you think of any concepts that would be beyond a being who was confined to sensation alone?

2 Could the statue develop into a being with a fully fledged belief system like your own? What problems would it face? Are there things you believe or know that such a statue could not?

Some would argue that Condillac's whole approach is doomed. The statue would just receive a flow of uninterpreted sensations: noises, shapes, colours and tastes. But to begin to form concepts, the statue would have, at the very least, to recognise that two sensations are similar. How could it do this without a prior concept of similarity? In order to compare and contrast, for example, we need common features, such as size or quantity or speed with which to compare the different sensations. But how are these concepts to arise in the first place if we have no prior way of categorising and storing the information? Would the statue be able even to recall its ideas if some form of classification had not taken place first?

To explore the problem further, consider an analogy with a storage system in an office. Imagine you have just got a new job in a busy office. The workers in the office (representing the senses) generate lots of complicated letters, files, faxes and correspondence. Your job is to file these away (a process akin to that of the mind turning impressions into ideas). For the purposes of this analogy, imagine too that you are quite forgetful and have a poor memory (as otherwise we will end up using your memory to explain the memory system of the office). The office has no prior system for filing and will not let you set one up. All you can do is place the files in the drawers in the order they were given to you. Two months later, thousands of pieces of paper fill umpteen drawers. Suppose you were then asked to retrieve a particular letter. How would you go about it with no system to guide you?

Most would say that in these circumstances you wouldn't be able to find the letter. But isn't this what we were asking of the statue? If the statue just receives raw data, how is it to recognise and store these data without having some prior classification system in place? How could the statue use the concepts it had acquired from its experience to think without there being a system for organising them or without any common classifications of the sensations to think about?

Many would reject this approach. Human beings are not like Condillac's statue and the mind is not like a *tabula rasa*. Rather the mind at birth is at least partially formed and has a structure or architecture that enables it to make sense of the raw sense data it receives.

It seems that to make sense of experience some system of classification of sense impressions – some conceptual scheme – is necessary. Where might such a scheme come from? For Condillac any conceptual organisation must originate in experience *a posteriori* and perhaps the obvious place to look for a system which labels, organises and categorises experience is language. Certainly the development of a complex network of beliefs about the world, including beliefs about the past and future of the sort enjoyed by adults relies on the possession of a vast array of concepts that depend on language. For this reason Condillac was interested to uncover the origins of language and attempted to show how the mind would be able to develop a system of signs by which to transform raw sensation into organised experience and ultimately developed thought. The task of the empiricist must be to show how we can generate a language to organise experience out of that very experience. But the difficulty is that it is hard to see how we can begin to organise the data of sense if we don't already have some means of doing so which precede experience. If I don't already possess a conceptual scheme with which to organise my experience, then the data of our senses will remain confused.

No experience without categorisation

Earlier we discussed whether it was possible to experience raw sense impressions prior to any classification by the mind. William James proposed that such an undifferentiated stream of sensations would be a 'blooming, buzzing confusion'. One suggestion was that there is no such thing as a simple sense impression that we experience directly. The very act of experiencing the sense impression is an act of interpreting. It is not a question of a 'given' or set experience that we then interpret, but rather the interpretation is already required for anything to enter into experience. This amounts to saying that there is no such thing as a 'fixed' world that we all experience; the world as we experience it necessarily involves an act of interpretation by the mind (see pages 485–87).

One consequence of this claim is that the human mind must have some sort conceptual scheme already in place in order for any data received by the body to be classed as an experience of some kind. So the very possibility of having experiences at all depends upon us possessing some conceptual apparatus from the beginning, which is to say innately. If this is the case then not all of our concepts can be derived from sense experience as some must have existed in order for anything to count as an experience in the first place.

This is more or less the claim made by Immanuel Kant. As we saw above (on page 279), he claimed that 'Thoughts without content are empty; intuitions without concepts are blind' and suggested that there is no such thing as sense experience that is raw or uncategorised. (Kant uses the term *intuition* to mean roughly the same thing as an *impression* but we will stick with Hume's terminology for the sake of consistency.) Kant argued this by claiming that having a concept in place is a precondition of any experience. As we saw above, this is a transcendental argument as it seeks to suggest that something is necessary for the possibility of something else.

For Kant this is not a conscious process, and so is to be contrasted with the sort of classification or conceptual scheme that we develop through experience *a posteriori*. For example, after tasting some food we might subsequently classify the experience in various ways – tasty, exotic or expensive. These ways may vary from individual to individual and from culture to culture. Indeed it is often suggested that speakers of different languages conceive their worlds differently because of the difference in the concepts behind their language. To some extent, learning a language is learning how to classify the world: for example, 'we call *these* sense experiences snow and *these* ones slush' and such conceptual schemes are probably derived from experience.

Kant is not talking about these types of concept. Rather, he suggests that there are fundamental categories that are applied to the raw data we receive and these combine to give us our sense experience of the world. This process is carried out automatically by the mind and, he suggests, must happen for any mind to have an experience of the world. These categories are *a priori* as they are not derived from experience. Indeed they are the precondition of any experience happening in the first place.

Some categories are not derived from experience

So what are these categories that are not derived from experience? Well, we have met one of them already. Hume points out that we do not derive our concept of causation from any specific sense experience. When we stop and carefully think about it we only see one ball approach another, hear a sound and then see another ball move. We do not see any sense impression that might be termed a cause. Hume then suggests that the idea of cause arises when we repeatedly see events following from other events. He suggests that our idea of cause is brought about by a habit of the mind through experience and so is developed *a posteriori*.

Kant agrees that our idea of cause is not derived from any particular impression. However, he argues that causation is one of the categories by which the raw data from the world are turned into an intelligible experience in the mind. Causation is one of the *a priori* concepts needed for any experience to occur. Because of this we cannot help but view the world as a sequence of causes and effects rather than a series of unconnected events with nothing tying them together. We experience the world as causal because the data from the world has been categorised using the concept of cause. The concept of cause is a necessary part of our conceptual scheme and without it our experience of the world would be unintelligible; it would not form part of a coherent structure.

We discuss in Chapter 7 the view that the concept of matter or material substance is also not derived directly from our sense experience. We experience colours, sounds, tastes, smells and textures but do not actually perceive matter itself. Matter is what is assumed to be lurking behind all of these impressions. The fact that we do not directly perceive matter can be seen in the thought experiment of the brain in a vat, which suggests that our experiences might not be caused by matter itself, but by a computer. If we could perceive matter directly then this thought experiment would not work. So for empiricists such as Condillac it would always be problematic to explain the origin of our concept of matter as distinct from our sense impressions. How can it be derived from experience if there can be no impression of it? Indeed these considerations lead some philosophers – IDEALISTS – to give up on the concept of matter completely. Kant agrees that the concept of matter is not directly derived from any one sense impression; however, at the same time we undeniably perceive that world as being filled with material objects, and, as with causation, this is because our mind categorises the raw data with the concept of substance. Once more without this our experience of the world would be, in part, unintelligible.

For Kant these are the categories by which the mind organises the raw data and so makes experience possible:

a) Categories of quantity: Unity, Plurality, Totality
b) Categories of quality: Reality, Negation, Limitation
c) Categories of relation: Substance and Accident, Causality and Dependence, Community or Interaction
d) Categories of modality: Possibility–Impossibility, Existence–Non-existence, Necessity–Contingency

This is quite a complex looking list and you do not need to come to grips with it all for the purposes of understanding the essential thrust of Kant's argument. None the less, we will pause here to examine one further example, the concept of unity. The modern scientific view of the world is of a huge mass of energy constantly shifting and changing. However, we do not perceive the world like this: we perceive an ordered world with objects made of matter that cause events. And part of this order is because our minds impose the category of unity on our perceptions. To see how this might work, consider how a computer perceives the world.

Computers are very good at doing some things we tend to find very difficult, such as playing chess or finding square roots. However, computers have a great deal of difficulty in doing something that we find automatic, such as perceiving objects in the world. For example, I am looking now at a table in front of me and can clearly pick out the objects resting on the top and can easily distinguish these objects from the table itself. The computer reading information from a digital camera does not know where the coffee cup begins and where the table ends or even that they are separate objects; and programming a computer to recognise such things is proving very difficult indeed. Many websites, to stop computers from automatically registering in place of real people, use this very difficulty as the basis of their security measures. You may be familiar with being asked to key in the hidden word in images like this.

■ Figure 4.15

A human finds the word easy to pick out, whereas a computer with dedicated software finds this difficult

The point of such measures is that humans find it very easy to see the word and this ensures that each registration is carried out by a human typing on a keyboard, rather than by an automated computer program. This works because the computer does not 'perceive' the picture as a series of distinct letters on a background of scratches. It simply perceives a series of marks and blanks and has great difficult in picking out the letters, let alone the word. This shows that a conceptual scheme is required for the way we experience our sense impressions. Our perception is altered because we have the concept of a letter and so experience the image as a word. Our concept of letter has changed the experience we have. Of course, the concept of letter is empirical. It is derived from experience but Kant's point is even more fundamental; the concept of letter can only be formed in the first place because we already innately possess the category of unity, which is the idea that there are discrete entities separate from other entities. Without this idea, our experiences of the world would, in part, be unintelligible.

In addition to the categories above, there are two more important features that the mind adds to the raw data in order to make an experience. *Space*, Kant claims, is the form of our outer impressions, meaning everything we experience of the physical world is automatically in space. The events we experience in our mind, such as happiness, or memory, are non-spatial as the concept of space is not applied in these cases. However, these do occur in time, and so *time* is the form that all impressions, both inner and outer, are bound by.

One final way of helping to understand Kant's claim is to consider how different the five senses really are. (Please note that this is not a point that Kant actually makes, more a way of helping to understand his theory). We have five different senses but yet are able to merge all of these into a single conscious experience of the world. How is this possible? Sounds have nothing in common with smells or colours; they are different sorts of things entirely. There is no overlap in their features that could enable us to combine them into a single experience. Why then don't we have five separate consciousnesses each revealing a different aspect of the world (like a security guard having five different monitor systems each picking up a different sense)? One possible way of explaining this is to see that the unity of consciousness is enabled by these *a priori* categories. Sight, sound, tastes and so on are linked via the common concepts of substance, causation and unity and so on, and by the forms of space and time. It is these concepts that provide the glue that enables the different senses of the world to stick together and form a single unified experience.

Copernican revolution

Through these considerations a Kantian theory of perception emerges. Look around the space you are in now and try to soak up the experience for a few moments. Now consider what Kant is really saying. He is suggesting that some aspects of this scene that you are experiencing have been added by your mind. Your brain has taken the raw data and applied various forms and categories and the result is what you are experiencing now.

To the casual observer when looking at the room it may appear as if you are peering out at the world and seeing it as it is. For many reasons this naïve realist approach for perception is not a workable theory. (See Chapter 7 for a fuller account of different theories of perception.) We know from basic science that the idea of peering out is wrong. Light bounces off objects and enters your eyes and so when you put your hand in front of your eyes this does not stop you peering *out* at the world, rather it stops the light from entering *in*. Now, if this is the case, then we have to acknowledge that the information that reaches our eyes is somehow processed by the brain to produce our perception and this producing alters the information that you receive. The world you are now experiencing is a result of raw data plus the processing of the brain. This much is fairly uncontroversial. However, this scientific account generates a two-world view of perception. There is the world that causes the data to reach our brain (the real world) and there is the world we experience after our brains have done some processing (the perceptual world).

What Kant is attempting to do is to articulate the ways in which the mind must categorise and structure the data in order for an intelligible experience to occur. In doing this Kant is likewise proposing a two-world view. There is the world itself – which Kant calls the *noumenal* world – and there is the world we experience – which Kant calls the *phenomenal* world (see Figure 4.16).

■ **Figure 4.16 The mind structures the experience of the world**

Kant noted that the way in which we observe the world is organised by our sensory and cognitive apparatus. The way our sense organs and our brains arrange the data they receive determines how we perceive the world. This means we cannot hope to know the world as it is in itself, but only describe the structural conditions under which it appears.

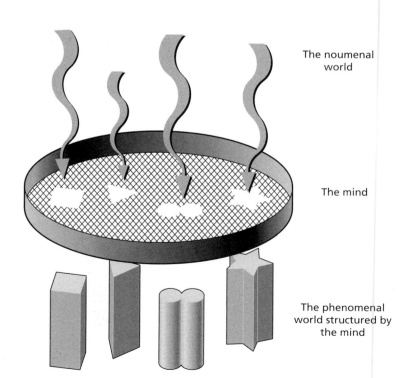

The noumenal world

The mind

The phenomenal world structured by the mind

Figure 4.17
The Copernican revolution

It appears that the sun is going round the earth (a) but this illusion is caused by the earth spinning; in fact the earth is going round the sun (b). For Kant, his account of the reality that we perceive requires a similar mental switch. It appears as if we perceive a given world and derive our concepts from it. However, Kant suggests that it is in fact our concepts that create the world we perceive. Our concepts do not conform to the world – instead, it is the world that conforms to our concepts.

(a)   (b)

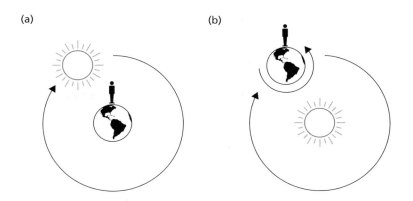

To reiterate the point: what you now perceive, the world around you, has been structured by your mind. Imagine there are four other people with you in the same room. It is tempting to think of you all peering out of your eyes and looking at the same room. However, in Kant's version, in five different people's minds five different rooms are projected, each of which has been structured, in part, by the individual's mind. However, the basic structures in each mind will be the same, as Kant claimed these were the preconditions of all conscious experience.

Kant regarded the significance of this claim as profound and termed it his Copernican revolution in philosophy. Copernicus was a Polish astronomer and one of the first in the modern era to argue that the earth revolves around the sun, rejecting the orthodox earth-centred view of the universe. Such a concept revolutionised the way we think of the world. Every day we talk of the sun rising and going down, and to the observer it does indeed appear that the sun is travelling around the earth. However, Copernicus suggested

Figure 4.18
Kant's Copernican revolution

It appears as if we perceive the world and derive our concepts from it. For Kant, however, our mind structures the world according to our concepts.

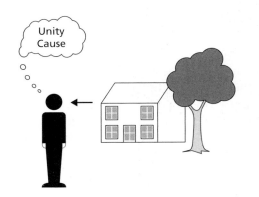

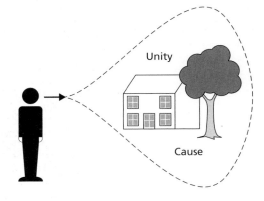

(a)   We derive our concepts from the world   (b)   Our concepts shape our world

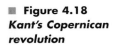

this is not true: rather, it is the earth that is going round the sun, and the spinning of the earth gives rise to the illusion of the sun moving. In some senses nothing has changed for the observer, but in another sense everything has changed. The Copernican revolution involves a switch in understanding whereby our view of the universe changes forever.

Kant's proof

more difficult

Kant's attempt to prove that the categories must exist in order for experience to exist are highly complex and quite questionable, and yet we can leave the details of these arguments aside without losing sight of the essence of his approach.

Kant argues that for our experiences to count as knowledge there must be self-consciousness, which in turn requires thought, which itself is the application of rules to content, which in turn require the categories.

As a specific example, Kant argues that the category of substance is needed for intelligible experience. His argument runs roughly like this: I am aware of myself existing in time. A precondition of this is that I have changing impressions (inner and outer). However, simply having changing impressions alone would not allow me to distinguish myself in time as I would not be able to distinguish myself from my thoughts. So an idea is required of an enduring substance that can remain the same throughout change. This enables me to distinguish myself when moving in relation to an unchanging substance (a bit like being a raft on a river – you need the unmoving bank to be aware that you are in fact moving with the river).

Kant

In other words, the awareness of my existence is at the same time an immediate awareness of the existence of other things outside me.[20]

So the concept of an enduring substance, argues Kant, is a precondition of being aware of the self in time. Such transcendental arguments are obscure and difficult to follow. However, Kant provides other supporting evidence for his claims. The Greek philosopher Aristotle some two thousand years earlier suggested that there were ten different ways in which we can speak about the world. All sentences are analysable in terms of ten basic categories. For example, consider the following sentences:

The cat pushed the ball.
John hit Kevin.

Both sentences can be seen as having the form that a *substance* carried out an *action* to another *substance* and so are of the same basic type. In the same way, the following sentences:

> The cat sat on the blue mat.
> John was by the old tree.

are of the same category in that they are both saying that a *substance* is in a *spatial relation* to another *substance* that has a *quality*.

This is quite a profound thought – that we can analyse all sentences using just ten basic categories. Kant claimed there was a reason for this, which was that these categories are the basic ways in which the mind categorises the world prior to experience. (Note that for Kant there were 14 ways, 12 categories plus the forms of space and time, so he disagreed slightly with Aristotle.)

■ Summary

So Kant suggests that it is impossible to experience raw sense impressions. Impressions can only be experienced after the mind has applied basic concepts, our innate conceptual scheme, which make the experience intelligible. Kant thought that we could work out what these categories were through a series of transcendental deductions, and it turns out that these categories were more or less the same as the ones Aristotle suggested are needed to explain all sentences. In explaining the basic concepts underpinning all sentences Aristotle is also explaining the basic concepts underpinning our thoughts – as sentences are the expressions of these thoughts. Likewise Kant is explaining the fundamental ways in which we categorise the world – all subsequent categorisation will be subsets of these more basic sets. So once again he is explaining the basic concepts of thoughts, and these should be the same as Aristotle's.

We will now turn to the implications of these ideas for the *tabula rasa* theory and the claim that deductive reasoning can only yield analytic truths.

Synthetic *a priori*

Kant was raised in the rationalist tradition, assuming that reason could provide truths about the world. However, he was awoken from his 'dogmatic slumbers' upon reading Hume, and was particularly puzzled by Hume's claim that we cannot have knowledge of the world which can be acquired *a priori*. Hume's argument was that all *a priori* truths are analytic; meaning that the only thoughts that deductive reasoning alone can establish are those that are true by definition. They can be recognised as true independently of experience only because they are tautological, and so don't go beyond unpacking the definitions of the terms they use. A proposition such as 'All bachelors are unmarried' can be recognised as true simply by analysing the meanings of the terms involved, in other words it can be reduced to saying that 'All unmarried men are unmarried'. Such propositions cannot tell us anything new or anything about the world of experience precisely because they can only inform us about the meanings of terms.

It was in fact Immanuel Kant who introduced the terms 'analytic' and 'synthetic' to describe two categories of propositions. Kant divided propositions into two parts, the subject and the predicate. The subject part is the thing the proposition is about. For example, in 'All bachelors are unmarried' the subject term is 'All bachelors'. The predicate is the part of the proposition which tells you about the subject. In this case, the predicate is 'are unmarried'. Now Kant defined analytic propositions as those for which the predicate is 'contained within' the subject, by which he meant that analysis of the meaning of the predicate would reveal that it was already there in the subject.

For this reason the truth of an analytic proposition can be established *a priori* since one need do no more than analyse the meanings of the terms involved. Synthetic propositions, by contrast, are those where the predicate is not contained within the subject and so they cannot be known to be true by analysis alone. Their truth, therefore, depends on the way the world happens to be. For example, we would not be able to establish the truth of the proposition 'All bachelors are untidy' by analysing the meanings of the words involved, and so we have to appeal to experience. Knowledge of synthetic propositions therefore can only be established *a posteriori*.

This, then, gives us the following picture of different types of proposition and how they can be known.

	A posteriori	**A priori**
Analytic	✗	✓
Synthetic	✓	✗

Analytic propositions are knowable *a priori* and not *a posteriori*, and synthetic propositions are knowable only *a posteriori* and cannot be established *a priori*. This view is often known as Hume's Law and is a central plank of much empiricist thinking from Hume's time and into the twentieth century. To say that synthetic *a priori* knowledge is impossible means that we cannot discover substantive truths about the world by the use of reason alone.

Kant's efforts to clarify this point, however, were ultimately in the service of an attempt to question it. He wanted to establish that synthetic *a priori* knowledge is possible. He wanted to show that we could establish truths about the world, using reason, that were not simply true by definition. For example, Hume claimed that we cannot know *a priori* that every event has a cause; we only work out so-called causes by seeing events which regularly follow other events. Kant, however, claimed that we could know *a priori* that every event has a cause. This is not true by definition. It is not part of the meaning of the word 'event' that it is something which must be caused. But this, for Kant, is an example of a synthetic judgement that can be known *a priori*. How did he hope to show that such synthetic judgements were *a priori*?

As we have seen, Kant attempted to turn the empiricist approach on its head. Rather than ask the traditional question of how we can come to know that our understanding of the world accurately reflects reality, he claimed that reality reflects our understanding. What we can know of the world is not a simple matter of passively receiving sense impressions; the mind actively orders our experience and so gives it the particular structure it has. If he could unearth this structure Kant could establish substantive truths about the way experience must be organised, truths which would be necessarily true of the world as it appears to us.

Now, as we have seen, Kant explored what the conditions for the possibility of our experience might be. Such an investigation can be conducted *a priori*, by analysing experience and working out what has to be the case in order for us to enjoy the type of experience that we do. And if such analysis can unearth transcendental conditions which are necessary for experience to occur at all, then these conditions might tell us something substantive about the world as we conceive it; it would, in other words, establish certain synthetic *a priori* truths.

So we can know *a priori* that every event has a cause because we know that we must experience the world causally. We know that every object is a substance because we are bound to experience the world consisting of substance. As an analogy, imagine you have a black and white TV. Now you don't know for sure what picture you will see when you turn on the TV, as the schedules may change, for example. However, you do know that whatever you see will be in black and white as this is the way that the TV has structured the experience. This you can know *a priori*.

In the same way, for Kant it was possible to know things about the world (or the way we perceive the world) that are not true by definition (synthetic) but could be discovered by reason alone by transcendental arguments (*a priori*). In this way Kant could overcome the scepticism of Hume concerning causation, since, by uncovering the way we structure our experiences, for example causally, we can then be sure that every event we experience will be a causal one.

Consider the following passage:

Suppose your car stalls every time you stop. You bring it into the car repair shop, and when you return the repairman tells you he hasn't fixed it.
'Why not?' you ask.
'There isn't any reason why it's stalling,' he replies.
'You mean, you haven't found the cause?' you say, getting annoyed.
'No, I've taken everything apart and examined it very carefully,' he says. 'There isn't any cause for that stalling.'
At this point you should find a different repairman. You think that something must be causing that stalling; he simply hasn't found it. Why do you think this? Not because you know more about cars than he does. It's because you think that everything has a cause.[21]

Can you think of something happening without a cause, even a hidden cause?

It is not easy to do, although it may be possible. However, this does not really undermine Kant's point. We may, upon reflection, be able to imagine something without a cause, but this is not how we experience the world. Our experience is of a world where events cause other events, even if the cause is sometimes hidden.

▶ criticism ◀ **Does Kant really prove his theory?**

Kant's argumentation is obscure and hard to follow. It is certainly not clear that he succeeds in establishing the existence of the 12 categories as preconditions of experience.

Indeed subsequent philosophers have disagreed about the nature of the categories – Schopenhauer, for example, claimed that we only needed causation and substance. On a similar point, Peter Strawson argued that it is perfectly possible to imagine having experiences of the world without some of the Kantian categories. For example, he articulates what an understanding of the world without the form of space might be like and suggests that this is intelligible. If so, Kant can't claim that the form of space is a necessary condition of all conscious experience. Indeed it is hard to see how Kant can argue anything beyond what might be the case in his own mind. As he does not have access to other minds, he cannot really be certain that he is articulating the preconditions for all intelligible experience.

Does Kant's *a priori* knowledge apply to the real world?

We only know *a priori* certain features of the world as we perceive it, not as it really is. Since we receive data and then the mind adds the categories, we cannot know that our concepts apply to the real world. As such, Kant cannot claim that we can *have a priori* knowledge of the real world, only of the world we perceive.

Much depends on which we call the real world. The world that our mind receives the data from is called the *noumenal* world by Kant. Kant also refers to the noumenal world as 'things-in-themselves' as opposed to 'things as they appear'. What we perceive, which he terms the *phenomenal* world, has been processed by the mind. This post-processed world is all we have access to. We can never perceive the noumenal world and so the categories themselves, as far as we know, only apply to the world as we perceive it – the world of causes and substances etc.

For example, it is tempting to think that the *objects* in the noumenal world *cause* our sensations. However, can we really say this? After all, the concept of causation is a concept that (as far as we can know) applies only to the world of sense experience. It is only within our experience that we observe one event causing another, but we can't observe the real world causing the perceived world, nor can we suppose the real world exhibits causal relations at all. The same applies to space and time. All of our sensations appear to us in space and time, but we cannot know whether the real world is spatio-temporal. We, of course, can't imagine what a world would be like that did not involve space, time or causality. But that is to be expected, since we can only understand and imagine the world of our experience. The real world lies totally beyond our comprehension. We shouldn't even call it a world at all. We should say nothing about it whatsoever. Kant suggests that we should call the world we experience – the phenomenal world – the real world, as this is the world we inhabit and is the only world of which we can meaningfully speak. In this sense he claims that we can have synthetic *a priori* knowledge of the real world, but only by redefining what the real world is.

The world as it is in itself, independently of our perception of it, is not something we can have any knowledge of anyway since knowledge is confined to what it is possible to experience. Human enquiry, in other words, is delimited by our conceptual scheme and we cannot think outside of this conceptual scheme.

Science disproves Euclidean geometry

Kant's arguments offer an interesting explanation of why mathematics and geometry seem to apply so well to the world. This is because they are derived from the categories that our minds apply to the world. So naturally space will have certain features as these are the features that the mind imposes. Kant also argues that mathematical propositions are not analytic, so they count as synthetic *a priori* knowledge. Focusing on geometry, however, it seems that science has disproved Kant's claims.

Is science exploring the phenomenal world or the noumenal world? There is no easy answer to this. Interestingly the concepts we apply to the phenomenal world seem to break down in the world of quantum mechanics. It is not clear that the concept of object or even cause meaningfully apply to sub-atomic particles. To some extent this would prove Kant's point – which is that the concepts only apply to the world of appearance, and not to theories that go beyond this. However, it also appears that the world we experience is not Euclidean (see above) although it does appear that way to us in the scale at which we can observe things. So Kant's claims that we can have synthetic *a priori* knowledge of Euclidean geometry is not true.

Kant's legacy

Kant's idea that experience has to be organised by some set of pre-existing concepts, or 'conceptual scheme', in order for it to have any form and so be intelligible has been extremely influential. Later thinkers have reflected on whether there is just one set of concepts common to all humanity, or whether the way different cultures and periods in history conceive the world might be governed by distinct conceptual schemes. Such schemes are not innate or part of our biology, but are acquired as we learn how to classify elements of our experience according to the framework used by the culture we are born into. On this way of thinking the way we cut the world up or codify the flux of sense experience is a function of our conceptual scheme and is not imposed upon us by the way the world is. So the types of things we are capable of noticing in the world are as much a product of our culture as of the nature of reality.

One consequence of this is that people operating with different conceptual schemes will have different views about what kinds of things there are in the world and how they fit together. In one culture certain things will be regarded as important and so will have a rich vocabulary relating to them, meaning that people from that culture will make fine distinctions which would be lost on people from another culture. The example often used to illustrate this point is that peoples from the arctic have many words for snow, whereas in English there is just one. Where English speakers see just one kind of white stuff, it is claimed, Inuits perceive a whole range.

Different conceptual schemes are normally thought to be the product of different languages. This idea is given expression in the so-called Sapir-Whorf hypothesis, which is that the grammatical structure and vocabulary of the language you speak determines how you structure experience. The American linguist Benjamin Whorf (1897–1941) formulated this hypothesis studying the American Hopi Indians who have no words for time, past and future, and speculated that they must therefore have radically different conceptions and experience of time from English speakers.[22]

The idea that language delimits what it is possible for us to think finds literary expression in George Orwell's dystopian vision in *1984*. In the novel the government has introduced a new vocabulary, called Newspeak, which eliminates words which might enable people to think of subversive thoughts. If there are no words for 'oppression' or 'revolution' then the people won't notice they are being oppressed or think of rebelling. Orwell's concerns about our thoughts being controlled by our political masters through restricting our vocabulary depend on the view that language completely determines what it is possible to think. However, while it is clear that language has an influence on thought it is far from obvious that it constrains what we can think in the way Orwell and Whorf imagine.

In the philosophy of science the idea of conceptual schemes has also had a significant impact. Thomas Kuhn (1922–1996) famously argued that scientists in a given field operate within a theoretical framework or 'paradigm' – in other words a conceptual scheme – which determines their world view, the kinds of questions that they ask and the sorts of experiments they conduct.[23] Scientists operating within different paradigms find it difficult – if not impossible – to communicate with each other because the ways in which they understand the world are radically different. And yet paradigms can often explain and make sense of the experimental data equally well; it's just that they explain them in very different ways. Scientific revolutions occur when one paradigm gives way to a new one, as for example when Einstein's physics took over from Newton's or Copernicus' sun-centred model of the planetary system took over from the earth-centred model.

This way of thinking readily leads to the idea that two different languages might be incompatible in the sense that we can never translate concepts of one into those of the other. This claim in its most radical form implies that different people's view of the world may be so radically different that there can be no basis for them to communicate; they would appear almost literally to inhabit different worlds. Such 'conceptual relativism' threatens to lead into an extreme scepticism about the possibility of any objective or true interpretation of the world since it suggests that there is no basis for determining which if any conceptual schemes are an accurate representation of reality.

The idea of conceptual schemes, as well as the conceptual relativism it seems to invite, were the subject of much critical attention in the latter part of the last century with important arguments being put forward to reject the very idea.[24] Nonetheless Kant's insight, which for the first time put our own faculties under the spotlight in order to examine the way we perceive and understand our world, has been one of revolutionary significance and one which continues to attract considerable philosophical attention.

Key points: Chapter 4

What you need to know about **reason and experience:**

1 The idea of *tabula rasa* is that our minds are born as 'blank slates' and that all subsequent ideas and knowledge must come from experience. This view is associated with a branch of philosophy known as empiricism.
2 The empiricists claim that all of our ideas, both simple and complex, must be derived from our sense impressions of the world.

3 Hume claims that ideas that don't relate to sense impressions should be treated with suspicion. On a similar note, logical positivists claim that propositions, to be meaningful, must be hypothetically verifiable.

4 Foundationalism is the claim that our knowledge must be based on a set of foundational beliefs that themselves cannot be questioned. The empiricist version of foundationalism claims that our sense impressions are indubitable and so form a bedrock that the rest of our knowledge can be inferred from.

5 The claims of the empiricist philosophy are open to a host of criticisms including the claims that:

- some ideas can't be traced back to impressions
- our knowledge of the world cannot be safely inferred from impressions as we don't know with certainty what causes the impressions, for example we could be brains in a vat
- impressions require classifying in order to be understood and that this may mean that they are either no longer so certain, and can be mistaken, or that, before classification, they are not the sorts of things that can be meaningfully called 'certain' in the first place.

6 An innate idea is one that is not derived from experience, and the existence of such ideas would undermine the *tabula rasa* principle. There are a variety of ideas which different philosophers have claimed are innate.

7 The truths of mathematics would seem be strong candidates for examples of innate knowledge of the world. The empiricist, however, can claim that such truths do not add to our knowledge of the world. They are either true by definition and not about the world or they are the deduced implications of truths that are already known through experience.

8 Rationalist philosophers have sought to establish other truths, independently of the senses, through reason. Descartes, for example, establishes the *cogito* – which proves that he exists.

9 Beyond the *cogito* there seems little that can be found out about the world via reason alone. One suggestion is that this is because the truths of the world are synthetic and that *a priori* we can only establish analytic truths.

10 The amount we can know for certain seems limited. However, various arguments suggest that this body of certain knowledge can be extended beyond the realm of introspection and the analytic or tautological.

11 Kant claims that experience is only possible because the mind categorises the raw data in certain ways. A conceptual scheme is a set of concepts which organise experience. He claims that if we can work out the ways in which the mind categorises the data then we can know *a priori* how the world will appear to us. In this way he claims that we can have synthetic *a priori* knowledge.

5 The debate over free will and determinism

Introduction

I think I know the delights of freedom.[1]

Charles Dickens

More precious than all worldly riches is freedom.[2]

Walt Whitman

The feeling of freedom can be an overwhelming experience. When it fully hits us, as it does every now and then on our journeys to death, it is intoxicating; as the American poet Walt Whitman puts it 'I have felt to soar in freedom and in the fullness of power, joy, volition.'[3] Freedom brings with it the opening up of our futures, liberation from our past, the sense that anything is possible, that living is a wondrous thing. It can also be an unsettling and fearful experience, one that we wish to avoid so that we can continue in our safe lives, doing the same thing we have always done, without having to consider the possibility that we are free to leave our jobs suddenly, to give up college, to walk out on our families. But freedom is something rarely felt. More often than not we find ourselves on 'automatic pilot', slotted into a routine, compelled to eat, to sleep, to watch television, unable to escape our rut. Worryingly, like badly programmed machines, we seem to make the same mistakes we've always done, to choose the same things we've always chosen, to repeat ourselves, to think the same thoughts over and over again, and to have preferences, desires, even addictions, that we can't seem to shake. So, what are we: Are we free? Are we machines? Or are we something in between (although what type of thing that could be is hard to imagine, as freedom seems to be something you either have or don't have – it doesn't admit of degrees.)

The debate over FREE WILL and DETERMINISM is a classic problem of philosophy. Sometimes philosophy is accused of discussing matters that seem far removed from ordinary experience or everyday concerns. However, in this debate one of the central features of human existence is under scrutiny. The different answers to this question seem to put forward starkly contrasting views of what it is to be human. On the one hand, it is possible to view humans merely as complex machines operating with no more freedom than say that of a snooker ball. On the other hand, the human spirit can be seen as transcending the physical world, free from the laws of nature. Between these two extremes there are many other views of human nature, all depending on the answer taken to the debate over free will and determinism.

Whether we are free or not matters. It makes a difference to how we approach our lives, whether we attempt to reinvent ourselves, or whether we try to analyse our pasts for clues as to what our futures will bring. It makes a difference as to whether we hold criminals responsible for their actions, or whether we treat them as malfunctioning machines who could not avoid acting the way they did. Free will and determinism is a significant philosophical problem in its own right, but it also raises questions in several different areas of philosophy, for example:

- Metaphysical questions such as: what is the nature of causation? And what is the nature of the human mind?
- Moral questions such as: can we really ever blame anyone for their actions?
- Questions about the theory of language: what is the meaning of the word 'free'?

The breadth of topics covered makes this an excellent area to study in an introduction to the world of philosophy. This chapter examines these issues as they arise from each of the following questions:

1 What is determinism?
2 What is free will?
2 What are the implications of determinism?

One of the hardest things with the debate about freedom, as with most philosophical debates, is determining exactly what it is about. To do this we will first try to establish what the debate is *not* about – it is not about political freedom.

Political freedom

Most of the time when the word 'freedom' is used in literature, in the media or in everyday speech it is referring to political freedom. This is the freedom to go about your daily business unimpeded by others and in particular by the state: for example, the freedom to smoke outdoors, or the freedom to travel on a bus. Different countries allow different amounts of freedom. Some countries allow alcohol to be drunk whereas other countries don't. The types of freedom citizens should have is often hotly debated in the media, with the political parties all offering different suggestions on different issues. However this is *not* the kind of freedom that we are primarily discussing in this chapter. We are concerned with a different kind of freedom, sometimes called metaphysical freedom.

Consider a man in each of the following situations, and then answer the questions below.

1 He is living in England with no criminal convictions.
2 He is living in England but has a driving ban and his passport withheld.
3 He is living in an open prison.
4 He is in prison, but is confined to his cell.
5 He is in prison, confined to his cell and strapped to his chair

For each situation:
a) Consider what can the man do, and what he can't do.
b) Do you think the man is free, or not free?
c) What is it that determines whether the man is free?

We can see in each of these successive instances that the number of available options that a person is at liberty to do seems to decrease in each case. This means that the amount of *political freedom* diminishes, meaning the freedom to go about your business unimpeded by obstacles or restrictions. Here, the term 'political' isn't being used simply in relation to party politics and voting in general elections; its meaning is far more fundamental. Politics is essentially the discussion of how we should live collectively, so political freedom is the freedom we have in relation to other people's freedoms. If you were stranded on a desert island all by yourself, with no laws governing you, then you would have a maximum amount of political freedom. However, as soon as other people start to join you, the idea of rules and rights will enter the equation and consequently the amount of political freedom you have will diminish.

It is worth noting that this is only a very simple definition of political freedom and what has been defined here is something called 'negative' liberty, which is the freedom from the interference of others.[4] The nature of political freedom is another keenly contested philosophical idea, but that is not the focus of this chapter. Here we are concerned with free will or what is sometimes called metaphysical freedom. Consider the five cases in the activity above: the amount of political freedom decreases in each case from 1 to 5 but, according to some philosophers, our freedom to choose remains the same in each instance.

Sartre

We shall not say that a prisoner is always free to go out of prison, which would be absurd . . . but that he is always free to try to escape (or get himself liberated). [5]

So what is this alleged 'metaphysical' freedom that somehow remains with us even while we are locked up in chains?

Metaphysical freedom

Metaphysical freedom or free will, as we shall refer to it, is hard to describe precisely because competing theories offer different accounts of what it is. For the time being, however, let us say it is *the ability to make choices*. In each of the cases above, the number of actual choices *available* to the man diminishes in each case; however, the *ability* to make choices remains the same. A man confined to a prison cell can still choose to sit down, stand up, walk to the window or close his eyes. Even the man strapped in the chair, although he has fewer choices available, can still choose whether to open or close his eyes and is free to choose what to think about. The *ability* to make free choices remains and has not been removed; it is the availability of actual options to choose from that has diminished.

Consider the scenarios listed below.
a) Do you think each entity has any free choice about what it does?
b) Why might you claim that certain entities had no free choice?

1 A **snooker ball** is struck by another and moves across the table.
2 A **leaf** falls off a tree, swinging one way then the other before reaching the ground.
3 **Two dice** are thrown in the air and land on the ground.
4 A **lump of ice** melts in the sun.
5 A **man** in a prison cell selects a book from a book shelf.
6 A **teenager** surfs the internet.

Most people would claim that only 5 and 6 have free choice, and that the entities in 1–4 had no free choice. The considerations for the snooker ball might have involved some of these:

A The snooker ball has no mind and, having no mind, the ball cannot 'choose' between different options.
B The ball is simply a collection of atoms which all react to the impact of the other ball in accordance with the laws of nature and so has no choice.
C If repeated again with exactly the same impact the ball would always do the same thing, so the ball had no choice.

D The snooker ball is responding in a straightforward way to external causes, and so is caused to move in a particular way.

D The snooker ball is responding in a straightforward way to external causes, and so is caused to move in a particular way.
E The snooker ball is forced to move.
F The movement of the second ball is a necessary consequence of the movement of the first.
G It would be fairly easy to predict with some accuracy the movement of the snooker ball in advance.
H The snooker ball could not have done otherwise.

Regarding 5 and 6 most would believe that the man and the teenager have free choice. Having the ability to make free choices is what we will term 'free will' for the time being. If you consider the arguments A–H above and apply them to the man and the teenager you may be inclined to think that some or all of the following apply, and this is what enables free will in cases 5 and 6 but not in cases 1–4 (the arguments below are just the opposites of the arguments above).

A The man has a mind and is able to choose between different options.
B The man is more than a simple collection of atoms and is not bound by the laws of nature.
C If repeated again the man might choose a different book.
D The man is not being caused to choose a particular book by external causes; the reason for the choice is largely internal to the man.
E The man is not forced to choose a particular book.
F The choice of book is not a necessary consequence of prior events.
G It would be fairly difficult, if not impossible, to predict with accuracy which book the man would choose.
H The man could have acted otherwise.

You may not agree with all of these arguments, but if you believed that the man and the teenager had free will then you will probably go along with at least one of them.

Some people argue that there are two types of entity: those with free will, such as humans, and those without, such as inanimate objects. However, others argue that cases 5 and 6 are in key respects that same as 1–4 and that none of the entities in question has so-called free will. Some say humans have free will and others say we don't – hence the 'debate' about free will that forms the title of this chapter.

First we will turn our attention to the theory of determinism, which is the name given to the group of theories which claim that humans do *not* have free will.

However before we do this, to provide some fuel for future discussions, consider the following scenario.

experimenting with ideas

Read through the following description of a typical day in the life of Billy, and answer the questions below.

On Thursday morning Billy came back from the shops with some milk for his breakfast, to replace the off-milk that had been left in his broken-down fridge. He had four different kinds of cereal lined up on a shelf: Rice Crisps, Weet-bix, Kornflakes and a Crunchy Oat-based cereal that tended to stick in his teeth. He thought for a few moments about what particular combination of texture, flavour and sweetness he fancied, and eventually went for the Rice Crisps. He decided not to get them too wet, putting only a little milk in the bottom so that the snaps and pops could be distinctly heard. He got a spoon from the drawer to eat the cereal, but it slipped from his fingers and landed on the floor. He decided to use it anyway as it had bounced the right way up. He then made a cup of tea, which he made slightly stronger than normal, as he wanted to be alert for the next hour or so. He took his cup of tea and went upstairs to dress properly. He had already laid out his clothes, having decided what to wear yesterday, although he still had to choose a tie. As he knew he was appearing in court as a defence witness, he opted for a dark blue tie which he thought gave an air of seriousness – without being too sombre. There was a fly buzzing round the room, darting at a carton of old milk. He usually enjoyed a bit of fly-swatting action but looked at his watch and realised he wouldn't have time to really get his eye in – he was late. He left the house and walked quickly to the crown court. En route he did some serious thinking. His friend, who was a borderline psychopath, was up on a charge of minor shoplifting, which Billy knew he was guilty of. He had agreed to speak on behalf of the defence to testify that he was with Bob most of the day in question, which was true, and to confirm that Bob didn't mention or speak about shoplifting all day, which was not true, as Bob had been going on all that day about 'nicking that baseball bat so he could really do some damage'. It was a bit of a dilemma. Billy's dad, who had died two years ago, had a saying 'you never snitch on your mates' and had repeated this to Billy on many occasions and it echoed round his head loudly today. Billy decided that he would lie to the court although he was under oath.

1 Identify all the decisions that are clearly stated in the passage.
2 For each decision you have identified, would Billy have felt as if it were freely made?
3 For each decision you have identified, did Billy make it freely?
4 Do you think Billy has free will? Explain why/why not.

What is determinism?

There are many different forms of determinism but they all hold in common that the future is somehow *determined*. This could mean that the future is already pre-determined or that at every moment the future is created as an inevitable consequence of the past, in other words that the past determines the future. Either way, the future is inevitable and this would seem to imply that humans have no free will. It may appear as if we have lots of choices at any given moment, but if the future is inevitable then it would seem to be the case that we are determined to pick one particular option.

The inevitability of the future could be caused by a number of different things: fate, God or the laws of nature. Each of these possibilities represents a different form of determinism which we will explore in turn.

Logical determinism and fatalism

Que sera sera
Whatever will be, will be[6]

Logical determinism is one of the oldest ideas on record, dating back to the pre-Socratic period, and addressed in detail by Aristotle.[7] At the heart of the theory is a very simple idea. Imagine a middle-aged man called Casper Thimble who is alive and fairly healthy. Recently though he has been putting on a bit of weight and, given that his family has a tradition of heart problems, he is considering going on a diet for health reasons.

Now consider the following two statements.

    A   Casper Thimble will die of a heart attack.
    B   Casper Thimble will not die of a heart attack.

It would appear that one of A or B must be true. In logic this is known as the law of the excluded middle, because there is no third 'middle' option. Either a proposition is true or not; there is no middle ground. For example, 'there are two chairs in a room or there are not two chairs in the room'.

So it seems that one of A or B above must be true, although we may not actually know which one until poor Casper dies. Let us for the moment assume it is A and that Casper will die of a heart attack. If that is the case then there seems little point in his eating healthily. He might as well enjoy eating butter, drinking beer and not bother exercising.

After all, there seems no point in being healthy if he's going to die of a heart attack anyway. Now consider B, that Casper will not die of heart attack. Once again, if this is the case there seems little point in Casper worrying about the quality of his intake because, after all, he won't actually die of a heart attack.

If A is true then Casper doesn't have to start his diet and if B is true then he doesn't have to start his diet. It would seem that, either way, there is little point in Casper starting a diet; he might as well eat what he likes and resign himself to whichever of either A or B is true. This was the view taken by the Stoics in ancient Greece. Being stoical, even today, means to take misfortune or even good fortune in your stride as there is little that you can do about it.

Logical determinism claims that, because there must be a truth or falsity regarding the future, there is little that we can do to avoid it now. The future is determined and will occur *regardless* of what you do. The more common term for logical determinism is *fatalism*: the idea that the future is determined and will occur regardless of your actions, so you might as well resign yourself to your *fate*. 'So it goes' is the fatalist refrain occurring throughout Kurt Vonnegut's novel *Slaughterhouse 5* about the firebombing of Dresden by the Allies on 14 February 1944: every death in the novel, whether of individuals or the 30,000 people who died that day, is punctuated by the phrase 'so it goes' – that's just the way it is.

And the dancing girl said:
'What I say is
If there's a bomb made for YOU
You're going to get it.' [8]

Some people adopted a fatalistic outlook during the Second World War, like the dancing girl in Desmond Hawkins" poem 'Night raid'. For a period, London was being heavily bombed by German planes, and people had a choice whether to stay in the bomb shelters or go out to communal areas. It was tempting for some people to reason as follows: either they would be hit by a bomb and die, or they wouldn't. If it was the case that they would be hit by a bomb, then they might as well go out on the street during a blitz to dance and enjoy themselves. If it was *not* the case that they would be hit by a bomb, then again they might as well go out on the street dancing and enjoying themselves. Either way, there seemed little point in sheltering.

This view seems obviously false, and you would predict that the death rates of people who reasoned along these lines and went out dancing while the bombs were falling would be greater than the death rates of the people who stayed in the underground shelters. However, pinpointing exactly what the error is has taken a great deal of time on behalf of a great many philosophers.

▶ criticism ◀   One problem with logical determinism is that we shouldn't regard statements about the future as being true or false until they actually happen. Consider the proposition:

The Third World War will start in 2021.

Now it would seem that this statement must be either true or false. Imagine two friends Kate and Amy disagreeing over the matter, with Kate believing it will indeed start that year and Amy saying it won't. Imagine we zoomed forward in time to 2022 and there was in fact no Third World War. With hindsight we can easily say that Kate's belief was true and Amy's was false. Even now, it seems tempting to say, with no knowledge of the future, that either the statement is true or it is false. We could, however, take another position, which is to say that the sentence is neither true nor false, as the truth of the matter has yet to be determined. If this seems reasonable then it undermines the logic behind the fatalist argument. The fatalist can no longer reason as follows 'it's either true or false that I will die of a heart attack so either way I might as well keep eating cakes' as they should not regard any claims about the future as either true or false.

    The fatalist, however, could always amend their claim and argue the following 'well, imagine that in the future it turns out to be true that I die of a heart attack' etc. So instead of saying it *is* either true or false that they will have a heart attack, as from the perspective of the present it is neither true nor false, they say instead that in the future it *will* turn out that either they will or won't die that way. However, in this rephrased version the subsequent conclusion 'so I might as well keep eating cakes' seems to be far less persuasive, since from the perspective of the future it seems more obvious that the eating of the cakes might indeed be the cause of the heart attack, just as dancing while the bombs drop might be a contributing cause of your limbs being violently and suddenly removed from your body.

▶ criticism ◀   Another objection is to suggest that the fatalist is confused about the idea of 'necessity'. It may seem that for any proposition (let's call this proposition 'A') then 'either A or not-A' must necessarily be true. However, it does not follow from this that either A will occur out of necessity or that not-A will occur out of necessity. For example 'either it will rain today or it won't rain today' seems to be necessarily true. However, it does not follow that it will necessarily rain or that it will necessarily stay dry. One of the two will necessarily happen, but that does not mean that either of them will occur with necessity.

One way of seeing this is by introducing additional facts into the case. Consider Casper and his diet options. It may be true that Casper will not die of a heart attack but it may also be true that he won't die of a heart attack only if he keeps fit etc. If we accept that this is the case then the idea that he will not have a heart attack, regardless of what he does, can be seen to be false. In other words his heart attack is not a necessary event and of course will depend on the actions that Casper takes.

---

experimenting with ideas

Consider Nadia, who has just started at university. In her first year Nadia was living on the top floor of a big hall of residence. Getting to her room involved going up five flights of steps. On her first day at college Nadia reasoned as follows.

'By the time I leave these halls of residence in a year's time there will be a specific number of steps that I will have walked up – it might be 10,521 steps, it might be 15,316 steps or whatever. Given that there are a specific number, then I might as well try to eat into this total early on before the workload kicks in.'

So indeed Nadia spent the first week at university running up and down the steps in an attempt to reduce the final tally of steps she would eventually walk up.

1 Put into your own words how Nadia's reasoning led her to run up and down steps at the beginning of her course.
2 Is Nadia's reasoning valid?
3 If it is not valid, then what is the error that Nadia is making?

One way of looking at the flaw is that Nadia is assuming that the finite number of steps that will be taken is independent of her actions, which of course is blatantly false. The exact number is entirely dependent on the choices that Nadia makes. Nadia has made the mistake outlined in the criticism above. Although it is necessarily true that there will be a specific number of steps trodden by the time Nadia leaves, this does not mean that any particular number will be necessarily true. The finally tally will be entirely dependent on her actions.

Another way of seeing the flaw will be to say, as in the first criticism, that at this point there is no true number of steps that will be climbed. As the final count hasn't happened no number can be said to be true or false

So we can see that logical determinism, or fatalism, is flawed. It views the future as determined and that the future outcomes will occur regardless of your actions in between. However, fatalism in some form or other is quite widely believed. The popularity of astrology, tarot cards and fortune-telling reveals a belief in many people that the future will somehow occur regardless of what they do.

Although generally false, there may be occasions where fatalism is justified, for example when dealing with the movement of planets or far-off events. These *will* occur regardless of your actions. You might as well resign yourself to the fact that sun will rise tomorrow as this will occur regardless of whatever you do; but this doesn't mean you should resign yourself to everything. This type of 'qualified fatalism' is captured on the walls of toilets throughout the country in the cheesy platitude of the Serenity Prayer,[9] and less cheesily in the philosopher Bill Bartley's rhyme:

For every ailment under the sun
There be a remedy, or there is none;
If there be one, try to find it
If there be none, never mind it.[10]

Religious predestination

We know that God is always at work for the good of everyone who loves him. They are the ones God has chosen for his purpose, and he has always known who his chosen ones would be.

Romans 8:28

The idea of fate for many people is closely bound up with the idea of God, perhaps via a belief that God has a specific path in store for them, as the passage above from the Bible seems to imply. Somewhat like fatalism this is a belief that regardless of what they do God may intervene and bring about certain events in their lives. The idea that God controls aspects of the future is certainly not a new idea, indeed it probably ranks amongst the earliest of all philosophical beliefs. However, when medieval Christian philosophers started to articulate the concept of God in more detail other problems arose in regard to human free will (see Chapter 6, pages 480–83).

We should first note that many religious thinkers believe that humans do indeed have free will and that the future is not determined. Human free will plays an important role in the defence against the challenge to belief in God called the 'PROBLEM OF EVIL' (see page 461 for more detail). In short the problem of evil is as follows. If God is all-good and all-powerful then why is there suffering and evil in the world? Why didn't God simply create a world in which everyone is happy and there is no disease, famine and war? If he is all-powerful then God is capable of creating such a world and if he is all-good then surely he *must* create such a world; otherwise he is deliberately creating suffering. The most common defence to this problem is to say that that God gave humans free will and that most of the problems in the world result from humans using their free will to bad ends, starting with choosing to eat the apple from the tree of knowledge.

The problem of evil is revived if, as John Calvin (1509–1564) and his followers argue, God has already decided who will go to heaven and who will not (as suggested in the quote from the Bible above). In this case of predestination God's goodness needs to be reconciled with the eternal suffering of people who had no choice in whether they were destined to go to heaven or hell. The question we can then ask is whether such a God (one who knows in advance that people will suffer, possibly for eternity, in the afterlife and that they can do nothing about this) can really be called 'good'. (For more on the discussion of the afterlife in relation to the problem of evil see pages 473–75.)

So, for many religious thinkers, human free will plays an important role in their religious belief. But is it really possible to believe in God *and* human free will? We have just seen that God is typically characterised as all-good (BENEVOLENT) and all-powerful (OMNIPOTENT). For many believers it is also important that God is conceived as being all-knowing (OMNISCIENT). In other words, God knows everything there is to know: the history of the world; everything that is occurring in the present and presumably everything that will happen in the future as well. But this presents a problem, indeed more than one problem. The first problem is this. If God knows the future then he knows what I will do. For example, today I got up and I am undecided whether to go to the park or the cinema in the afternoon. But if God knows which of these I will choose then it appears that I have no choice at all. It may appear to me as if there were two options but I was always going to choose one of them. If the future is known now by God then it seems that the future will occur regardless of what I do. It may appear that I am unable to change the future. One of the key concepts in free will is that I am able to choose between different possibilities, such as whether to go to the cinema or not. If it turns out that there is only one possibility then God's omniscience would seem to make free will problematic.

One way of reconciling God's omniscience with our free will is to view God as standing outside of time (see pages 96–98 for more). If God is part of the temporal process and has knowledge of the future events that are yet to happen in both our and God's existence, then free will can seem to be problematic. However, if God stands outside of time and can somehow view the whole of human existence and see what individual humans do, in fact, from their own free will go on to choose then this might provide a solution. God has simply looked at the result of our choices from the vantage point of the future.

■ **Figure 5.1 God in time**

God existing, like us, in the present and so looking forward to what the future is.

■ **Figure 5.2 God outside of time**

God standing outside time and looking at the free choices that were made.

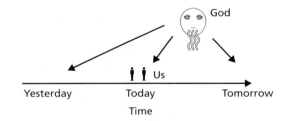

Another problem thrown up by God's omniscience is the problem of God's own free will. Are God's actions determined? Does God inevitably know what he will choose? A similar, related problem also rises with the assumption that God is *all-powerful* and *all good*. If so, on every single occasion it would appear that God only has one choice and that is to act so as to maximise the *goodness* in the world. For more on these and other related problems with the concept of God see pages 100–112.

We can see that the existence of an omniscient God might raise questions about human free will, but these questions are not likely to be taken seriously by the non-believer, and so will not be explored in any more depth here. However, some of these concerns can be re-expressed in a non-religious context. For example, what would happen if a very powerful computer were able to successfully predict the behaviour of a human being? Such an idea will be discussed in more detail later on.

Physical determinism

Rock-a-bye baby
On the treetop
When the wind blows the baby will rock
When the bough breaks the cradle will fall
Down will come baby, cradle and all

Children's nursery rhyme

This is the form of determinism that is at the centre of the free will–determinism debate and is the type of determinism that we will focus on for the rest of this chapter. According to this theory, determinism is operating in everything that happens, even in the nursery rhyme above: the baby's cradle is hung from the branch of a tree; the wind blows causing the cradle to rock; the wind blows a bit more, causing the branch to snap, and the baby, cradle and branch hit the ground at 20 miles an hour – it's a Health and Safety nightmare. In short, physical determinism is the view that all events in the universe are caused by the immediately preceding events.

This idea of causal or physical determinism gained momentum during the sixteenth and seventeenth centuries, although it has an even longer tradition in philosophy. Around the time of Galileo (1564–1642) and Isaac Newton (1643–1727) scientists started to be able to predict the movements of planets and objects with great accuracy. Newton produced several elegant, mathematical 'laws of nature'. These meant that if the starting conditions related to an object were known and the relevant law applied then it was possible to work out what would happen to the object next. These laws applied equally to apples, or cradles falling from trees, as they did to the planets and moons whose movements could be predicated with incredible accuracy. The universal nature of these laws helped to give rise to the idea of a 'clockwork' universe which worked with precise order.

Since those early days, science has delved further into the workings of nature, and many areas that were once mysterious can now be explained and predicted by various laws and theories in the branches of physics, chemistry and biology. For many aspects of nature it appears if we know the starting conditions and the relevant law we can work out and predict with accuracy what will happen next. For example, if we know the initial position, speed and direction at which a snooker ball is moving across a table then we can predict the direction and speed at which the target ball that it hits will move. We know the starting conditions and the relevant laws of nature that apply to the movement of snooker balls, so we are able to predict the outcome.

From such examples a general principle of prediction emerges:

Knowledge of starting conditions

+

Knowledge of relevant laws

=

Successful prediction of outcome

This general principle of prediction, which is an *epistemic* principle as it concerns human knowledge, is used to support a very broad theory about the nature of the universe, an ONTOLOGICAL theory. This is the claim that that every state of affairs in the universe has been casually determined by the previous state of affairs.

■ **Figure 5.3**
Physical determinism

Each state of affairs is determined by the preceding state of affairs

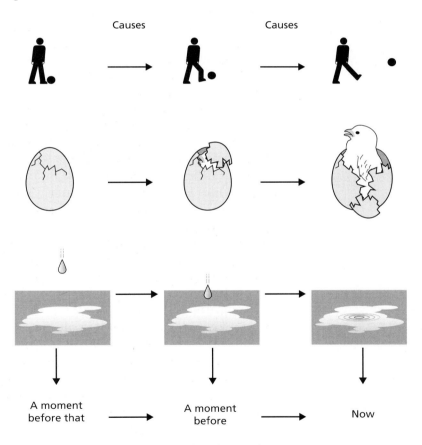

| Causes | Causes |

A moment before that → A moment before → Now

The theory that the present is completely determined by the past is the theory of *physical determinism*. It is this theory that explains how we can predict the future. We are able to predict how events will turn out *because* events are determined by the past in the ways sets in the laws of nature.

From the theory of physical determinism emerge the ideas that it might be possible to know in advance what exactly will happen in the universe. This idea was considered by the philosopher Pierre Laplace (1749–1827). Laplace strongly believed in physical determinism, as is apparent from the following quote:

Laplace

We may regard the present state of the universe as the effect of its past and the cause of its future. An intellect which at a certain moment would know all forces that set nature in motion, and all positions of all items of which nature is composed, if this intellect were also vast enough to submit these data to analysis, it would embrace in a single formula the movements of the greatest bodies of the universe and those of the tiniest atom; for such an intellect nothing would be uncertain and the future just like the past would be present before its eyes.[11]

The idea here is that a vast intellect, given the precise details of the universe at any given state, would be able to work out precisely what will happen next. And also work out precisely what has happened in the past. The idea of such a vast intellect is known as Laplace's demon, although this expression was coined later and not by Laplace himself. (In Chapter 6 we discuss the reaction to Laplace's claim that he had no need for the 'God hypothesis' in his mechanistic theory of the universe – see page 502.)

This idea is no longer pure fantasy. At present, computers are able to predict solar eclipses for the next 10,000 years at least down to the very second. Some computers can even model the start of the universe. If we imagine such technology improving in the future then is it such a far-fetched idea that a computer might be able to work out what will happen next on the earth?

As a small aside, it can be argued that such a machine would be impossible as, if it could predict the future, humans would use this knowledge and the future would be changed – as happens in *Back to the Future*, *Bill And Ted's Excellent Adventure* and Hollywood's numerous other time-travel films. Perhaps it would only work if humans could not access the computer, if it were sealed in a room and after a period of time its earlier predictions were checked to see if they turned out to be true. But in this scenario we would be unable to peer into the future ourselves via the machine.

Is physical determinism true?

Physical determinism is a simple and to some extent 'catchy' idea. But is it true that every event in the universe is caused by the preceding events? You may be able to think of at least one exception to this claim: namely that some events are just random and are not determined at all. Perhaps humans' minds are another exception, somehow escaping the chain of cause and effect. In either case the computer outlined above wouldn't be able to predict the future, even when locked in a room by itself.

The truth of physical determinism cannot be completely demonstrated, as it is impossible to observe every event in the universe. So we will never know whether all events are determined. The whole premise of the theory of determinism is based on the relatively small number of events that scientists can correctly predict. The correctness of predictions leads people to assume that there is an underlying mechanism whereby one event causes another and from this the assumption is made that the underlying mechanisms apply to every aspect of the universe. So to some extent the theory of physical determinism is a leap of faith – it is an inductive argument from a restricted set of cases to the assumption that the theory applies in all cases. The argument for physical determinism would seem to run something along these lines.

1 We can predict many events.
2 This suggests there is an underlying mechanism, 'a necessary cause', which makes these events occur.
3 Therefore all events are caused by the preceding events.

We should note that the 'therefore' in line 3 is not a DEDUCTIVE 'therefore'. The truth of the CONCLUSION (line 3) is not guaranteed by the PREMISES (1 and 2) as this is an INDUCTIVE ARGUMENT not a deductive argument (see pages 114–17 for more detail on the differences between these two types of arguments). So the argument does not act as conclusive proof of the theory. Nevertheless, many inductive arguments are very persuasive and seem reasonable to believe.

We should also note that for the first time we have introduced the idea of necessity into the formulation of physical determinism. This is not some sleight of hand. The idea that one event is *determined* by the other, is the same as the idea that one event followed *necessarily* from the other. This means that, given the first event, the second event *had* to occur.

To explore physical determinism in more depth we will examine some contentious areas about the theory. This will involve considering the nature of causation, the uncertainty of predictions and the idea of a random universe. After these explorations we will look at how physical determinism might apply to humans and what implications this might have for the idea of free will.

more difficult

Causation

One of the fundamental concepts behind the principle of determinism is the idea that one event causes another, and that it causes the second event in such a way that the second event had to happen. In other words, the second event necessarily followed the first.

Initially this seems an intuitive idea. However, once we begin to look more closely at it, the concept of cause begins to appear rather elusive. What exactly do we *mean* when we say that one event *causes* another?

We surely see events causing other events in the world every day, much as we see colours and so it would seem to be that causation is a concept that is directly derived directly from the senses, much like the colour red. But is it?

(Please note that much of the following section is repeated from Chapter 4.) The philosopher David Hume suggests that we don't actually perceive 'causes' via the senses at all. Using Hume's example, it is certainly true that we *seem* to see objects cause one another to move all the time. One billiard ball approaches another, hits the second and the second moves off – it seems obvious that we have just experienced one ball *causing* another to move. But when we look more closely can we actually pinpoint where we saw the cause? We certainly saw one ball approach another ball and we heard a sound and the saw the second ball move off (see Figure 5.4). But we did not actually witness any cause, just movements and sounds.

■ **Figure 5.4** *Are we seeing the first ball cause the second ball to move?*

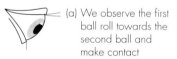 (a) We observe the first ball roll towards the second ball and make contact

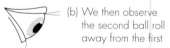 (b) We then observe the second ball roll away from the first

Imagine that all the time there were elaborate magnets under the table and that these moved the first ball up to the second, and then a separate magnet moved the second ball away, such that the first ball did not cause the second to move at all, but the magnets made it appear to. Would this look any different to the casual observer? The answer is surely no. But if there is no observable difference between the magnet scenario and the first case then we must conclude that indeed a cause is not something we actually experience in the SENSE IMPRESSIONS, as the sense impressions are the same whether or not there was a cause.

So it seems that the concept of cause is not directly drawn from the senses. So what do we mean by a cause? Hume claims that we tend to use the word 'cause' to link patterns of experience that frequently occur together. This is something that our minds automatically do for us. Imagine your friend clapped her hands and a split second later you heard thunder in the distance. You would to probably think nothing of it. Imagine the same thing happened again a minute later; again you would put it down to coincidence. But imagine this happened a third, fourth, fifth and sixth time. Your mind would automatically start assuming that your friend's clapping caused the thunder. But this inference cannot be based simply on the sense data involved for there was nothing different about the first clap than there was about the sixth; the only difference is in the repetition, the constant occurrence of the two events. By the sixth clap your experience of the event feels very different; it now starts to feel like a causal event. Thus Hume suggests that what we mean and experience as cause and effect is really just the constant conjunction of events (constant = repeated, conjunction = joining together). It is the repetition of these conjunctions that make us believe that one event causes the other.

We know nothing farther of causation of any kind than merely the constant conjunction of objects.[12]

Hume

So it is contended that we don't actually experience causes as such, only repeating patterns. As causes are not directly perceived it would be dangerous for us to say with any confidence that any event caused another. We should note here that Hume is not really doubting whether events are caused or not. His primary concern is to examine some of the key philosophical terms we use (in this case 'causation') and investigate how the concept relates to our sense experience. Hume is sometimes termed an epistemic sceptic as his doubt concerns what we know and mean by causation (EPISTEMOLOGY) rather than whether such a thing really exists (ONTOLOGY). What are the consequences of Hume's analysis of causation for the theory of physical determinism?

Hume's theory of causation does not radically change the way we might view the theory of physical determinism, although it might help us be clearer about what is being claimed. Earlier we characterised the argument for physical determinism as follows.

1 We can predict many events (an epistemic claim).
2 This suggests there is an underlying mechanism, 'a necessary cause', which makes these events occur (an ontological claim).
3 Therefore all events are caused by the preceding events (an ontological claim).

Hume would suggest that the idea of a 'necessary cause' in line 2 is derived from the fact that we can indeed predict many events (they are constantly conjoined). It has no basis in experience beyond the constant conjunction of events. So, for Hume, the argument might read a bit differently, like this:

1 We observe that many events follow from other events with regularity, and sometimes can predict them correctly (an epistemic claim).
2 This is what we mean when we say the second event was necessarily caused by the first (an epistemic claim).
3 Therefore all events are caused by the preceding events (an ontological claim).

For Hume, the added element of necessary causation takes us no closer to the final conclusion that every event has a cause: you might as well jump from the regularity of the universe to the claim that all events are caused, as the regularity is what we mean by 'events being caused'. Hume believes the regularity of the universe is the start and end of the claims we can make about physical determinism.

Hume's analysis of causation, which itself is open to criticism, does not destroy the idea of physical determinism. However, it does perhaps make us think about what we mean by the idea of universal causation and the corresponding idea of a necessary cause, and that we should not use these words without being clear about what we mean.

Some philosophers are not convinced by Hume: after all, what if the regularity of the universe were one big coincidence as opposed to there being an underlying mechanism? This is what the ancient Greek philosopher Epicurus (341–270 BCE) claimed (for more on the Epicurean hypothesis see Chapter 6, page 456). Hume rightly points out there would be no observable difference if the Epicurean Hypothesis were true, but it is surely reasonable to believe in an underlying mechanism. It could be that every event in the universe is completely random and unrelated. Imagine that every atom acts entirely independently of every other atom and simply moves randomly. It could so happen, via incredible coincidence or divine creation, as suggested by Leibniz in his theory of pre-established harmony,[13] that every atom moves independently but in such a way that it makes the universe look as if one event 'causes' another. This theory of coincidence claims that, although one thing *looks* as if it causes another, they are actually two unrelated events that coincide. To make this clearer, we can picture two clocks placed side by side, one with hands but no chime, and the other with a chime but no hands. These two clocks could be synchronised so whenever the one with hands marks '12' the other clock chimes twelve times and so on. To the observer it would look as if the first clock causes the chimes in the second. The same principle applies to things we might observe in real life, for example a toy doll melting on a fire. According to this theory of coincidence, the atoms of the toy in the flame randomly move so as to, by coincidence, look as if they have melted. But the doll is not *caused* to melt by the flame, it just looks that way: the movement of the atoms and the proximity of the fire are independent of one another. This is admittedly a rather strange theory, but it does show that it is theoretically possible that all the events in the known universe have taken place not as a result of causal necessity but as a result of atoms moving randomly.

However, it is surely simpler to believe that any event occurring always happens for a reason. A ball moved because it was pushed, a toy melted because it was burned. So although Hume might be right in saying that belief in an underlying mechanism termed 'causation' is not derived from experience, it seems a reasonable leap to make – as otherwise we are simply left with the regularity of the universe and nothing to explain the regularity.

■ Hume on free will

The conjunction between motives and voluntary actions is as regular and uniform as that between cause and effect in any part of nature.[14]

Hume

Although we are not yet examining physical determinism in relation to humans it is worth briefly examining what Hume had to say on the matter while his ideas on causation are still fresh in our minds. Hume notes, in Section 8 of *An Enquiry Concerning Human Understanding*, that when we examine our minds we do not feel any 'necessity' about our choice. We feel no force that might make our choices inevitably follow from other events. As there is no feeling of force some people are inclined to believe there is no a 'necessary connection' between our actions and our stimulus.

Hume, however, points out that the same is true of the physical world. We do not actually experience any force or 'necessary connection' between physical events. We sometimes imagine that we do but this is the mind adding to the event after experiencing many similarly conjoined events. So, according to Hume, the lack of a feeling of necessity is no reason to believe we have free will, as this is the same in all such cases of 'causation'.

Hume claims that it is clear that human action follows the same patterns of conjunction that we see in the physical world. Events such as winning money are conjoined with behaviour such as smiling and whooping, time and time again. Indeed our very ability to understand human emotions and actions is premised on our being able to conjoin similar sorts of effect with similar sorts of cause. In this sense our actions are 'necessarily caused' by the preceding events every bit as much as in the physical world. So Hume claims that our actions are determined, albeit in his sense of causally determined. Indeed he asks us to imagine the opposite – that our behaviour was not conjoined to our emotions or desires. Hume suggests that this leads to problems for morality because if our actions are not caused by our emotions and thoughts then how can we be held morally responsible for them? Hume suggests that morality *requires* us to believe in determinism.

Lastly Hume analyses the concept of free will. As with causation, he seeks to analyse when we use this word and see what sense experiences it might relate to. He suggests that the sense data that we typically associate with the term 'free will' is that of a lack of force or coercion. In other words we call an act a *free* act if the person was able to act on their own desires and was not physically forced to carry out the action. So I am free as long as I have choices and am not forced to act or not act by others.

By liberty, then, we can only mean a power of acting or not acting, according to the determinations of the will.[15]

Hume

Overall Hume is a COMPATIBILIST as he believes that humans both have free will and are determined. He believes in determinism – which he claims simply means that particular human actions are constantly conjoined with particular effects. He also believes that free will can only mean freedom to act on your desires free from coercion and restraint, which is perfectly compatible with determinism.

So underlying the theory of physical determinism is the idea of universal causation, of a necessary connection between events. However, Hume's analysis suggests that we should be wary of claiming a special necessary connection between any events, as such an element is not present in our experience of the world. Our belief in such a connection only occurs out of constantly seeing particular effects follow particular causes.

For want of a nail the shoe was lost.
For want of a shoe the horse was lost.
For want of a horse the rider was lost.
For want of a rider the battle was lost.
For want of a battle the kingdom was lost.
And all for the want of a horseshoe nail.

Children's nursery rhyme

Another element that might make us somewhat wary of the theory of physical determinism is the difficulty of prediction – military strategists and quarter masters do all they can to ensure the right equipment is with the right soldiers at the right time etc. But could they predict, and prevent, an event as small as the loss of a horseshoe nail, which could result in the toppling of a kingdom?

It seems impossible to predict everything. A quick argument against physical determinism would be to point out that not every event can be predicted. For example, if I shake a six-sided die in a cup then throw it high in the air it is impossible to be absolutely certain as to what number it will land on (given that the die is not loaded). Unpredictability is not just confined to die: as we all know, the weather, at least in the United Kingdom, can't be predicted very well, and humans are especially tricky to gauge. For example, it would be hard to predict what a particular person might say if you approached them pretending to be a rabbit. Much in life is unpredictable, hence the existence and continued success of betting shops and online gambling sites. So the determinist assumption that all events are physically caused may not be justified, as many events cannot be accurately predicted. In other words premise 1 of the argument for determinism (see page 357) is not valid.

Let us, however, reconsider the die. Imagine we had a machine that shook the die in *exactly* the same way and that the die started in *exactly* the same position, then might we be able to predict the outcome? Even with such a machine we may not be able to record the starting conditions accurately enough to predict the outcome with regular accuracy. For example, the die could have picked up some microscopic bits of dust from the previous roll which might affect its spin, speed or trajectory and hence affect the final outcome.

Small differences in starting conditions can sometimes mean very big differences in later outcomes. Ray Bradbury's short story 'A sound of thunder' unravels how the killing of a butterfly millions of years ago causes ripples of effects that eventually change the course of human history. In a brief talk given in 1972 the mathematician and meteorologist Edward Lorenz popularised the idea that small, insignificant, events could be amplified until they had global impact – the lecture was entitled 'Predictability: Does the flap of a butterfly's wings in Brazil lead to a tornado in Texas?'.[16] These ideas became known as *chaos theory* and are summed up by the idea of the 'butterfly effect'. This is Lorenz's idea that even something as small as the flap of a butterfly's wings might have an impact on whether there is a tornado or not in another part of the world. Going back to the die thrown in the air, very small differences in starting conditions can mean widely different outcomes later on, and often these starting conditions cannot accurately be determined. A small amount of dust on the die, or even the very gentlest of breezes in the room (perhaps caused by a butterfly!) might lead to a different number landing face up.

Does chaos theory offer a helping hand towards those who believe in free will? After all, it seems to suggest that not everything in the universe is simply one predictable event after another. Perhaps free will is to be located in our brains as a 'random generator', liberated from the deterministic world. But this doesn't seem to be what we would be looking for in genuine free will for two reasons: first, we would hope that free will tie our decisions in such a way as to make us morally responsible (see pages 406–26 below); secondly, a random generator in our brain would still work according to the laws of physics, and would still *cause* us to act. As Steven Pinker writes:

Pinker

> *A butterfly's flutter can set off a cascade of events culminating in a hurricane. A fluttering in the brain that causes a hurricane of behaviour, if it were ever found, would still be a cause of behaviour and would not fit the concept of uncaused free will that underlies moral responsibility.*[17]

The issue here is the complexity of the factors. All of the conditions are not known with complete accuracy, and this means that we cannot predict the event with complete accuracy. However, again this does *not* mean that there is no causal necessity at play – only that as humans we are limited in our ability to determine the exact initial conditions. It could be argued that, at every stage, the movement in the die was caused by the state of affairs in the preceding stage and follows necessarily from it. There is no randomness or even free will at play, only matter and the laws of physics. So the principle of physical determinism may still apply; it is only our ability to predict the outcome that is affected.

Our capacity to predict certain events does not really alter the argument for physical determinism. The first line of the argument (page 357 above) states that

1) We can predict many events.

It does not state that we can predict *all* events and nor does it need to. As long as some events are predictable this might give us grounds to claim that there is an underlying mechanism that causes each event to occur.

It seems that determinism and chance are perfectly compatible as long as we see chance as resulting from a shortfall in our knowledge; in other words, as long as chance is the result of an epistemic deficit. However, what if chance were an inherent feature of the world? In other words, what if chance were an ontological part of the world, rather than just a gap in our knowledge? If true, this may well undermine the theory of physical determinism.

A random world

Well, got to go – the dice told me to go shoot the pet of my neighbour. [18]

Luke Rhinehart

We return to the random actions of Luke Rhinehart below, but first let us consider how randomness fits into the universe as described in classical physics. The rise of physical determinism occurred in part because of the success of Isaac Newton's theories in predicting the movements of objects and planets. His theories are known as Newtonian mechanics and explain very well how large and medium-sized objects behave (i.e. things that are easy for humans to see, like planets and snooker balls). However, the problem is more complex when we are dealing with the behaviour of very small objects such as atoms and electrons.

In this microscopic arena Newtonian mechanics no longer apply. A different set of physical laws and theories come into play to try to predict the movements and behaviour of these small objects. The set of theories is known as quantum mechanics. Newtonian mechanics points to a future where events are determined by what has just happened, combined with the laws of physics; but the position is not so clear with quantum mechanics. Many physicists believe that quantum mechanics shows that at this very small level (for example, the rate of decay of an atom) the universe is not determined and the best we can do is produce probabilities concerning the future.

It seems that sub-atomic elements such as protons and electrons sometimes behave as if they were discrete particles existing at a particular point in space, and at other times experiments show that they act more like all waves and cannot be localised at any one point. In order to make sense of the various experiments, in 1927 the physicists Niels Bohr and Werner Heisenberg proposed the 'Copenhagen interpretation' of quantum mechanics, which suggests that the position and the momentum of sub-atomic particles are best described by probability fields. For example, over a given area we can only describe the probability that a particle is at any one point. The Copenhagen interpretation is probably the most widely accepted explanation of experimental data in quantum mechanics and although there are many different variations within this interpretation most suggest that that quantum mechanics can only give probabilistic predictions because the world itself is not determined but is probabilistic. In other words, our inability to predict how particles behave is because there *is* no underlying mechanism.

Above we saw that chaos theory does not really affect physical determinism as it is based on our inability to predict the world, an *epistemic* deficit, rather than any feature of the world, an *ontological* deficit. However quantum mechanics is different. The Copenhagen interpretation suggests that our inability to predict is precisely because the world itself is probabilistic. And this is a big problem for the theory of physical determinism: the conclusion that the sub-atomic world is probabilistic has caused great concern amongst scientists and non-scientists.

Quantum mechanics is certainly imposing. But an inner voice tells me that it is not yet the real thing . . . I, at any rate, am convinced that He [God] does not throw dice.[19]

Einstein

Einstein, amongst others, was convinced that the uncertainty at the heart of quantum mechanics was due to hidden variables in particles that had not yet been discovered and that when these were known we would be able to predict the behaviour of sub-atomic particles with certainty. His view is encapsulated in his claim that God 'does not throw dice' which means that the world itself is not random or probabilistic. (Note that Einstein was not referring to God in any theistic sense.)

In theory the principles of quantum mechanics should apply to all aspects of the world, as ultimately everything is made of sub-atomic particles. However, although each particle may behave probabilistically, when they are joined up with other particles the interaction makes the probabilities much easier to predict. In theory it is possible that every atom in the apple on the table in front of me might suddenly shift two centimetres to the left, but this is so unlikely as to be virtually impossible. The bonds between atoms mean that they would all have to shift at once, a bit like everyone in China shaking two dice at the same time and everyone throwing two sixes. The big numbers of particles involved in most objects means that their behaviour can be predicted with accuracy and traditional Newtonian laws can be applied.

Where does all this leave the theory of physical determinism? Let us revisit the suggested argument for the theory.

1 We can predict many events.
2 This suggests there is an underlying mechanism, 'a necessary cause', which makes these events occur.
3 Therefore all events are the inevitable result of the preceding set of events.

According to quantum mechanics, number 1 is not true of the microscopic world. We cannot predict with complete accuracy the behaviour of small particles. Number 2 is problematic: it seems that there is no one particular event that might follow another. Instead there are probabilities of different events occurring and this is because there is no precise underlying mechanism in the world. Number 3 would also need revisiting, as it may be true that all events are affected by other preceding events, but this is not to say there is a prior cause that *necessitates* a particular outcome.

As we can see, if the Copenhagen interpretation of quantum mechanics is true then the theory of physical determinism is left in tatters. Or at the very least it doesn't apply to the very small building blocks of the universe. Quite where this leaves humans is unclear for two reasons. First, most would claim that quantum mechanics only really applies to very small objects such as electrons. The human brain, it is claimed, operates on a larger scale and so the probabilistic thinking of quantum theory does not apply to humans.

Secondly, even if quantum mechanics did apply to human brains, this would not necessarily give humans free will. If effects are not linked to causes, then it can be argued humans cannot have free will. As Hume suggests earlier, if my moving my arm was not related to my wanting to move my arm then I can't really be held responsible for moving my arm. It is precisely because there *is* an underlying link between causes and effects that humans are able to have free will. To use a metaphor – imagine a ship that been damaged and is being towed towards a dock. The ship would have no choice in the direction it went, its path being determined by the tugboat (determinism). However, a ship that has no oars, sails or motor and is just at the mercy of the chopping and changing of the waves also has no choice in the direction it goes (randomness).

Randomness doesn't offer an escape to the person seeking to salvage their free will. In George Cockcroft's novel *The Dice Man* (published under the pseudonym Luke Rhinehart), the protagonist decides that he will live his life according to the roll of dice. He assigns actions, of random significance, to each of the six numbers on a die (1 eat an apple, 2 carry on with my writing, 3 shoot the neighbour's pet, etc.) and then throws the die and does *whatever* it has told him to do. His life is ruled by the randomness of the die. This process might make his life more interesting, but it doesn't make him any freer.

■ Summary of the theory of physical determinism

So far we have looked at the theory of physical determinism in general, at how it applies, or not, to all objects in the universe. We have seen that the concept of causation lying at the heart of the theory is far from clear. We have seen that our inability to predict so-called chance events such as the throwing of dice is perfectly compatible with the theory. However, we have also seen that quantum mechanics may throw the theory into disarray when applied to very small objects. We will now turn our attention to physical determinism as it relates to humans in particular.

Determinism and humans

Pinker

Should we go even farther than the National Rifle Association bumper sticker – GUNS DON'T KILL; PEOPLE KILL – and say that not even people kill, because people are just as mechanical as guns?[20]

Once the idea of physical determinism and the clockwork universe took hold, an inevitable question followed. If all events in the universe are caused by preceding events, is the same true of human action? Are humans simply like complicated pieces of clockwork as the quote above suggests? Inside the brain are various atoms formed into cells which interact with each other, all in keeping with the laws of the universe. Although the brain is very complicated it is made of the same sort of stuff as snooker balls and computers. We do not think that snooker balls and computers have free will so why should we think it of humans?

In the novel *A Clockwork Orange* Alex, a sociopathic gang-member, is put onto an experimental crime prevention programme by the government: he is to be conditioned to behave in an appropriately moral way. This conditioning means that, although he still wants to lie, steal and kill, he can't because of the physical sickness that envelops him when he tries to do these things. If he behaves in the opposite way (even though he has no natural inclination to do so) and is honest, respectful etc., then he feels a lot better. Once this conditioning is complete Alex is put on display as the future of crime prevention; he is now a 'clockwork orange', physically incapable of doing any harm. He now grovels in front of the man he wishes to slice up with his knife. One observer questions the success of this experiment; to him Alex is no longer a moral agent:

Choice . . . He has no real choice, has he? Self-interest, fear of physical pain, drove him to that grotesque act of self-abasement. Its insincerity was clearly to be seen. He ceases to be a wrongdoer. He ceases also to be a creature capable of moral choice.[21]

We will return to the issue of determinism and morality later.

An initial quick criticism of the idea that humans are determined is that physical determinism is premised on our ability to predict aspects of the world yet we cannot predict human behaviour. On one level this is a true claim – we are a very long way off from being able to predict human behaviour accurately. However, if we overlook brain chemistry and instead turn to folk psychology (that is, the ordinary everyday psychological theories that we use to make sense of the behaviour of people) on the whole the behaviour of others is not *that* difficult to predict. People get angry when wronged; they cry when they lose a loved one; they smile when they win money. Certain events tend to cause certain behaviour. As David Hume says, if you want to know how the ancient Greeks and Romans behaved, then simply study the emotions and actions of contemporary French and English folk.[22] By analysing likely human desires and intentions (sometimes described as taking an intentional stance) we can make reasonable predictions about how people might behave in given situations. Such predictions are, however, a long way from being certain.

The 'scientific' route of predicting behaviour, perhaps by analysing brain chemistry, is far from being able to calculate specific actions. We may be able to state that certain chemicals or drugs may make us happy or inclined to act in certain ways. However, when it comes to specific acts such as which book the prisoner would pick from the library (page 344), brain chemistry, as yet, is silent. So we still lack the power to calculate and predict human behaviour in a scientific way, even though our understanding is increasing all the time. But this is an epistemological concern, about what we are and are not capable of knowing – the main point is that the human brain is part of the same deterministic universe that atoms and planets are part of (which is an ontological claim). This claim can be turned into a more formal argument:

1 In other parts of the world physical objects behave as if determined by the laws of nature.
2 The human brain is made of the same physical stuff as these objects.
3 Therefore the human brain too must be determined by the laws of nature.

This is the general argument which suggests that the theory of physical determinism must apply to humans too. Before we look at any criticisms of it we will consider whether there is any other supporting evidence to suggest the argument is true.

The first sort of evidence is to point out the general success of a reductivist approach in science. REDUCTIONISM is the attempt to explain more complex phenomena by reference to simpler phenomena. The natural sciences offer many forms of reductionism. For example, the behaviour of cells can be explained in terms of the 'behaviour' of the chemicals they are composed of; the properties of chemicals such as alcohol or water can be explained in terms of the structure and properties of the basic elements, hydrogen, oxygen etc. In turn the properties of the various elements can be explained in terms of the properties of the three basic sub-atomic particles, electrons, neutrons and protons. Such a progression might look something like Figure 5.5.

This is just to give a basic idea and is not a fully fledged account of the route of scientific explanation. Each element in the diagram can be explained, in principle, in terms of the element below it: for example, cells in terms of chemicals, and society in terms of human thought. In other words, the more complex elements (higher up) can be explained in terms of the simpler elements (lower down): the process known as reductionism. We should also note that scientists are nowhere near being able to actually provide such reductivist accounts in all cases, and that further up the table the very principle of reductionism is disputed by some. For example, it is claimed that at certain levels of complexity new properties can emerge, for example consciousness, which cannot be explained in terms of the properties of the constituent parts. Also we might want to question whether social phenomena such as the results of elections could be predicted in theory

■ Figure 5.5
Reductionism

Reductionism is the process of explaining each stage in terms of the stage below.

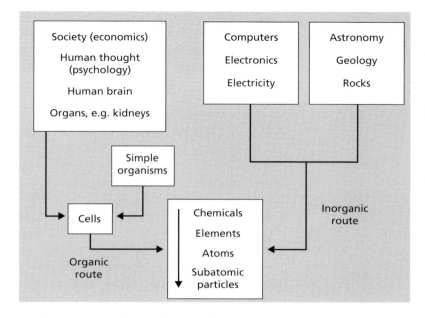

on the basis of the studying of atoms alone. It may not be simply a question of mind-boggling complexity but might be impossible in principle. However, lower down the diagram few would doubt the success of the reductionist approach – for example, scientists are able to show how the properties of molecules can be derived from the properties of the atoms that constitute them.

The success of reductionism as a whole might be used as supporting evidence for the theory of physical determinism since it shows how increasingly complex behaviour of objects can be explained in terms of the behaviour of their components. This might persuade some that the principle of physical determinism also applies to human behaviour. But what of the sceptic who claims that human behaviour is an emergent property that will never be explained in terms of simpler phenomena? Is there evidence that might shed light on the debate one way or the other?

■ Biological determinism

Biological determinism is the name of the theory that claims that many aspects of our behaviour are shaped by our genetic make-up. Such a theory is of course part of the broader theory of physical determinism. As yet genetics is a long way off being able to explain human behaviour. The most that can be claimed is that our genes may be one determinate factor in certain behaviour traits. For example, it might turn out that a certain set of genes will make people score highly in IQ tests (although it might not). Studies of identical twins have suggested that there is some basis for such claims, not specifically relating to IQ – but more broadly to behaviour traits. However, even if such sets of genes were found to exist, we would still be nowhere near being able use the idea of genes to account for specific behaviour rather than just general traits.

Cultural/environmental determinism

Cultural determinism is the name for those who believe that our experiences and environment shape our behaviour. Again this is a variation of the more general theory of physical determinism. The empirical evidence for cultural determinism is far stronger than for biological determinism, in part because we are only just beginning to understand our genetic make-up. However, for a dramatic example of cultural determinism, we need look no further than religion. Is it a coincidence that people in Islamic countries grow up to be Muslims or that people in Utah grow up to be Mormons? It is easy to see that whole patterns of belief and behaviour are perhaps not freely chosen but rather culturally acquired. At a personal level it is possible to trace many of our our own interests and hobbies back to elements from our childhood.

You may be familiar with the great nature–nurture debate: what is more important in the formation of the human mind? Is it the genetic inheritance from our parents or is it the environment that they provide and the experiences we undergo? Those favouring nature lean towards biological determinism; those favouring nurture lean towards environmental determinism. Most opt for a bit of both (although the current work of evolutionary psychologists such as Steven Pinker[23] seem to be tipping the scales of evidence towards biological determinism). Indeed any teacher who has attended parents' evenings will know all too well that many of the behavioural manifestations of the pupils are inherent either in the genes or in the behaviour of their parents.

For the physical determinist, however, the question of which is more important doesn't really matter as nature and nurture are both accounts of how we can explain human behaviour in reference to the preceding set of conditions that necessitated it.

ACTIVITY   Revisit the example of Billy on page 346.

1 How many of his decisions might be related to either his genetic make-up or his upbringing?
2 What about yourself: do you find yourself acting in ways in which your parents and friends do?
3 If so do you think this adds weight to the claim that our actions are causally determined?

■ Brain chemistry

Another area that might add credence to the claim that physical determinism applies to humans is our increasing understanding of the brain. We are able to locate the regions of the brain that play the primary role in elements of cognition, such as sight and speech. We are aware of how chemicals can affect the brain. Certain drugs such as anti-depressants clearly have an effect on our mood and behaviour. The more we know about how the brain works, the more, it is argued, we are entitled so see human behaviour in terms of the brain chemistry that causes it. This in turn gives rise to the idea that physical determinism applies to humans as much as it does to any other aspect of the physical universe.

All of this evidence – genetics, nurture and brain chemistry – adds weight to the claim that humans are another part of the universal chain of cause and effect. However, this does not necessarily mean that humans have no free will. For example, if you dangled a £50 note in front of 100 people's noses and said they could take it and keep it with no catches, how many people would take up the offer? Probably 100. However, we could still claim that each of these choices was free; it was just that the attractiveness of the £50 note made the option of taking it an appealing and sensible one. It can be argued (see the section on Sartre below) that the same is true of our genetic and cultural make-up: these elements make certain actions seem more tempting to us as they provide the desires and urges that might incline us to act one way or the other. However, this can be metaphorically seen as the dangling a £50 inside someone's mind. It makes a certain course of action seem like the best one to take. However, as with the £50 in front of your nose, this does not mean you are not free to refuse; you could override the biologically determined desires and urges in the same way that you could refuse the £50.

Physical determinism and free will

So far we have explored the theory of physical determinism and looked at the arguments and evidence to suggest it applies to humans. If you believe that it does then that makes you a determinist. However, does being a determinist mean that you have to believe that humans have no free will? Not necessarily, as it will depend on how you define free will. Some determinists believe humans have free will, others that they don't. *Soft determinism* is the term used to summarise the belief that free will and determinism are compatible (sometimes called compatibilism). *Hard determinism* is the name of the theory which holds that physical determinism is true and that therefore humans do have not free will. In this section we will examine hard determinism. We will return to soft determinism in the next section when we examine free will in general.

■ Hard determinism

For some hard determinists there is no need to try to prove that humans have no free will, since it follows inevitably from the principle of physical determinism. Snooker balls have no free will; and in the same way that movement of the snooker ball is determined by starting conditions and the laws of nature, so the human brain is determined by *its* starting conditions every time it makes a decision. On this view, determinism is the default position of all objects in the universe and so the onus is on those who believe in free will to show why humans should be an exception to the rule.

Some hard determinists are happy to go further than this and to specify exactly what it is about physical determinism that makes the idea of human free will impossible. On page 344 above we outlined different answers that could be given to explain why the snooker ball has no free will; these included:

■ The ball is simply a collection of atoms which all react to the impact of the other ball in accordance with the laws of nature and so it has no choice.
■ If repeated again with exactly the same impact the ball would always do the same thing, so the ball had no choice.
■ The movement of the second ball is a necessary consequence of the movement of the first.
■ The snooker ball could not have done otherwise.

Although there is some overlap in these answers each of them can be put forward by the hard determinist to suggest that humans equally have no free will.

■ Humans are a collection of atoms each of which is determined by the laws of nature.
■ If repeated again, with the same starting conditions, humans would make the same choice in any given instant.
■ The decisions/choices we make are a necessary result of who we are and the stimulus we have received.
■ For any action the person could not have done otherwise.

All of these arguments seem to point to humans not having free will. It is sometimes suggested that free will can exist only if it is possible on some occasions to have acted otherwise, and the hard determinist would claim that this is not possible.

Earlier we considered the typical responses that people might give as to why humans were different from snooker balls and so have free will. We looked at the example of a prisoner choosing a book from a shelf. Below are some reasons that suggest that the prisoner's action was freely chosen. Read through these reasons and briefly state what a hard determinist might say in response to each of these claims made by the supporter of free will.

1 The man has a mind and is able to choose between different options.

2 The man is more than a simple collection of atoms and is not bound by the laws of nature.

3 If repeated again the man might choose a different book.

4 The man is not being caused to choose a particular book by external causes; the reason for the choice is largely internal to the man.

5 The man is not forced to choose a particular book.

6 The choice of book is not a necessary consequence of prior events.

7 It would be fairly difficult, if not impossible, to predict with accuracy which book the man would choose.

8 The man could have acted otherwise.

We will indirectly explore criticisms of hard determinism later when looking at what can be said in favour of the opposing theories of libertarianism and soft determinism. We should also note that one of the biggest problems with hard determinism is that, if true, it would appear to have major implications for other areas of human life such as morality and rationality. These consequences are explored in the final section of this chapter. In the meantime we have given some short responses that a hard determinist might make against each of the claims made in the activity above:

1 Yes, the man does have a mind but the choice is still determined.

2 No, a man *is* a collection of atoms.

3 Not true, if everything were identical then the same book would be chosen again.

4 True, but the choice was determined by neural events in brain.

5 Possibly true but irrelevant – the choice is still determined by the starting conditions.

6 Yes it is. The choice of book is a necessary consequence of events in the man's brain.

7 True, but again not relevant. It is difficult to predict the weather but this does not have free will.

8 No, the man could not have acted otherwise.

Later we will explore some of the consequences of hard determinism, however by way of a taster, imagine that it is true and that on any occasion it is impossible for a human to act in any other way than they do.

Read through the following emotional responses, and answer the question below:

1 Getting irritated with a friend for being late
2 Being outraged with someone for stealing your wallet
3 Getting angry over the decision to invade Iraq
4 Blaming the manager when England lose a game of football
5 Being thankful that someone has returned your wallet

If we discover that hard determinism is true, how might this alter the emotions we felt in each of the situations above?

Of course if hard determinism is true then you would have no choice but to feel such emotions on such occasions.

The illusion of free will

According to hard determinism our actions are causally determined and there is no such thing as free will. However, hard determinists would acknowledge that it *appears* to the individual, when making a decision, that he or she does have free will. It is hard to deny the appearance of free will, on the grounds that a person cannot be wrong about how their mind appears to them. If we return to the scenario on page 346 above, we can see that Billy thought he was making lots of decisions, just as we all do every day. Consider the case of choosing the cereal.

1 It certainly appeared as if Billy had a choice of four cereals.
2 He was not forced by any external agency to choose a particular cereal.
3 He would have felt no 'guiding force' or necessary causation that led to a particular cereal.
4 Billy would have felt as if he could have chosen any of them.

These are some of the elements that make us feel as if we have free will, and even most hard determinists would agree to all of these claims. The hard determinist must therefore give some account of why it appears to us as if we have free will. If they are not able to account for this feeling, then the supporter of free will might claim these feelings as strong evidence that we do in fact have free will (for some philosophers this is the only evidence we need; see the sections on Sartre and phenomenology below).

Imagine you are a hard determinist, denying humans have free will. How would explain the four factors listed above – factors which collectively lead to the appearance of free will?

1 The existence of choices is not a necessary indicator of free will. A chess computer has several choices available to select from in most instances and chooses one of the possibilities. However, few would credit the computer with free will, so the existence of choices alone is not evidence of free will – even though it may lead to the illusion of free will.

2 It is true that no one overtly made Billy choose the Rice Crisps (although certain advertising/marketing people may disagree!). Billy was not forced by another person to make a decision. Or, in an extreme example, his hand was not, against his will, physically forced to grab the box. However, each stage of the decision-making process was still determined by the preceding stage and so no free will exists. Defenders of free will might claim that if we have no free will then there can be no real difference between Billy choosing a particular box and his hand being made by someone else to reach out and grab. In both cases there was only one outcome which could occur. Hard determinists must account for the fact that we do treat such cases differently – which we do – particularly when morality is concerned. Someone whose finger was physically forced to pull a trigger and kill someone is treated very differently in law from someone who had no other hand forcing their own hands onto the gun. However, why should this be? In both cases there was only one outcome that could follow, given the relevant set of conditions. The defence of this point is treated in the section on morality (pages 406–11).

3 As discussed earlier on page 359, Hume suggests that we do not actually experience any guiding hand or necessary causation when witnessing any example of causation in the world, as when one snooker ball moves another. So the absence of the feeling of any guiding hand or compulsion in our decision-making should be no cause for concern.

4 This is as the crux of the illusion of free will and the hard determinist needs to give an account. Why should we feel as if we could choose otherwise when in fact we can't? To some extent the answers given in the previous three points might explain why. However, more can be offered by way of explanation. It has been claimed that the illusion of free will may arise out of a combination of a) our incomplete access to brain processes, b) the complexity of the decision-making process.

First, the illusion that we have free will may be the consequence of not having complete access in our consciousness to all the workings of our brain. The human brain is one of the most complex objects in the known universe: there may be more *potential* connections between the 100 billion or so neurons in the brain than there are atoms in the entire universe. So decision-making is a very complex process involving many different areas of the brain, very few of which we have conscious access to. Each area of the brain may be computing facts in quite a straightforward way, according to simple rules or procedures or events that most would concede are deterministic. However, we do not have conscious access to these processes. We might be aware of small urges or prompts toward a particular cereal, perhaps based on the unconscious processing of the colour of the packaging, smells, desire for certain tastes, the desire for variety, the mood we are in. These urges will then determine the one we 'fancy' today. Each of these factors may be 'computed' by the brain in a deterministic way. However, as we don't have access to these causal processes, it can feel as if the decision was freely made.

A criticism of this claim is that this may be true if we *only* acted on the first desire that popped into our head. However, often we consciously deliberate decisions, weigh up the pros and cons (the textures, flavours and relative sweetness of each cereal) and we appear to have some access to this process.

Secondly the illusion that we have free will may be because of the complexity of process. Even though there are only four cereals to choose from there are a large number of factors to compute. A bit like with chess, there may only be four realistic moves at any stage, and the rules involved may be simple and deterministic, but this can generate an enormous amount of computational analysis. Chess, however, only has one set of rules to follow. In the decision about cereals there may be lots of different 'rules' from different domains – cost of the cereal, how full you feel, taste in your mouth, childhood memories and so on – not all of which will be consciously processed. The number of different rules in play, combined with the complexity these rules can generate, leads to a sense of freedom at play, or at least masks the determined nature of the decision.

So the large number of factors and choices, together with the fact that we do not have access to all the computational brain processes, combine to make the process of deciding seem open and free, as opposed to closed and determined. However, being unaware of the cause of our choice is not the same as being aware of no cause.

What is free will?

Introduction

I am a free man. All entangling alliances ceased about a month ago . . . I'm now free to do whatever I want. Go wherever I want and have all the time in the world to develop into some kind of writer.[24]

Ernest Hemingway

So far we have explored the idea of physical determinism and seen that for certain people – hard determinists – this would imply that humans have no free will. What then can be said in defence of the idea that humans have free will, that Hemingway's dreams as a young man of becoming a novelist were in his power to achieve? First, we should remember that philosophers who claim that humans have free will, along with philosophers who claim we are determined, fall into two camps: those who believe that free will is compatible with physical determinism and those who don't. Those who do are called compatibilists or soft determinists, and those who don't are incompatibilists and could be either hard determinists or libertarians.

Table 5.1 *Varieties of free will and determinism*

Free will	Physical determinism	Name	Name 2
✓	✓	Soft determinism	Compatabilism
✓	✗	Libertarianism incompatabilism	A type of
✗	✓	Hard determinism incompatabilism	A type of

First we will explore the case of the libertarians, i.e. those who seek to argue that physical determinism does not apply to humans.

Libertarianism

The most common form of LIBERTARIANISM is that which is implicitly or explicitly contained in a broader theory of the mind called DUALISM. For many people, including a large number of those who believe in God, the human mind is not seen as a part of the physical world. It is therefore argued that the human mind is not bound by the laws of nature.

The general term applied to people who believe that the universe is made entirely of physical matter is, unsurprisingly, MATERIALISM. Materialism (sometimes called physicalism) is one of the varieties of monism ('mono' meaning one in Latin – referring to a single type of substance). Monists believe that the universe is made of only one type of thing and in the case of materialism this is physical substance – matter. (There is also another kind of monism which claims that the entire universe is just made of thoughts or ideas. This is known as IDEALISM. See pages 541–56.)

■ Table 5.2 The basic ontological theories

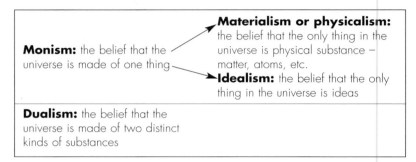

Monism: the belief that the universe is made of one thing

Materialism or physicalism: the belief that the only thing in the universe is physical substance – matter, atoms, etc.

Idealism: the belief that the only thing in the universe is ideas

Dualism: the belief that the universe is made of two distinct kinds of substances

In contrast to materialism, mind–body dualism is the belief that the physical world is made of physical substance but that the mind is non-physical and made up of a different kind of substance. This type of dualism would seem to offer those believing in free will an escape route from physical determinism. To explore this we need to consider three questions: What is dualism? How strong are its foundations? Does it offer an escape from physical determinism?

Dualism

Versions of dualism are implicit in the beliefs of many societies since earliest times. Ceremonial burial, for example, can be construed as a belief in a spiritual afterlife, the existence of another realm separate from the physical world. In cases of 'folk philosophy' these dualistic beliefs were not formally articulated as theories to be discussed and analysed. Plato believed in the existence of an immortal soul (see Chapter 2, pages 87–88), as did many of the Christian philosophers of the Middle Ages. Probably the most important articulation of dualism is in the work of René Descartes (1596–1650) and is known as Cartesian dualism – after the author. Descartes believed that the mind and body were two very different substances. He believed that physical bodies, including the brain, were made of physical substance. This substance is extended (i.e. it occupies space) and unthinking in its nature. The mind or soul, however, is made of a very different substance, which is in essence unextended (it does not occupy space) and thinking. In other words, thoughts in the mind do not occupy physical space whereas physical matter exists in space but is not capable of thought. To some extent this accords with our intuitions. If you were thinking of a green elephant and your brain was somehow instantly frozen and carefully sliced open, then we would find nothing green or elephant-shaped in there. The thought of the green elephant does not *seem* to occupy physical space; it somehow occupies 'mind space'.

Descartes

because on the one hand, I have a clear and distinct idea of myself in so far as I am a thinking and unextended thing, and because, on the other hand I have a distinct idea of the body in so far as it is an unextended thing but which does not think, it is certain that I, that is to say my mind . . . is entirely and truly distinct from my body.[25]

Descartes believed that these two elements, the mind and the brain, constantly interact with each other. For example, I may see a wasp walking across my desk. This involves light from the window reflecting off the wasp into my eye causing 'yellow-and-black-striped-insect' information to register in my brain. The brain then interacts with the mind, which then perceives the wasp. The interaction works the other way too: let's say I decide to swat the wasp. This thought, which takes place in my mind, then affects certain brain cells (although Descartes wouldn't have phrased it like that) which then cause my hand to move. Most people believing in dualism will want this form of two-way interaction between the brain, which occupies physical space, and the mind, which does not occupy physical space.

This account of dualism would seem to provide humans with the possibility of free will. The physical world, of which the brain is a part, is determined by the laws of nature and so is not free. The mind is not part of the physical universe and so is free to make choices unaffected by the laws of nature. But is this a convincing solution?

Criticism 1: Incoherence of interactionism

An obvious problem for Descartes' dualism is how the two substances are supposed to interact, given that they have such radically different natures. How can my desire to scratch my nose, which it is claimed takes place in my mind and totally outside the physical universe, cause the brute matter of my arm to move? If the mind does not exist in space *where* does it come into contact with the brain? If ordinary matter in space can only be moved by the impact of some other moving object, how is some immaterial thinking substance to influence it? It seems as if the idea of a non-physical mind operating in a physical universe, as if it were part of a physical process yet being somehow a different kind of substance, is incoherent.

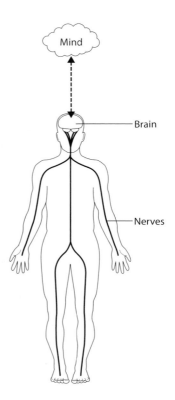

Mind

Brain

Nerves

Criticism 2: Violation of the law of conservation of energy

Another criticism is that the account provided by Descartes is at odds with the well-established physical laws about the conservation of energy and momentum. The first law of thermodynamics states that, in a closed system, energy cannot be created or destroyed – which means that the total energy in the universe must always remain the same.

But if human minds are interacting with our brains then this will require energy, which must be coming from outside of the physical world. This would contravene the law of the conservation of energy. Consider the case of a woman who sees a bull charging towards her and wisely turns to flee. If physical determinism is true then theoretically we should be able to give a complete causal explanation of how this happens and be able to account for all the energy involved in the process. We should be able to give an account of the light waves from the sun bouncing off the skin of the bull and hitting the retina in the eyes of the woman. We could then give a casual account of the light waves hitting the rods and cones in the back of the eye and these in turn causing chemical/electrical impulses to travel along axons to different neurons in the brain. It should be possible to carry on and give a complete causal account of what happens in the brain, ending up with the nerves in the leg causing the muscles to contract and hence the woman fleeing from the bull. Although such an account is beyond present science, it is theoretically possible if physical determinism is true.

However, if Descartes' dualism is true then our causal account must break down somewhere and new energy will either be lost from or added to the system. At some stage a neuron will 'fire' in the brain and it will not have been caused by the firing of any preceding neuron. To the scientist observing this event it will appear to fire for no reason, and the energy required will seem to have been instantly created. The firing of the neuron will have been caused by the mind, which is of course not in physical space and so beyond the prying eye of the scientists. If Descartes' account of the mind is true then there will be gaps in chains of cause and effect in the physical world. It would mean that the physical world itself is not fully determined since certain events in the brain will occur that cannot be explained purely by reference to other events in the preceding causal chain.

So dualism implies that there is a gap in the universal causality of the physical universe. It would also contravene the theory of the conservation of energy, as a small amount energy would have entered the brain that could not be accounted for in terms of the amount of energy in the brain before the intervention of the mind.

Criticism 3: Neural dependence
A final difficulty for dualism concerns the fact that our minds appear to be heavily reliant on our brains. Damage to the brain seems to have a direct impact on mental functioning. If there is alcohol in the blood coursing round my brain, I have trouble doing arithmetic. A sharp blow to the head can produce unconsciousness, and also leads to trouble doing arithmetic. Further evidence of the brain's involvement in our thinking comes from modern magnetic resonance imaging techniques, which show that specific parts of the brain are active when we are engaged in specific sorts of mental activity from doing philosophy or mathematics, to willing, imagining and sensing.

Dualists can defend themselves here by emphasising that the mind is, in this life, intimately conjoined to the body and so the mind's functioning is affected by contact with the brain. Still, why should unconsciousness follow from a blow to the head? Surely the brain might suffer trauma and we should remain conscious, since our conscious mind is supposed to be indestructible.

In sum, the neural dependence of the mind is far better explained if we suppose that the mind is really something to do with the brain. The most common version of this view – that the mind is in the final analysis explicable in purely material terms – is known as materialism, and it is perhaps the standard view of the nature of mind today. So although dualism may seem an attractive option for those wishing to defend human free will, there are problems with the theory, in particular in articulating the relationship between the mind and the brain.

Criticism 4: Can dualism deliver free will?

We noted earlier that many who believe in dualism may also believe in God – Descartes was no exception. Dualism involves the belief in a non-physical dimension to the universe and such dimensions are often associated with the belief that humans have an immortal soul and that there is life after death. Religious dualists face additional problems to the ones already outlined above, namely the incompatibility of free will with the existence of an omnipotent and omniscient God. The existence of an omniscient (all-knowing) God is a problem for the dualist, because if God knows what we are going to do before we have actually done it then it's hard to see how we are free to do anything other than what God has foreseen (see pages 352–53 above). The existence of an omnipotent God is also a problem, because if God is all-powerful then he has control over everything, in which case he also has control over us – and this too seems to contradict the idea of genuine free will.

So the escape route that dualism offers free will may not be straightforward. Furthermore, on a broader level, escaping from physical causation may not provide a full explanation of free will. Some would hold that physical determinism is just one example (albeit an important one) of a broader principle – which Leibniz called the principle of sufficient reason. This is the idea that everything that happens must happen for a reason.

Let's say dualism is true and that Billy (page 346) has a non-spatial mind which is exempt from the laws of nature. Billy still has to choose a cereal. His brain will feed him some information – for example smells, colours and sense of hunger – and then it is up to Billy to 'freely' choose his cereal – in this case Rice Crisps. Now imagine that we rewind time and replay the scene again. Everything being the same, Billy's brain will receive and send the same information to the mind and then it is up to Billy to make a decision. What will he do? The first time Billy chose, presumably he did so for a reason – for example, his sense of hunger and perhaps the stress of the day ahead meant that he wanted something light like Rice

Crisps, rather than something heavy like the crunchy oat-based option. Presumably if we played the scene again then Billy would reason again the same way. If he chose the Rice Crisps the first time for a particular reason, and everything is identical the second time around, then presumably the same reason will apply.

For some people, the idea that if you rewound time, and each time the same result followed, would imply that Billy had no free will. So, although a non-spatial mind can escape the physical laws of nature that might determine decisions, it can be argued that such a mind cannot escape the more general principle of sufficient reason.

If dualism does not offer a route for libertarians, are there other alternatives?

Jean-Paul Sartre and existentialist freedom

Sartre

Man is free, Man is Freedom.[26]

Jean-Paul Sartre (1905–1980) was a famous existentialist philosopher, novelist and playwright. EXISTENTIALISM is a difficult philosophical movement to define but some of its key concerns revolve around the *individual*, the range of *human experience* and the significance of choice or *free will*. Existentialism is often grounded in a philosophical approach called PHENOMENOLOGY, which tries to make sense of the world, starting from the elements of experience that are most real, certain and central to the life of the individual. For Sartre the most central and defining feature of human experience was free will.

The need to make decisions and choices is present with us at nearly all times. Every minute of every day we are required to make decisions: what to wear, how to walk, what to say, what to buy. Even when not making decisions the possibility of choice is ever-present in our thoughts. Shall I finish reading this sentence? Maybe I should stop and get a biscuit? What shall I do tomorrow evening? We cannot escape choice as it is required in our every action, and we cannot avoid actions. Even doing nothing is a choice. We cannot even choose not to make choices, as even this is a choice. Obviously, the decisions we make shape our lives in sometimes small, sometimes big ways. However, how we *respond* to the constant need to make decisions is also a key part of our lives, and Sartre builds his philosophy around this issue.

Along with other existentialists, Sartre does not give a rigorous proof of human free will. To some extent it is simply assumed as one of the starting points of his philosophy. He does, however, articulate some of the conditions he thinks are necessary for humans to have free will.

All physical objects have an essence. For Sartre this is such things as their weight, shape and size. This essence determines how the object behaves – whether it breaks when it drops or burns when thrown in a fire etc. Such objects have no freedom; their essence determines how they behave at every instant. In Sartre's terms their essence precedes and determines how they exist.

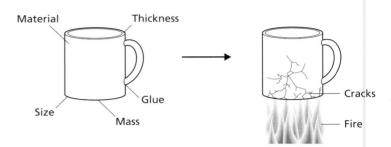

■ **Figure 5.7 The essence of a cup determines how it behaves**

Humans, however, have no such essence (although some people crave one) – our existence precedes our essence. If we did have an essence then, in common with other objects, it would determine how we behaved at every moment. In other words, determinism would be true and we would be no different from other physical objects. The fact that we have no essence gives us our free will. We exist first and make choices. We are each the author of the book of our own lives, and we are making up the chapters as we go along.

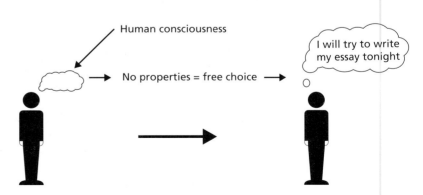

■ **Figure 5.8 Humans have no essence**

As humans have no essence, their essence does not determine the action and so they are free.

Sartre was disappointed by those philosophers (Plato, Aristotle, Hume, and most of the modern philosophers examined in this book) who believed that there was a certain nature which is common to all men and fixed for all time.

This view of human beings requires that 'the wild man of the woods, man in the state of nature and the bourgeois are all contained in the same definition and have the same fundamental qualities'.[27] Such a view, according to Sartre, simply reinstates the religious attitude that the essence of man precedes his existence. Many philosophers have talked about human nature. For example, Aristotle sees us as essentially political animals, Plato as essentially rational; Christians see our essence as one of having sinned; Freud talks of our Id, Ego and Superego; Hobbes sees us as selfish; some humanists see us as essentially good. Similarly, scientists claim that we have a biological nature which determines what we are as human beings. What such views have in common is that they believe us to be defined by our essence. But Sartre sees us as essentially *nothing* – for him, every philosopher prior to existentialism was missing the point. We have no essence, we have nothing at our core, we are bound to nothing, fixed by nothing, determined by nothing.

There is no human nature, according to Sartre, that can give us an essence. Nor is there any fixed personality, or inner self or soul that can give us an essence. Any attempt to fix someone's character or personality by labelling them as 'cowardly' or 'criminal' is to deny the truth about their being, namely their lack of essence. No name-calling or assignment of roles can determine what we may become; no description of our past lives captures what we could be in the future. The description 'coward' necessarily comes after the fact, and the individual can always redefine herself by changing her actions. Unlike physical objects, which Sartre terms beings-in-themselves, humans are essentially indefinable. It is not until we die, and can no longer act, that we can be defined, and we become a being-in-itself with an essence.

To illustrate his point that we have no essence Sartre gives the example of the French novelist Marcel Proust, a writer considered by many to be a genius because of the psychological and emotional depth of his novels.[28] But this genius was not something that he was born with, or that preceded his novels. According to Sartre, Proust did not possess any essential genius that was the cause of his great works. Instead, Sartre says his genius *is* his works, or his genius is constituted through his works.[29] If Proust had died and had only written sketchy ideas on the backs of envelopes, but hadn't got round to writing his novels, then he would not have been a genius. Proust defined himself as a genius by writing works of genius. This goes for all of us, we create ourselves (our essence if you like) through what we do.

Sartre

Man is nothing else but the sum of his actions.[30]

If we have no essence what then are we? Sartre claims that we are not what we have been in the past, even though it might appear that way. Whenever we search into ourselves to what we are we cannot find anything permanent that might answer the question, just a sequence of fleeting thoughts and feelings. At this very moment you may be angry or confused, but that is not a permanent part of you as the next minute you might not be angry and confused. You might see a blue sky, but the next moment you see a green tree. Nothing permanent remains in your consciousness that might constitute an answer to the question of what you are. You only know that you are not the confusion or the anger or the blueness or the greenness. We only know what we are not, not what we are. On this basis Sartre claims that we are not nothing, but something he terms *nothingness*.

This lack of an essence, the uncertainty of what we are and the constant need to create our own lives can be unsettling for some. So people convince themselves that they have an essence and in doing so relinquish their free will. I can't play the piano as I'm not musical. I can't eat pizza as I don't like tomatoes. Somehow their imagined essence provides them with definite positions to take and hence they don't actually need to make a decision. For many readers approaching this topic of free will the problem is one of 'it seems we are determined; how is free will possible?' For Sartre the common experience for many is: it appears I am free, how can I pretend to myself that I am determined!

As mentioned, most people find the responsibility of making decisions, especially decisions about their own life, overwhelming and convince themselves they have no freedom. For example, I can't do my homework tonight because I need to look after my sick dog. In this case Sartre would say that no, you could do your homework tonight but you *choose* to look after your sick dog – which indeed may be a good choice to make. But don't pretend you cannot do it; it is a *choice* not to do it. You could try to learn the piano but you choose not to. You could stop reading this book at this point and spend all your money on an expensive collection of kites but you *choose* not to do this. For Sartre, we often delude ourselves that we have no choice, but in fact we nearly always do. He calls this delusion *mauvaise foi*, translated as 'bad faith' or 'self-deception' – it means believing and pretending to be determined, to have an essence, when in fact we are absolutely free.

Of course you are not free to do *anything* you choose. You are not free to jump 100 feet in the air, as this is beyond the ability of your body, although you are of course free to try. Your body, along with other features of the world, dictates the boundaries and limits of your possible choices. Your body can also factor into your positive decision-making. Sartre invites us to consider the example of a man walking up a hill.[31] As he walks further and further up the hill he becomes increasingly tired. At some point the man stops and says he *cannot* go on. This is perhaps an experience familiar to many of us – we stop when we feel a bit tired or our legs hurt a bit. However, in nearly all cases we *could* have gone on but we *chose* not to. Our body would have carried us further but the pain in our legs or in our lungs was such that we made a decision to stop. Sartre would emphasise that this is still a free choice. The pain from our bodies makes the choice to stop a very tempting one, but it is still a choice. You did not *have* to stop; you could have run on until your legs literally would not carry you any more and you fell over – not through choice but through the failings of your legs. Sartre's point is that the tiredness did not cause the hiker to give up; he *chose* to stop walking. Giving up was his response to this particular obstacle – but he could have chosen to have carried on walking, to have been spurred on by his fatigue, rather than crushed by it.

experimenting with ideas

Read through the following situations and then answer the questions below for each one.

1 You want to go on holiday with your friends, but you've just lost your job.
2 You have been in a car accident and lost the use of one leg.
3 Your country goes to war and you are conscripted into the army.
4 You've become addicted to pain killers, and can no longer function without them.
5 You are carrying an injured friend through the wilderness to find help, but every step you take hurts you more and more.

   a) Given these obstacles/events, what are all the possible options that you have?
   b) What would your response to these obstacles/events be?

Through analysis such as this, Sartre can defend the idea of free will from claims of biological or cultural determinism. Our genes provide us with a certain physical constitution; this constitution may in turn provide us with certain desires. Perhaps people with gene C1276 are more inclined to drink alcohol. Likewise with environmental inputs: a child exposed to swimming pools may enjoy swimming as an adult, whereas a child who had a bad experience with crisps may avoid potato snacks later in life. However, for Sartre, such desires are similar to our desire to stop when walking up the hill. Our genetic make-up may incline us towards certain behaviours but it is still our free choice to carry out those behaviours. It's just that many people will, understandably, give in to their desires. So the statistical correlations between genes and behaviour or between upbringing and behaviour will exist. For Sartre, however, this does not rule out free will; it simply suggests that many of us do not embrace freedom as much as we could and perhaps go along with our impulses a touch too easily.

▶ criticism ◀ An obvious criticism is simply to deny the claim that we have no essence. A materialist would state that you have a brain and this defines how you behave. Your brain is your essence and this determines your existence and hence you have no freedom.

A further criticism arises from the lack of clarity in Sartre's account as to what happens to the chains of cause and effect when it comes to making decisions. It is not clear whether the 'nothingness' that makes humans is part of the physical world or not. However, if it is part of the physical world, then the most that can be argued for it is compatabilism not libertarianism. If it is not part of the physical world then the problem of interaction and the break in the laws of nature (outlined above) will once again apply.

Phenomenology

In Sartre's defence he does not claim to provide a proof for free will. It is presumed as one of the starting points of his philosophy. It appears to be such a central feature of human existence that it can be assumed as a given.

As mentioned, Sartre's philosophy is part of a wider philosophical movement known as phenomenology. The movement takes its lead from the approach taken by Descartes in his book the *Meditations*. Descartes sought to find what can be known for certain, and to do this imagined that there was an evil demon setting out to deceive him (see page 304). If there was, perhaps everything was just an illusion created by the demon and the world does not exist, a bit like in the film *The Matrix*. Descartes concludes that he can at least be certain he exists: if there is a deceiver there must be someone existing to be deceived (I think therefore I am – he claims). From this Descartes tries to build a philosophy based on the certainty of his existence.

Other people have tried this general approach. Like

Descartes they take as the starting point the immediate experiences of the senses and of the mind – those elements that cannot really be doubted. For example, I am now looking at a pair of red curtains. It may be possible that there are no actual red curtains and that I am deluded. However, what is *undeniable* is that I am having a red-curtain-like experience. This is true whether this is a dream, a delusion, a hallucination or (far more likely) caused by seeing an actual pair of red curtains. Phenomenology is not really concerned with what causes our experiences; in this regard it is said to 'bracket off' the question of what exists. Instead it focuses on our subjective sensations, emotions and thoughts and tries to give a philosophical account of our experiences in life.

A very basic phenomenological account of science would proceed like this. We are aware via the senses of various colours, shapes and sounds and we call these things objects. We notice that there are regular patterns or sequences of events whereby one object or event follows another. I throw an object in the air, it falls to the ground. I put fire near paper and notice it burns. We then come up with mathematical laws that help us to understand these patterns of data and help us to predict the future. In this brief account, the task of science has been constructed from that which we are immediately and undeniably aware of – the experience of the senses.

For some phenomenologists, physical determinism seems to proceed the wrong way round. It starts with the theory of universal causation – something that is not an immediate or a basic experience but is a highly generalised abstract theory – and uses this to claim that something that is immediate and undeniable – the feeling of free will – must be wrong. For the phenomenologist this is methodologically an inappropriate way of seeking certainty. The determinist is starting with something that is itself not certain, and is in turn derived from more basic elements of experience – the theory of universal causation. They then use this to claim that something that feels very certain and basic (free will) is in fact wrong.

For some phenomenologists the debate about free will is ultimately one of method or approach. Do we:

a) believe in our experience of free will and so assume that there is something wrong with the unproven theory of universal causation

or

b) believe in the theory of universal causation and assume that something is wrong with our experience of free will – that it is illusory?

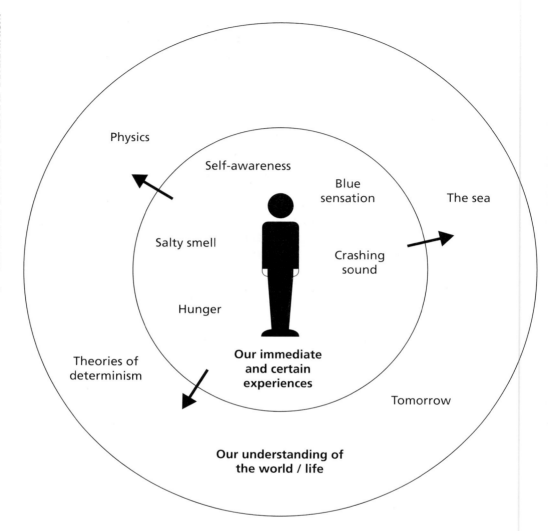

Physics

Self-awareness

Blue sensation

The sea

Salty smell

Crashing sound

Hunger

Our immediate and certain experiences

Theories of determinism

Tomorrow

Our understanding of the world / life

■ **Figure 5.9**
Phenomenology

The phenomenologist starts with what is most certain to them: their feelings and ideas about how the world appears. From here they proceed outwards to explain and understand themselves and their surroundings.

For the phenomenologist the first choice is the obvious one. They claim the best philosophical method is to start from certainties and move outwards. The scientist, however, might prefer the second approach.

On one level phenomenologists are not very concerned with the debate about free will. They can still meaningfully write about the world as it appears to us even if we have no free will, for it is undeniable that we have the feeling of free will, and how we react to and deal with this is important to discuss in its own right. Indeed it could be argued that little would change in the phenomenologists' philosophies if it turns out that we don't have free will, as our experience of the world would be the same either way, and phenomenology takes as its starting point our experience of the world. In the same vein it can be argued that existentialism would be completely compatible with soft determinism. In other words existentialists can claim we have free will; they do not actually need to deny physical determinism for their theories to work.

Primary mover unmoved

Determinism is based on the idea that every state of affairs is caused by the preceding state of affairs. This idea seems plausible but when and how did this whole process of causation begin? Perhaps the chain of causes and effects goes back forever, perhaps there always was a universe with events caused by the preceding events. On the other hand, perhaps there was a beginning. If the universe did have a beginning then it would seem to be the case that there must have been some events that happened that were not caused by the preceding events. The first event could not have been caused by any previous event, otherwise it would not, by definition, be the *first* event.

If this did happen – a first event spontaneously occurring with no cause – then we have a case of *causa sui* (meaning the cause of itself). Some people claim that God may have started the universe, but that in turn leads to the question of what caused God to act. A common answer would be to claim that god can act *causa sui* – meaning that God can cause things, without himself being caused to do things. Another term for this is to say that God is a primary mover – unmoved (see Plato and Aristotle's influence on this concept, page 88). God can be the initial cause of chains and cause and effect (he is a *primary mover*) but is not caused to do things by other causes (he is *unmoved*). Now if the universe did have a beginning it can be argued that there is at least one case of *causa sui* or of a primary mover unmoved. If there is one, perhaps there are more cases? Perhaps humans too are primary movers unmoved?

Gap in universal causation

Something along the lines of a gap in universal causation must be the case in all forms of libertarianism. Both the dualist and the existentialist claim that humans can act, and the act is not the result of previous causes. Both theories require a gap in the chain of universal causality, and such a gap underlies the very premise of a primary mover unmoved (see Figure 5.10).

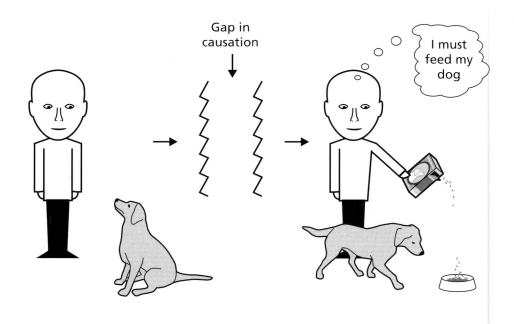

Gap in causation

I must feed my dog

Moments before

Decision to feed dog

■ Figure 5.10
Primary mover unmoved

Here the man makes a decision to feed the dog. However, this choice was not caused by the preceding events; there was a gap in the chain of causes and effects. The man is a primary mover unmoved and so is free.

For the dualists, the gap occurs because events are caused by the mind or the soul. Such events are not determined by physical events (they are unmoved) but themselves set off a new chain of cause and effect in the physical world (they are primary movers). For Sartre, the account is less clear, but our nothingness, the fact that we have no essence, must mean that we are able to act on the world (primary movers) without such actions being caused by an essence (unmoved).

Such approaches require a gap in the idea of universal causation, in which case they are, in theory, empirically verifiable. In other words, they are testable. As we saw in the instance of the woman fleeing the bull above (page 382), if physical determinism is true and applies to humans then the scientist should be able to give a full account of how the woman sees the bull and turns to run, every single stage being completely determined by the stage before it. However, if the dualist or existentialist is right then at some point the account will fail because at some stage an event will occur that has not been caused by any previous event, and this is because it has been caused by a primary mover, unmoved.

So it is in theory scientifically testable to see whether or not a gap in universal causation has occurred. In practice, however, this matter will not be settled one way or another by science as we are a long way off the sorts of technologies and techniques required.

Soft determinism

Aristotle

> *The movement of the limbs that are the instruments of action has its origin in the agent, and where this is so it is in his power either to act or not to act. Therefore such actions are voluntary.*[32]

Not all accounts of free will require there to be a gap in universal causation. Indeed the libertarian approach of denying that physical determinism applies to humans can actually cause problems for those wishing to claim free will. As discussed earlier, for some it is important that our desires and thoughts cause our actions, as otherwise we can't be held responsible for them. The majority of philosophers, including Aristotle and David Hume, believe that physical determinism is true *and* that humans have free will. Such thinkers hold a version of *soft determinism* to be true. In the table on page 379 we equated soft determinism with *compatibilism*, the idea that determinism and human free will are compatible. There is, however, a very small difference between the two positions. Technically a soft determinist believes that physical determinism is actually true, whereas a compatibilist believes that physical determinism and free will are compatible, but might not actually believe that either of them is true – just that they are compatible. In reality, however, most compatibilists do believe in the truth of both, and so are soft determinists.

There are different variations of soft determinism and we will start by exploring an argument attempting to outline the case for free will.

Ifs and coulds

> *Rita, if you only had one day to live – what would you do with it?*[33]
>
> *Groundhog Day*

Earlier on we looked at different answers that could be given to explain why a prisoner choosing a book had free will:

1 The man has a mind and is able to choose between different options.
2 The man is more than a simple collection of atoms and is not bound by the laws of nature.
3 If repeated again the man might choose a different book.
4 The man is not being caused to choose a particular book by external causes; the reason for the choice is largely internal to the man.

5 The man is not forced to choose a particular book.

6 The choice of book is not a necessary consequence of prior events.

7 It would be fairly difficult, if not impossible, to predict with accuracy which book the man would choose.

8 The man could have acted otherwise.

Many of these answers overlap and to some extent make the same point. The libertarian positions of dualism and existentialism discussed above claim 2 and 6 to be the key reasons why we have free will. However, to explore the first variant of soft determinism, we will begin by focusing on 8, the claim that 'the man could have acted otherwise'. For many, if this is true then we have free will. Snooker balls and rain drops could *not* have acted otherwise, which means that they have no free will. We humans could have acted otherwise and so we are free. The proof of the pudding might be to rewind time and see whether we could, in fact, behave any differently. In the film *Groundhog Day* the actor Bill Murray plays TV weatherman Phil Connors who gets to enact this fantasy, or nightmare, over and over again. He is trapped by a snowstorm in a small town and, at the end of the day, while he is asleep, time is rewound by 24 hours. So day after day he wakes up only to find it is the identical day, 2 February, as the day before. Everyone around him acts in the same way as they did yesterday, whereas he has the power to change the way he behaves, to try out different ways of living: stealing money, learning the piano, getting chased by the police, seducing beautiful women, committing suicide, taking French lessons. The film offers a very funny test case for free will, proposing that we are free to behave in different ways and, more cheesily, suggesting that we are free to change ourselves to become good people. However, this is not a strict case of rewinding time as, in each instance of the day starting again, Phil is able to remember what happened the previous times that the same day started. The real question would be what would Phil do if every single aspect of the day was the same each time, *including* the content of his mind?

Let us explore this idea in more detail. Cast your mind back once again to Billy's morning (page 346). If we were to ask Billy whether it were possible that he *could* have eaten say the crunchy oat cereal instead of the Rice Crisps then Billy would probably say 'Yes, I *could* have easily chosen that.' There was nothing to stop him picking a different cereal and if he had felt differently then he would have chosen differently. Likewise with the tie Billy chose, he would probably admit that he could have chosen differently. We could, though, invent a scenario in which his tie choice was less free. Imagine that two men, acting on behalf of the prosecution, had kidnapped Billy. Against his will they dressed him for his appearance at court in a jaunty yellow Homer Simpson tie in a desperate effort to undermine his credibility. After such a kidnapping, if you then asked Billy if he could have chosen differently when the tie was thrust on him, he would probably have said no.

So most of the time we could have done otherwise and so act out of free will. But sometimes, when we are physically (or perhaps psychologically) constrained, we could not have acted otherwise so did not have free will. Here we seem to have an answer to the problem of free will. Billy had free will in choosing his cereal because he could have done otherwise, which is to say he was not constrained in his actions.

This is more or less the position put forward by Hume on page 362. Free will really just means freedom from physical constraint. This certainly accords with our use of the word freedom in everyday speech. It also is in tune with the way we use moral concepts – we don't morally blame someone for an action they were physically forced to do. We only blame people if they could have done otherwise. Relating these to the explanations above, the suggestion here is that humans have free will because of 8, and 8 means the same as 5.

Some soft determinists are happy to stop the discussion at this point, whereas others are not satisfied. After all, many entities are free from physical constraint, but yet we would be wary of granting them free will. No one is forcing the mould to grow on my bread, or the ant to collect food. Yet would we grant these two free will? We could argue that the laws of nature are 'forcing' them to act in a particular way and so they are physically constrained and hence not free. But, if so, doesn't that also apply to me? It seems that if we construe physical constraint in too loose a way then we seem to be granting a lot things free will, because they are free from constraint. However, if we construe constraint in too tight a way then it appears that humans too have no free will.

Perhaps freedom from constraint is only part of the picture, and we need to add the ability to choose. Perhaps a phrase such as:

A Billy could have done otherwise.

means something like this:

B Billy would have done otherwise if he had so chosen.

This second formulation implies that there was nothing to stop the Billy from choosing differently. It states that if he had chosen differently then he would have done differently – which is not the case if he was forced to act. If forced he would have done the same regardless of how he had chosen. It also implies that Billy has the ability to choose, which perhaps ants and mould lack. Relating these to the explanations above, humans have free will because of 8, and 8 means the same as 1 and 5.

However, the hard determinist, who denies that humans still have free will, might still interject. They might agree that Billy *would* have done otherwise if he had so chosen. They agree with B, above. But they would deny that Billy *could* have chosen otherwise. In other words they deny that B is the same as A. They want an extra clause added to the definition— *that Billy could have chosen differently,* and they would deny this clause is true.

> A Billy could have done otherwise.
>
> =
>
> B Billy would have done otherwise if he had so chosen.
>
> +
>
> C Billy could have chosen otherwise.

The hard determinist would claim that Billy's choice was determined by such things as his genetics, upbringing, memories and feelings on that day. If we were to rewind time so that the whole scene and everything in it was the same in Billy's life up to that point, then, unlike Phil Connors in *Groundhog Day*, Billy would choose to do the same things, select the same tie, the same cereal, say the same things. According to hard determinism, Billy could not have chosen otherwise and so had no free will. In terms of the list above, 3 is not true, so 8 is not true.

We need to be clear about what is being stated here. For if the claim is that:

> X: If we rewound time and everything was the same *including* Billy's choice . . .

then it is obvious that Billy could not have chosen otherwise, as Billy's choice is one of the things stated that cannot change. So this is a bit of an unfair thought experiment. However, the question might be this:

> Y: What if we rewound time and everything was exactly the same right up to the moment that Billy chose his cereal, then what would he choose?

The claim of the hard determinist is that he always would choose Rice Crisps, and this means that he could not have chosen otherwise. However, the soft determinist has a range of different responses she could make to this claim. She could:

1 Disagree and claim that Billy could still choose otherwise.
2 Claim that the question is unfair. Choices are not really made in a single moment, they draw together lots of factors that may be mulled over in the background, so question Y above is really just another version of the unfair thought experiment X.
3 Agree that Billy would always choose Rice Crisps, but still maintain that it is true that he could have done otherwise if he had so chosen, and this implies he could have done otherwise, which implies he has free will. In other words, deny that extra clause C above is needed.
4 Agree with the hard determinist but maintain that this doesn't mean we don't have free will and try another way of showing that free will and determinism are compatible.

ACTIVITY **1** Re-read through the soft determinist's responses in 1–4 above.
2 Which of these responses do you agree with and why?

So this version of soft determinism claims that, by analysing what we mean by free will, it is possible to show that having free will simply means acting when not physically or psychologically constrained. The hard determinist, however, would disagree with the analysis. At this stage we will leave this discussion and follow option 4 above: try another route.

The type of cause

As we saw above, much is made of the idea of time being rewound. Such an idea is probably a familiar element in most of our inner lives. We might replay a situation in our minds and think *if only I had done this or that*. However, when considering this we tend to impose the mind we have now on the situation back then, and of course if this were the case we would act differently. But to imagine the scenario properly we must imagine that our minds have also been rewound and that our thoughts and feelings were the same as they were back then. If this was the case could you really have acted differently?

Consider Billy's cereal choice. On this occasion Billy chose Rice Crisps because he liked the texture, taste and sweetness – but he was also feeling a bit nervous and was having some slight butterflies in his tummy and didn't really fancy any food. He realised that he would need to eat otherwise he might feel faint later so decided to go for Rice Crisps as they are light on the tummy and quite appetisingly tasty. Presumably if Billy was in exactly the same situation and everything leading up to the event had been the same it is tempting to think that he will have chosen Rice Crisps again as his reasoning would have been the same.

Some compatibilists, like Hume, would say that, even if true, this wouldn't restrict our free will. It is merely to say that often we do things for reasons and that if we are in similar circumstances and similar events occur then we would do things for similar reasons. In fact consider the opposite – that our actions are not based on reasons at all. Imagine we could run an experiment whereby we rewound the scene four times and found that Billy chose a different cereal each time – even though his thought processes up to that point had been exactly the same. This might suggest that our decisions are not based on our thinking at all. They are either random or based on something other than our thinking. Either way, it might imply that our actions are not determined by us. So the problem with defence 1 given on page 399 above is that it comes close to indeterminism, the idea that physical determinism is not true. And this might be considered akin to claiming that our choices are random.

So perhaps we should embrace the idea that we would do the same thing again. The key is that the choice was made by Billy and by no one else. For Aristotle this is the crucial point: were a person's actions determined internally (by beliefs, hopes, desires, etc.) or were they determined externally (by someone controlling my arms using string or a remote control)?[34] If they were determined internally, then the person is choosing freely and must bear full responsibility for their actions. Billy determined his actions and, yes, if time were rewound he would do the same thing again. This does not imply that there is some invisible hand guiding us, or using a remote control to move our limbs in a particular way. It simply means that we make our own free choices and would do the same thing again for the same freely chosen reasons. It just shows that we are consistent as well as being free!

In this analysis it is not the *ifs* and the *coulds* of the situation that provide the freedom. It is the *who* we are that counts.

■ **Figure 5.11 *The snooker ball***

The second snooker ball moves primarily because of the first snooker ball; because of causes external to it.

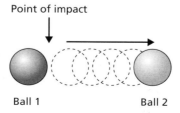

Point of impact

Ball 1   Ball 2

Snooker ball 2 in Figure 5.11, like all snooker balls, has no mind and so has no options to consider. Its behaviour is caused as much by the stimulus as by the ball itself. The same ball will always respond in the same way to the same stimulus on different days. This is sometimes referred to as event causation or transient causation, whereby one event causes another.

In Figure 5.12 we see that the human mind can conceive of different options and chooses one of them. Although the stimulus plays a key role, the event can be said to be caused

■ Figure 5.12 *The human*

The man chooses which cereal to eat primarily because of the content of his mind: because of causes internal to him.

by the agent rather than by the stimulus. Factors such as the mood, memories and hopes would cause different responses to the same stimulus on different days. This is sometimes referred to as AGENT causation or IMMANENT causation – whereby the agent causes an event through processes internal to herself. This idea that the *agent* causes the behaviour provides another version of soft determinism. An argument such as this could be made:

1 The mind determines the action.
2 You are your mind.
3 Therefore you determine your actions.
4 Therefore you have free will.

Referring to the list (pages 395–96) above, in this version 4 and 1 are the key to free will, with lack of constraint thrown in too (5), as no one else is determining your actions. This seems a simple and intuitive way of arguing for free will. However, the exact nature of the relationship between the stimulus, agent and action must be tightened up, as not all cases of such a relationship might be classed as examples of free will.

Consider the following occurrences and answer the questions below.

1 A dog chasing a rabbit in a field
2 A man unwillingly being pushed off a cliff
3 An ant collecting food
4 A student wanting to be rich and buying a lottery ticket
5 Someone with Tourette's syndrome swearing in public
6 Someone with obsessive compulsive disorder washing his hands for the 209th time that day
7 A hypnotised woman acting like a cat via the suggestion of the hypnotist
8 A man feeling ill and being sick in the toilet
9 A one-year-old baby screaming
10 A teenager, having watched a 'slick' ad for trainers, going out and buying the same pair the next day
11 An alcoholic buying an alcoholic drink

a) For each situation write down what the internal desires of the agent are.
b) Rank the relevant agent's free will on a scale of 1 to 10, whereby 10 is fully free and 1 is not free.

Earlier we suggested that free will is absolute – you either have it or you don't – this was the position taken by existentialists like Jean-Paul Sartre. If this is so, all of the cases above should be ranked either 1 or 10, with nothing in between. These examples, however, might make us question this idea. Indeed, this whole agent-centred approach might make us question the absoluteness of free will as the conditions for being a suitably free agent might not be so clear-cut.

- For case 2, a man pushed from a cliff, most would say that this was not agent-caused and so is not a free act, although the pusher might be classed as freely acting.
- Some would argue that 1, 3 and 9 are not suitably complex agents and so don't have free will. But if 9 is not an agent, at what age or in what circumstances do we have free will?
- In case 8 the act is not caused by the agent's mind, so might not be classed as a free choice.
- In case 7 some would argue that the woman is acting on her desires to be a cat and so it is a free act; others would argue that she is psychologically constrained and that the desires are not hers – in which case she is not free. However, what about in 4, 10 and 11: are these agents psychologically restrained? Whose desires are these? If a desire implanted by a hypnosis does not 'belong' to the agent, then what about desires produced by addiction, advertising, or even by upbringing?

▶ criticism ◀ A quick analysis of these scenarios suggests that this agent-caused version of soft determinism needs refining to cope with some of these issues. Such considerations as above, in particular the last point, lead to one of the main criticisms of this approach. It can be conceded that entities in your mind, such as desires or beliefs, determine the action (see Figure 5.12). It might also be conceded that this implies that you determine your actions. However, as you did not determine what was in the desires, hopes and dreams then you cannot claim to be free. In terms of the arguments on page 401 the first three lines are true but because you can't control your desires then line 4 does not follow.

To consider this version of soft determinism further we will look at a particular account held by a philosopher called Harry Frankfurt.

Second-order desires

Frankfurt suggests that humans, as opposed to other animals, possess free will and he claims this is because of a different *kind* of desire that humans are capable of having. He suggests that both animals and humans desire lots of things in the world. For example, I might want money, or cheese on my toast, or a cigarette. When the object of our desire is something in the world then he calls such urges *first-order desires.*

■ **Figure 5.13**
First-order desires
When the object of our desire is in the world this is termed a first-order desire.

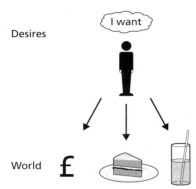

Frankfurt claims that humans have the capacity for self-awareness, which involves being aware of our thoughts. This mean we are able to have thoughts, beliefs and indeed desires about our first-order desires. I may want a cigarette but may want to *not want* a cigarette. So my first-order desire is for a cigarette but my second-order desire is to want to not want a cigarette. The object of my first-order desire is something in the world; the object of my second-order desire is a first-order desire.

■ **Figure 5.14**
Second-order desires
When the object of our desire is itself a desire about the world then this is termed a second-order desire.

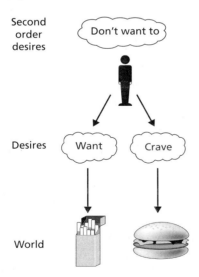

It is possible, of course, for someone to be satisfied with his first-order desires without in any way considering whether to endorse them. In that case he is identified with his first-order desires. But insofar as his desires are utterly unreflective, he is to that extent not genuinely a person at all. He is a wanton.[35]

Harry Frankfurt

Frankfurt suggests that most animals only have first-order desires and this means they have no free will. He also suggests that if humans acted on their first-order desires all the time then they would be to be determined by their desires. He calls such a person a *wanton*. A drug addict would fit the bill: they want drugs, but might not care about this first-order desire, not reflect on whether they want to want drugs.

Other drug addicts are genuine agents, in other words they may want to end their addiction – in Frankfurt's terms they 'identify' with their second-order preference (to kick the habit), not their first-order preference (to take the drugs). Most of us, however, can on some occasions resist our first-order desires and impose our second-order desires. We still acknowledge that we may want a piece of cake or a cigarette but we have a different set of desires, second-order desires, that are able to trump the first-order desires. Frankfurt identifies the set of second-order desires with the vision we have for our ideal self and these are more strongly associated with *you*. This is the view taken by Plato and Aristotle (see page 36) when they emphasise the rational control over our desires in people who are truly flourishing. It is precisely the ability to impose your second-order desires first that Frankfurt (and Plato and Aristotle) believes allows humans to have free will. Only then do *you* determine your action, as opposed to your *desires* determining them.

Frankfurt's approach has several redeeming features. It seems to allow humans to have free will, in contrast with animals who are determined by their first-order preferences, which for many seems intuitive. It also seems to allow for the limited success of biological and cultural determinism as our genes and our environment will indeed dictate our first-order desires, and so can be used with some accuracy to predict human behaviour. The theory implies that free will may not be absolute, which accords with the findings of the activity on page 401. If we unthinkingly act on our first-order desires then we may not be acting freely. Sometimes we act freely and sometimes we might not.

Finally it might also overcome the criticism outlined on page 402, which claims that, as we don't choose our desires, we don't have free will. Frankfurt suggests that, although we can't choose our desires, we can choose whether to act on them. We might go even further and claim that to some extent we are able to choose our desires. For example, you might not like art but you have a second-order desire to want to like art (possibly motivated by the fact that there is someone you fancy in your philosophy class who also likes art) and so do lots of reading up on the subject and spend time in galleries. In time you may well start liking art and through this process you have chosen your desire. Aristotle calls this 'habituation', in other words the development of our character (our habits, dispositions and desires) through constant training, until we end up genuinely wanting to do the thing that we originally had to force ourselves to do. Learning to play the guitar is a good practical example of Aristotelian habituation, painful, enforced practice at first, then later mastery and global rockgod-dom. For Aristotle it is not just practical skills but moral and emotional habits (and the second-order desires which accompany them) that can be usefully developed in this way:

Aristotle

Moral goodness is the result of habit . . . Anything we have to learn to do we learn by the actual doing of it: people become builders by building and musicians by playing instruments. Similarly we become just be performing just acts . . . brave by performing brave acts.[36]

► criticism ◄

However, does Frankfurt's theory really answer the criticism that we don't choose our desires? Frankfurt equates the self with a set of second-order desires, but it is not so clear why this should be the case. Why should your desires about your desires represent *you* any more than your plain own first-order desires? Crucially, where do the second-order desires come from? The criticism of the agent-caused approach is that as we didn't choose our desires then acting on them is not acting out of free choice. However, to what extent do we choose our second-order desires? I may want to be a certain kind of person, i.e. non-smoking, healthy, loving of the arts, and so on, but where did these second-order desires come from?

You could argue that these again are desires derived from our genetic make-up and our environment; in other words, they were determined by something other than you. Even Aristotle acknowledges that we can't go against our natural tendencies, but can only further develop what is already innate in us:

Aristotle

We are constituted by nature to receive [our virtues], but their full development is in us due to habit.[37]

For Aristotle, just as we cannot train a stone to move upwards simply by throwing it in the air a few thousand times, so we cannot train ourselves to be truly courageous if we were born a coward (although we might train ourselves to over-ride our cowardice, we might never actually have the desire to be courageous or the pleasure accompanying courage). But if we don't determine our desires, including our second-order desires, then can we really claim that acting on our desires constitutes free will? It may be true that you determine your actions, but if you don't determine who you are then you still don't have free will. Only something that genuinely created all relevant aspects of itself – a primary mover unmoved – can claim to have free will.

To further illustrate this criticism consider the question of intelligence. This surely is a factor in much of our decision-making. However, you do not appear to choose how intelligent you are; this seems to be determined by other factors. So, even though your decisions are primarily determined by internal factors of the mind, such as intelligence, as you didn't choose these, then you cant really claim to be making free choices.

Summary

So we have seen that there are different ways of reconciling physical determinism and human free will. One way is to analyse the language surrounding free will and suggest that it is meaningful, and true, to claim that 'on most occasions we could have acted otherwise and so are free'. Another way is to look at the agent who causes the actions and argue that if certain conditions are met then an act is free. Both lines of argument run into some difficulty. However, these are only some of the approaches to soft determinism; there are others. Some philosophers, such as Plato and Aristotle, have claimed that it is only when we act out of reason, as opposed to desires, that we have free will. Others have claimed that is our ability to think about the future and so conceive of different possibilities that sets us apart from other animals and gives us free will. Some claim that it is only when we consider moral actions and make a specific moral decision that we act freely. Perhaps you also have a suggestion for how free will and physical determinism can live happily side by side?

What are the implications of determinism?

Moral responsibility and choice

'One is soon very bored with everything my angel; it is a law of nature. It is not my fault . . .
It follows that for some time I have been deceiving you, but then your relentless tenderness forced me in some sort to do so! It is not my fault.

A woman that I madly love now insists that I give you up for her sake. It is not my fault.

Goodbye, my angel. I took you with pleasure: I leave you with regret . . . Such is life. It is not my fault.[338]

In Laclos' novel *Dangerous Liaisons*, the character Valmont breaks off his affair with a virtuous and devout woman by copying the letter above and sending it to her. In his letter he repeats throughout that it is not his fault; each reason for breaking this woman's heart lies beyond his control. Valmont knows that the woman will be destroyed by this letter, but he denies any responsibility: he has distanced himself from his action, he is driven by external circumstances that he has no power over. And to some extent he is right, it isn't his fault – he doesn't want to write the letter but is driven to write it by his love for another woman; it was she who suggested the wording in the first instance. It is a chilling letter, from a chilling man. If, as Valmont writes, the causes of our action are beyond our control, then the consequences are not our fault, we are not responsible. In this section we look at some of the implications of determinism on our moral responsibility.

Morality plays an important part in all of our lives. In small and big ways we often think about what we ought to do. Should I spend my money on downloads or get them for free? Should I go out tonight or stay in and work? Should I still be friends with Alice after I find out she has said rude and nasty things behind my back? Should I give more money to charity? All these questions and countless others form part of our moral lives. Morality at its most basic is a quest to answer the question 'how should I live my life?' The questions in the paragraph above simply reflect different aspects of this broader quest. Another way of viewing the moral arena is to see science as attempting to *describe* how the world is, and so is *descriptive*, whereas morality is concerned with how the world *should* be and how we ought to behave, and so is termed *prescriptive*. (We look in detail at the question of why we should be moral in Chapter 1.)

Herein lies a possible problem for the hard determinist. The soft determinist claims that we have free will because we meaningfully could have acted otherwise. The hard determinist denies this and claims that for any action we could not have acted otherwise. The moral concept of *ought* would seem to be logically linked to the concept of *could* or *can*, insomuch as we can only say someone ought to have done something if it is something they *could* have actually done.

Consider the following:

> Albert is pushed off a small cliff and lands on a dog being taken for a walk on the beach below. The dog is killed and Albert sustains a minor injury.

Let us ignore the question of who did the pushing for now, but focus on Albert instead. Is it right for us to get morally outraged by Albert's action? Should we say that what Albert did was wrong? Should Albert be sent to prison? The answer is surely no. Albert had no choice; he could not have done otherwise and an action can only be morally wrong if the person could have done otherwise. We can only berate a person for what they ought to have done if they could have done otherwise.

To look at this again, consider Albert's true position. Albert hated the owner of the dog, Clive. Ten years ago Clive got a promotion at work that Albert thought was rightfully his. The anger has boiled up inside him all this time and now he wants to exact revenge. He watches Clive walk his dog every Sunday on the beach and works out a cunning, yet risky, plan. He has arranged the event to look as if he was mugged by robbers who pushed him over the edge of a small cliff. In fact, the robbers were friends who, on Albert's instructions, pushed him off the cliff so as to land on and kill the dog below. Would you now blame Albert for his actions? Should we punish him? We would say yes, because Albert had a choice; he could have done otherwise.

It seems that we need choice, the ability to do otherwise, in order to morally blame or praise people for their actions. To further explore the link between choice and moral blame, examine the scenarios in the next activity.

Consider the following cases, and answer the questions below.

1 A woman sets up a fake website and takes money from customers for new televisions that don't actually exist.

2 A man violently mugs another man for money and keeps kicking the man even after he's got the wallet.

3 A man is forced at knifepoint to throw a brick off a motorway bridge. The brick smashes a windscreen on a car travelling at high speed, killing the driver.

4 A hypnotised woman steals from a friend after a suggestion was put into her head.

5 A six-year-old child throws a brick at a shop window.

6 A heroin addict steals a wallet from a student to get drugs.

7 A woman who was beaten as a child starts to beat her own child.

a) How much free will would you accord each person on a scale of 1 to 10?

b) How much moral blame would you accord each person on a scale of 1 to 10?

You might have made the following observations:

- In cases 1 and 2, most people would morally blame the perpetrator and would accord them plenty of free will.
- Case 3 is a bit more ambiguous as in theory the person had a choice not to throw the brick. However, most people would sympathise and not attribute any blame as there was great psychological pressure, namely the terror of what would happen if he did not carry out the act. So there was only a little choice and so, it would seem, only a little, if any blame.
- In case 4, although the woman was not physically constrained, most would claim she had no choice as she was psychologically constrained, so most would not accord much blame.
- In cases 5 to 7 the person would seem to have some degree of choice, and again they would all seem to have some degree of blame.

These scenarios would seem to accord with our intuitions that the proportion of blame is linked to the proportion of freedom. And if a person could not have done otherwise then they have no moral blame. This is Aristotle's conclusion in Book 3 of the *Ethics*: an agent can only be blamed (or praised) for an action if it had its origins in the agent (i.e. in the person carrying out the act). Where an action has its origin external to the agent, in the case of compulsory acts where someone is literally controlling my limbs or my mind, then the agent has no responsibility.

These findings present a problem for the hard determinist. He would claim that we could never do otherwise, in which case all our acts are compulsory and it would seem as if we can never be morally blamed for our actions. More formally stated the problem is this:

1 The hard determinist claims that for every occasion every human could not have done otherwise.
2 If a person could not have done otherwise then they cannot be considered to be morally wrong in their action.
3 If the hard determinist is right then on no occasion can any human be considered morally wrong for their action.

We should also note that it is not just morality but a whole range of other emotional responses that would seem to have their premise in the idea that humans have free will. For example, regret – what would be the point in this if you could not have done otherwise? Gratitude – why thank a person for their kindness if they had no choice but to act that way? Guilt – why beat yourself up about some behaviour that your genes, environment and neurological make-up compelled you to do?

If hard determinism is true, then are we mistaken in our approach to moral blame? Imagine we applied morality only to chemistry and made such judgements as *it was wrong of the salt to dissolve in water* or *that naughty acid really shouldn't have neutralised that alkaline*. This would seem to be a mistaken use of moral language. We are simply making an error in applying the concept of moral blame to chemicals. If hard determinism is true, could it be argued that we must also be mistaken in applying moral blame to humans?

Here is another way of making the same point. Suppose that there is indeed a God and that hard determinism is true. Good people go to heaven, bad people go to a life of endless suffering in hell. It seems a bit harsh of God to create a person who, entirely because of the way they are made, cannot help but make certain choices in life and so is sent to suffer in hell (we look at this idea in more detail in Chapter 6, pages 473–75). It would be wrong for God to sit in moral judgement if we could not have done otherwise. However, we can re-imagine the scenario without God. It seems very harsh for any of us to sit in moral judgement if a person could not have done otherwise.

So it does seem that we can only morally blame people if they could have done otherwise – if they had free will. This might seem to suggest that we can in fact do otherwise and so we do actually have free will. Or perhaps it suggests that all of our moral blame is somehow false or misplaced. One defence available to the hard determinist is to go for this latter option, to agree that we are mistaken in morally blaming humans for their actions, but to explain how moral blame and praise persist. The claim is that as long as behaviour changes in response to moral concepts such as praise and blame then we have a reason to use such concepts. People may have no free will; however, they still make decisions on the basis of desires, beliefs, fears *and* moral concepts. They may not have been able to choose otherwise but that does not mean that the process of coming to a decision was not an involved one. As long as moral concepts are involved in this process and so affect behaviour then we can understand and explain why moral blame exists.

The idea is that if we morally vilify someone then we might stop the person and others from carrying out such an action again. As long as people factor moral concepts in to their decision-making then these concepts will have their use and value. Someone might give money to a charity because they want to be seen to do the right thing and raise the esteem in which they are held. Another person may give money because they believe it is the right thing to do. In both cases our moral concepts have an effect on behaviour and this would be the case even if we are determined.

■ **Figure 5.15**
Morality is a factor in our decision-making

The man making the decision whether to steal the dog considers the fact that many people would think this to be a bad thing. Moral considerations are part of his decision-making process and so might affect his behaviour.

As long as moral concepts have a potential effect on behaviour then we can understand why they are used. Note also that we don't, as a general rule, use moral concepts on inanimate objects or on animals. This is because they would not respond or change their behaviour if we did. So, although it is as mistaken to morally blame chemicals for their action as it is to blame humans, we can understand why we blame humans – because it can change future behaviour – whereas it would have no impact on the way chemicals behaved.

ACTIVITY   Revisit the cases above (page 408). Would morally blaming the person in question have any impact on whether they or others carried out similar acts again? Might this explain why sometimes we blame and sometimes we don't?

It can be argued that in cases 1 and 2 some people might be dissuaded from carrying out the actions again: for example, if people close to them thought that the actions were morally wrong and expressed their views strongly. Other people of course would not undertake such actions in the first place because they thought they were wrong. So in these cases it can be argued that moral blame has its use in as much as it can affect future behaviour and this is the reason why we pour our moral scorn on people who do something wrong. In cases 3 and 4 it can be argued that the person or similar persons would not be susceptible to moral concepts. The person throwing a brick off a bridge under knifepoint, or stealing while hypnotised, is not less likely to do the same thing again if the action was called wrong. The hard determinist claims that we do not consider the behaviour of either of these people to be morally wrong as labelling such behaviour would not change their, or others', behaviour. So although we are mistaken to morally blame individuals, we can understand why we do so.

► criticism ◄ ## Explaining and explaining away
One criticism of this defence is that the hard determinist has not explained moral blame, but simply explained it away.

ACTIVITY   Read the following strange events:

1 Derek used magic to cure his wife's cold.
2 Finbar walked aboard a UFO.
3 God answered Ian's prayers and he got a pay rise.

How might you explain the occurrence of each of these events?

Did your answer explain what happened or explain away what happened? Consider the example of the magic that Derek used. An explanation for what happened might be something like this: 'Magic describes those situations when spells and incantations along with special ingredients affect the world. They work because invisible pixies, or spirits, or energies respond to the incantations and, unseen, change the world in particular ways – in this case by curing Derek's wife.' Note that in the explanation the existence of magic is still preserved. However, another answer could be given: 'Derek spent the evening chanting, but this was unrelated to his wife's recovery, which would have happened anyway. The fact that they occurred together made Derek believe that it was indeed magic at work.' In this explanation magic does not exist – what has been explained is Derek's belief in magic. Regarding the UFO, one explanation might be that a vehicle from another planet landed, and Finbar, who was nearby, walked on to it. In this case the existence of the UFO is preserved. An alternative account is to say that Finbar was very tired after drinking too much absinthe, and mistook some bright lights for a UFO; he fell asleep and convinced himself he had walked aboard. Here the UFO no longer exists; it has been explained away. Sociologists can provide a very convincing account of why we believe in magic, UFOs and Gods (see Chapter 6 pages 509–12 for a variety of explanations as to why we believe in God). They may be able to convincingly explain why some people continue to use these concepts and suggest how they play a useful role in some societies or in individuals' lives – but such explanations often explain away the relevant phenomena.

This seems to have happened with the idea of moral blame. The hard determinist has not explained moral blame, in the sense that we use it, but rather explained why moral blame exists and is useful. To some extent it has been explained away as morality as we know it is no longer preserved in the determinist's account. According to most folk, we blame people because they should not have carried out such an act and should have done otherwise. According to the hard determinist, the placing of moral blame is mistaken as the person could not have done otherwise. So although we cannot *really* blame someone for their action, doing so may be of some longer-term benefit. It seems the hard determinist has explained away morality. Both camps might agree about what we should describe as good and bad actions. It's just that the determinist believes we are mistaken in blaming people for carrying out the bad ones.

This may not be problematic. Most people reading this book no longer believe in magic and so are happy with the idea that it can be explained away. However, some people are very religious and would not accept sociological explanations of their belief in God. Their belief in God is so certain that they would reject such accounts as wrong.

For some, the same is true of morality. They are not prepared to accept that we are mistaken in attributing moral blame and so believe that hard determinism, or at least this account of the use of moral language, must be wrong.

Sentencing and determinism

If we are wrong to morally blame people for their actions are we wrong to send then to prison? The law and the court system to some extent mirror our moral thinking. A starting point is to note that crimes that are more morally serious tend to have longer sentences, which is an example of how the law reflects our moral indignation. But moral indignation is not the only reason to send people to prison. The four main justifications for incarceration are as follows.

1 Prevention – to stop that person committing any more crimes
2 Rehabilitation – to encourage that person to become a useful member of society

3 Deterrence – to stop people in general from committing that crime

4 Retribution – to simply punish that person for their wrong-doing.

Most would claim that we send people to jail for a mixture of the reasons above, although different people and different political parties might emphasise different reasons.

Read through the following crimes and answer the questions below.

1 Murder

2 Shoplifting (a fifth similar offence)

3 Driving under the influence of alcohol

For each of the crimes rank the different reasons for punishment in order of importance.

a) Does the order change for different crimes?

b) Does your ordering reflect your belief in free will/determinism?

c) Imagine you believed in determinism. Which of the reasons for punishment above would still have validity and why?

Even if you believe that humans are completely determined, most of the reasons for punishing would still hold. You would want to keep those likely to commit offences off the street (prevention); you would hope to make that person less likely to commit the crime in the future (rehabilitation); you would hope to make all people less likely to commit such crimes in the first place (deterrence). The difference for the determinist lies in idea of retribution. The hard determinist does not believe that the person carrying out the crime had any moral responsibility as they had no freedom to do otherwise. Punishing someone solely for their moral wrong-doing would seem to be misplaced – like punishing the rain for falling. However, as discussed above, moral concepts can still have their use if they affect behaviour, so the concept of moral retribution may still be of value or purpose. Instead of saying someone is morally guilty and so should be punished, the determinist is in effect saying that the decision-making process that led to the crime is susceptible to moral concepts, and so calling a person who commits a crime morally guilty may lead to this person or others not committing such crimes in the future. However, this would be to effectively re-label retribution, saying that it acts as a form of deterrence, or as rehabilitation.

So the reasons for sentencing stay largely intact whether you believe in free will or not, although the determinist may

have to recast retribution as a subtler form of deterrence or
rehabilitation.

Courts and determinism

The courtroom is an obvious place where battles are carried
out over the morality of human actions. However, the
courtroom is also host to this very question of free will and
determinism. In some cases the defence team are, in effect,
trying to show that the defendant, though guilty of the crime,
is not morally guilty because they had no free will and their
action was a result of physical determinism. In such cases the
defence may offer a plea of diminished responsibility. This
might be because the person in question had a mental illness
that prevented them from thinking clearly. It might be
because the person was under the influence of drugs. Perhaps
the person's upbringing might be brought into the picture to
suggest that they were environmentally determined. In the
future someone's genetic make-up may even be used in
defence.

One famous example of a plea for lack of free will is the
notorious 'Twinkie defence'. In 1978 in America, Dan White
was charged and tried for the murder of two people who had
been shot. There was no question that Dan White was the
man who had shot the people. The defence team called in an
expert witness who claimed that the defendant's eating of
junk food (including cheap cake-bars called Twinkies) made
him depressed which in turn led to diminished mental
capacity and resulted in his decision to shoot the victims. The
defendant was only convicted of voluntary manslaughter as
opposed to murder. After this case limits were set on the
types of evidence that could be used to claim mitigating
circumstances.

Such claims are increasingly common and they seem to be
increasing in line with our understanding of how the brain
works. Is it so hard to imagine a future where moral blame is
shown to be mistaken in the courtroom? Expert teams show
that the defendant could not have done otherwise – perhaps
through a thorough analysis of brain chemistry. As a result,
prisons might focus much more on rehabilitation to ensure
the prisoner does not re-offend. And if this is not deemed
likely then the prisoner would be held in jail longer for
purposes of prevention. Such a future, it could be argued, is a
future in which the courts have proved the truth of hard
determinism and shown that the concept of moral blame is in
fact mistaken.

Agent-centred morality

Another way the hard determinist can interpret morality is not to focus on individual actions, but to focus on the moral character of a person. As stated, the problem for the hard determinist is that we cannot really blame someone for their action if they could not have done otherwise. So if we side step the issue of *actions* then this may disappear. The claim goes that when people do morally nice or nasty things and we berate them, we are really passing judgement on their character, not their action. Sometimes this is exactly what we do. We might call a cold-blooded killer evil, or hold up someone like Ghandi or Nelson Mandela as a moral role model. The moral judgements here don't focus on specific actions, but on their general character.

Labelling *someone*, as opposed to some *act*, as good or bad makes sense from both the free will and determinist perspectives. Imagine you bought a cheap bunch of snooker balls and some of them didn't roll in a straight line. You would want to know which ones were good and which were bad, so that you could fix or remove the bad ones. But it would be silly to blame the ball for its wonky roll. Labelling the balls as good and bad makes sense, but blaming the ball for its roll does not make sense, as it has no choice.

So the hard determinist can defend our use of moral blame by re-interpreting the praise or blame as a comment on the moral character of the person. As with the example of Ghandi, this defence has the benefit of fitting in with much of our existing practice in morality. Indeed independent of this debate there is a whole philosophical movement which argues that agent-centred morality is a more useful general approach than act-centred models of morality (see pages 23–48).

Those favouring the act-centred approach might still claim that this re-interpreting of moral blame is yet another case of explaining away the phenomena. They would still assert that blaming someone for their *action* is meaningful, and it must be hard determinism itself that is wrong.

Criticisms of the determinist's defence: it is dehumanising

Imagine that the truth of hard determinism is somehow proved and blaming people for their actions is shown to be mistaken. Beyond the feelings of blame, other sentiments that rely on the concept of free will would also need to be re-interpreted. For example, gratitude may also need an overhaul. Imagine a friend, thinking you are feeling a bit low, pops round with a cake they baked to cheer you up. You are touched by the thoughtfulness of the act and feel grateful. This is like feeling grateful for a lump of sugar dissolving in a cup of tea. You may feel pleased that this happened, but gratitude towards the sugar is misplaced as it has no choice. So why might we use such a term? As with blame, perhaps the explanation is that people adapt their behaviour on account of the concept. Maybe the friend will be more likely to repeat such an act if you show gratitude this time. Hence we use the term gratitude.

If hard determinism is true what does all this mean for the way we view each other? Am I to see my gratitude as a way of squeezing more out of my friend? Am I to see moral blame as a way of somehow reprogramming broken human machines to make them less likely to repeat again? If we realise the truth of hard determinism surely this would mean re-evaluating the way we interact with friends. We might argue, with David Hume, that our moral feelings of sympathy and other sentiments towards each other are what make us *human*. They separate us from the more mechanical side of nature and provide us with our humanity. If we have to explain away such concepts as simply being instrumental to some or other end, then this takes away our humanity from us.

Other philosophers, such as Peter Strawson, have suggested that nothing would change.[39] The fact that we need to see ourselves as humans, as people as opposed to machines, would mean that our moral concepts would live on as they are. For Strawson, we may not be able to stop the psychological process which leads to feelings of praise or blame but, even if we could, we would not wish to abandon these reactive attitudes anyway, as they are such an important part of what it is to be human. To a similar end, others have suggested that the sheer complexity of man as a machine would mean that we still have to interact with each other as if we had free will, as this would still be the most effective way of helping to understand and predict behaviour. In other words, nothing would change if hard determinism were shown to be true.

Physical determinism and human rationality

Another possible consequence of determinism is that, if true, it might undermine human rationality.

Determinism is premised on the idea that events in the world can be explained in terms of prior events with reference to the laws of nature. For many events in the world these explanations seem to work very well. Imagine we have to give a causal account of how a car started. We might talk about the fuel in the pistons combusting as a result of being ignited by the spark plugs. And in turn explain the spark plugs' firing in terms of the electricity in the battery flowing through the circuit, as a result of a the key being turned. Scientists may be able to give a more detailed account of every stage and supply the relevant laws of nature for electricity and combustion etc. For our purposes, however, the principle is enough, and this is that a causal account of the car's starting can be given in terms of the prior state of the engine, prior events such as the turning of the key and the relevant laws of nature. Such an explanation uses a scientific methodology and seeks to outline a sequence of causes and effects leading up to and so causing the event, and we call such an explanation a *mechanical* account.

For humans, however, it seems that we can supply competing accounts of how an event occurred. Consider an everyday scenario whereby you enter the kitchen and turn on the kettle, which causes the water to boil. As with the explanation of the car above, we can supply a causal account of the events leading up to the water boiling in *mechanical terms*, which might read something like this:

> In the brain, various electro-chemical reactions occurred, some of which caused the muscles in the legs to move others, which caused more brain events to occur. Eventually neuron 234 fired, which caused the nerve in the finger to contract the muscle, which moved with enough force to depress a switch, which completed a circuit, which allowed electricity to flow to the base under the kettle.

However, we can also give an account of the events leading up to the water boiling in terms of *reasons* and *intentions*.

> The person entered the room and upon seeing the kettle realised they were thirsty so walked up to the kettle and turned it on with the plan of making a cup of tea.

So for humans there are two, possibly competing, accounts that can be given of how an event came to pass. One account, the *mechanical* account is couched in terms of atoms and cells; the other account, the *intentional* account, is couched in terms of reasons and intentions. Some philosophers, such as Daniel Dennett, would claim that these two accounts are very different stances that we take to the world (for more on Dennett's account of stances see pages 172 and 424).

In the second account it seems the kettle was turned on because of our intention to make a cup of tea. In other words, the explanation contains a reference to a possible future event – the cup of tea. (Such explanations are described as TELEOLOGICAL, as they point towards the goal or purpose of the event.) However, in the first account no future event needs be referred to. Each stage is simply caused by the preceding stage. Atoms after all are essentially 'blind' about the future and, individually, would know nothing about the impending cup of tea.

It has been claimed that the first mechanical account may explain *how* an event occurs but only the intentional account can explain *why*. On a related point it is claimed that the first account can only explain human *movement*; the second account can explain human *actions*.

Any explanation of actions, it is claimed, must contain concepts that are familiar to (or logically connected to terms that are familiar to) the person carrying out the action. To see this more clearly, imagine a game of football. Player A makes a telling pass to player B only for the referee to blow the whistle for offside. Out of frustration player B then kicks the ball into the stands, where the supporters watch the match, and gets a yellow card (a bad thing in footballing terms). A mechanical account of these events would be able to explain all the muscle movements of the players up to the angry kick and then the brain and muscle movement of the referee as he pulled out the card. However, it can plausibly be argued that something crucial is missing from this account. Surely we can only understand the action (as opposed to the movement) if our account, at some point, explains what football is (e.g. that the aim is to kick the ball in the goal not the stand) and perhaps explains what sport is in general, and most importantly explains what the notoriously complex offside rule is! Any account that lacks these features will have failed to explain the action. Human action can be seen as governed by a range of formal and informal rules and practices, and failing to state the relevant ones would be to fail to explain the action.

The point can also be seen if we consider something completely alien to us. Imagine that in the future we discover a planet with intelligent spider-like creatures. They frequently meet in groups and seemingly fight until just one spider dies. By studying their anatomy we can explain exactly how the spiders move and so can give a mechanical account of how the spider comes to die. However, it would be very hard for us to really explain what is going on when the spiders meet and fight: it might be a dance, a sport, a punishment or a religious sacrifice. And these are just guessing along the lines of the things that humans do. Perhaps the spiders have their own forms of pastimes, activities that bear no relation to our human concepts. It seems then we would be unable to explain their actions as we do not know the rules and practices that govern the activity. We would know how they are moving but not what they are doing; we would be able to explain the movement but not the action. (In Chapter 6, pages 503–08, we look at Wittgenstein's discussion of how essential the understanding of rules and practices is to understanding what people believe.)

So it might be suggested that the mechanical account of human action is not a complete account. The mechanical account might seem to imply that hard determinism is true and that humans have no free will. Might such an account be missing something? After all it seems to fail to explain the nature of the action, which might be an important element in considering whether an action is free.

However, it can also be claimed that the mechanical account is missing nothing – it all depends on how the event being explained is described. Looking back at the yellow card incident above, if we want to explain how the booking occurred then we would need to refer to the rules of football. If we are to explain how the referee waved the card then the mechanical account seems to do the job with no bits missing. The mechanical account can explain events perfectly as long as they are couched in mechanical terms. But once again this might imply some form of limitation of the mechanical account, and perhaps that the reductivist approach to science might falter when it comes to explaining human action (see pages 370-71).

Reasons, causes and free will

So we have two competing accounts of how an event occurs. Which one is the true account? Did I turn the kettle on because I wanted a cup of tea or because neuron 234 fired? Perhaps because of both? It can be argued that these different accounts lie at the heart of the free will debate. Imagine a woman jumping into to a river to rescue a drowning puppy. We could give two accounts of the action (see Figure 5.16), one from the mechanical stance, and one from the intentional stance.

Viewed from the mechanical stance it seems quite obvious that the action was entirely determined, just a question of the atoms and cells all behaving in accordance with the laws of nature. However, this is not a stance that we generally apply to our own actions. After all, we are unaware of the cells and axons in our brain. As individuals making choices we are only aware of reasons, morality and desires and so forth. From the intentional stance, also shown in Figure 5.16, it feels to us as if we do have free will and we have a strong feeling that we could have acted otherwise.

■ **Figure 5.16** *The mechanical stance compared with the intentional stance*

In the mechanical stance the laws relating to physical matter are used to explain the movement of the person. In the intentional stance the thoughts and desires are used to explain the action.

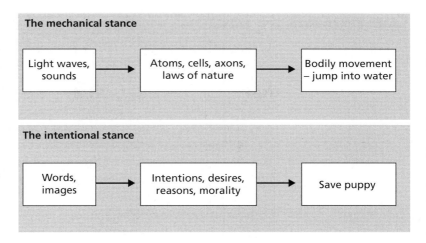

Note also that as far as we are aware a computer lacks this second 'inside' perspective. Although we are able to treat the computer as if it had such a stance, we do not actually believe that it does. Perhaps this is the reason why we are far less willing to concede free will to a machine, however sophisticated.

So if we take the mechanical stance as the true account then we appear to be determined; if we take the intentional stance we appear to have free will. What is the true account? Going back to the example of the kettle, what really caused the kettle to be turned on: cells and atoms, or the desire for a hot cuppa? At stake perhaps is more than the debate over free will, for by adopting a mechanical stance we are undermining the rationality of the action. If we are able to entirely explain human movements in terms of scientific terms then what role do our reasons play? Do they simply accompany all the goings-on in the brain, but themselves have no *causal* role in human behaviour? (The theory that claims this is the case is called epiphenomenalism.) If they play no causal role then we can't really be said to do things for a reason. Reasons belong to the order of exploration associated with the intentional stance. Atoms themselves viewed from a mechanistic stance simply obey the laws of nature and do not do things for 'reasons'. So if we were to only adopt this stance in explaining human behaviour then it would seem that human behaviour is not rational.

Some physical determinists would say that only physical events can cause other physical events. It is impossible for a reason to cause a physical event. Reasons may play a role in explaining human *action*, which is perhaps the account we tell ourselves about events in the world, but they have no role in giving a causal account of human *movement*.

Can reasons be causes?

Imagine that someone who likes cheese is in a queue to get a burger at a non-franchised chain. The person gets to the front and asks for the cheeseburger as opposed to the regular burger. Can their reason, the liking of cheese, help in giving a causal account of the event? On the face of it, it does seem to play a role. The person had a *desire* for cheese; they looked at the options on the board, saw the cheeseburger option and this *caused* them to ask for the cheeseburger. It would seem at first sight that the desire for cheese caused the request for a cheeseburger. So on a straightforward level is seems that reasons do cause events.

However, there are powerful considerations to suggest that 'reasons' cannot provide a causal account of behaviour: first, because only physical events can cause physical events and secondly because 'reasons' lack the law-like nature of scientific causal accounts. We cannot make a simple law that 'every one who likes cheese will buy a cheeseburger' as this simply isn't true. We might try to complicate the law to allow for some exceptions. For example, 'anyone who likes cheese and isn't worried about the extra money and isn't concerned by the extra fat content will choose a cheeseburger over a burger'. However, what if the person simply doesn't fancy the cheese option at that moment, or if they're a vegetarian? And so on. Compare this to a law such as 'at normal atmospheric pressure, at ground level, water heated to 100 degrees centigrade will boil and turn to vapour'. This law has no exceptions and so can play a valid role in causal explanation of the world. A law outlines a necessary connection between events, and this connection explains what causes things to happen. If we cannot provide laws involving reasons then they cannot play a role in the causal explanation of the world.

ACTIVITY   Try to come up with a law relating reason to actions:

1 People will always choose a cheeseburger over a burger if . . .
2 People will always give money to charity if . . .

It would seem to be impossible to actually provide law-like accounts of how reasons cause behaviour. It is always easy to imagine a scenario where a person meets all of the reasons for actions, but still does not act that way anyway. Remember also that people are not themselves always good at 'reasons' and may do things for the wrong, mistaken or silly reasons: for example 'I thought that by denying myself the cheese in the burger my pet hamster might get better'.

We should also note that if it were possible to provide law-like accounts of how reasons cause behaviour then this might also imply that humans have no free will. If statements such as 'If reasons x, y and z are present then all people will always choose x' are true then it seems as if you have to choose x given that x, y and z. We would be determined by the laws governing reasons as opposed to just the laws governing atoms.

It used to be something of a consensus that reasons could not cause physical events. However, this view was challenged in an important paper by Donald Davidson.[40] One of his key points is that we don't need to establish law-like statements for reasons to be causes; it is enough if we can show that on this particular occasion Jenny's desire for cheese was the cause of her asking for the cheeseburger – and indeed we can convincingly argue such a case. He also suggests that we do not need to see the mechanical and the intentional stances as competing. They are explanations of the same event, but from different perspectives. He suggests that every desire, belief or intention is identical to some particular brain state. So it is not a question of either that neuron 234 causes my hand to move or my desire for a cup of tea causes my hand to move. It is more the case that the neuron firing and my desire are different expressions of the same event so both can act as causal accounts for my behaviour.

If Davidson is right then we don't need to see determinism with its mechanical stance as undermining rationality. For every action we can also provide an intentional explanation which involves reasons, and this can be validly seen as the cause of the behaviour.

Different stances

Pinker

A human being is simultaneously a machine and a sentient free agent, depending on the purpose of the discussion, just as he is also a taxpayer, an insurance salesman, and two hundred pounds of ballast on a commuter airplane . . . The mechanistic stance allows us to understand what makes us tick and how we fit into the physical universe. When those discussions wind down for the day, we go back to talking about each other as free and dignified human beings.[41]

The concept of using different stances to understand and explain behaviour can be a useful lens with which to study the debate about free will. We tend to explain human behaviour in terms of the intentional stance. If we observed someone putting the kettle on we would naturally explain the behaviour in terms of intentions: for example, 'perhaps they want a cup of tea?' We don't tend to use the mechanical stance – 'perhaps neuron 234 fired?' This, in part, is because we naturally think of humans as having reasons for their actions. Conversely we tend to explain the behaviour of physical objects by reference to a mechanical stance. If a tile blows off my roof in a gale I do not try to explain it in terms of the tile wanting to jump off the roof, or no longer liking the roof. I would refer to such physical elements as wind speed, wobbly nails and gravity. I explain the behaviour of the tile from a mechanical stance.

These are not the only stances we can use. Sometimes we explain features of physical objects by reference to what Daniel Dennett calls the *design* stance – by considering what it is designed for.[42] In these cases we do not use intentions nor go down to the level of mechanics, but instead focus on that the object was designed to do. For example, I'm considering hitting the print button on my new printer and trying to guess about what will happen next. I naturally assume that if I hit the button on my printer it will print the pages I am now writing as the printer is attached to the computer. This is not because I think the printer *wants* to print these pages (the intentional stance). Nor do I resort to thinking about circuits and electricity (the mechanical stance). Rather I think in terms of the general idea of printers being designed to print, and the print button having its function so as to print whatever is on the screen.

When trying to predict the behaviour of certain objects we might perhaps use any one of these three stances (see page 172). It is suggested, however, that the more complex the object the more we are likely to use the intentional stance, even if the object itself doesn't operate on that level.

Imagine you are playing a sophisticated computer game which involves killing lots of different monsters with a sword. You enter a large room and can hear two scary monsters in the far corner facing away from you. You might start by thinking that the monsters may be interested in the food they can smell in your backpack. So if you quietly take it off, leave it on the floor and hide then, while the monsters are investigating the backpack, you can kill them with an element of surprise. In other words, you use the intentional stance. With a less sophisticated game you might use the design stance, for example you may think that these monsters are designed to wander around these two rooms and fight me and when I get a bit close this will trigger the sub-program to attack. In this case it would be virtually impossible to adopt the mechanistic stance without a PhD in programming and electronics.

So we might use the intentional stance, even if the computer itself lacks intentions. We said above that the more complex the object the more we are likely to use the intentional stance. For example, on page 156 we discuss Hume's suggestion that humans introduced the idea of gods and hence intentionality as a way of dealing with the complexity and unpredictability of the world. It was easier to explain lightning and other phenomena with recourse to intentions as the mechanical stance was not available. If it is true that the intentional stance is of particular use to us in making sense of the world, then it might help to shed light on the discussion of morality above. In the future even if hard determinism is shown true, concepts such as moral responsibility may still be used as a way of dealing with the sheer complexity of human behaviour.

Another interesting feature of the stance approach is that we tend to turn to the mechanistic stance when machines and people seem to 'break down'. If someone is behaving irrationally, perhaps banging their head against a wall or smearing themselves with strawberry jam, then we might start to explain their behaviour in terms of chemical imbalances in their brain rather than looking for suitable motivational reasons.

This switch of stances is increasingly used in courts. Sometimes people commit crimes that most of us would find hard to understand on an intentional stance: *why would someone do something like that?* In such cases we might refer to the mechanics of the brain, for example drug addiction or emotional imbalance. The 'Twinkie defence', which we mentioned above on page 415, can be seen as such an attempt to use the mechanical stance to explain behaviour. It is also suggested that the more we know about the mechanical explanation for an act or event the more we are inclined to believe that that takes precedent over the intentional explanation. Perhaps as we understand the brain more we will increasingly turn to this stance. Indeed even in the space of the last few years people are increasingly using phrases like *adrenalin rush, caffeine buzz* and *endorphin high* to express their thoughts and feelings instead of saying such things as 'Crikey, I must say that bungee jump has made me rather excited.'

Finally, we should note that the different methodological approaches taken by the phenomenologists and the scientists can be couched in the language of stances. The hard determinist scientist sees the mechanical stance as the starting point for explaining the world. The phenomenologist claims that the intentional stance must be the route by which all explanations of the world are ultimately founded. Of course it may not be necessary to see either as the correct starting point.

Conclusion

This debate over free will and determinism has been raging for over two thousand years, and it would seem that it will not be settled in a hurry. We might be tempted to freely admit that we cannot reconcile our belief in human free will and our belief in physical determinism and resign ourselves to leaving this particular philosophical arena none the wiser. This approach has been taken by many philosophers.

But at the core of this problem is an even more fundamental question. The determinist may claim that snooker balls are made of atoms, they have no free will; humans are made of atoms so they have no free will. But there is a key difference. Humans are conscious and snooker balls are not (as far as we know). At present there is no generally accepted explanation of why and how certain collections of atoms, such as the brain, are conscious. Why and how have some elements of the physical universe developed self-awareness?

In other words why does the intentional stance exist at all? Why are we not simply biological machines that unconsciously make decisions? One could argue that consciousness itself is bound up with process of decision-making. Such an account might be put forward by existentialists and evolutionary psychologists alike. If so, it suggests that the riddle of free will and choice is closely bound up with the riddle of consciousness.

Perhaps the question of whether we have free will cannot be solved until we answer the puzzle of how seemingly non-conscious matter can generate consciousness.

Key points: Chapter 5

What you need to know about **the debate over free will and determinism:**

1 Metaphysical freedom or free will is different from political freedom.

2 Determinism is the view that the future happens necessarily. This could be because fate, God or the laws of nature are determining events.

3 Physical determinism is the theory that every state of the universe is caused necessarily by the preceding state of the universe and the laws of nature.

4 Chance events that arise out of our lack of knowledge do not challenge this theory. However, if some aspects of the universe are genuinely random this would challenge the theory, although it is unlikely to provide an account of free will.

5 Hard determinism is the theory that physical determinism applies to humans, and this means that humans have no free will.

6 The hard determinist needs to provide an account of why we have the illusion of free will.

7 Libertarians deny that physical determinism applies to humans. Dualists see free will as resulting from a non-physical mind. Existentialists see our lack of essence as the key to free will. Both views require a gap in universal causality.

8 Soft determinists believe that physical determinism applies to humans *and* that we have free will.

9 Some argue that if we are free from physical and psychological constraint then we *could have done otherwise* and so have free will. This view is rejected by the hard determinist as you could not choose otherwise so cannot meaningfully claim that you could have acted otherwise.

10 Other soft determinists claim that, because your actions are largely determined by you, you have free will. The hard determinist rejects this by claming that we don't choose who we are and so are not free.

11 Moral blame seems to require the ability to do otherwise.

12 Hard determinism may mean we are mistaken in attributing moral blame. However, the hard determinist can explain why we might use the concept of moral blame.

13 If reasons cannot cause behaviour then we cannot be said to do things for a reason. This would undermine human rationality. It can be reasonably claimed, though, that reasons do cause actions.

God and the world

Introduction

What could be more clear or obvious when we look up to the sky and contemplate the heavens, than that there is some divinity of superior intelligence?[1]

Cicero

Darwin

I cannot see as plainly as others do, and as I should wish to do, evidence of design and beneficence on all sides of us. There seems to me too much misery in the world.[2]

Darwin

People with faith in God see the world very differently from the way ATHEISTS see the world. Believers might experience the beauty of a sunset as filled with the love and light of God; they look at the stars and see evidence of a divine intelligence; they see the hand of a designer at work in the stunning precision of the eye. But, for non-believers, stars, sunsets and eyeballs are not indications of a superior, supernatural intelligence; moreover their observations about the world point to the very opposite conclusion: that there is no God. Charles Darwin, in his letter to Asa Gray quoted above, gives as an example of 'misery in the world' the stomach-churning nesting instincts of the Ichneumon wasp. Rather than create a snug and cosy nursery for their babies, perhaps decorated with a few tasteful mobiles, these wasps inject their eggs directly into the larvae of other insects, such as caterpillars; when the wasp larva hatches inside its host, it then eats its way out of the caterpillar.[3] Darwin writes 'I cannot persuade myself that a beneficent and omnipotent God would have designedly created Ichneumonidae with the express intention of their feeding within the living bodies of caterpillars.'

ACTIVITY Read through the following observations made about the world and answer the questions below.

1 The discovery by Mary Anning in 1811 of the fossilised skeleton of a dinosaur in the cliffs of Charmouth

2 The massacres of thousands of men, women and children in churches throughout Rwanda between April and July 1994

3 The overwhelming sensations of sublime beauty that eighteenth-century travellers experienced as they passed through the Alps from France to Italy

4 The observation (made by Charles Darwin in Chapter 7 of *The Descent of Man*) that the brains of humans and of apes resemble one another in their fundamental character

5 The invisible hand that wrote a terrible warning on the walls to King Belshazzar as he was feasting with all his nobles, wives and concubines in the sixth century BCE

6 The measurement of 'redshift' in the light from distant galaxies by Edwin Hubble in 1929, which supported the conclusion that the universe was expanding from an original Big Bang

7 The evidence published by William Ryan and Walter Pitman in 1998 that there had been a 'great flood' from the Mediterranean into the Black Sea circa 5600 BCE – with water pouring across the landscape at 200 times the rate of the Niagara Falls

8 The testimony by Professor Michael Behe under oath to a court of law in the United States that certain features of the world, such as the eye, are irreducibly complex and could not be the product of evolution

9 The lifelong charity work of Mother Teresa throughout the last century which helped thousands of the poorest people of the world to stay alive and die in relative peace

10 The fact that the universe exists at all.

For each observation:

a) Does it support the claim that God exists?

b) If it does, how might an atheist account for this observation?

c) Does it support the claim that God doesn't exist?

d) If it does, how might a believer account for this observation?

Can we look to the world for proof of God's existence, or will our observations point towards the opposite conclusion, that there is no God? In this chapter we look first at the claim that the world provides evidence for God, in particular that the universe and everything in it seems to have been designed by a supernatural designer. This type of argument is known as the design argument. In the second section we examine claims that belief in God is incompatible with the horror, cruelty and suffering that are a daily occurrence amongst humans and every other creature in the world. This challenge to the belief in God is known as the PROBLEM OF EVIL. In the final section we ask why believers and non-believers see the world in such different ways. How can completely different conclusions (that there is/isn't a God) be drawn from the same available evidence? Perhaps the disagreement between atheists and believers isn't a disagreement about whether God exists or not, but is instead merely an expression of differing feelings or attitudes.

The Design Argument

Introduction

Thou dost cause the grass to grow for the cattle, and plants for man to cultivate . . . Thou hast made the moon to mark the seasons, the sun knows its time for setting.

Psalms 104: 14, 19

All things bright and beautiful, all creatures great and small. All things wise and wonderful, the Lord God made them all.[4]

Anglican hymn

To the writer of Psalm 104, and to millions of others throughout history who looked up at their surroundings and wondered, the universe looks as if it has been deliberately made. From the features of earthly creatures, great and small, to the order and regularity of planetary motion, there seems to be every sign of a supernatural craftsman or artist at work – a designer, in fact, who 'made them all'. These types of arguments are known as design arguments or TELEOLOGICAL ARGUMENTS. They are probably the most commonly cited type of argument, as anyone who has ever talked to a door-to-door evangelist will know. As Kant says:

This proof always deserves to be mentioned with respect. It is the oldest, the clearest, and the most accordant with the common reason of mankind.[5]

Kant

Design arguments are concerned with the specific details of the universe: why does the universe possess the particular qualities that it does and how can we best explain them? [6] These qualities include many puzzling features that scientists, philosophers and theologians have noted, including:

- the regularity and order of the world
- the way that everything in the world seems to be designed for some purpose
- the way that living things appear constructed so as to suit their environment
- the fact that that life developed in the world at all
- the fact that conscious beings exist.

Before we look at the different types of teleological arguments which account for these features, we should first revisit some of the technical terms that we examined in Chapter 2.

- *Teleological arguments are* A POSTERIORI. Because teleological arguments are based on our experience of the universe they can be categorised as *a posteriori* proofs, in contrast to ontological arguments which are A PRIORI (see pages 119–37). The observations that form the basis of design arguments include specific observations about the way animals have been put together, the way they fit into their environments, as well as more general observations about how the earth is so suitable for life.

- *Teleological arguments are* INDUCTIVE. Design arguments move from particular observations to a general conclusion about the whole world. Deductive arguments, like the ontological proofs of God's existence attempted by St Anselm and Descartes, are capable of providing a conclusive proof, so long as the PREMISES are true and the argument is a valid one. In contrast an inductive argument, such as a teleological argument, cannot conclusively prove the existence of God even if it is based on true premises. At best a teleological argument can only show that God's existence is probable.

- *'Teleology' has its origins in ancient Greek thought.* The word 'teleological' comes from the Greek *telos*, which means end or goal, and *logos*, which means 'an account of' or 'study of'. Hence 'teleology' literally means 'the study of final ends'. (On page 35 above we looked at Aristotle's teleological perspective of the universe.) The term has also come to refer to the view that everything has a purpose and is aimed at some goal. So teleological or design arguments draw on evidence that the world has been designed and has a purpose in order to conclude that God exists.

Sometimes teleological arguments are referred to simply as 'arguments from design'. However, as Antony Flew and others have pointed out, the label 'argument from design' is an unhappy one.[7] The term 'from design' suggests that the conclusion (that the world has been designed) is already assumed in the premises, and hence there's hardly much argument that needs to be done. Flew proposes 'argument to design' as a better label for this cluster of arguments, and this is certainly less of a mouthful than Kant's suggestion which was the 'physico-theological' arguments. We shall stick with using the terms 'teleological' and 'design argument', but we can identify two main types of design arguments.

■ Arguments from analogy

There is a tradition of teleological arguments which compare certain features of the universe with similar features of designed objects. These proofs argue from design in that they begin by examining design in human artefacts (in this sense then they are arguments *from* design). Similarities, or analogies, can be found between these designed objects and the world around us, and this leads to an intermediate conclusion that the world has also been designed. From here it is a short step to the final conclusion that God is the designer. In the sections below we examine Aquinas' and William Paley's arguments from analogy and the criticisms of these made by David Hume.

■ Arguments to the best explanation

There is another type of teleological argument which seeks a different path to the conclusion that the world has been designed. Such proofs begin by noticing certain unusual properties of the universe in particular, its apparent order and purpose. They aim to show that naturalistic explanations for these properties are inadequate, and that the existence of a supernatural designer is the best explanation of these features. We can think of these as the arguments *to* design that Flew mentions, in that they try to demonstrate that these features are not the result of chance, but point strongly towards the existence of a designer-God. In the sections below we examine proofs which infer that God is the best explanation for the order and regularity of the universe as well as being the best explanation for the existence of conscious human life.

Aquinas' argument from analogy

In his book the *Summa Theologica* Aquinas offers five ways in which God's existence can be demonstrated. The first three ways are all forms of cosmological argument;[8] the fourth way is an argument from morality, and in his fifth way Aquinas offers a version of an argument from design. It is an argument by analogy, in that it compares the natural world (the fact that it appears to have a purpose and goal) with human activity (which does have a purpose and a goal). The example Aquinas uses in his argument by analogy is that of an archer:

1 Things that lack intelligence, such as living organisms, have an end (a purpose).
2 Things that lack intelligence cannot move towards their end unless they are directed by someone with knowledge and intelligence.

3 For example, an arrow does not direct itself towards its target, but needs an archer to direct it.

4 (Conclusion) Therefore (by analogy) there must be some intelligent being which directs all unintelligent natural things towards their end. This being we call God.

This argument makes use of a belief that Aristotle held (you may remember that Aquinas was a big fan of Aristotle), namely the view that everything in the universe has an end or purpose. Aquinas himself does not give any illustrations from nature to support this 'teleological view' of the world, but we can use any number of Aristotle's observations. For example, Aristotle notices that ducks have webbed feet, [9] and he argues that the reason for this is so that they might swim better. Every living organism, and nearly every part of a living organism, has a function aimed at some purpose according to Aristotle. For Aristotle this is not an indication of any plan or design; it is simply a fact about the nature of things.

Aquinas accepts Aristotle's belief that organisms have a purpose or function, but he rejects the Aristotelian view that this teleology (i.e. this purposefulness) could come about naturally. Instead he argues that there must be an intelligence lying behind the function of organisms: someone must have arranged the world so that ducks ended up with an efficient paddling mechanism. So Aquinas claims that unintelligent objects (such as an arrow) can only be aimed towards a goal (such as a target) with the guiding hand of an intelligent being (such as an archer).

However, the analogy of the archer aiming the arrow has two functions in Aquinas' argument from design. Not only does it illustrate Aquinas' view that unintelligent objects can only reach their goal with the help of a guiding intelligence but it also represents a stepping-stone to the conclusion that a guiding intelligence must lie behind the universe. It is only in another work, *De Veritate*, that Aquinas makes this second function clear. In this work, Aquinas expands on his archer example, and says, 'Similarly, philosophers call every work of nature the work of intelligence.'[10] The key word here is 'similarly', as it suggests that Aquinas thinks we can use the archer example as an analogy for the whole universe. His conclusion is that the universe, which is unintelligent yet goal-directed like the arrow, must have a guiding intelligence behind it, just as the archer aims and fires the arrow. This intelligent being, Aquinas concludes, we call God.

► criticism ◄ The key premise in Aquinas' argument is the claim that 'things that lack intelligence cannot move towards their end unless they are directed by someone with knowledge and intelligence'. However, this is a controversial premise in so far as it very nearly assumes what the argument is setting out to prove, namely that there is an intelligent being who created the universe. If the argument were to succeed, a supporter of Aquinas would need to bolster this premise with further evidence and justification. There may well be good reasons for believing that (a) all living organisms and parts of organisms have a function, and (b) these functions must be the result of the actions of an intelligent being. But Aquinas hasn't provided us with these reasons, and his argument needs fleshing out.

Moreover, as Flew points out,[11] the appealing suggestion that natural organisms have been designed seems to go against all available evidence. It is pretty clear that when an archer fires an arrow, or when an architect designs a house, there is direction in the process stemming from some intelligent being. Yet we observe that most ducklings, acorns, embryos, etc. grow and develop very successfully without any interference from an intelligent being. And so the claim that some intelligent hand must directly shape the natural world simply isn't supported by our observations of it. In the five hundred years after Aquinas the success of science changed the way people saw the universe. The traditional Aristotelian view of the universe, which placed the earth at the centre surrounded by unchanging heavenly bodies, was undermined by the work of Copernicus (1473–1543) and Galileo (1564–1642). The new discoveries showed that the earth was just one planet amongst many revolving around the sun. Isaac Newton (1642–1727) claimed to have discovered the laws of motion that governed the movement of all objects, and the universe came to be viewed as a complex machine. Some thinkers saw these breakthroughs as a threat to Christianity – indeed the new discoveries did undermine much traditional Church teaching – but others used the new science as evidence that the universe was a glorious work of divine craftsmanship. If the universe is machine-like then it needs a designer, just as an ordinary machine such as a watch needs a designer. This analogy between the universe and a watch was the basis for an argument from design put forward by William Paley.

In Figure 6.1 there are five boxes, each containing an object. Boxes 1–4 contain a wrist watch, a pebble, a honeycomb, a coin; Box 5 contains an unknown object.

1 Which of the objects in Boxes 1–4 would you say have been designed?

2 What do the designed objects have in common?

3 List all the things you would be looking for in the fifth object, in order to determine whether it had been designed.

■ **Figure 6.1 What's in the mystery box? How could we tell it had been designed?**

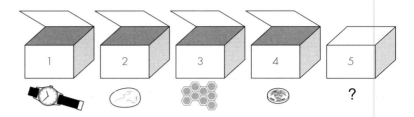

William Paley's argument from analogy

The Archdeacon of Carlisle, William Paley (1743–1805), put forward a very popular argument from design in his book *Natural Theology* (1802). Paley imagines himself walking across a heath and first coming across a stone, which he strikes with his foot, then finding a watch on the ground. The same question occurs to him on both occasions: 'how did that object come to be here?'. In the case of the stone, for all Paley knows it may have lain there forever. However, in the case of the watch such an answer is unsatisfactory: there is something about the presence of the watch on the heath that demands further explanation.

So what is the difference between a watch and a stone in this case? What Paley actually notices about the watch is that:

- it has several parts
- the parts are framed and work together for a purpose
- the parts have been made with specific material, appropriate to their action
- together the parts produce regulated motion
- if the parts had been different in any way, such motion would not be produced.

In the activity above you might have found further features that indicate some sort of design in a watch: e.g. its aesthetic appearance, or its complexity. We might think of this list as Paley's criteria for (or indicators of) design, and if an object meets these criteria then Paley will take it as evidence that the object has been designed. For Paley the watch on the heath has all the evidence of what he terms 'contrivance', i.e.

design, and where there is design or contrivance there must be a designer or 'contriver'. [12] He concludes that the watch must have had a maker.

Draw a table like the one below.

1 Along the top, write in your criteria for design, referring to either
   a) the list you established in part 3 of the activity above, or
   b) the criteria Paley proposes.
2 For all the natural features listed, decide which criteria they meet.
3 Are there any natural features you can think of that don't meet any of the criteria?

Natural features	Criteria				
	1	**2**	**3**	**4**	**5**
A snake's eye					
A peacock's tail					
The changing of the seasons					
The 'flu virus					
The solar system					

Paley

Every indication of contrivance, every manifestation of design, which existed in the watch, exists in the works of nature.[13]

Having examined the watch and thereby established some criteria with which to determine whether something has been designed, Paley turns his attention to the natural world. He finds that all the indicators of design that we observed in the watch we can also observe in nature, except that the works of nature actually surpass any human design. This leads him to the conclusion that nature must have a designer wondrous enough to have designed such a universe.

We can summarise Paley's argument in the following way.

1 A watch has certain complex features (e.g. it consists of parts, each of which has a function, and they work together for a specific purpose).
2 Anything which exhibits these features must have been designed.
3 (From 1 and 2) Therefore the watch has been designed by a designer.
4 The universe is like the watch in that it possesses the same features, except on a far more wondrous scale.
5 (From 4 and 2) Therefore the universe, like the watch, has been designed, except by a wondrous universe maker – God.

Like Aquinas' fifth way, Paley's teleological argument is an ARGUMENT FROM ANALOGY. Remember these arguments work by comparing two things, and by arguing that because they are alike in one (observed) respect they are also alike in another (unobserved) respect. Paley's analogy between the watch and the natural world works like this.

Figure 6.2 Paley's analogy between the watch and the universe

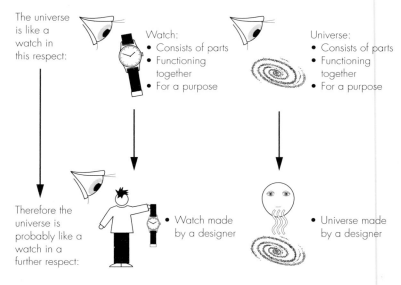

The universe is like a watch in this respect:

Watch:
• Consists of parts
• Functioning together
• For a purpose

Universe:
• Consists of parts
• Functioning together
• For a purpose

Therefore the universe is probably like a watch in a further respect:

• Watch made by a designer

• Universe made by a designer

experimenting with ideas

Read through the following arguments from analogy and answer the questions below.

a) In many ways a dog is like a cat, for example they both are warm-blooded mammals. Dogs give birth to live young, therefore cats do too.

b) A dog is like a duck-billed platypus, in that they are both warm-blooded mammals. Dogs give birth to live young, therefore duck-billed platypuses do too.

c) Just as a curry is a more stimulating dish if it contains a variety of flavours, so a nation will be more stimulating if it contains a variety of cultures.

d) Just as a window box is more interesting if it contains a variety of flowers, so a garden will be more interesting if it contains a variety of plants and trees.

e) We wouldn't let a wild animal control its owner, because the owner knows better than the animal what's in its interests. Therefore we shouldn't let the common people control the government because the rulers know better than the people what's in their interests.

f) We wouldn't let a child control its parents because the parents know better than the child what's in its interests. Therefore we shouldn't let students control an A level class, because the teacher knows better than the students what's in their interests.

g) If you suddenly found yourself being used, against your will, as a life-support device for a famous violinist and knew it would last nine months, you would not have a moral obligation to keep the violinist alive. Similarly, if you suddenly found that you were pregnant, against your will, you would not have a moral obligation to see the pregnancy through to birth.

h) If you suddenly found yourself attached to a stranger who was acting as your life-support machine for nine months, and they're the only person who can keep you alive, then you have a right to be kept alive by that stranger. Similarly a foetus, whilst in the womb, has a right to be kept alive until birth by its mother.

1 What words or phrases indicate that an argument uses an analogy?
2 Which of the above did you think were strong analogies, and which were weak?
3 What do you think makes an analogy a strong or successful one?

► criticism ◄

William Paley takes great care in *Natural Theology* to outline, and then respond to, a number of criticisms people might make of his argument from design. Here are some of the criticisms Paley anticipates:

A We may be in ignorance about how watches are made.
B The watch may sometimes go wrong.
C Some parts of the watch may appear to have no purpose.
D The watch might have come together by chance.

All of these criticisms would go some way to undermining Paley's claim that we know, just by examining a watch, that it has been designed. By implication of the analogy, they would also undermine Paley's claim that by examining the universe we can conclude it has been designed. Some of these criticisms are ones that David Hume wrote 30 years *before* Paley, and we examine these problems overleaf.

In the meantime let us look briefly at criticism C. When Paley finds the stone on the heath he dismisses it out of hand: it doesn't seem to have any purpose, and certainly offers no evidence that the universe has been designed. It seems that if parts of the watch, or the universe, have no purpose then the conclusion that they have been designed is weakened. After all a designer wouldn't include pointless parts.

Paley's response to criticism C is as follows. He argues that there may be parts whose purpose we have not yet discovered, or that we don't understand and perhaps never will understand. It may well be that the stone is only a small piece in a wider puzzle, and we need to view the whole before we can see where the stone fits in.

David Hume's critique of arguments from analogy

David Hume offered some of the most memorable criticisms of the arguments from design in his *Dialogues Concerning Natural Religion* published in 1779. In this book we listen in on three fictional philosophers discussing the nature of God:

- Philo (characterised by his 'careless scepticism')
- Cleanthes (characterised by his 'accurate philosophical turn')
- Demea (characterised by his 'inflexible orthodoxy').

Near the beginning Cleanthes suggests a teleological argument that takes a similar form to Paley's version. Cleanthes argues that we can see the same effects in the world as we see in all manner of machines, namely that all the parts are finely adjusted to fit each other and work towards some definite purpose. Working through the analogy, Cleanthes' conclusion is that the cause of these effects must also be similar: just as the design of a machine is caused by human intelligence, so the design of the world is caused by divine intelligence. We can see that, as with Paley's version, this argument is based on an analogy (between a machine and the world), and as with Paley it moves backwards from observation of the effect (the machine/the world) to a conclusion about the cause (the designer/God).

Philo responds to Cleanthes' argument with a barrage of objections, many of which are also applicable to Paley's argument written 30 years later. Hume was an empiricist, and believed that all our justifiable beliefs come from observation and experience: 'a wise man proportions his belief to the evidence' was his guiding principle.[14] Such a starting point is very close to the critical scepticism of Philo, and many commentators assume that Philo's position is also Hume's.[15] We can classify the problems Philo/Hume raises with this teleological argument into three main types.

Problem 1: We have no experience of world-making

► criticism ◄

We can only recognise that certain sorts of objects, such as machines, have an intelligent designer because we have had direct or indirect experience of such objects being designed and manufactured. So it is by observation of the way in which watches, for example, come into being in our world that we learn that they require a designer. But if we had never had any experience of manufacture, engineering or design, then we would never suppose that an object such as a watch had been designed. Hume's point is that to know what has brought something about we have to have experience of its being brought about. So unless we have had some experience of other universes being made we cannot reasonably claim to know whether our own universe has been made.[16]

Paley may have been thinking of Hume's attack when he responded to criticism A above. Paley thinks that it does not matter if we have never seen a watch being made, and have no understanding of how it is manufactured. Paley asks 'Does one man in a million know how oval frames are turned?'[17] Since the answer is doubtless 'no', then how is it we nonetheless are certain that they have been designed? His answer is that there are certain intrinsic features possessed by certain objects which show that they are designed.

► criticism ◄ Hume's point cuts deeper than this though. It is indeed possible, as Paley says, for us successfully to infer that some unfamiliar object has been designed. But this is only because we can compare it to other manufactured objects that we've previously encountered. If we had absolutely no experience, direct or indirect, of the manufacturing process, then the object would remain a mystery to us. Yet we have no experience of the process that causes universes to come into being, as the universe is unique and there is nothing we can compare it to. The only experiences we have of the universe are of its separate parts, and these parts on their own cannot tell us about the origin of the whole. As Philo says, 'from observing the growth of a hair, can we learn anything concerning the generation of a man?'.[18] For Hume, if we have no experience of this universe being designed, and if we cannot compare it to other universes that have been designed, then we have no grounds for concluding that God or anyone else has designed it.

experimenting with ideas

The arguments in the activity above (pages 438–39) all relied on analogies. However, although two things might be similar in some respects, they might be very dissimilar in other respects.

1 Examine the table overleaf. List the similarities and dissimilarities between each pair of things listed.
2 How might the dissimilarities you've listed damage the arguments on pages 438–39?

	Similarities	Dissimilarities
a) A dog *and* a cat		
b) A dog *and* a duck-billed platypus		
c) A curry *and* a nation		
d) A window-box *and* a garden		
e) A wild animal *and* the common people		
f) The child–parent relationship *and* the student–teacher relationship		
g) Acting as a life-support machine for a violinist *and* carrying an unborn child		
h) A machine *and* the universe		

■ Problem 2: Arguments from analogy are weak

An argument from analogy claims that, because X is like Y in one (observed) respect, they are therefore probably alike in some other (hidden) respect. However, arguments like this are only reliable when the two things being compared have lots of relevant similarities. A reliable example of an argument from analogy might be this: I notice that you and I behave in similar ways when we miss the nails we are hammering and hit our thumb; from this I infer that you and I have similar sensations following thumb-hammering incidents. I conclude, by analogy with my own case, that when you smash your thumb with a hammer you feel pain. This conclusion seems justified even though it is impossible for me to feel your pain. It is justified because you and I are similar in at least one important way: we both share a similar human physiology. The question is: does a machine have enough relevant similarities with the universe to support the conclusion that they were both designed?

▶ criticism ◀ Hume (through the character of Philo) argues that the universe is not at all like a machine, not even a vast and complex one. Hume suggests that the universe resembles something more organic than mechanical; it is far more like an animal or vegetable than 'a watch or a knitting-loom'. [19] If so, the appearance of function and purpose amongst the parts of the universe is due more to 'generation or vegetation than to reason or design'. And since a vegetable does not have any designer; since its organisation appears to develop by some blind natural process, we have no reason to suppose that the universe is designed. Perhaps it simply grew! Now, it may seem rather absurd to compare the universe to a giant vegetable, but this is partly Hume's point: it is only as absurd as comparing the universe to a machine. For Hume there is nothing to choose between the world–machine analogy and the world–vegetable analogy: both are equally flawed comparisons. Flawed because, as we've said, for an argument from analogy to be reliable the two things being compared need to be alike in all the relevant ways. Unfortunately in both Cleanthes' and Paley's teleological arguments the two things being compared (a man-made object and the universe) are hardly like each other at all. Therefore Cleanthes (and Paley) cannot conclude, on the basis of the analogy with a machine, that the universe has a designer.

Think about how you might reason backwards from the cause to the effect. Have a look at the list of effects (in the left-hand column), and the list of possible causes (in the right-hand column), and then answer questions 1–3 below.

Effect	Cause
a) A stylish and ergonomic wooden shelving unit	A) A five-year-old girl
b) Concentration camps	B) An unshaven and smelly carpenter
c) A simple metal ruler	C) A murderer and common thief
d) A classic racing car	D) An engineer working from his London garage
e) A miniature cottage made from small plastic building blocks	E) A power-hungry megalomaniac
f) A shoddy, badly made, wooden table	F) A team of world-class designers
g) One small piece of a quilt	G) A vegetarian who hates the sight of blood
h) A stunning sixteenth-century painting of Jesus being entombed	H) A 90-year-old woman
i) An efficient legal system	I) A smart and trendy carpenter

1 For each effect try to work out who created (or caused) it. We have connected one as an example.

2 What reasons can you give for each decision you've made?

3 What problems are there with reasoning backwards from effects to causes in this way? (Hint: G is a possible description of Adolf Hitler.)

■ Problem 3: The argument does not demonstrate the existence of God

One of the main assumptions on which Cleanthes' teleological argument rests is that 'like effects have like causes',[20] i.e. two things that are similar in their effects have similar causes. Both Cleanthes and William Paley must make this assumption if they are to conclude that the universe has a designer:

> 1 Machines and the universe exhibit similar features of design ('like effects').
> 2 Therefore they have both been designed by some intelligent being ('like causes').

Yet neither Cleanthes nor Paley examines in detail how far the likeness of causes can extend, both being happy to move quickly to the conclusion that the designer of the universe is God.

▶ criticism ◀ Philo, however, takes the idea of 'like causes' and gleefully runs with it, bringing out some potential absurdities in comparing the universe with machines. He finds that by staying true to the analogy he arrives at possible causes of the universe that are nothing like a perfect, unique God. So he makes the following points.

1 Complex machines are not usually the product of a single brilliant designer. Instead teams of people are involved in their design and construction. So, by the 'like causes' principle, the universe may also have been designed and created by many gods, not by a single deity.

2 We can take the analogy to its extreme by fully 'anthropomorphising' the designers of the universe, i.e. making them very similar to humans. For example, the designers and constructors of complex machines are often foolish and morally weak people. In the same way the gods who built the universe may well be foolish and morally weak. Humans involved in manufacture are both male and female, and reproduce in the usual fashion; so perhaps the deities are gendered and also engage in reproduction (like the gods of ancient Greece and Rome).

3 In most cases complex machines are the product of many years of trial and error, with each new generation of machine an improvement on its predecessors. By the 'like causes' principle then 'many worlds might have been botched and bungled' (as Philo says) before this one was created. In other words this universe may be the product of trial and error, one in a long line of 'draft' universes, and may well be superseded by a better one in the future.

4 Where there are design faults in a machine we usually infer that the designer lacked resources or skills, or simply didn't care. The universe appears to contain many design faults (particularly those that cause needless pain and suffering). For all we know this is because it was created by a God who lacked the power, skill or love to create something better (or perhaps, Philo muses, it was created by an infant or a senile God). As Philo says, the most reasonable conclusion of this argument is that the designer of the universe 'is entirely indifferent . . . and has no more regard to good above ill than to heat above cold or drought above moisture'. [21] This is a far cry from the all-loving God envisaged by Cleanthes and Paley.

This last objection, which draws on the problem of evil (see page 461), may not be fatal for a teleological argument. Paley acknowledges the possibility of an attack from this quarter in the criticism above. But Paley argues that it is not necessary that a machine be perfect in order to be designed; all that is important is that the machine exhibits some sort of purpose. We shall see when we examine the problem of evil that the existence of God isn't necessarily incompatible with the presence of apparent design flaws (like unnecessary pain and suffering) in the universe.

It may also be possible to side-step Philo's criticisms by conceding that we can say very little about the designer of the universe purely on the basis of a teleological argument. This would take the sting out of Philo's attacks, as the conclusion of such an argument would simply be that a designer of the universe exists and would make no claims about what such a designer is like. In this case Cleanthes and Paley need only show a common thread of intent in the design of a machine and of the universe: just as the machine's design is the result of intentional action so is the universe's design. For Robert Hambourger, a modern supporter of teleological arguments, so long as we concede that the universe exhibits elements of design, even if only in parts and even if other parts are flawed, then this 'would be enough to show that something was seriously wrong with the atheist's standard picture of the universe'.[22] If we admit the possibility of design then we also admit the idea of an intentional act lying behind the design, and this would undermine the atheist's position.

► criticism ◄ However, we have now moved a long way from the optimistic claims, made by supporters of the arguments from design, that we can see God's handiworks in nature just as we see evidence of an artisan in an artefact. Hume's Philo concludes that the very most that arguments from design are able to establish is 'that the cause or causes of the universe probably bear some remote analogy to human intelligence'.[23] Such a tentative conclusion is unlikely to persuade anyone of the existence of God, unless they already believe in him.

ACTIVITY   Re-read Paley's teleological argument. Where do you think Hume's criticisms really hit home? For each proposed criticism decide:

a) whether it undermines a premise, and, if so, identify which premise
or
b) whether it undermines the structure of the argument, i.e. the steps it takes towards the conclusion.

The challenge of Darwin

Traditional arguments from design, based on the analogy made between the natural world and human artefacts, were faced with further criticism when Charles Darwin's (1809–1882) work on natural selection was published. We have already met with Darwin's theory of evolution, in Chapter 2, when we examined the evolutionary psychologist's explanation of the origins of 'God' (pages 168–75).

Much of the persuasive power of an argument like Paley's lay in examples of design taken from the natural world: it seemed obvious that the intricacy of a human eye and the beauty of a peacock's tail could not have come about by chance; they must have been designed. However, Darwin's *Origin of Species* (1859) provided an account of how such perfectly adapted features could and did come about, not by intelligent design, but by the struggle of every generation of species to compete, survive and reproduce. Darwin's theory of evolution became widely accepted as the best explanation of the features that William Paley puzzled over, namely that:

- living organisms consist of individual parts
- these parts are framed and work together for a purpose
- they have been made with specific material, appropriate to their action
- together they produce regulated motion
- if the parts had been different in any way such motion would not be produced.

ACTIVITY
1 Revisit the explanation of how evolution works (above page 168).
2 How might evolution account for the puzzling features (ones that suggest design) listed above?

Darwin

The old argument from design in nature, as given by Paley . . . fails now that the law of natural selection has been discovered. We can no longer argue that, for instance, the beautiful hinge of a bivalve shell must have been made by an intelligent being, like the hinge of a door by man. There seems to be no more design in the variability of organic beings . . . than in the course which the wind blows.[24]

Nevertheless, we should give Paley's argument its due. The eye seems to be a precision organ precisely put together to perform a particular function. Before Darwin, the only explanation going for the existence of such features was the existence of a designer. What Darwin did was to give us an alternative account of how such design can appear. Random mutation plus the pressures of natural selection is the designer of all living organisms: it is not an intelligent or purposeful designer, but a blind unthinking mechanism.

Darwin's theory did not extinguish arguments from design altogether. Some philosophers incorporated evolution into their arguments; Richard Swinburne, for example, assimilates evolution into the 'machine-making' nature of this mechanical universe.[25] So those features of design in the natural universe, although not directly caused by God as previously suggested by Paley and others, are still the result of the evolutionary mechanism built into the universe by God. Other theologians reject Darwin and argue instead for INTELLIGENT DESIGN, which we shall examine below. So teleological arguments have proved to be extraordinarily robust in the face of other challenges from naturalism (theories that claim the universe can be explained in a fully naturalistic, non-supernatural, way); this is despite the success of modern physics and biology in explaining the apparent order and purpose the universe.

Recent design arguments have moved away from simplistic arguments from analogy, but instead argue that naturalistic explanations are inadequate, and that God is the best hypothesis explaining why the world is the way it is. These more modern arguments for design include:

- Arguments for Intelligent Design – which draw on the principle of 'irreducible complexity' as a response to the theory of evolution
- Arguments to the best explanation – which use the method of abduction, to propose God as a hypothesis that best accounts for all the features of the universe
- Arguments responding to the ANTHROPIC PRINCIPLE – which assess the likelihood of two possibilities: first, the probability of the universe being the way it is (and of conscious beings coming into existence) through chance; secondly, the probability of the universe being as it is by design.

Arguments for Intelligent Design

Thus we can say today with a new certitude and joyousness that the human being is indeed a divine project, which only the creating Intelligence was strong and great and audacious enough to conceive of.[26]

Cardinal Ratzinger

In recent years American theologians have responded vigorously to Darwinian claims by putting forward an alternative that they believe provides a better account of why living organisms appear so well adapted to their environments. According to its critics, Darwin's theory of evolution and modern versions of it (such as that put forward by Richard Dawkins) simply cannot explain how certain features of animals evolved. The alternative theory that they propose is termed Intelligent Design, and its supporters present it as a scientific project aimed at demonstrating that living things have been designed by an intelligent designer, and are not simply the result of the improbable processes of evolution.

According to supporters of Intelligent Design, such as Michael Behe and William Dembski, science can only go so far in its understanding of how organisms developed over time. Darwinian theory, they argue, becomes unstuck when it tries to give details of how an organ as complex, yet perfectly adapted, as the eye evolved. Charles Darwin himself admitted as much, when he acknowledged that it seemed 'absurd in the highest degree' that something as sophisticated as an eye could have evolved through natural selection.[27] There just doesn't seem to be any way that an eye could have evolved from something more primitive; as Richard Dawkins puts it (when summarising this criticism), 'what use is half an eye?'[28] The answer provided by Intelligent Design supporters is 'none'; in which case evolutionary theory, which tries to show how an eye might have evolved from more primitive light-detectors, is dramatically undermined.

> *How did a spot become innervated and thereby light-sensitive? How did a lens form within a pinhole camera? . . . None of these questions receives an answer purely in Darwinian terms. Darwinian just-so stories have no more scientific content than Rudyard Kipling's original just-so stories.*[29]
>
> Dembski

We saw in Chapter 2 (page 173) that a just-so story is a backwards-looking explanation that isn't supported by any evidence – it's just a neat and tidy explanation that fits in with the theory. Dembski's criticism of evolutionary theory is that it makes lots of noise about how things like eyes evolved, but that it cannot substantiate these claims by showing how the parts of an eye might have evolved and come together with such spectacular success across the animal kingdom. Michael Behe uses the term 'irreducible complexity' to refer to those features of nature which are so complex that they cannot be explained in evolutionary terms. Behe does not believe that evolutionists have shown how imperfect and simple light-detectors gradually become complex and perfect eyes. Behe's claim is that irreducibly complex features such as the eye are made up of parts (lens, retina, rods, cones) that form a highly successful unit – but that these parts on their own would be useless in evolutionary terms; they would not lead to success. The only explanation for their existence is that these units came into being fully formed as a whole, and did not go through any evolutionary process.

Behe gives an analogy to help us understand irreducible complexity. He asks us to consider a mouse-trap, and how the various parts of it work together to create a functioning whole unit: the base, the metal spring, the holding bar, the catch. If any one of these parts were missing or worked less efficiently, then the mouse-trap would fail to work. The mouse-trap only functions when all its parts are in place, and we know that this is how the designer designed it. In the same way, a complex feature like an eye only functions when all its parts are in place. Working backwards from this complex unit towards a simpler one, as evolutionary explanations do, results in these parts being removed or made less efficient, and the eye would cease to function. Evolutionary theory, therefore, fails to explain how well-adapted features like the eye came about.

It turns out that irreducibly complex systems are headaches for Darwinian theory, because they are resistant to being produced in the gradual, step-by-step manner, that Darwin envisaged.[30]

Behe

The conclusion drawn by Behe, Dembski and their colleagues is that complex features such as the eye can be explained only if we posit the existence of an intelligent designer, God, who deliberately created these units with a specific function in mind. Saying that there exists an intelligent designer still allows for a scientific research programme, as proposed by Behe, that seeks to identify the irreducibly complex component parts, to analyse them and determine their functions and interrelationships.

Because of the scientific presentation of Intelligent Design theory there were campaigns across the United States to introduce Intelligent Design into the science curriculum to be taught alongside evolution. In 2005 a significant test case was brought to court by the parents from the Dover Area School in Pennsylvania. The parents objected to the teaching of Intelligent Design alongside evolutionary biology in science classes – they argued it was a form of creationism and had no place in science. The court heard evidence from a number of adaptationists (supporters of Darwin's theory) and from Intelligent Design supporters, including Michael Behe. After several months the judge ruled that Intelligent Design was not a science and he barred its teaching from science classes. Let us now briefly look at some of the problems with Intelligent Design.

► criticism ◄

One significant problem with Intelligent Design is that it has had difficulties identifying a clear instance of a feature which is irreducibly complex. The eye is often given as a paradigm example of irreducible complexity, and supporters of Intelligent Design refer to Darwin's own difficulties in explaining how 'half an eye' (as Dawkins put it) could be evolutionary successful. Darwin wrote that the claim that an eye is a product of evolution seemed 'absurd in the highest degree' – although he does then go on to explain in painstaking details how the eye could have evolved by gradual degrees. Dawkins attacks the assumption (made as part of the principle of 'irreducible complexity') that features like eyes cease to function if a part of them is removed. Someone who has their sight damaged might not be able to drive a car, but may be able to see well enough not to walk into a tree or over a cliff. Partial sight is useful and it gives an evolutionary advantage over competitors who are unsighted. Hence, in organisms which lack sight, a gene sequence that results in partial-sightedness will be more successful in reproducing than their zero-sighted competitors, and the genes will spread through the population. Each mutation that leads to a refinement and improvement in the eye will spread through the population in the same way. We would expect to see, in nature, a range of more-or-less sophisticated sight detectors, and this is what biologists have found: primitive photoreceptors (flat 'eyespots' simply detecting light and dark) in unicellular *euglena*; cupped pit-eyes in *planaria*, which can detect the direction of the light; pin-hole camera eyes in *nautilus* which register an image; and so on through to the incredible vision of birds of prey. With the evidence stacking up in favour of an evolutionary explanation for the eye, Intelligent Design has had to look elsewhere for examples of irreducible complexity – mindful of Dawkins' warning:

Do not just declare things to be irreducibly complex; the chances are that you haven't looked carefully enough at the details.[31]

► criticism ◄

Currently none of the features suggested by supporters of Intelligent Design has been accepted as an example of irreducible complexity, either by the scientific community, or by the US judge in the Dover school trial. But a more damaging criticism of Intelligent Design is that it is not a science at all. It has not been accepted by the scientific community (many of whom are religious) in so far as no research carried out under the banner of Intelligent Design has been accepted into a peer-reviewed academic journal – the key marker of respect from the scientific community. It might be objected that there is a global conspiracy against Intelligent Design, but the explanation given by editors is that Intelligent Design does not follow scientific methodology: it does not carry out rigorous testing in tightly controlled experiments, or make definite predictions based on its theory; it lacks consistency and generally any scientific utility. The defence offered by supporters of Intelligent Design is that it is still in its infancy. But until it publishes some original, peer-reviewed, research it looks like remaining very much a non-science.

Tennant's argument to the best explanation

experimenting with ideas

For each of the following situations, decide whether a), b) or c) is the best explanation for what happened. Then:

i) For each situation explain (ideally to someone else) why you have selected a), b) or c). What made your selection the best explanation?

ii) Make a list of all the things that make an explanation strong.

1 Ilham has been all around the world, studying thousands of birds, but he has never seen a white raven. This is because:
   a) All ravens are in fact black.
   b) All ravens are in fact black up until the year 2010, after which they might become any colour of the rainbow.
   c) All ravens that Ilham is about to see quickly change their colour, like chameleons, so that they appear black to him.

2 People in Cadiz harbour see the masts of ships disappear as they move away from port towards the horizon. This is because:
   a) The human eye is limited in its range: it can only see up to 29 miles in the distance.
   b) The earth is round.
   c) The masts don't actually disappear. It's the heavy mists in the air above the Atlantic Ocean around the coast of Spain that makes them seem to disappear.

3 Hayley found a rock on a heath, and brought it home as an ornament. But she found it interfered with the digital radio that it was placed next to. This is because:
   a) The rock is a magical stone, out to take vengeance on humanity for its destruction of Mother Earth.
   b) The rock is a lodestone, and has strong electro-magnetic fields that interfere with other magnetic fields such as those in digital radios.
   c) It was sheer coincidence that the radio broke soon after the rock was put next to it: there is no connection between the two events.

4 Blaine needs to throw six 6s in a dice game in order to win – he picks up the dice and rolls exactly six 6s. This is because:
   a) Blaine is a cheat and switched the ordinary dice for loaded dice when it came to his turn.
   b) It is entirely possible to roll six 6s purely by chance, and that's just what happened here.
   c) Blaine is naturally lucky: good fortune has shone on him throughout his life, and this is just another example of his good luck.

5 Hudson watches a cuckoo lay an egg in the nest of a robin. The cuckoo chick hatches and shifts itself around until all the robin eggs have fallen out of the nest. Eventually only the cuckoo is left, and the robin spends all day foraging for food to feed this parasitic bird. This is because:

a) The cuckoo egg was laid in the robin's nest by accident, and when it hatched it moved around too vigorously, which unfortunately knocked the robin eggs out of the nest.

b) God designed cuckoos as parasitic birds in order to destroy the eggs and chicks of unsuspecting robins.

c) Cuckoos have evolved behaviour over millions of years which exploits the maternal instincts in other bird species like robins.

6 Elias discovered a strange object in an ancient wreck at the bottom of the seabed near the island of Antikythera. The object looked like a rock with a complex metal wheel embedded in it. This is because:

a) Someone had thrown a piece of machinery overboard from their fishing boat and it happened to land at the bottom of the sea near an ancient wreck

b) The ship had been carrying an ancient stone chariot with metal wheels, but on its way to Crete, where it was going to sell the chariot, the ship had sunk under the weight.

c) The object was part of an ancient machine designed to show the movements of the sun, the earth and the moon.

All teleological arguments begin by asking why the universe contains the specific features that it does: regularity, beauty, order and purpose. We have seen that some teleological arguments proceed by analogy to show that these features were designed by God, just as machines were designed by humans. Other teleological arguments advance in a different way, by asking how these features can be explained and concluding that God is the best explanation. This is a type of reverse engineering (of the kind we saw undertaken by evolutionary biologists on page 169 above). In other words, when we are confronted with something that seems to require an explanation but for which the original cause is no longer observable, we try to trace the causal chain backwards in order to arrive at the best explanation for its existence. So, for example, the scientists and engineers who have studied the famous Antikythera mechanism, described in **6** in the activity above, have looked in great detail at the grooves, the cogs and the dials. Using reverse engineering they have concluded that the mechanism is in fact part of an orrery – a model of the solar system – and have even reconstructed this model and all its parts.

■ **Figure 6.3**
Reverse engineering to determine the function of the Antikytheran mechanism

Existing fragment of
the Antikythera

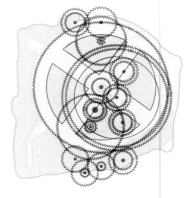

Reversed engineered
orrery built from the
Antikythera fragment

Teleological arguments to the best explanation typically use reverse engineering by proceeding along the following lines.

1   We see in the universe the presence of certain special features (orderliness, regularity, beauty, life, self-conscious beings, etc.).
2   These features, either collectively or individually, cannot be adequately explained by the natural sciences such as physics or biology.
3   The presence of these features (both collectively and individually) can be made sense of by the existence of God.
4   Where an explanation makes sense of certain features that cannot be accounted for by any other explanation, then we can conclude it is probably right.
5   Therefore God exists.

The fourth premise stems from an idea known as 'inference to the best explanation'. This was termed 'abduction' by the American philosopher C.S. Pierce (1839–1914) as an alternative to induction and deduction, and he claims that by using abduction we arrive at the hypothesis that God exists. Abductive arguments proceed by arguing that we should believe in whichever hypothesis best explains the data – i.e. whichever explanation is strongest. From engaging in the activity above you will have drawn up your own list of what makes an explanation a strong one, but it may have included the following.

■   Simplicity: we should favour simple explanations over more complex ones, if they explain the same thing equally well (this is known as Ockham's Razor).
■   Explanatory power: we should favour the explanation that is able to account for the greatest amount of the data.
■   Predictive power: we should favour explanations that can be used to make predictions that can then be tested.

- Cohesiveness: we should favour explanations that best fit with those tried-and-tested beliefs that we currently hold.

The question is, when it comes to accounting for the orderliness, regularity, beauty, etc. of the universe, is God the strongest hypothesis? (We ask below whether God is a hypothesis at all.)

Design arguments to the best explanation are able to build a cumulative case for the existence of God. F.R. Tennant (in *Philosophical Teleology*, 1930) draws on a range of features that we observe in the universe, all of which seem to demand an explanation; he concludes that God is the best hypothesis we have to explain their occurrence. Tennant recognises that each feature on its own may be explicable through the natural sciences, but together they form an overwhelming case for God's existence. He includes the following features as ones that are best explained by the existence of God.

- The intelligibility of the universe to humans: because it is ordered and regular rather than chaotic, our scientific investigations are able to unravel its laws.
- The possibility of organic adaptation: the process of evolution enables beings to adapt to their environment.
- The adaptation of the inorganic world to life: this planet is able to generate and support life, through its geology, climate, atmosphere, position in the solar system, etc.
- The beauty of nature: from the microscopic to the astromonical, the natural world astounds believers and non-believers alike with its beauty and sublimity.
- The existence of morality: humans are able to identify good from evil and to work to achieve the good.
- The emergence of human beings: evolution has progressed to produce humans who have the ability to contemplate the universe, appreciate its beauty and seek what is good within it.

For Tennant, each of these features taken individually is very difficult to explain from a naturalistic perspective, i.e. one that remains only within the realms of the world of nature. When we consider the existence of all of them collectively, then the task of explaining them naturalistically becomes even harder. Only God provides an adequate explanation of why a barren, inanimate world gave rise, first to life, then to human beings capable of contemplating the universe and reflecting on their place within it. Tennant believes that the world is the way it is, and we are the way we are, because of God's guiding intelligence behind his creation.

ACTIVITY **1** How might an atheist scientist seek to explain each of the features mentioned by Tennant?

2 Without referring to God, how else is it possible that all of these features could occur together in a single universe?

▶ *criticism* ◀ David Hume suggests an alternative to teleological explanations in his *Dialogues Concerning Natural Religion.* Hume argues that it is at least possible that the universe is ordered and life-supporting as a result of chance and not intelligence.[32] This theory is often referred to as the Epicurean Hypothesis, after the ancient Greek philosopher Epicurus (341–270 BCE) who proposed that the universe exists in the way it does as a result of the random movements of a finite number of atoms. Over an infinite period of time these atoms will take every possible position, some of them ordered, some of them chaotic. It just so happens that the physical universe is currently in a state of order, and that, by chance, beings have evolved that are capable of reflecting on the universe and why it is here. Hume argues that, although this may be a remote possibility, it cannot be disregarded as a possible explanation for the appearance of design in the universe.

The Epicurean Hypothesis, unsurprisingly, has not found favour with theologians, who continue to look for scientific grounds for saying that God, not chance, is the best explanation for design in the universe.

 *experimenting with ideas*

A long time ago in a universe far away there lived the Yahoos, a species of self-conscious, carbon-based alien life forms. At a certain point in their intellectual evolution the Yahoos began to ponder the mysteries of the universe, where it came from and why they were here. Some of them argued that the universe was purposeful, with each part contriving to enable the evolution of the Yahoos themselves. The Yahoos believed that such a finely adjusted universe, which had resulted in the existence of Yahoos, clearly required an explanation.

1 Which explanation best accounts for the existence of the Yahoos: a) a teleological explanation, relying on the guiding intelligence of God; or b) an 'Epicurean' explanation, relying on blind chance?

2 Are there any other explanations that might account for the existence of the Yahoos?

3 Are the Yahoos justified in their belief that the universe has been perfectly adjusted so that they might come into existence? Why/Why not?

Anthropic design arguments and the Anthropic Principle

What strikes Tennant as most odd about the universe is the extraordinary list of physical conditions that have to be in place for human life to be possible. Human life is only possible because the universe exhibits very precise chemical, thermal and astronomical features, whose origin can be traced back to the Big Bang.[33] According to this way of thinking, the likelihood that this chain of events (extending over billions of years and culminating in the appearance of life on Earth and conscious intelligent beings) could occur by pure chance is so unimaginably low that we are forced to conclude that there must be a guiding hand behind the process. It is this that leads him to the conclusion that it is no coincidence that everything on Earth is just right for human existence; God intended it to be that way.

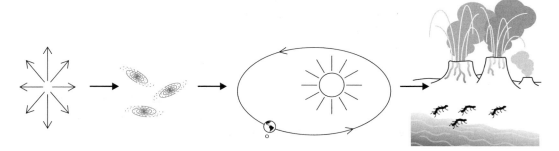

■ **Figure 6.4 The long chain of events leading to life on Earth and eventually human beings**

From the THEISTS' perspective the work done by scientists on the Big Bang in the past fifty years has actually strengthened their case for God's existence. After all for even the most primitive of life to occur billions of years after the Big Bang certain very precise and unusual conditions need to be met. Is it really conceivable that it was pure chance that brought about these conditions? And it is not just the conditions for life on Earth that are incredibly unlikely. Below is a list of some of the conditions that have been cited as necessary for the emergence of human beings.

■ The Big Bang had to occur exactly as it happened, without variation. The scientist Paul Davies has maintained that if the strength of the initial event had varied by one part in 10^{60} (that's a 10 followed by 60 noughts!) then there would have been no Big Bang. This is analogous to the accuracy an archer would have to have in order to hit a one-inch target from twenty billion light years away.[34]

- There needs to be a precise balance in the values of constants that govern gravitational force and the weak nuclear force in every atom. Without this there would be no expansion of the universe, and so no formation of stars or planets. Yet it's been speculated that the two forces need to be balanced to an accuracy of one part in ten thousand billion, billion, billion, billion. [35]
- Stars must have formed, and within them carbon atoms created from the fusion of hydrogen and helium atoms (carbon is an essential component of organic matter).
- A life-containing planet, such as Earth, needs to be at a precise distance from the sun in order to have just enough light and heat to maintain life once it has emerged.
- There must be the development of self-replicating DNA in the 'primeval soup' on the planet.
- There must take place the same random mutations that led to the natural selection of mammals, and eventually the emergence of our ancestors on the African plains.[36]

In fact when we consider all the physical conditions that the universe had to possess for humans to evolve then, as Russell Stannard puts it, 'there seems to be a conspiracy to fix the conditions'.[37] But, by positing the existence of God, this series of amazing coincidences is explained in one fell swoop: they are not coincidences, but the product of God's design. We can build up the argument as follows:

1 For human life to come into existence certain very specific, and unconnected, physical conditions need to be in place.
2 All these physical features are found to be in place in this universe.
3 Either these special features have occurred by chance (the 'Epicurean Hypothesis') or by Intelligent Design (the 'God Hypothesis').
4 The probability of all these features occurring by coincidence is incredibly small.
5 Therefore the most likely explanation for these life-enabling features is Intelligent Design (the God Hypothesis).
6 Therefore God exists.

This type of argument can be described as an 'anthropic teleological argument', because its premises explore those special features of the universe needed to produce *human beings* – 'anthropic' means 'relating to human beings' (from the Greek *anthropos* meaning man or human).

▶ criticism ◀ Discussions of the 'God Hypothesis', which explains why the universe seems so finely tuned for human existence, have led to the construction of the so-called Anthropic Principle (AP). There have been many formulations of the AP, and this has led to confusion about its exact meaning. Different versions of the AP have been developed both to support (e.g. by Tennant) and undermine (e.g. by Carter) the belief in God. But the original version of the AP, proposed by Brandon Carter in 1974, says that we have no reason to be surprised that the universe is the way it is, because if it were any different then we would not be around to be surprised. [38] It is only when explanation-seeking creatures like humans evolve that they start seeing the features that led to their own existence as special. It is true that the particular way that the universe did turn out was incredibly unlikely, but that doesn't mean that we can turn around and say that it couldn't have happened by chance. After all, it had to turn out one way or another and whichever way it did turn out would appear incredibly unlikely after the fact. If the initial conditions had been different the universe would have turned out very different. It could have resulted in the evolution of Yahoos or Houyhnhnms, instead of humans. It would then be the Yahoos or Houyhnhnms who marvelled at the amazing contrivances of the universe that led to their existence. It might have evolved without any intelligent life. In such a case the way it turned out would have been just as incredibly unlikely, the only difference would be that there would have been no one around to be surprised. This implies there is nothing inherently special about the features that led to life, and there is no need to posit God in order to explain them. The problem with the anthropic teleological argument is that it treats our own existence as of prime importance, as the most remarkable thing that requires explaining. But humans are only one of a great number of incredible things that the universe has thrown up, and only one of an even greater number of things that it might have thrown up had it been slightly different.

▶ criticism ◀   A less respectful criticism of anthropic-type teleological arguments comes from the American writer Mark Twain. Twain's short and scathing article 'Was the World made for Man?' attacks the human-centred view of the universe that he felt some theologians held. He takes great delight in imagining how millions of years of evolution were needed to make oysters and fish (and coal for the fire) just so that we might have a light and tasty snack for tea. He concludes his article with the following sarcastic observation:

Man has been here 32,000 years. That it took a hundred million years to prepare the world for him is proof that is what it was done for . . . If the Eiffel tower were now representing the world's age, the skin of paint on the pinnacle-knob at its summit would represent man's share of that age; and anybody would perceive that that skin was what the tower was built for. I reckon they would.[39]

▶ criticism ◀ The question we have been addressing is whether God is the most probable explanation for the special features of the universe that resulted in human existence. However, it only makes sense to talk about probabilities where we are able to compare the chances each outcome has of taking place. For example, when we flick a coin a few hundred times we can work out that there is a 50 per cent chance that the coin lands heads side up. But Hume has already pointed out that this universe, or at very least our experience of this universe, is unique. We are therefore in no position to calculate the probability that this particular universe has of existing; we just don't have any other universes to compare it to. Thus we are also in no position to conclude whether God, or pure chance, is the most likely explanation for this universe.

Of all the proofs of God's existence, teleological arguments are the most reliant on empirical observation and scientific theories. For this reason we might think that they would be the most vulnerable to scientific criticism; and yet they have consistently proved to be resilient and adaptive. Teleological arguments have managed to incorporate developments like the mechanical universe of Galileo and Newton, Darwin's theory of evolution and recently the Big Bang theory. As they respond to science, so teleological arguments have shifted their focus from one special feature of the universe to another: from wondering at the place of the Earth at the centre of the universe, to puzzling over the perfect spiral of a snail's shell, to calculating the probability of carbon atoms forming.

An atheist might find this unacceptable. After all a theory that shifts and adjusts according to the prevailing intellectual wind seems to be unfalsifiable, that is to say, there would appear to be no way of demonstrating that it is false. Theories that cannot be falsified are regarded by some thinkers as meaningless, and this is an idea we will be examining more closely when we look at Flew below (page 491). However, the popularity of teleological arguments with ordinary believers and religious philosophers is undiminished. We are still struck by the beauty and orderliness of the universe, whether in the equations of theoretical physics, or in watching a thunderstorm in the mountains. To the atheist, it is a wonder that chance has led to such things and to our being here to appreciate them. But the atheist also looks at other features of the world and asks 'how can you believe in God when *this* is the world we live in?' It is not the order and regularity of the natural world that strikes many atheists, but the disorder and disharmony that creates so much pain, suffering and misery.

The problem of evil

I didn't want to harm the man. I thought he was a very nice gentleman. Soft-spoken. I thought so right up to the moment I cut his throat.[40]

The multiple killer, Perry Smith

I form light and create darkness, I make peace and create evil, I the Lord, do all these things.

Isaiah 45:7

1 Write down a list of ten things that have happened in the world in the last fifteen years that you regard as evil – try to be as specific as you can.

2 What do these things have in common, i.e. what makes them evil?

3 Can you categorise your examples into different types of evil?

What is meant by 'evil'?

The problem of evil remains one of the most contentious and unsettling areas in the philosophy of religion. The problem is important to believers and non-believers alike: believers because they have to reconcile their belief in God with their day-to-day encounter with pain and suffering in the world; non-believers because the existence of evil is often cited as evidence against the existence of God. Unlike some of the other theological issues that we have encountered (What are the attributes of God? Can his existence be proved? Is he a necessary being?) the problem of evil is generated through our experience of life, and not simply through intellectual investigation. Before we outline the problem of evil in more detail we should first examine what is meant by 'evil' in this context.

At a very general level, 'evil' is taken to refer to those concrete and negative experiences that sentient beings have of the world. These negative experiences can be grouped into the physical (including hunger, cold, pain) and the mental (including misery, anguish, terror), and we can summarise these two types of experience as pain and suffering.[41] Pain and suffering are commonplace amongst sentient beings on this planet, and so evil confronts us on a daily basis.

Theologians have offered other, more technical, definitions of evil. For example, St Augustine defines evil as that 'which we fear, or the act of fearing itself'.[42] The idea of fear as an evil in itself is echoed in Truman Capote's account of a horrific multiple murder (by two drifters, Perry Smith and Dick Hickock) and its aftermath in a sleepy mid-west American town in 1959. In the townspeople's panic following the murders there was a rush to buy locks and bolts to protect their homes:

Folks ain't particular what brand they buy; they just want them to hold. Imagination of course can open any door – turn the key and let terror walk right in.[43]

If we apply Augustine's account of evil to the situation that these townsfolk found themselves in, then we can identify both the cold-blooded murderers and the terror they leave behind as evil. But Augustine and Aquinas are careful to argue that evil is not a 'thing' (a mysterious substance or presence, for example) but is the absence of goodness. Their account of goodness was strongly influenced by Plato and Aristotle's understanding of 'good', which contained the idea of goal or purpose. For Aristotle 'good' refers to the complete fulfilment of a thing's natural potential. So a good can-opener is one that is excellent at opening cans, it possesses all the relevant features (the Greeks would call them 'virtues') necessary for opening cans safely and efficiently. Similarly a good oak tree is one that has all the virtues of an oak tree (it has strong roots, is disease free, efficiently photosynthesises and produces numerous acorns).

Augustine

[Evil is] nothing but the corruption of natural measure, form or order. What is called an evil nature is a corrupt nature . . . It is bad only so far as it has been corrupted.[44]

So, for Augustine, and Aquinas, evil is not a concrete presence or substance, it is simply the 'privation of good', i.e. a lack of goodness, a failure to flourish or fulfil a natural purpose. We shall see later that this account of evil is fundamental to Augustine's explanation of why it exists. Augustine sees the world, as created by God, in terms of goodness; evil is introduced only later as some disorder within the goodness of God's creation.

Two types of evil

In the activity above you might well have found that your examples of evil fell easily into two types: 'pain and suffering caused by humans' and 'pain and suffering caused by nature'. Philosophers of religion have traditionally identified two sources of evil: natural and moral.[45] 'Natural evil' refers to the pain and suffering of sentient beings that occurs independently of human actions. On the morning of All Saints' Day (1 November) 1755 the city of Lisbon in Portugal was hit by an earthquake that wrenched streets apart by 5 metre fissures and turned the city into ruins. Soon afterwards a massive tsunami swept into the remains of the city, as a result of the earthquake, and in the areas not destroyed by earth or water, fire broke out that lasted for days. Around a third of all inhabitants of Lisbon were burned, drowned or crushed – 90,000 people. When the French philosopher Voltaire heard the news he wrote his 'Poem on the Disaster of Lisbon' (see extract below) that had a huge impact on European intellectuals of the day.

Oh unhappy mortals! Oh wretched earth!
Oh dreadful gathering of so many dead!
The eternal sport of fruitless griefs!
Mistaken philosophers who cry: 'All is well',
Approach, look upon these frightful ruins,
This debris, these shreds, these unhappy ashes,
These scattered limbs beneath these broken marbles;
A hundred thousand wretches swallowed by the earth,
Bleeding, torn, with hearts still beating,
Buried beneath their roofs, ended without help
Their lamentable days in the horrors of their suffering!

For Voltaire, the immense and pointless suffering of innocent people caused by the Lisbon earthquake was a troubling sign that this was not, after all, the 'best possible world'. The Boxing Day tsunami in 2004 that killed 230,000 people around the Indian Ocean is another instance of a disaster that would fall under the heading 'natural evil'. There are countless other examples of pain and suffering that could be given: the 'cloaking' device of cancerous cells that enables them to stay hidden from our immune systems and multiply their cancer unchecked; the habits of certain types of wasps to lay their eggs in caterpillars which are then eaten alive from the inside out; the mass extinction of dinosaurs 65 million years ago; the human and non-human victims of viruses, bacteria and other microscopic killers.

'Moral evil' refers to those acts of cruelty, viciousness and injustice carried out by humans upon fellow humans and other creatures, and which, for theologians, includes the concept of 'sin'. According to the American scientist and writer Jared Diamond, since the murderous genocides of Hitler and Stalin in the 1930s and 1940s, in which tens of millions of people were killed, there have been a further seventeen known genocides across the world. The soul-searching and hand-wringing after the Second World War, the creation of the United Nations, the pursuit of democracy and global capitalism have been accompanied by an *increase*, rather than a decrease, in the number of politicised mass murders around the world. For Jared Diamond these genocides have a close connection with tensions arising in society for geopolitical reasons: there are not enough resources to go round an increasing population and the situation is set to get worse.[46] But it was humans, not nature, who in 1994 executed by knife and machete around 800,000 people of Rwanda in a few weeks. As with natural evil the suffering on this vast scale is more than matched by the daily torture and abuse of individuals around the world that goes unnoticed, unpublicised and unpunished.

What is the relationship between natural and moral evil? For some, natural evil might be seen as a consequence of human action or inaction, and hence as a subset, of moral evil. For example, crop failure, drought and starvation are often brought about by overpopulation, over-farming, the destruction of the environment, etc. So these 'natural evils' might be read as 'moral evils', but there are other, more problematic examples for this reading. The human immunodeficiency virus (HIV), which has killed over 25 million people in the past 25 years, has been seen by some as a punishment for human sinfulness. St Augustine argued that the once perfect world of the Garden of Eden has been made imperfect by the 'original sin' of Adam (pages 469–70) and that the suffering caused by natural disasters and disease is God's punishment for this original moral evil.

It is also possible to regard moral evil as a form of natural evil, although this involves a philosophical view of human nature and freedom that is far removed from the teachings of Western religious traditions: namely the view that humans do not hold a privileged position within the natural world. If humans lie on a continuum with the rest of nature, then 'moral evil' is not distinct from the 'natural' pain and suffering caused by earthquakes, rabid dogs and malaria-carrying mosquitos. If our species is governed by the same principles as all other forms of life, then moral evil is just one local example of the pain and suffering that all animals inevitably endure. John Stuart Mill (in _Three Essays on Religion_, 1874) argued that natural evil arose from the malfunctioning of the universe, which was originally intended for the preservation, not destruction, of life. If we assume, as Mill and Darwin did, that humans do not have a divine purpose or privileged place in the hierarchy of animals, then it is easier to see moral evil as a form of natural evil. Humans are jealous, live in close social groups, compete with one another for food, resources and mates, and have trouble controlling their violent and sometimes murderous impulses. Without any theological scaffolding, such as that of original sin, it is possible to view human actions that cause pain and suffering ('moral evil') as simply an extreme case of the 'natural' pain and suffering inflicted in the rest of the animal kingdom.

The problem of evil outlined

Refer to the examples of evil you gave in the activity on page 461.

1 Which of these evils would you prevent if:
   a) you were a billionaire
   b) you were Superman
   c) you were even more powerful than Superman?

2 In the case of c) are there any evils you would allow to persist – why/why not?

The problem of evil affects all the theistic religions, which have as their object of worship a God who is the all-powerful creator of the world, and who cares deeply for his creation. We find the problem clearly stated in the works of both St Augustine and Aquinas,[47] but we can also find earlier versions dating back to Epicurus (341–270 BCE). This is how Epicurus puts it:

God either wishes to take away evils, and is unable; or he is able, and is unwilling; or he is neither willing nor able; or he is both willing and able. If he is willing and is unable, he is feeble, which is not in accordance with the character of God; if he is able and unwilling, he is envious, which is equally at variance with God; if he is neither willing nor able, he is both envious and feeble, and therefore not God; if he is both willing and able . . . from what source then are evils? Or why does he not remove them? [48]

As John Hick (1922–) puts it: 'Can the presence of evil in the world be reconciled with the existence of a God who is unlimited both in goodness and in power?'[49] More recently philosophers have identified at least two different formulations of the problem of evil: the *logical problem* and the *evidential problem*.

The logical problem of evil

The logical problem of evil asserts that believers are committed to holding two apparently inconsistent beliefs:

1 God is the all-powerful, wholly good and all-knowing creator of the universe.
2 Evil exists in the universe.

We can find one of the clearest statements of the logical problem of evil in J.L. Mackie's paper 'Evil and omnipotence'.[50] Mackie tightens up the problem by adding a third proposition that really brings out the contradiction:

3 A wholly good being eliminates evil as far as it can.

ACTIVITY

i) Using these three propositions do you think it's possible for an atheist to construct an argument to prove that God cannot exist?
ii) Write down any additional premises that would be needed to make the argument watertight.
iii) How might believers criticise such an argument (which premises or steps would they deny)?

For Mackie, propositions 1, 2 and 3 cannot be held to be true simultaneously, so believers must give up at least one of them. It seems undeniable that there is pain and suffering in

■ **Figure 6.5**

It appears that not all of these beliefs can be true at once. Yet evil certainly seems to be real, so, does God not know about it? Does he not care about it? Is he unable to stop it? If we opt for any of these it seems that the God of the philosophers does not exist.

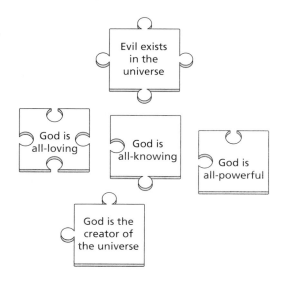

the universe, and thus 2 is true. [51] What about 1? The contradiction would disappear if believers jettisoned some, or all, of the qualities of God, as either he wouldn't be able to do anything about evil, or he wouldn't care. But as Epicurus points out, if God does not have the will to eradicate evil (he is not all-loving) or if he does not have the power to do so (he is not omnipotent) then he would no longer be God at all. We shall see that many proposed solutions to the problem of evil argue that evil is in some way good, or contributes to something good, in which case 3 can be surrendered without abandoning theism. It remains to be seen whether these solutions are successful.

The evidential problem of evil

Darwin

God who could create the universe, is to our finite minds omnipotent and omniscient, and it revolts our understanding to suppose that his benevolence is not unbounded, for what advantage can there be in the sufferings of millions of the lower animals throughout almost endless time?[52]

Darwin's experiences as a biologist brought him face to face with the daily pain and suffering of animals. For many thinkers, including Darwin, David Hume and the contemporary philosopher William Rowe, the sheer amount of evil in the world weighs against there being a God who is omnipotent and wholly good. After all, would an almighty, all-knowing, all-loving God allow such extraordinary pain and suffering to exist? Why doesn't he intervene to prevent earthquakes that kill tens of thousands, or viruses that kill millions? Why does he allow psychopaths and serial killers to unleash their cruelty onto innocent people? Why has he permitted genocide after genocide in the past hundred years?

This is not a logical argument, as it does not aim to show that the theist holds a set of inconsistent beliefs. Instead it is posing a question: Given the existence of evil, which of the following is the more reasonable hypothesis?

H1 There is an infinitely powerful, wholly good God who created the world.

or

H2 There is no such God.

For Hume and Rowe, the existence of evil is clear evidence in favour of the second hypothesis. As Hume says:

Hume

> *We must forever find it impossible to reconcile any mixture of evil in the universe with infinite attributes . . . But supposing the Author of nature to be finitely perfect, though far exceeding mankind, a satisfactory account may then be given of natural and moral evil.*[53]

William Rowe cites gratuitous and pointless evil as evidence that a theistic God doesn't exist at all.[54] As an example of gratuitous evil, Rowe describes the suffering of a deer, trapped and horribly burned by a forest fire, which lies in agony for several days before dying. The agony endured by the deer seems to be pointless, and preventable, but Rowe accepts that such an example does not *prove* that God doesn't exist. However, he does maintain that such gratuitous evil makes it reasonable to believe in H2 and reject H1.

ACTIVITY   Refer to the examples of evil you gave in the activity on page 461. Think of as many reasons as you can why God might permit such evils to exist (write down every reason, no matter how absurd, or whether or not you believe it to be true).

Resolving the problem of evil

Since the problem of evil was first posed, theists have sought to resolve it without abandoning their belief in an all-powerful, all-knowing and all-loving God. There have been many proposed solutions to the problem of evil, but we can group the main ones into five types:

- the view that traditional theism should be abandoned
- evil is necessary for good
- evil needs to be seen in a wider context (life after death)
- evil is a means to a greater good (soul making, the best of all possible worlds)
- evil is the responsibility of humans (the free will defence).

Of these, the last four preserve theism as a religious system, and solutions of this type have come to be termed THEODICIES.[55] We might further categorise such solutions as either 'strong' or 'weak' theodicies. A strong theodicy provides an explanation or justification of why God permits the existence of evil within his creation. A weak theodicy (or a 'defence') may not venture to explain why evil exists, but it does offer a defence of theism and shows that the existence of God is not incompatible with the existence of evil as the atheist claims.

■ Solution 1: Traditional theism should be abandoned

In the twentieth century some theologians proposed a radically different interpretation of what it means to believe in God. Two such revisionist theories stand out as offering potential solutions to the problem of evil: *theological* ANTI-REALISM and *process theology*. We return to theological anti-realism on page 507 when we look at the philosophy of Wittgenstein. In brief it is the claim that religious beliefs do not refer to anything in the real world. So, for example, belief in God does not imply belief in a being who exists 'out there' in the real world. Anti-realists differ as to what belief in God does imply, but it might include a commitment to a moral way of life, a cultural tradition, or a certain attitude and approach to the world.[56] From an anti-realist point of view the problem of evil is no longer a problem, as God is not a real being existing independently of our minds, and so could not have made the world differently or have intervened to prevent evil from happening.

Process theology, as inspired by A.N. Whitehead (1861–1947) and Charles Hartshorne (1897–2000), suggests that God is not omnipotent, as has been traditionally claimed within theism. In Whitehead's words, God is 'the great companion – the fellow-sufferer who understands', so he is not separate from his creation, but a part of it and developing with it, influencing events but not determining them. Process theology, far removed from standard Christian theology, is able to solve the problem of evil by surrendering God's omnipotence. God remains able to affect his creation through his infinite persuasive powers, but he cannot eradicate evil or prevent evil from happening. [57]

A third solution to the problem of evil might be found amongst the religious sects who proposed that God is not the only powerful deity. In the Persian traditions of the Zoroastrians (founded in the sixth century BCE) and the Manicheans (founded in the fourth century AD) a benevolent God vies with a malicious devil for control of the world. St Augustine himself was a Manichean for about nine years before converting to Christianity. Within these religions evil exists because of an evil deity, and it is not the responsibility of the benevolent God. However, as Augustine realised, such a dualist perspective undermines the absolute power of God, and is at variance with much that is written in the Bible. However, there is an ambiguity in the Old Testament as to whether God or the devil is the source of evil, and in some passages, for example the book of Job, the devil seems to carry out evil acts on behalf of God.[58]

▶ criticism ◀   It is clear that these types of solutions lead in a direction often far away from Christian teachings, and so they are unacceptable to many believers. However, for those who are attempting to make sense of the universe and of evil from a position outside traditional theism such solutions may be reasonable and plausible.

■ Solution 2: Evil is necessary for good

Augustine's 'aesthetic' theodicy

St Augustine provides one of the best-known theodicies, and argues that God is good and powerful, and created a perfect world. Evil was then introduced into the world because some of his creatures turned away from God. Augustine places particular blame on the fall of the angel Satan from heaven and on the failure of Adam and Eve to resist temptation in the garden of Eden. This, for Augustine, constitutes the original sin of humans. Through these sins God's creation was corrupted, and the natural goodness of the world disappeared: there was a 'privation' of the good. Augustine's theodicy thus places the blame for moral and natural evil on the freely chosen acts of God's creatures (humans and angels). We shall return to this when we review the free will defence below.

In addition to his 'free will' theodicy, Augustine also offers an explanation which suggests that evil is part of the natural balance of the universe. This is an aesthetic argument, an argument for the beauty of the universe, and Augustine draws an analogy with the use an artist makes of light and dark shades that create harmony and balance in a painting.

Augustine

For as the beauty of a picture is increased by well-managed shadows so, to the eye that has skill to discern it, the universe is beautified even by sinners, though, considered by themselves, their deformity is a sad blemish.[59]

How does this description of the world as being perfectly balanced fit in with the idea of original sin, and the imperfection that we have brought into the world? Well, Augustine says that this is a matter of perspective. It may seem to us, at a local level, that there is imbalance in God's creation: there is too much pain and suffering, and too much evil that goes unpunished. But Augustine claims that our sinful acts are ultimately balanced by the justice of God: after we die we are all judged, and sinners atone for their sins by being punished. So the beauty that Augustine is talking about is a kind of 'moral beauty' where ultimately justice is done, and the moral balance of the universe is restored.

But in parts of creation, some things, because they do not harmonise with others, are considered evil. Yet those same things harmonise with others and are good. [60]

Augustine

ACTIVITY   Do you agree with Augustine's comparison between the universe and a work of art? What problems are there with this analogy?

► criticism ◄   There are at least two pressing problems with Augustine's aesthetic theodicy. First, as Darwin pointed out, there is a vast amount of suffering undergone by animals which doesn't seem to be balanced by anything, even after the animals die. Augustine isn't really concerned with this type of suffering, and doesn't have much to say on it, except to suggest that nature needs to change and progress, and somehow the deaths of animals helps this to happen. Secondly, and more seriously, Augustine is left with having to justify the eternal pain of humans who are punished and go to hell. By explaining how the suffering caused on this Earth is balanced by the suffering of the wrong-doers in hell, Augustine has simply moved the problem of evil to the next life. Why does a benevolent, omnipotent, omniscient creator allow eternal pain and suffering to exist for those in hell?

1 In a world where everything is red, would it be possible to appreciate, or even recognise, the redness of the universe? If it is possible, how is it possible?

2 How might you go about teaching someone the meaning of the following terms *without* referring to the words in brackets:
a) down (up)
b) hard (soft)
c) sad (happy)
d) tall (short)
e) good (evil)?

There is another way in which evil might be seen as necessary for good. This is the so-called 'contrast' theory. At some points in his theodicy Augustine seems to be hinting at something along these lines, but, as Hick points out, such a theory is in no way central to Augustine's theodicy. [61] The contrast theory is the idea that good only makes sense in contrast to evil; the two concepts trade off each other and so evil is actually necessary for good. If this is right we couldn't have a concept of good without a concept of evil, and we would be unable to recognise the good things and actions in the world without also perceiving the evil things and actions with which they are contrasted. Part of the implication is that in a world without any pain or suffering we would not recognise good acts and so would not applaud, or strive towards them. To use an analogy, a world without evil would be similar to a world with no colours other than red: we wouldn't be able to see the redness because we would have no (non-red) point of reference, nothing to compare it to. [62]

▶ criticism ◀ However, as Mackie points out[63] the contrast theory seems to set limits on what God can and can't do: he can't create good, or make us aware of good, without simultaneously creating evil. So if we wish to maintain that God is omnipotent then the contrast theory of evil must be abandoned. Because of this, a theist committed to God's omnipotence will probably not be tempted by this solution to the problem of evil.

▶ criticism ◀ However, there is a far stronger argument against the contrast theory: namely, that the two concepts don't in fact trade off against each other in the way they'd have to for the contrast theory to work. Good and evil are not opposites in the same way that 'up' and 'down' are. With these latter you clearly cannot have one without the other. But the concept of good has certain intrinsic features which are not defined simply by opposition to evil. It is true that on the Augustine–Aquinas interpretation of evil they are logical opposites: evil means 'lack of goodness', and so is the exact counterpart to 'goodness'. However, by the more common understanding of 'evil' as being 'pain and suffering', good and evil are not opposites. As Hick points out, pain has a very different physiological structure and cause to pleasure, and it doesn't make sense to think of pleasure and pain as opposites. [64] Moreover, we can imagine a world in which everyone is good (perhaps a communist utopia, or a Christian Kingdom of God) and where no one does anyone else wrong. There is nothing inconsistent in the idea of such a world. It may be true that the people in it would have no need of the *concepts* good and evil, and might not recognise acts they performed as 'good'. But this is not the same as saying that they are not actually good, and, most importantly, is not the same as saying that their world would not be *better* than this world.

■ Solution 3: Evil needs to be seen in a wider context

A different response to the problem of evil invites us to consider pain and suffering in a much broader theological context. One of the features common to all the major world religions is the belief in the possibility of life after death (we saw above, on pages 156 and 165, how Hume and Freud both interpreted the fear of death as one of the causes of belief in God). Survival after our physical death is usually thought to involve survival of an immortal soul. Plato, for example, believed that our soul existed before we were born and both Buddhism and Hinduism concur. By contrast the monotheistic religions of Judaism, Christianity and Islam claim that our souls are created at conception, or thereabouts. However, all are agreed that there is some form of life after death, whether it be by surviving as purely spiritual beings, being born into a new body or by resurrection (Woody Allen was leaning towards the latter possibility when he said 'I don't believe in an afterlife, although I am bringing a change of underwear'[65]).

The belief in life after death is one of the fundamental tenets of Christianity; it recurs throughout the New Testament, and finds support from the traditional view of God, the 'God of the philosophers' (see pages 92–99). As Hick argues, an omnipotent, personal creator would not allow his human creations to cease to exist while his aspirations and purpose for them had not been met.[66] So how does belief in life after death resolve the problem of evil? Or to put it another way: is the existence of a benevolent God compatible with a world in which there is a finite amount of suffering in this life, but an infinite amount of happiness in the next life?

If there is any eventual resolution of the interplay between good and evil, any decisive bringing of good out of evil, it must lie beyond this world and beyond the enigma of death.[67]

John Hick

■ **Figure 6.6 Putting pain and suffering into a wider context**

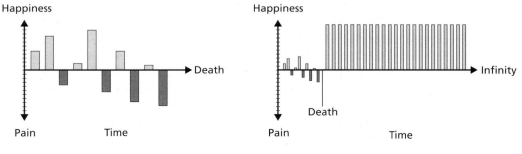

(a) Happiness and suffering in the context of a lifetime

(b) Happiness and suffering in the context of eternity

The graphs in Figure 6.6 show how putting pain and suffering into the context of eternal life makes the problem of evil much easier to resolve. It might be true that, from the perspective of life in this world, the cruelties and horrors seem very difficult, if not impossible, to reconcile with the existence of a loving, caring God. However, from the perspective of eternity a limited amount of suffering becomes infinitesimal compared with the potential for unlimited happiness in the next life.

Blessed is the man who will eat at the feast in the Kingdom of Heaven.

Luke 14:15

The teachings of Jesus suggest that the afterlife will be like a joyous banquet, where all who have accepted the invitation will rejoice together. The eternal happiness and spiritual satisfaction that will be found in the afterlife must render irrelevant the suffering of this life.

Jesus talks about the positive aspects of life after death for those who are 'invited to the banquet'. But what about those who are not invited: what happens to the souls of people who have rejected God, or have done terrible deeds, or who have never even heard of God? Socrates, in Plato's dialogue the *Gorgias*, describes how in the afterlife our souls, which have been stripped bare, will be judged and those souls who have led an unjust life will be punished in Hades with painful and terrifying suffering (*Gorgias* 525a–e). Jesus is very clear about what will happen to those who reject the offer of eternal salvation:

Angels will come and separate the wicked from the righteous and throw them into the fiery furnace, where there will be weeping and gnashing of teeth.

Matthew 13:50

This message, about the suffering endured by those in hell, is repeated throughout the gospels. There is a sense of satisfaction knowing that the people who inflict injustice and suffering on us in this life will be punished in the next life. The possibility of justice in the future goes part way to resolving the moral problem of evil for some people: vicious people will get their comeuppance, virtuous people will be rewarded.

► criticism ◄ However, it seems as if the existence of hell simply defers the problem of evil to the next life, and amplifies it. If we found it difficult to reconcile the existence of a benevolent God with the existence of (limited) suffering in this life, how much more difficult are we going to find it reconciling such a God with the unlimited suffering of hell in the next life? Why would God, who loves the world, create a person with free will, knowing that the person would abuse their free will and end up being tortured for all eternity? There may be an answer to this question, but the question is recognisable as one raised by the problem of evil – positing the existence of hell has not helped resolve the problem.

With some nifty metaphysical footwork, theologians have come up with various responses to this criticism. Perhaps hell is a 'halfway house' (in Roman Catholicism this is called Purgatory) where punishment is meted out before entry into heaven. Or perhaps hell is a metaphor, and there is no torture, there is just the absence of God for those who have rejected him. Or perhaps there is no hell at all, not even the absence of God, and everyone goes to heaven (this thesis is known as 'universalism'). But in this case there must be a radical re-reading of the New Testament, for Jesus is very clear on the fact that some people are invited to the banquet, to heaven, and some are not.

▶ criticism ◀   There are problems in general with the claim that there is life after death. For many theologians it is our immortal soul that survives our death, with the possibility of physical resurrection at some future point (following judgement day). However, distinguishing between the soul and body in this way is a form of DUALISM, and mind–body dualism has had a troubled history ever since it was clearly proposed in its modern form by Descartes in the sixteenth century (see Chapter 5, page 380). The main problem with dualism is the problem of interaction – it is not clear how two substances (the mental/spiritual and the physical) can interact, as they are so radically different. No satisfactory philosophical solution has been found for this, and most philosophers have now abandoned dualism as a plausible theory of the mind.

A further problem is the issue of whether, if we survive our bodily death in some form, we will be the same person as we once were. This is a problem of personal identity, and we address it in Chapter 3, pages 208–13, as well as below when we come to look at John Hick's parable of the celestial city (page 498).

■ Solution 4: Evil is a means to a greater good

One of the most appealing solutions to the problem of evil is to see evil as having some purpose and contributing to a greater or higher good. This could mean that evil is an enabler for other goods which wouldn't exist without evil. Or it could mean that the universe is in some way a better place because of the existence of evil.

experimenting with ideas

You have a summer job as a shop assistant in Worlds 'R' Us – the Ultimate in Universe Shopping. One day God walks in and says he wants to buy a universe. More specifically he wants to buy the best possible universe (which he can easily do, given he is God). He browses through the billions of shelves, which contain every possible universe, and then asks you for more details of their specifications: the quantity of pain and suffering, the extent of free will, the level of determinism, the degree of order and regularity, the balance and beauty in each universe. Eventually, after examining all the billions of universes in the shop, God comes up to the counter and says 'I'll take this one'; and that is the universe we now live in.

1 What 'health warnings' or 'unique selling points' would you have told God about when selling him this universe?
2 Do you think God made a good choice? Why/Why not?
3 Was there a better universe on offer? In what way would it have been better?
4 What do you think God was looking for in a universe (what 'specifications')?

Leibniz's theodicy

Leibniz

This supreme wisdom, united to a goodness that is no less infinite, cannot but have chosen the best . . . So it may be said that if this were not the best of all possible worlds, God would not have chosen any . . . There is an infinitude of possible worlds amongst which God must needs have chosen the best.[68]

Gottfried Leibniz (1646–1716) asks us to consider the situation of God as one of an all-powerful and good being whose task it is to select, from amongst all the possible universes that he could create, the one he will actually create. Now, given that God knows the whole histories of all the possible universes, and is wholly good, then the one he selected to create must be the very best one possible. As this universe is the one that God chose to create, it follows that, despite appearances to the contrary, it must be the best universe going, and every feature in it is an essential part of the divine plan. Therefore the pain and suffering of this world are just some of the many essential ingredients which go into the construction of the best possible world. This means that all the evil which exists in this universe, must, in some way, contribute to making it a better place than every other possible universe. And if any particular occasion of pain or suffering were to be different from the way it actually is, then the world would overall be worse off. In other words, every single piece of evil, from the suffering of innocent children, to all the millions of people dying horrible and painful deaths from disease, famine and war, is all for the best. Of course, we are not able to see why each local instance of evil is necessary to the divine plan, and it is inexplicable to us why God should allow this or that person to suffer. But, as Augustine argued before him, for Leibniz this is because we do not have God's perspective on the whole of creation, and neither are we able to understand what the other options, the possible worlds rejected by God, are.

► criticism ◄

Leibniz's position has had many critics, and the French philosopher and writer Voltaire (1694–1778) was one of the first to attack Leibniz's theodicy. In Voltaire's novel *Candide,* the character Dr Pangloss regularly announces that this is the best of all possible worlds. As the eponymous hero is tortured by religious fanatics, and as he watches his mentor Dr Pangloss hanged, Candide wonders to himself: 'if this is the best of all possible worlds, what can the others be like?'[69] What Voltaire does is to confront the cool intellectual approach that Leibniz takes to the problem of evil with the pain and suffering of the world. In so doing, he does not really refute Leibniz's theodicy, but it is certainly not easy to support it when faced with the concrete reality of pain and suffering.

Swinburne's theodicy
Richard Swinburne (1934–) argues that some forms of evil are the means to certain goods.[70] Swinburne accepts that God is omnipotent and could stop evil, but only at the price of sacrificing the virtuous acts which are the noble human response to its presence. So the existence of suffering makes higher-order goods possible. For example, courage and charity would not exist if there were no one in danger or in need. Swinburne has gone so far as to say that even the existence of Nazi concentration camps can be justified if they

led to greater goods, such as acts of sympathy, cooperation and benevolence. He argues that it is better that we live in a world where we can work to reach these goods than in a 'toy world' where nothing threatens us and human actions have no significant consequences. After all, if there were no obstacles to our desires, no possibility of suffering, never the threat that our actions might produce evil outcomes, then our actions would be devoid of meaning; there would be no moral dimension to anything we did. So if there is to be any point to human agency and any space within the universe for making moral decisions, we need to live in a world where there are real challenges and our actions matter. Swinburne's conclusion is that God created a 'half-finished' universe (neither free from evil nor full of evil) which gives humans the opportunity to improve it from within. This does rely on the assumption that humans are free, and we shall examine this assumption when we look at the free will defence below.

For each of the evils outlined below, think about what good could come of them.

1 Children starve in drought-ridden central Africa.
2 Homeless people, who are sleeping rough, freeze on the winter streets of New York.
3 Forest fires sweep round the outskirts of an Australian town, burning livestock and choking people.
4 A tidal wave destroys all the coastal villages of Indonesia.
5 The bubonic plague wipes out half the population of Europe in the fifteenth century.
6 A ruthless dictator sends his enemies to die in labour camps.

Swinburne's theory also goes some way to solving the problem of natural evil. If human actions are to have consequences that we can learn from and build on, then the world needs to be law-abiding. If God intervened with a minor miracle every time someone fell from a building, or cut themselves with a knife, then humans would not be able to anticipate consequences of their actions, nor formulate general laws of nature. It is only within a law-abiding universe that humans can learn from experience; and a law-abiding universe will contain natural disasters and all the pain and suffering of the fight for survival.

St Irenaeus (AD 130–202) and more recently John Hick have argued, along with Swinburne, that God allowed evil in his creation for a reason: so that we might make a journey towards the good.

Irenaeus' theodicy

It was possible for God himself to have made man perfect from the first, but man could not receive this [perfection], being as yet an infant.

Against Heresies 4.39.1

Unlike Augustine, St Irenaeus does not take the view that human free will (initially through the choices of Satan, Adam and Eve) caused evil to 'seep into' a perfect world. Irenaeus argues that humans must use their free will to work towards moral and spiritual understanding, eventually achieving perfection in the next life. So, for Augustine, perfection existed in the past, at the moment of creation, and we have fallen from this state of grace; whereas, for Irenaeus, perfection will come in the future at the end of time.

■ **Figure 6.7a**
The Augustinian theodicy

■ **Figure 6.7b**
The Irenaean theodicy

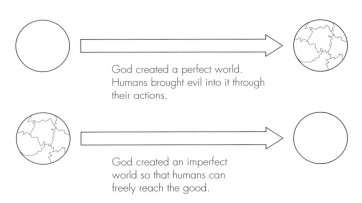

God created a perfect world. Humans brought evil into it through their actions.

God created an imperfect world so that humans can freely reach the good.

John Hick also takes a teleological approach, that is to say, he also argues that the imperfections and suffering of this world will eventually lead to a better state. For Hick the world is a 'vale of soul-making'[71] in which our souls are strengthened and matured by the struggle and suffering of this life. God maintains an 'epistemic distance' from us (that is to say, he doesn't provide us with the knowledge of what our destiny or purpose in this life is) so that we do not know what our purpose is and must exercise our genuine free will in order to approach the good (a state of holiness).[72]

▶ criticism ◀ The claim that evil exists as a means to some other good (such as spiritual maturity or noble virtues) has been bitterly contested. Hick himself acknowledges that the distribution of misery in the world seems to be random and meaningless, so that it may be heaped upon those who seem least deserving.[73] In such cases it is hard to see what good can come of such evil. Dostoyevsky put forward a series of particularly painful examples of evil in his novel *The Brothers Karamazov*. The character Ivan Karamazov cites three cases of appalling and pointless cruelty to Russian children (to which could be added the holocaust in Belorussia in 1942,[74] or the Beslan school massacre of 2004), which in his view clearly give reason to reject God and the world he has created. Ivan does not deny the existence of God, but instead, disgusted at the universe God has created, he rejects God as a being who is worthy of worship.[75]

Read through the following two examples given by Ivan Karamazov and answer the questions below.

1 A young girl, abused by her parents, wets her bed and is forced by her mother to eat her own excrement, before she is made to sleep in a freezing cold shed.

2 A boy throws a stone and injures a General's dog. The boy is stripped and sent out as quarry for a hunt. He is eventually caught and torn to pieces by dogs in front of his mother.

a) How might these examples of evil be explained within Swinburne's theodicy and St Irenaeus' theodicy?

b) Do you think these explanations are satisfactory?

► criticism ◄

The problem Dostoyevsky poses is a question about whether the outcome justifies the method. For any theodicy that views the existence of evil as a means to an end we can ask 'is the end worth it?' In other words is God justified in creating a world that contains so much pointless and gratuitous evil in order to attain certain goals? For Ivan Karamazov the answer is no – there can be no goal so worth having that young children are allowed to be tortured in order that this goal might one day be reached.

◼ Solution 5: Evil is the responsibility of humans – the free will defence

In many of the most influential explanations of the existence of evil, particularly in St Augustine's and St Irenaeus' theodicies, human free will is an essential element. We have seen that St Augustine argues that it was free will that led to the original sin of Adam and Eve. This resulted in their subsequent expulsion from paradise by God, and the introduction of pain and suffering into their lives and the lives of all their progeny.[76] Augustine maintains that, although God created a perfect world, evil was introduced by the choices humans made, and thus it is the responsibility of humans not of God.

For St Irenaeus (and modern supporters such as Swinburne and Hick) free will is necessary if we are to improve ourselves and the world, and to work towards spiritual maturity and noble actions. With this type of theodicy, evil is thus an unfortunate side effect of God granting us free will. But it is a price worth paying if there is also the possibility that human free will can lead to salvation and redemption. In this sense then, solution 5 (the free will defence) is connected to solution 4 (evil ultimately makes the world a better place).

Both the Augustinian and Irenaean 'free will defences' view moral evil as stemming from the free choices of humans. They also both view free will as a positive quality that is a gift from God to humans. Peter Vardy offers a summary of the free will defence as follows: [77]

1   The highest good for humans is a loving relationship with God.
2   Love must be freely chosen.
3   So God, who is all-powerful and loving, gave humans free will (in order to achieve 1).
4   Genuine free will means that humans will sometimes choose good, and sometimes evil (cruelty, viciousness, greed, etc.).
5   Therefore evil exists in order that humans may choose a loving relationship with God.

As both Hick and Swinburne point out, God does not wish to create a cosy 'toy world' for his human 'pets' to live in. So it is a mistake to look at the world and wonder why it isn't more pleasant for humans. A much greater good than pleasure is the relationship humans can have with God, and this can only be a genuine relationship if we have free will. And, as we have seen, freely chosen evil is a terrible side effect of free will, but one that is worth it.

Let us now look at some of the most important criticisms that have been made of the free will defence.

▶ criticism ◀ St Augustine's account of original sin is problematic in that it depends upon a literal interpretation of the first book of the Bible. For Augustine, the succumbing to temptation by Eve and then Adam in the Garden of Eden is the real origin of sin and evil. Many believers do not now read the account of what happened in the Garden of Eden as literally true, preferring to read it symbolically. Nor do many modern believers subscribe to the view that the angel Satan turned away from God, and that this too introduced evil into the world.

▶ criticism ◀ Antony Flew criticises the free will defence on the basis of the very meaning of 'free will'.[78] For Flew, freely chosen actions are ones that have their causes within the persons themselves, rather than externally. For example, when you have the chance to marry the person you love, your decision to do so will ultimately stem from the type of person you are: whether you find them funny, whether you fancy them, whether you 'click' with them, whether you trust them, etc. As long as your choice to marry is internal to you, that is to say, powered by your own character and desires, then it is freely chosen. Flew then goes on to say that God could have created a possible world in which all humans had a nature that was good, and yet in which they were free in Flew's sense. In such a world, humans would always freely choose to do the right thing. And such a world would surely be a better one than this.

However, Flew's attack on the free will defence may be objected to on the following grounds. What would be the difference between Flew's 'naturally good' people, and automata or mere puppets who had been created always to act in a good way? It is important to theistic belief that God gave humans the freedom to choose to worship and love him, or the freedom to turn away from him. But, in Flew's world, God seems to have manipulated the key parts of his creation (humans) in order to bring about his desired results. Imagine a hypnotist persuading someone they were in love: what would be the worth of this love? Just as we would question the value of the feelings manipulated in someone by a hypnotist, so we might question the value of the love felt for God by the 'naturally good' humans in Flew's world. Moreover, is a God who manipulates the end-results in the way Flew describes a God who is worthy of worship?

▶ criticism ◀ J.L. Mackie offers another version of Flew's criticism, presenting it as a logical possibility, perfectly within God's omnipotent powers.[79] He argues that:

1　It is logically possible for me to choose to do good on any one occasion.
2　It is logically possible for me to choose to do good on every occasion.
3　It is logically possible for any individual to choose to do good throughout their life.
4　God is omnipotent and can create any logically possible world.
5　Therefore God could have created a world in which we were all genuinely free, yet we all chose to do good.
6　God did not create such a world.
7　Therefore either God is not omnipotent, or he is not wholly good.

So Mackie's attack on the free will defence leads to a restatement of the logical problem of evil.

However, in recent years the logical problem of evil, as presented by Mackie and others, has been rigorously attacked by theistic philosophers, and the free will defence remounted. Alvin Plantinga (1932–) rejects the idea that God can create an *infinite* number of possible worlds. For example, God cannot create a world in which humans aren't created by God. And even within the possible worlds that God could create there are limitations. For example, it is possible that there is some person (Plantinga names him Curly Smith) who has a corrupt nature such that, in every possible world that God could create, he will always choose to do at least one evil action. In this case, it is not possible for God (even an infinitely powerful and loving one) to create a world in which Curly is free yet always does good actions. Plantinga is offering a defence (what we called above a 'weak' theodicy) of evil, showing that the existence of evil is compatible with a wholly good and all-powerful God.

Our position on the problem of evil may come down to our prior beliefs about the universe. If we are committed atheists, then we may use the existence of evil to justify our atheism. However, it does not seem as if evil proves the non-existence of God. The most evil does is to show that belief in the non-existence of God is rational. From the believer's point of view the existence of evil is a lived and agonising problem. The Book of Job in the Bible underpins this, as God proves to the devil that Job will love him whatever his circumstances. The devil destroys Job's life, family, livestock, leaving him with nothing. Job's friends argue that he must have done something wrong. But throughout his trials, Job maintains his faith in God's righteousness, despite being in ignorance about why he is suffering so much. This story of faith in God, in the face of pain and suffering, is an inspiration to many believers. But the story of Job does not solve the problem of evil, it merely tells us how it is possible to live with evil and yet still believe in God. The story reassures believers, but frustrates atheists who will continue to ask how such a juggling act is possible.

The religious point of view

Rows and flows of angel hair
And ice cream castles in the air
And feather canyons everywhere
I've looked at clouds that way

But now they only block the sun
They rain and snow on everyone
So many things I would have done
But clouds got in my way

Joni Mitchell

We have been examining in this chapter evidence for or against the existence of God in the world. Not evidence that is mysterious or subjective such as that drawn from religious experience and miracles. Instead we have been examining evidence that is plain for all to see and that both sides agree on:

- that there is order and regularity in the universe and its laws
- that living creatures are amazingly well suited to their environment
- that the individual parts of these living creatures appear to have a function and purpose
- that the presence of conscious human life on Earth appears to be incredibly unlikely
- that humans suffer a random and unpredictable degree of pain and suffering during their lives, regardless of whether they believe in God or not
- that wicked people sometimes go unpunished and good people are wrongly persecuted
- that nature is unpredictable and uncontrollable and is frequently destructive to human and non-human animals.

Both believers and non-believers are looking at the same facts, and yet their interpretation of that evidence could not be more different. What is going on here? Is it the case, as with Joni Mitchell's clouds, that they are each looking at two sides of the same thing except one group can only see the amazing beauty of the world, while the other group can only see the empty meaninglessness of the world? Is it that both groups are wearing a set of 'mental spectacles' that prevent them from seeing what the other group sees? Is it that one group is right about what is actually there, and the other group is simply mistaken? Or is it that one group is actually talking about the world, what is out there, while the other group is simply expressing the way they feel about the world?

In this final section we look at what underpins these two opposing perspectives on the world, and what they are in opposition to. First we examine the claim that the way we see the world is not a straightforward process – seeing is an interpretative process, it means seeing something *as* something (seeing-as) – and this is dependent upon our beliefs, expectations, feelings and so on. Secondly we ask whether the religious hypothesis (that there is a God) is a genuine and meaningful hypothesis. For it to be meaningful, it must consist of statements that genuinely refer to the world. But is the believer making claims about the world, or are they doing something else entirely? Perhaps religious claims are about attitudes and commitments rather than facts.

Seeing-as

The way we see the world is not a straightforward process – it is not simply the case that light bouncing off an object hits our eyes, an image is registered on the back, rotated around in our minds somewhere and then flashes up as pictures of the world. Artists such as M.C. Escher (see the front cover of this book) enjoy creating and playing with illusions that confound our attempts to see an image simply as one thing, such as a staircase going up. We first see one staircase going up, then see it going down, and we are able to flick between the two ways of seeing without the thing we're looking at changing at all. The same switch in perception is possible with every philosopher's favourite illusion, the duck–rabbit:[80]

■ **Figure 6.8** *Do you see this as a duck or a rabbit?*

What determines whether we see the figure as a duck or a rabbit? Or the clouds as ice-cream castles, feather canyons or simply as rain-carrying annoyances? Or the world as filled with God's love, or emptied of all meaning? Ludwig Wittgenstein (1889–1951), used the duck–rabbit example to suggest that seeing is an interpretative act.

We can also see the illustration now as one thing now as another. So we interpret it and see it as we interpret it.[81]

Wittgenstein

The words surrounding an image, or playing in our head when we look at the world, seem to have a profound impact on our interpretation and hence on what we see. John Berger, in his book *Ways of Seeing* invites us to look at a picture of some crows flying over a cornfield, beneath a brooding sky. He then re-prints the picture with the words handwritten underneath it 'This is the last picture painted by Van Gogh before he killed himself'.[82] This suggestion means that we now see a picture of a man's impending death, and the dark clouds and jagged crows become more disturbing and sinister. We are suggestable creatures – we have, consciously or unconsciously, a tendency to believe other people's suggestions (in Chapter 2, page 171, we saw that Richard Dawkins believed this was a product of evolution). Magicians, hypnotists and con-artists all over the world make their living from the fact that people are suggestable. A less interesting example of the effect that words have on interpretation can be seen in Figure 6.9. With our attention drawn to the duck's tongue we find it easier to see the image as a picture of a duck.

■ **Figure 6.9 A picture of a duck**

A mallard duck's tongue contains tiny spikes for gripping food

There are other factors that influence interpretation; consider another simple example in Figure 6.10. Most people see this image as a staircase going away from us, up to the left, perhaps because we are used to seeing staircases from this angle. But it can just as well be seen as a staircase going down to the right and viewed from beneath. Now since whichever we happen to be seeing the sensory input must remain unchanged, it seems that what we see is determined, at least in part, by what we are *expecting* to see. And this implies that seeing is not a straightforward absorption of information, but instead that observations are influenced by our surrounding beliefs about the world.

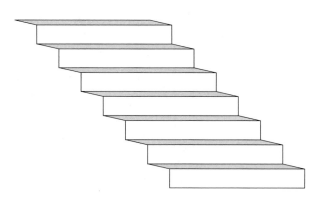

Figure 6.10 *What we see depends on what we expect*

Another example of someone's expectations influencing what they see can be found in Leonardo Da Vinci's drawings of the human heart.[83] These detailed drawings show only three ventricles. How could a draughtsman of Da Vinci's calibre not see the four ventricles that we now know the heart to contain? One answer is that what we see is in a large part determined by our background assumptions. Only once people recognised the heart to be a kind of pump were they able to see that it had four chambers.

'Seeing-as' means seeing something and interpreting it, either consciously or unconsciously. There are many different factors that affect the way we see things, including: our prior expectations; the beliefs we currently hold about the world; our emotional state; our cultural concepts; and our conceptual scheme (see Chapter 4, pages 321–34). So how does this impact on the dispute between believers and non-believers regarding what they see in the world?

John Wisdom's parable of the gardener

John Wisdom was interested in what is going on when two people disagree as to whether there is a God. In particular Wisdom wants to know whether the disagreement is a dispute about the facts of the matter; or about what explains those facts (the 'god hypothesis' versus the atheist's hypothesis); or about how we see the world.

Wisdom invites us to consider the following parable: two people return to their neglected garden. One person notices the flowers and the organisation of the plants and takes this as evidence that someone has been caring for the garden. The other person notices the weeds and the disorder and concludes that no one has been tending the garden (Figure 6.11). The second also points out that none of the neighbours has seen any gardener, although the first responds by suggesting that the gardener comes at night.

*Each learns all the other learns . . . about the garden.
Consequently, when after all this, one says 'I still believe a
gardener comes' while the other says 'I don't' their different
words now reflect no difference as to what they have found
in the garden, [or] would find in the garden if they looked
further.*[84]

John Wisdom

Wisdom's point is that although two people can be presented
with exactly the same empirical evidence – it is the self-same
garden that both have returned to – but their perspectives can
be completely different. One person sees the garden as
neglected, the other sees the garden as cared for by a
gardener. In the same way the atheist sees the universe as a
place without God (she points to natural disasters, to terrible
injustices, to pointless suffering); but the believer points to
the order and beauty of the world and sees this as evidence of
the work of a divine intelligence. The difference between this
example of 'seeing-as' and the example of the duck–rabbit or
the staircase is that the optical illusions have been deliberately
designed to be ambiguous, to enable the observer to see it as
a rabbit in one instance, as a duck in the next. So the
question as to whether Figure 6.8 is 'really' a duck or 'really'
a rabbit could be resolved empirically – we can discover
whether the intentions of the artist (Joseph Jastrow) were to
draw something that looked like both a duck and a rabbit.

But, for Wisdom, in the case of the believer and the atheist
there is no further empirical evidence that could be used to
say which perspective is correct. Wisdom argues that the two
are not disagreeing about the facts they observe, nor about
any future observations. There is nothing, no experiment or
observation, that could verify and confirm either of their

■ **Figure 6.11** *Is
there a gardener or
not?*

claims. But in this case their claims that there is or is not a god cannot be claims that are straightforwardly about the world. As with the examples we looked at above (clouds, duck–rabbits, and staircases), whether someone sees the world as a divine creation, or a meaningless lump of rock, emerges from their existing set of beliefs, from their expectations, from the suggestions of other people's words and thoughts, and from their current emotional state.

Why do you think some people see the world as a divine creation and others as a meaningless lump of rock?

1 Read through Paley's design argument (pages 436–39) above. Think about the way that William Paley sees the world as he walks across the hills with a friend looking at the landscape, the sun setting, the birds of prey hunting. Describe how each of the following affects what he sees.
    a) His existing set of beliefs (what do you think he believes?)
    b) His expectations as to what he might observe
    c) The suggestions that might have been made to him
    d) His emotional states
    e) The culture he's grown up in

2 Read through Richard Dawkins' evolutionary explanation for why we might believe in God (Chapter 2, pages 168–71 above). Think about Dawkins walking through the same hills, observing the same features as Paley had done two hundred years before. Describe how **a)–e)** affect what Dawkins sees.

However, Wisdom does *not* believe that this means believers and atheists are simply reporting their feelings about the world. If the difference were simply a difference of feelings, then there would be no genuine dispute – as the difference would no longer concern what is or is not the case in the world, but rather the emotional state of the observers. But Wisdom believes that there is more bite to the dispute than this, and that the believers and non-believers are genuinely talking about the world, and not simply about their feelings.

So Wisdom is arguing that believers and atheists are not making 'experimental hypotheses' that can be tested against empirical observations. They observe the same facts about the world but have different perspectives on the world and draw different conclusions. Believers see the world as evidence for the existence of God, atheists see the world as evidence for the non-existence of God. But for Wisdom, even though their dispute is not like a scientific dispute, they are still talking about the world, and what is needed is a procedure for settling the issue.

To help determine what that procedure might be Wisdom gives another example, of two people looking at a piece of art – one says it is beautiful the other says 'I don't see it that way'.[85] Here, as with the garden and as with religion, the two people are encountering the same thing but seeing it in different ways. But the debate can shift, and people's beliefs can change, according to the power of the different connections, patterns and relationships with other things that can be brought to bear on the debate. Our opinions about a work of art can be changed when someone draws out connections we hadn't previously seen; or enables us to see a relationship with another picture or theory; or forces us to abandon a set of prejudices or bad reasoning. For Wisdom the procedure needed to resolve the dispute between the believer and atheist is similar to that needed in the dispute over the work of art. The procedure will involve further discussion between the two, with the aims of *connecting* and *disconnecting* their current observations to and from other beliefs and observations, each person 'presenting and representing the features favouring his hypothesis . . . each emphasising the pattern he wishes to emphasise'.[86] Wisdom, himself a believer (although not apparently in a conventional Christian sense), is making the assumption that through this type of discussion the atheist will gradually come to see the world as having been created by God.

▶ criticism ◀

Wisdom opened up a theological can of worms by proposing that religious claims about the world (such as that there is a God) are not claims that have any empirical basis, but are an individual's perspective on the world. This seems to undermine both the teleological argument (which makes the claim that observations about the world support the hypothesis that God exists) and the problem of evil (which claims that observations about the world support the hypothesis that God does not exist). The atheist might not be too fussed if it turns out they can't say anything meaningful about God, as they don't believe in God in the first place and would be glad for a release from these kinds of never-ending discussions. But for the believer the consequences of Wisdom's argument are very worrying. If Wisdom is correct and if religious claims cannot be shown to be true or false according to any facts, then there is a question about whether religious statements and discussions have any meaning at all. Wisdom does not accept that religious statements are meaningless – but Antony Flew thinks this is exactly where Wisdom's approach is heading.

Antony Flew: the rejection of the religious hypothesis

In his 1955 lecture 'Theology and Falsification', Antony Flew (1923–) used Wisdom's parable to draw the conclusion that religious claims about the world are not only unverifiable (as Wisdom acknowledged), they are also unfalsifiable. For Flew this means that religious claims are meaningless and they tell us nothing about the world. A similar attack had been made earlier in the twentieth century by A.J. Ayer (1910–1989) in his book *Language, Truth and Logic* (as we saw in Chapter 1 and Chapter 4 earlier). Ayer argued for a strictly empirical understanding of what was 'meaningful'. In other words, if a statement cannot be shown to be true (either by definition or by observations of the world), and we can't imagine any circumstances under which it might be shown to be true, then it is meaningless. The religious hypothesis (that God exists) clearly falls into this category because it is about something transcendent and refers to objects which lie beyond human experience, for example God, heaven, or life after death. There are no experiments we could carry out, or observations we could make, which prove them, and so such statements are not meaningful. There are many problems with Ayer's VERIFICATION PRINCIPLE, as it is referred to. It rules out as meaningless much of what we speak about (poetry, metaphors, art and music, ethics, political values). It is also unclear how the Verification Principle itself has any meaning (it's not true by definition, nor can it be verified), and philosophers have moved away from verification as a tool with which to attack theologians.

However, in 'Theology and Falsification' Antony Flew revives the attack on the meaningfulness of religious language by borrowing the gardener parable from John Wisdom, and adapting it to make his case. In Flew's reworking of the parable, the two people spend some days in the garden. Unlike in Wisdom's parable, Flew's sceptic (who doesn't see any evidence of a gardener) regards the claim that there is a gardener as a *hypothesis* that needs to be tested. Since they do not observe any gardener visiting the garden, the sceptic reckons there must be no gardener. However, his companion, rather than give up her belief that there is a gardener, concludes that one must come at night. So the two of them stay up all night keeping vigil, hoping to spot the mysterious gardener, but none appears. Again the sceptic takes this as evidence that there is no gardener, but the believer stubbornly responds that the gardener must be invisible. So they put up an electric fence around the garden and guard it with sniffer-dogs, but still they find no evidence of a gardener sneaking in to tend the land. Despite this the believer continues to maintain that there is a gardener, but now claims he is not only invisible, but also odourless and intangible, which accounts for why they have so far been unable to find direct evidence of his activity. Eventually the sceptic despairs and asks the believer 'how does your claim that there is an invisible, odourless, intangible gardener differ from the claim that there is no gardener at all?' Because the believer holds onto the belief that there is a gardener, despite the failure to see one, she has shown that no evidence at all will make her surrender her belief. Each time their effort to find the gardener fails, the believer simply modifies her belief so that it isn't falsified. Thus her belief is effectively unfalsifiable.

ACTIVITY   In Flew and Wisdom's parables what do the following represent:

1 The garden
2 The flowerbed
3 The weeds
4 The differences in belief between the two people in the garden?

Flew is arguing that a statement, such as 'there is a gardener', is only meaningful if it is a genuine claim about the world. But it is only a genuine claim (in technical terms 'factually significant') if the person making the statement can imagine being wrong, in other words if there is a possibility of the statement being falsified. This is because someone who refuses to give up their belief, no matter what is discovered about the world, is not really talking about the world at all. When presented with evidence showing that their statement is false, they add to and qualify it so that the new evidence no longer refutes it. In other words, they move the goal posts to accommodate the new evidence.

An example of how this happens with the religious hypothesis might be the Biblical story about the creation. Traditionally, Christians believed it to be literally true that God created the universe in six days, and that he created humans out of earth. Modern cosmology and evolutionary theory have cast serious doubts on such claims, and most theists nowadays have qualified their belief in God, so that it can accommodate such scientific advances. So, instead of saying that the fact that humans have evolved from other life forms shows that God doesn't really exist, they have qualified their beliefs. God, it is now urged, created humans by using evolution in the modified form proposed by Intelligent Design theory (see above pages 448–51). But such manoeuvrings don't impress Flew. If one repeatedly qualifies one's belief in the light of the new evidence to avoid having to give it up, then one's belief suffers what Flew calls 'death by a thousand qualifications'. Through constant qualification and amendment the original statement is shown to be unfalsifiable and therefore it is not about the world and according to Flew is not meaningful.

Let's look at another example. Imagine you have a friend who is convinced that Jennifer Lopez has romantic feelings for him. He sees all the evidence as pointing towards this conclusion. More than this, he claims that Jennifer Lopez loves him. So his claim is:

> Jennifer Lopez loves me.

In questioning this claim you point out that Ms Lopez' agent called your friend recently, and told him to stop sending flowers, love poems and personal effects. The agent made it very clear that Ms Lopez was not interested. But your friend explained to you that the agent was merely protecting his client from the damaging effects of her passion. Eventually Ms Lopez herself calls to tell your friend that if his pestering doesn't stop she will call her lawyers. Your friend tells you that she is just playing hard-to-get. His original claim is now qualified as follows:

> Jennifer Lopez loves me (but she is playing hard-to-get).

You explain patiently that she doesn't even know him; that she has never even seen him; and that she is known to be in love with someone else. However, your friend claims that this is because she has to keep her love for him a secret in order to avoid a scandal in the tabloid newspapers. You realise that he's made a further adjustment to his claim:

> Jennifer Lopez loves me (but she is playing hard-to-get and it is a deeply secret love).

Even when the court order arrives forcing your friend to keep at least 2 miles away from Ms Lopez, your friend explains to you that her entourage don't want her to become romantically involved with someone so young.

> Jennifer Lopez loves me (but she is playing hard-to-get, it is a deeply secret love and her entourage is conspiring to prevent us from getting together).

Eventually you ask him if there is anything that anyone could say or do, anything that could happen that would demonstrate to him that Jennifer Lopez doesn't love him. He confesses that nothing could come between him and J-Lo, that her love for him is forever, and, even if she doesn't yet realise it, deep down she will always be in love with him.

Ian McEwan's novel *Enduring Love* ends on a similar, and sinister, one-sided declaration of love. A stalker, who has finally been imprisoned, continues to write passionate letters to his victim, finding in his prison cell all sorts of signs that his victim returns this love. His thousandth letter ends as follows: 'Thank you for loving me, thank you for accepting me, thank you for recognising what I am doing for our love. Send me a new message soon.' The 'message' the deluded man is referring to is simply the sun rising over the prison.

Antony Flew would argue that these claims to enduring love are empirically empty because for the person who makes them they cannot be falsified by any evidence. If the evidence merely leads to an adjustment (or qualification) in the claim, so that it remains immune to falsification, then the belief is not sensitive to the facts. For Flew the consistent failure of someone to alter their belief in accordance with new information that is made available to them suggests that the belief isn't actually about the world at all. And if it is not about facts (i.e. it's not factually significant) then for Flew the belief is meaningless.

Flew is particularly interested in the religious hypothesis, and argues that believers hold on to it no matter what. Flew uses the example of the belief that God loves us like a father loves his children. If we point out to believers that no father would let his children suffer what humans suffer, they typically respond by qualifying their statement and saying that God's love is a mysterious love. So, Flew asks, how much suffering and evil must there be before the believer will admit that either God doesn't exist, or he doesn't love us? Flew is probably right when he says that nothing will count as evidence against this belief (in other words, that no amount of suffering will ever lead believers to give up belief in God). After all, in one of the most important books of the Old Testament, Job, who has lost everything (his family, livelihood, friends, health) and who is sitting on a dungheap wondering what on earth he's done to deserve this (nothing, actually) still asserts that 'I know my redeemer liveth.'[87]

For Flew, if nothing counts against the belief, if it is unfalsifiable, then the religious hypothesis and its associated claims (e.g. that 'God loves us') should be rejected. The theist may qualify their belief in God's love, but they won't ever give it up no matter what horrors humans suffer, and so it is unfalsifiable and meaningless. If the believer does accept that the suffering of humanity could, in principle, establish that God doesn't love us, then Flew claims they should give up their belief now, since the amount of suffering clearly suggests that no loving God exists.

Imagine the following pairs of people are having a conversation, and construct a dialogue that might take place between them:

Person A	Person B
has an unshakeable belief that they will never give up no matter what the evidence.	**wishes to provide evidence that shows person A they are wrong.**
1 The Prime Minister believes that a certain country in the Middle East has weapons of mass destruction.	1 The United Nations chief weapons inspector is carrying out thorough inspections and finds nothing.
2 Someone from the Flat-Earth Society sincerely believes that the earth is flat and there is a conspiracy to 'prove' it is round.	2 A specialist in astronomy and geography is out to disband the Flat-Earth Society.
3 A child believes that there are monsters under their bed.	3 A mother is trying to reassure her child to help him get to sleep.
4 A fanatical England football supporter believes that the England team play the best football in the world.	4 A football historian wants to show this fan that all the evidence of past tournaments show England are simply average.
5 A student is convinced that all her lecturers are out to ruin her life, no matter how helpful they might appear.	5 A helpful student counsellor is trying to help this student, so that she might rejoin her classes.
6 A believer is convinced that God loves the world.	6 An atheist is convinced that a loving God does not exist, because of the amount of suffering in the world.

Basil Mitchell and Richard Hare's criticisms of Flew

Two philosophers gave their responses following directly on from Flew's lecture 'Theology and Falsification'. Both Richard Hare and Basil Mitchell tried to show that, even though religious statements were not claims about the world (they weren't factually significant) they were still meaningful. Hare and Mitchell both take as their starting point the idea that we can see the same things from very different perspectives, just as Wisdom and Flew did (and as in the case of the duck–rabbit). Let us take Hare's response first.

Hare gives his own parable to help us to understand the strange nature of religious statements, which we can call the parable of the Paranoid Student:

A certain lunatic is convinced that all dons want to murder him. His friends introduce him to all the mildest and most respectable dons that they can find, and after each of them has retired, they say, 'You see, he doesn't really want to murder you; he spoke to you in a most cordial manner; surely you are convinced now?' But the lunatic replies 'Yes, but that was only his diabolical cunning; he's really plotting against me the whole time, like the rest of them; I know it I tell you.' However many kindly dons are produced, the reaction is still the same.[88]

Like the person who believes in the invisible gardener, or Calvin in the cartoon below, the paranoid student cannot imagine being wrong, his statement 'my teachers are out to get me' is unfalsifiable. And yet Hare argues that this belief remains very meaningful. After all, it has a deep influence on how the student approaches the world, how he forms other beliefs and how he lives his life. It is true that it operates so centrally within his belief system that it cannot be falisified, and all evidence is twisted to fit with this fundamental belief; but the very centrality of the belief means that it is deeply meaningful, contrary to what Flew has argued.

■ **Figure 6.12 *The paranoid six-year-old***

So Hare argues that it is possible to assent to a proposition which is not falsifiable but which is none the less meaningful. And such beliefs are not confined to the unusual case of paranoia. According to Hare we are all in some ways like the student: we *all* have fundamental beliefs or principles on which we base our actions and which we will never give up. These thoughts and principles often form the very basis for our other beliefs, and they are both unverifiable and unfalsifiable. For example, most of us believe that all events have a cause. Imagine that a sceptic tried to falsify this belief. They might point to events for which no cause could be observed, such as the unexpected disappearance of your cat, or the sudden appearance of a puncture in your bicycle tyre. We can suppose that you had spent months trying to find out how or why your cat disappeared, or hours looking for the offending object that had penetrated your tyre, but had found nothing. Would you accept such failure as evidence that these events just happened without any reason or cause? Probably not. For what you would try to do instead is hold on to your belief that everything has a cause, and explain your failure to find any in these cases as related to the fact that you didn't search long or hard enough. If you had had the time, perhaps you would indeed have found the cause. And no matter how many events the sceptic might describe that appear to lack a cause, you may well respond in the same way: refusing to give up your belief that all events have causes despite the mounting number of events cited where no cause is forthcoming.

Hare thinks that beliefs like this are perfectly meaningful, even though unfalsifiable. He invented the word 'blik' to refer to such foundational thoughts and principles and argued that many religious beliefs fall into this category. For example, when believers say that 'God exists' they are expressing a *blik*: it is a belief that informs their perspective on the world, and in terms of which they interpret their whole lives. They may never be prepared to give it up, but the fundamental nature of the belief ensures that it remains important to them, and distinctly meaningful. So if *bliks* have meaning it is an error to suppose, as Flew does, that all our meaningful beliefs are falsifiable.

Basil Mitchell also criticises Flew, but from a different angle to Hare. He disagrees with the view that religious beliefs are unfalsifiable and he tells another parable to make his point, this time about a resistance leader.[89]

Imagine your country has been invaded and a resistance movement develops to overthrow the occupiers. One night you meet a man claiming to be a resistance leader, and he convinces you to put your trust in him and the movement. Over the months you sometimes see the man act for the resistance, but sometimes you also see him act against the movement. This troubles you: you worry that he might be a traitor, but your trust in him eventually overcomes your concerns and you continue to believe in him. Your belief that 'the stranger is on your side' is one that you don't give up, even though you see many things that suggest you are wrong.

Mitchell argues that this belief in the resistance leader is meaningful, even though you refuse to give it up. He does not think that it is a *blik*, however, because there are many occasions in which you do doubt your own belief. This doubt shows that your belief is falsifiable, i.e. that you can imagine circumstances under which you would give up your belief. Mitchell's parable reflects the doubts that religious believers sometimes have when they encounter great suffering in their lives (see the problem of evil earlier in this chapter). These 'trials of faith' show that Flew is wrong to think that believers simply shrug off evidence that goes against their beliefs. Some believers, after all, do lose their faith in the face of painful and apparently senseless episodes in their lives. Mitchell also thinks that one day the truth will be revealed – in the parable this happens when the war is over; in real life this will happen after we die. (John Hick adheres to this belief that life after death can verify the truth of religious statements and we look at his theory below.) So, for Mitchell, a belief that 'God exists' is both falsifiable (there are trials of faith) and verifiable (after we die), and therefore religious statements are meaningful.

John Hick and the revival of the religious hypothesis

We began this section by looking at the duck–rabbit: at how it raised issues regarding the ambiguity of observation, about how different people with different expectations and beliefs might see the world differently, and about how the world seems to accommodate these different perspectives. But we saw that philosophers are not satisfied with a 'live and let live' approach to beliefs: Wisdom, Flew, Mitchell and Hare all think that one set of beliefs is the correct set: either the believer or the atheist is correct in their interpretation of the world; either there is a God or there isn't; either the religious hypothesis is true or it isn't. However, there is a problem here, as Flew pointed out – if there are no facts and no observations that will change the minds, and the statements, of religious believers then isn't what they say simply meaningless?

The philosopher John Hick responded to this attack by reviving the idea of verification (see above page 491). Hick, like Wisdom, acknowledged the ambiguous nature of the world, and that observations appear to support *both* the claim that God does exist *and* that he does not. But Hick tries to show that ultimately the ambiguity disappears, and that in the afterlife religious statements can be verified and therefore the religious hypothesis is genuine. We examine three main features of Hick's approach:

1 his definition of 'verification', which is different from A.J. Ayer's;
2 his parable of the Celestial City, showing that verification of religious statements is possible and reasonably straightforward;
3 his account of personal identity after death, showing that resurrection is possible.

Let us deal with each part in turn.

Hick agrees with Ayer that only statements that make claims about the world (i.e. are factually significant) are meaningful, and that factual significance is judged by whether the truth or falsity of an assertion makes a difference to our experience of the world. For example, whether the statement 'there is an invisible, odourless, intangible rabbit in this room' is true or is false makes no difference to our experience. Hence the statement is not factually significant; it tells us nothing about the world and is not meaningful. Like Ayer, Hick proposes that the factual significance of an assertion is best assessed by whether it can be verified. Hick goes on to say that verifiability should be judged by whether it is possible to remove the grounds for rational doubt about the truth of the claim in question. For example, claiming that there is a family of foxes living at the bottom of the garden can be verified if you keep finding mutilated squirrels on the lawn, if you have seen a red furry tail sticking out from a hole under the shed, and if your night-vision goggles reveal frolicking fox cubs. Such evidence would effectively remove any serious doubts about the matter.

Now, Hick accepts that religious propositions cannot be falsified. They cannot be falsified because, if there is no God, then after we die we will just be dead and we won't be able to say 'ah-ha – there is no God, those believers were all wrong!' But Hick's argument is that although religious statements may never be falsified they *can* be verified, in the sense that rational doubt can be removed about their truth. For Hick it is the potential verifiability of religious statements that makes them meaningful. To illustrate how such verification is possible he offers his parable of the Celestial City:

Two men are travelling together along a road. One of them believes that it leads to the Celestial City, the other that it leads nowhere; but since this is the only road there is, both must travel it . . . During the journey they meet with moments of refreshment and delight, and with moments of hardship and danger. All the time one of them thinks of his journey as a pilgrimage to the Celestial City. He interprets the pleasant parts of the journey as encouragements and the obstacles as trials of his purpose . . . The other, however, believes none of this . . . Since he has no choice in the matter he enjoys the good and endures the bad . . . When they do turn the last corner it will be apparent that one of them has been right all the time and the other wrong.[90]

1 Revisit the section on 'Seeing-as', on pages 485–87 above. What factors influence the way that these travellers see the world?
2 What differences and similarities are there between this parable and the parables of Flew, Mitchell and Hare?

This parable points to the possibility of what Hick calls 'ESCHATOLOGICAL verification', that is to say verification after our death in the next life ('eschatology' concerns what happens at the end of things, for instance at the last judgement). Hick is arguing that many religious statements, particularly in Christianity, rest on the claim that there is an afterlife, and they are meaningful because they can be verified in the afterlife. I can verify whether there is a heaven or not if, after I die, I find myself in heaven. For Hick such experience would remove grounds for rational doubt about the existence of heaven.

Hick recognises that the possibility of eschatological verification relies on the possibility of my retaining my personal identity through the processes of death, but there are certain difficulties with this idea (we raised this issue earlier on page 196). One difficulty is that we all know that when people die their bodies quickly decompose. How, if the body of which you are made has dissipated, can you possibly be thought to have survived? If someone subsequently appears in heaven, in what sense can it be said to be me? If I am resurrected how can this new body be thought of as still me?

To answer such questions, Hick presents three separate 'thought experiments' which try to show that a person appearing in an afterlife can meaningfully be considered as the same person as someone who had lived and died in this life.

1 First Hick asks us to imagine a person, X, disappearing in America, while at the very same moment someone else, who is the exact double of X (same physical features, the same memory, etc.) appears in Australia. If this happened would you consider the person appearing in Australia to be the same as X? Hick thinks that we would.
2 Now imagine that person X, instead of disappearing, dies in America, and at the very same moment their double appears in Australia. Wouldn't we still say they were the same person? Hick thinks that if we accept that it is the same person in the first scenario, we would have to accept that it is the same person in this scenario.
3 Finally, imagine that person X dies in America, and their double now appears, not in Australia, but in heaven. Again Hick thinks that if we accept that it is the same person in scenarios 1 and 2, then we must accept it is the same in this scenario too. And if we accept that it is the same person,

then we are accepting that it makes sense to talk about surviving one's death and preserving one's personal identity.

What these thought experiments are supposed to show is that resurrection is at least possible. And if we are resurrected in heaven, we (or at least some of us) will be in no doubt that it is heaven that we are in. For Hick there are two factors that will remove all rational doubt that we are in heaven: firstly our final understanding of the purpose and destiny given to us by God; and secondly our encountering our saviour Jesus Christ. Note that Hick says that only some of us may be able to verify this, namely those who already believe in God. But, none the less, if it is logically possible that at least someone will be able to verify (remove rational doubt from) the hypothesis that 'God exists', then this claim is meaningful.

▶ criticism ◀ One line of criticism against Hick is to question the conclusions he draws from his thought experiments. Each scenario, it may be urged, really produces a duplicate person in a new location, and so not really the self-same person who disappeared or died. To see this, consider altering the scenarios slightly, such that in each case the original person remains alongside the double appearing in Australia or heaven. In such cases we would be inclined to think the double was a different person from the original. However, this alteration to the scenario has not changed the status of the double itself, and so the double cannot be the same as the original. God could certainly create a duplicate of me in heaven on my death, but a duplicate of me is not me. Our intuitions appear to suggest that for my personal identity to survive the process of death, there would have to be some form of bodily continuity. Simply rebuilding a perfect copy is not resurrecting the self same person. (This, the duplication problem, is discussed in greater detail in Chapter 3.)

A second difficulty concerns whether we truly can verify through our post-mortem experience the various religious claims in question. Consider the most obvious claims that God and heaven exist. Now in order to verify that we are now in heaven, or are now experiencing God, we need to first recognise that this vision in front of us is heaven (or God). However, there is a difficulty with the subjective nature of religious experiences: it may not be possible to recognise something we have never seen before and that lies beyond our understanding. So if, as some philosophers say, God is beyond our comprehension, then perhaps it won't be possible to recognise, or verify, that this is God or heaven we see before us.

We have now moved a long way from the type of discussions that arose in the sections on the design arguments and on the problem of evil. These arguments took religious belief roughly at face value: religious claims were supposed, on both sides, to be hypotheses about the world and the arguments proceeded from there. John Wisdom doubted whether religious arguments could be settled by making new observations of the world and consequently, whether he intended to or not, revived the issue as to whether religious language is meaningful. What Wisdom wanted to do was to show that two people could see the same thing from very different perspectives (what Wittgenstein called 'seeing-as'). But the issues he raised led to the troubling attack by Antony Flew on the very meaning of religious language, namely that because it can never be falsified it isn't making any claims about the world at all. We now need to meet head on the issue of whether religious claims reflect genuine beliefs about the world, or whether religious expressions and statements are doing something else entirely.

Is religion a hypothesis at all?

There is a story told of how the French scientist Pierre Laplace (1749–1827) gave the Emperor Napoleon a copy of his book *Système du Monde* (we look at Laplace's theory in Chapter 5). Napoleon said that he had heard that Laplace had written a large book on the system of the universe, but that it had no mention of the Creator. To which Laplace replied:

I have no need of that hypothesis.[91]

Laplace

William James (1842–1910) took a very different view:

What then do we now mean by the religious hypothesis? . . . First, that the best things are the more eternal things . . . an affirmation which obviously cannot yet be verified scientifically at all. The second affirmation of religion is that we are better off even now if we believe [the] first affirmation to be true.[92]

William James

A hypothesis is a proposed solution to a problem, for example an event that needs explaining, but it is a proposal that requires further evidence. The religious 'hypothesis' that Laplace and James are referring to is the claim that God exists and is the best explanation for the existence and special properties of the world. The best examples of the religious hypothesis in action can be found in the various design arguments for the existence of God. These arguments begin with a number of features that need explaining, the order, regularity and apparent function of things in nature, and they conclude that these features are best accounted for by the existence of God.

For Laplace, the universe can be adequately explained without introducing the idea of God. But, for William James, there is much more ambiguity in the world – there is not enough evidence to demonstrate either that God exists or that he doesn't exist. For James, the religious hypothesis – that belief in God offers eternal life – cannot be verified (this is in contrast to Hick whom we looked at above). James says that we do not have time to wait for evidence; we are like a traveller on a mountain pass, surrounded by swirling snow – if we stand still then we will freeze to death. So we are faced with an urgent and momentous choice: to have faith in God or not; to believe in the religious hypothesis or, like Laplace, to reject it.

But there is a question as to whether religion should be taken to be a hypothesis at all. Perhaps it is a mistake to even think of religious statements in this way. Perhaps religious claims are not claims about the world, are not hypotheses to compete with scientific hypotheses, but are something else entirely. In the final section of this chapter we ask what the status of religious belief and religious language is; and if they are not directed towards making claims about the world then what is their function?

Wittgenstein and the rejection of the religious hypothesis

Ludwig Wittgenstein (1889–1951) was one of the most significant philosophers of the last century. He was primarily a philosopher of language, and it was his reflections on the nature of meaning that led him to the conclusion that religious claims are not claims about the world in the same way that scientific claims are. Wittgenstein believes that to treat religious claims as hypotheses is to seriously misunderstand the meaning of religious language. But before we come to look at what Wittgenstein had to say about expressions of religious conviction, we should first sketch the philosophy of language that lies behind his thoughts on religion.

Wittgenstein put forward two distinct theories of meaning, one when he was young and the other towards the end of his career. Wittgenstein in both his early and later phases believed that the heart of philosophy lay in the study of language and that by studying language we could clear up many of the disputes of philosophers and perhaps even make philosophy no longer necessary. The early Wittgenstein adopted a 'picture theory' of meaning, arguing that language is a way of representing facts. So a sentence like *The cat is on the mat* is meaningful because it represents or pictures some state of affairs in the world. Wittgenstein argued that when we attempt to use language to do anything other than to say things about the world we stray into the realm of nonsense. This picture theory of meaning was influential to A.J. Ayer and to the Vienna Circle (a group of philosophers active in the 1930s, whose ideas were based on logical positivism: see Chapter 4, pages 254–57).

However, the later Wittgenstein was one of the foremost critics of this simplistic view of meaning. He attacked the logical positivists and his own early work, arguing that it utterly failed to capture the complexity of language. For Ayer and his associates the only meaningful statements were ones about science or about the world we see, or ones that were true by definition. But Wittgenstein realised that our language was so much richer and more varied and this, and it was a ridiculous mistake for philosophers to rule out the rest of language because it couldn't be true or false. For example, when we talk about beauty, or love, or poetry, or religion, or art, or the meaning of life we seem to understand one another – yet Ayer tells us that we are talking nonsense. So Wittgenstein searched for a new way of understanding the nature of meaning.

ACTIVITY

1 Construct as many different sentences as you can that contain the word 'down'.

2 How many different meanings of the word 'down' have you used?

From this simple exercise you can immediately see that words don't have a single meaning. There are many, many different meanings of the word 'down', over twenty if you include slang and colloquial uses. The later Wittgenstein argued that there was no such thing as 'the' meaning of a word or sentence, since there are many different ways in which language can be meaningful. He rejected the idea that a single theory of meaning was possible. Presuming that words must have some specific meaning, he argued, is the source of many philosophical difficulties. What we need to do is to be alive to the vagueness of words, to the great variety of different meanings they can have, and to the many ways they can be used.

Go back to the ways in which the word 'down' can be used. In the context of rambling (the South Down Way); of upholstery (down as in duck feathers); of giving directions (you go down the road); of dog training (a command for a dog to grovel); of crosswords (down clues); of emotions (feeling down); of dancing (get on down); of drinking (down in one) and there are many, many more. And the nature of meaning itself is as variegated as the meanings or uses of words. Understanding the meaning of a word is not a matter of catching hold of some abstract idea which is *the* meaning, but is a practical matter of being able to use the word appropriately in a variety of contexts. So you know the meaning of the word 'down' just because you can use it, but this doesn't mean that there is one thing, the word's *meaning*, which you have in your head.

The meaning of a word is its use in the language,[93]

Wittgenstein

So Wittgenstein's later theory of meaning denied that the meaning of language could be reduced to how it pictured the world. This may be one function of language, but it is certainly not the only one. Language can be used to do so many more things than this, and Wittgenstein cites the following as some examples of the multiplicity of language use: to give orders, to describe an object, to report an event, to make up a story, to tell a joke, to ask, thank, curse, greet, pray, etc.[94] All these uses are legitimate. So if we wish to know the meaning of a word we should look for how it is used, according to Wittgenstein, and this view is sometimes condensed into the phrase 'meaning is use'.

The term 'language-game' is meant to bring into prominence the fact that the speaking of language is part of an activity.[95]

Wittgenstein

The different uses of language are activities that take place in different social contexts, which Wittgenstein famously termed language games. He did not mean 'game' in a flippant or competitive sense, but in the sense that language use is an activity governed by certain rules, and these rules vary from context to context. For example, the rules governing the use of the word 'experience' in science are very different from those governing this word in a religious context. But Wittgenstein argued that it was a mistake to think that one use of a word was better than or more fundamental than another.

How many different types of language games can you think of? Can you describe how some of the rules of these language games differ?

Remember what Ayer and Flew claimed: that for a statement to be meaningful it must refer to the world. But Wittgenstein is now suggesting that statements are meaningful so long as they are understood by other language users in a specific context. He therefore thinks (unlike Ayer) that morality, art, poetry, etc. are all meaningful, they are all language games. Now, when it comes to religious statements and concepts, according to Wittgenstein's approach, they are meaningful because they form part of a religious language game. Believers are users of this language; they are immersed in the practice of following its rules and, if we consider meaning to be equated with use, then such a language is meaningful to whoever is able to use the language appropriately, that is to say, to 'players' of the game.

So to understand religious statements we need to be a part of the religious language game; as Wittgenstein said, we need to be immersed in the religious 'Form of Life'. If we are not immersed in that particularly way of living, if we don't share those beliefs, or use those concepts in a familiar and regular way then we cannot understand religious statements. This is the problem with philosophers like Ayer and Flew. They think that there is only one way language can be meaningful, namely if it is factually significant; so when religious language fails to be factually significant they accuse it of being meaningless. But the error is to think that meaning lies in factual significance, i.e. in statements that describe the world. The fundamental mistake made by Ayer and Flew is to treat statements from one language game (expressions of religious faith), as if they came from another (descriptions of the world): in other words to treat religious talk as if it were scientific talk and as if it were a hypothesis.

Wittgenstein

Suppose someone were a believer and said: 'I believe in a Last Judgement', and I said: 'Well, I'm not so sure. Possibly.' You would say that there is an enormous gulf between us. If he said 'There is a German aeroplane overhead', and I said 'Possibly, I'm not so sure' you'd say we were fairly near.[96]

For Wittgenstein, science and religion are two different language games, they are not in competition with one another, and neither can help solve the problems of the other. According to Wittgenstein, it might be appropriate for us to take a hard-nosed approach to the meaning of scientific statements, in the way Ayer and Flew suggest: scientific claims are hypotheses that need to be verified or falsified. However, religious claims about God and the Creation or Last Judgement are not hypotheses and are not subject to the same rules as scientific claims.

When a believer says 'The Creator exists' they are not using 'exists' in the same way as when a scientist says 'duck-billed platypuses exist'. For when a believer is talking about the Creator they are also being reverential; they are expressing their faith and their understanding of the purpose of life. Although 'the Creator exists' looks very similar to a statement like 'the chairs exist', it is a much richer and resonant phrase, and is an expression of faith, of belief in the grace of God and of salvation. Atheists just don't get it, and they can't get it unless they become involved in a religious way of life.

▶ criticism ◀ However, there are problems with Wittgenstein's theory. The most fundamental problem arises because a meaningful statement (within a religious language game) no longer has to be connected to the world, it no longer has to be true or false. So we can imagine a group of religious language users who can talk meaningfully about the existence of goblins, elves and pixies so long as they have a consistent set of rules governing their concepts. The fact that there aren't any such creatures is irrelevant to the meaningfulness of the language game. This view about the nature of language, that it doesn't refer to the world, is termed anti-realism (see page 73). However, being anti-realist about religious language doesn't sit well with what most believers think they are doing when they talk, for example, of God or the afterlife. Making religious statements does appear to involve making claims about what does and doesn't exist in reality. So there is a problem in supposing, as Wittgenstein does, that religion is nothing other than a game played in words and deeds by a community of people. The religious language game includes a set of substantive metaphysical claims, regarding the existence of God, heaven, Jesus, the afterlife, the creation, etc. So many believers would disagree with Wittgenstein's point that religion is different from science. For believers the Creator is real, and not simply another piece in a complicated language game.

Other philosophers have agreed with Wittgenstein, and see religious belief not as a competing theory alongside science, but as something else entirely. We look below at two alternative accounts of the function of religious belief: the first, proposed by Richard Braithwaite, is that we should understand religious claims to be expressions of a commitment to a certain (moral) way of life; the second is the claim that religious belief is an attitude that we adopt in relation to God and the world.

Religious belief as a moral commitment

Richard Braithwaite was influenced by Wittgenstein's theory. Like Wittgenstein he rejected a theory of meaning (embraced by Flew and Ayer) which tied the meaningfulness of a statement to whether it was true or false. Like Wittgenstein he argued that the meaning of statements, including religious statements, was determined by their use. Braithwaite proposed that religious statements are used by believers to express a commitment to a certain way of life, in other words to a certain morality.[97]

Although Braithwaite's essay is called 'An empiricist's view' his analysis of religious language differs from that of other empiricists, such as Ayer and the Vienna Circle. Empiricism is a type of philosophy that considers observation and experience to be the foundation of all our concepts. And, as we have seen, for Ayer statements must refer to something empirically verifiable if they are to be meaningful. However, Braithwaite argues that we must consider the empirical *use* of a statement, as well as its verifiability, when looking at its meaning. Braithwaite believes that empiricism, through observing how religious statements are used, can uncover their meaning.

His basic argument is that religious statements work in the same way as moral statements. According to Braithwaite when we look at how moral statements are used we find they are expressions of an attitude towards life, and a commitment to a certain way of behaving. So when I say 'killing animals is wrong' what I mean is that I will never kill an animal, and will discourage other people from doing so. Religious statements are also expressions of a commitment to a certain way of life, and Braithwaite identifies the statement 'God is love' as meaning 'I will act in an agapeistic way' (agapeistic is from the ancient Greek word *AGAPE* for selfless love).

Braithwaite recognises that there might be a number of religions which recommend similar ways of living, but this does not make them identical. What differentiates one religion from another is not just the actions of its believers, but also the set of stories in which it is embedded. These background stories, such as the Flood and Noah's Ark, or the exodus from Egypt by the Hebrews, also distinguish religious statements from moral statements (as moral statements have no such attached stories).

► criticism ◄ The problem is Braithwaite's account of the meaning of religious propositions doesn't really capture what believers think they are saying when they talk about God, Jesus, etc. Most believers do not simply think of their beliefs as a type of morality embedded in a set of myths. Nor do believers think that when they say that 'God is love' they are using this statement to prescribe a course of action. Most believers would hold that they are talking in a literal way about the universe, and referring to a literal God, a literal Creation, a literal Resurrection, etc. In some way it belittles religious language to reduce it to the 'intention to carry out a certain behaviour policy', as Braithwaite claims.[98]

Religious belief as an attitude

We have now looked at the claims that religious belief is a hypothesis (supporters of the Design Argument view it this way) that can be verified. We have seen how Wittgenstein and his followers reject the claim that religious belief is a hypothesis – Braithwaite suggesting that it is a moral commitment. We now turn to the claim that religious belief should be seen in the context of faith – as an expression of an attitude towards God and the world.

Some religious philosophers (St Thomas Aquinas, Alvin Plantinga and William James) view religious faith as a special kind of belief because it lacks evidence or because it doesn't need any evidence. These interpretations offer 'propositional' accounts of religious faith, i.e. the belief that the proposition 'God exists' is true. On this view, faith or religious belief enables us to plug the gaps in the evidence, and so we can agree that 'God exists' is true. But there is another account of religious belief that makes more of an effort to understand the attitudes to faith that ordinary believers possess. This account focuses on the existential concern of what living faith is like, and is more about an attitude to God rather than about the belief that God exists.

The Protestant Reformation of the sixteenth century, driven by the reformers Martin Luther and John Calvin, marked a switch away from a relationship with God mediated through the Church, towards an emphasis on the direct personal relationship believers can have with God. In this new protestant tradition, faith was not about assenting to certain propositions (as Aquinas claimed), but instead was a way of experiencing and being in a relationship with God. To understand the difference between this new understanding of faith and the 'propositional' interpretation that sees religious belief as a kind of scientific hypothesis, we shall draw on the distinction between two kinds of belief: 'believing that' and 'believing in'.

Let us examine the first kind of belief. 'Believing that . . . ' entails believing certain propositions to be true. Take the example:

> I believe Aretha Franklin is the greatest soul singer ever.

Now what this means is:

> I believe that the proposition 'Aretha Franklin is the greatest soul singer ever' is true.

Most of the time when philosophers are talking about belief they are talking about this kind of propositional belief, i.e. belief about the truth (or falsity) of propositions. On this view religious beliefs are simply beliefs about special kinds of propositions: propositions about certain supernatural facts, such as that Christ rose from the dead, or that God loves us.

There is another way in which we use the word 'belief', and that is when we say that we BELIEVE IN something. H.H. Price (1899–1985) raised the question of whether all statements about 'believing in something' could be reduced to, or translated into, statements about 'believing that' something was the case.[99]

a) 'Translate' the following statements from a 'believe in' statement to a 'believe that' statement. For example, 'I believe in invisible pixies' can be translated as 'I believe that invisible pixies exist.'

b) Which of your translations have resulted in a change in meaning of the original statements? Which of your translations have preserved the meaning of the original?

1 I believe in miracles.
2 believe in the Loch Ness Monster.
3 I believe in lifelong learning.
4 I don't believe in aliens.
5 I believe in most conspiracy theories.
6 I believe in the survival of the fittest.
7 I believe in doctors.
8 I don't believe in Robin Hood.
9 I don't believe in ice cold baths.
10 I believe in equality of opportunity.

From the activity you might have shown that there are difficulties in rendering all 'belief in' statements as 'belief that' statements, without changing the meaning of the sentence. Price argues that there are two different senses of 'belief in'. The first sense is a *factual* sense, and sentences that use 'belief in' in this way can be translated into 'belief that' without any real loss of meaning. So when someone says they believe in ghosts or UFOs what they really mean is that they believe that ghosts or UFOs exist. It may even be the case that when some philosophers talk about 'believing in God' what they really mean is 'believing that God exists' or 'believing that the proposition "God exists" is true'.[100]

However, there is another sense of 'belief in', which Price calls the *evaluative* sense, that cannot be translated into 'belief that'. So people say they believe in an institution (e.g. the government) or a theory (e.g. evolution) or a course of action (e.g. seeing dentists). Price argues that this sense of 'belief in' captures an attitude of trust, commitment and belief in the value of the institution, theory, course of action, etc. We also talk about believing *in* a specific person, and this is being used in the evaluative sense too. For example, the statement 'Gary believes in the Prime Minister' might mean that in his heart Gary trusts and values the Prime Minister and feels that she will govern the country in the best possible way. However, it clearly does not mean that he believes that the Prime Minister exists. So when we talk about belief in a person we are talking about a particular kind of attitude we have to that person, and the question of their existence doesn't even come into it; it is assumed. To believe in someone means to trust them, to commit to them, to rely on them, and to have confidence in them.

Belief in God means trusting God, accepting God, accepting his purposes, committing one's life to him and living in his presence.[101]

Alvin Plantinga

Plantinga

Price says that it is the *evaluative* sense of 'belief in' that people use when they say 'I believe in God';[102] and this means more than simply 'I believe that God exists'. To someone with religious faith, someone who believes in God, the existence of God is a given. God is a given because to the believer God is part of their way of seeing the world, the 'mental spectacles' they wear which helps them make sense of the world, and within which their other beliefs have meaning and a place (compare this thought with R.M. Hare's concept of 'bliks' discussed above on page 497).

On this account then, religious faith, or belief in God, goes far beyond discussions about God's existence, and instead encompasses an attitude towards a being, God, who is already present in the believer's life. So religious faith also describes the experience that believers have of God, and the spectrum of emotions that accompany this experience. For John Hick, belief in God is an awareness of God, which means 'to see oneself as a created, dependent creature, receiving life and well-being from a higher source . . . the only appropriate attitude is one of grateful worship and obedience'.[103]

Summary

We began this chapter by looking at the design argument, and whether there was sufficient evidence in the world to support the claim that God exists. This approach views God's existence as a hypothesis about the world that can be proved to be true through the gathering of evidence. The sorts of evidence that believers point towards include the order and regularity of the universe, and the way that organisms are so well suited to their environment – as if they had been designed. However, atheists can point to evidence against this hypothesis, namely the extent of pain and suffering that humans and other creatures have experienced throughout history.

John Wisdom suggests that the disagreement between believers and atheists is a disagreement between different perspectives on the world. The believer sees the world as God's creation while the atheist sees the world as one without God. So for Wisdom the disagreement isn't about a factual hypothesis (is there a world or isn't there?) but about a difference in perspective. Antony Flew seizes upon Wisdom's analogy (of the Invisible Gardener) to show that the believer isn't making a genuine hypothesis about the world at all – their claims are actually meaningless, because there is no evidence that would falsify them.

Wittgenstein also argues that religion is not a hypothesis – but for very different reasons. For Wittgenstein religious claims should not be read as if they were scientific claims. Scientists make hypotheses; believers do not. However, this argument would sit uncomfortably with many believers who feel they are making meaningful statements that are genuinely about the world. John Hick recognises this when he proposes that religious claims can be verified, but that this is only possibly in the next life (although there are many problems with Hick's argument).

Finally we looked at the claims that religious beliefs are not beliefs about the world at all. For Braithwaite, a follower of Wittgenstein, religious belief is an expression of an attitude to God and to the world – as Plantinga said, committing your life to God and living in his presence.

Key points: Chapter 6

What you need to know about **God and the world:**

1 Teleological arguments are inductive proofs of the existence of God based on observations about specific features of the universe, namely the ordered, regular and purposive appearance of the world and its inhabitants. Some of the most influential teleological arguments have rested on an analogy with designed objects. Many features of designed objects (having parts which work together, functioning to fulfil a purpose) seem to be shared with living creatures and their environment. It is therefore supposed that living creatures were also designed, along with their environments. However, arguments based on analogy are most reliable when the two things being compared are very similar; but does the universe resemble a watch closely enough for us to be able to draw any conclusion about whether it was designed? Other teleological arguments rely on showing that God is the best explanation for why the world is the way it is. This may involve building up a cumulative case for the existence of God. It may also involve arguing that modern science cannot adequately explain things like 'intelligent design' or the improbable existence of human beings.

2 The greatest challenge facing the belief in God is the problem of evil. Evil comes in two forms, natural evil (the pain and suffering caused by natural events) and moral evil (the pain and suffering caused by human beings). How can an all-powerful, all-knowing and benevolent God create a universe in which so much suffering exists? To some atheists, like J.L. Mackie, this problem demonstrates that an omnipotent, omniscient and benevolent Creator does not exist. Various solutions, known as *theodicies*, have been proposed to the problem of evil. Perhaps Augustine is right and God is striving for a beautiful universe in which there is a balance of light and dark, good and evil; perhaps evil enables people to act in a good or saintly way, as Swinburne suggests; perhaps humans become stronger and better people through their struggle to overcome and cope with evil, as Hick and Irenaeus propose; or perhaps there will be justice in the next life, with evil-doers being punished and good people going to heaven. Underpinning many solutions to the problem of evil is the free will defence. Humans were given the freedom to choose between good and evil, and our decision to choose evil is our responsibility, not God's.

3 There is a vast difference between the way that the atheist sees the world and the way that a believer sees the world. John Wisdom used an analogy of two people recently returning to a garden: one person sees the weeds growing everywhere, while the other notices the careful arrangements of flowers. In the case of the world, the believer notices the order and design of the universe, the atheist notices the pain, chaos and suffering. Whether or not there is a God cannot be determined from observation, since the atheist and believer observe exactly the same things. For Antony Flew the problem raised by the believer's continuous claim that there is a God, in spite of all the evidence against his existence, is an indicator that religious claims are unfalsifiable and therefore meaningless. No matter what happens a believer will never retract their belief that God exists, and will keep adding qualifications in order to save it. Recently the issue has arisen as to whether God or religion is a hypothesis or not. A hypothesis is a suggested explanation that accounts for the data we've derived from our observations. Wittgenstein argued that it was absurd for us to compare a religious framework with a scientific framework – the two things are entirely separate. Other philosophers have argued that belief in the existence of God is not a hypothesis about the universe, but is actually just the expression of a commitment to a moral way of life, or an attitude of faith that we adopt to the world.

Knowledge of the external world

Introduction

How do we acquire knowledge of the world? An obvious answer is that we learn about it through our senses. We know that the cat is on the mat because we can *see* it there. We know that it is a hot day because we can *feel* the warmth of the sun on our backs. However, in Chapter 4 we have already had occasion to raise doubts about the reliability of our senses in telling us about the world. So just how accurate are the human sense organs as indicators of the way the world really is? It is interesting to observe in this connection that other animals have senses that are far more sensitive than our own. Dogs, for example, can hear sounds that are too high for us to hear, and they can smell all kinds of things that we can't. Does this mean they are perceiving the world more accurately than us? Other creatures have senses completely different from ours. The ability of sharks to sense the electric field created by living things, or of bats to use sound to navigate, raises the question of what the world must seem like to these animals. How do their senses represent the world in their minds? In colours and shapes? In textures and sounds? Or in some way we simply cannot imagine? Perhaps these animals have a truer perception of the world than we do. Or perhaps no animal sees the world as it truly is.

1 **a)** Do you think your favourite food tastes the same to a dog as it does to you?
   b) Do you think dog food tastes the same to you as to a dog?
   c) Who has a truer perception of the world: dogs or humans?
2 Some creatures lack the senses we have. They may be blind or deaf. Others have senses that we don't have. They may detect electricity or magnetic fields. How many senses must a creature have for it to get a true picture of the world? Make a list of the necessary senses.
3 Dogs can hear high frequency sound waves that we do not register. Likewise, elephants hear frequencies lower than we can register. Does it follow that all humans are partially deaf? Are some sounds so low and others so high that no creature can hear them?

4 As with sound waves we only perceive light waves within a particular bandwidth. Imagine meeting an alien who does not perceive the frequencies of light that we do, but perceives a whole set of higher ones such as ultra violet and beyond. The alien represents these waves in a range of colours much as we do. Who sees the true colours of the world: humans or aliens? If neither of us does, does that mean that no colours are the real colours?

5 Can you be sure that, when you and your friend share a piece of chicken, the flavour you experience is actually the same for both of you? Similarly, is there any way of telling that you are seeing exactly the same colours as someone else?

6 Sound is caused by compression waves of air hitting your ear drum. If a tree fell down in a forest and there were no ears around (human or otherwise), would it:

a) make a sound?

b) just produce airwaves?

7 Where are rainbows? Are they in the sky, in rain droplets, in people's minds or nowhere?

These questions raise all sorts of puzzles about how perception works and what it can tell us about the world. What should be evident from having considered them is that we need to be clear about what is going on in perception before we can be completely confident about our answers. In other words we need to develop some kind of theory of perception. In this chapter we will consider some of the main philosophical theories of perception which, in turn, give different accounts of our knowledge of the world around us.

Realism

When the doors of perception are cleansed, man will see things as they truly are: Infinite.[1]

William Blake

Much of the debate on perception hinges on the question of how much of what we perceive is really a feature of the world and how much is a feature of our minds. In other words, how much of what we are perceiving is really out there? This question of what is real or not is also central to many other areas of philosophy. If you are a REALIST about something, then you believe it exists independently of our minds. If you are an ANTI-REALIST about something, you think it is mind-dependent. The following activity reveals on which topics you are a realist and on which you take an anti-realist stance.

ACTIVITY For each of the following, consider whether the object or topic in question is real or not. For this exercise, take 'real' to mean 'has an existence independent of minds – human or otherwise'. Copy and complete the table.

	Real	**Not real**	**Don't know**
1 Numbers e.g. number 7			
2 Your reflection in the mirror			
3 Colours, e.g. red			
4 Smells			
5 Morality			
6 Electrons			
7 Scientific laws, e.g. $e = mc^2$			
8 Ghosts			
9 Matter			
10 Beauty			

Real or not?

1 Numbers, e.g. the number 7. Whether numbers are real or not has vexed many a philosopher and is still a current debate. Plato famously thought that numbers existed independently of humans, not in the world that we see and touch, but in a world we can only perceive with our minds; a world of ideas or 'forms'. He in turn was greatly influenced by another ancient Greek philosopher, Pythagoras, who thought that to understand the world truly one must look for the mathematical structures that lie behind appearances. Pythagoras sought to uncover these structures and, among other things, revealed how music and harmony have a mathematical basis.

2 Your reflection in the mirror. Is your reflection behind the mirror, in the mirror, in your mind or nowhere? Is your reflection a part of the physical world? The mirror seems to be a window into another world but one that doesn't exist in real physical space. Is this world just an illusion in the mind?

3 Colours, e.g. red. Some will argue that the word 'red' refers to the way humans see a particular wavelength of light when it hits their retinas. Others see it as the name for the particular wavelength itself. It could also be the name for a physical object's propensity to bounce back visible light at a particular frequency. So red could be in the head, in the air or on the tomato. The same is true of the colour green and trees (see Figure 7.1).

■ Figure 7.1 *Where is the green of the tree?*

The word 'green' appears to have various meanings. It can refer to something in the leaves themselves: the objective property that the naïve realist says they have. It can refer to the power the leaves have to absorb and emit various wavelengths of light. It can refer to the specific wavelength itself that leaves typically emit. Or it can refer to the experience of the colour as it appears to us in our minds.

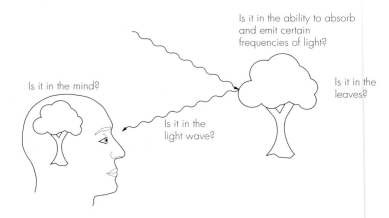

Is it in the ability to absorb and emit certain frequencies of light?

Is it in the mind?

Is it in the leaves?

Is it in the light wave?

4 Smell. This is discussed on page 527.

5 Morality. Are good and evil objectively real? This is a key question in moral philosophy. Those who think that morality exists independently of human minds, perhaps as a creation of God or as an objective moral law, are ethical realists. Those who think that morality is in some sense a product of human minds are ethical anti-realists.

6 Electrons. Some take the view that electrons and other such entities that cannot be directly observed are just a useful story we invent to make sense of experimental data. Others believe that such objects do exist and exist as we conceive them.

7 Scientific laws. These are formulated in the minds of humans, but to be successful they must be able to explain and predict aspects of the world. This raises the question of how real they are and whether there is something out there to which the law could correspond. Some anti-realists take the view that the laws do not correspond to anything and cannot really be said to be true or false – they are merely instrumental in helping humans manipulate the world. A realist may take the view that scientific laws, as they slowly evolve, edge ever closer to the truth – that is, to matching the laws of the universe.

8 Ghosts. We leave this for you to decide.

9 Matter. Some argue that the only thing of which we are ever aware are ideas or sensations in our minds and that matter is just a convenient way of talking about these sensations. Most people believe that there is a material universe that we perceive all around us.

10 Beauty. Some may argue that the concept of beauty – whether in the setting of the sun or the song of the nightingale – is so universal that there must be an external standard of beauty to which these things refer. Others think that beauty is subjective – or at most culturally ingrained – and is thus solely in the eye of the beholder.

Realist theories of perception

■ Naïve (or direct) realism

The DIRECT REALIST, or common-sense theory of perception is the kind of view people tend to have before they have thought much about the issues. It is, in other words, the position of common sense. For this reason it is often, and rather unfairly, termed NAÏVE REALISM, despite the fact that it can be supported by sophisticated philosophical arguments. So let's outline its main theses.

Naïve realism claims that the world is pretty much as it appears to our senses. All objects are composed of matter; they occupy space, and have properties such as size, shape, texture, smell, taste and colour. These properties are perceived directly. In other words, when we look at and touch things we see and feel those things themselves and so perceive them as they really are. Objects continue to observe the laws of physics and retain their properties whether or not there is anyone present to observe them doing so. So, when we leave the room the objects in it remain and retain all the properties we perceive them to have.

■ **Figure 7.2 Naïve realism**

The common-sense view of perception says that we see, hear and smell things directly as they are. Our sense organs detect properties of objects which exist out there in the world, and all of us perceive the same objects with the same properties.

Someone's sense organs

Physical object

Someone else's sense organs

ACTIVITY Question: If a tree falls in a forest and no sentient beings are there to hear it, then does it make a noise?
a) What do you personally think?
b) What would a naïve realist say?

The naïve realist would say that the tree does make a noise. The world is exactly how is appears to be and it appears to us that trees make a noise when they fall down. If trees make a noise when they fall down then they will make a noise whether there is anyone or anything there to hear them or not.

In sum, the naïve realist is saying that we perceive objects with certain properties because they are there and have those properties, and we know they are there and have the properties they do because we perceive them.

■ Criticisms of naïve realism

Most philosophers have felt that naïve realism cannot be maintained. David Hume, for example, claimed that once one had engaged in 'the slightest philosophy'[2] one would be forced to give it up.

Criticism 1: What about perspective?

To take one immediate problem, consider perspective. As objects move away from us they appear much smaller. Likewise the gap between railway lines seems to narrow as we gaze into the distance. However, we know that objects do not actually get smaller as they get further away and we know, by travelling beside a track, that the gap between the lines remains the same. So straight away we can conclude that the world cannot be exactly as it appears to us, for it appears that objects get smaller when, in fact, they do not. To avoid having to construct some strange theory about how objects actually shrink as they move further away, it seems that the out-and-out realist must concede defeat. Objects cannot be exactly as we perceive them to be. It can be argued that our minds do take account of this; we are somehow automatically aware that we view the world from a particular angle or from a particular distance and that we are not fooled as to the *real* size or shapes of objects. However this would be to admit some form of defeat, it would be to acknowledge that the *real* world is different from the world as it *appears* and so the world cannot be *exactly* as it appears.

Criticism2: What is the real colour of objects?

There are further and related difficulties that direct realism faces, many of which were highlighted by the great British empiricist philosopher, George Berkeley (1685–1753) in one of his *Three Dialogues between Hylas and Philonous* (1713). The character of Philonous, Berkeley's spokesman, asks Hylas to consider what the colour of some distant clouds is.

Philonous: *Let me know, whether the same colours which we see, exist in external bodies, or some other.*
Hylas: *The very same.*
Philonous: *What! Are then the beautiful red and purple we see on yonder clouds, really in them? Or do you imagine they have in themselves any other form than that of a dark mist or vapour?*
Hylas: *I must own, Philonous, those colours are not really in the clouds as they seem to be at this distance. They are only apparent colours.*
Philonous: *Apparent call you them? How shall we distinguish these apparent colours from real?*

Hylas:	*Very easily. Those are to be thought apparent which, appearing only at a distance, vanish upon a nearer approach.*
Philonous:	*And those I suppose are to be thought real which are discovered by the most near and exact survey.*
Hylas:	*Right.*
Philonous:	*Is the nearest and exactest survey made by the help of a microscope, or by the naked eye?*
Hylas:	*By a microscope doubtless.*
Philonous:	*But a microscope often discovers colours in an object different from those perceived by the unassisted sight. And in case we had microscopes magnifying to any assigned degree; it is certain, that no object whatsoever viewed through them, would appear in the same colour which it exhibits to the naked eye.*
Hylas:	*And what will you conclude from all this? You cannot argue that there are really and naturally no colours on objects; because by artificial managements they may be altered, or made to vanish.*
Philonous:	*I think it may evidently be concluded from your own concessions, that all the colours we see with our naked eyes, are only apparent as those on the clouds, since they vanish upon a more close and accurate inspection, which is afforded us by a microscope.[3]*

Since the clouds may appear red from a distance, and any number of colours from different perspectives, according to Berkeley it makes no sense to suppose that they have any *real* colour. This goes just as well for any objects. If we look closely at a flower through a microscope its colour will be different from how it looks with the naked eye. So we are forced to say that the colour is merely an effect made upon us by physical things, and not something in the objects themselves. In other words, colour is an appearance to us, not something objectively real.

■ **Figure 7.3**
Berkeley's example of observing clouds

The clouds appear different colours to different observers. But who is right? No one has any privileged perspective, and so no one can observe the true colour. Therefore colour is an appearance to observers, and not something real.

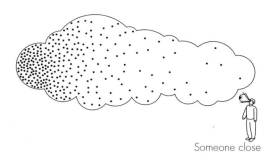

Someone close

Someone far off

You might be tempted to claim that the real colour is the colour as seen by a person standing near the object. But even this attempt to shore up naïve realism fails as the colour of the object changes throughout the day, from the bright light of noon to the soft light of the evening. Do we really believe that something in the object actually changes as the light does? And again what is the real colour of the object?

Another of Berkeley's examples is that of putting a hot hand and a cold hand into the same bucket of lukewarm water. The water then feels cold to one hand and hot to the other. But clearly the same small area of water cannot really be both hot and cold at the same time. This would be a contradiction. So the conclusion follows that it must merely appear to be hot and cold. Heat and cold, therefore, are not real properties of objects but effects such objects have on observers like us.[4]

Criticism 3: Circular justification

Another problem with naïve realism is that the justification for the theory appears circular. To see this consider how the sceptical philosopher might question the naïve realist:

Sceptic:	*So how do we know what the world around us is really like? Couldn't it be very different from the way it seems to us?*
Naïve realist:	*Don't be silly. Our senses reveal the world directly to us. They enable us to perceive the world with all its properties. So what you perceive is what there is.*
Sceptic:	*But how can you be sure that we perceive it as it really is? It could be that the senses distort the world and that objects don't really have the properties they seem to.*
Naïve realist:	*But we can tell that objects have various properties, colours, smells, tastes and so on, because we can perceive them. If they weren't there we wouldn't be able to see them, would we? So we perceive what we perceive because it is there, and so obviously we see things as they really are.*

The problem here is that the naïve realist's claim that we know what physical objects are like by perceiving them relies on the claim that we perceive things as they are. However, the claim that we perceive things as they are presupposes that we know what they are like. So the naïve realist is arguing in a circle.

In short, that justification goes:

> Question. *How do you know that the world is as it appears to be?*
> Answer. *Because it appears to be that way.*

Circular arguments are not convincing as they fail to give any independent justification by which we might believe in the conclusion. Consider the following exchange:

The Bible is true because it is the word of God
How do you know it is the word of God?
Because it says so in the Bible.

The truth of the Bible is being established by the content of the Bible itself. If the Bible is not true then this argument fails. Ideally you would have some independent evidence for the truth of the Bible, or for the claim that it is the word of God.

Likewise with the naïve realist. If the world is not how it appears, then appealing to its appearance to justify your belief that it is that way does not hold much force. An obvious response to this complaint is for the naïve realist to say that we can know that what we are perceiving really is there by appealing to the testimony of other people. If everyone perceives the world in the same way as me then I have some other evidence that the world is exactly how it appears.

So if I see a banana as yellow, and you see it as yellow, then one would think that it must be yellow. However, the sceptic may not be impressed by such a line of defence. The difficulty is that the perception of the second observer is plagued by the same difficulty as mine. If the human perceptual system distorts reality, then it will distort it in the same way for all humans. The fact that we both see a banana as yellow tells us about the way we see bananas, rather than the way bananas are. Using another human doesn't get round the question of whether humans perceive things as they are.

Recall the film *The Matrix*. This is premised on the idea that everyone is connected to a vast super-computer that feeds data directly to the human brain in such a way that the humans consider what is portrayed to be reality. In many ways this idea is similar to that presented by Descartes' demon (page 304), although the whole of humanity is being deceived this time, not just one person. For those in the 'matrix' there is a big difference between reality and what appears to them to be real. This difference arises because their perceptions are not caused by what they think is reality but by a machine. For the people in the matrix, appealing to fellow matrix 'dwellers' to confirm that what they see is real is futile, for they too are being deceived. Likewise, without needing to resort to the idea of a deceptive matrix, if somehow the human experience in general doesn't mirror reality exactly, for example if colours aren't real, then the testimony of others will not help us one jot.

Criticism 4: We perceive the world differently
The testimony of others can help to establish that, on any one occasion, you are not having a dream or hallucination since other people would be able to correct you. In this sense the

testimony of others can help to confirm that you are not alone in having a particular perception. However, it will not alert us to any problems that might affect us all in matching perceptions to reality. In fact the testimony of others is another problem for the naïve realist.

We know that some people perceive the world differently, perhaps because of colour-blindness, so the world cannot be exactly how it appears to everyone. We ourselves also perceive the world differently at different times. A red object may change in tone as the light changes; an object may appear smaller than it really is if observed at a distance. If the naïve realist concedes that the 'real' colour or size is different from how it appears, she will have to drop her claim always to perceive things directly as they are.

Criticism 5: Hallucinations

On some occasions we are subject to illusions and hallucinations. Such deceptive perceptions show not just that we don't always see things as they truly are but, worse, that we can even seem to see things that are not there. The problem for the naïve realist is that if the world is exactly as it appears then hallucinations and illusion must, contrary to popular belief, actually be a part of the world. The naïve realist cannot seem to distinguish between perceiving something which is there and seeming to perceive something which in reality is not there, as they are not prepared to admit that reality might in any way be different from the appearance of reality.

Criticism 6: Lag in time

You see lightening and a few seconds later hear the thunder. In the distance you see someone hit a golf ball and a few seconds later hear the thwack. For the naïve realist this represents another problem, as if the world is exactly as it appears then there must in fact be a delay from the time of the striking of the ball to the sound of the ball. But we all know there isn't really one, or if there is one it is negligible for the person hitting the ball.

Criticism 7: The homunculus and the brain

Perhaps the most naïve version of naïve realism is to think that perception involves looking out of our eyes and simply seeing the world as it is. Our eyes are like clear windows and we simply peer out at the world which is full of colours, shapes and so on. There is a certainly a sense in which this is what perceiving the external world *feels like*. However this account will not do. Not only for all the reasons outlined above, but for two more reasons:

a) *The problem of the homunculus.* If our eyes are like windows and we peer out of them, then who is doing the peering? Presumably someone that also has eyes. One silly idea is to posit a small person (known as a homunculus) that lives in your head and does the peering out through your eyes. However, such an explanation, as well as being silly, is also misconceived as presumably the homunculus has eyes too, so there must be someone inside him also peering out. And what about this second homunculus, surely he has eyes too? . . . And so on. The 'eyes as windows which we peer through' account of visual perception simply won't do – it leads to an infinite regress.

b) *The problem of brain processing.* We know from basic science that the idea of peering out is wrong. Light bounces off objects and enters your eyes. When you put your hand in front of your eyes this does not stop you peering *out* at the world, rather it stops the light from entering *in*. Now if this is the case then we may have to acknowledge that the information/data that reaches our eyes is somehow processed by the brain and then perceived. This processing may well alter the information that you receive. Indeed it can be easily shown that that the brain sometimes adds information.

ACTIVITY   There is a 'blind spot' in your vision. This is caused by an area on the retina without light receptors where the optic nerve takes the information to the brain. To find your blind spot, follow these instructions.

In the margin on page 524 we have printed a circle and a square. In a moment:

- Tip the book on its side so that the square is on the right of the paper and the circle on the left.
- Close your right eye.
- Hold the book at arm's length and focus on the square.
- Move the book slowly toward you.
- At some point the circle will 'disappear' as the light bouncing off it falls on your blind spot.

So you can see that you have a blind spot. However, when you are walking around with only one eye open there is not a constant gap in your visual field and this is because the brain fills in this gap for you. The brain adds missing information from your eyes in other ways too so that what is perceived is a less patchy view of the world. Now if we accept that the brain is processing information before you perceive it then it would appear that there must be at least two elements involved in perception: 1) the world as it is and 2) the world as it appears to the perceiver after the processing of the brain. It is precisely this account of perception that we will explore in the next section.

■ Primary and secondary qualities

Many of the arguments against naïve realism hinge on the idea that some of the properties we perceive, such as colours, tastes and smells, are not actually properties of the objects themselves. However, objects must have some properties that are real otherwise they wouldn't exist. Perhaps objects indeed possess certain properties such as size and shape but other properties such as colour and taste are more subjective in that they rely on a mind being present.

ACTIVITY

Imagine that an intelligent alien lands on Earth. The alien has a very different set of senses to the ones we use to navigate reality. He has a sonic sense like a bat, and an electric sense like a dolphin. He has no colour vision and can only see in black and white. When he touches objects his nerves and brain translate the touches into noises that he hears in his mind. The alien is about to examine some objects from Earth and see what properties the objects have.

What would the alien write down as the real properties of the following objects?

1 A one pound coin

2 A cup of tea

3 A piece of sand paper

Consider the property of value. Does a one pound coin actually have that property? Could an alien place the coin under the microscope and discern that it has the property of value? 'No' is the obvious answer. The alien would be able to tell its size, the metals from which it is composed and its density but would not be able to measure its value. Value does not actually inhere in the object itself but is caused by the role the object plays in a human society. So while we talk of the coin having a value, its value is not strictly a real property of the coin at all.

The same can be said for other supposed properties of the coin. Consider its colour. Remember the alien only perceives light in black and white. The alien would measure the pound coin, would know all of its physical properties and would know how it absorbs and emits light waves. But the alien would not know that humans perceive this coin as golden-coloured as it would not know how humans perceive the various wavelengths of light, nor would the alien even have the concept of gold-coloured. So even if the alien produced a complete physical description of the coin it would not include the colour of the coin, only the wavelength of light the coin bounces back. Yet the alien's description would not be lacking in any important way, so it seems we must conclude that the coin does not have the property of being coloured in the same way that it has other properties such as shape and density.

Now consider smell. Current science suggests that smell is actually caused by the shapes of molecules. On the inside of our noses are thousands of receptors of different shapes and sizes. When we inhale, millions of molecules whizz up through our noses and, if they are the right shape and size, some of these molecules will lodge briefly in these receptors. If enough molecules of the same type do this then we perceive a smell. So the smell really represents the shape of a molecule. Molecules are not coated with a smelly property that we somehow perceive. They merely have a shape which, in humans, causes the subjective experience of a smell.

Thus it would seem that objects physically possess some properties, whereas other properties are related to the minds experiencing them. The technical terms for the real properties of objects and the somehow less 'real' properties are PRIMARY AND SECONDARY QUALITIES respectively.

ACTIVITY Here are some possible properties of things. Which of these properties do you think are primary – properties that actually belong to objects? Which are secondary – in some sense reliant on humans or minds?

Possible properties of things	Primary: property of object	Secondary: combination of object and mind
1 Mass		
2 Fun		
3 Yellow		
4 Bitterness		
5 10 metres wide		
6 Density		
7 Smell		
8 Motion		
9 Roughness		
10 Circular		
11 Vibration		
12 Dangerous		
13 Loud		
14 Sweet-smelling		
15 Importance		

Primary and secondary qualities are not always defined or divided up in precisely the same way by philosophers. But a traditional division is set out in the table below. Did you agree? How would you place these various qualities?

Primary qualities, i.e. real, physical qualities	Secondary qualities, i.e. the 'powers' of the object that produce experiences in humans (and other animals)	Other associated properties, often a social concept but in part a result of the primary or secondary qualities
• Position (i.e. where the object is) • Number (i.e. how many there are) • Shape • Size (i.e. how big it is) • Motion (i.e. how fast it is moving)	• Colour • Heat and cold • Smell • Sound • Taste	• Beauty • Value • Addictive • Important • Disposable

People often find it difficult to recall which are the primary and which the secondary qualities. One way to think about the difference and so remember the terminology is to regard the primary qualities as those that are in objects from the *beginning* or *primarily*, that is before anyone comes along to perceive them. By contrast, the secondary qualities are those which appear only *secondarily*, when minds arrive on the scene to perceive things. In a world without perceivers there would be lots of objects with primary qualities reacting to each other; they would collide, melt, dissolve and so forth. The objects in this world can also be said to have secondary qualities as they would still have the potential to produce subjective experiences in perceivers should any appear. But without the perceivers there would be no experiences of the secondary qualities and no sensations of colour, sound or smell.

Another way of conceiving the difference between primary and secondary qualities is to consider how physical objects behave. Physical objects act and interact with one another purely on the basis of their primary qualities. The outcome of a collision between two moving objects, say billiard balls, depends on their mass, direction of movement, speed, and how they are held together by the atoms that compose them. In other words, the outcome depends entirely on the primary qualities of the objects involved. Secondary qualities have nothing to do with how objects behave. Secondary qualities are just the powers of an object to produce experiences in perceivers. This cannot have an effect on how physical objects interact with each other.

Also, note that secondary qualities ultimately boil down to primary qualities. Consider the example of smell given above. A smell is a secondary quality – a power of a molecule to produce a subjective experience in a perceiver. However, a molecule has this power in virtue of the organisation of its parts and this organisation is a matter of the primary qualities (shape, size and so on) alone. So although objects can be said to have secondary qualities, in terms of physics alone they have only primary qualities. These primary qualities have the potential to cause specific experiences in humans, and it is this potential we term a secondary quality. Thus it can be said that a secondary quality is simply the potential of a primary quality to produce an experience in a perceiver.

There are other considerations which have led philosophers to draw the primary/secondary quality distinction.

1 All the primary qualities lend themselves readily to mathematical or geometric description. They are readily *measurable*. The positions of any objects relative to any others can be precisely described, as can their number, shape, speed and so forth. So I can say that one object is moving three times as fast as another, that it is twice as big and so on. And I can meaningfully say that a hexagon has twice the number of sides as a triangle. However, subjectively experienced smells, colours and so on just don't behave like this. Cheese and onion flavour could never be twice salt and vinegar or any other flavour. I can't subtract the smell of lavender from that of thyme. I can't weigh the taste of coffee, or calculate the inertia of the smell of bacon. We can't add, subtract, divide or multiply tastes, flavours, colours, touches or smells in the same way that we can sizes, shapes, speeds, masses and quantities. So it seems that secondary qualities are less amenable to being represented mathematically.

If you have studied Descartes' *Meditations* you will notice that he makes much of this way of thinking about the physical world in drawing his own primary/secondary quality distinction in *Meditation 6*. However, for him, only those qualities that can be represented geometrically are real and this leads him to exclude weight and hardness which have no shape, position or size. Locke draws the distinction slightly differently and includes these two in the list of primary qualities.[5]

2 The discoveries of the natural sciences may also lead us to suppose that the world cannot be precisely as it appears to be. For example, physics tells us that light is a form of electromagnetic radiation and that what we perceive as different colours are in reality simply light waves of different lengths. Light in itself, in other words, is not coloured. In reality it possesses only the primary qualities of having a certain magnitude of wavelength, of travelling at a particular speed, and so on. Similarly, heat in objects cannot properly be said to be hot or cold. Rather our experience of hot and cold is produced by our coming into contact with physical objects with differing mean kinetic energy levels among their component atoms and molecules. The sounds we experience are also not things with independent existences. Rather they are produced in us by compression waves of air impacting on our eardrums.

In general the approach of science is to try to establish an objective view of the world. Our own subjective viewpoints can only access the world as it appears to us. Science, however, tries to gain a view of the world that is not based on any particular perspective. It tries to see the world from a vantage point which the philosopher Thomas Nagel calls 'the view from nowhere'.[6] In doing so we should expect the view of the world presented by science *not* to include those elements that exist only in the human mind or that are caused in the mind by objects, as these are part of the subjective experience of the world and not part of the objective world. This indeed seems to be the case. Or rather we should say that science conforms to the primary/secondary quality distinction and only ascribes primary properties to objects.

3 Some philosophers have argued that certain properties are essential to objects while others are not. They have then used this distinction to argue that the essential ones must be primary, while the inessential ones are secondary. There are different ways of distinguishing the essential from the inessential properties of an object. One method involves simply working out which ones we can and cannot conceive of an object's lacking. Inessential properties are those that you can imagine an object without, while it remains the object in question. Essential properties are those you cannot imagine the thing without, while it remains the same thing.

To illustrate this point, consider the following thought experiment about a bachelor. Can you imagine a bachelor who is hungry? Would he still be a bachelor if he were bald? Clearly yes. So being well fed and having a full head of hair are not essential properties of a bachelor. However, would a man still be a bachelor if he got married? Clearly not. You can't be a married bachelor. Such a thing is inconceivable. Would he still be a bachelor if he had a sex change? No. You can't be a bachelor unless you are male. So being unmarried and being male are essential properties of being a bachelor.[7]

Now let's apply this same method to physical objects and their properties. Think of an object, say an apple. If you imagine it is making no sound (which is not difficult to do) then you are still thinking of an object (a silent apple). So making a noise cannot be an essential property of an object like an apple. Similarly, if you suppose it to have no odour, then you are still thinking of an object. Next subtract its flavour. Still you are thinking of an object, albeit not a very appetising one. You may say that it is no longer an apple, but certainly it is still an object of some sort. But now let's go further and imagine it without any colour. Again, it is plausible to argue that you are still thinking of an object, only now it is invisible. Perhaps it has been 'cloaked' by some alien technology that bends the light waves around its surface so that our eyes cannot detect it. So here we have subtracted sound, odour, flavour and colour but we are still thinking of an object. This suggests that these qualities are inessential and so that it is possible for an object to exist without them. Many objects would appear to fall into this category such as certain gases (at least when motionless), bacteria, and perhaps ghosts.

But let us return to our apple and imagine it devoid of any shape, size, position or motion, either still or moving. Here, it seems our imagination fails us. An object cannot lack these properties and remain an object. An object cannot be neither moving nor still. It cannot be completely without shape. It must have a particular size and occupy a specific position in space. It would seem, then, that these properties are not properties an object could lack in reality. If they are essential to the object they cannot be properties that we merely perceive in it, but which aren't really there. It follows that they must be primary qualities. At the same time, those qualities that we can imagine an object doing without must be inessential, and so plausibly they exist only through their relations with perceiving beings like ourselves. (Does this example convince you? We will return to it later.)

So there are many reasons to suggest that we should hold some sort of primary/secondary quality distinction, and it appears we must make a distinction between how the world appears to us and how it really is. But if the world is not exactly as it appears, then we can no longer hold onto a naïve realist position. We must therefore look to another theory to explain what is going on when we perceive the world.

Representative realism

Having done the 'slightest philosophy' (as Hume said earlier) it seems we can no longer hold on to the idea that we perceive things directly as they are. Having recognised a distinction between appearance and reality, the natural next step is towards a REPRESENTATIVE REALIST theory of perception (or INDIRECT REALISM). The representative realist agrees with the naïve realist that the world consists of material objects which occupy a public space and that these material objects possess certain independently existing properties. This commitment to the real existence of matter with real properties is what makes them both realists. However, the representative realist disagrees with her naïve realist counterpart over whether we perceive the properties of matter directly and as they are. She distinguishes our sensations (sometimes called SENSE IMPRESSIONS or SENSE DATA) from the objects perceived. In other words, the claim is that there is, on the one hand, a mental component – namely the way the object appears to the observer – and, on the other, the object as it is in reality. For the representative realist, sensations are a REPRESENTATION or image of the world. It's as if we had pictures in our minds which represent to us the real world outside of our minds.

■ **Figure 7.4 Representative realism**

Representative realism distinguishes our sensations from the thing perceived. The physical object causes a sensation in us which is a representation of the real thing. So we now have two worlds: the world as it is in itself, and a picture of the world as it appears to our minds. But how accurate is our representation of the world? According to representative realism, some aspects of our sensations are accurate while others are not. So, our representation of the so-called primary qualities of size, shape, position, and motion represent accurately what is out there. Physical objects really have these properties. But our experiences of colour, sound, smell, taste and so on, do not. These properties do not exist in the objects themselves in the same way that primary qualities do. Rather such sensations are imperfect representations produced in us by the secondary qualities of objects. So our different experiences of smells represent different shapes of molecules, for example.

Perceived object

Real object

By using this distinction the representative realist hopes to explain sense deception. Deception occurs when the sense impressions do not match up with the object. When the image I have in my mind, for whatever reason, does not accurately correspond to the way things are in the world, I am subject to some sort of illusion. It can also explain how hallucinations are possible. They occur when a sensation occurs in the mind but there is nothing corresponding to it in the world.

The representative realist also explains the difference between primary and secondary qualities. Some of those properties that we perceive to be in objects really are there, and some are not. So the former are accurate reflections of the way the world is in reality and should form the basis for our knowledge of the world, while the latter are not real and, to some extent, are illusions.

This is not to say they aren't useful illusions. Matter might not be coloured in the sense that my experience of red is out there on the surfaces of things. But an apple does have certain properties that we succeed in picking out by seeing it as red, and it is often useful to be able to recognise these properties. For example, the ability to see red helps up pick out ripe fruits from a leafy background. Similarly food stuffs might not be objectively bitter, but foods that taste bitter may often be poisonous to us.

Also, calling our experience of secondary qualities an illusion is not to class them as completely fictional and unrelated to the world. Indeed they are related to objects in the world because they are caused by them. As Locke explains, the primary qualities are 'utterly inseparable from . . . body' while secondary qualities are 'nothing in objects themselves, but powers to produce various sensations in us'.[8] So our sensations of colour, sound, smell and so on are not completely misleading, since they do map onto real differences in the objects but at a scale too small for us to detect. So, for example, colour, a sensation in the mind, represents certain secondary qualities the surface of an object has, namely its ability to absorb, emit and reflect light. In other words, the wavelengths of light get 'translated' or interpreted by us into our experience of colour. Similarly, smell represents the shape of a molecule: our nose and brain somehow translate the molecule into the smell. So the molecule itself isn't smelly. This is just an effect the molecule makes on us. In this way, the real world of primary qualities is represented to us as a world of colour, smells, tastes and so on.

In the paragraph above we used the idea of our sensations 'mapping' onto the real world, and this is another useful way of understanding representative realism. A geographical map represents a physical area in the world. Some elements in the map such as contour lines and the symbol for a church do not resemble the world exactly but represent the world in such a way that we are able to use the map to navigate in the world. Changes in the terrain are represented by changes in the map so the symbols in the map are not illusions as they represent reality. However, they are illusory in as much as they do not really resemble the objects they represent.

One final way to understand what the representative realist is saying is to imagine yourself reduced to the size of a molecule of air with some special ship in which to get around the world. Imagine observing what happens when a person smells a smell, hears a sound or sees a colour. Nothing in what you observe would be smelly, noisy or colourful. The molecules producing the smell wouldn't themselves smell, nor would the compression waves of air you observe have any sound. The wavelengths of light entering someone's eyes would have a particular length, but no colour; and the surfaces of the things that reflect these wavelengths would also have no colour. (How precisely one would observe the real world if so reduced in size is a difficulty we will ignore.) So, in this account, the real world is odourless, colourless and silent: a world describable only in the language of matter in motion. However, you would be able to see how the arrangements of the normally invisible parts which compose physical objects produce certain reactions in human sense organs. The powers to produce these reactions are the secondary qualities.

Representative realism is the preferred view of most modern philosophers since Descartes, including Descartes himself and Locke. Locke distinguished between internal, private sensations (sense impressions) and external, publicly observable physical objects. We can only come to know about the latter through observation of the former, and so long as we know when and which aspects of our sense impressions are accurate representations of the external world we can use our senses to build up an accurate picture of it. Representative realism also fits in very well with the current scientific view of the world. As we saw above, scientists these days tell us that colours, smells, sounds and so forth don't exist in the world as it is in itself. What really exists are light waves, chemicals and compression waves of air, all of which can be described in geometric and mathematical terms.

The strength of representative realism as a theory is its ability to explain all the criticisms of naïve realism; changes in perspective, the shifting colours of objects, hallucinations, the colourless world of the scientist, time lags and so on. That is not to say it is without criticisms of its own as we will explore below.

Finally, let us return to the question on page 519.

ACTIVITY   Question: If a tree falls in a forest with no one there to hear it, then does it make a noise?
a) Having done a little philosophy, what do you now believe?
b) What would a representative realist say?

According to a representative realist the answer to the question is yes and no! Yes, in as much as the noise is a secondary quality, i.e. a power to produce an experience in humans. But no, in the sense that if there were no perceivers then there would be no subjective experience of a noise, but only compression waves of air. The same must also go for the colours, smells and tastes of the tree.

Criticisms of representative realism

However, as we might have expected, difficulties arise. Representative realism has set up a sort of two-world view to explain perception. There is world number one – the world as it really is. Here, objects with primary qualities happily obey the laws of physics in their colourless, soundless, tasteless and odour-free world. It is this world, in conjunction with our human brains that causes us to perceive world number two – the colourful, smelly, tasty world we experience around us. Of course, these two worlds are not really separate: world number two, the world we perceive, is simply a representation of world number one, the world as it is.

Criticism 1: How do we really know what the real world is like?
Once this two-world account of perception has been established, serious philosophical problems arise. One crucial difficulty concerns how we are to tell when our senses are and are not deceiving us.

Unlike naïve realism representative realism is able to account for the fact that on any one particular occasion our senses may be deceiving us. Because the theory does not claim the world is exactly as it appears then it is comfortable with the idea that sometimes our mind may play tricks on us or that optical illusions, such as the narrowing of railway lines, do not match reality. As the theory posits two elements – the world and sense impressions (also known as sense data) – it can provide an account of what hallucinations are. They occur when the sense impressions fail to represent the world accurately. Individual or 'local' hallucinations can be corrected by the testimony of others, who can point out that the pink elephant you are seeing floating in the sky is not actually there.

However there is the much tougher issue of general or widespread misrepresentations. Indeed if, as the name of the theory suggests, what we perceive is a kind of *representation* of the world, how do we know how accurate that representation is? In other words, how can we be sure that the human perception of the world (world two) in any way resembles the world as it is (world one)? Critics of representative realism would claim that we are only ever aware of secondary qualities; we never perceive primary qualities directly. Everything we perceive must come from our five senses and these produce all the colours, sounds, tastes, smells and touches associated with secondary qualities. So we have to infer the existence of an independent object with primary qualities purely from our awareness of our sense impressions. But if the existence of physical objects is just inferred from our sensations, how can we be sure they are accurate in their representation? Without independent access we cannot place our sensations and the physical objects side by side in order to make a comparison. In other words, we can't get out of our own minds and adopt a God's-eye view, as it were, from which to observe both our sense impressions and the world. But without such a point of view we cannot establish when we are being deceived or how accurate our representations are.

Another way to see this point is to imagine that you were born and raised inside a cinema. Suppose that you spent all your days watching movies, but were never allowed to leave to visit the outside world. Living such a restricted life you would doubtless have dreams of escaping. You would wonder what it was like beyond the walls of your prison. But imagine what a distorted picture you would have of life outside the cinema. Given that all you had to go on would be the films you had seen you would doubtless fantasise about meeting the likes of Indiana Jones and Buzz Lightyear. Because you could never compare reality with the movies, you would be in no position to judge what was fact and what was fiction. But you are already in this position with regard to your sense experience. You can't escape the prison of your own mind to discover how accurate your sensations are.

A final way of making this point is to return to the analogy of the map above. Maps help us to find our way in the world precisely because we are able to compare both the map and the area that it represents and see how closely the one resembles the other. Some features of the map such as the spatial relationship of the symbols on the map closely

■ **Figure 7.5**
Representative realism faces a problem

To determine how accurate our perception of the world is, we would have to compare our representations of it in our minds with the world as it is in itself. But to do this we would need to get out of our own mind and adopt a 'God's-eye' point of view. This, of course, is impossible.

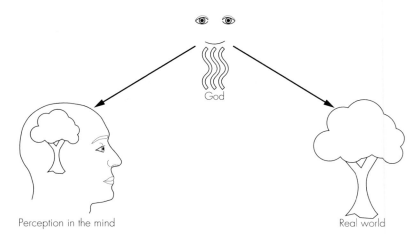

God

Perception in the mind

Real world

resemble the spatial relationship of the real objects in the world, only on a smaller scale. Other elements such as the contour lines do not really resemble the features – in this case the slopes. The representation here is more abstract. With maps we are able to find these things out because we can compare the map with reality. With perception, however, we are unable to do this. We only have access to the sense impressions (the map) and can never see the real world to see how closely it might resemble it.

Criticism 2: The veil of perception

In separating the world as it appears from the world as it really is, representative realism has made this latter world seemingly inaccessible to our senses. The two-world account of perception has created a gap between the world as it appears and the world as it really is, and this gap seems to be an insurmountable chasm. A *veil of perception* has dropped down between us and the world, meaning that we only ever have access to our representations and cannot peer beyond the veil to see the world as it really is (see Figure 7.6).

So it appears we cannot know whether the world we perceive is an accurate representation of the world as it really is. The real world could be radically different from the way it appears to us and, because we can't penetrate the veil, we will never be able to know what it is really like. One line of defence against this objection is that if the world we perceive did not, in important ways, match the world as it really is, then we would not survive. We would have been unable to hunt and catch animals, or find the nuts and berries needed to nourish and sustain ourselves, and would have died out long ago. We have survived, so our representation of the world must be fairly accurate. Our senses have evolved precisely to give us an accurate representation of the world as it is, so the relationship between the two worlds must be sound.

This defence may well satisfy some. It suggests that our representations are correlated systematically with the world and so seem to provide some assurance that they represent something real. However, it still doesn't tell us how accurate our perception is. It could well be that our senses are rigged up to help us survive in the world, but that in the process they distort it completely. There is no guarantee that the best way of ensuring a species' survival is for it to evolve an accurate perception of its environment. The way it is useful to perceive things need not be a good indication of the way things are.

But there are worse problems for this line of defence. Recall how in Chapter 4 the sceptic raised powerful doubts about the nature of the external world, claiming that our present sensations could be caused by something entirely different – a dream, a powerful demon, a virtual reality machine or by being a brain in a vat (see page 258). Now, even if these possibilities are far-fetched, the very fact that they are conceivable shows that we have no way of verifying that it is in fact the real world – world number one – we are perceiving. Such doubts will always be possible so long as there remains a gap between the world we perceive and the world as it is. If we could verify the accuracy of our sensations by comparing them with the actual physical objects themselves, then such scepticism could be refuted instantly. But there can be no way of doing this. So even if, as above, we try to infer the existence of a material world by the fact that we are alive, such an inference can always be called into question; for we would still be making such an inference if there were no such world.

So the problem remains: if we perceive the world only indirectly, as representative realism claims, then we can never be absolutely sure of what the world is really like, or even if it is really out there at all.

■ **Figure 7.6 The veil of perception and the trap of solipsism**

All we have direct access to are our own sensations. We cannot peer beyond the veil of perception to perceive the world as it really is. But if we can't penetrate the veil of perception, then not only can we not know what the world is really like, but we can never know that the real world exists at all. Perhaps something else entirely is causing our sensations (see Figure 4.9, page 275).

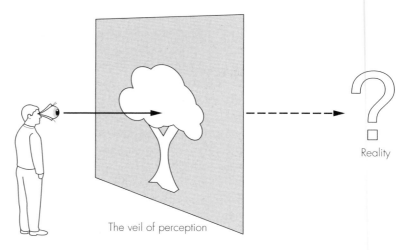

Reality

The veil of perception

Criticism 3: We cannot even talk about the real world

Some philosophers have gone further still in analysing the consequences of this gap between sensation and reality.[9] As we saw in Chapter 4, the philosopher Immanuel Kant argued that we can't know anything about the 'real' world (which he called the *noumenal* world). Our mind receives data from this world, which it then processes. What we perceive (which he termed the *phenomenal* world) has been processed by the mind. This post-processed world is all we have access to. All the words and concepts we learn during our lives are learned by dealing with the world as we perceive it: the world of colours, smells, tastes and textures. As such, our concepts are designed to match and apply to this world of sensation. If this is the case, then there is no reason at all why our concepts should apply to the noumenal world – the world as it really is. For example, earlier we said that real world is the *cause* of our sensations. However, can we really say this? After all, causation is a concept that (as far as we can know) applies only to the world of sense experience. It is only within our experience that we observe one event causing another, but we can't observe the real world causing the perceived world, nor can we suppose the real world exhibits causal relations at all. The same applies to space and time. All of our sensations appear to us in space and time, but we cannot know whether the real world behind the veil is spatio-temporal. We, of course, can't imagine what a world would be like that did not involve space, time or causality. But that is to be expected, since we can only understand and imagine the world of our experience. The real world lies totally beyond our comprehension. We shouldn't even call it a world at all. We should say nothing about it whatsoever.

Kant suggests that we should call the world we experience – the phenomenological world – the real world, as this is the world we inhabit and is the only world of which we can meaningfully speak.

Is there a physical world?

What if everything is an illusion and nothing exists? In that case, I definitely overpaid for my carpet.[10]

Woody Allen

We have seen the representative realist introduce a gap between the nature of our experiences and the nature of the physical world in order to account for the possibility of sense-deception and the apparent fact that not everything we perceive is real. But in the process it has become unclear how to justify our claims to know things about a physical world that is supposed to exist independently of our experience. Sceptical doubts have forced us to retreat behind the veil of perception. If direct knowledge of the physical world is impossible and we can find no good reason to suppose that the world exists at all, then belief in the external world begins to look like an irrational superstition, which any serious thinker must reject. This is the position of the *solipsist*. The solipsist has a rich interior life of her own sense experiences, but denies that anything exists other than such experiences. The universe of the solipsist is a purely mental universe of one.

Few, if any, philosophers have defended SOLIPSISM. This may be because any sincere solipsists would have no reason to write down their arguments since they would not believe there was anyone else around to read them. If I were ever to encounter someone defending solipsism I could be sure that they were mistaken since if I could understand their arguments then someone other than the solipsist (namely myself) must exist. But just because no one else could be correct in their solipsism doesn't refute it as a philosophical position. The possibility that no external world and no other minds exist remains a possibility for me, that is, for the subject of experience. If solipsism is true, then what you are reading wasn't written by someone else – it is nothing more than an aspect of your consciousness.

The quote from Woody Allen above highlights one apparent implication of solipsism – if your carpet doesn't exist then clearly whatever you paid for it was too much. The joke relies in part on the juxtaposition of philosophical concerns with more mundane worries (in any case, if nothing exists then you didn't pay anything for your non-existent carpet). However, philosophical doubt is not the same as genuine doubt and serves a different purpose, in this case to test theories and try to establish certainty.

ACTIVITY   Imagine you actually believe that you are the only being in existence and everything else is some kind of illusion.

1 Would you change your life?
2 What would you do?
3 Can you think of a specific action that you might do differently?
4 Would you still have a morality?
5 Is there a difference between genuine doubt and philosophical doubt?

Anti-realist theories of perception

How are we going to react to the possibility of solipsism? An important line of response to the representative realist's problem is to swallow the sceptical conclusion, accepting that there is no reality existing independently of our experience. Anti-realists hope to overcome the sceptical impasse by denying that there is any material world the existence of which we need to establish. The only reality is that of which we are *directly* aware, or what appears immediately to us; that is to say, sense data. Other than these apparent objects there is nothing left over, no EXTERNAL WORLD, for us to perceive indirectly. We will now look at two related anti-realist theories of perception – IDEALISM and PHENOMENALISM.

Idealism

Reality leaves a lot to the imagination.[11]

John Lennon

Idealism is not simply a theory of perception. It is also an *ontology* – that is, a theory of being or of what exists. Ontology is the branch of philosophy concerned with working out what kinds of things there are, or of categorising the main ways or types of being. Although the idea of forming a theory of 'being' sounds daunting, it is plausible to hold that all of us have some implicit ontology, even if in most cases it is not well formalised. To try to work out what your ontology is, work through the following steps.

ACTIVITY

1 The first step is to think of everything that exists. Begin writing down everything you can think of. For example, you may begin like this:

My pen, my headache, myself, my neighbour's chickens, chicken pox, Chicken Tikka Massala, China, chamber music, fairies, . . .

Now, obviously it is going to take too long to list literally everything, so to speed things along:

2 Try to lump similar types of thing together to produce different classes. Then make a list of the different classes you've created. For example, you may want to divide things into: physical objects, people, concepts, sensations, animals, countries, spirits, . . .

3 Once you've got what you think is an exhaustive list of the types of things there are, think about what each item on the list is ultimately made of, and write a list of the constituent ingredients. Keep reducing this list to the fewest basic ingredients. For example, you may find that ultimately:

all these things are made of physical matter, or spiritual matter

4 When you have reduced this list to a few core ingredients and can reduce it no further then you are well on the way to formalising your own ontology. This ontology tells you what everything is ultimately made of.

As various philosophers over the ages have completed something akin to the above, three major ontologies have emerged:

- *Materialism* is the view that everything in the world is made of matter. Dreams, countries, ideas, numbers, colours, and so on all boil down to matter in its various guises, interacting with other bits of matter.
- *Dualism* claims that the list of things that exist can ultimately be reduced to two classes: *matter*, which occupies physical space; and *spirit or mind*, which is of a fundamentally different nature. This is, perhaps, the prevalent view on the planet, since many people believe that we, as humans, are made of a combination of a material body and a spiritual mind. Dualism's origins extend back before recorded history but it was Descartes in the modern era who gave it its most forceful philosophical expression.
- *Idealism* is the view that what is real depends upon the mind, and in the philosophy of perception it amounts to the claim that the material world does not exist outside of the mind. According to the idealist Berkeley, all that exists are minds and their ideas, sensations and thoughts. We know we have a mind, we know we perceive various colours and shapes, and so on. But to suppose that there is a material world that causes these sensations is a leap of faith that we do not need to make. To be an idealist is to take an anti-realist stance regarding matter.

Berkeley's idealism

Bishop George Berkeley was born in Ireland in 1685 and died in Oxford in 1753. During his life he made important contributions in the fields of philosophy, mathematics and economics. In philosophy he is considered the second of the three great British empiricists (the first being the Englishman John Locke and the third the Scot David Hume). He is most famous for founding the philosophy of idealism although his last writings were on the medicinal benefits of tar-water!

Berkeley termed sense impressions (and the other contents of the mind) IDEAS and claimed that physical objects don't exist independently of the mind, but in reality are collections of such ideas. This position he termed *idealism*.[12] Berkeley advanced several arguments for this position. The first follows from the empiricist principle he shared with Locke, namely that all the contents of our minds must come from experience.[13] Concepts, Berkeley is saying, have their origin in experience of sense impressions or 'ideas'. This means that if we think we have a concept, but can't find anything in experience from which it could have come, then we don't really have the concept at all. For example, a blind person, the empiricist argues, cannot have the concept of the colour red, since they have not had any experience of red.

With this point in view, let's consider the concept of matter. Where could this concept have come from? What is its basis in experience? Well, according to the representative realist, matter is something that we cannot experience since it lies beyond the veil of perception. It is the cause of our experience, but not something we can actually experience directly. But, Berkeley argues, if we accept that we cannot experience matter, then it follows from the empiricist principle that we cannot have a concept of it. In other words, the concept 'material object' is empty of content, for there is no possible experience, no possible sensation, from which we could have acquired it. For this reason he claimed that the representative realist's talk about 'matter' was literally meaningless and that the idea of an unperceivable thing was a contradiction in terms. From the claim that an object cannot exist unperceived, Berkeley concluded that its being or existence consists solely in its being perceived, or as he put it in Latin in his famous slogan: *esse est percipi*, meaning 'to be (or to exist) is to be perceived'.[14]

It is important to recognise that Berkeley did not intend to deny the existence of what we ordinarily think of as physical objects. Rather he is denying that they have an existence independent of sensation. He denies the existence of what the representative realist terms 'matter': some mysterious stuff which it is impossible to perceive. So an object, on Berkeley's account, is no more and no less than a cluster of ideas or sense impressions. An apple is a certain smell, taste, colour, shape, position and size, somehow bundled together before the mind. This is not the same as saying that we imagine the apple. Perception is clearly different from imagination; after all you cannot choose what you are going to perceive next, no matter how hard you try. Perception is still the passive receiving of sense impressions.

On page 531 we suggested that one way of determining whether a quality was primary as opposed to a secondary was to see if we can conceive of the object without that quality. We gave the example of an apple and suggested that it could be imagined without its colour, smell, taste, feel and noise (secondary qualities) but not without its shape, size, position or motion (primary qualities). Did you find this argument convincing?

An idealist would claim that we only know of the apple via the five senses and if we take those away then we know nothing of the apple – indeed there is no apple as far as our possible knowledge is concerned. An apple that has no touch or colour and so on is not an apple. What remains after these secondary qualities have been mentally removed is just the idea of matter – a sort of empty vessel that can contain the secondary qualities we experience. Even Locke, one of the first philosophers to put forward an account of the primary/secondary quality distinction, admitted that the idea of matter, stripped of the secondary qualities, was hard to imagine. He called it something but admitted 'I know not what'. For the idealist there is no need to retain this extra, empty idea of matter that exists over and above the various sensations that we experience.

Let's now return to the question of the tree in the forest.

ACTIVITY Question: If a tree falls in a forest and no one is there to hear it, then does it make a noise?
a) What do you personally think now?
b) What would an idealist say?

Berkeley would claim that the tree makes no noise. Noises are ideas or sense impressions. They exist only in minds, and so if no mind is perceiving one, it does not exist. For similar reasons, there will be no colours, smells or tastes. However, Berkeley goes further and claims that there would be no actual tree falling at all unless someone experienced it. It's not just the noise which is perceived, but also the very event of the tree falling itself, consisting purely of the colours, the smells, the vibrations, and so on. The tree falling is no less something perceived than the noise we suppose it to make. We like to imagine that such a tree could still fall down unobserved, but when we do so we always do it from the point of view of an imaginary observer. To imagine the tree falling unobserved is implicitly to imagine its being observed. We are incapable of conceiving of the tree falling without at the same time conceiving the experience of the tree falling. For Berkeley this reinforces his point that to be is simply to be perceived.

■ Criticisms of idealism

Criticism 1: Hallucinations
An initial difficulty with idealism is that it seems unable to explain the distinction between perceptual error and *veridical*, i.e. truthful or accurate, perception. If everything we perceive is a kind of dream, as the idealist seems to be saying, then there would appear to be no difference between seeing something as it really is, and being mistaken; or between hallucinating and actually seeing something. But before we

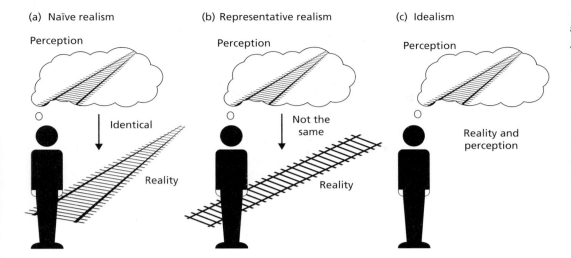

(a) Naïve realism

Perception

Identical

Reality

(b) Representative realism

Perception

Not the same

Reality

(c) Idealism

Perception

Reality and perception

■ **Figure 7.7 The problem of hallucinations**

For (a) the naïve realist and (c) the idealist, reality is identical with perception. This makes it conceptually difficult to account for perceptual errors such as hallucinations. The representative realist (b) posits a perception of reality and a reality distinct from the perception. This allows for a conceptual account of perceptual error – which occurs when the perception does not match reality.

get too carried away with this apparent flaw, note that perceptual error is somewhat of a problem for the representative realist too. The representative realist admits that we cannot distinguish hallucinations or errors from veridical (i.e. truthful) perception by appeal to the way the world really is in itself, since we have no access to such a world. This means that the distinction has to be made from within one's experience. Somehow or other we must make the distinction by examining the world of sense impressions or ideas, that is, by examining the contents of our own minds. In admitting this, the representative realist is obliged to give a similar solution to the idealist. However, at least the representative realist can make sense of the concept of perceptual error, as in their account there is a real physical world that our ideas represent with fluctuating degrees of accuracy – hence error. The idealist does not have a 'real world' that can feature in their account of perceptual error.

Given this, how can the idealist make sense of perceptual error? The basic answer concerns the regularity that we observe in our past experience. We regard as real or veridical those features of what we perceive which fit well with the regularities displayed in our past experience, while those features which do not fit in well may be regarded as aberrations or errors. So, for example, if I perceive a pink elephant floating across my field of vision, I have a choice: I can regard it either as a veridical experience or as a hallucination. But I cannot determine this by comparing my sensations with the way the world is (as both idealist and representative realist admit). So I have to ask myself how well this experience fits in with my past experiences. Is this the kind of experience which coheres well with the way my world has been up to now? Clearly not, and so this is not to be regarded as a real feature of the world.

Criticism 2: The continued existence of things

While the idealist seems to have explained the difference between illusions and veridical experiences, she still faces an obvious difficulty: what happens to objects when no one is perceiving them? The answer seems to be that they cease to exist. An apple, for example, no longer exists as soon as I hide it in a drawer, and yet, no sooner do I open the drawer once again than it miraculously returns to existence. Similarly, the apple has no smell or taste until someone smells and tastes it. Indeed, before someone bites into it it has no inside at all! But doesn't this seem patently absurd? You light a fire and it roars into life. You leave the room and thus it ceases to exist. You come back in the room and, lo and behold, it exists again. Idealism seems to imply there are 'gaps' in the fire's existence when it is not perceived. But if fires are so 'gappy' how come the fire has dwindled as if it had existed all the time? What can the idealist say to explain this? Consider also the tree which falls unobserved in the forest. If we saw it standing one day, and on the ground the next, how did it get there? How do we explain this if there has been no process, no unobserved falling-over that brought the tree to the ground? Finally consider the blind spot experiment on page 525. The idealist must claim that the spot comes in and out of existence as the book is moved. There can be no independent spot still there when the book is in a certain position, which realists would call the blind spot.

It seems that the world inhabited by the idealist is very different from the one to which we are used. Physical things have no hidden sides, no interiors and no secret aspects. They disappear and reappear without explanation, and there are no unobserved processes going on to explain the changes they undergo in the interim.

Criticism 3: Regularity of the universe

A related difficulty is that idealism appears not to be able to give any explanation of why there is such regularity and predictability in our experience, nor where our ideas come from. Why, for example, do I expect to see the apple once again on reopening the drawer? Why can I be pretty sure of how this apple will taste? Indeed why do I see and hear things at all? The realist, of whatever stripe, claims to have a good explanation of why we have the sense impressions we do and why they are so regular and predictable. There exist material objects which impact upon our sense organs and cause us to see, hear or taste them. Matter retains certain properties when we are not perceiving it, so when we do come to perceive it we can expect it to produce the same sensations in us. It is because of the independent existence of matter that our experience hangs together as it does. Idealism appears to have no parallel explanation, and the whole world of ideas we inhabit appears nothing short of miraculous.

■ Berkeley's defence

In response to the complaint that idealism cannot explain the regularity of our experience, Berkeley would simply question the materialist's use of matter to this end. Why, he would ask, should we suppose matter to behave in a regular way? What account does the materialist have of this? Isn't this at least as miraculous as Berkeley's claim that our sensations exhibit regularity? So when it comes to explaining regularity, materialism and idealism are in the same boat.

■ Figure 7.8
Idealism

Nothing can exist unperceived. So physical objects are just collections of 'ideas' or sense data appearing to minds. God plants these ideas in all of us and perceives the world, thereby keeping it in existence.

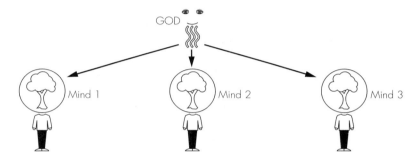

But what of the gappiness of objects? Berkeley's idealism as so far characterised appears to fly in the face of our common-sense understanding of the nature of physical things, and threatens to reduce idealism to absurdity. Berkeley takes the challenge seriously and salvages his account by supposing that there is an all-powerful God who is a permanent perceiver of all possible ideas. By perceiving everything when no humans or animals are perceiving them, Berkeley's God ensures that physical objects retain the kind of continuous existence that realists and common sense would claim for them. This also explains both the origin and regularity of our sense data. Berkeley's defence is neatly summed up in a limerick by Ronald Knox:[15]

There was a young man who said, 'God
Must think it exceedingly odd
If he finds that this tree
Continues to be
When there is no one around in the Quad.'

to which the reply is:

Dear Sir:
Your astonishment's odd:
I am always around in the <u>Quad</u>,
And that's why the tree
Will continue to be
Since observed by
Yours faithfully
God.

■ Criticisms of Berkeley's defence

The use of God to shore up a philosophical position is often regarded as evidence that there is something seriously wrong with it. God helps Berkeley out of his difficulties but we have no independent reason to suppose either that there is a God or, if there is, that he plays the role Berkeley casts him in. To use God in this way to expressly solve a problem is often regarded as intellectually dishonest since it masquerades as an explanation while in fact it explains nothing. If whenever there is something that we can't explain we turn to divine intervention then we could eliminate all mysteries. All philosophical difficulties could be explained away as miracles, a bit like 'solving' a puzzle about the world by explaining sagely that God moves in mysterious ways.

Before moving on let's allow Berkeley the last word in his defence. While the materialist thinks his use of God is dishonest, at least God is supposed to be an intelligence, and so it makes sense that he would do things in an orderly way. So he provides a good explanation of the regularity and predictability of experience. The idea that some mindless substance called matter should behave in a regular and orderly fashion and so account for the origin and regularity of experience is, according to Berkeley, a far bigger cop-out than an appeal to God. In fact, it's worth noting that, as far as Berkeley is concerned, God doesn't enter his theory to save it. Rather Berkeley's whole argument amounts to a demonstration of God's existence. If his arguments succeed in showing that matter cannot exist, then the only way to explain the orderly appearance of sense impressions is by positing the existence of some intelligence producing them.

▶ criticism ◀

more difficult

Criticism 4: Confusion over the term 'ideas'

This is a criticism stemming from Russell and others claiming that idealism is based on a confusion over the meaning of the term *idea*.

According to the realist, some ideas such as such as pain and desire are entirely mental. They are mental in *essence* as they are *acts* of the mind. Other ideas such as colours and sounds may rely on the perceiver; they are in part mental, but they are not acts of the mind, they are *objects* of the mind. The claim is that the idealist has not recognised this distinction. They have confused objects of the mind (sense impressions) with acts of the mind (desires) and so claim that what we perceive is entirely mental or ideas. Specifically the charge is that the idealist has not distinguished between the act of perception (wholly mental) with the objects of perception (in part mental) and so believes she is justified in claming the world is not physical, but somehow mental. In short the criticism is that idealism is based on a confusion of two senses of the term 'idea'.

Berkeley, however, was aware of this criticism. He claimed that the only true mental act is an act of the will. Perception, he claimed, is not such an act as we cannot will what we want to perceive. Perception, he claimed, is passive and so not an act. As perception is not an act of the mind there can be no confusion between the act and the object of that act.

Indeed this whole criticism relies on there being a difference between an act of perception and the object of the act and it's not clear what this difference is. What is an act of perception over and above an awareness of the objects of perception? Is there really a difference? Also, the claim that the objects of perception are not essentially mental is a bit suspect. What are the objects of perception? They are not the objects in the world, as this would be to believe in naïve realism. The representative realist claims the objects of perception are sense impressions. But in what sense is this not essentially mental? Sense impressions could not exist without a mind – and they are all we are aware of when perceiving. This criticism itself is deemed to have failed as it relied on a distinction that can't be properly articulated, and even Russell later rejected it.

ACTIVITY   Below are four well-known objections to Berkeley's idealism.

1 Read through each quotation in turn and see if you can work out what objection is being made.
2 Ask yourself how Berkeley might respond.
3 Finally decide who you think is right.

> **a)** From James Boswell's *Life of Johnson*
> *After we came out of the church, we stood talking for some time together of Bishop Berkeley's ingenious sophistry to prove the non-existence of matter, and that every thing in the universe is merely ideal. I observed that though we are satisfied his doctrine is not true, it is impossible to refute it. I never shall forget the alacrity with which Johnson answered, striking his foot with mighty force against a large stone, till he rebounded from it, 'I refute it thus.'*[16]

b) From James Boswell's *Life of Johnson*
Being in company with a gentleman who thought fit to maintain Dr Berkeley's ingenious philosophy, that nothing exists but as perceived by some mind; when the gentleman was going away, Johnson said to him, 'Pray, Sir, don't leave us; for we may perhaps forget to think of you, and then you will cease to exist.' [17]

c) From G.E. Moore's 'Proof of an external world'
I can now give a large number of different proofs [of the existence of things outside of us], each of which is a perfectly rigorous proof . . . I can prove now, for instance, that two human hands exist. How? By holding up my two hands, and saying, as I make a certain gesture with the right hand, 'Here is one hand', and adding, as I make a certain gesture with the left, 'and here is another'. And if, by doing this, I have proved ipso facto the existence of external things, you will all see that I can also do it now in numbers of other ways: there is no need to multiply examples. [18]

d) From David Hume's *A Treatise on Human Nature*
Thus the sceptic still continues to reason and believe, even tho' he asserts that he cannot defend his reason by reason; and by the same rule he must assent to the principle concerning the existence of body, tho' he cannot pretend by any argument of philosophy to maintain its veracity. Nature has not left this to his choice, and has doubtless esteem'd it of far too great importance to be trusted to our uncertain reasonings and speculations. We may well ask, What causes induce us to believe in the existence of body? But 'tis in vain to ask, Whether there be body or not? That is a point, which we must take for granted in all our reasonings. [19]

Phenomenalism

more difficult

Although not on the AS level syllabus, phenomenalism is a twentieth-century attempt to account for our knowledge of the external world that has much in common with idealism and so is worth having some knowledge of, if only as a way of defending a version of idealism. However, if this does not appeal then feel free to skip to the conclusion of the chapter on page 555.

One variation of phenomenalism that gained particular favour is *linguistic phenomenalism*. Linguistic phenomenalism is primarily a theory of meaning: it's a theory about what we really mean when we talk about physical objects. The linguistic phenomenalist claims that, although we talk quite happily about physical objects as if they exist, when we do so we are in fact referring to various patterns of sense impressions that we experience. Talk of physical objects is just a shorthand way of talking about collections of sense impressions or phenomena. As such, linguistic phenomenalism claims that, although useful, talk of physical objects can technically be avoided as it is only really sense impressions to which we are referring. So linguistic phenomenalism amounts to the claim that all talk of independently existing objects can be translated into talk about sense impressions without any loss of meaning.

Such a claim is backed up by considering how we learn language. We are born and slowly start to perceive lots of strange shapes, colours, noises and tastes. As young babies we start to recognise familiar patterns in these colours and shapes and eventually we learn to associate a word with these patterns, such as 'apple', 'dog' or 'shoe horn'. Slowly our vocabulary increases, but ultimately all the words we learn for the objects around us are really just words for regular and consistent patterns of sense impressions. Talk about physical objects is thus just shorthand for talk about sense impressions. So the word 'apple' doesn't really refer to some independent material object, it really means something like 'a round, red and green, hard, sweet, slightly sharp, crunchy, collection of potential sense impressions'.

To illustrate this, consider a character such as Buzz Lightyear from the computer-animated film *Toy Story*. We have no difficulty in talking about him or about other characters in the film, and yet we are simply referring to a particular collection of coloured shapes on the screen and the sounds that accompany them. 'Buzz Lightyear' is just the name for this collection of colours and sounds, and he has no existence independently of it. The phenomenalist is saying that the same principle applies to everything you perceive. All objects are just collections of sense impressions. There is no need to posit an independent existence.

If talk about objects is really just talk about sense impressions then we should be able to 'translate' our talk about physical objects into talk about sense impressions with no loss of meaning. Here is an example of how a phenomenal translation might work. The physical object expression:

The melon rolls across the wooden table and knocks over a glass.

becomes:

A round yellow patch rotates and moves left across the brown expanse reaching a transparent, hard container-shaped collection of sense impressions which turns suddenly downwards.

The first phrase features the word 'melon', 'table' and 'glass'. These could be construed as referring to independently existing objects, whereas in the translation we are clearly referring only to patterns of sense impressions, and at no point does the existence of independent objects seem to be implied. Note that phenomenalists are not saying that we should all start talking in *phenomenalese*. Obviously this would be impractical since it would take too long and communication would break down. Rather they are arguing that it is possible to remove all talk of physical objects from our speech with no loss of meaning. It may be long-winded and unwieldy, but ultimately it means exactly the same. If this is right it shows that belief in the existence of independent physical objects is redundant. In principle at least we can make do with sense impressions alone.

ACTIVITY

1 a) To get the hang of this idea, try your hand at your own translations of the following terms into phenomenalese:
- boiled egg
- water
- banana

b) What difficulties did you encounter?

While long-winded, you probably found that translating a single word is relatively easy.

2 Now consider translating a full sentence:

The boiled egg fell into the bowl of water with a splash.

How did you do?

The linguistic phenomenalist can also deal with the problem faced by idealism of explaining what we mean when we talk about objects that are not currently being perceived. We really mean that they would be perceived if there were someone suitably placed to perceive them. For example, the sentence:

There is an unobserved tree falling in the forest.

really means something like:

If you approached the large green and brown expanse (the forest) and walked into it for a while, then a small brown and green patch (the tree) would shift in relation to the other brown and green patches and a roaring noise and shaking would also be experienced.

The phenomenalist is saying that, instead of explaining perception by reference to the independent existence of material objects as the realist does, we should appeal to continuing possibilities of experience, possibilities which will be triggered by the occurrence of suitable conditions. If someone happens to be in the right place at the right time they will have experiences of a certain sort. This remains true whether or not anyone is in such a time and place. This means that the phenomenalist explains my seeing a tree by appealing to the statement that '*if* suitable conditions were to obtain (the tree is before me, the lighting conditions are good, I have normal vision, etc.), *then* I would have tree-seeing-experiences, *and* those conditions do obtain'. It is the truth of this statement that explains why I have the sense experiences I do. Similarly, she explains my *not* seeing the tree, although it continues to exist hidden in the forest, by claiming that this simply means that *if* suitable conditions were to obtain (if I were to go to the forest, stand before the tree, in good lighting conditions, with good eyesight, etc.), *then* I would see the tree, but currently these conditions do not obtain.

One benefit of phenomenalism is that its anti-realist position makes it resistant to sceptical attack since it closes the gap between our experience and the world. For the realist there is always the lurking sceptical question 'How can I be sure there really is a table in this room?' or 'Perhaps I am being deceived or having a dream?' Phenomenalism can dismiss such worries. In saying 'there is a table in the room' the phenomenalist simply means: 'If I were to look in the room, then I would have table-like experiences' and this is true whether dreaming or not. The sceptic can only make hay if there is a possible gap between conscious experience and the world on which to cast doubt. But the phenomenalist is saying that all talk about the world is really talk about experience, so there is no gap for the sceptic to exploit.

Criticisms of phenomenalism

Criticism 1: Persistence of objects and their regularity

Despite its advantages, we may still harbour the same worries with this form of anti-realism as we did with idealism over why objects seem to persist and why they behave with such regularity. Why should possible sense experience behave in this way? Surely the realists' explanation still has the advantage, since they claim that as well as the possibility of experiences there is something permanent that allows for that possibility, something distinct from and supporting it – namely the material world.

The standard phenomenalist reply is to appeal to regularities in past experience. The hypothetical statement that someone would see the tree if they looked in the forest is justified by the regular ways in which trees have been experienced in the past. In other words, if every time in the past that you've gone for a walk in the forest you've had the same pattern of tree-like experiences, then this justifies you in making the general hypothetical claim that if you were to go once more to the forest you would once again have the same tree-like experiences.

However, such a response may still strike us as an inadequate account of the actual nature of our perceptual experience, as it has failed to provide any causal explanation of why the tree should appear. The reason why the tree reappears every time I go on the same walk in the forest cannot be that it has appeared in the past under similar circumstances. This may be the evidence we would appeal to in order to justify our expectation that it will reappear, but it is not an explanation of why it will: it is not the underlying cause. Instead, says the realist, the independent existence of the object explains the regularities. So the tree doesn't reappear because it has reappeared in the past, rather it has reappeared in the past because it was there all along.

Once again, the phenomenalist has a reply. She may seek to question whether the realists' appeal to material objects is really any better as an explanation of regularity. Can't we ask the same questions of matter as the realist asks of phenomena? Why should matter retain the properties it does so as to be ready on occasion to provide us with predictable sense impressions? Isn't the appeal to matter with its regular properties just as miraculous as an appeal to regularities in possible sense impressions? The only possible justification for supposing that matter will retain its properties unperceived is because of past regularities, and so the realist is in the same boat as the phenomenalist when it comes to explaining why experience is as it is.

■ Criticism 2: Impossibility of removing physical objects from 'translations'

Another criticism of phenomenalism concerns the impossibility of translating all talk about objects into talk about sense impressions. The previous explanation we gave of a melon rolling across a wooden table and knocking over a glass would translate as:

> A round yellow patch rotates and moves left across the brown expanse reaching a transparent, hard container-shaped collection of sense impressions which turns suddenly downwards.

However, this statement still relies on the existence of physical objects as it includes spatial relations, such as moves left and downwards. Moving left in relation to what? Presumably another object?

The observer has to be in some appropriate position in order to perceive, and this means being spatially related to the object in question and using one's physical sense organs. Whatever we try, it seems we are going to end up reintroducing spatial relations and our own bodies into the translation. So any phenomenal translation will be not only infinitely complex and long but also impossible, even in principle, to complete since it must reintroduce physical object language at each turn. This seems to show that our language is dependent on the assumption of an independently existing world and cannot be translated into statements about actual and potential sense impressions.

Conclusion

One might have thought that there could be nothing easier in life than simply sensing and experiencing the world. Opening our eyes to see or our ears to hear normally requires no real effort. However, we have seen that trying to account for the relationship between our sense experiences and the world is far from easy. The natural view – the view of common sense or naïve realism – that we peer out through our eyes and listen through our ears and simply see and hear the world around us as it is, turned out not to hold water. Having done what Hume calls 'the slightest philosophy', we saw that the world cannot be exactly as it appears and that perception is a complex affair. Our eyes receive light reflected off objects and this triggers a complex chain of events involving the optic nerve and the visual cortex (at the back of the head), which culminates in the experience of seeing an object. In the process our senses interpret the world for us and present us with a picture of it, which may be accurate in some respects but deceptive in others. This recognition appeared to lead us to the view that these experiences or sense impressions exist only in our minds, that they are representations of the world which enable us to interact with it. This is the view of representative realism.

But such a view drives a wedge between our sensations and reality (see Figure 7.7). Now there seem to be two worlds involved: the world as we perceive it, full of colours and sounds, and the world as it really is in itself, a bumbling mass of colourless, soundless matter or energy. It appears that we can no longer be certain that our senses give us genuine knowledge of the world, as we can never check our sensations against reality. Any attempt to do so can only give us further sensations. A 'veil of perception' has descended between us and the world which it seems impossible to remove.

This difficulty led some thinkers to suggest that the very belief that there is an independent world causing our sensations is the problem. Idealists hope to do away with belief in matter, regarding it is as a leap of faith that we do not need to make. However, idealism itself seems to rely on a leap of religious faith. As we saw, Berkeley is forced to rely on God to explain why it is that we have the regular experiences that we do, and why we suppose objects to exist when no one perceives them. Phenomenalism seems to fare better, but still the worry remains that we need some explanation of the regularity and predictability of experience. Moreover, as we argued, the project to translate all talk about physical objects into sense impressions needs to reintroduce a commitment to a physical world. Matter, it seems, is not so easily dismissed.

It seems that any account of perception runs into profound difficulty. The simple act of perceiving the world turns out to be one of the hardest for which to give a coherent account.

Key points: Chapter 7

What you need to know about **knowledge of the external world:**

1 Naïve realism is the common-sense view of perception. It is a realist theory because it claims that physical objects exist independently of our perception of them. The properties of objects, from their size and shape through to colours, smells and textures, also have independent existence and are perceived directly by us.

2 The key features of naïve realism are:
- Physical objects exist in space and have the properties we perceive them to have.
- We perceive physical objects directly because they are there and we know they are there because we perceive them directly.
- When no one is perceiving an object it continues to exist along with all its properties.

3 However, naïve realism finds it difficult to account for sense deception, and the apparent fact that physical objects often appear different from how they really are. Also, some of the properties perceived in objects seem not to be really out there, but are effects on perceiving beings like ourselves.

4 Various considerations lead philosophers to draw a distinction between properties that actually exist in objects themselves, and the powers these objects have to produce sensations of various sorts in us. Those such as size, position and shape are real and are known as primary qualities. Those such as colour, sound and smell are called secondary qualities.

5 Representative realism claims that physical objects impact upon our sense organs, causing us to experience sensations. These sensations are akin to pictures which represent the objects that cause them. So we don't perceive the world directly, but indirectly, via our sensations.

6 The key features of representative realism are:
- Physical objects exist in space and have only some of the properties we perceive them to have.
- We perceive our own sense impressions directly, and physical objects only indirectly.
- When no one is perceiving an object it continues to exist along with some of its properties.

7 This view, however, also leads into difficulties. If we are directly acquainted only with our own sensations, and have only indirect access to the real world, the question arises of how we can be certain that we are perceiving the world accurately. Moreover, as we are caught behind the veil of perception, the trap of solipsism looms.

8 Berkeley tried to deal with the problems of representative realism by denying that there is any material world about which doubt might arise. True to his empiricist principles, he argued that the concept of something which cannot be experienced is incoherent, and so the idea of a material world lying beyond the veil of perception had to be dismissed. To exist, something has to be perceived, and so physical things can exist only when perceived by some mind.

9 Berkeley's idealism faces an immediate difficulty, namely how to account for our ordinary sense that physical objects continue to exist when no one is perceiving them. Berkeley's answer is that God perceives everything and so sustains the universe in existence.

10 The key features of Berkeley's idealism are:
- Physical objects are clusters of sense impressions or ideas existing in minds.
- An object exists only when someone is perceiving it.
- God perceives everything and so sustains the universe in existence.

11 Berkeley's use of God, however, looks like a desperate measure to save his theory.

12 The key features of phenomenalism are:
- Physical objects are permanent possibilities of sensation.
- All talk about physical objects can be reduced to talk about sense impressions without loss of meaning.
- We are able to predict what sense data we will perceive because of past regularities in experience.

13 However, the theory still has some difficulties in accounting for the persistence of objects in a satisfactory way. Also it seems to be impossible to turn sentences about physical objects into sentences purely about sense impressions, as the existence of objects will be implied somewhere in the translation.

Glossary

Aesthetic   Beautiful, concerning the beauty of things. Part of St Augustine's **theodicy** was that evil might exist in order to balance goodness, and so make for a more aesthetic and balanced universe.

Agape   The ancient Greek word for thoughtful or selfless love, sometimes translated in the Bible as 'charity'.

Agent   A being who is capable of action. Agency and action are typically restricted to **persons**, because they have the capacity to reason, make a choice between two courses of action, then do what they have chosen.

Alienation   The state of being estranged from something that should belong to us, be a part of us, or with which we should be in harmony. Alienation implies a damaging or harmful separation, even though people are often unaware that they are in an alienated state. For Feuerbach we are alienated from our own humanity; for Marx we are alienated from our own work and labour.

Altruism   The view that at least some of our actions are selfless, and are intended to benefit other people rather than ourselves. See also **egoism**.

Analogical   According to Aquinas, a word is used analogically in different contexts when there is an imperfect likeness in the meaning of the two words: 'imperfect', because the two things are different, but 'likeness' because the two things have something in common. Aquinas believed that we could only talk about God analogically.

Analytic   A term that describes the manner in which a proposition is true. An analytic truth is a proposition that is true in virtue of the meanings of the words alone. In other words an analytic truth is one that is true by definition, for example 'A bachelor is an unmarried man.' Analytic truths are contrasted with **synthetic** truths – truths that can not be determined simply by analysing the meanings of the terms used. For example, 'All bachelors

have the use of at least one kidney' is a synthetic truth.

Anthropic Principle   Confusingly, the Anthropic Principle is not a single principle, but has been used both to support and undermine the belief in God. Both sides acknowledge that the existence of self-conscious life – i.e. of humans – in the universe seems to be astonishingly improbable and requires an explanation. (Anthropic stems from the Greek word for 'human being'.) Believers (such as Tennant) have framed the Anthropic Principle so that it seems impossible to believe that humans could come to exist by chance; hence there must be a guiding hand behind the development of the universe. Non-believers (such as Brandon Carter) have developed the Anthropic Principle to show that humans should not be surprised that the universe has led to our existence, because if it hadn't led to our existence we wouldn't have been around to be surprised.

Anti-realism   If you are a realist about something, then you believe it exists independently of our minds. If you are an anti-realist about something you think it is mind dependent. For example, in **epistemology**, anti-realists about perception think that material objects exist only for minds and that a mind-independent world is non-existent (Berkeley summed up this **idealist** position by saying that to be is to be perceived). An example of anti-realism from moral philosophy is **emotivism**: the claim that moral terms do not refer to anything real, but are merely the expressions of feelings. See also **realism**.

A posteriori   A Latin term that describes a belief that can only be known via experience of the world: for example, that 'snow is white' or that 'the Atlantic is smaller than the Pacific'. *A posteriori* beliefs are contrasted with ***a priori*** beliefs.

A priori   A Latin term that describes knowledge that is known prior to or independently from experience. For example, that '1,000,000 + 1 = 1,000,001' can be known independently of counting a million apples, adding another one, and then recounting them. *A priori* beliefs are contrasted with *a posteriori* beliefs, which are ones derived from experience.

Argument   An argument is a series of propositions intended to support a conclusion. The propositions offered in support of the conclusion are termed **premises**.

Argument from analogy   See **inductive argument**.

Argument from design   See **teleological argument**.

Atemporal   Outside of time. It is generally agreed that God is eternal, but some theologians maintain that this means that God exists outside of time: he has no past, present or future.

Atheism/Atheist   In the tradition of Western philosophy, atheism generally refers to the belief that there is no God in a Christian (or Jewish, or Islamic) sense. In contrast to **theism**.

Autonomy   (From the Greek *auto* – self, and *nomos* – law) An **agent** has autonomy in so far as it is rational and free, that is insofar as it is in control of its self and its actions. Autonomy is often regarded as an essential characteristic of personhood. For Kant moral autonomy was only achieved through following the **categorical imperative**.

Belief   A belief is a state of mind or thought which is about the world. It is a mental representation which claims that something is the case, or that a proposition is true. For example, you may have the belief that Highgate is in London or that cod liver oil is good for your health. A belief will have some degree of evidence in support of it but is normally regarded as weaker than **knowledge**, either because knowledge cannot turn out to be false, or because it requires stronger evidence.

Belief in…Belief that…   Ordinarily when we talk about beliefs we are talking about beliefs *that* certain things are true (for example you might believe that Media Studies AS Level is easier than Philosophy AS Level). Sometimes we talk about beliefs *in* certain things (for example, belief in God, or in the new England football coach). To believe *in* something means not only believing that it exists, but

also having a certain confidence in that person or process – we adopt a positive attitude towards that person or process and are committed to it.

Benevolence   The desire and disposition to do good for others. Christian philosophers maintain that God has the property of benevolence.

Camera obscura   Latin for 'dark room' and referring to a room with one small aperture covered by a lens which allows the scene outside to be projected inside onto a screen by the same mechanism as a modern camera. Locke uses the device as an analogy for how the mind works. Sensations are representations of things in the physical world which are projected into the mind as they are into a camera. All our concepts and beliefs are formed out of the sensations in our minds. We have direct access only to sensations and we make judgements about the nature of the physical world on the basis of them. So our beliefs about the world are justified in terms of beliefs about our sense experiences. The *camera obscura* analogy expresses Locke's empiricist conviction that all our concepts derive from sensation, that all knowledge is justified in terms of experience and his representative realism about perception.

Categorical imperative   See **imperative**.

Clear and distinct ideas   The basic or self-justifying beliefs that Descartes hopes to use as foundations for his system of knowledge. Clear and distinct ideas, we are told, are those which can be 'intuited' by the mind by what he calls the 'light of reason'. In other words, they are truths of **reason**, truths that can be known with the mind alone. Descartes' examples of clear and distinct ideas are the basic claims of logic, geometry and mathematics. Knowledge of truths of reason, it is claimed, resists any **sceptical** attack, since we recognise its truth immediately. Our faculty of 'intuition' permits us to recognise the truth without allowing any room for doubt or error. For example, it is in vain to ask how I know that triangles have three sides. Such knowledge is given in the very act of understanding the terms involved. There is no further evidence I need appeal to in order to justify such knowledge.

Cogito   Latin for 'I think', and shorthand for Descartes' famous argument to prove his own existence. Descartes attempted to doubt that he existed, but realised that, in order to doubt this, he must exist. So his own existence was indubitable.

Cognitivism/Non-cognitivism   Cognitivism is a position in the philosophy of language which holds that judgements or statements must be true or false if they are to mean anything. Cognitivist perspectives on religious language include **verificationism** and **falsificationism**. Non-cognitivism is the position that statements can be meaningful, even if they don't refer to the world and the concepts of 'truth' and 'falsity' don't apply to them. An example of a non-cognitivist perspective in religious language comes from Wittgenstein.

Coherentism   A view about the structure of justification which claims that no beliefs are foundational and therefore that all beliefs need justification in terms of further beliefs. On this account beliefs are more or less well justified to the extent that they fit in or cohere with other beliefs in the system.

Compatibilism   See **free will**.

Concept   Having a concept of something is what enables one to recognise it, distinguish it from other things and think about it. So, if I have the concept of a hedgehog, I can think about hedgehogs, and recognise them when I encounter them, and tell the difference between them and hogs or hedges. Similarly, to have a concept of red is to be able to think about it, recognise it and to distinguish it from other colours. According to traditional empiricism, all our concepts are formed as kinds of 'copy' of the original sensations.

Conclusion   A statement that comes at the end of an argument and that is supported by the reasons given in the argument. If an argument is sound or valid and all of the **premises** are true, then the conclusion will also be true.

Contingent   A contingent truth is one which happens to be true, but which may not have been. In other words, it is a truth for which it is logically possible that it be false. The opposite of a contingent truth is a **necessary** one, i.e. one which has to be true and couldn't be otherwise, or for which it is logically impossible that it be false. For example, it is a contingent truth that daffodils are yellow, since it is conceivable that they might have been blue.

Corporeal   Made of matter. In contrast to **incorporeal**.

Cosmological arguments   Cosmology is the study of the universe as whole. Cosmological arguments for the existence of God operate by claiming that there must be some ultimate cause or reason for the existence of the universe. This explanation cannot be found within the universe and so must be found in some supernatural being, namely God.

Deductive argument   A deductive argument is one where the truth of the conclusion is guaranteed by the truth of the premises. In other words it is an argument in which the premises entail the conclusion. So if one accepts the truth of the premises one must, as a matter of logical necessity, accept the conclusion. For example: Either you'll become a fireman or a doctor. But you can only become a doctor with a medical degree which you'll never get. So you'll become a fireman. A deductive argument is in contrast to an **inductive argument**. **Ontological arguments** are deductive proofs of God's existence.

Deontological ethics   A type of **normative** moral theory which views the moral value of an action to lie in the action itself. So an action is right or wrong in itself, whatever the consequences. Generally deontologists (like Kant) propose certain rules or principles that guide us as to which actions are right and which are wrong. See also **Kantian ethics**.

Determinism   See **free will**.

Direct realism   Another term for **naïve realism**.

Disposition   Our tendency to behave in certain ways, our character traits. This term is used by **virtue ethicists**, who believe we ought to develop virtuous dispositions.

Dualism   Dualism about mind and body is the claim that humans are made of two distinct kinds of stuff: a material body and a spiritual mind.

Duty   An action which we are required or impelled to carry out. Kant's deontological theory places duty at its centre. For Kant duties are experienced as imperatives. See also **prima facie duty**.

Egoism   The view that our actions are essentially self-interested. Psychological egoism claims that it is a matter of fact that humans are motivated solely by self-interest. Ethical egoism goes a stage further and claims that we ought to do whatever is in our self-interest. See also **altruism**.

Emotivism An **anti-realist** position in moral philosophy, made popular by A. J. Ayer, which claims that moral judgements do not refer to anything in the world, but are expressions of our feelings of approval and disapproval.

Empiricism An **epistemological** position which holds that our **beliefs**, and knowledge, must be based on experience. David Hume was one philosopher who rigorously applied his empiricist approach to questions in the philosophy of religion.

Enlightenment Also known as the Age of Reason. The period of European history in the eighteenth century in which thinkers and writers were optimistic about the progress that humans could make in different fields. It was characterised by critical and analytic thinking, and meant a break with the past, including a break with Christian thinking. Some of this optimism arose from the scientific discoveries of Sir Isaac Newton, which led to the belief that similar theories and laws could be developed in other areas of human thought. Famous enlightenment philosophers include Voltaire and Hume.

Epistemology One of the three main areas of philosophical study and analysis (see also **ethics** and **metaphysics**). Epistemology, or the theory of knowledge, looks at questions of what it is possible to know, what grounds our claims to knowledge are based on, what is true, what is the distinction between knowledge and belief. (The term is derived the ancient Greek words *episteme* meaning 'knowledge' and *logos* meaning 'account', or 'rationale'.)

Eschatological Eschatology is the study of the 'end of things' or the 'last things' as described from a religious perspective: this includes death, what happens after we die, the end of time, the last judgement, etc. Eschatological verification is a term used by John Hick to describe the process by which religious statements can (in theory) be shown to be meaningful: if they are true then they can be shown to be true (verified) after we die.

Ethical egoism See **egoism**.

Ethics One of the three main areas of philosophical study and analysis (see also **epistemology** and **metaphysics**). Ethics, or moral philosophy, is concerned with questions of how we should live, what rules we should follow, how should we act, what sort of person we should try to be. Practical, or applied,

ethics looks at particular issues and dilemmas that face us in the real world. **Normative ethics** examines the rules and principles that have been proposed to govern and judge our actions. Meta-ethics assesses the status of these rules, and at the meaning of moral claims and judgements.

Eudaimonia According to many ancient Greek philosophers *eudaimonia* is the goal or 'good' we are all striving for. Sometimes translated as 'happiness', it is probably closer in meaning to 'flourishing'. Aristotle's virtue ethics is centred around *eudaimonia*.

Euthyphro Dilemma In the philosophy of religion this dilemma raises the question 'in what way are God's commands good?' and offers two problematic options. The first option is that whatever God commands is good, in which case his commands to commit genocide (Deuteronomy 3:2) or infanticide (Genesis 22:2), for example, are good. The second option is that God's commands are good because they conform to some external moral law, in which case we should pay attention to this moral law, rather than God.

Evidence The reasons for holding a belief.

Evil Philosophers usually distinguish between moral evil, which is the suffering caused by humans, and Natural evil, which is the suffering brought about by natural events such as earthquakes. The existence of evil in the universe presents a challenge to believers known as the **problem of evil**.

Evil demon A device used by Descartes to generate a sceptical argument about the possibility of knowledge of the external world and of basic propositions of arithmetic and geometry. It is conceivable that there exists an extremely powerful spirit or demon bent on deceiving me. If this were the case then all my perceptions of the world around me could be an illusion produced in my mind by the demon. Even my own body could be a part of the illusion. Moreover, the demon could cause me to make mistakes even about the most simple judgements of maths and geometry so that I go wrong when adding 2 to 3 or counting the sides of a square.

Evolution Evolution is the process, described as **natural selection** by Charles Darwin, by which organisms gradually change over time according to changes in their environment and genetic mutations. Some mutations lead to traits or characteristics which make an organism better suited to an environment and more successful in having offspring that also survive and reproduce; some environmental changes mean that an organism is less suited to its environment and its offspring are less successful in surviving and reproducing. Over long periods of time, and in environmentally stable conditions, the characteristics of an organism become highly adapted to its environment and have all the appearance of being designed for that environment.

Existential change See **numerical change**.

Existentialism The name for a group of related philosophies which focus on describing and explaining what it feels like to exist as a human. Some of the key concerns revolve around the individual, the range of human experience and the significance of choice or **free will**.

External world All that exists outside of or independently of the mind; the physical world.

Fact Something which is the case. For example, it is a fact that the earth revolves around the sun.

Factual significance A statement has factual significance if it tells us something about the real world. Some theories of meaning (such as **verificationism**) maintain that a sentence is only meaningful if it is factually significant.

Fallacy An argument which is flawed either because a mistake has been made, rendering the argument invalid; or because the argument has a form, or structure, which is always invalid.

False A term used of beliefs and propositions. A false belief is one which is not true. One account of what makes a belief or proposition false is that it fails to correspond with the facts. So, for example, the belief that humans are descended from apes will be false if in fact they are descended from dolphins.

Falsificationism A philosophical theory about the nature of meaning. Closely related to **verificationism**, falsificationism claims that for a proposition to be meaningful we must be able to understand what would count as proving the proposition false (i.e. what would falsify it).

Forms (theory of) Plato's theory of forms is a theory about types or classes of thing. The word 'form' is used to translate Plato's use of the Greek word 'idea' with which he refers to the type or class to which a thing belongs. Plato argues that over and above the realm of physical objects there is a realm of 'forms' to which individual physical things belong. So in the physical realm there are many tables, but there is also the single form of the table, the ideal or blueprint of the table, which we recognise not with our senses, but with the mind.

Foundationalism A view about the structure of justification which claims that there are two sorts of belief: those which are basic or foundational and which require no justification (or which are self-justifying), and those which are built on top of the foundations and justified in terms of them.

Free will Also known as metaphysical freedom. The idea of free will is that the self controls aspects of its own life, such as bodily movements like picking up a pencil. Many religious philosophers believe that God granted humans free will. Free will can be contrasted with **determinism**, which is the belief that all events in the universe are the necessary consequence of physical laws, and these laws apply to human actions as well. A determinist might claim that humans are like complex pieces of biological machinery with no real freedom of will. Some philosophers believe that these two positions (free will versus determinism) are compatible with each other, and claim that humans can have free will but are also subject to deterministic laws; such a view is known as compatibilism.

Given The given is the raw and immediate element of experience prior to any judgement. What is given to us immediately are often termed **sense data** and such experience is thought to be known for certain and **incorrigibly**.

Golden rule Versions of this rule have appeared at various points within different religions and philosophies (including Confucius, Jesus, Hobbes and Kant). The basic idea is that we should be impartial, and not afford ourselves special treatment: we should treat others as we should like to be treated. See also **universalisability**.

Good Actions are good according to whether they bring about certain positive outcomes – these may be pleasure or happiness, or something more intangible. But 'good' also has a functional meaning, in the sense that 'good' means 'fulfilling your function well'. Aristotle believed that we have a function and hence can be good in both senses: by being good (fulfilling our function) we can reach the good (*eudaimonia*).

Hedonism   The claim that pleasure is the **good**. Many **utilitarians** are hedonists, in that they believe we ought to try to maximise pleasure (for the majority).

Holy   The concept of 'Holy' is used to encapsulate everything that is special and sacred about God. It can also be used to describe religious objects which share in this sacredness. Rudolf Otto described the overpowering experience of God's holiness as **numinous**.

Hypothetical imperative   See **imperative**.

Hypothetical statements: '*If. . . then*' statements which make claims about states of affairs which are not actual, but which would be *if* certain conditions were satisfied. Hypothetical statements are used to translate physical object language into phenomenal language in linguistic **phenomenalism**.

Idea   The uses of the word 'idea' are various within the philosophical literature, as well as in ordinary parlance. Here the word is not used in a technical or precise sense, except when in italics where it refers to Locke's use of the word to mean anything of which the mind is conscious, including **sense data**, **concepts** and **beliefs**.

Idealism   Idealism as discussed here is an **anti-realist** theory of perception. Put forward by Berkeley, it is the view that matter does not exist independently of the mind and that all that exists are minds and their ideas. Physical objects are no more than collections of sensations appearing in minds. Objects which are not currently being perceived by any creature are sustained in existence by being perceived in the mind of God.

Ideology   In Marxist thought, the complex of ideas and shared beliefs of a society which arises from particular economic and political conditions, and which justify, explain and support these conditions. The philosophical ideas, ethics, religion, culture, and arts of a particular society are all part of its ideology, and cannot claim to have a 'neutral' or objective status.

Immanent   The opposite of **transcendent**. Existing, or immersed, in something. So to say

that God is immanent is to say that God continues to be present in and exist in his creation.

Immaterial   Not made of matter. According to Descartes this would mean not occupying physical space. God is said to be immaterial in this sense.

Immutable   Something that can never change. God is said to be immutable, and this is bound up with the idea that God is simple (he is one thing, and his attributes such as **benevolence** and **omnipotence** cannot be separated from one another).

Imperative   In Kantian ethics we experience our duties as commands (imperatives) which are categorical, or absolute. These categorical imperatives are commands that we are obliged to follow no matter what, and according to Kant only these are moral imperatives. As rational agents we can work out the categorical imperative by asking whether the maxim that lies behind our action is **universalisable**. Other imperatives, things we should do in order to achieve some goal, are conditional or hypothetical imperatives, and they are not moral according to Kant.

Incorporeal   Not made of matter, non-material. God is said to be incorporeal.

Incorrigibility   To call a belief incorrigible is to say that it cannot be corrected or changed. Someone who honestly holds a belief which is incorrigible cannot be mistaken about it. Beliefs about our own **sense data** are often thought to be incorrigible since there appears to be no way in which I can be mistaken about my own experiences and there appears to be no further evidence that could be brought to bear to make me change my mind about what I'm experiencing. For this reason such beliefs are often taken to be immune to sceptical attack.

Indirect realism   Another term for **representative realism**. The view that the immediate objects of perception are **sense data** or representations and that the physical world is perceived only indirectly via these representations.

Indubitable   Not doubtable. A belief which it is not possible to doubt is indubitable.

Inductive argument   An inductive argument is one where the truth of the conclusion is not fully guaranteed by the truth of the premises. For example: moving from particular examples (every raven I've seen has been black) to a generalisation (all ravens are black); or moving from our experience of the past (day has always followed night) to a prediction about the future (day will always follow night). Arguments from analogy are also inductive: they compare two things, and move from what these two things are known to have in common to draw a conclusion about other (unknown) things they are supposed to have in common. The **cosmological** and **teleological arguments** are inductive arguments for God's existence.

Inference   The move in an argument from the **premises** or reasons to the **conclusion**. For example, in the argument 'Moriarty had blood on his hands, therefore he must be the murderer' the inference is the move made from the premise that Moriarty had blood on his hands *to* the conclusion that he is the murderer.

Infinite regress   A regress is a process of reasoning from effect to cause, or of going backwards in a chain of explanations. An infinite regress is one where the process never stops, where it is repeated endlessly. This is generally considered problematic in a philosophical argument, and a sign that a mistake has been made.

Innate ideas   Ideas that exist in the mind which are not acquired from experience. Plato, for example, argued that all **ideas** or **concepts** are innate and that the process of acquiring knowledge is not one of learning in the strict sense, but rather of recollecting what we already implicitly know. So we are all born with innate knowledge of the '**forms**' and it is this knowledge which enables us to recognise individual exemplars of the forms in this life. **Rationalists** traditionally favoured the belief that we possess such ideas. Leibniz, for example, argued that such ideas exist implicitly within the mind and that they are brought to the surface of consciousness through experience. Rationalists often use the doctrine of innate ideas to explain the possibility of *a priori* knowledge. Descartes argued that knowledge of mathematics is innate and that the discovery of mathematical truths involves the mind looking into itself to uncover them. Knowledge of the existence of God is also possible, according to Descartes, because we can look into our own mind to discover the idea and deduce his existence in an *a priori* manner simply through careful mental scrutiny of the idea. Opposed to the doctrine of innate

ideas are the **empiricists** and in particular John Locke who devoted the first Book of his *Essay Concerning Human Understanding* to their repudiation. Locke argued that all the contents of the mind can be reduced to sensation variously transformed and that the mind at birth is akin to a blank paper.

Intelligent Design   A modern version of the **teleological argument** couched in scientific terminology. It claims that certain characteristics of living things cannot be explained through evolution – they are 'irreducibly complex' – and that only the existence of an intelligent designer (God) can explain them. Although it presents itself as a science, it has no recognised or published research within the scientific community, and is best seen as a theological argument for God's existence. See also **evolution**.

Intuition   A kind of mental seeing by which rational truths can be recognised. For Descartes, the mind deploys the faculty of intuition when it sees by the 'light of reason' that $2 + 2 = 4$ or that a sphere is bounded by one surface.

Intuitionism   A **realist** theory of morality which claims that we can determine what is right or good according to our moral intuitions. For intuitionists, the terms 'right' and 'good' refer to something objective, but they cannot be reduced to natural facts.

Judgement   A moral judgement is a decision made (in advance or retrospectively) about the rightness or goodness of a course of action (our own or someone else's,) or, for **virtue** theorists, of someone's character.

Justification   The support or grounds for holding a belief, which gives someone a reason for believing it or makes them justified in believing it. The process of justifying a belief is by offering evidence. The traditional analysis of knowledge sees justification as necessary for knowledge.

Kantian ethics   A **deontological** ethical theory developed by Kant or influenced by Kant. At the heart of Kantian ethics is the claim that we can determine what is right, and what our duties are, through the categorical imperative.

Knowledge   There are three sorts of knowledge: practical knowledge, knowledge by acquaintance, and factual knowledge. The traditional account of factual knowledge claims that it is justified true **belief**.

Language-game   The phrase used by Wittgenstein to convey the idea that language has meaning within a particular social context, and that these contexts are governed by rules (in the same way that different games are governed by different rules). The way in which a sentence is meaningful therefore varies according to the context in which it occurs.

Libertarianism   A term used for the theory that humans have free will. See **free will**.

Logical positivism   See **verificationism**.

Material   Made of physical matter. According to Descartes this involved occupying physical space. In contrast, God is thought of by Christian philosophers as **immaterial**.

Materialism   The view that everything in the world is made of matter and that ultimately all mental or apparently spiritual entities can be given a purely material explanation.

Maxim   A rule that guides action or moral behaviour, for example, 'don't lie'. In **Kantian ethics** a maxim that is **universalisable** is a moral duty.

Meta-ethics   Sometimes called 'second order ethics' this is the study by philosophers of the meaning of moral statements and concepts. This covers issues of **realism** and **anti-realism** in ethics.

Metaphysics   One of the three main areas of philosophical study and analysis (see also **epistemology** and **ethics**). Metaphysics is concerned with determining what sorts of things really exist, what is the ultimate nature of reality, where does the world come from, what is the relationship of our mind to the world. (It is said that the term 'metaphysics' came about because in ancient catalogues of Aristotle's work his books on the nature of reality came after (in Greek 'meta') his books on physics – hence metaphysics.)

Method of doubt   Descartes' sceptical method used to find certainty. Descartes found that many of his beliefs had turned out to be false, and to remedy this situation he elected to cast doubt upon all his beliefs. If any beliefs showed themselves to be **indubitable**, and could survive the most radical **scepticism**, then they would have established themselves as absolutely certain. Once he had discovered such beliefs, Descartes hoped to rebuild a body of knowledge based on them which would be free from error.

Mitigated scepticism   Hume's expression meaning literally 'moderated' scepticism. Hume argued that radical scepticism in the manner of Descartes could lead only to a dead end in which nothing could be known. To be of any practical use to the philosopher, therefore, scepticism should be used more moderately so as not to destroy one's belief system completely. Scepticism is useful when it is used to reject beliefs which it is unreasonable to hold, but not when used indiscriminately to destroy all one's beliefs.

Naïve realism   The common-sense view of how perception works. Physical objects have an independent existence in space, they follow the laws of physics and possess certain properties, ranging from size and shape through to colour, smell and texture. When humans are in the presence of such objects under appropriate conditions they are able to perceive them along with all these properties.

Natural selection   See **evolution**.

Natural theology   Gaining an understanding of God through the use of our reason. This may be through an examination of the world around us (which leads, for example, to the **teleological argument**), or through an analysis of concepts (which leads, for example, to the **ontological argument**). This is in contrast to **revealed theology**.

Necessary   A necessary truth is one which has to be true and couldn't be otherwise. It is one that is true in all possible worlds.

Necessary/contingent   'Necessary' and 'contingent' are opposing terms. It is generally agreed that there can be necessary and **contingent** truths; but some philosophers have also used the terms to apply to beings in the world.

Necessary/contingent beings   A contingent being is one whose existence depends on something else (e.g. humans are contingent because their existence depends on the existence of parents, oxygen, food, etc.) A necessary being is one that does not depend upon anything else for its existence. There are both **cosmological** and **ontological arguments** that hold God to be a necessary being.

Necessary/contingent truths   In the most restricted sense, a necessary truth is one where the opposite is logically impossible; e.g. that a triangle has three sides (a two-sided triangle is logically impossible and cannot be imagined).

A contingent truth is one where the opposite is logically possible, for example it's true that Winston Churchill was once the Prime Minister of the United Kingdom (but it's entirely possible that this may never have happened). It is supposed by some philosophers that the proposition 'God exists' is a necessary truth, because the concept of 'God' already contains the idea of 'a being who must exist'. This claim lies at the heart of some **ontological arguments**.

Necessary/sufficient conditions   A is a necessary condition for B when you have to have A in order to have B. In other words, if you don't have A you can't have B. By contrast A is a sufficient condition for B when if you have A you must have B too. In other words, having A is enough or sufficient to guarantee that you have B.

Non-cognitivism   See **cognitivism**.

Normative ethics   Sometimes called 'first order ethics' this term covers moral theories that offer action-guides. These are rules, principles or standards by which we make moral judgements, and according to which our conduct is directed. There are three general forms of normative theory: **deontological**, **utilitarian** and **virtue ethics**.

Numerical change   When an object undergoes such radical alteration that it is no longer the object in question, for example, a chair being burnt and reduced to a pile of ashes. This is in contrast to **qualitative identity**.

Numerical identity   The identity an object retains throughout other changes. For example, a chair may be painted a different colour but still remain the same chair. This is in contrast to **qualitative identity**. In discussions of personal identity over time personal survival is normally thought to require the numerical identity of the person.

Numinous   A term invented by Rudolf Otto to describe the overwhelming experiences of an encounter with God. These experiences combine terror and dread with awe and wonder.

Omnipotent   All-powerful. Along with **benevolence** this is one of the main attributes of God.

Omnipresent   Everywhere at once. Like **benevolence** and **omnipotence** this is one of the attributes of God.

Omniscient   All-knowing. As with **benevolence**, **omnipotence** and **omnipresence**, this is one of the attributes of God. However, it is important to remember that these attributes cannot be separated from one another in God, because God is simple and **immutable**.

Ontological arguments   Ontology is the study of existence. If you were to write down everything you thought existed (cats, dogs, electrons, aliens, etc.), then this list would form your own personal ontology. If aliens were present on the list then you could be said to be making be making an ontological commitment to the existence of aliens (in other words you claim they exist). All believers (except **anti-realists**) include God in their ontology. The ontological argument is a particular proof of God's existence, and tries to show that the very meaning of the concept 'God' implies that he must exist.

Ontology   The study of being in general or of what there is.

Ordinary-language philosophy   Ordinary language doesn't have all the fine distinctions or precise meanings that are often necessary in philosophical argument. For this reason philosophical discourse is often conducted in a language which is very different from that of ordinary life. However, this departure from ordinary discourse brings with it its own problems. By using words in their own peculiar way, philosophers can often create unnecessary bewilderment and confusion. According to ordinary-language philosophers, by paying attention to the way terms are ordinarily used some, if not all, philosophical puzzles can be dissolved.

Pantheism   The view that God is the same thing as the universe itself.

Paradox   An apparently contradictory statement or one which goes against common-sense opinion.

Perception   The process by which we become aware of physical objects including our own body.

Person   In ordinary language this refers to human beings, but recently some philosophers have asked what is special about persons and whether a) all human beings are persons and b) some non-human beings might count as persons. The sorts of qualities that characterise persons might include agency, autonomy, rationality, self-consciousness, etc.

Phenomenalism An **anti-realist** theory of perception distinguished from **idealism** in that it claims that physical objects are collections not just of actual **sense data** but also of potential sense data. Physical objects continue to exist unperceived since they retain the potential to be perceived.

Phenomenology A philosophical approach which tries to make sense of the world starting from the elements of experience that are most real, certain and central to the life of the individual.

Physico-theological A term used by the philosopher Immanuel Kant to describe an argument for God's existence based on particular features of the world (e.g. order, regularity, design). The phrase didn't catch on, and we now refer to these arguments as **teleological**.

Polytheism The belief that there are many gods (as held, for example, in most ancient societies, including those in India, Egypt, Greece, Rome and much of the rest of Europe and the Middle East).

Practical ethics Like **normative ethics** this is also a type of 'first order' theory. It looks at the application of ethical theories to concrete situations and moral dilemmas that people face, such as abortion, euthanasia and the treatment of animals.

Predicate Many propositions can be divided into a **subject** and a predicate, where the subject is the thing that the sentence is about and the predicate gives us information about the subject. For example, in the sentence 'The balloon is red' the expression 'is red' is the predicate, the term 'balloon' the subject. Some philosophers argued that in the sentence 'God exists', 'exists' is a predicate applying to 'God'. However, philosophers from Kant onwards have doubted whether existence is a genuine predicate.

Premise Any reason given (usually in the form of a statement or claim) to support the conclusion of an argument.

Prescriptive/descriptive A prescriptive statement is one that guides action, it tells us what to do. A descriptive statement on the other hand simply tells us the way things are.

Prima facie duty *Prima facie* is a Latin term that means roughly 'at first sight' or 'as things first appear'. A *prima facie* duty is a term used by W.D. Ross to describe the 'rough and ready' obligations that we know that we have in advance of any particular situation (such as the obligations to be honest, keep promises, not harm others). Sometimes we face dilemmas where our *prima facie* duties clash, and we have to decide what our actual duties are in these circumstances, i.e. which duty has the stronger claim over us.

Primary and secondary qualities According to **representative realism** physical objects have certain primary qualities such as size and shape which we are able to perceive. At the same time we also seem to perceive objects to have a set of secondary qualities such us colours, sounds and smells. However, these qualities are not actually in the objects themselves, but rather are powers to produce these sensations in us. Such powers are a product of the arrangement of the parts of the object which are too small for us to observe.

Prisoner's Dilemma A fictional thought experiment, in which two prisoners are offered various rewards (for cooperating) and punishments (for not cooperating). Two key features of this thought experiment are: that the outcomes are dependent on the choices that the other prisoner makes; and that the best outcome for each prisoner is one that goes against their immediate self-interest.

Problem of evil A problem recognised by both believers and **atheists**: how can an all-powerful, all-loving and all-knowing creator have created a world which seems to contain so much unnecessary pain and suffering?

Proposition A proposition is a sentence that makes a claim about the way the world actually is: for example, 'there is a cat on my mat' or 'I am thinking about a dragon'. Like beliefs, propositions can be true or false. Other sentences can play different roles, for example 'Sit down NOW' or 'What are you looking at?' Such sentences (commands, questions, exclamations) do not make specific claims about the way the world is, and hence are not propositions.

Propositional content The thought expressed by a proposition. A proposition or belief has propositional content just if it expresses some thought or proposition. Many linguistic expressions may fail to express a proposition and so have no propositional content; for example expletives, warnings or expressions of attitude.

Pyrrhonism   Extreme scepticism. Named after Pyrrho (4th–3rd century BCE), a sceptical philosopher, who maintained that there is always as much evidence against as for any belief, and that it is therefore sensible not to commit oneself to any positive belief.

Qualitative change   Changes in an object's properties, for example, a chair being painted a different colour. This is in contrast to **numerical change**.

Qualitative identity   When two objects have the same properties, for example, two brand new cars which are of the same make, model and colour. This is in contrast to **numerical identity**.

Rationalism   The tendency in philosophy to regard reason, as opposed to sense experience, as the primary source of the important knowledge of which we are capable. Rationalists are typically impressed by the systematic nature of mathematical knowledge and the possibility of certainty that it affords. Using mathematics as the ideal of how knowledge should be, rationalists typically attempt to extend this type of knowledge into other areas of human inquiry, such as to knowledge of the physical world, or to **ethics**. Rationalism is traditionally contrasted with **empiricism**: the view that most of what we know is acquired through experience.

Rationality   The capacity, supposedly possessed by most adult human beings, to reason and to use reason to guide one's actions. Rationality is often cited as a distinguishing feature of being a person.

Realism   If you are a realist about something, then you believe it exists independently of our minds. If you are an anti-realist about something you think it is mind dependent. Examples of realist positions from **epistemology** are **naïve realism** and **representative realism**. What they have in common is the conviction that physical objects are real, that is, that they have an existence independently of our perception of them. An example of realism in moral philosophy is Kant's belief that the moral law exists independently of human beings and that we can discover its rules. See also **anti-realism**.

Reason   The capacity for rational argument and judgement. The process by which we are able to discover the truth of things by pure thought by inferring conclusions from **premises**. Often contrasted with instinct, emotion or imagination.

Reductio ad absurdum   A method of **argument** by which you prove that a claim is false by first supposing it to be true and then drawing out the logical consequences. If these consequences can be shown to be false or absurd then the original claim cannot be true. Aquinas uses a *reductio ad absurdum* in his **cosmological arguments**.

Reductionism   The attempt to explain more complex phenomena by reference to simpler, or more basic phenomena. For example to explain the properties of a chemical by reference to the properties of its constituent atoms.

Reformed epistemology   A term used by Plantinga and his followers to describe the revival of the protestant approach of the sixteenth-century Reformation to belief about God. Plantinga argues that it is perfectly reasonable to believe that God exists, even though there may not be sufficient evidence for this belief. This is because belief in God is a *basic* **belief**, and, like other basic beliefs, it doesn't need sufficient evidence.

Representation   In the philosophy of perception a representation is a sense experience or collection of **sense data** which appears to picture some aspect of the physical world, such as an object. See also **representative realism**.

Representative realism   A realist theory of perception which claims that physical objects impact upon our sense organs causing us to experience sensations. These sensations are akin to pictures which represent the objects which cause them.

Revealed theology   Gaining an understanding of God through the revelations of sacred texts and prophets. This is in contrast to **natural theology**, although to Aquinas the two approaches are compatible with each other.

Revelation   Information that is revealed, or disclosed, to humans by a supernatural source, such as God or angels. The Bible is regarded as a work of revelation, and it forms the basis of **revealed theology**.

Right Actions are right according to whether they ought to be done, irrespective of the particular situation, or the consequences that result from a course of action. **Deontological** theorists believe that moral value lies solely in what is right (rather than in what is good) and that we have obligations or duties to do what is right. However, consequentialist theorists are quite happy to redefine 'right' to mean 'actions that bring about the good'.

Rights A right is an entitlement that I have to the protection of certain powers, interests or privileges. It is debatable whether we can only have rights because we make a contract within society, or whether we have 'natural rights' which exist independently of any contract. Rights may be seen as the converse of duties; thus, if I have a right to X, then you have a **duty** to promote X or at least not interfere in my access to X.

Scepticism Philosophical scepticism entails raising doubts about our claims to know. Global scepticism directs its doubts at all knowledge claims and argues that we can know nothing. Scepticism can also have a more limited application to some subset of our knowledge claims, for example concerning the possibility of knowledge of the claims of religion or of **ethics**. The purpose of scepticism in philosophy is firstly to test our knowledge claims. If they can survive the sceptic's attack, then they may vindicate themselves as genuine knowledge. Descartes used scepticism in this way so that he could isolate a few certainties which he felt could be used as a foundation to rebuild a body of knowledge free from doubt or error. Scepticism is also used as a tool for distinguishing which types of belief can be treated as known and which cannot, thereby delimiting those areas where knowledge is possible. In this way philosophers often exclude certain regions of human enquiry as fruitless since they cannot lead to knowledge. **Empiricists**, for example, often argue that knowledge of religious claims is impossible since they cannot be verified in terms of experience.

Seeing-as A phrase which captures the idea that seeing is an activity (it is not just the result of light waves hitting our eyes). What we see depends upon many things including the **beliefs** we currently hold; what we expect to see; what we have been told we are seeing; our emotional state, etc. Seeing is an act of interpreting the world, and this means that people with different beliefs, expectations, emotions, etc. might observe the world differently.

Self What the word 'I' refers to. The essence of the person and what many philosophers, most notably Descartes, have argued we are directly aware of through introspection.

Self-interest This can be understood in two senses. First, as a motivation to action – namely that we are each selfishly motivated to act so that we achieve our own goals, fulfil our own desires and preserve our own futures. Secondly, as an analysis of what is really in the interests of the self: not just what appears to us to be so (according to our immediate desires and preferences), but what is for our own good objectively.

Sensation The subjective experience we have as a consequence of perceiving physical objects including our own bodies, such as the experience of smelling a rose, or of feeling hungry.

Sense data What one is directly aware of in perception. The subjective elements which constitute experience. For example, when perceiving a banana, what I actually sense is a collection of sense data, the way the banana seems to me, including a distinctive smell, a crescent-shaped yellow expanse, a certain texture and taste. According to sense data theorists, we make judgements about the nature of the physical world on the basis of immediate awareness of these sense data. So, on the basis of my awareness of the sense datum of a yellow expanse, plus that of a banana smell, etc. I judge that I am in the presence of a banana. In this way, we build up a picture of the physical world and so all **empirical** knowledge can rest on the foundation of sense data.

Sense impressions The colours, noises, tastes, sounds and smells that one is aware of when perceiving the world. Also known as **sense data**.

Social contract A fictional device that shows how it is possible for self-interested individuals to live together in society, and how moral rules and obligations might emerge from self-interested behaviour. If we all pursued our own selfish interests, irrespective of the damage this did to others, then we would find it very difficult to achieve our goals, and would be in constant danger from others. It makes sense for all of us to have limits placed on what we can do to achieve our self-interests, and this means each of us agreeing on these restrictions, on who should police these restrictions, and what form the restrictions should take. In other words we submit to a kind of social contract so that we may all pursue our goals as safely as possible.

Solipsism The view that all that can be known to exist is my own mind. This is not normally a position defended by philosophers, but rather a **sceptical** trap into which certain ways of thinking appear to lead. For example, if it is urged that all that can be truly known is what one is directly aware of oneself, then it follows that one *cannot* know anything of which one is *not* directly aware. This might include the minds of other people (which one can only learn about via their behaviour), or, more radically, the very existence of the physical world, including one's own body (which one can only learn about via one's sense experience of them).

Sophists The sophists are literally 'wise ones', freelance teachers in ancient Greece who would give lectures or take on the education of nobles for a fee.

Soul There are many different philosophical accounts of the soul. In some accounts it is what gives life to the human being. In others it is the **immaterial** part of us: that which constitutes the essence of the individual person. It is also seen as that which can survive the death of the body and so guarantee the continued existence of the person after physical death.

Statement Indicative sentence.

Subject In grammar, the part of a proposition that picks out the main object which is being described or discussed: for example, in 'the red balloon popped' the subject is 'the balloon'. In the sentence 'God is the greatest conceivable being', 'God' is the subject.

Sufficient condition See **necessary condition**.

Superstructural beliefs The superstructure of a building is the part which rests on the foundations. According to **foundationalism** our beliefs fall into two categories, the foundational ones and the superstructural ones. The foundational beliefs justify themselves while the superstructural ones are justified by (rest on) the foundational ones.

Sympathy Hume believed that we could give a psychological account of morality, through understanding moral judgements in terms of the feelings certain actions or characteristics arouse in us. It is through sympathy (in modern terms empathy) that we feel the pains and pleasures of others and that we then judge others as virtuous or vicious.

Synthetic See **analytic**.

Teleological Deriving from the Greek word *telos* meaning purpose, goal or end. A teleological explanation is a way of accounting for events by reference to their purpose or ultimate goal. For example, you notice a green shoot emerging from an acorn. A teleological explanation will refer to the purpose of this event, or to a future state that needs to be attained: 'because it is trying to grow into a tree', or 'it is searching for soil and water'. Such a teleological approach may be contrasted with efficient or mechanical explanations, which explain events only by making reference to physical factors leading up to the event. So the green shoot emerges because of certain changes in temperature and the production of enzymes, which lead to the growth of certain cells, which eventually shatters the acorn shell etc.

Teleological arguments Arguments which propose that God exists on the basis of certain **teleological** features of the universe: for example, observations concerning its ordered nature, or concerning the apparent design and purpose of the parts of living organisms. Such arguments are also known as arguments from design.

Theism/theist Belief in one God, who is a person, who is generally held to be perfect, who is the creator of the universe, and who has a relationship with that universe. This is in contrast to **atheism** (the belief that there is no such God) and agnosticism (refusing to commit to either atheism or theism).

Theodicy The attempt to justify God's actions, and to show why, for example, a perfect God has created an imperfect world. The most common forms of theodicy are responses to the **problem of evil** that explain why God allows pain and suffering to exist.

Theology The study of God from a religious perspective. This is in contrast to the philosophy of religion, which starts from a philosophical perspective.

Theory of Forms   See **World of Forms**.

Transcendent   To be outside, beyond, or removed from something. So to say that God is transcendent is to say that he exists outside of his creation, outside of space and time.

Transcendental   A term coined by Kant to describe a certain form of anti-sceptical argument. A transcendental argument operates by showing that the **sceptic** must presuppose what she attempts to deny in order for her argument to make sense. For example, to defeat the sceptic's claim that we cannot know that the physical universe exists beyond our own minds we would need to show that the existence of that world is presupposed in the formulation of the sceptical argument itself. How this might be done is discussed in more detail in the text.

True   A term used of **beliefs** and **propositions**. There are different theories of what makes a belief or proposition true. For the sake of simplicity, in this book we have been operating with the so called correspondence theory of truth which says that beliefs and propositions are true when they correspond with the facts, that is, when what they say about the world is the case.

Universalisability   A fundamental feature of most ethical theories, and a version of the **golden rule**. A principle is universalisable if it is applied to all people equally and in the same way. Some philosophers have seen this as part of the very meaning of a moral judgement – it applies to everyone in the same situation. **Utilitarians** (Bentham and Mill), **deontologists** (Kant) and even **existentialists** (Sartre) have all appealed to universalisability at some point in their theories. For Kantians the principle of universalisability has to be a more rigorous version of the golden rule: it says that we should only act on those rules which we can will to be universal laws (i.e. without contradiction or inconsistency).

Utilitarian/utilitarianism   A **normative** moral theory, perhaps inspired by Hume and developed first by Bentham and then by Mill and Sidgwick. In most of its forms it is a **hedonistic** theory claiming that what is good (i.e. what we ought to strive to bring about) is as much pleasure or happiness as possible for most people. In its negative forms it says we ought to strive to reduce pain or harm to most people.

Utility   Welfare or use for the majority of people. For Bentham and Mill utility came to mean 'pleasure' or 'happiness'.

Verificationism   A philosophical belief about the nature of meaning. **Logical positivism** claims that for a proposition to be meaningful it must be (hypothetically) verifiable or true by definition. Other than truths by definition most **propositions** make a specific claim about the universe – that it is this way or that – for example, that 'there is a cat on my mat' or that the 'leaves on my tree are green'. In such cases it is easy for us to imagine how such claims could be verified or not. However, take the claim that 'God loves the world'. How could we verify this claim? What could we look for in the world to see whether that claim is true or not? If it is not clear how the universe would look if the claim were true or not, then it is not clear what it is asserting and thus logical positivists might claim that the proposition is not meaningful.

Verification principle   The rule put forward by **verificationists** that a statement is only meaningful if it can be shown to be true (verified): either empirically (e.g. by observation) or because it is true by definition.

Via negativa   A Latin term meaning 'the negative way'. It refers to the claim by Maimonides, and others, that we can only come to understand God by knowing what he is not.

Virtue   A character trait or disposition which is to be valued (for the ancient Greeks, it is a disposition which is excellent). Common virtues include wisdom, courage, self-control, honesty, generosity, compassion, kindness, etc.

Virtue ethics   A **normative** ethical theory which locates value not in an action or its consequences, but in the agent performing the act. Virtue ethicists stress the need to develop virtuous dispositions, and to judge actions within the broader context of what someone is inclined to do. So a person may be judged to be virtuous or vicious through noting how they are disposed to act. Frustratingly, for many people, virtue ethicists fail to give us a formula (unlike **consequentialists** and **deontologists**) that guides us in what we ought to do in any particular situation.

World of Forms   Plato's theory that universal concepts such as Beauty and Justice exist independently of human minds, in another realm. Plato called such concepts 'forms'.

Notes

Chapter 1

1 The founder of utilitarianism, Jeremy Bentham, claimed that these two types of reasons (both positive and negative) were fundamental to human motivation: 'Nature has placed mankind under the governance of two sovereign masters, *pain* and *pleasure* . . . They govern us in all we do, in all we say, in all we think.' Jeremy Bentham, 'Introduction to the principles of morals and legislation', in John Stuart Mill, *Utilitarianism*, ed. Mary Warnock, Fontana 1985, p. 33.

2 Other enlightenment thinkers who used the social contract device to explore the origins of our ethical obligations include Locke (1632–1704), Rousseau (1712–1778), Thomas Paine (1737–1809) and J. S. Mill (1806–1873). For all these thinkers, morality is grounded in mutual agreement designed to overcome our natural selfishness or to help us to promote our natural altruism.

3 Thomas Hobbes, *Leviathan, English Works* 3, Wilder 2007, p. 75.

4 Ian McEwan, *Enduring Love*, Vintage 1998, pp. 14–15.

5 *Second Treatise of Government*, Section 6, Hackett 1980, p. 9. Thus on Locke's account the state of nature was pre-political but not pre-moral and so his account does not explain morality so much as explain why moral beings would band together to form a political entity: the state.

6 David Gauthier, 'Morality and advantage', *Philosophical Review*, Vol. 76 (1961), 460–475.

7 See, for example, Richard Dawkins, *The Selfish Gene*, Oxford University Press 1999, pp. 228–233.

8 John Rawls, *A Theory of Justice*, Oxford University Press 1971.

9 Thomas Hobbes, *Leviathan*, Part 1, Chapter xiii.

10 Ibid., Part 1, Chapter 6.

11 The ancient Greeks used their own alphabet, and the terms given in italics are transcriptions from the ancient Greek script, so *ergon* (which we translate as 'function') was written as εργον, and *eudaimonia* ('happiness') would have been written as ευδαιμονια.

12 Julia Annas, *An Introduction to Plato's Republic*, Oxford University Press 1981, p. 157.

13 Plato, *Euthydemus*, 278e6.

14 Aristotle, *Ethics*, 1095a16, Penguin 1988, p. 66.

15 Plato, *Gorgias*, 492c, Clarendon Press 1995, p. 66.

16 Aristotle, *Ethics*, 1095b25, p. 68.

17 Aristotle, *Ethics*, 1095b16, p. 68 and 1098a1, p. 75.

18 Plato, *Gorgias*, 494d, p. 68.

19 Plato, *Republic* 344c, Penguin 1987 p. 86.

20 Plato, *Republic*, 352d, p. 98.

21 Aristotle, *Ethics*, 1102a17, p. 88.

22 Plato, *The Republic*, 434e–441c, pp. 208–217.

23 Plato, *Phaedrus*, 253d, Oxford University Press 2002, p. 202.

24 Aristotle, *Ethics*, 1102a30–1103a10, pp. 88–90.

25 Aristotle, *Ethics*, 1097b22–1098a15, pp. 76–77.

26 Ibid., p. 76.

27 Plato, *The Republic*, 441d, p. 218.

28 Ibid., 442b, p. 219.

29 Aristotle, *Ethics*, 1106b20, p. 101.

30 Aristotle, *Ethics*, 1106a22–1106b33, pp. 100–101.

31 For a more complete list see Aristotle, *Ethics*, p. 104.

32 Aristotle, *Ethics*, 1098a15, p. 76.

33 Plato, *The Republic*, 514a–517c.

34 Plato, *Protagoras*, 358c–d, Hackett 1992, p. 55.

35 Aristotle, *Ethics*, 1096a10ff, pp. 69–72.

36 Immanuel Kant, *Critique of Practical Reason*, Cambridge University Press 1999, p. 133.

37 Bill Watterson, *The Indispensable Calvin and Hobbes*, Warner Books 2004, p. 69.

38 Kant, *Foundations of the Metaphysics of Morals*, Section II, 415–419, in H. J. Paton, *The Moral Law*, Hutchinson 1972, p. 63.

39 Ibid., p. 66.

40 Immanuel Kant, *Groundwork for the Metaphysic of Morals*, in Paton, *The Moral Law*, p. 78.

41 Heinrich Hoffman, *Struwwelpeter or Pretty Stories and Funny Pictures*, Belitha Press 1997.

42 In H. J. Paton, *The Moral Law*, p. 65.

43 Kant, *Foundations of the Metaphysics of Morals*, trans. L. W. Beck, in O.A. Johnson, *Ethics*, Harcourt Brace College 1998, p. 198.

44 For example see the Bible, Matthew 7:12 and Luke 6:31. Another version of the Golden Rule can be found in the writings of K'ung Ch'iu (Confucius): 'What you do not like when done to yourself do not do to others' in *Analects* Book 15:3.

45 Kant, *Foundations of the Metaphysics of Morals*, in Johnson, *Ethics*, p. 190.

46 Kant, in Paton, *The Moral Law*, pp. 85–86.

47 Ibid., p. 95.

48 See Plato, *The Republic*, 331c, Penguin 1987, p. 66, and Kant's essay 'On a supposed right to lie from altruistic motives', extract in Christine Korsgaard, 'Kant on dealing with evil', in James Sterba (ed.), *Ethics: The Big Questions*, Blackwell 2004, p. 199.

49 W.D. Ross, *The Right and the Good*, Oxford University Press 2002.

50 Bernard Williams, *Ethics and the Limits of Philosophy*, Fontana 1985, pp. 66–69.

51 David Hume, *Treatise of Human Nature*, Book II, Part 3, Section 6 (II.3.6), Dover 2004, p. 440.

52 Ibid., II.3.3, p. 295.

53 Ibid., II.3.3, p. 296.

54 Although perhaps we shouldn't expect so much of moral philosophers, as Nicholson Baker writes 'you can be eloquently virtuous in one sphere while tolerant of nastiness, or even nasty yourself, in another', *The Mezzanine*, Granta 1998, p. 121.

55 David Hume, *Treatise of Human Nature*, III.1.1, p. 333.

56 David Hume, *An Enquiry Concerning the Principles of Morals*, p. 114.

57 Choderlos de Laclos, *Dangerous Liaisons*, Penguin 1989, p. 58.

58 David Hume, *An Enquiry Concerning the Principles of Morals*, p. 156.

59 Ibid., p. 145.

60 Ibid., p. 146.

61 Wallace Matson draws a similar distinction between morality which is common to all humans because we are social animals, and morality which is constructed by individual cultures. The former he calls 'low morality' and the latter 'high morality'. See Wallace Matson, 'The expiration of morality', in E.F. Paul, F.D. Miller and J. Paul (eds), *Cultural Pluralism and Moral Knowledge*, Cambridge University Press 1994, pp. 159–178.

62 Ibid., p. 77.

63 But the twentieth century is not unique. Such has been the frequency of genocide throughout human history that Jared Diamond identifies genocide as one of the 'hallmarks' of human beings – i.e. what distinguishes us as animals from other animals. Jared Diamond, *The Rise and Fall of the Third Chimpanzee*, Vintage 1992, pp. 250–276.

64 William Golding, *Lord of the Flies*, Faber and Faber 1958, pp. 98–99.

65 Hume, *Treatise*, Book II, Part 3, Section 3, p. 296.

66 Ibid., Book III, Part 1, Section 1.

67 A.J. Ayer, *Language, Truth and Logic*, Penguin 1980, p. 143.

68 Ibid., p. 142.

69 C.K. Ogden and I.A. Richards, *The Meaning of Meaning*, Kegan Paul 1923, p. 125.

Chapter 2

1 Blaise Pascal, *Pensées*, no. 230, Penguin 1995, p. 245.

2 David Hume, *Dialogues Concerning Natural Religion*, Oxford University Press 1998, p. 43.

3 Plato, *Laws*, Nuvision Publications 2006, p. 239.

4 Aristotle, *Metaphysics*, Beta 4, 999b, University of Michigan Press 1952, p. 51.

5 For a very clear account of the threat Aristotle posed to Christian thought and of the assimilation of Aristotelian philosophy into Christian theology by Aquinas, see F.C. Copleston, *Aquinas*, Penguin 1965, pp. 63–69.

6 Plato, *Timaeus*, 41a, Penguin 1965, p. 56.

7 Reprinted in C. Taliaferro and P.J. Griffiths (eds), *The Philosophy of Religion*, Blackwell 2003, pp. 146–161.

8 Colin Gunton, *Act and Being: Towards a Theology of the Divine Attributes*, Eerdmans 2003, p. 9.

9 St Augustine, *City of God*, Book 8, Ch. 2, trans. Henry Bettenson, Penguin 1984, pp. 312–313.

10 St Anselm, *Proslogion*, Ch. 2 in Alvin Plantinga (ed.), *The Ontological Argument*, Macmillan 1968, p. 4.

11 René Descartes, *Meditation 3*, *Descartes – Selected Philosophical Writings*, Cambridge University Press 1993, p. 93.

12 Richard Swinburne, *The Coherence of Theism*, Clarendon Press 1977, p. 2.

13 Blaise Pascal, *Pensées,* Penguin 1985, p. 150.

14 J.L. Mackie, 'Evil and omnipotence' in Basil Mitchell (ed.), *The Philosophy of Religion*, Oxford University Press 1971, pp. 101–104.

15 See George Mavrodes, 'Omniscience', in C. Taliaferro and P.J. Griffiths (eds), *Philosophy of Religion*, Blackwell 2003, pp. 236–237.

16 St Augustine, *De Trinitate*, 8.3.

17 St Thomas Aquinas, *Summa Theologica* 1:14:13 (reply to objection 3). Aquinas borrows this analogy from Boethius: Book 5 of his *Consolation of Philosophy*.

18 Kurt Vonnegut, *Slaughterhouse 5*, Vintage 2000, p. 83.

19 Augustine, *Confessions*, XI, vii.

20 Mackie, 'Evil and omnipotence', in Mitchell, *The Philosophy of Religion*, pp. 102–104.

21 Søren Kierkegaard, *Fear and Trembling*, trans. Alastair Hannay, Penguin 1985, pp. 83–95.

22 Anselm, *Proslogion*, Ch.19, in *Anselm of Canterbury: The Major Works*, Oxford University Press 1998, p. 98.

23 Psalm 31:3.

24 Exodus 15:3.

25 Thomas Aquinas, 'The words we use for God' from *Summa Theologica*, reprinted in Brian Davies (ed.), *Philosophy of Religion*, Oxford University Press 2000, pp. 156–167.

26 Ibid., p. 164.

27 Stanislaw Lem, *Solaris*, Faber and Faber 1991, p. 172.

28 Woody Allen, 'Mr Big' in *Complete Prose*, Picador 1997, p. 285.

29 First Vatican Council, 1869–1870, Chapter 2.1.

30 St Thomas Aquinas, *Summa Theologica* 1:2:2.

31 In eighteenth-century France, scientists and naturalists attempted to discover whether the Beast of Gevaudan (a creature that had apparently killed 140 people) really existed. For a stylish fictionalised version of their attempts see the film *Brotherhood of the Wolf* directed by Christopher Gans (2001).

32 The philosopher J.N. Findlay argues that this definition is correct as it arises out of a genuinely religious attitude. To a believer the object of worship 'should have an *unsurpassable* supremacy along all avenues [and] tower *infinitely* above all other objects' (J.N. Findlay, 'Can God's existence be disproved?', in A. Flew and A. MacIntyre (eds), *New Essays on Philosophical Theology*, Macmillan 1955, p. 51). However, Findlay then goes on to to disprove God's existence in order to show the absurdity of the ontological argument!

33 Alvin Plantinga would add to these attributes 'worthy of worship'. An imaginary God is not worthy of worship, but the supreme being must be at the very least worthy of worship, and so must exist (Alvin Plantinga (ed.), *The Ontological Argument: From St Anselm to Contemporary Philosophers*, Macmillan 1968, p. *x*).

34 Gaunilo's 'On Behalf of the Fool' is reprinted in Plantinga, *The Ontological Argument*, pp. 6–13. Some philosophers have had a lot of fun with the ontological argument. For example D. and M. Haight used it to prove the existence of the greatest conceivable evil being ('An ontological argument for the devil', *The Monist*, no. 54, 1970).

35 F.C. Copleston sees Aquinas' rejection of the ontological argument as evidence of his 'empiricism' (F.C. Copleston, *Aquinas,* Penguin 1965, p. 113). Aquinas does offer five alternative proofs of God's existence, all of them based on our experience of the effects of God's existence – namely the world we see around us.

36 *Descartes – Selected Philosophical Writings*, Meditations 5, p. 107. For a more detailed expansion and analysis of Descartes' ontological argument, read Clement Dore, 'Ontological arguments', in P.L. Quinn and C. Taliaferro (eds), *A Companion to Philosophy of Religion*, Blackwell 1999, pp. 323–329.

37 Kant, *Critique of Pure Reason*, Macmillan 1980, pp. 500 ff.

38 This is a position also taken by David Hume in his *Dialogues Concerning Natural Religion,* Oxford University Press 1998, p. 91. For both Hume and Kant a proposition is a necessary truth if, when we reject the predicate, a contradiction results. So 'Bachelors are unmarried men' is necessarily true because when we reject the predicate, and suggest that 'Bachelors are married men', then we have a contradiction. However, for Hume and Kant no statement about existence can be necessary, as it is always possible to deny something exists, without that statement being contradictory. So to say 'God does not exist' is not a contradiction, which means 'God exists' is not a necessary truth.

39 Kant calls propositions that are true by definition, and known to be true *a priori*, 'analytic' propositions (e.g. all bachelors are unmarried). This is in contrast to what he calls 'synthetic' propositions; these are statements that tell us something new about the world (e.g. some bachelors eat baked beans straight from the tin).

40 The Dutch theologian Johan de Kater (Caterus) made a similar criticism of Descartes' argument, and this was included in the first published edition of the Meditations as 'The First Set of Objections'. See *Descartes – Selected Philosophical Writings*, Cambridge University Press 1988, p. 136.

41 Kant, *Critique of Pure Reason*, p. 504.

42 Bertrand Russell, *Why I am Not a Christian*, Routledge 1996, p. 137.

43 Alvin Plantinga, 'A valid ontological argument?' reprinted in A. Plantinga (ed.), *The Ontological Argument: From St Anselm to Contemporary Philosophers*, Macmillan 1968, pp. 161–171.

44 René Descartes, *Discourse on Method and the Meditations*, Penguin Classics 1968.

45 Descartes, *Discourse on Method and the Meditations*, Penguin Classics 1968, p. 115. All page references given for further quotations are to this edition.

46 Here we can ignore Descartes' distinction between 'actual or formal' and 'eminent' reality, the difference being that to possess something actually or formally is to actually possess it, while to possess something eminently is to be able to produce it in something else, because one possesses more reality than what one would produce.

47 Euripides, *Sisyphus*, as translated for W.G. Benham's *Book of Quotations, Proverbs and Household words*, Putnam 1949. This quote from a fragment of the play *Sisyphus* has also been widely attributed to Critias, the uncle of Plato. A more common, although not as succinct, translation of the lines is: 'Some shrewd man first, a man in judgment wise, found for mortals the fear of gods, thereby to frighten the wicked' (as translated by R.G. Bury, revised by J. Garrett in *Aristotle and the Theology of the Living Immortals*, University of New York 2000).

48 Bertrand Russell, *Why I am Not a Christian*, Routledge 1996, p. 25.

49 Recent years have seen the publication of a number of high-profile books, critical of religion, that are a response to the rise of fundamentalism in both Islam and Christianity: Daniel Dennett, *Breaking the Spell: Religion as a Natural Phenomenon*, Allen Lane 2006; Richard Dawkins, *The God Delusion*, Houghton Mifflin 2006; Christopher Hitchens, *God Is Not Great: How Religion Poisons Everything*, Allen and Unwin 2007.

50 David Hume, *Dialogues and Natural History of Religion*, ed. J.C.A. Gaskin, Oxford University Press 1998, p. 176.

51 Ibid., p. 140.

52 Ibid., p. 155.

53 Ludwig Feuerbach, *The Essence of Christianity*, trans. George Eliot, Prometheus Books 1989, p. 159.

54 Karl Marx, introduction of *Toward a Critique of Hegel's Philosophy of Right*, in *Marx – Selections*, ed. Allen Wood, Macmillan 1988, p. 23.

55 Karl Marx and Friedrich Engels, *Theses on Feuerbach*, in *Marx – Selections*, p. 82.

56 Karl Marx, preface to *Toward a Critique of Political Economy*, in *Marx – Selections*, p. 134.

57 Marx and Engels, *Manifesto of the Communist Party*, in *Marx – Selections*, p. 142.

58 In Plato's masterpiece, *The Republic*, Socrates suggests that the ideal state, as he's described it, needs a myth that everyone can buy into and which justifies the clear hierarchy of the state. Plato, *The Republic*, 415a–d.

59 Aldous Huxley, *Brave New World*, Penguin 1959, p. 33.

60 See, for example, Antoinette Renouf's 'Tracing lexical productivity and creativity in the British media', in Judith Munat (ed.), *Lexical Creativity: Texts and Contexts*, John Benjamin Publishers 2007.

61 Marx, introduction to *Toward a Critique of Hegel's Philosophy of Right*, in *Marx – Selections*, p. 24.

62 Ibid., p. 24

63 Karl Popper, *Conjectures and Refutations*, Routledge 2002, p. 45.

64 Sigmund Freud, *Civilisation and its Discontents*, Pelican Freud Library 1976, Vol. 12, p. 260.

65 Sigmund Freud, *The Future of an Illusion*, Doubleday 1957, p. 36.

66 Ibid., p. 51.

67 *The Sopranos*, 'Pax Soprano' Episode 6, Season 1, HBO productions.

68 Bronislaw Malinowski, *Sex and Repression in Savage Society*, Harcourt Brace 1927.

69 Karl Popper, *Conjectures and Refutations*, Routledge 2002, p. 50.

70 Richard Dawkins, *The God Delusion*, Houghton Mifflin 2006, p. 172.

71 Ibid., p. 172.

72 Steven Pinker, *How the Mind Works*, Penguin 1997, p. 556

73 Dawkins, *The God Delusion*, p. 165.

74 Ibid., p. 174.

75 Daniel Dennett, 'Intentional systems', in *Brainstorms: Philosophical Essays on Mind and Psychology*, MIT Press 1980, pp. 3–7.

76 See, for example, William Dembski, *No Free Lunch: Why Specified Complexity cannot be Purchased without Intelligence*, Rowman and Littlefield 2006, p. 368.

77 Richard Dawkins, *The Extended Phenotype*, Oxford 1999, p. 42.

78 Steven Pinker, quoting Cecil Adams, in *How the Mind Works*, p. 36.

79 Dawkins, *The God Delusion*, p. 283.

Chapter 3

1 John Locke, 'Of identity and diversity', *Essay Concerning Human Understanding*, Book II, Ch. 27, Section 8, reprinted in J. Perry (ed.), *Personal Identity*, University of California Press 1992, pp. 33–52.

2 Aristotle, *Politics*, 1253a, Penguin 1992, p. 59.

3 D. Dennet, *Consciousness Explained*, Allen Lane The Penguin Press 1991, p. 416; J. Glover, *I: The Philosophy and Psychology of Personal Identity*, Penguin 1988, pp.131–153.

4 Based on an idea by Jonathan Glover in *I: The Philosophy and Psychology of Personal Identity*, Penguin 1988, p.132.

5 We see similar claims made by Sartre, see pages 385–90.

6 Donald Davidson, *Inquiries into Truth and Interpretation*, Oxford University Press 2001.

7 René Descartes, *Discourse on the Method*, in P. Geach and E. Anscombe (eds), *Descartes: Philosophical Writings*, Nelson 1966, pp. 41–42.

8 John Locke, *Essay on Human Understanding*, Book II, Chapter 27, Section 9, reprinted in Perry, *Personal Identity*, pp. 33–52.

9 Bernard Williams, 'Personal identity and individuation' (1956–57), reprinted in *Problems of the Self*, Cambridge University Press 1973.

10 P.F. Strawson, 'Persons' (1958), reprinted in *Individuals*, Methuen 1959, pp. 101–102.

11 David Wiggins, *Sameness and Substance*, Section on personal identity, Basil Blackwell 1980.

12 David Hume, *A Treatise of Human Nature* [1739], ed. L.A. Selby-Bigge, Oxford University Press 1960, p.176.

13 Ibid., p. 177.

14 John Locke, *Essay Concerning Human Understanding*, Book II, Ch. 27, Section 8, reprinted in Perry, *Personal Identity*, pp. 33–52.

15 Dr Roger S. Fouts and Deborah H. Fouts, Project Washoe, Chimpanzee and Human Communication Institute: Central Washington University, 1996: accessed at: http://www.cwu.edu/%7Ecwuchci/faq.html

16 G.E.M. Anscombe (tr.), *Philosophical Investigations*, Blackwell 1958, p. 223.

17 Part of Wittgenstein's point is that we need to be wary of anthropomorphising animals, that is interpreting them in terms of ourselves when they are very different. Indeed, humans may be inclined to interpret more than just other animals in terms of themselves. We personify trees, the wind, sun and stars, sometimes regarding these as owners of beliefs and desires. But this is surely a mistake, and we need to be wary of this tendency when it comes to higher animals as well.

18 Alan Turing, 'Computing, machinery and intelligence', *Mind*, 59 (1950) 433–460.

19 John Locke, *Essay Concerning Human Understanding*, Book II, Ch. 27, Section 15, ed. J.V. Yolton, Everyman 1961, pp. 33–52.

20 R.W. Sperry, 'Hemisphere deconnection and unity in conscious awareness', *American Psychologist* 23 (1968), 723–733. See also Thomas Nagel, 'Brain bisection and the unity of consciousness', *Synthese* 22(3–4) (1971), 396–413.

21 John Locke, *Essay Concerning Human Understanding*, Book II, Chapter 27, Section 14, p. 285. Compare this with Leibniz: 'Let us suppose that some individual were to become the King of China at one stroke, but on condition of forgetting what he had been, as if he had been born anew, is it not as much in practice, or as regards the effects which one can perceive, as if he were to be annihilated and a King of China to be created in his place at the same instant? Which this individual has no reason to desire', *Discourse on Metaphysics*, trans. P. Lucas and L. Grint, Manchester University Press 1953, p. 58.

22 Ibid., Section 19, p. 287.

23 Ibid., Section 16, p. 286.

24 Ibid., Section 20.

25 Thomas Reid, 'Of Mr. Locke's account of our personal identity', in *Essays on the Intellectual Powers of Man* [1785], reprinted in J. Perry (ed.), *Personal Identity*, University of California Press 1992, pp. 114–115.

26 A version of this criterion is offered by A. Quinton, 'The soul', in Perry, *Personal Identity*, pp. 53–72.

27 D. Parfit, *Reasons and Persons*, Clarendon Press 1994.

28 J. Butler, 'Of personal identity', originally published as the first appendix to Butler, *The Analogy of Religion* [1736], reprinted in Perry, *Personal Identity*, pp.99–105.

29 Reid, 'Of Mr. Locke's account of our personal identity', in Perry, *Personal Identity*, pp. 113–119.

30 B. Williams, 'Personal identity and individuation' [1956–57], reprinted in B. Williams, *Problems of the Self*, Cambridge University Press 1973.

31 Ibid., pp. 7–9.

32 David Hume, *A Treatise of Human Nature*, I.iv.6, ed. L.A. Selby-Bigge, Clarendon Press 1978, pp. 251, 252.

33 See Thomas Nagel, 'Brain bisection and the unity of consciousness', in Perry, *Personal Identity*, pp. 227–245.

34 Thinkers such as Irenaeus (130?–203?), Minucius Felix (fl. 200) and Tertullian (160?–230?).

35 See Sydney Shoemaker, *Self-knowledge and Self-identity*, Cornell University Press 1963, for discussion of brain transplantation.

36 One way of dealing with the reduplication argument is to insist that it does matter what happens to the second half of your brain, that is, that you would survive if only half your brain were transplanted and the other destroyed, but not if both were.

37 D. Parfit, 'Personal identity', *Philosophical Review* 80 (1971) 3–27, and *Reasons and Persons*, Clarendon Press 1984.

Chapter 4

1 Aristotle, *On the Soul*, 3.4.430ᵃ.

2 This passage is repeated in the chapter on Free Will.

3 Descartes, *Meditations on First Philosophy*, in Sutcliffe, F.E. (trans.), *Discourse on Method and the Meditations*, Penguin 1968, p. 107.

4 Immanuel Kant, *Critique of Pure Reason*, B.75, trans. N. Kemp Smith, Macmillan Education 1989 [1929], p. 93.

5 Locke, *Essay Concerning Human Understanding*, Book I, 2.1, p. 48.

6 It is important to distinguish sentences from the propositions they may be used to express. This is because, on the one hand, different sentences can express the same proposition. For example consider the two different sentences: 'Romeo loves Juliet' and 'Juliet is loved by Romeo'. Both clearly have the same meaning and assert the same thought. In other words they express the same proposition. Similarly sentences in different languages can be used to express the same proposition. 'Je cherche mon chapeau' and 'I'm looking for my hat' are clearly different sentences, but they express the same proposition. On the other hand, the *same* sentence can be used to express *different* propositions, depending on the context. So the sentence 'I love you' as spoken by Romeo to Juliet expresses the proposition that Romeo loves Juliet, but if spoken by Jack to Jill expresses the proposition that Jack loves Jill. Finally it is important to note that not all sentences express a proposition. Sentences can also be used to ask questions, to express an attitude, to make an exclamation, issue a command and so on. What distinguishes propositions from other uses of language is that they can be either true or false. In other words, propositions can be asserted or denied.

7 G.E. Moore, *Principia Ethica*, Cambridge University Press 1986, p. 15.

8 *Discourse 2, Discourse on Method* in René Descartes, *Philosophical Writings*, trans. and ed. Elizabeth Anscombe and Peter Thomas Geach, Nelson's University Paperbacks 1977.

9 René Descartes, *Discourse on Method and the Meditations*, Penguin Classics 1968, p. 96.

10 René Descartes, *Principles of Philosophy* 1, vii, in E.S. Haldene and G.T.R. Ross (trans.), *The Philosophical Works of Descartes*, Cambridge University Press 1911.

11 Descartes, *Meditations*, p. 103.

12 See, for example, David Hume, *Treatise of Human Nature*, Book I, Part 4, Section 6 (I.4.6), Dover 2004; Ludwig Wittgenstein, *Tractatus Logico-Philosophicus*, 5.621–5.6331, trans. David Pears and Brian McGuiness, Routledge Classics 2001.

13 Plato, *Meno*, Penguin 1956, pp. 82–85.

14 Plato, *The Republic*, Penguin 1987, 485b.

15 For example, Plato, *The Republic*, 475–476d.

16 Leibniz's view that we live in the best possible world has caused a fair amount of controversy and it was savagely satirised by the French writer Voltaire (1694–1778) in his novel *Candide*.

17 Note that this position raises difficulties for our ordinary, common-sense view that in all kinds of situations we could do otherwise

than we actually did. In other words, it seems to deny that we have free will. Both Leibniz and Spinoza are aware of this apparent implication and have complex and ingenious ways of dealing with it, which we have no space to go into here.

18 *The Philosophical Writings of Descartes*, Volume 1, trans. J. Cottingham, R. Stoothoff and M. Dugald, Cambridge University Press 1991, para 421 p. 46.

19 Extract quoted in Brand Blanshard, *On Philosophical Style*, Manchester University Press 1954, p. 1.

20 Kant, *Critique of Pure Reason*, B276, trans. N. Kemp Smith, Palgrave Macmillan 2003.

21 Robert Martin, *There are Two Mistakes in the the title of this Book*, Broadview Press 1998, p. 121.

22 Benjamin Whorf (ed. John Carroll), *Language, Thought and Reality: Selected Writings of Benjamin Lee Whorf*, MIT Press 1956.

23 *The Structure of Scientific Revolutions*, University of Chicago Press 1962.

24 In particular Donald Davidson in 'On the very idea of a conceptual scheme' in *Inquiries into Truth and Interpretation*, Clarendon Press 1984.

Chapter 5

1 Charles Dickens, *Great Expectations*, Chapter 54, Penguin Classics 2003, p. 437.

2 Walt Whitman, 'A Lincoln Reminiscence', in *Complete Prose Works*, Kessinger Publishers 2004, p. 362.

3 Walt Whitman,'Old Age Echoes', in *The Works of Whitman*, Wordsworth Press 1998, p. 496.

4 The ideas of 'negative' and 'positive' liberty were first proposed by Isaiah Berlin in his essay 'The two concepts of liberty', reprinted in *Freedom: An Introduction with Readings*, ed. Nigel Warburton, Routledge 2001.

5 For example, Jean Paul Sartre (1905–1980) in *Being and Nothingness*, Methuen 1977, p. 483.

6 From the song 'Que sera sera (Whatever will be, will be)' first published in 1956 by Jay Livingston and Ray Evans.

7 Aristotle, *De Interpretatione*, Ch. 9, trans. C.H.A. Whittaker, Clarendon Press 2002.

8 Desmond Hawkins, 'Night raid', in B. Gardner (ed.), *The Terrible Rain: War Poets, 1939–45*, Methuen 1987, p. 57.

9 'God, grant me the serenity to accept the things I cannot change; the courage to change the things I can; and the wisdom to know the difference', attributed to the theologian Reinhold Niebuhr (1892–1971).

10 W.W. Bartley, *The Retreat to Commitment*, Knopf 1964, p. 35.

11 Pierre Laplace, introduction to *Philosophical Essay on Probabilities*, trans. Andrew Dal, Springer-Verlag 1998, p. 2.

12 David Hume, *An Enquiry Concerning Human Understanding*, Section 8, Part 1, Oxford University Press 1988, p. 92.

13 Gottfried Leibniz, 'New system of nature', in *Leibniz's New System and Associated Contemporary Texts*, Oxford University Press 2006, pp. 10–27.

14 Hume, *An Enquiry Concerning Human Understanding*, Section 7, Part 1, p. 88.

15 Ibid., p. 95.

16 Edward Lorenz, 'A butterfly effect', reprinted in R.H. Abraham and Y. Ueda (eds), *The Chaos Avant-Garde: Memories of the Early Days of Chaos Theory*, World Scientific Publishers 2001, pp. 91–95.

17 Steven Pinker, *How the Mind Works*, Penguin 1998, p. 55.

18 Luke Rhinehart, *The Dice Man*, Hart-Davis MacGibbon 1978, p. 358.

19 Albert Einstein, in a letter to Max Born in 1926, reprinted in Ronald Clark, *Einstein: The Life and Times*, Hodder and Stoughton 1979, p. 340.

20 Steven Pinker, *The Blank Slate*, Penguin 2002, p. 176.

21 Anthony Burgess, *A Clockwork Orange*, Penguin 1972, pp. 99–100.

22 Hume, *An Enquiry Concerning Human Understanding*, p. 83.

23 See, for example, Pinker, *The Blank Slate*.

24 Ernest Hemingway, letter to James Gamble, April 1919 in *Along with Youth: Hemingway, the Early Years*, Oxford University Press 1985, p. 117.

25 René Descartes, *Meditation 3*, in *Descartes – Selected Philosophical Writings*, Cambridge University Press 1993, p. 156.

26 Jean-Paul Sartre, *Existentialism and Humanism*, Methuen 1987, p. 34.

27 Sartre, *Existentialism and Humanism*, p. 27.

28 He wrote several volumes of his masterpiece *A la recherche du temps perdu* (translated into English as *In Search Of Lost Time*, Penguin 2002).

29 Sartre, *Existentialism and Humanism*, pp. 41–42.

30 Ibid., p. 41.

31 Ibid., pp. 453–456.

32 Aristotle, *Ethics*, Penguin 1988, pp. 111–112.

33 From the film *Groundhog Day*, directed by Harold Ramis, 1993.

34 Aristotle, *Ethics*, Chapter 3.

35 Harry Frankfurt, *Necessity, Volition and Love*, Cambridge University Press 1998, p. 105.

36 Aristotle, *Ethics*, pp. 91–92.

37 Ibid., p. 91.

38 Choderlos de Laclos, *Dangerous Liaisons*, Penguin 1961, pp. 335–336.

39 Peter Strawson, 'Freedom and resentment', reprinted in J.M. Fischer and M. Ravizza (eds), *Essays on Moral Responsibility*, Cornell University Press 1993, pp. 45–66.

40 Donald Davidson, 'Actions, reasons and causes', in *The Essential Davidson*, Oxford University Press 2006, pp. 23–37.

41 Steven Pinker, *How the Mind Works*, p. 56.

42 Daniel Dennett, 'Intentional systems', in *Brainstorms: Philosophical Essays on Mind and Psychology*, MIT Press 1980, pp. 3–7.

Chapter 6

1 The character Lucilius in Cicero's *On the Nature of the Gods*, Book II, 3–5, Penguin Classics 1972, p. 124.

2 Charles Darwin, *The Autobiography of Charles Darwin*, Barnes & Noble 2005, p. 261.

3 The film *Alien*, directed by Ridley Scott, uses a creature with similarly parasitic tendencies whose off-spring are planted as eggs inside the human 'hosts', before exploding from the stomachs of their hosts once they've hatched.

4 Written by Cecil Alexander in 1848.

5 Immanuel Kant, *Critique of Pure Reason*, trans. Norman Kemp Smith, Macmillan 1980, p. 520.

6 Terence Penelhum thinks of cosmological arguments as 'existential' arguments, and teleological arguments as 'qualitative' arguments'. See 'Divine necessity', in Basil Mitchell (ed.), *The Philosophy of Religion*, Oxford University Press 1971, pp. 180–181.

7 Antony Flew, *An Introduction to Western Philosophy*, Thames & Hudson 1978, p. 206.

8 Aquinas, *Summa Theologica*, 1:2:3.

9 Jonathan Barnes analyses this, and other passages from Aristotle's *Parts of Animals*, in *Aristotle*, Oxford University Press 1982, pp. 73–77.

10 Aquinas, 'Is the world ruled by providence', extract in Brian Davies (ed.), *Philosophy of Religion: A Guide and Anthology*, Oxford University Press 2000, pp. 251–252. Aquinas gives other analogies in this passage, for example between the governance by God of the universe, and the governance by a ruler of a kingdom.

11 Flew, *Introduction to Western Philosophy*, p. 207.

12 William Paley, *Natural Theology*, extract reprinted in Davies (ed.), *Philosophy of Religion*, p. 257.

13 Ibid., p. 259.

14 David Hume, *An Enquiry Concerning Human Understanding*, Section 10, Part 1, Oxford University Press 1982, p. 110.

15 Although Hume is usually read as an out-and-out atheist, this over-simplifies his beliefs. For a lively account of Hume's occupation of the 'borderlands between belief and unbelief' see Stewart Sutherland, *Faith and Ambiguity*, SCM Press 1984, pp. 28–41.

16 Hume, *Dialogues Concerning Natural Religion*, Oxford University Press 1998, pp. 51–52.

17 William Paley, *Natural Theology*, in Davies (ed.), *Philosophy of Religion*, p. 254.

18 Hume, *Dialogues Concerning Natural Religion*, p. 49.

19 Ibid., p. 78.

20 Ibid., p. 67.

21 Ibid,. p. 114.

22 Robert Hambourger, 'Can design arguments be defended today?', reprinted in Davies (ed.), *Philosophy of Religion*, p. 286.

23 Hume, *Dialogues Concerning Natural Religion*, p. 129.

24 Quoted in E.S. De Beer, *Charles Darwin and T. H. Huxley: Autobiographies*, Oxford University Press 1974, p. 50f.

25 Richard Swinburne, *The Existence of God*, Clarendon Press 1979, p. 135.

26 Cardinal Ratzinger, quoted in Michael Behe, William Dembski and Stephen Meyer, *Science and Evidence for Design in the Universe*, Ignatius Press 2000, p. 114.

27 Charles Darwin, *Origin of Species*, Hayes Barton Press 2007, p. 153.

28 Richard Dawkins, *The God Delusion*, Houghton Mifflin 2006, p. 123.

29 William Dembski, *No Free Lunch: Why Specified Complexity cannot be Purchased without Intelligence*, Rowman and Littlefield 2002, p. 368.

30 Behe, Dembski and Meyer, *Science and Evidence for Design in the Universe*, p. 134.

31 Richard Dawkins, *The God Delusion*, p. 124.

32 Hume, *Dialogues Concerning Natural Religion*, pp. 84ff.

33 Ibid.

34 Paul Davies, *God and the New Physics*, Penguin 1990, p.179. However, it has been pointed out that the beginning of the Big Bang 'is so poorly understood that it has been

aptly compared with the regions of maps of ancient cartographers marked "Here there be dragons" – it can be filled with all sorts of fantasies.' William Craig, 'Theism and physical cosmology', in P.L. Quinn and C. Taliaferro (eds), *A Companion to Philosophy of Religion*, Blackwell 1999, p. 420.

35 Paul Davies, *The Accidental Universe*, Cambridge University Press 1982, p. 95.

36 For an interesting speculative account of how intelligent primates like humans might have emerged, see Steven Pinker. 'Revenge of the Nerds', *How the Mind Works*, Penguin 1997.

37 Russell Stannard, *Grounds for Reasonable Belief*, Scottish Academic Press 1989; quoted in Stuart Brown (ed.), *Philosophy of Religion – An introduction with Readings*, Routledge 2001, p. 141.

38 Brandon Carter, 'Large number coincidences and the Anthropic Principle in cosmology', *Confrontation of Cosmological Theories with Observational Data*, Reidel 1974, pp. 291–298.

39 Mark Twain, 'Was the world made for man' in John Carey (ed.), *The Faber Book of Science*, Faber & Faber 1995, p. 250.

40 Truman Capote, *In Cold Blood*, Penguin 2000, p. 237.

41 For a more detailed analysis of pain and suffering in relation to evil see John Hick, *Evil and the God of Love*, Fontana 1968, pp. 328–372.

42 St Augustine, *Confessions*, Book 7, Ch 5.

43 Capote, *In Cold Blood*, p. 84.

44 St Augustine, *The Nature of Good*, 4.

45 See, for example, John Hick, *Evil and the God of Love*, p. 18.

46 Jared Diamond, *The Rise and Fall of the Third Chimpanzee*, Vintage 1992, Ch. 16.

47 St Augustine: 'Good is good, yea most mightily better than all his works . . . Where, then, is evil, and whence does it come and how has it crept in?' in *Confessions*, Book 7, Ch 5. Aquinas: 'If, therefore, God existed there would be no evil discoverable; but there is evil in the world. Therefore God does not exist', in *Summa Theologica* 1:2:3.

48 Quoted in Hick, *Evil and the God of Love*, p. 4.

49 Ibid., p. 3.

50 Reprinted in Mitchell, *The Philosophy of Religion*, pp. 92–93.

51 Although Mary Baker Eddy, the Christian Scientist, did claim that evil is an illusion in *Science and Health*, Christian Science Publishing 1934, p. 480.

52 Quoted in E.S. De Beer, *Charles Darwin and T. H. Huxley: Autobiographies*, p. 52.

53 Hume, *Dialogues Concerning Natural Religion*, p. 105.

54 William Rowe, 'The problem of evil and some varieties of atheism', in C. Taliaferro and P.J. Griffiths (eds), *Philosophy of Religion*, Blackwell 2003, pp. 306–373.

55 Hume, *Dialogues Concerning Natural Religion*, p. 105.

56 Significant theological anti-realists include Don Cuppit and followers of Ludwig Wittgenstein, such as D.Z. Phillips. For a brief introduction to some of the issues around anti-realism see Roger Trigg 'Realism and anti-realism', in Quinn and Taliaferro (eds), *A Companion to the Philosophy of Religion*, pp. 213–220.

57 For a succinct account of a new process theodicy as proposed by David Griffin see John Hick, *Philosophy of Religion*, Prentice Hall 1990, pp. 48–55.

58 Job 1:12 and 2:6.

59 Augustine, *City of God*, 11:23.

60 Augustine, *Confessions*, 7:13, quoted in Hick, *Evil and the God of Love*, p. 90.

61 Hick, *Evil and the God of Love*, p. 95.

62 Mackie, 'Evil and omnipotence', in Mitchell, *Philosophy of Religion*, p. 96.

63 Ibid., p. 95.

64 Hick, *Evil and the God of Love*, pp. 328–329.

65 Woody Allen, *Getting Even*, Vintage 1978, p. 91.

66 Hick, *Evil and the God of Love*, p. 374.

67 Ibid., p. 375.

68 Leibniz, *Theodicy*, Book 1, Section 8.

69 Voltaire, *Candide*, Wordsworth Classics 1996, p. 12.

70 Richard Swinburne, 'The problem of evil', quoted in Davies, *Philosophy of Religion*, pp. 610–611.

71 Hick, *Evil and the God of Love*, p. 370.

72 Ibid., pp. 322–323.

73 Ibid., p. 369.

74 Elim Klimov's film *Come and See* (1985) offers a compelling and graphic account of these atrocities from a child's perspective.

75 Fyodor Dostoyevsky, *The Brothers Karamazov*, Bantam 1970, pp. 295–296.

76 Genesis 3:14–20.

77 Peter Vardy, *The Puzzle of Evil*, Fount Press 1992, pp. 38–39.

78 Antony Flew, 'Divine omnipotence and human freedom', in A. Flew and A. MacIntyre (eds), *New Essays in Philosophical Theology*, SCM 1955.

79 Mackie, 'Evil and omnipotence', in Mitchell, *Philosophy of Religion*, pp. 100–101.

80 The American psychologist Joseph Jastrow (1863–1944) created this figure. Philosophers who have used it include Ludwig Wittgenstein, *Philosophical Investigations*, Blackwell 1981, II xi, and E.H. Gombrich, 'Psychology and the riddle of style', in Richard Woolfield (ed.), *The Essential Gombrich*, Phaidon 1996.

81 Wittgenstein, *Philosophical Investigations*, Blackwell 1981, II xi, 193e.

82 John Berger, *Ways of Seeing*, Penguin 1973, p. 30.

83 These examples are from A.F. Chalmers, *What is this Thing called Science?* Open University Press 1987, 2nd edition.

84 John Wisdom, 'Gods', in John Cottingham (ed.), *Western Philosophy: An Anthology*, Blackwell 1996, p. 291.

85 Wisdom, 'Gods', p. 292.

86 Ibid., p. 292.

87 Job 19:25.

88 Richard Hare, in Mitchell (ed.), *Philosophy of Religion*, p. 16.

89 Ibid., pp. 18–19.

90 John Hick, 'Theology and verification', in Mitchell, *Philosophy of Religion*, pp. 59–60.

91 Pierre Laplace, quoted in Fred Shapiro (ed.), *The Yale Book of Quotations*, Yale University Press 2007, p. 443.

92 William James, *The Will to Believe*, in John Cottingham (ed.), *Western Philosophy: An Anthology*, 2nd edition, Blackwell 2007, pp. 285–286.

93 Ludwig Wittgenstein, *Philosophical Investigations*, no. 43, Blackwell 1981, p. 20.

94 Ibid., no. 23, pp. 11–12.

95 Ibid., no. 23, p. 11.

96 Ludwig Wittgenstein, *Lectures and Conversations on Aesthetics, Psychology and Religious Belief*, Blackwell 1970, p. 53.

97 R.B. Braithwaite, 'An empiricist's view of the nature of religious language', in Mitchell, *The Philosophy of Religion*, pp. 72–91.

98 Ibid., p. 89.

99 H.H. Price, 'Belief in and belief that', in Mitchell, *The Philosophy of Religion*, pp. 143–167.

100 See, for example, Alvin Plantinga in Davies, *Philosophy of Religion*, p. 44.

101 Ibid., p. 44.

102 Price, 'Belief in and belief that', p. 166.

103 Hick, *Philosophy of Religion*, p. 65.

Chapter 7

1 William Blake, 'The marriage of heaven and hell', plate 14, *A Memorable Fancy*, (c. 1793), reprinted in *Complete Writings*, ed. Geoffrey Keynes, Oxford University Press 1957.

2 David Hume, *An Enquiry Concerning Human Understanding*, Oxford University Press 1999, I, xii, p. 118.

3 George Berkeley, *First Dialogue* in *Three Dialogues* in *A New Theory of Vision and Other Writings*, Everyman 1963, p. 214.

4 Ibid., p. 208.

5 John Locke, *An Essay Concerning Human Understanding*, Oxford University Press 1999, Book II, ch. 8.

6 Thomas Nagel, *The View from Nowhere*, Oxford University Press 1986.

7 For those studying dualism, Descartes uses this argument to establish the nature of matter and mind/spirit (Descartes, *Meditations on First Philosophy*, in F.E. Sutcliffe (tr.), *Discourse on Method and the Meditations*, Penguin 1968, *Meditation 6*, p. 156). He claims that extension (occupying space) is the only property we can't conceive matter without. So that must be its essential feature. And the one thing you can't conceive a mind without is thought, so thought is the essential property of mind. Some philosophers, however, have criticised this whole method of establishing essential and non-essential properties. It seems to rely on what humans can and cannot imagine, and this would seem to introduce a subjective element into the proceedings. For example, perhaps matter can exist without extension – but humans simply can't conceive of it as such.

8 Locke, *Essay Concerning Human Understanding*, II, viii, 10.

9 Immanuel Kant (1724–1804) argued along these lines in his revolutionary work *The Critique of Pure Reason* (1781). Kant's big idea was that we should give up being concerned with trying to prove that the way we perceive and understand the world conforms to reality (world one), since this is impossible. Instead he tried to demonstrate that the only 'reality' we can know is the one which conforms to our perception and understanding, i.e. world two. Since all objects of experience must, he argued, appear in space and time and are subject to causality, this is the only world we can know. Knowledge is limited to appearances: to world two. Nothing can be known about the real world: world one.

10 Woody Allen, *Without Feathers*, Ballantine Books 1986.

11 John Lennon (1940–1980), British rock musician, *The Way It Is*, CBC-TV, June 1969.

12 The meaning of the term 'idea' as used by the

empiricists of the eighteenth century is notoriously difficult to pin down. Berkeley's use follows Locke's for whom the term means whatever one is conscious of. So, while including what we are here calling sense data, it would also include beliefs and concepts. Note also that Berkeley's arguments discussed above concerning the distinction between primary and secondary qualities are in fact strategic ones, and his considered position actually denies that there is any such distinction.

13 A second argument involves showing that if secondary qualities exist only in the mind of the perceiver, then so do primary qualities of figure, extension, motion and solidity. See Berkeley, *First Dialogue* in *Three Dialogues*, pp. 218–222.

14 This argument has much in common with those of Hume, who uses the empiricist claim that all genuine ideas must derive from experience to argue that we don't really have an idea of self, for example.

15 Ronald Knox, in *The Complete Limerick Book*, Langford Reed, 1924. The second part of the limerick (the answer) is thought to be either by an anonymous author or by Bertrand Russell (because he uses them in several books).

16 James Boswell, *Life of Samuel Johnson*, Clarendon Press, 1804, I, p. 471.

17 Ibid., p. 27.

18 G.E. Moore, 'Proof of an External World' in *Philosophical Papers*, Muirhead Library of Philosophy, 1959, p. 145.

19 Hume, *A Treatise on Human Nature*, Oxford University Press, 1978, p. 187.

Selected bibliography

Recommended reading, Chapter 1 – Moral philosophy

Aristotle, *Ethics*, Penguin 1988

Blackburn, Simon, *Being Good*, Oxford University Press 2001

Frankena, William, *Ethics*, Prentice Hall 1973

Hume, David, *An Enquiry Concerning the Principles of Morals*, ed. Tom Beauchamp, Oxford University Press 1998

Kant, Immanuel, *Groundwork for the Metaphysic of Morals*, in H.J. Paton, *The Moral Law*, Hutchinson 1972

MacIntyre, Alasdair, *A Short History of Ethics*, Routledge 1967

Mackie, J.L., *Ethics: Inventing Right and Wrong*, Penguin 1977

Plato, *Gorgias,* Clarendon Press 1995

Plato, *The Republic*, Penguin 1987

Singer, Peter (ed.), *A Companion to Ethics*, Blackwell 1997

Sterba, James (ed.), *Ethics: The Big Questions*, Blackwell 2004

Weston, Anthony, *A 21st Century Ethical Toolbox*, Oxford University Press 2001

Williams, Bernard, *Morality*, Cambridge University Press 1980

Recommended reading, Chapters 2 and 6 – Philosophy of religion

Davies, Brian, *Introduction to the Philosophy of Religion*, Oxford University Press 1993

Davies, Brian (ed.), *Philosophy of Religion: A Guide and Anthology*, Oxford University Press 2000

Hick, John, *Evil and the God of Love*, Fontana 1968

Hick, John, *Philosophy of Religion*, Prentice Hall 1990

Hick, John (ed.), *The Existence of God*, Macmillan 1964

Hitchens, Christopher, *The Portable Atheist*, Da Capo Press 2007

Hume, David, *Dialogues Concerning Natural Religion*, Oxford University Press 1998

Mackie, J.L., *The Miracle of Theism*, Oxford University Press 1982

Mitchell, Basil (ed.), *The Philosophy of Religion*, Oxford University Press 1971

Quinn, P.L. and Taliaferro, C. (eds), *A Companion to Philosophy of Religion*, Blackwell 1999

Swinburne, Richard, *The Existence of God*, Clarendon Press 1979

Taliaferro, C. and Griffiths, P.J. (eds), *Philosophy of Religion*, Blackwell 2003

Recommended reading, Chapter 3 – Persons

Hume, David, 'Of personal identity', in *Treatise of Human Nature*, Penguin 1985

Locke, John, 'Of identity and diversity', in *Essay Concerning Human Understanding*, Penguin 1997

Perry, John (ed.), *Personal Identity*, University of California Press 1975

Reid, Thomas, 'Of Mr. Locke's account of personal identity', in *Essay on the Intellectual Powers of Man*, reprinted in Perry, *Personal Identity*

Recommended reading, Chapters 4 and 7 – Epistemology

Audi, Robert, *Epistemology: A Contemporary Introduction to the Theory of Knowledge*, Routledge 1998

Cole, Peter, *Theory of Knowledge*, Hodder & Stoughton 2002

Descartes, René, *Meditations on First Philosophy*, Cambridge University Press 1996

Everitt, Nicholas and Fisher, Alec, *Modern Epistemology: A New Introduction*, McGraw-Hill 1995

Morton, Adam, *A Guide through the Theory of Knowledge*, Blackwell 1977

Russell, Bertrand, *The Problems of Philosophy*, Oxford University Press 1986

Trusted, Jennifer, *An Introduction to the Philosophy of Knowledge*, Palgrave 1997

Recommended reading, Chapter 5 – Free will and determinism

Dennett, Daniel, *Elbow Room: The Varieties of Free Will Worth Wanting*, Oxford University Press 1985
Glover, Jonathan, *I: The Philosophy and Psychology of Personal Identity*, Penguin 1988
Honderich, Ted, *How Free Are You?*, Oxford University Press 1993
Sartre, Jean-Paul, *Existentialism and Humanism*, Methuen 1987
Watson, Gary (ed.), *Free Will*, Oxford University Press 1982
Frankfurt, Harry, *Necessity, Volition and Love*, Cambridge University Press 1998

Recommended reading – general

Blackburn, Simon, *Think*, Oxford University Press 2001
Honderich, Ted (ed.), *The Oxford Companion to Philosophy*, Oxford University Press 1995
Hospers, John, *An Introduction to Philosophical Analysis*, Routledge 1997
Martin, Robert, *There are Two Errors in The The Title of this Book*, Broadview 1998
Morton, Adam, *Philosophy in Practice*, Blackwell 1998
Rosenberg, Jay, *The Practice of Philosophy*, Prentice Hall 1976
Warburton, Nigel, *Philosophy: The Essential Study Guide*, Routledge 2004

Index